HEIDEGGER AND HOMECOMING: THE LEITMOTIF IN THE LATER WRITINGS

Martin Heidegger devoted himself to challenging previously held ontological notions of what constitutes 'being,' and much of his work focused on how beings interact within particular spatial locations. Heidegger frequently used the motifs of homelessness and homecoming in order to express such spatial interactions, but despite early and continued recognition of the importance of homelessness and homecoming, this is the first sustained study of these motifs in his later works.

Utilizing both literary and philosophical analysis, *Heidegger and Homecoming* reveals the deep figural unity of the German philosopher's writings, by exploring not only these homecoming and homelessness motifs, but also the six distinctive voices that structure the apparent disorder of his works. In this illuminating and comprehensive study, Robert Mugerauer argues that these motifs and Heidegger's many voices are required to overcome and replace conventional and linear methods of logic and representation.

Making use of material that has been neglected and is yet to be translated into English, *Heidegger and Homecoming* explains the elaborate means by which Heidegger proposed that humans are able to open themselves to others, while at the same time preserving their self-identity.

(New Studies in Phenomenology and Hermeneutics)

ROBERT MUGERAUER is a professor and dean emeritus in the College of Architecture and Urban Design at the University of Washington.

New Studies in Phenomenology and Hermeneutics

Kenneth Maly, General Editor

New Studies in Phenomenology and Hermeneutics aims to open up new approaches to classical issues in phenomenology and hermeneutics. Thus its intentions are the following: to further the work of Edmund Husserl, Maurice Merleau-Ponty, and Martin Heidegger – as well as that of Paul Ricoeur, Hans-Georg Gadamer, and Emmanuel Levinas; to enhance phenomenological thinking today by means of insightful interpretations of texts in phenomenology as they inform current issues in philosophical study; to inquire into the role of interpretation in phenomenological thinking; to take seriously Husserl's term *phenomenology* as 'a science which is intended to supply the basic instrument for a rigorously scientific philosophy and, in its consequent application, to make possible a methodical reform of all the sciences'; to take up Heidegger's claim that 'what is own to phenomenology, as a philosophical "direction," does not rest in being *real.* Higher than reality stands *possibility.* Understanding phenomenology consists solely in grasping it as possibility'; to practise *phenomenology* as 'underway,' as 'the *praxis* of the self-showing of the matter for thinking,' as 'entering into the movement of enactment-thinking.'

The commitment of this book series is also to provide English translations of significant works from other languages. In summary, **New Studies in Phenomenology and Hermeneutics** intends to provide a forum for a full and fresh thinking and rethinking of the way of phenomenology and interpretive phenomenology, that is, hermeneutics.

ROBERT MUGERAUER

Heidegger and Homecoming

The Leitmotif in the Later Writings

UNIVERSITY OF TORONTO PRESS
Toronto Buffalo London

Toronto Buffalo London
www.utppublishing.com

Reprinted in paperback 2014

ISBN 978-0-8020-9810-8 (cloth)
ISBN 978-1-4426-2681-2 (paper)

Library and Archives Canada Cataloguing in Publication

Mugerauer, Robert
Heidegger and homecoming : the leitmotif in the later writings / Robert Mugerauer.

(New studies in phenomenology and hermeneutics)
Includes bibliographical references and index.
ISBN 978-0-8020-9810-8 (bound). – ISBN 978-1-4426-2681-2 (pbk.)

1. Heidegger, Martin, 1889–1976. 2. Homecoming – Philosophy. 3. Homelessness – Philosophy. I. Title. II. Series: New studies in phenomenology and hermeneutics (Toronto, Ont.)

B3279.H49.M84 2008 193 C2008-903790-1

University of Toronto Press acknowledges the financial assistance to its publishing program of the Canada Council for the Arts and the Ontario Arts Council.

Canada Council for the Arts Conseil des Arts du Canada

University of Toronto Press acknowledges the financial support of the Government of Canada through the Canada Book Fund for its publishing activities.

For my parents,
Viola Virginia Stietz Mugerauer and Robert Mugerauer

The coming to be at home in one's own in itself entails that human beings are initially, and for a long time, and sometimes forever, not at home. And this in turn entails that human beings fail to recognize, that they deny, and perhaps even have to deny and flee what belongs to the home. Coming to be at home is thus a passage through the foreign. And if the becoming homely of a particular humankind sustains the historicality of its history, then the law of the encounter between the foreign and one's own is the fundamental truth of history, a truth from out of which the essence of history must unveil itself. For this reason, the poetic meditation on becoming homely must also for its part be of a historical nature and, as poetic, demand a historical dialogue with foreign poets.

Heidegger, *Hölderlin's Hymn 'The Ister'*

The hardest lesson in life is 'that when things are gone they're gone. They aint comin' back.'

Cormac McCarthy, *All the Pretty Horses*

Contents

Abbreviations

Abbreviations for Heidegger's works frequently cited, followed by year of original, German publication (see the bibliography)

A	'Andenken,' 1943
AaSC	'Über Abrahim a Santa Clara,' 1964
AF	'The Anaximander Fragment,' 1946
Al	'Aletheia (Heraklit, Fragment 16),' 1943
aOWA	Addendum to 'The Origin of the Work of Art,' 1956
AS	'Art and Space,' 1969
AWP	'Age of the World Picture,' 1938
Az80	*Ansprachen zum 80 Geburtstag (am 26 September 1969 in Meßkirch)*, 1969
BDT	'Building Dwelling Thinking,' 1951
BPP	*The Basic Problems of Phenomenology*, 1927
BT	*Being and Time*, 1927
CMH	'Conversation with Martin Heidegger,' 1953
CCP	'Conversation on a Country Path,' 1944–5
CP	*Contributions to Philosophy (From Enowning)*, 1936–8
DHP	'Dank bei der Verleihung des staatlichen Hebelgedenkpreises,' 1960
DL	'A Dialogue on Language,' 1953–4
DM	'Dankansprache am 26 September 1969 in Meßkirch,' 1969
EP	'The End of Philosophy and the Task of Thinking,' 1966
ET	'On the Essence of Truth,' 1930
FHT	'Festansprache beim Heimatfest in Todtnauberg,' 1966
FS	*Four Seminars*, 1966–73
G	'Das Gedicht,' 1968

GG	'Vom Geheimnis des Glockenturms,' 1954
HEH	'Hölderlin's Erde und Himmel,' 1960
HEP	'Hölderlin and the Essence of Poetry,' 1936
HFH	'Hebel – Friend of the House,' 1957
ID	*Identity and Difference*, 1957
IM	*An Introduction to Metaphysics*, 1935
JPHZ	'Johann Peter Hebel: Zähringer Rede,' 1954
K	'Das "Kuinzige,"' 1954
La	'Language,' 1950
Lo	'Logos,' 1944
LH	'Letter on Humanism,' 1947
LP	'Language in the Poem,' 1953
M	'Moira (Parmenides, Fragment VIII, 34–41),' 1951–2
MA	'Memorial Address,' 1955 ('Gelassenheit')
MHB	'Metaphysics as History of Being,' 1941
N	*Nietzsche*, 1936–40
NL	'The Nature of Language,' 1957–8
OM	'Overcoming Metaphysics,' 1936–46
OtlCM	'Onto-theo-logical Constitution of Metaphysics,' 1956–7
OWA	'The Origin of the Work of Art,' 1935–6
P	'Pathway,' 1947–8 ('Der Feldweg')
PI	'The Principle of Identity,' 1957
PMD	'Poetically Man Dwells,' 1951
PN-oTS	'Problem of Non-objectifying Thinking and Speaking in Today's Theology,' 1964
PR	*The Principle of Reason*, 1953–6
PT	'Principles of Thinking,' 1958
pWM	'Postscript to "What Is Metaphysics,"' 1943
QB	*The Question of Being*, 1955
QCT	'The Question Concerning Technology,' 1949/53
RM	'Recollection in Metaphysics,' 1941
RP	'Remembrance of the Poet,' 1943
S	*Sojourns: The Journey to Greece*, 1989
SeR	'Statt einer Rede,' 1973
700YM	'700 Years of Meßkirch,' 1961 ('700 Jahre Meßkirch')
sHBM	'Sketches for a History of Being as Metaphysics,' 1941
SG	'Der Satz vom Grund,' 1953–6
SH	'Sprache und Heimat,' 1960
SJPH	'Die Sprache Johann Peter Hebels,' 1955
SR	'Science and Reflection,' 1953

sTB	'Protocol to a Seminar on "Time and Being,"' 1962
T	'The Thing,' 1949–50
TB	'Time and Being,' 1962
Tu	'The Turning,' 1949
VH	'Verlust der Heimat,' 1966
W	'Words,' 1958
WCT	*What Is Called Thinking?*, 1951–2
WD	'Ein Wort des Dankes,' 1959 (aka, 'Dank an die Heimatstadt Meßkirch' [1959])
WISP	'Why Do I Stay in the Provinces?,' 1933–4
WL	'The Way to Language,' 1959
WM	'What Is Metaphysics?' 1929
WN	'The Word of Nietzsche: "God Is Dead,"' 1936–40, 1943
WP	*What Is Philosophy?* 1955
WPF	'What Are Poets For?' 1946
WWAF	'Wie wenn am Feiertage,' 1939 ('As If on a Holiday')

Preface

Given how hard Heidegger is to read and how apparently arcane his topics might seem (being and beings, appropriation/enowning and unconcealment), even before considering what approach or tactics might prove useful we need to ask, 'Why read Heidegger at all?' In fact, we will see that Heidegger's deepest subject matter is not exotic. Quite the opposite. Though indeed subtly and complexly, he basically thinks and writes about what lies closest to us here and now: the loss and attempted recovery of home – specifically, the trajectories of individual, historical-cultural, and epochal-cosmic homelessness and homecoming.

In the broadest terms, he joins a long tradition of conversation about the human condition and prospect, about what might be our relation to 'ultimate reality' or to what grounds us (God, being, human society, the material universe) if there is such a thing; if there is not, then the discussion turns to whether and how we would need to let go of such supposedly transcendental foundations to overcome our childish need for an impossible security. Not surprisingly, for thousands of years the topic has been the subject of highly diverse, imaginative, and analytic approaches (literary, dramatic, cinematic, musical, religious, philosophical, scientific, architectural, planning, historical, sociological, geographical, and ecological). Even doing no more than beginning a list of worldwide 'classics' testifies to the power of the phenomena 'of homelessness and homecoming': *The Gilgamesh Epic*, Genesis and Exodus, Homer's *Odyssey*, St Bonaventure's *Itinerarium Mentis ad Deum* (*The Mind's Road to God*), Dante's *Divine Comedy*, Tao-Chi's *Returning Home: Album of Landscapes and Flowers* from the end of the Ming Dynasty (seventeenth-century China), the Mexica (Aztec) *La Tira de la Peregrinacion – Codice Botarini* (*The Peregrination Scroll*) (early sixteenth-century Mexico), and African-American spirituals such as 'Deep River,' 'Roll, Jordan, Roll,' and 'Steal Away to Jesus.'

Across time and space, and by way of differences, we still respond to the perennial traumas of the human condition that we hear in Io's lament in Aeschylus' *Prometheus Bound*, when exiled from her polis; in Pascal's cry in *Pensées,* when he finds himself in a material universe described by science as dizzyingly infinite, and which knows him not; and, when African American slaves sought the strength to endure their situation in this world, in their songs of hope and trust that God would carry them home in the next. These great human concerns and the works engaging them continue to merit sustained reflection, not despite differences across times, spaces, and situations, but because of that very fact. Today, we continue to face the mysteries of the unexpected, resisted, or regretted loss of home; the achievement or attempted recovery of the sense of place and identity; and the anticipated phases of change, escape, or growth during the course of life.

At the same time, we also have our own particular historical ways of understanding the challenges (to which Heidegger demonstrably makes extraordinary contributions). How to deal with the placeless realm of contemporary homogeneous housing and cities, of shopping and tourist sites, of technological and bureaucratic systems that seem so different from, and so indifferent to, the unique sites and ways of life associated with home as one's birthplace, the family household into which one is born (for better or worse), the homes that one tries to make in one's adult life? Or, on larger scales, that placelessness in the absence of a homeland (whether or not 'nation') or (in the case of the most inclusive realm) of being with God or within some sort of coherent universe in which we might genuinely belong.

Even before he published anything significant, Heidegger became famous because he powerfully addressed how we might live meaningfully in the face of the massive destruction and death wrought by technological warfare, how we might act authentically when the power of the subject is either exaggerated into the cult of egoism or annihilated before impersonal systems of power (or the power of systems), and how we might hope appropriately in the time of nihilism that rises as traditional beliefs, norms, and customs fail. Here too his philosophical work joins or is followed by worldwide contemporary attempts to work through the loss and recovery of home. Specifically, as we will see in the course of the book and explicitly treat at the end, Heidegger either directly addresses or clearly implies how we can approach at least the following four major problems facing us today:

- The existential problems of each individual person – how to live, how to face life's challenges of meaningfulness in our cynical postmodern era
- Massive forced emigration-immigration and refugee displacement around the world, for example as witnessed in the literature and film of exile and diaspora and in the work of international relief organizations
- Technologies consuming and controlling life itself: genetically engineering crops, patenting the agricultural patrimony of marginalized peoples, developing an international economy marketing organs and transplants
- Ecological disasters on a global scale: the destruction of the earth, the oceans, and the atmosphere – *our home of homes.*

The transnational trauma of homelessness shows the continuing ripples of displacement operating at the largest historical, geographical, and social scales. Begun in time immemorial, but exacerbated and shifted by modernity and subsequent technological-economic modernization, the problem now takes new forms with globalization, post- and then re-nationalization, ethnic and religious warfare, and environmental disasters. Certainly the formation of the Americas resulted from sequences of dispossession and attempted recovery of place – ranging across indigenous peoples, the African diaspora, European and Asian immigrants. The same would seem to be true of most colonial and post-colonial dynamics.[1]

Postmodern analyses of globalization also focus on mass displacement, diaspora, and exile, on emigration and immigration that are in effect everywhere. That the problems are widespread and pressing is witnessed by the rapid production of whole literatures and film cultures that wrestle with the complexities of these phenomena, not so much to solve them in any way, but at least to articulate the dilemmas, to generate a sense of shared situatedness among different groups in a given place, among those sharing a language but spread across the world, or sometimes even in broader human solidarity.[2] The problem seems unresolvable: the older philosophical views of the Enlightenment that theoretically posited universal human nature and thus human rights actually led to further colonial political and economic domination by those who initially might have exercised their superiority in the name of liberating and aiding those 'not yet illuminated' or self-determining, but who in fact finally contributed to destroying local knowledge and practices by imposing technology-rationalism and by delivering over the peoples wrongly deemed 'inferior' according to such measures to nationalist and capitalist domination.

Yet, neither the fall of Enlightenment foundations, resulting from post-structuralist attacks on the possibility of objective knowledge and principled-grounded political determination, nor the radical affirmation of difference has led to the hoped-for liberation. To the contrary, it is increasingly apparent that constituting identity by way of difference from groups holding power actually endangers the disempowered, endangering them either physically or by exclusion from the flows of capital. It would seem there is no way out of this double bind: no way back to a discredited modern view of rationality and universal, essential human nature and no way forward with the denial of 'essences' in favour of emphasis on difference, since it would appear that the rejection of one pole of difference in favour of its opposite (or simply, another) leads to nothing except a different regime of bio-techno-power. The latter change would merely shift who is oppressed and oppressor, but not eliminate the deadly binary of arbitrarily dominating-dominated. Even so, given the obvious need to provide for human rights, theorists on the left are re-exploring a 'new universalism' in an effort to purchase a hold for arguments effective at least locally, while maintaining distance from delegitimized origins.[3]

Two further forms of homelessness appear in our separation from the natural world. Biotechnologies move beyond shaping the world to make it more productive or suited to our desires, to the point where they are already consuming and controlling life itself. Many hold that, even with reservations about some dimensions of past technologies – which in any case appear inseparable from human life – we are moving into newly dangerous hubris and alienation from the natural biological processes of which we are a part. Again, there appears no agreed-upon, non-arbitrary measure – or none other than control and capital gain – with which to evaluate genetic engineering of crops or even animals and humans. Nor in regard to patenting the agricultural heritage of indigenous peoples, as happens now when the Indian government has to undertake years of international lawsuits to contest the corporate patenting of Basmati rice and turmeric, which threatens to bar free use of what has long been part of regional culture, just as hybrid corn must already be purchased anew each year by farmers all over the world. Or, beyond the problematic capitalization and control of human blood, tissues, and cell lines, there is the still darker side of transplant practices involving controversial procedures such as harvesting and selling organs removed by state surgeons from executed prisoners, illicitly gleaned from hospital morgues, or systematically solicited from the poor in distressed areas of the world, who are induced by what amounts to a great deal of money for them.[4]

In addition, environmentally, we are unquestionably destroying our home of homes – the earth itself – as we contribute to climate change on a global scale. We are burning fossil fuels in our factories, power plants, homes, and cars, releasing so much CO_2 that we have changed the atmosphere and the oceans (which absorb it). As a result, the earth's polar ice caps are melting at an alarming rate, raising the level of the oceans, which could dislocate millions of people (nearly 39 percent of the world's populations live within 100 kilometres of a coastline).[5] Urbanization continues at a pace that clearly is not sustainable: from 1950 to 1990 the population of the world's cities rose from 200 million to over 2 billion, with 3 billion expected by 2025; each year 20 million people migrate to cities. Already the world has twenty 'mega-cities,' those of over 10 million people; nineteen of the world's twenty largest cities are in developing countries. Cities' consumption of energy and production of waste is colossal; the overcrowded squatter camps of minimal shelters are built on rubbish dumps, polluted brownfield sites, and areas prone to flooding or landslide; the unprecedented air pollution is so serious that a fifth of the world's population lives in mega-cities where the air is not fit to breathe because it causes respiratory infection and other illnesses.[6] Nor are rural areas exempt from impending disaster: dramatic shifts in rainfall and temperature are causing new patterns of drought and flooding, resulting in crop failure in traditional agricultural areas, shortages of safe drinking water, and ultimately the collapse of economically and culturally fragile ways of life, for centuries already the scene of the poverty and isolation that drives people to the cities. All this, of course, does not even broach the irreparable damage to the earth's ecosystems and to the inherently valuable complex webs of organisms that are faced with scandalous waves of extinction a thousand times greater than historically precedented.[7]

Though resolving or even mitigating these problems will obviously not follow directly from what Heidegger says, his complex and profound insights into homelessness and the barriers to the possibility of homecoming (both in what lies within our power and, just as crucially, in understanding what lies beyond it in the epochal developments of differing worlds) can help us to lean to think and act appropriately. In the end, he does articulate a substantial understanding of how we might come to our own. This could occur, however, only as we actually participate in a specific historical gathering-together of humans, earth, and the sacred, if there is such – an event in which the other dimensions would simultaneously come to their own. The first task on the way toward such a homecoming is to become open to what gives itself, and for that we need to learn to better think and speak about our current homelessness, a task for which Heidegger will prove to be a consummate guide.

Before we begin, a few practical notes. My belief that a thorough, close reading of Heidegger lay before me as the primary task should not in the least be taken to indicate any disinterest in or lack of appreciation for previous scholarship. To the contrary, this book was written to follow and unfold a motif long recognized by readers of Heidegger, but surprisingly never fully explored. The importance of homelessness and home in Heidegger's approach to the world and to the history of philosophy was pointed out to English-speaking readers by early guides such as William J. Richardson (1961) and J.L. Mehta (1967), though they did not extensively develop their insights.[8] Very specific facets of Heidegger's language about homelessness were then explored by scholars such as John Sallis (1969, 1970), Reiner Schürmann (1987 [1982]), and Axel Beelemann (1994); recently, fresh readings of works now appearing via the *Gesamtausgabe* use the motif to interpret critical details (Crownfield 2001) while historical research has traced the theme in Heidegger's cultural context (Bambach 2003).[9] But because the attempt to think along with Heidegger by focusing on this leitmotif has been more than enough of a project for me, I do not intend in this book to take up such technical and historical debates about the development of Heidegger's thought or his social-political errancies. My direction and strategy of reading simply derived from the conviction that before I could really appreciate and benefit from the work of so many others, I first needed to focus on what Heidegger himself was saying concerning the complex dynamic of home, homelessness, and homecoming.

I have confined my explication to the 'later' works only because choices had to be made: I could not treat everything Heidegger wrote with the detail required, because the manuscript was already way too long and I was afraid that editors would forget I was working on the project. Given this limitation, the later publications seemed richer and were more compelling to me than the earlier (though I know that the opposite holds true for many). Even insofar as my approach results in a fruitful interpretation, since my project could not cover a larger field of writings, I hope that what lies beyond me might be done by others.[10]

Obviously, I regret that I have not been able to do all the work related to this leitmotif. I do trust, though, that following and complementing those who have taken up the topic before me, I show that there is yet another way to read Heidegger – that his many voices need not be taken as a cacophony but can be heard as a polymorphous chorus, thoughtfully celebrating the multiple, often simultaneous, meanings of the unfolding of our world.

A Note on References and Translations

For references to Heidegger's works, I use the abbreviations noted at the front of the volume; for other works a short version of the title is cited – as usual, the bibliography contains the full information. Where relevant, I indicate the German edition page number in square brackets at the end of the citation: '... a region [*eine Gegend*] ...' (CCP 65 [38]). Note, the convention with translations of *Being and Time* is that the original German page numbers are printed in the margins, and it is to the latter that all references are made.

Generally I have used existing English translations but have made certain systematic modifications because of widespread disagreement among translators about how to translate critical terms, and even about whether to capitalize central words ('Being' or 'being'), which leads to confusion and, often, mistakes. Both in translating passages myself and in using existing English translations, I have followed the convention of using lower case for key words to avoid the misleading traditional transcendental, metaphysical meanings and to steer clear of reifying the supposed referents. Thus, following the recent trend to de-emphasize the substantive (unless in a given case specifically marking the opposite, metaphysical tradition), in the many English translations used I change translations without additional notice to uniformly read 'being,' 'the serene,' 'the holy,' 'saying,' 'appropriation,' 'open,' 'owning,' 'enframing,' and so on. For the same reason, to show Heidegger's intention to think the dynamic, I also systematically use (substitute) 'sending,' not 'destiny,' for *Geshick* and replace many occurrences of 'essence' (*Wesen*) with phrases such as 'what is ownmost to ...', 'manner of abiding (or enduring),' 'a way of being,' '(way in which something) holds sway,' and 'essential sway.' The specific problems associated with '*Ereignis*' as 'en-owning' or 'appropriation' are dealt with in the text and notes along the way.

I, the several reviewers, and the Press's editors have done our best to eliminate the gender bias of Heidegger's references to the poet. But, since he refers only to male poets, and regularly conflates himself with Hölderlin, there are only so many alternative wordings that are not annoyingly contrived. Thus, I agree with Jennifer Anna Golsetti-Ferencei that the general solution is to 'maintain Heidegger's use of the masculine poet (*der Dichter*), his (*sein, seine*) and him (*ihn, ihm*)' and to defer concerning the issue to the specialized literature on the gendered subject and on Heidegger's language.'[11]

Translations of the following are mine:

- 'Andenken'
- 'Hölderlin's Erde und Himmel'
- 'Dank bei der Verleihung des staatlichen Hebelgedenkpreises'
- 'Dankansprache am 26 September 1969 in Meßkirch'
- 'Das Gedicht'
- 'Vom Geheimnis des Glockenturms'
- 'Festansprache beim Heimatfest in Todtnauberg'
- 'Johann Peter Hebel: Zahringer Rede'
- 'Das "Kuinzige"'
- 'Sprache und Heimat'
- 'Statt einer Rede'
- 'Die Sprache Johann Peter Hebel'
- 'Verlust der Heimat'
- 'Ein Wort des Dankes' (aka 'Dank an die Heimatstadt Meßkirch')
- 'Wie wenn am Feiertag'
- 'Über Abrahim a Santa Clara.'

I used the *Gesamtausgabe* as I wrote, but much was done from earlier editions (before the *Gesamtausgabe* was available), as indicated in the bibliography.

Acknowledgments

Support for publication was provided by a grant from the Graham Foundation for Advanced Studies in the Fine Arts.

Additional support was provided by the University of Washington Graduate School Fund for Excellence and Innovation (GSFEI), under the leadership of Dean Suzanne Ortega, for which I am most grateful.

The project started in a previous life, with a National Endowment for the Humanities fellowship in 1979–80 to study Heidegger and homelessness, which took me for the first time to Freiburg im Breisgau and Heidegger's home places. I like to believe that the twenty-nine years spent on the project have benefited from both sustained and matured reflection and from the continually interesting unfolding of Heidegger's work through the *Gesamtausgabe* and the worldwide dialogue stimulated by it. I want to thank Professor Phil Hopkins for invaluable consultation on the Greek, especially that of Heraclitus, and Professor Monika Kaup for always helpful advice on the subtleties of the German and for lively, open discussion.

I want to thank series editor Kenn Maly for his encouraging response to the manuscript, expert negotiations with presses, and mindfulness to the nuances of Heidegger's texts and ways that I might become more responsive to them. I am very grateful for the exceptional time and energy the anonymous readers spent in closely reading the manuscript and making positive suggestions that I was glad to embrace. It was a pleasure working with the University of Toronto Press – Assistant Managing Editor Richard Ratzlaff, who saw me through the final editing processes, and especially Humanities Editor Len Husband, who supported the project from the beginning, gave sound professional advice, and exercised great skill and care in seeing such a long manuscript through to publication.

HEIDEGGER AND HOMECOMING

Introduction

How to understand Heidegger, and through him, the world? The contention of this book is that the leitmotif of homelessness and homecoming not only provides Heidegger with a subject matter of the greatest human importance, but also the means to think and say that phenomenon. The latter includes both (*i*) the figure through which to interpret the historical giving-withdrawing of being, including that to come, and (*ii*) the very language and strategic movement or style of the thinking and saying by means of which to fruitfully explore and successfully articulate that subject matter.

Insofar as Heidegger has much to tell us about the loss and attempted recovery of home, the question of how to understand what he says is all the more pressing. That his individual works are notoriously difficult because of their apparent subject matter and his complex (often idiosyncratic) language is compounded by the fact that he seems to write in a number of different styles, not only across his corpus, but even within single essays and books. This makes it difficult to discern what he actually intends to say; it is hard to find any consistency or final direction in his many publications.

However, it is a testimony to the depth and importance of Heidegger's thinking that there continue to be new phases to interpreting him. To note several, there was substantial early analysis and critique (that ranged from emphasizing existential and ontological issues to exploring his interaction with theology); a subsequent energetic wave, when the 'later Heidegger' appeared after what seemed a dramatic turn; and more recently the requisite comprehensive rereading and reappraisal, after we learned more about the full extent of his entanglement with National Socialism. Now yet another reading all over again is underway, not only as his youthful works become available, but because of the explosive release of *Contributions to Philosophy (From Enowning)*, seen by many as the long-hidden master work and more radical twin to *Being and Time*. In short, it seems that Heidegger has many voices; and that there also are many pulses of Heidegger interpretation.

It is easy to see that Heidegger thinks and writes focally and profoundly about home, homelessness, and homecoming, not only in his more generally known works such as 'Letter on Humanism,' where he speaks of 'the house of being,' or in 'Poetically Man Dwells' and 'Building Dwelling Thinking,' but most everywhere.[1] To cite but one example, in the generative *Contributions* the language of paths, line, map, territory, stages on the way, and ground elaborates into enacting a 'crossing from metaphysics into be-ing historical thinking,' where the 'crossing to the other beginning' (CP 3) through a 'leap into the between' (CP 11) is necessary to go from our currently 'growing uprootedness' (CP 85) through the uncanny/strange (CP 77) and the displacement hidden by the familiar (CP 10–11) toward a revival of be-ing (CP 81). But only the great turning around (coming back) of be-ing itself (CP 129) would be the ground that would allow human being, *Da-sein*, gods, earth and world, to belong with enowning. Thus, abiding in *Ereignis* (CP 19), they would be let come into their ownmost, so that 'uprooting is … overcome by way of a new rooting' (CP 82) in the between. Not only is *Ereignis*' 'turning a counter-turning' (*Wider-Kehre*), but the human being is the returner (*Zurückkehrer*), who, in throwing himself free and then returning from the free throw – that he might 'come to stand in enowning and [have] his abode in the truth of be-ing' (CP 19) – responds to a call that is a calling to homecoming.

Rather than proceeding by raising (much less attempting to answer) questions about what we supposedly know on the basis of previous scholarship or the research literature, we first – more simply – need to try to open to what Heidegger says with this family of words (*Heimat* (homeland), *Heim* (home or abode), homelessness, homecoming, dwelling, site, place, mystery or secret (*Geheimnis*), rootedness (*Bodenständigkeit*), and rootlessness (*Bodenlosigkeit*), attending to that which is given to us and attempting to follow the threads of the network of connections. At times this requires letting the 'key terms' slip into the periphery, so that whatever is laid before us is let come forward. It turns out that in the course of the attempt to so attend, several correlate insights emerge. The first, obviously, is that we do not clearly accumulate correspondences between terms in the vocabulary of home and items of Heidegger's personal life or his 'ideas,' as we might in an intellectual autobiography. In addition, his thinking's constant movements to and fro do not 'develop' or progress in any simple sense, much less in some order that would match the chronology of the works' publication, or even composition; indeed the way his thinking goes back and forth subverts the importance of sequence in 'the linear flow of time.' As a result, Heidegger's work needs to be (seen as) gathered into and followed in some other constellations. Even more importantly, the apparently disorderly unfolding of his corpus (where the works simultaneously, or non-sequentially, develop multiple themes and strategies of inquiry) indicates that the phenomena he explores – metaphysical and non-metaphysical worlds, homelessness and homecoming – may be going on at the same time, in the same place.

Though what I lay out here at the start will have to be shown to be trustworthy and fruitful, it is useful to provide at least a provisional roadmap at the beginning, given the almost bewildering complexity of what Heidegger does and says. Here, then, is a note on how the book is organized, that is, on the way it moves through Heidegger's corpus to follow what he says concerning homelessness and homecoming. I have attempted to listen closely and long (for over thirty years) to Heidegger to discern the way he actually goes about exploring the topic. Now, with so many notes and possible ways to weave together the rich material, I am confident that I can at least present it faithfully to Heidegger's own modes of operation.

The chief principle of interpretation for this book derives from discerning and arranging the many voices with which Heidegger speaks. Employing a literary critical method of analysis and the hermeneutical assumption – as others have also argued and as I have shown in a previous work (*Heidegger's Language and Thinking*) – that Heidegger's thinking belongs inseparably to the language in which it occurs and to the manner in which the thinking and saying are laid before us.

In discovering the way homelessness, homecoming, and home provide the theme and strategy-means to think, we arrive at a key to the inner dynamic of his works. As he moves, in philosophical and poetic language, and across the pre-metaphysical, metaphysical, and post-metaphysical epochs, he acquires distinct, multiple voices. In a discussion with other thinkers and times, he plays out various parts; or, better put, he comes to speak polyphonically. When we set these voices out, the order and relationships among works (sometimes even within a given work) become much clearer. The patterns in Heidegger's thought are not only obscured by the complexities noted above, but occur because he, as a finite learner, does not, cannot, run through the issues in an unidirectional way. He can only say things to us as he learns them – a lifelong process, full of changes, errors, reversals, and dead ends, as he repeatedly tells us. Further, given the character of the phenomena, none of what is found, or needs be said, goes away, as in linear logic or mathematical formulae, which run to an 'end' in the form of a conclusion or sum. What is important in the historical epochs remains, though variously disclosed or concealed over time; in the inner movement of thought, or what is given over for thought, much continues to bear on us today, and enters into the future. As Foucault calls it, it is 'effective history,' still forming part of our live alternatives. Thus, the voices neither succeed one another nor pass away once and for all; rather, they come to the fore or recede to the background; they may be heard solo, then in chorus (in varying combinations). The multiple voices and their stopping and starting are not so hard to hear 'after the fact,' as it were. Once they are pointed out they may even seem to be obvious, as happens when we learn to see the face of the 'man in the moon' or the Big Dipper, or that *lethe* is unsaid, hidden within *aletheia*.

After sustained analysis I discern at least six major story- or song lines – six voices, we can say – running through Heidegger's corpus. That is, if we investigate how what Heidegger says and the mode of saying it are the same and we are alert to how he employs a figural principle of organization rather than a linear logic, we find six voices emerging as he thinks through and tells the story of human and 'ontological' homelessness and homecoming. I ask of you, 'Trust me.' Suppose with me – for the sake of reading, for the adventure of finding intelligible what otherwise (and perhaps in any case) is too confusing. Suppose there are six major voices that form discernable patterns, though in complex ways.

The clearest way to show the patterns is to start by presenting the six modes in schematic form, first describing the basic kinds of language-style and theme for each voice and then adding textual examples. Note that after the third movement (itself a turning) completes a whole 'pulse,' Heidegger 'begins again,' generating another entire phase of three more movements that return to 'repeat' the pattern of the first three.

The Six Modes of Style and Subject Matter

First Cycle

1 Fairly straightforward *representational language*, treating *metaphysical issues* (being, beings, etc.)

2 *Poetically informed language*, explicating *poetizing* and the *holy*
3 (Combining modes 1 and 2) still *direct*, but *poetically informed vocabulary-movement*, transferring to thinking *being*, *language*, *and world*

Second Cycle

4 Two-track thinking, both *clear narrative* (cf. mode 1) and *high originary saying* (cf. modes 2 and 3), swinging to and fro across the history of the A) *not-yet-metaphysical;* B) *metaphysical* (five phases); C) *no-longer-metaphysical*
5 *Originary-poetic musing* (cf. modes 2 and 3) on *disclosure of world by saying* and on what he himself has experienced
6 *Originary, plain, and dialectal saying*, focusing explicitly on *dwelling and place*

A First Cycle of Three Voices

The first cycle is constituted by three sets of works, works of three voices, each with its own combination of mode of language and subject matter.

First Voice

- Language and style – relatively straightforward conceptual explication
- subject matter – traditional metaphysical issues

Heidegger was renowned as a great teacher. But for all his ability to create a new kind of language or, as a kind of Zen master, to awaken us with a slap from what we take for granted, being a brilliant teacher requires being able to present clear explications in traditional representational language that serious listeners can follow.

In the works considered here, Heidegger's focus on and basic concerns with these traditional topics or phenomena are in no way odd, though he teases out the problematic, concealed, hitherto unthought aspects of being, beings, time, knowledge, death, and the history of philosophy. Indeed, these are especially important books to many who read Heidegger as one in a long line of metaphysicians, to many who are interested in his contributions to traditional problems (but not in his other, 'weird' works), to those who seek to understand something about the history of metaphysics that is profound but neither controversial nor likely to elicit unexpected critique or disapproval in the course of obtaining a degree, tenure, publication contracts, or acceptance by the broad philosophical community of those other than Heideggerians. Thus, for example, though Heidegger's *An Introduction to Metaphysics* is certainly not an easy book, a recent commentator could quite correctly say it remains one of his most popular.[2] It is not merely that his metaphysical theme is traditional. So too is his basic mode of analysis and historical narrative. He successfully works to show how ideas develop or change so as to lose meaning between major figures or epochs. Indeed, his explications have been so powerful and convincing that we have absorbed them, often not realizing how much of what we believe stems from Heidegger and how much has not always been held to be so. Especially important is the fact that his vocabulary largely consists of concepts that are familiar and are used in the usual manner. To be sure, he does introduce novel terms and categories that he would like to add to the accepted vocabulary – or even to supplant terms he finds especially problematic. But he is trying hard to clarify a traditional subject matter. As a specific example, he gives us ideas and language such as the following: 'But if we consider the question of being in the sense of an inquiry into being as such, it becomes clear to anyone who follows our thinking that being as such is precisely hidden from metaphysics, and remains forgotten – and so radically that the forgetfulness of being, which itself falls into forgetfullness, is the unknown but enduring impetus to metaphysical questioning' (IM 15–16).

Second Voice

- Language and style – poetically informed language
- subject matter – poetry itself, the poetic approach and language, and the holy

Heidegger was not only a great teacher but also – and surely because he was a great teacher – a great learner. As he struggled to rethink traditional metaphysical topics and representational language he realized that those twinned dimensions were together a major part of the problem. He came to see that there were powerful insights into what he sought to articulate, and even before that, he came to discern poetry in what was often derided as the opposite, or absence, of philosophy. So, he carefully read and reflected upon what poetry had to say on its own: how its proper focus seemed to be, not being, but the holy; how its language was distinct from the concepts of philosophy, yet having its own kind of precision; how the poetic approach was distinct, often circling about its theme or devolving from a figural unity rather than moving as a linear flow (*dis-cursis*) of logical discourse; how poetic language pushed beyond the descriptive or analytic norms of the language intended to correctly represent the way things are or ought to be.

It is not that Heidegger himself speaks on poetic topics here. He reads and explicates the poetic and acquires what might be called a poetically informed language. It is as if he learns to think and speak with a kind of poetic accent, while following what the poets say and how they say it. In these works we can hear Heidegger taking up and practising – even echoing – poetic language and a poetic way of reflecting. He provides explications, but the explications are not translations into clear representational concepts; rather, in an almost old-fashioned manner they explicate in a language that unfolds in the same terms as the poetic theme. They operate in a mode that in the end seems almost to consist of paraphrases, as the commentator thinks a text through and leads the reader along in the poet's own language. This is one reason why works of the second set, those of the second voice, have substantially influenced literary criticism. Those looking for deeper understanding, especially of Hölderlin, are not especially looking for a translation into philosophical terms. For the same reason, many philosophers are dismayed or disinterested in these works, seeing them as weak attempts to speak as a poet. I contend, though, that here we find the voice of Heidegger as he begins to learn, not as a logician-metaphysician, but as another, just-emerging sort of thinker, exploring a non-metaphysical theme by learning to hear and speak in a poetic mode and with a poetic vocabulary. For example, Heidegger writes, 'The joyous is the serene. We call this also "the spatially-ordered" ... The spatially-ordered is, within its spatiality, freed, clarified, and integrated. The serene, the spatially-ordered, is alone able to house everything in its proper place. The joyous has its being in the serene, which serenifies ... While the serenification makes everything clear, the serene allots each thing to that place of existence whereby in its nature it belongs, so that it may stand there in the brightness of the serene, like a still light, proportionate to its own being' (RP 247). Clearly we have two distinctive voices thus far.

Third Voice

- Language and style – poetic vocabulary and movement
- subject matter – transferred to philosophical issues of being, language, and world

- As a result, Heidegger, no longer just practising, actually arrives at a new competence and a fresh realm

Here we find works that reap the benefits of simultaneously working in voices 1 and 2. By means of learning how the poetic Hölderlin thought and spoke about his proper subject matter (the holy) and by pushing to the limits how representational philosophical concepts clarify and obscure being and beings, Heidegger passes beyond practising for what might be his especially distinctive contribution. That is, he begins to come to his own with a new, clear role – neither traditional metaphysical thinker working in a representational conceptual vocabulary and logical analytic approach nor an apprentice poet attempting to speak of the holy. Creating a hybrid, he addresses being, human being, and language in a vocabulary largely derived from Hölderlin and in a style that variously lays down sentence after sentence as a poem sets out images and lines, not running from premise to conclusion but setting each into place with the others so that all remain in sight, connected as much with what came before as to what follows. Here, relationships either emerge as explicit or call on us to make them so in our reading and response. (Especially in the last of these works the features commonly associated with the 'later Heidegger' begin to appear – a point to be developed as we go.)

For instance, he writes, 'Man is not the lord of beings. Man is the shepherd of being. Man loses nothing in this "less"; rather, he gains in that he attains the truth of being. He gains the essential poverty of the shepherd, whose dignity consists in being called by being itself into the preservation of being's truth' (LH 221). 'Thinking gathers language into simple saying. In this way language is the language of being, as clouds are the clouds of the sky. With its saying, thinking lays inconspicuous furrows in language. They are still more inconspicuous than the furrows that the farmer, slow of step, draws through the field' (LH 242). Here we clearly have a third voice, the fusion of philosophical subject matter and poetic language.

Toward a Second Cycle of Three Voices

Insofar as he has developed an increasingly originary vocabulary and reflective mode he might be able to stop speaking in voices 1 and 2. But lest the seemingly innocent word 'insofar' cover up a multitude of successful and limited efforts, of which Heidegger is far more aware than we, the learning and doing remains underway. Further, since this third voice is a new and distinctive mode in which to think and write it would inform but not replace the first and second voices. Since what is thought coincides with how it is thought, Heidegger's success thus far makes him strong and confident enough to further develop both the philosophical analysis of being and the appropriate attention to the poet's celebration of the holy. With the accomplishment of speaking with these first three voices, each of which has its place and critical contribution to make, Heidegger wants to press even further, to realize the most that might come from what is given to him and to which he can more fully respond with his increasing capacity. Thus, he does not so much pause and consolidate as launch into a full second cycle of the three distinct modes of thinking and saying.

Informed by what has been learned – and integrated – in the first three modes of thinking and speaking, he returns to *repeat* the entire threefold process, now (he tells us) with a deeper experience and a *newly developing originary manner of thinking and saying* with which to *recover,* and again *span across the history of metaphysics,* the relationship of *poetizing language and world,* and the focal phenomena of *dwelling, region, building.* In the following robust works, Heidegger's thinking becomes even subtler and more complex as the play among the various dimensions to be thought unfolds. In this second cycle he more often than not is doing several things at once, allowing several voices to be heard in the same set of writings or even within a particular essay or book.

Fourth Voice

- Language and style – doubled, two-track thinking: clear analytic and narrative (cf. voice 1) and high originary saying (cf. voices 2 and 3), moving to and fro across, etc.
- subject matter – the three great epochs:
  - The not-yet-metaphysical
  - The metaphysical (with five subphases)
  - The no-longer-metaphysical.

Continuing from, but beyond, what he began in the first voice, Heidegger further delineates the history of metaphysics, which amounts to the history of the disclosure and concealment of being. Since he has already found that neither the history of being itself nor our partial, finite understanding occurs in a singular, linear flow, he has to find a way to doubly think the three epochs all at the same time, as it were, that is, all in one complex motion. Again, we can appreciate that his writing would need to be even more complex than before (elsewhere). However, he resumes a *fairly direct treatment* of the unfolding of the three historical-epochal streams. Indeed, some of his most insightful analysis and clearest narrative occur in these works; as we see with *What Is Called Thinking?*, he also more fully develops his distinctive vocabulary and movement to and fro – culminating in *his 'high originary' mode of meditative thinking* (which exemplifies the style perhaps most readily associated with the 'later Heidegger'). Here he explicitly practises a two-track thinking that intertwines representational or calculative thinking with non-representational meanings that are thinking's proper analogue to poetry and mysticism.

Since one of the great insights from the first cycle was that such meditative thinking was an appropriate mode to appreciate – even to recover – the non-linear historical unfolding of being in the three major epochs, he can see and say how the not-yet-metaphysical yielded to and was obscured by the metaphysical, which transforms through at least five discernable subphases (consisting of the Greek, Roman, medieval, modern, and current technological eras, the latter inaugurated in the last century) and which may yet be 'countered' by the no-longer-metaphysical. The latter would arrive, not by succeeding or replacing the metaphysical, since the metaphysical has just begun its long reign, but by triply *leaping* from where we are (in the *metaphysical*) over to the *not-yet-metaphysical*, and thence into the *no-longer-metaphysical – then continuing to move to and fro among these realms.* In this complex meditative retrieval, Heidegger crosses back and forth over the history of metaphysics (a project he clearly already set out as a major task in the revolutionary *Contributions*).

This set of works, then, has its own mini-chorus of voices, as *the two-track thinking retrieves non-representational meanings and weaves those together with the representational* while passing back and forth from the early Greek, through all the phases of metaphysics, and to the originary, no-longer-metaphysical alternative. In two examples of his two-track thinking, both from the same work, *What Is Called Thinking?*, we first hear his clear, teacherly voice and then his meditative reflection, both 'explaining' what thinking is. In clear, representational language:

> Is there anyone among us who does not know what it is to form an idea? When we form an idea of something – of a text if we are philologists, or a work of art if we are art historians, a combustion process if we are chemists

> – we have a representational idea of those objects. Where do we have those ideas? We have them in our head. We have them in our consciousness. We have them in our soul. We have the ideas inside ourselves, these ideas of objects. (WCT 39)

As non-representational, recollective saying:

> The *thanc* means man's inmost mind, the heart, the heart's core, that innermost essence of man which reaches outward most fully and to the outermost limits, and so decisively that, rightly considered, the idea of an inner and an outer word does not arise. The *thanc*, the heart's core, is the gathering of all that concerns us, all that we care for, all that touches us insofar as we are, as human beings. (WCT 144)

Finally, as an example of how the latter evolves into his high originary mode of meditative retrieval:

> Nestling, malleable, pliant, compliant, nimble – in old German these are called *ring* and *gering*. The mirror-play of the worlding world, as the ringing of the ring, wrests free the united four in their own compliancy, the circling compliancy of their presence. So nestling, they join together, worlding, the world. (T 179–80)

It might seem as if this were more than enough: the whole history of metaphysics, of being's unfolding, in two modes, representational-conceptual and originary-recollective thinking. Yet Heidegger has arrived at what could be considered the 'height of his powers' and has more to say.

Fifth Voice

- Language and style – high originary-poetic musing (cf. voices 2, 3, and 4)
- subject matter – the disclosure of world by saying what he himself has experienced

Having arrived at his own voice and experience, in a way that he could not have before the dialogue with the poets, Heidegger's originary stance and mode of speaking rejoin with the poets'. Now he no longer learns from them by explicating them in a way that is heavily accented by their mode of thinking and speaking; rather, he meditates poetically on his own. Even compared with the high originary tone of the fourth voice, here his movement is notably slower, denser still, even more hesitant and careful. His words often come in short phrases, one quietly placed after the other, with few connective terms. As a result, this voice seldom speaks in long, smoothly flowing sentences. Instead we have a series of 'sayings' alternating with gently forced pauses. I do not mean to exaggerate, since it is not so dramatic as 'phrase,' stop (and think the phenomena), 'phrase,' stop (and think the phenomena). There are sentences that are fairly normal, but the effect is that he is speaking very deliberately with a slow tempo, such that we are meant not to run along at speed, but to respond by slowing ourselves down in receiving what is given.

An additional difference in the fifth voice is that, unlike the fourth one, which does also use a high originary manner of thinking beyond being, here the subject is again poetic saying itself (as with voice 2). Heidegger does continue to explicate, but as just noted, not as a learner. Now he participates as a full partner in meditating on what it is that the poets show. With them he continues to go beyond being to consider the relationship between language-saying-poetizing and world disclosure. Thus, whereas voice 4 reached a high originary thinking (intertwined with clear narrative) that, for all its newness, still said what was the thinker's 'proper' concern, in the fifth voice Heidegger passes over into a poetic musing on the poetic.

For instance, in the fifth voice Heidegger says, 'Language is the tongue ... Language is the flower of the mouth. In language the earth blossoms toward the bloom of the sky ... When the word is called the mouth's flower and its blossom, we hear the sound of language rising like the earth. From whence? From saying in which it comes to pass that world is made to appear' (NL 97, 99, 101). Here we can especially understand the divided opinion about his work. Those who would have someone who is supposedly a philosopher utilize analytic, logical language and stick to properly philosophical topics would have little patience either with what Heidegger says or with how he says it. Clearly, the works operating with the fifth voice would be unattractive given such expectations (of course, Heidegger has long since ceased to call himself a philosopher for just such reasons).

Finally, just as in his long apprenticeship of the first set of works, where he fused the metaphysical-representational dimension of the first voice with the poetic dimension of the second to achieve an initial competence to speak with a poetic inflection about being, in this fully mature second cycle, he can unify the fourth voice's already complex clear narrative and high originary saying of what comes after being with the fifth voice's poetic saying of language to create a sixth voice that explicitly focuses on dwelling and place.

Sixth Voice

- Languages and style – after continuing originary, then plain and dialectal saying
- subject matter – dwelling, place, abiding, building

As he concentrates on the intricate knot, or mystery, of the complex gathering and interplay of the multiple dimensions that constitute cultural and personal dwelling within the opening and closing of historical worlds, over the years Heidegger generates a diverse set of works *that focus explicitly on dwelling, place, region, abiding, and building.* In setting forth this specific subject matter, Heidegger shifts across several distinct sorts of language and style, the first of which continues the *high originary mode* developed in voices 4 and 5, again combining what he gained from the movement across the history of metaphysics and what he has been able to say originarily about the unfolding of a fourfold world by way of things and words.

However, Heidegger comes to appreciate that for all the lessons of the poets leading to his high originary voice, there are other poetic modes too, modes that correlate more closely with the language of the place from which they spring and the simplicity of the ordinary but remain crucially far removed from the trivializing 'average everyday.' Insofar as this manner of saying is familiar to us, it is likely as the mode of thinking and saying which the meditative masters practise and commend. Returning to pick up a way of speaking that he heard early in life from country folk, Heidegger now *achieves an increasingly plain manner of delineating the splendour of 'the simple.'* One could almost say that this language and thinking are deceptively simple, except that there is no deception; there is only as much quiet reflexivity and resonance – disclosure – as Heidegger can manage, or that is given to him.

The difference between the plain talk we are now considering and the high originary mode of voice five (continued here) is striking. To note typical examples of each, whereas the latter says that dwelling means 'to remain at peace within the free, the preserve, the free sphere [the open] that safeguards each thing in its nature' (BDT 149), the former tells us, 'anyone can follow the path of meditative thinking in his own manner and within his own limits. Why? Because man is a thinking, that is, a meditating being. This meditative thinking need by no means be high-flown. It is enough if we dwell on what lies close and meditate on what is closest; upon that which concerns us, each one of us, here and now; here, on this patch of home ground; now, in the present hour of history' (MA 47).

Finally, Heidegger releases himself altogether from his own ventures in originary language, instead passing back not only to plain talk but to *dialect*, with the help of local neighbours who still speak it and a few select poets who hone it. Heidegger comes to abide in the stillest language and thought of all as, in the end, he enters into the yet-*vibrant mother tongue* of a given valley (or watershed), where the deepest origins of language are held and still may come forth. (We will need to wait to hear an example of this, since it needs significant preparation on our part.)

We have six voices, then, learned and developed over a lifetime, combined in various ways. Discerning this can significantly help us understand why Heidegger writes as he does, what he is doing in any specific work, and how the different works in fact form a complex whole, not a confusing or frustratingly inconsistent jumble.

As noted above, in the course of reading, rereading, and interpreting Heidegger's many essays and books, I have tried out a great many versions of how the works might go together if heard in their distinctive modes of writing and thinking. Extensive notes and analyses of each one led to considering multiple possible complexes. But no matter what the minor variations, even taking into account the fact that many works speak with several voices, we find the same basic pattern emerging again and again. I am not interested in 'proving' that there are these and only these six sets of writings, much less that precisely this arrangement of particular works into these six strands obtains, though I have made every effort to conscientiously discern and present the textual basis for such a reading (at least, as much as any non–hyper-specialized reader might be willing to consider). Indeed, as with any approach to a rich body of work, open to multiple interpretations from various and changing horizons, mine would welcome, and I would expect, alternative arrangements. For instance, there are, in fact, good reasons to consider the first part of the sixth set of works as a continuation of the fourth or fifth sets – though doing so would make it a bit more difficult to follow, while in no way changing the overall pattern.

To help keep matters straight, figure 1 gives a somewhat fuller version of the schema of where and how Heidegger goes, a map that will be delineated in detail by close readings as we go along. The diagram makes explicit the specific ways in which, over forty-five years, he develops the distinctive voices or styles through more than seventy-five books and essays (often in the same time period, and even simultaneously within a given work).

Yet, even discerning a major principle of organization of Heidegger's corpus does not make the most important point, that these six voices actually all think through and beyond the history of being – the unfolding of what is given and concealed – by means of the figural logic of homelessness and homecoming. The six voices play out the phases of the motif, precisely, though totally unpredictably, along the lines of the trajectory laid out by Hölderlin in his poetic *ur*-phenomenology of homecoming.

Insofar as Heidegger's thinking and saying are inseparable, his works would not always be traditionally linear and 'logical,' because in attempting to overcome and replace the representational, he needs to employ an alternative language and organization. The possibility becomes fulfilled, we will see, as he sets into work a figural unity – where the figure is none other than the dynamic complex of homelessness-homecoming-home. It turns out that many, if not most, of Heidegger's later works, and the overall chorus of his many voices, proceed from this wellspring. In other words, the leitmotif of homelessness-homecoming is a principle of organization of much of his corpus, as is shown by the chapter titles of my book, which are straightforwardly descriptive of the subject matter:

1 At Home in Metaphysics' Uncanny Homelessness
2 Poetic Wandering in the Foreign
3 Turning Toward the Overcoming of Homelessness
4 Originary Homecoming: The Moment of Arrival
5 Learning to Become at Home in Saying
6 Staying Near the Source

Further, and surprisingly, the explication will clarify that the six different modes which emerge in the works to be considered not only articulate different dimensions of the subject matter, but retrieve the same six phases of the phenomena that Hölderlin delineated (according to Heidegger's interpretation): 1) initial being at home (even though not at home there); 2) homelessness or wandering in the foreign; 3) turning toward home; 4) a moment of homecoming or arrival; 5) learning to become at home; 6) and abiding or dwelling near the primal source, the home. That this might be so, I discovered only lately, and then almost

Figure 1. The story of homelessness and homecoming.

Six voices in seventy-seven works, across forty-five years (see the abbreviations section for the titles of works). In terms of the entire body of works, the first and second sets of works generate the third; the fourth is like the first, and the fifth is like the second; the fourth and fifth generate the sixth; the sixth is like the third:

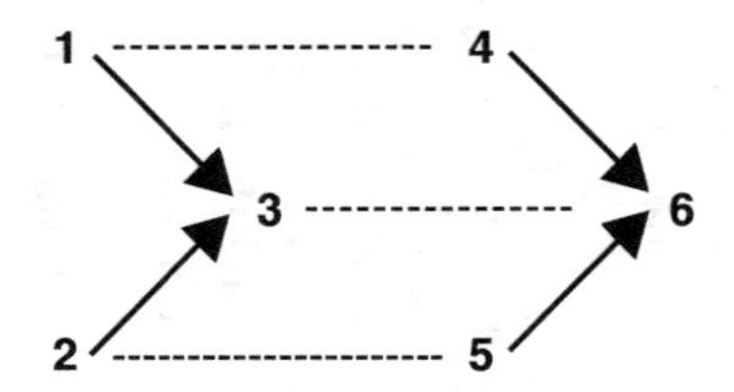

1927 28 29 30-35 36 37 38 39 40 41 42 43 44 45 46 47 48 49 50 51 52 53 54 55 56 57 58 59 60 61 62 63 64 65 66 67 68 69 70 71 72 73

1 BT WM IM AWP MHB WN OM
BPP ET N SHBM
RM

2 HEP WWAF A
RP

3 CP PWM OM LH TU
WN WPF

4 A) AL LO AF WCT M

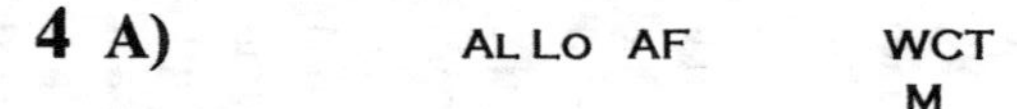

B)

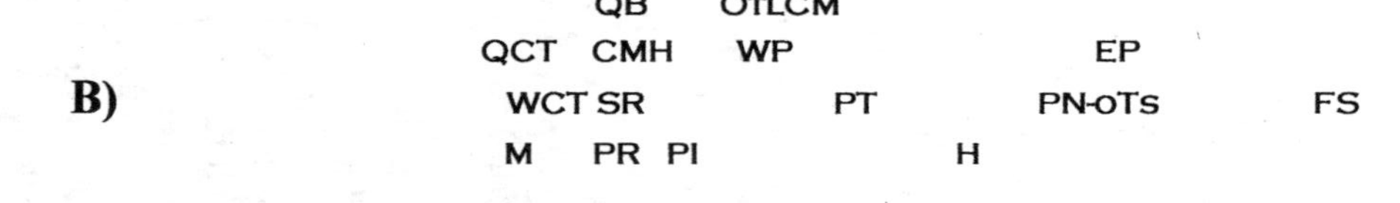

C) DL STB
TH WCT PI WL TB H

5

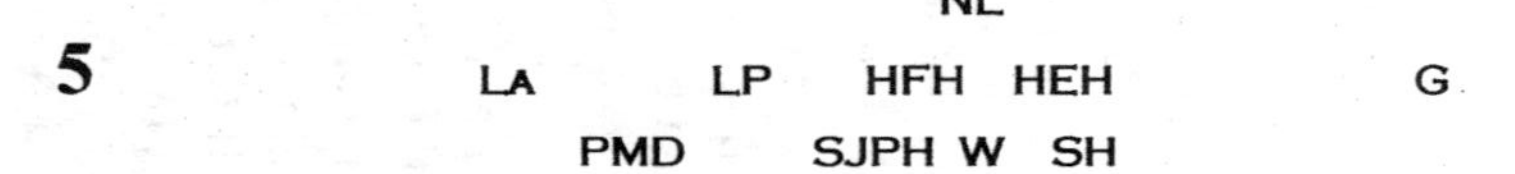

WISP ——→ **6** CCP TH BDT GG AOWA AASC AS
OWA P JPHZ WD 700M VH DM SER
MA DHP FHT

1927 28 29 30-35 36 37 38 39 40 4142 43 44 45 46 47 48 49 50 51 52 53 54 55 56 57 58 59 60 61 62 63 64 65 66 67 68 69 70 71 72 73

accidentally, after reading again and again and 'classifying' each work. Though readers, of course, will have to decide for themselves, this correlation is a further confirmation for me of the congruence, especially because I had made a mistake along the complicated way, generating notes that indicated that Hölderlin had seven stages in his homecoming. Thus, the six modes of Heidegger's writing and saying came forth quite independently of my having any focal awareness of Hölderlin's six stages.

But later in the process of writing and working out descriptive headings and titles for the six sets within the corpus, there was a 'click,' after which the correspondence between the style of the six distinctive sets and the anatomy of Hölderlin's stages seemed obvious. If this homology is so, either this is deliberate on Heidegger's part or it is unconscious but not surprising, insofar as such an archetypal pattern would be holistic, or in that 'reality will out.' If it is not so, nothing earth-shattering results; there is no loss of any crucial point beyond the loveliness of difference in unity. That is, this correlation is not any sort of hypothesis that I would prove, but a gestalt that seemed to emerge and add an additional dimension of meaning. In any case, the leitmotif of homelessness-homecoming can help us understand not only Heidegger's diversity of styles, but the inner structure and dynamic of a large part of his corpus, and thence the sense of the individual works and otherwise apparently disconnected facets of his writing.

Where does all this leave us? We have the story of how, hidden along the way, unfolding from the earliest Greek thinkers, an originary alternative to the increasingly metaphysical-technological world might yet be given to us. Such an originary dimension or possibility is articulated at the beginning by the early Greeks (for example, Heraclitus), during the long metaphysical epoch, by deviants (from *de-via,* literally, 'turned from the straight road') who go by another way – especially mystics and poets such as Meister Eckhart and Hölderlin, and today, as Heidegger would hope for the work of his best moments, by himself. That is why Heidegger gathers his thinking and saying together with Heraclitus' and Hölderlin's, meditating on homelessness and homecoming in an originary manner, as they did. Given his intimacy with, even imitation of, the language and movements of thinkers and poets such as Heraclitus and Hölderlin, it may be helpful if we start our exploration by first attending to what Heidegger does and says about them, and then staying appropriately alert to how this informs his work and subsequently tells us about him. Thus, in asking if, and how, Heidegger makes sense, we can take a clue from what he says about Heraclitus:

> He is called 'the Obscure' [ὁ Σκοτεινός] ... Heraclitus had this reputation even when his writings were preserved intact ... [We still do not have] what is essential: the definitive, all-articulating unity of the inner structure of Heraclitus' writing. Only a constantly advancing insight into this structure will reveal the point from which the individual fragments are speaking, and in what sense each of them, as a saying, must be heard. Because we can scarcely surmise what the well-spring is that gives the writing of Heraclitus its unity, and because we find this source so difficult to think, we are justified in calling this thinker 'the Obscure.' Even the inherent meaning of what this epithet says to us remains obscure.
>
> Heraclitus is called 'the Obscure.' But he is the Lucid. For he tells of the lighting whose shining he attempts to call forth into the language of thinking. Insofar as it illuminates, the lighting endures. We call its illumination the lighting [*die Lichtung*]. What belongs to it, and how and where it takes place, still remain to be considered ... Lighting bestows the shining, opens what shines to an appearance. The open is the realm of unconcealment and is governed by disclosure. What belongs to the latter, and whether and to what extent disclosing and lighting are the Same, remain to be asked. (Al 102–3)

Since we have the same kind of challenge in learning how to understand Heidegger, if we reflexively apply what he says about Heraclitus we find our task is actually also to discern 'the definitive, all-articulating unity of the inner structure of [Heidegger's] writing' because only insight into the wellspring that provides the unity of his writing will enable us to understand 'the point from which the individual fragments are speaking, and in what sense each of them, as a saying, must be heard.' Just as the source of Heraclitus' writing is difficult to think, so obviously is Heidegger's. Yet, it need not be so hard, as is often supposed. I contend that with homelessness and homecoming we discern a leitmotif that provides a figural unity to his life's work – a key that Heidegger has left hidden in plain sight.

To the extent that Heidegger begins to think explicitly what the Greeks – save perhaps Homer – did not, Heraclitus' lighting and Heidegger's homecoming would say the same. Hence, continuing to reflexively read what Heidegger said about Heraclitus in the quotation above, now substituting Heidegger's homecoming for Heraclitus' lighting, we find both paragraphs directly apply to and help us interpret Heidegger's work. The first paragraph correlates with my investigation of the leitmotif as the source of the figural unity and meaning of much of Heidegger's corpus; with the second paragraph, we would hear the following paraphrase:

> Heidegger too is called obscure, but he is also lucid. For he tells of the homecoming whose gathering together he attempts to call forth into the language of thinking. Insofar as it summons and assembles what belongs together even when apart, the homecoming endures. We call its assembling the homecoming. What belongs to it, and how and where it takes place, still remain to be considered ... Homecoming [endows, bestows] is the granting of the gathering together, letting what gathers together come into its own, all together and each. Home – also named *einräumen: roden* – is the region that allows [admits] arrival and abiding, and is governed by giving. What belongs to the latter, and whether and to what extent giving and homecoming are the Same, remain to be asked.

Here we find Heidegger's task, and mine. Perhaps, the readers' too.

1 At Home in Metaphysics' Uncanny Homelessness

When Heidegger begins to speak in his published writings, he already stands in the midst of that which he needs to think and say. Whatever he is able to see and to show us must first have given itself to him, and that means to us too. Supposedly, that single object of Heidegger's thought has been clearly identified: being. But do we know this? And how? And what does it mean? Alternatively, it is held that he tells us about our existence, about human being. But is this what he says? In what ways would he do so?

If we listen carefully to Heidegger, we find that he provides neither an analysis of being nor of human being singly, nor yet of the two simply conjoined. Rather, he tells us, over and over in various ways, the story of homelessness. This is a story of metaphysics, though not merely a metaphysical tale, because, though he relates the history of being which draws human being into its unfolding, the story strives to reach beyond metaphysics, both in its substance and in its mode of speaking. Indeed, that it is a story, a saying thinking, is part of the way it is no longer even philosophy, that is, metaphysical thought. Before we can understand how Heidegger's story is not about either being or human being, conceived as independent givens that are connected by certain relationships, we need to hear how he begins to talk about what he has seen and how he thinks and says what is unfolding, the *unheimlich*, which, at least to begin with, we can take to mean uncanny homelessness.

As noted in the introduction, I am not covering Heidegger's early work, including *Being and Time;* that is too huge a topic, calling for another volume (and is already treated by other scholarship).[1] But there is a fundamental point of departure in *Being and Time,* a point of critical disclosure, without which it is almost impossible to make sense of what follows. Why would homecoming be a compelling human and philosophical issue? In some sense it intuitively seems desirable to be 'at home.' Even before we begin to define what home means it seems to be taken for granted that home connotes a positively valorized place or condition in *Being and Time* (though that is often not the case in our experience). Insofar as we existentially lose home because of a natural disaster or war, because of a death or divorce, or because of some other personal, family, or cultural displacement, we usually, but not always, miss what is lost and desire some kind of return. Insofar as the displacement would be metaphysical, collapsing our grounding and orientation in the world/cosmos, it would seem that a recovery would require, or even amount to, an ontological homecoming. But matters are not so simple.

The Uncanny and Da-sein: Not Being-at-Home

Since Heidegger is a technically trained, professional philosopher who is focused on the question of being, it is not immediately clear why he approaches the subject matter as he does. He explores the most difficult, even austere, problems by way of a vocabulary of loss and recovery, of dwelling and displacement, of the familiar and the uncanny. Among the related terms, he uses home (*Heim*), Homeland, native place (*Heimat*), homeless (*heimatlos*), homey (*heimisch*), concealed, secret, hidden, snug (*heimlich*), at home, in one's own country (*daheim*), indigenous, native (*einheimisch*), secret, mysterious (*Geheimnis*), obscure, hidden (*geheimnisvoll*), being-at-home (*zuhause*), and not-being-at home and homelessness (*un-zuhause, Unheimlichkeit*); familiarity (*Vertrautheit*) and the uncanny (*unheimlich*) or strange or alien (*fremd*); dwelling, staying, holding open (*Aufenthalt, sich aufhalten*); rootedness (*Verwurzelung*) and uprooting (*Entwurzelung*); ground or foundation (*Grund, Boden*) and groundlessness (*Bodenlos*); autochthony (*Bodenständigkeit*) and primordial source or origin (*Ursprung, ursprünglich*); falling prey, entangled, and ensnared (*Verfallen*); belonging (*hin/zu-gehören*) and lostness (*Verlorenheit/sein*); return to the source (*Herkunft*) and retrieve or raise again (*wiederholen/ung*); flight and turning away (*Flucht, Abkehr*), as well as coming toward (*zukommen, Zu-kunft*), arrival (*Ankunft*), and return into (*Umkehr*), call back (*Rückruf*); world (*Welt*), surrounding world (*Umwelt*), and deworlding (*Entweltlichung*) or worldless (*Weltlos*); clearing (*Lichtung*) and Open (*Offenheit*); far and near (*Ferne* und *Nähe*); making room (*einräumen, verräumlichen*), place, location, locus (*Ort*), and region (*Gegend*).[2] Why does he proceed and speak this way?

The answer lies in his contention that there are two modes of access to being, which in the end take us along the same way of thinking. First, there is the philosophical tradition in which, in the West, philosophers have reflected on being and beings for over twenty-five hundred years. However, Heidegger argues that this tradition has in fact uprooted and obscured the important phenomena and is now a barrier that needs to be removed:

> The tradition that hereby gains dominance makes what it 'transmits' so little accessible that initially and for the most part it covers over instead. What has been handed down hands it over to obviousness; it bars access to those original 'wellsprings' out of which the traditional categories and concepts were in part genuinely drawn. The tradition even makes us forget such a provenance altogether. Indeed, it makes us wholly incapable of even understanding that such a return is necessary. The tradition uproots the historicity of Da-sein ... and ... tries to veil its own groundlessness ... Consequently ... Da-sein no longer understands the most elementary conditions which alone make a positive return to the past possible – in the sense of its productive appropriation. (BT 21)[3]

> ... the question of the meaning of being was not only unresolved, not only inadequately formulated, but in spite of all interest in 'metaphysics' has even been forgotten ... The ontology that thus arises is ensnared by the tradition, which allows it to sink to the level of the obvious and become mere material for reworking ... Greek ontology thus uprooted becomes a fixed body of doctrine in the Middle Ages ... The beings just cited remain unquestioned with respect to the being and structure of their being, which indicates the thorough neglect of the question of being ... If the question of being is to achieve clarity regarding its own history, a loosening of the sclerotic tradition and a dissolving of the concealments produced is necessary. We understand this task as a destructuring of the traditional content of ancient ontology which is to be carried out along the *guidelines of the question of being.* This destructuring is based upon the original experiences. (BT 21–2)

> The question of being attains true concreteness only when we carry out the destructuring of the ontological tradition. By so doing we can thoroughly demonstrate the inescapability of the question of the meaning of being and so demonstrate the meaning of our talk about a 'retrieve' of this question. (BT 26)

Heidegger not only points to the need to return to the original source and experience but contends that doing so requires radically taking the tradition apart: 'the task of a destructuring of the history of ontology' and basing a new start on an analysis of the phenomena of Da-sein, a term already used several times but not yet defined (BT 19). Here we find the second route to philosophizing adequately, which, Heidegger claims, is also the only way to deconstruct and reconstruct the first way. The short version of what Heidegger means is that humans directly provide access to being in their possibilities or dimensions as Da-sein. That, in fact, is the basic definition of Da-sein. Our human 'kind of being' is 'distinctively different from other beings' in that 'Da-sein is a being which is concerned in its being about that being' (BT 115, 82). Critically, this is not a matter of a being fixed or determined but of having open possibilities, which means that Da-sein is not only concerned about its being in understanding it, but also in choices and self-founding action. Hence, Heidegger also says, 'Da-sein is always essentially its possibility, it can "choose" itself in its being, it can win itself, it can lose itself, or it can never and only "apparently" win itself' (BT 42). According to Heidegger, by way of an adequate, never yet attempted, analysis of the structure of Da-sein in the world, we could recover the possibilities concealed in experience and the access to being that can be found therein. He speaks of this in terms of struggle and violence, and the reasons for his doing so need to be explored: 'The way of encountering being and the structures of being in the mode of phenomenon must first be wrested from the objects of phenomenology ... The idea of an "originary" and "intuitive" grasp and explication of phenomena must be opposed to the naïveté of an accidental, "immediate," and unreflective "beholding"' (BT 36–7); 'Truth (discoveredness) must always first be wrested from beings. Beings are torn from concealment,' which was originally articulated in the way the 'Greeks express themselves about the essence of truth with a privative expression [*a-letheia*] ... (taken out of hiding)' (BT 222). Nor is the task ever done with, once and for all; just the opposite, 'Da-sein must explicitly and essentially appropriate what has also already been discovered, defend it against illusion and distortion, and ensure itself of its discoveredness again and again' (BT 222).

There is a further consideration, however, because even if Da-sein exists in a special relation to being, our understanding not only of being but of Da-sein itself is prevented by the philosophical tradition because 'in its manner of existing at any given time, and accordingly also with the understanding of being that belongs to it, Da-sein grows into a customary interpretation of itself and grows up in that interpretation. It understands itself in terms of this interpretation' (BT 20): 'Da-sein not only has the inclination to be entangled in the world in which it is and to interpret itself in terms of that world by its reflected light; at the same time Da-sein is also entangled in a tradition which it more or less explicitly grasps. This tradition deprives Da-sein of its own leadership in questioning and choosing. This is especially true of that understanding (and its possible development) which is rooted in the most proper being of Da-sein – the ontological understanding' (BT 21).

How to break through to a new understanding of Da-sein and, thereby, of being? Here lies the project of *Being and Time* that justifiably made Heidegger famous. Were we to follow the tradition we would investigate human being from either of two points of view. We could focus on the internal, subjective dimensions of human life or we could turn to external, objective dimensions of the world, for example, the objects we encounter. Heidegger rejects both approaches, needing to find a way to free us from our ensnaring tradition. To begin again requires thinking in a way that is open to seeing human being and the world as given together, not as separated.

Properly understood, holding that Da-sein is the being uniquely oriented to understanding being is our starting point, which also requires bearing in mind a distinction between considering beings in their existence (the ontical) and their being – being itself (the ontological). Heidegger plays with the fact that the things nearest to us often are the hardest to see and with the problem that what is farthest nonetheless needs to be brought nearer. Da-sein is elusive, ambiguous in both respects: 'Da-sein is ontically not only what is near or even nearest – we ourselves *are* it, each of us. Nevertheless, or precisely for this reason, it is ontologically what is farthest removed'; 'Da-sein is ontically "nearest" to itself, ontologically farthest away; but pre-ontologically certainly not foreign to itself' (BT 15, see also 43–4). Thus, for all the complexity and difficulty, we do have a way to begin. To avoid becoming entangled in traditional metaphysics or science and even before attempting a new philosophical construction, Heidegger shows that we can gain an initial access to the phenomena at stake through the way Da-sein occurs and is given to itself pre-ontologically. We could say that it already happens in our everyday, pre-reflective life – if we but could see it and make it explicit: 'And because average everydayness constitutes the ontic immediacy of this being, it was and will be passed over again and again in the explication of Da-sein. What is ontically nearest and familiar is ontologically the farthest, unrecognized and constantly overlooked in its methodological significance. Augustine asks ... "But what is closer to me than 'myself?'"' (BT 44).

But the analysis into ourselves could not begin with introspection into our inner subjective processes, since we really find ourselves, see ourselves, by way of the outside world in which we live. As Heidegger puts it, 'Rather, in accordance with the kind of being belonging to it, Da-sein tends to understand its own being in terms of that being to which it is essentially, continually, and most closely related – the "world." In Da-sein itself and therewith in its own understanding of being, as we shall show, the way the world is understood is ontologically reflected back upon the interpretation of Da-sein' (BT 15). Complementarily, an understanding oriented to or from the outside does not imply that we proceed from objects as conceptually defined in the history of our culture, as with the concept of 'nature,' which actually blocks the intelligibility of the world, or in the scientific view of material extended in absolute, homogeneous space and experienced as something in a specific position (BT 65, 101–2, 361–2). Rather, Heidegger intends to show that these concepts and views depend upon a prior – and different – mode of engagement in which Da-sein is in the world, but not as a mere object in space, and where, in fact, the former generates the latter ordinary, taken-for-granted aspect: 'even one's own Da-sein initially becomes "discoverable" by looking away from its "experiences" ... Da-sein initially finds "itself" in what it does, needs, expects, has charge of, in the things at hand which it initially takes care of in the surrounding world' (BT 119).

What first shows itself to us, as nearest and pre-ontological, is Da-sein in everyday life and everydayness. According to Heidegger, 'The manner of access and interpretation ... should show that being as it is *initially and for the most part – in its average everydayness* [*Alltäglichkeit*]. Not arbitrary and accidental structures but essential ones are to be demonstrated in this everydayness, structures that remain determinative in every mode of being of factual Da-sein. By looking at the fundamental constitution of the everydayness of Da-sein we shall bring out in a preparatory way the being of this being' (BT 16–17).

Heidegger's analysis also proves to be a demonstration that everydayness substantially focuses on comfort and ease, on lack of distress, and thus amounts to dwelling in the familiar, convenient, and reliable (BT 137, 188–90). Though it is neither possible nor necessary to systematically consider the complexities of *Being and Time,* even without the details the thrust of the descriptions of Da-sein and its everyday mode of being comes across clearly. Admittedly, given the pointedness of the words chosen and the sharpness of the critique, it is hard to fully accept Heidegger's assertion that the descriptions of the everyday are not meant to be derogatory. In any case, they do provide the point of access to begin to uncover the structures of Da-sein, which subsequently leads to increasingly penetrating insights. At base, Heidegger means to explain that rather than amounting to absence or negation of human being, 'everydayness is also and precisely a kind of being of Da-sein' (BT 50). What everydayness shows is how Da-sein 'initially and for the most part' is in the world. I think it fair to say that Heidegger's analysis begins by describing the neutral dimensions and structures of everydayness, but soon takes up the ways that Da-sein usually fails to achieve itself therein (in his own terms, the 'indifferent' and 'deficient' modes, respectively); finally, through the analysis of the fallen condition, he turns to the manner in which Da-sein could positively come toward itself (BT 124).

Heidegger already has pointed out that Da-sein is what is nearest, since we are it. Nearness also characterizes Da-sein's relationship with the surrounding world (*Umwelt*). We bring the world to ourselves to live in it, use things in it, and understand it, in a process he calls de-distancing. 'We use the expression de-distancing in an active and transitive sense. It means a constitution of being of Da-sein of which de-distancing something, putting it away, is only a definite, factical mode. De-distancing means making distance disappear, making the being at a distance of something disappear, bringing it near. Da-sein is essentially de-distancing. As the being that it is, it lets beings be encountered in nearness' (BT 105). Da-sein's kind of spatiality and its relation to things in the world is not primarily a function of distance or space in the ordinary sense, measured in terms of two feet or a mile but a matter of presence to or within our lives. We experience the difference and the primacy of the non-physical when an absent lover or sick family member is immediately and constantly before us all day, even though thousands of miles away, in contrast to mere distance or familiarity, where ordinarily we 'initially always overlook and fail to hear what is measurably "nearest" to us,' as with our contact lenses or the chair on which I sit as I write (BT 107).

We have a pre-reflective relation to things and people in the surrounding world in that they are part of what we are about by virtue of being included in the sphere around us which we open up in order to do things. We make room for our projects and what is encountered in them. We establish specific locales and within those arrange 'the things at hand of everyday association,' where the latter 'do not simply have a place in space, objectively present somewhere, but as useful things are essentially installed, put in their place, set up, and put in order' (BT 102). 'Letting innerworldly beings be encountered, which is constitutive for being-in-the-world, is "giving space." This "giving space" which we call making room [*einräumen*], frees things at hand for their spatiality. As a way of discovering and presenting a possible totality of places relevantly determined, making room makes actual factical orientation possible. As circumspect taking care of things in the world, Da-sein can change things around, remove them or "make room" for them only because making room ... belongs to its being-in-the-world. But neither the previously discovered region nor the actual spatiality in general are explicitly in view' (BT 111).[4] Here the world surrounds us in its handiness, as happens for artisans with their tools and materials, or in our scholarly work with books and word processors (BT 117–18). We are always already in a surrounding world, where 'being-in is to be understood in terms of the over there of the world at hand where Da-sein dwells in taking care' – as we do with our food and clothing and the organization and upkeep of our buildings (BT 103–4, 119, 121). Through such examples, we can see that the surrounding world makes itself known in that it already is or has been disclosed, even if not, strictly speaking, seen (BT 75).

Indeed, Heidegger argues, it is because we first make room for habitation and activity in the surrounding world that measures such as distance from me (at the centre) to what is over there in my environment make any sense in the first place. In its difference Da-sein opens a region around it, establishing a place. 'Place is always the definite "over there" and the "there" of a useful thing belonging there ... But a whereto in general ... underlies the positional belonging somewhere ... as a condition of their possibility. We call this whereto of the possible belonging somewhere of useful things, circumspectly held in view in advance, and heedful association, the *region*' (BT 102–3). 'With what is encountered as things at hand, there is always relevance in a region. A regional spatial relevance belongs to the totality of relevance, which constitutes the being of things at hand in the surrounding world' (BT 111). Along with the de-distancing in which we gather things that are useful or otherwise important, we experience the world not only as over there, over here, but in terms of a valenced directionality, as established from my body: orientation is given in terms of front and back, up and down, left and right. Heidegger's analysis shows that the 'directional discovery of something like a region belongs to the making room of Da-sein. With this expression we mean initially the whereto of the possible belonging somewhere of useful things at hand in the surrounding world' (BT 368). Though we are not aware of the constitution as such, Da-sein unfolds an environment around itself, making an opening for the world to enter and a place for itself to operate – establishing a region: 'With the phenomenon of the region we have already indicated that for which space is discovered beforehand in Da-sein. We understand the region as that to which the context of useful things at hand possibly belongs, a context that can be encountered as something directional, that is, containing places and as de-distanced' (BT 110; see also 368). The surrounding world, then, is always already given as meaningfully organized and underway.

It has been there all along for us but not made explicit, not distanced enough to be adequately seen and analysed, since normally we unselfconsciously operate with circumspection and heedfulness (*Umsicht* and *Sorge*), looking around at what is appropriate to include in our placement and at that with which we should concern ourselves (BT 107). Heidegger develops the idea of region to explicate the phenomena: '"In the region of" means not only "in the direction of," but also in the orbit [*Umkreis*] of something that lies in that direction. The kind of place which is constituted by direction and remoteness – nearness is only a mode of the later – is already oriented toward a region and within that region. Something akin to a region must already be discovered if there is to be any possibility of referring and finding the places of a totality of useful things available to circumspection [*umsichtig verfügbaren*]. This regional orientation of the multiplicity of places of what is at hand constitutes the aroundness, the being around us of beings encountered initially in the surrounding world [*das Umhafte, das Um-uns-herum des umweltlich*]' (BT 103). Regioning is prior to the experience and codification of three-dimensionality by mathematics, science, technology, and philosophy, for example with Euclidean geometry or Renaissance theories of perspective (BT 110). Opposite what we take for granted because of a lack of critical historical knowledge and analytic phenomenology, 'Regions are not first formed by things objectively present together, but are always already at hand in individual places. The places themselves are assigned to what is at hand in the circumspection of taking care of things' (BT 103).

We now have at least a first understanding of why Heidegger freshly utilizes the vocabulary we remarked upon at the outset. To interpret being directly and in a new way, as well as to deconstruct and reconstruct the obscuring philosophical tradition, requires approaching matters by way of Da-sein. It turns out that our relationship with the tradition, with the world that surrounds us, and even with ourselves as Da-sein is substantially a matter of distancing and de-distancing, of uprootedness and retrieval, of making room, region, and place for the ordinary 'beings with which Da-sein initially and for the most part dwells, [for] "valuable" things' such as 'field, boat, book,' clock, and house (BT 63, 104, 118).

Indeed, the description and analysis of such useful things and our surrounding world already discloses a primary and unique dimension of Da-sein because, Heidegger contends, 'the analysis of the kind of being in which Da-sein, initially and for the most part, lives' shows that it is not of the same kind as the handiness of useful things and does not merely operate in a surrounding environment (BT 117): 'The world of Da-sein thus frees beings which are not only completely different from tools and things, but which themselves in accordance with their kind of being as Da-sein are themselves "in" the world as being-in-the-world in which they are at the same time encountered' (BT 118). Accordingly, he says that it is proper that 'our investigation takes its orientation from being-in-the-world' (BT 117). With the formal description of Da-sein as being-in-the-world, we come another step closer to the fundamental character of human being:

> being-in designates a constitution of being of Da-sein ... But we cannot understand by this the objective presence of a material thing (the human body) 'in' a being objectively present ... [nor] does the term designate a spatial 'in one another' of two things objectively present, any more than the word 'in' primordially means a spatial relation of this kind. 'In' stems from *innan-*, to live, *habitare*, to dwell. '*An*' means I am used to, familiar with, I take care of something. It has the meaning of *colo* in the sense of *habito* and *diligo*. We characterized this being to whom being-in belongs in this meaning as the being which I myself always am. The expression '*bin*' is connected with '*bei*.' '*Ich bin*' (I am) means I dwell, I stay near ... the world as something familiar in such and such a way. Being as the infinitive of 'I am': that is, understood as an existential, means to dwell near ... to be familiar with ... *being-in is thus the formal existential expression of the being of* Da-sein which has the essential constitution of being-in-the-world. (BT 54)[5]

It is crucial, then, to reject seeing Da-sein merely as useful, as reduced to having instrumental value. In an adequate interpretation of knowing 'when Da-sein dwells together with a being to be known and determines its character' (which also means where truthfulness is 'not representation, not correspondence'), 'looking itself becomes a mode of independent dwelling together with beings in the world. In this "dwelling" – as the refusal of every manipulation and use – the perception of what is objectively present takes place' (BT 61–2). With this we also come closer to the original source that we philosophically seek and need to recover: we find that '"being-in-the-world" is a structure that is primordial and constantly whole' (BT 180).

By now we may have a better sense of Heidegger's procedure, as well as of his vocabulary. Before deconstructing the tradition to return to the original source, he believes we first need to proceed by way of human being, which as Da-sein, the being concerned with its being, is nearest to us. By means of the phenomena in which Da-sein brings the world near he can describe a fundamental relation between humans and their surrounding worlds, since Da-sein is disclosed as being-in-the-world. But as noted, what this means still remains ontologically far away from us, and much more needs to be thought through.

Of course, we should not speak as if there were one human being for we are many together in the world. Da-sein is not solitary: 'the world of Da-sein is a *with-world*. Being-in is *being-with* others' (BT 118). And given Da-sein's special character, clearly human beings cannot be recognized as such, if treated functionally or pragmatically. As Heidegger puts it, the kind of being to which Da-sein 'is related as being-with does not, however, have the kind of being of useful things at hand; it is itself Da-sein' (BT 121): 'The others are not encountered by grasping and previously discriminating one's own subject, initially objectively present, from other subjects also present. They are not encountered by first looking at oneself and then ascertaining the opposite pole of a distinction. They are encountered from the world in which Da-sein, heedful and circumspect, essentially dwells ... We must hold fast to the phenomenal fact ... of their being encountered in the surrounding world' (BT 119). Since others are first found in the region of our practical daily concerns, we are likely involved in shared projects and have similar goals and values. Consequently, rather than being significantly different from us, they are 'those from whom one mostly does *not* distinguish oneself, those among whom one is, too. This being-there-too with them does not have the ontological character of being objectively present "with" them within a world. The "with" is of the character of Da-sein, the "also" means the sameness of being as circumspect, heedful being-in-the-world' (BT 118). Here another dimension of Da-sein is made explicit: 'Da-sein is itself essentially being-with,' being-together-with (*Mitda-sein*); further, as being-in-the-world, Da-sein also encounters the others as *Mitda-sien*–in-the-world (BT 120; see also 117–25).

Yet, in everydayness Da-sein does not exercise its full capacities but operates deficiently, for the most part precisely because of the mode of relation to others. Even more than when we are absorbed in the things and processes at hand in the course of daily activities, when we are immersed with others whom we meet 'at work' or in leisure time in the surrounding world, Da-sein does not stand back from itself and reflect on itself (BT 120, 123). Often Da-sein is not even engaged in significant activity at hand but is merely standing around. Indeed, Heidegger finds that '"standing around" is an existential mode of being, the lingering with everything and nothing which lacks heedfulness and circumspection' (BT 120). Even 'concern, initially and for the most part, dwells in the deficient or at least indifferent modes – in the indifference of passing-one-another-by' (BT 124).

The crucial point for us is that in everydayness the mode of being 'at home' (*zuhause*) does *not* realize Da-sein's full potential; indeed, it prevents it from coming to itself. Even without further explanation of the technical meanings or intricate relationships of the terms, the named deficient modes of concern convey straightforwardly enough the 'falling short' of what is possible: 'being for-, against-, and without-one-another, passing-one-another-by, not-mattering-to-one-another, are possible ways of concern. And precisely the last named modes of deficiency and indifference characterize the everyday and average being-with-one-another' (BT 121). The usual mode of being for Da-sein is 'uncovered in the indifferent way in which it is initially and for the most part. This indifference of the everydayness of Da-sein is not nothing ... All existing is how it is out of this kind of being, and back into it. We call this everyday indifference of Da-sein *averageness*' (BT 43). Though not nothing, nonetheless the 'creation of averageness' is not positive: the reign of others 'maintains itself factically in the averageness of what is proper, what is allowed, and what is not. Of what is granted success and what is not. This averageness, which prescribes what can and may not be ventured, watches over every exception ... Every priority is noiselessly squashed. Overnight, everything primordial is flattened down as something long since known. Everything gained by a struggle becomes something to be manipulated. Every mystery loses its power. The care of averageness reveals, in turn, an essential tendency of Da-sein, which we call the *leveling down* of all possibilities of being' (BT 127).

In such conditions 'Da-sein is not itself. Who is it, then, who has taken over being as everyday being-with-one-another' (BT 29)? Famously, Heidegger explores these questions with a focus on the relation of everyday being one's self and the they, arguing that 'as everyday being-with-one-another, Da-sein stands in subservience to the others ... The everyday possibilities of being of Da-sein are at the disposal of the whims of the others. These others are not definite others.' Heidegger pointedly explains that the 'they' so named appears to us in the form of the anonymous, but normative social force we reference when we observe, 'they say that ...,' 'it is not allowed' (that is, 'they do not allow it here'), 'one does not do such and such' (that is, 'they do not approve of that'). The ways of being of the they paradigmatically appear as 'everyday being-among-one-another, distantiality, averageness, leveling down, publicness, disburdening of one's being, and accommodation' (BT 127–8).

What is negative about this condition is that indifference (and even more so, deficiency) 'estranges Da-sein from its ownmost non-relational potentiality-of-being'; that is, here Da-sein 'drifts toward an alienation,' drifts away from what is its ownmost (BT 254, 178). Here Da-sein becomes so entangled in itself in its unmindful immersion in the everyday that it spirals in on itself, as it were. Heidegger says that 'We call this kind of "movement" of Da-sein in its own being the plunge. Da-sein plunges out of itself into itself, into the groundlessness and nothingness of inauthentic everydayness,' but this implosion is hidden from itself, since it is 'publicly interpreted as "getting ahead"' (BT 178).

Heidegger's deft descriptions, which he insists are not disparaging, because they properly reveal the structure of everyday Da-sein, show how we operate at the level of the they in our idle talk. For example, we convey and reinforce a common understanding in our ordinary gossiping and when we pass the word along ('I hear that ...'). Since what is said in such cases is not a matter of our own first-hand investigation or careful understanding, it is, in fact, groundless (*bodenlos*) (BT 168–9).

> Idle talk, which closes off in the way we described, is the mode of being of the uprooted [*entwurzelten*] understanding of Da-sein. However, it does not occur as the objectively present condition of something objectively present, but it is existentially uprooted, and this uprooting is constant. Ontologically, this means that when Da-sein maintains itself in idle talk, it is – as being-in-the-world – cut off from the primary and primordially genuine relations of being toward the world, toward Mitda-sein, toward being-in-itself. It keeps itself in suspension and yet in doing so it is still always together with the 'world,' with the others, and toward itself. Only those

> beings whose disclosedness is constituted by attuned and understanding discourse, that is, who are in this ontological constitution their there, who are 'in-the-world,' have the possibility of being of such uprooting, which, far from constituting a nonbeing of Da-sein, rather constitutes its most everyday and stubborn 'reality.'
>
> However, it is in the nature of the obviousness and self-assurance of the average way of being interpreted that under its protection, the uncanniness of the suspension in which Da-sein can drift toward an increasing groundlessness [*Bodenlosigkeit*] remains concealed to actual Da-sein itself. (BT 170)

Rather than leading to an individualized and accountable discovery, then, such chatter 'turns disclosing around into a closing off': 'by its very nature, idle talk is a closing off since it omits going back to the foundation of what is being talked about' (BT 169). Because such 'covering over' is precisely the opposite of keeping a phenomena open to understanding, with idle talk we discover that 'in the self-certainty and decisiveness of the they, it gets spread abroad increasingly that there is no need of authentic, attuned understanding ... The supposition of the they ... brings a *tranquilization* to Da-sein ... Entangled being-in-the-world, tempting itself, is at the same time *tranquilizing*' (BT 169, 177). Nor should it be supposed that we avoid such anaesthetization by keeping busy in our everyday activities: though it may be true that tranquilization 'drives one into busyness,' the latter is itself just another mode of escaping thoughtfulness, since it operates as curiosity abandoning itself into the flow of the world without comprehension and is a 'specific [kind of] non-staying [*Unverweilen*] with what is nearest' as it restlessly seeks excitement in continual novelty and distraction but avoids any deeper wondering (BT 178, 172). 'The two factors constitutive for curiosity: *non-staying* [*Unverweilen*] in the surrounding world taken care of and *distraction* [*Zerstreuung*] by new possibilities, are the basis of the third essential characteristic of this phenomenon, which we call *never dwelling anywhere* [*Aufenthaltslosigkeit*]. Curiosity is everywhere and nowhere. This mode of being-in-the-world reveals a new kind of being of everyday Da-sein, one in which it constantly uproots [*entwurzelt*] itself' (BT 172–3; see also 347).

Additionally, though the they is everywhere, it does not support Da-sein's actual engagement and understanding of what is at hand, much less of what is afar. That is not only because in the everyday 'a genuine understanding is suppressed' but because under the sway of the they, and deferring to it, 'Da-sein takes refuge in surrogates,' though not in others who are identifiable or accountable. We can now see part of the attraction and power of this mode of being-with: the they removes the burden of responsibility from Da-sein, so that 'no one has to vouch for anything' (BT 125, 127). As Heidegger puts it, 'the they disburdens Da-sein in its everydayness'; thus, in the end, 'the they accommodates Da-sein in its tendency to take things easily and make them easy' (BT 128).

Ordinarily, then, Da-sein has been, for the most part, completely taken in by the things and public realm of the surrounding world; it has 'fallen prey to the world,' which means that it has 'fallen away from itself' (BT 176). Heidegger calls this mode of being 'inauthenticity.' It should be noted at the outset that one of the most difficult aspects of understanding Heidegger lies in his use of 'authenticity.' Just as 'Da-sein' does not name our subjectivity, 'authenticity' does *not* mean the subjective, existential aspects of individual humans but indicates the ontological dimension. That is, as we will see, with 'authentic' (*eigentlich*) and 'authenticity' (*Eigentlichkeit*) Heidegger intends us to hear the root *eigen* – own – a term that will remain critical for him and play out in several powerful ways. For now, the point is that what is properly and uniquely Dasein's own is that its being, and thus being itself, is an issue for it. Dasein can be something of its own (*zueigen*) (BT 42).

Da-sein takes its possibilities from the discovered world with which it is always already together, but this happens 'initially in accordance with the interpretedness of the they. This interpretation has from the outset restricted the possible options of choice to the scope of what is familiar, attainable, feasible, to what is correct and proper. The leveling down of the possibilities of Da-sein to what is initially available in an everyday way at the same time results in a phasing out of the possible as such. The average everydayness of taking care of things becomes blind to possibility and gets tranquilized with what is merely "real." The tranquilization not only does not rule out a high degree of busyness in taking care of things, it arouses it. It is not the case that positive, new possibilities are then willed, but what is available is "tactically" changed in such a way that there is an illusion of something actually happening' (BT 194–5). Insofar as Da-sein becomes lost in the anaesthetized dimensions of the everyday and under the sway of the they, *it turns out, then, that being-at-home (zuhause) is negative, both in terms of Da-sein's potential to become itself and as a philosophical means to adequately move by way of Da-sein to the question of being* (BT 188–9, 276). The comfortable mode that obtains first and for the most part prevents Da-sein from thinking of itself and its being, much less from coming toward itself, toward its fullest potential. This condition is a kind of self-oblivion – not only is Da-sein unmindful of the meaning of itself and the world, but is unmindful of being unmindful – because, under the spell of the they, Da-sein 'does not get to "the heart of the matter," because it is insensitive to every difference of level and genuineness. Publicness obscures everything, and then claims that what has been thus covered over is what is familiar and accessible to everybody' (BT 127). That is, as we have heard, even when we dwell concernfully, it remains to press beyond the indifferent to a deeper understanding of what is far away: 'a nearest and essential knowing oneself is in need of a getting-to-know-oneself' (BT 124).

Further, behind the drive toward the comfortable and easy, there is an avoidance, which Heidegger characterizes as a flight: in 'the average everydayness of Da-sein' it 'is concerned with a particular mode of its being to which it is related in the way of average everydayness, if only in the way of fleeing from it and of forgetting it' (BT 44). He can also specify that from which we are fleeing in the rush toward the familiar useful objects and likeminded others in our surrounding world: 'In this entangled being-together-with, fleeing from uncanniness (which mostly remains covered over by latent Angst because the publicness of the they suppresses everything unfamiliar) announces itself' (BT 192). This is simultaneously a flight from our ownmost possibilities, that is, it is flight from ourselves, 'flight from the uncanniness that fundamentally determines individualized being-in-the-world' (BT 276).

Thus far, the initial analysis of Da-sein, and thus the approach to being through the way Da-sein is initially and usually in the world in inauthentic everydayness, not only discloses some of the essential structures of Da-sein and its being but also opens access to a second dimension, that of authenticity (BT 57). In any mode, Da-sein already reveals an ontological dimension beyond that of 'mere objects': 'ontologically there is an essential distinction between the "indifferent" being together of arbitrary things and the not-mattering-to-one-another of beings who are with one another' (BT 121). With Da-sein we find a realm that is open or undetermined in a dramatic way: Da-sein is its possibilities – thus requiring that it responsibly and decisively choose its course of action. Of course, as we have seen, insofar as it retreats to the comfortable being-at-home, it loses itself; insofar as it numbly follows the norms of the public, it is stranded in the 'groundlessness of idle talk': 'The average everydayness of Da-sein can thus be determined as entangled-disclosed, thrown-projecting being-in-the-world which is concerned with its ownmost potentiality in its being together with the "world" and in being-with the others' (BT 46, 181).

Here we find the positive characteristic of being directed by its potential, though of falling far short. But that means the alternative remains possible: 'The self of everyday Da-sein is the they-self which we distinguish from the authentic self, the self which has explicitly grasped itself' (BT 129). Where Da-sein would come to its own self, its way of being-with others would also open another sphere: 'when [human beings-with-one-another] devote themselves to the same thing in common, their doing so is determined by their Da-sein, which has been stirred. This authentic alliance' clears a more profound region for our lives (BT 122).

The fullest possibilities can be seen through the basic dimensions of Da-sein that have been disclosed: Da-sein's spatiality, temporality, and the freedom to choose would allow for authenticity and thereby for another return to what is most originary and grounding. Spatiality has already been discussed and seen to be not a matter of physical distance but of the opening of a region by Da-sein itself as it moves about the world, engaged in projects with the things that are at hand and with others: 'As being-in-the-world, Da-sein essentially dwells in de-distancing. This de-distancing, the farness from itself of what is at hand, is something that Da-sein can never cross over ... [Da-sein] is essentially de-distancing, that is, it is spatial,' as also is manifest in its directionality: 'locative adverbs ... the "here," "over there," "there" are ... characteristics of the primordial spatiality of Da-sein' (BT 108, 119). In short, 'correctly understood ontologically, Da-sein is spatial in a primordial sense' (BT 111).[6]

But space is coupled with time. Not only do we think and speak of them as interwoven – as with 'a span of time' – but just as Da-sein opens around itself a region that becomes space, so it also operates in a parallel 'horizon of time' that is grounded not only in waiting for things to be done in the surrounding world but finally in a deeper unity of temporality, so much so that Heidegger makes the striking assertion that 'the meaning of the being of that being we call Da-sein proves to be temporality' (BT 17, 235, 368). In the first place, Heidegger's analysis shows that the 'temporality of Da-sein [occurs] as everydayness, historicity, and within-time-ness' (BT 333). Where 'everydayness reveals itself as a mode of temporality,' parallel to making room, Da-sein gives itself its time. In the course of Da-sein's operating in the surrounding world 'care must need "time" and thus reckons with "time." The temporality of Da-sein develops a "time calculation"' (BT 235). Again, initially the measure unfolds from Da-sein's activities. Just as distance is a matter of 'a half-day's walk from here,' so a promised repair will 'take until sometime tomorrow' or a meeting will occur 'when the shadow is so many feet long,' according to what Heidegger calls 'the peasant's clock' (BT 413, 416). In the ordinary, original world of simple work, human activity followed the course of days and seasons, so that when the sun rose it was time for such and such, when the first day of spring came round, it again was time to do what was necessary for a new year's growth. Initially, we figured out daily, weekly, monthly, and seasonal time by the sun, as well as by the moon and stars. Heidegger notes, 'These regions of the sky which do not yet need to have any geographical meaning at all, give beforehand the whereto for every particular development of regions which can be occupied by places.' From our everyday activities we go on to discover the clock; from such activity 'originates the everyday, vulgar understanding of time. And that develops into the traditional concept of time' (BT 70–71, 235, 404, 412–14).

As we all know, in the course of going through life's tasks, we run out of time. In more formal terms, insofar as what we have and what we are is temporality, Heidegger says, 'Da-sein "uses itself up." Using itself up, Da-sein uses itself, that is, its time. Using its time, it reckons with it' (BT 332). Here we find the vulgar conception of time as a flow of 'nows' that stream out of the future, through the present, and irredeemably into the past. In the way Da-sein usually expends itself in everydayness, 'in living into its days, it stretches itself along "temporally" in the succession of its days. The monotony, the habit, the "like yesterday, so today and tomorrow," and the "for the most part" cannot be grasped without recourse to the "temporal" stretching along of Da-sein' (BT 371). Hence, Heidegger can conclude that 'basically nothing other is meant by the term everydayness than temporality' (BT 372).

But just as everyday being-at-home is an escape into the comfortable and away from what is challenging, so too the everyday mode of temporality is also a flight from what is disconcerting. The clearest instance of this is in the attempt to avoid the unavoidable: the running out of our time. Again, though we cannot follow his famous analysis here, Heidegger locates the core of Da-sein's temporality in its movement toward death, in its 'being toward death' (BT 234). Precisely in this fundamental characteristic in which Da-sein might find itself and its calling, we find 'a constant tranquilization about death' (BT 254). Nor is this something idiosyncratically or solipsistically brought about by this or that person. Rather, under the spell of the they, which 'does not permit the courage to have Angst about death,' the covering over is at the core of the way we live together with others (BT 254). We mutually comfort each other into numbness and avoidance of whatever is powerful and disconcerting: 'In this entangled being together with … the flight from uncanniness makes itself known, that is, the flight from its [Da-sein's] ownmost being-toward-death' (BT 252). As has often been remarked since Heidegger made the observation eighty years ago, we almost compulsively hide not only our mortality but all traces of death itself. Heidegger explains, 'the evasion of death which covers over, dominates everydayness so stubbornly that, in being-with-one-another, the "neighbors" often try to convince the "dying person" that he will escape death and soon return again to the tranquilized everydayness of his world taken care of. This "concern" has the intention of thus "comforting" the "dying person." Thus, the they makes sure of a *constant tranquilization about death*' (BT 253).

The shortfall and the flight of Da-sein in everyday temporality simultaneously discloses what makes it possible and provides a means of access to that to which we finally need arrive – or return. First of all, the core of Da-sein is uncovered: 'The primordial ontological ground of the existentiality of Da-sein … is temporality' (BT 234). Secondly – combining the spatial and the temporal – 'only in terms of the rootedness of Da-sein in temporality, do we gain insight into the existential *possibility* of the phenomena that we characterized … as the fundamental constitution of *being-in-the-world*' (BT 351). Where we face up to our finitude, we can recognize that because our temporality unfolds against the boundary of death and nothingness our decisions and actions concerning what is at stake in the decisive moment matter a great deal. How and when we act is of the essence. Indeed, decisiveness is a key to the further understanding of our possibilities. Hence, as with spatiality, it is in the unfolding of Da-sein that temporality has its meaning, and can appear in either of the two modes: either the inauthentic emerges, or with Da-sein-in-the-world the authentic can occur: 'Understanding is grounded primarily in the future (anticipation or awaiting). Attunement temporalizes itself primarily in having-been (retrieve or forgottenness). Falling prey is temporally rooted primarily in the present (making present or the Moment)' (BT 350). Thus, beyond the initial grounding of temporality in Da-sein's everyday being, a deeper foundation is reached in the disclosure of the unity of authentic temporality.

Specifically, the possibility of authenticity requires recovering from being lost in the tranquilization of being-at-home and in facing not-being-at-home. We need to move from numbing comfort to enlivening eeriness. In this regard, Heidegger has brought us to the *opposite* of what might appear to be the intuitive idea that home is existentially and ontologically positive; and the uncanny, the negative. To the contrary, *it turns out that being-at-home is tranquilizing and stifling, whereas the uncanny is liberating for us because in it and through it we can be called to and find a way to recover what has gone missing, to come back into what is our own and to find a new ground in place of the groundlessness of the they.*

Because 'uncanniness pursues Da-sein and threatens its self-forgetful lostness,' Da-sein must be called back to itself. But nothing otherworldly or 'spooky' need be inferred here, for it is nothing other than Da-sein itself that calls itself: 'the caller and he who is summoned are *themselves at the same time* one's own Da-sein' (BT 277, 279). The call of Da-sein which summons itself to its own possibility Heidegger names the 'call of conscience,' where 'conscience reveals itself as the call of care': 'summoning the they-self means calling forth the authentic self to its potentiality-of-being, as Da-sein, that is, being-in-the-world taking care of things and being-with-others' (BT 276–7, 280). Clearly, this is not possible so long as Da-sein is obliviously immersed in the everyday. Only when '*Da-sein, find*[*s*] *itself in the ground of its uncanniness' could it become* '*the caller of the call of conscience*' (BT 276). 'The call directs Da-sein *forward toward* its potentiality-of-being, as a call *out of* uncanniness. The caller is indeed indefinite, but where it calls from is not indifferent for the calling. Where it comes from – the uncanniness of thrown individuation – is also called in the calling, that is, is also disclosed. Where the call comes from in calling forth to … is that to which it is called back. The call does not give us to understand an ideal, universal potentiality-of-being; it discloses it as what is actually individualized in that particular Da-sein. The disclosive character of the call has not been completely determined until we understand it as a calling back that calls forth. Only if we are oriented toward the call thus understood, may we ask *what* it gives to understand' (BT 280).

Heidegger contends that speaking this way also makes sense because, rather than seeing truth as a matter of the correspondence of an internal or verbal representation with an object encountered, more primordially, just as with space, it needs to be traced back to the opening that happens with, that is nothing other than, Da-sein. Heidegger thus speaks of 'the clearing of Da-sein': 'To say that' human being ('which is in its mode of being its there') is '"illuminated" means that it is cleared in itself as being-in-the-world, not by another being, but in such a way that it is itself the clearing … Da-sein is its disclosure' (BT 133). The issue of understanding, then, just as of spatiality and temporality, is one of the openness of the there, of Da-sein, which Heidegger has at least approached preliminarily: 'What essentially clears this being, that is, makes it "open" as well as "bright" for itself, was defined as care, before any "temporal" interpretation' (BT 351).

Heidegger is moving from an analysis of the everyday to open up a more profound possibility as the fully positive goal to be sought, and to explicating how a transformation from the everyday might come about. As a first step, he has established that 'this flight as the flight from the uncanniness that fundamentally determines individualized being-in-the-world' needs to be checked and reversed; we need to stand firm and engage it (BT 276). Thus we have the combination of directions of movement: we are called forward, out of our entanglement and obliviousness, to a return to openness and our possibilities. 'The call is the call of care ... Da-sein stands primordially together with itself in uncanniness. Uncanniness brings this being face to face with its undisguised nullity, which belongs to the possibility of its ownmost potentiality-of-being. In that Da-sein as care is concerned about its being, it calls itself as a they that has factically fallen prey, and calls itself from its uncanniness to its potentiality-of-being. The summons calls back by calling forth; *forth* to the possibility of taking over in existence the thrown being that it is, *back* to thrownness in order to understand it as the null ground that it has to take up into existence ... Da-sein itself ... must bring itself back to itself from its lostness in the they' (BT 287).

Here we can see more fully the relevance of home and homelessness to the question of the nature of Da-sein and to that of being, as well as that of *how homecoming would be called for, and, 'oddly' enough, how genuine homecoming would amount to a refusal of the comfortable being-at-home* (*zuhause*) *and instead enter into not-being-at-home in the uncanny* (*unheimlich*): 'In its who, the caller is definable by *nothing* "worldly." It is Da-sein in its uncanniness, primordially thrown being-in-the-world, as not-at-home, the naked 'that' in the nothingness of the world. The caller is unfamiliar to the everyday they-self, it is something like an *alien* voice. What could be more alien to the they, lost in the manifold "world" of its heedfulness, than the self-individualized to itself in uncanniness thrown into nothingness?' (BT 277). Heidegger names the positive stance on behalf of our authentic possibility 'resoluteness,' which 'means letting oneself be summoned out of one's lostness in the they' (BT 299). 'As *authentic being a self*, resoluteness does not detach Da-sein from its world, nor does it isolate it as free floating ego. How could it, if resoluteness as authentic disclosedness is, after all, nothing other than *authentically being-in-the-world?*' (BT 298). 'Resoluteness brings Da-sein back to its ownmost potentiality-of-being-a-self. One's own potentiality-of-being becomes authentic and transparent in the understanding being-toward-death as the *ownmost* possibility' (BT 307).

Answering the call requires standing our ground to face the uncanny and uncovering what has been pushed into oblivion, which would open the possibility of facing toward (so that moving into and dwelling in the uncanny is not a negative movement but positively avoids the wrong way of the self-numbing being-at-home [*zuhause*]). 'Initially, factical Da-sein is in the with-world, discovered in an average way. Initially, "I" "am" not in the sense of my own self, but I am the others in the mode of the they. In terms of the they, and as the they, I am initially "given" to "myself." Initially, Da-sein is the they and for the most part it remains so. If Da-sein explicitly discovers the world and brings it near, if it discloses its authentic being to itself, this discovering of "world" and disclosing of Da-sein always comes about by clearing away coverings and obscurities, by breaking up the disguises with which Da-sein cuts itself off from itself' (BT 129). In what he says here about facing the eeriness and groundlessness of our uncanny being-in-the-world, we hear an echo of what Nietzsche said about Greek tragedy not teaching resignation but coming face to face with and saying 'yes' to all aspects of life: 'But at this juncture, when the will is most imperilled, art approaches, as a redeeming and healing enchantress; she alone may transform these horrible reflections on the terror and absurdity of existence into [imaginations] with which man may live. These are the [imaginations] of the sublime as the artistic conquest of the awful, and of the comic as the artistic release from the nausea of the absurd.'[7]

The next step would be to show specifically how the uncanny might be faced, and generally how authenticity might be possible. One of the most striking ways in which Da-sein can avoid fleeing into the comfortable and instead face the uncanny is disclosed by way of Angst. Angst is distinct from fear, in that the latter is of something definite. What is feared is what is specifically harmful, such as being bitten by a snake or losing one's job during an economic depression (BT 140). In contrast, 'Angst first makes fear possible' because more fundamentally it is a response to the 'completely indefinite': 'what threatens in Angst is already there and yet nowhere' (BT 186). Of course, Da-sein prudently 'shrinks back from what fear discloses'; but in the case of Angst, what Da-sein shrinks back from is itself and its own ground (or groundlessness in the uncanny) because the indefinite that operates is nothing other than the world as such: 'that about which Angst is anxious is being-in-the-world itself' (BT 185–7).

Angst is highly disclosive, then, not despite, but because of, its 'indefiniteness: the nothing and the nowhere' (BT 188). Heidegger finds that 'in Angst one has an "uncanny" feeling.' Since being-in-Angst is 'defined,' in this analysis, 'as dwelling with ... being familiar with,' where 'uncanniness means at the same time not-being-at-home,' we encounter the eerie condition of 'dwelling in not-being-at-home' (BT 188). Heidegger's bold conclusions are worth citing at some length:

> The they ... brings tranquilized self-assurance, 'being-at-home' with all its obviousness, into the average everydayness of Da-sein. *Angst*, on the other hand, fetches Da-sein back out of its entangled absorption in the 'world.' Everyday familiarity collapses. Da-sein is individualized, but as being-in-the-world. Being-in enters the existential 'mode' of *not-being-at-home.* The talk about 'uncanniness' means nothing other than this.
>
> Now, however, what falling prey, as flight, is fleeing from becomes phenomenally visible. It is not a flight *from* inner-worldly things, but precisely *toward* them as the beings among which taking care of things, lost in the they, can linger in tranquilized familiarity. Estranged flight *into* the being at home of publicness is flight *from* not-being-at-home, that is, from the uncanniness which lies in Da-sein ... as being-in-the-world entrusted to itself in its being ... The everyday way in which Da-sein understands uncanniness is the entangled turning away which 'phases out' not-being-at-home ... Tranquilized, familiar being-in-the-world is a mode of the uncanniness of Da-sein, not the other way around. *Not-being-at-home [Un-zuhause] must be conceived existentially and ontologically as the more primordial phenomenon.* (BT 189)

Hence, Heidegger goes on, 'in Angst there lies the possibility of a distinctive disclosure, since Angst individualizes. This individualizing fetches Da-sein back from its falling prey and reveals to it authenticity and inauthenticity as possibilities of its being. The fundamental possibilities of Da-sein, which is always my own, show themselves in Angst as they are, undistorted by inner-worldly beings to which Da-sein, initially and for the most part, clings' (BT 190). This is quite a contrast to what happens in the first place and for the most part in everydayness, where we normally operate in an awareness that is, in fact, a form of oblivion, since as Heidegger has shown, 'Everyday Da-sein derives the pre-ontological interpretation of its being from the nearest kind of being of the they' (BT 130).

Now Heidegger arrives at the alternative to everydayness. In the indifference and averageness of the everyday, we find tranquilization, estrangement, groundlessness, the closed off and covered over, and the removal of responsibility. The opposites would be alertness, engagement, groundedness, openness to understanding, and responsibility – all of which, according to Heidegger's analysis of Angst, might occur if Dasein faces and enters into the realm of the uncanny. That is why he says, 'Being free for its ownmost potentiality-for-being, and thus for the possibility of authenticity and inauthenticity, shows itself in a primordial, elemental concretion in Angst,' and that 'as attunement, being anxious is a way of being-in-the-world; that for which we have Angst is our potentiality-for-being-in-the-world. The complete phenomenon of Angst thus shows Da-sein as factical, existing being-in-the-world' (BT 191).

Seemingly, we have arrived at the threshold of a positive prospect: at 'the existential and ontological condition of the possibility of being free for authentic existentiell possibilities' (BT 193). Yet, the radical openness of the possibility of authenticity – or inauthenticity – cannot be overstressed. Nothing is guaranteed or certain; there is no sure route which automatically leads Da-sein to self-fulfilment. The conditional governs what Heidegger says here, for at any moment Da-sein can win or lose itself. Indeed, in the strategy he often employs to show foundations in originary possibility, Heidegger contends that it is precisely 'because it [Da-sein] is essentially possible as authentic, that is, it belongs to itself,' that it 'can be inauthentic' (BT 43). Responsible and appropriate action has no clear and distinct definition or measure; understanding, no royal road of methodology. As we see in *Being and Time*'s critique of the tradition, the understanding of being that belongs to Da-sein develops or decays. In everyday life – the alternate route to understanding human being and being – matters are normally concealed or covered up. 'It is possible for every phenomenological concept and proposition drawn from genuine origins to degenerate when communicated as a statement. It gets circulated in a vacuous fashion, loses its autochthony [*Bodenständigkeit*], and becomes a free floating thesis' (BT 36, 43).

Given that freedom and openness obtain, and that understanding at least is possible, there remains the issue of responsible action, which is also a matter of temporality, since what is decisive is not only proper in direction but occurs at the proper moment. Indeed, freedom is intimately bound up with timely action. Heidegger continues to develop the implications of the differences between what is initially and for the most part the case and what can happen at the plane of authenticity. In regard to our current issues, he says that for being-in-the-world 'taking care of things is guided by circumspection ... [that] gives to all our teaching and performing its routine of procedure, the means of doing something, the right opportunity, the proper moment.' Yet, crucially, it can be that 'circumspection becomes free ... no longer bound to the work-world.' Where care turned into circumspection is genuinely free, open, and 'essentially de-distancing, it provides new possibilities of de-distancing for itself, that is, it tends to leave the things nearest at hand for a distant and strange land' (*ferne und fremde Welt*) (BT 172). That is, it leaves the comfortable being-at-home, wherein it is ensnared and lost from itself, for the eerie and uncanny, where it may come toward its ownmost self.

When dealing with authentic temporality and facing the uncanny, Heidegger is involved in a double retrieval. He is not merely going back into the uncanny and thereby attempting to become open to discerning Da-sein's deepest potential for itself, but is (as we have since come to understand) engaged in retrieving the primordial sense of temporality by going back behind the history of metaphysics to thinking *Augenblick*. Though *Augenblick* is variously translated – usually as 'the Moment' or 'moment of vision' – since those terms may still lead to confusing it with 'a now' or 'that instant' in the flow of time, it is more helpful to keep in mind that Heidegger accomplished his originary retrieval of the meaning and experience of *Augenblick* by way of Aristotle's and St Paul's *kairos*, 'the decisive moment.'[8]

> What is projected in the primordial existential project of existence revealed itself as anticipatory resoluteness ... [that] is the *being toward* one' [*sic;* one's] ownmost, eminent potentiality-of-being. Something like this is possible only in such a way that Da-sein *can* come toward itself *at all* in its ownmost possibility and perdure the possibility as possibility in this letting-itself-come-toward itself, that is, that it exists. Letting-*come-toward-itself* that perdures the eminent possibility is the primordial phenomenon of the future ... Here future does not mean a now that has *not yet* become 'actual' and that sometime *will be* for the first time, but the coming in which Da-sein comes toward itself in its ownmost potentiality-of-being. Anticipation makes Da-sein *authentically* futural in such a way that anticipation itself is possible only in that Da-sein, as *existing*, always already comes toward itself, that is, is futural in its being in general. (BT 325)

Because Heidegger contrasts the everyday conception of time as the mere flow of successive 'nows' from the future, through the present, into the past with authentic temporality in which the possible stands before us, undecided, two differences simultaneously come to the fore. The inauthentic focuses on the present, both spatially and temporally, whereas Da-sein exists in a different dimension; in addition, the making-room of Da-sein is what is primary, for it opens for what subsequently becomes experienced as 'ordinary' space and time. In terms of the objects that we take up in space, Heidegger argues, 'The being of beings, which is there, too, is understood as objective presence ... [But] we have made possible the insight into the root of missing the ontological interpretation of this constitution of being. In itself, in its everyday kind of being, is what initially misses itself and covers itself over' (BT 130). What so misses itself is Da-sein, whose own mode of spatiality and being there is completely different from such objective presence (BT 117–18). Parallel,

> In resoluteness, the present is not only brought back from the dispersion in what is taken care of nearest at hand, but is held in the future and having-been. We call the *present* that is held in authentic temporality, and is thus *authentic*, the *Moment*. This term must be understood in the active sense of an ecstasy ... The phenomena of the Moment can *in principle not* be clarified in terms of the *now*. The now is a temporal phenomenon that belongs to time as within-time-ness: the now 'in which' something comes into being, passes away, or is objectively present. 'In the moment' nothing can happen, but as authentic present it lets us *encounter for the first time* what can be 'in a time' as something at hand or objectively present.
>
> In contrast to the Moment as authentic present, we shall call the inauthentic present *making present* ... The Moment, on the other hand, temporalizes itself out of the authentic future. (BT 338)

In the decisive Moment we find a vivid concentration quite in contrast with the 'gray everyday' in which it is impossible to find a fundamental temporal meaning (BT 345). Rather than the mere flow of 'present nows,' authentic temporality concentrates its tri-dimensionally in and into Da-sein as it engages its possibilities: 'Future, having-been, and present show the phenomenal characteristics of "toward itself," "back to," "letting something be encountered"' (BT 328). Da-sein is futural, or comes toward itself, in that it moves toward its possibilities from what it chooses. But in coming toward itself Da-sein takes responsibility for and brings along the being that it is (that it already has been). Thus in making a choice in the present, in the decisive moment, it has to come back to itself, bringing along all that it is into what it can become. In short, a profound unity occurs in the decisive moment (BT 324–31; see also BPP 287).

The primordial unity of future, having-been, and present can be better seen if we appreciate that all the dimensions of the German words *Aufenthalt* and *sich aufhalten* are at work where Heidegger writes that authentically Da-sein can 'stay, dwell, stop, stem, and hold or keep open' in temporality (though naturally translations choose one or another meaning). 'Making present is left more and more to itself as it is modified by the awaiting that pursues. It makes present for the sake of the present. Thus tangled up in itself, the dispersed not-staying turns into the *inability to stay at all.* This mode of the present is the most extreme opposite phenomenon to the *Moment.* In this inability Da-sein is everywhere and nowhere. The *Moment* brings existence to the situation and discloses the authentic "There"' (BT 347). In authentic temporality, Da-sein can stay in the sense of remaining with itself and what is about it, not busily rushing from one novelty to another; it can hold what needs to be faced, including holding itself in the uncanny; it can dwell, not uprooted in the tranquilized where it does not even realize its uprootedness, but in the uncanny homelessness where it may come to its ownmost possibilities. Hence, what happens does not pass away into the past, with ourselves being either amused, weary, or anxious spectators. Rather, what matters is summoned up, gathered around us, in temporalizing. We bring ourselves back to what is at stake; we bring what is at stake back before us and hold it there. Heidegger thus speaks of a 'back and forth' for temporality as well as for spatiality. 'The authentic coming-toward-itself of anticipatory resoluteness is at the same time a coming back to the ownmost self thrown into its individuation ... In anticipation, Da-sein *brings* itself *forth again* to its ownmost potentiality-of-being. We call authentic having-*been retrieve*' (BT 339). 'Angst is anxious about naked Da-sein thrown into uncanniness. It brings one back to the pure That of one's own-most, individuated thrownness ... back to thrownness as something to be *possibly retrieved*' (BT 343).

What comes toward itself is not a 'moment of time,' but Da-sein itself, its own uncertain prospect that has neither a guaranteed ground nor a sure outcome: 'Resolute, Da-sein has brought itself back out of falling prey in order to be all the more authentically "there" for the disclosed situation in the "Moment" [*Augenblick*]' (BT 328). The question is 'how the coming-toward-oneself is itself to be primordially determined *as such.* Its finitude does not primarily mean a stopping but is a characteristic of temporalizing itself. The primordial and authentic future is the toward-oneself, toward *oneself,* existing as the possibility of a nullity not-to-be-surpassed ... Primordial and authentic coming-toward-oneself is the meaning of existing in one's ownmost nullity' (BT 330).

There is, then, a double recovery and regathering, especially as a movement beyond that which is apparently in oblivion in the everyday. First, what is Da-sein's own comes back before Da-sein to stand as yet possible: 'Authentic historicity understands history as the "recurrence" of what is possible and knows that a possibility recurs only when existence is open for it fatefully, in the Moment, in resolute retrieve' (BT 391–2). Second, the three dimensions of temporality are brought together, where in the decisive Moment, what is possible is focused between what-has-been and the 'terminus' of death: 'The present ... never acquires another ecstatic horizon of its own accord, unless it is brought back from its lostness by a resolution so that both the actual situation and thus the primordial "boundary situation" of being-toward-death are disclosed as the held Moment' (BT 320).

Being and Time demonstrates that the question of being needs to be analysed in terms of dwelling and displacement because both the tradition that needs to be deconstructed and reconstructed and the character of Da-sein (that would lead us to being and to the lost primordial origins of philosophizing) are encountered as an 'uprooted everywhere and nowhere' and 'groundless floating' (BT 177). Here the most critical dimensions of ourselves, others, and the world are covered over and closed off. We are tranquilized and stand by as matters slip past into the past. In our usual immersion in the familiar and comfortable, and in our entanglement in projects at hand, spatially and temporally, as far as placement and coming toward ourselves are concerned, we fail at understanding, fail at decisive action. 'What is discovered and disclosed stands in the mode in which it has been disguised and closed off by idle talk, curiosity, and ambiguity. Being toward beings has not been extinguished but uprooted. Beings are not completely concealed, but precisely discovered, and at the same time distorted. They show themselves, but in the mode of illusion. Similarly, what was previously discovered sinks back again into disguise and concealment. *Because it essentially falls prey to the world, Da-sein is in "untruth" in accordance with its constitution of being*' (BT 222). One coherent way to say much of what *Being and Time* discloses is that what we most take for granted is precisely the *opposite* of what is true. We take for granted that we are somewhat successful in achieving a proper human belonging when we are at-home (*zuhause*), and that therein we might develop our potential to become fully ourselves. In fact, *when so 'at home' we are most alienated from ourselves, most homeless:* 'Uncanniness is the fundamental kind of being-in-the-world, although it is covered over in everydayness' (BT 277).

The possibility of an alternative to our everyday oblivion and impotent inaction lies in calling ourselves out from the they and into the possibilities of our ownmost selves, which requires leaving being-at-home (*zuhause*) and entering the uncanny, dwelling therein to face the groundlessness that is, that we are. *Thus, what is needed and sought after if we are to deal with the question of being and with our own Da-sein needs to be thought and enacted in retrieval, retrieval of a homecoming that would allow us to hold before us our ownmost potential and the primordial.*

Being and Da-sein are the same phenomena and are to be encountered in the same question because the '*understanding of being is itself a determination of being of Da-sein*' (BT 12). What is needed, then, is the way of being underway, since, in any case, 'Da-sein is always somehow directed and underway' as a 'specifically "spatial" being-in-the-world' (BT 79). The same is true insofar as we are essentially temporal beings, needing to find a way to come toward ourselves by coming back to our ownmost possibility, that is, to move by way of a retrieval (BT 328). Heidegger now needs to go along a braided pathway, where one strand inquires into the meaning of being, and travels back and forth along the metaphysical tradition, and the other continues to investigate the existential mode in which humans have their being as they live together in the world. He follows the former trajectory in works such as 'What Is Metaphysics?,' 'On the Essence of Truth,' and *An Introduction to Metaphysics* in the 1930s, to which we will turn shortly. But before we take up the large question of metaphysics and homelessness, the second direction also merits consideration, for example, as it occurs in *The Basic Problems of Phenomenology*, a lecture course Heidegger delivered in the summer of 1927, the same year in the spring of which *Being and Time* appeared.

We have heard in *Being and Time* how Da-sein makes room for what becomes space and time in the traditional sense, by opening a region that occurs in our de-distancing and directionality. This happens for temporality by the way we pace our activities according to the placement and movement of the sun, moon, or constellations of the sky and impacts the way we live and build, for example, as we work to make use of the sun's light and warmth or its shade and coolness (BT 412–13). This happens in the case of how we organize our houses: 'The house has its sunny side and its shady side. This provides the orientation for dividing up the "rooms" and "arranging" them according to their useful character' (BT 103). The same could be said concerning churches and graves, which are laid out according to the pathway of the sun, which delineates what are taken to be the regions of life and death and humans' temporal movement toward it (BT 104).

Da-sein first finds an understanding of itself in its surroundings, as we have heard in *Being and Time.* In *Basic Problems,* Heidegger explains that this occurs by way of beings that are intra-worldly, though initially the description and analysis amounts to seeing Da-sein's inauthenticity (BPP 171). Even for such self-discovery to be possible it is necessary that it occur within an already given world. Again, as Heidegger says in *Being and Time,* the phenomena happen within the world wherein Da-sein already has made room and cleared an opening as temporality, that is, within which there is already being-with-others-in-the-world (BPP 170–1). From this analysis of what appears in the everyday, we find that initially and for the most part, we do not see what is closest, such as the world presupposed, since that is covered up by our immersion in it (BPP 172), for example in the handiness or usefulness of things in the surrounding environment. It is possible to go more deeply, to de-distance such phenomena by exploring the ruptures in the familiar and closed off, so that by facing the uncanny (and not just comfortably dwelling in 'being-at-home'), we can uncover the spatiality and temporality within which Da-sein is being-in-the-world.

Heidegger pursues the issue of how Da-sein 'discovers beforehand the regions which are each in a decisive relevance,' through attention to what ordinarily appears in its 'character of an inconspicuous familiarity': 'The familiarity itself becomes visible in a conspicuous manner only when what is at hand is discovered circumspectly in the deficient mode of taking care of things. When we do not find something in its place, the region of that place often becomes explicitly accessible as such for the first time' (BT 104). In *Being and Time* Heidegger deployed the strategy of opening a deeper analysis by starting with what is 'out of place,' 'disturbed,' or 'not as usual' (for example, the uncanny and Angst) to catch off guard, as it were, the phenomena that are usually concealed in everydayness.

We have seen how, in *Being and Time,* Heidegger moves from describing and analysing the *Umwelt* to focusing on being-in-the-world. But even knowing what must be done, how could Heidegger come to see what is not ordinarily, not otherwise disclosed? How could he discover that to which we are normally oblivious? How could he so vividly and movingly describe, so appropriately deal with it? No doubt in large part through his own considerable powers of observation and reflection. But as Heidegger points out in *Basic Problems,* there are also others dedicated to bringing what is usually hidden into the light and toward understanding. Artists and writers, for example, are 'original enough still to *see* on [their] own the world that is always already unveiled with its existence, to verbalize it, and thereby to make it expressly visible for others' (BPP 171). Hence Heidegger's glad appreciation of literature as 'the elementary emergence into words, the becoming uncovered of existence as being-in-the-world' (BPP 171–2).

He cites a source (Rainer Maria Rilke's *The Notebooks of Malte Laurids Brigge*) that provides 'testimony on this point,' quoting it at some length, an exceptional indication by Heidegger that it warrants our doing the same:

> Houses? But, to be precise, they were houses that no longer existed. Houses that were torn down from top to bottom. What was there was the other houses, the ones that had stood alongside them, tall neighboring houses. They were obviously in danger of collapsing after everything next to them had been removed, for a whole framework of long tarred poles was rammed aslant between the ground of the rubble-strewn lot and the exposed wall. I don't know whether I've already said that I mean this wall. But it was, so to speak, not the first wall of the present houses (which nevertheless had to be assumed) but the last one of the earlier ones. You could see their inner side. You could see the walls of rooms on different stories, to which the wallpaper was still attached, and here and there the place where the floor or ceiling began. Along the whole wall, next to the walls of the rooms, there still remained a dirty-white area, and the open rust-stained furrow of the toilet pipe crept through it in unspeakably nauseating movements, soft, like those of a digesting worm. Of the paths taken by the illuminating gas, grey dusty traces were left at the edges of the ceilings, and here and there, quite unexpectedly, they bent round about and came running into the colored wall and into a black hole that had been ruthlessly ripped out. But most unforgettable were the walls themselves. The tenacious life of those rooms refused to let itself be trampled down. It was still there; it clung to the nails that had remained; it stood on the handsbreadth remnant of the floor; it had crept together there among the onsets of the corners where there was still a tiny bit of interior space. You could see that it was in the paint, which it had changed slowly year by year: from blue to an unpleasant green, from green to grey, and from yellow to an old decayed white that was now rotting away. But it was also in the fresher places that had been preserved behind mirrors, pictures, and in cupboards; for it had drawn and redrawn their contours and had also been in these hidden places, with the spiders and the

> dust, which now lay bare. It was in every streak that had been trashed off; it was in the moist blisters at the lower edge of the wall-hangings; it tosses in the torn-off tatters, and it sweated out of all the ugly stains that had been made so long ago. And from these walls, once blue, green, and yellow, which were framed by the tracks of the fractures of the intervening walls that had been destroyed, the breath of this life stood out, the tough, sluggish, musty breath which no wind had yet dispersed. There stood the noondays and the illnesses, and the expirings and the smoke of years and the sweat that breaks out under the armpits and makes the clothes heavy, and the stale breath of the mouths and the fuel-oil smell of fermenting feet. There stood the pungency of urine and the burning of soot and the grey reek of potatoes and the strong oily stench of decaying grease. The sweet lingering aroma of neglected suckling infants was there and the anguished odor of children going to school and the sultriness from the beds of pubescent boys. And much had joined this company, coming from below, evaporating upward from the abyss of the streets, and much else had seeped down with the rain, unclean, above the towns. And the domestic winds, weak and grown tame, which stay always in the same street, had brought much along with them, and there was much more too coming from no one knows where. But I've said, haven't I, that all the walls had been broken off, up to this last one? Well, I've been talking all along about this wall. You'll say that I stood in front of it for a long time, but I'll take an oath that I began to run as soon as I recognized the wall. For that's what's terrible – that I recognized it. I recognize all of it here, and that's why it goes right into me: it's at home in me. (BP 172–3)[9]

We find here that Rilke, just as Heidegger in *Being and Time*, moves through four levels of description. First, there are descriptions of things that appear simply as objects, laid bare to our view in their almost nauseating facticity; then there are things that are connected with their functions in the buildings and with human uses (within the surrounding world); next the encompassing environment is explicitly evoked; finally, the ground in being-in-the-world, in *Mitda-sein*, is disclosed. From there the speaker moves back to reinterpret and understand the houses as being of the world that happens with Da-sein – human life in the fullest sense – and thus the speaker experiences belonging together not only with the place but with the other people who had lived there, as being-with-in-the-world. Rilke's writing shows how, just as Heidegger's phenomenological description indicates, human understanding first unfolds from the things, then next from 'the others, the fellow humans, [who] are also there in immediately tangible proximity. In the way they are there with the Da-sein they are also jointly understood with it via things' (BPP 289). The upsurge of the experience conveyed by the speaker is precisely the encounter of Da-sein with itself, a case of Da-sein coming 'toward itself from out of things,' as we see in the end of the cited passage: the speaker 'recognize[s] all of it here, and that's why it goes right into me: it's at home in me.' Here he is called on to deal with the moment, though given that he flees from what he finds, here he may not have been up to the challenge.

Heidegger clearly appreciates the parallel between what Rilke and he are up to: 'Notice here in how elemental a way the world, being-in-the-world – Rilke calls it life – leaps toward us from things. What Rilke reads here in his sentences from the exposed wall is not imagined into the wall, but, quite to the contrary, the description is possible only as an interpretation and elucidation of what is "actually" in this wall, which leaps forth from it in our natural comportmental relationship to it. Not only is the writer able to see this original world, even though it has been unconsidered and not at all theoretically discovered, but Rilke also understands the philosophical concept of life ... which we have formulated with the aid of the concept of existence as being-in-the-world' (BPP 173). That is, with what Rilke shows us, we have moved from the vivid description of a destroyed home and of the spectre of homelessness to a disclosure of being-in-the-world: Da-sein. What then of being?

It might seem peculiar that in *Basic Problems* Heidegger says almost nothing explicitly about home or homelessness, yet presents an intensely vivid articulation of experiencing them. That is because, 'for the others who before were blind, the world first becomes visible by what is thus spoken' (BPP 172). If ordinarily we are separated from being because it remains covered over, we have the question of how to open the ontological questioning in the first place. If what is disclosed in literary works such as Rilke's and then analysed by Heidegger gives us half of what we need – access to being by way of Da-sein as being-in-the-world – then it becomes possible to continue on the way, through the uncanny, to move to the ontological analysis of being itself.

The Question Concerning Homelessness and Being

In 'What is Metaphysics?,' published in 1929, Heidegger asks traditional questions, questions for which he since has become famous. What is being? What is human being? How are the two thought together metaphysically? In asking these questions he is not focusing on anything distant from our lives or remote from his own task. Indeed, to ask them, he must first of all, before all else, think about how matters stand in our world and time. That is, in genuinely questioning metaphysics, 'the questioner as such is by his very questioning involved in the question' (WM 325).

Heidegger would have us understand an experience that is essential to our human being and at the same time is nothing merely human. That is, his story does not concern itself with an account of what we invent or with our subjective psychological feelings. Rather, it attempts to speak of what shows itself to us through our experience. We find ourselves, for example, caught up in anxiety, in dread. 'In anxiety, we say, "one feels ill at ease"'; '"one feels something uncanny"' (WM 103 and 336).[10] The German says, '*es ist einem unheimlich.*' Here the use of the dative *einem* directionally emphasizes that the uncanny, the experience of dis-ease, befalls or is given *to* one.

In this occurrence there is a wrench out of the everyday. That is why *unheimlich* means uncanny and not-at-home. In dread we experience something weird and therefore dangerous, and what we experience seems to come from beyond what is normal and natural. Indeed, it appears as dangerous precisely because it forces us away from what we are used to, from all that is comfortable and familiar. At base, then, we are touched by the uncanny just where we are not-at-home. Here we are not grounded in our own human-being, nor even in what we might suppose would be the basis for our being: being itself. Heidegger names the mysterious source of the *unheimlich:* 'Anxiety reveals the nothing' (WM 336). Heidegger's story, then, involves human being; but where we would also expect to hear of being, we instead hear of nothing. His tale apparently helps us think how we are 'caught in the uncanniness of dread' (WM 336).

Before Heidegger says any more, he makes clear that as human beings we face in two directions simultaneously. On the one side we have the everyday realm of our being and, as we metaphysically understand the state of affairs, being; on the other, we are not-at-home in the uncanny nothing which opens up before us. For a long time we have understood ourselves as attempting to move closer to our metaphysical ground. This would be the end of our philosophical thinking. We move toward being by way of truth. Or, perhaps better put, by 'truth' we mean our progression toward being. Accordingly, just as he tells us the story of being and nothing, Heidegger also tells us the story of this journey. He focuses on this in an address delivered in the 1930s, 'On the Essence of Truth.'

If we take up the story of our experience of the uncanny, we find ourselves moving along a different road than that of truth. Heidegger calls this opposite not simply falsity, but untruth. In terms of our movement, untruth is thought of by Heidegger as errancy (ET, sec. 7). The German word he uses is *das Irren*. It might seem that he means 'error,' since falsity is falling into the erroneous or committing an error in thinking. Yet, that is not what he says. He takes the movement, the turning experienced in being no longer at home, as his guiding thought.

Since the Latin root *errare* means 'to wander from the right way,'[11] the story thus far apparently tells us that the untruth is a wandering from the familiar human being, being, and truth, toward the uncanny and perhaps toward something not human. This is only apparently so. We are called to face up to the experience of the *unheimlich* and, ontologically, no-thing. To turn back toward what is everyday and comfortably normal would, in fact, be to turn away from what comes toward us. If our concern is to seek the shelter of what obliterates our dread, according to Heidegger, we have taken the wrong turn. Untruth, then, would be a flight seeking refuge from what shows itself to us, for example, in dread. If we are not careful, we can turn away from being along the way of untruth, that is, avoiding the uncanny and the not being at home.

Undoubtedly we do take the wrong way. After all, the uncanny is puzzling, uncomfortable, dangerous, even uninteresting. We prefer the familiar and our normal routine. Hence, Heidegger says, 'humanity is turned away from the mystery. The insistent turning toward what is readily available and the ek-sistent turning away from the mystery belong together. They are one and the same' (ET 135). We should not suppose, though, that this movement away from what concerns us is anything accidental or that it only occurs now and then to those who do not have sufficient philosophical discipline. Heidegger goes on to say that both the experience of the uncanny and the turning away from it, even the wrench away from the familiar which is at the heart of the uncanny, is essential to humans. To be human is to move toward both the homely and the not at home; it is to move along the right way and the wrong way too. 'Yet turning toward and away from is based on a turning to and fro proper to Dasein. Man's flight from the mystery toward what is readily available, onward from one current thing to the next, passing the mystery by – this is erring' (ET 135).

Somehow, to be human means that we can move either way. We have the possibility of both truth and untruth, as part of the free space of our turning and journey, because 'errancy belongs to the inner constitution of Da-sein' (ET 135–6). Again, Heidegger's tale presents errancy as a movement in which we unavoidably are engaged. It too must be faced as it is given to us. This means that truth and untruth are not reducable to the subjectively human and an interior anthropology. Rather, humans in their journey amidst mystery and the readily available can turn to and away from both. More complexly, to turn any way is both to turn toward and away from: 'In the simultaneity of disclosure and concealing errancy holds sway' (ET 136–7).

At this point, Heidegger's story is incomplete and the meaning of what he says is far from obvious. Still, it is clear that the saga is one of movement into a realm in which we are and are not at home, and that human being is caught up in this movement in regard to being that occurs amidst the uncanny and ordinary, disclosure and concealment. Since, according to the tale, 'in the ek-sistence of his Da-sein man is *especially* subjected to the rule of mystery and the oppression of errancy' (ET 136), we need to think 'the rule of mystery in errancy' (ET 137). To do this requires that we stay on the way which we unavoidably travel: the way which is *unheimlich.*

Since, as we saw with *Being and Time,* he needs to follow a complex pathway traversing both our essential mode and our metaphysical tradition, Heidegger continues his story of our not being at home along with his questioning of being, nothing, and human being. Indeed, the story of homelessness and the question of being are the same story, as told in *An Introduction to Metaphysics,* a lecture course of 1935. Recall that the attempt to face the subject matter does not amount to achieving some objective distance from existential or metaphysical phenomena. Heidegger insists all along that insofar as we genuinely think, and that means question, we also call ourselves into question. We must, therefore, attend to our own place in these issues, to our assumptions and desires, and to the very means by which we think.

When we attempt such questioning we find ourselves forced out of the familiar. As we have seen, if we attempt to stay on the right way, for example in looking for the truth about homelessness, being, nothing, and humans, we have to allow the *unheimlich* to stay before us. To stay within the uncanny, where we experience not being at home, means to refuse refuge in comfortable ways of living and thinking, in comfortable realms which might contain us, or in comfortable goals and hopes. But this has a far-reaching consequence. It means that to think and question is to hold ourselves in not being at home. The more fully we exercise our human capacities the more radically we have to endure homelessness. 'When in our thinking we open our minds, we first of all cease to dwell in any of the familiar realms' (IM 10).

It might seem some comfort that this is an essential human characteristic. We would not be alone in our questioning, since we would be part of a long tradition which seriously asks such questions. We could think of the Western philosophical tradition as a home, even if the whole of this movement finds itself homeless in regard to being, and before nothing. Yet, Heidegger tells us that the matter is neither this simple nor comforting. When, for example, we attempt to understand being along with or by way of philosophy, we can do so only through the language and texts which bind us to those who have thought before us. To understand would require that we have the same language and think in the same way, or that, at least, we have a means of access to being which binds us together with past philosophers. Closer inspection reveals that the ways in which the early Greeks thought beings, for instance, was changed in Roman philosophical thought and language, changed again in the Christian middle ages and in modern philosophy. It is not just that we have different languages and therefore require translations. Rather, meanings were dropped and added in the changes from one term to the others. Thus, we are involved in a long, complex 'process by which we cut ourselves off and alienated ourselves from the original essence of Greek philosophy' (IM 11).

We are doubly not at home: human beings are essentially not at home, because of our experiences of the uncanny; and we are not at home, even in a shared, historical understanding. Of course, if our questioning attempts to recover from this condition, it can do so only by starting from the closest point, that is, with the translation, language, and questioning in which we are engaged. The first step toward any being at home again would be to move out of 'this whole process of deformation and decay and attempt to regain the unimpaired strength of language and words' (IM 11). The aim of this effort needs to be clear. We do not seek a historical recovery of lost languages and meanings because we want the certainty of linguistic science or historiography established. We want to find a way of being at home with the language and the questions of earlier philosophers and thereby with what really concerns us – that which we question – being, nothing, and ourselves.

Heidegger says that the two sorts of not being at home go together. If we ask why we lose touch with previous language and thought and thereby with earlier understandings of how we are or are not at home, we find that we are questioning how it is that being and homelessness are inseparable. That is, our initial concern with the experience of the *unheimlich* is nothing other than a concern with being and nothing.

Two of the principal ways of experiencing and speaking of being in our tradition are poetry and philosophy. 'Only poetry stands in the same order as philosophy and its thinking, though poetry and thought are not the same thing' (IM 21; see also 12). It might be objected that science and scientific logic also have a place here, as a third way of thinking, but Heidegger argues that science is not of equal rank because all scientific thought is derived from philosophy (IM 21). Indeed, it is within philosophy that 'logic has its very home' (IM 19). Further, as he will show later, there is a kind of apparent comfort and familiarity in science which is a blindness or refusal of the not being at home that we must face up to. Heidegger, then, refuses to adopt the stance of scientific thought because that would be to turn from homelessness prematurely.

What does authentic poetry tell us about the extraordinary? Above all, it places it before us and tells us that the unfamiliar is of the utmost importance. For example, Heidegger cites works which show us 'the uprooted modern man who can do everything equally well yet who cannot lose his ties with the extraordinary' (IM 22). Before all else, poetry witnesses the nothingness that opens beneath us, the essential meaningfulness of the uncanny and its sway between being and non-being. Not that this poetry is thereby negative, dwelling only on human misery. As we have seen, it is by facing such not being at home that even in 'weakness and despair' we can remain authentic (IM 22). The value of poetry or other art partially lies in its power to involve us in its questioning, and that means in the questioning of not being at home and in the attempt to recover a home. For example, in a painting of peasant shoes by van Gogh, 'you are immediately alone with it as though you yourself were making your way wearily homeward' (IM 29).

Both poetry and philosophy present our not being at home and our desire to be at home again, and both show us beings and non-being. If we call our situation one of homelessness, this homelessness needs to be thought more deeply. What is homelessness? What are its essential movements and basic characteristics? Heidegger tells us that homelessness involves both apartness and togetherness. A stone might be dislodged from its place on a mountain and tumble to the valley below, but it is not thereby homeless. Homelessness is more than mere location. It is bound up with a deeper union, one which persists in some way, even when it is not fulfilled. For example, when we are away from home, at school or in the army perhaps, we are still bound up with our homes, even though we are dislocated. Or, if we should be exiled from our homes or driven out of our homeland by a disaster, we are only homeless because we are still connected with our homes, though far from them, even irretrievably. That is, only what has been or has the possibility of being at home can lose it; only what has had or might have a home is homeless. While homeless, we are connected with the no-longer-at-home and not-yet-at-home. Thus, to question homelessness is to question humans and that in respect to their being no longer or not yet at home. It is to question apartness and togetherness as occurring at the same time.

Heidegger says that we are not at home with being in the sense that we have forgotten being. Forgetting is our mode of turning away from being. Of course, it might seem that the entire metaphysical tradition has attended almost exclusively to being. Heidegger, though, is making the strong claim that our entire philosophical movement has itself been a forgetting of being, even as it talked of little else. 'But if we consider the question of being in the sense of an inquiry into being as such, it becomes clear to anyone who follows our thinking that being *as such* is precisely hidden from metaphysics, and remains forgotten – and so radically that the forgetfulness of being, which itself falls into forgetfulness, is the unknown but enduring impetus to metaphysical questioning' (IM 15–16; see also 20).

According to Heidegger, then, we are at a double remove from being. Not only are we no longer at home with being because we have forgotten being, but we have even forgotten that we are not at home.[12] Hence, Heidegger's insistence that we face up to not being at home. It is what we must endure and question if we are to see anything and move anywhere; it is our situation in regard to being and our own nature. The story of being and human being, and that also means the history of Western philosophy, is the story of how 'we have fallen out of being' (IM 30).[13] 'What if it were possible that humans, that nations in their greatest movements and traditions, are linked to being and yet had long fallen out of being, without knowing it? ... (See *Sein und Zeit,* section 38 in particular, pp. 179ff.)' (IM 30).

Notice that even as we have forgotten being and so are not at home in it, we are still linked to it, as now separated. We find an echo of this in our word 'being,' which seems, if we are honest, at once empty and trivial and yet is at the centre of our thought and tradition. Recall that Heidegger spoke of literature where we saw that modern human being 'cannot [yet] lose his ties with the extraordinary' (IM 22). Heidegger's story of contemporary not being at home spreads out. It moves back to the realm where we once were at home and from there shows us the present as a sphere where we are no longer at home. The story also moves forward, beyond our once being at home with being, through our current no longer being at home with being, to a future homecoming with being. 'For ultimately what matters is not that the word "being" remains a mere sound and its meanings vapor, but that we have fallen away from what this word says and for the moment cannot find our way back' (IM 33).

Our project, then, is to face up to not being at home, to think how this has occurred, and to attempt a new being at home. To ask 'How does it stand with being?' means nothing less than to recapture, to repeat (*wieder-holen*), the beginning of our historical-spiritual existence, in order to transform it into a new beginning. This is possible ... But we do not repeat a beginning by reducing it to something past and now known, which need merely be imitated; no, the beginning must be begun again, more radically, with all the strangeness, darkness, insecurity that attend a true beginning' (IM, 32).

By now it should be clear that, though humans are homeless in being, homelessness is not some merely human affair. The story of homelessness is the story of human beings and being all at once; the movements to and fro which are made in language and thought involve both humans and being at the same time. That is why Heidegger says, 'In this questioning we seem to belong entirely to ourselves. Yet it is this questioning that moves us into the open, provided that in questioning it transforms itself (which all true questioning does), and casts a new space over everything and into everything' (IM 24).

The question concerning homelessness and being is asked in two dimensions. First, Heidegger thinks through concrete historical situations of being once-at-home, no-longer-at-home, not-yet-at-home by considering the history of Western philosophy. In the story of being and our homelessness from it, we find 'the spiritual destiny of the Western world' (IM 31). Second, he investigates the modes of apartness and togetherness which unfold between being and human being, thinking, and language. Note that homelessness holds both these dimensions within itself. Homelessness involves a past home, present homelessness, and future homecoming; homelessness involves both separation from and connection with the no-longer-home and not-yet-home. Thus, the story of two-dimensional homelessness is nothing other than the story of being and temporality (where the history of being involves the essence of human being). A basic movement throughout the history of being emphasizes separation in the present metaphysical period and unity in the original Greek phase and in the anticipated future. Thus, for example, though being and thinking are always both in some way apart and together, Heidegger traces how they were originally closely bound, then fell apart, and may yet move back together.

Section 4 of *An Introduction to Metaphysics*, entitled 'The Limitation of Being,' investigates being and that which 'differentiated from being somehow belongs intrinsically to being' (IM 79). Specifically, Heidegger inquires about being and becoming, being and appearance, being and thinking, and being and the ought. He will return later to fill in how and why these become opposite in the metaphysical tradition. Here, he emphasizes the original state and touches upon the future. He begins by emphasizing that the origin of these differentiations is found in the early thinking of the Greeks. But seeking after origin is not merely looking for what always was apart. 'These distinctions are by no means accidental. What is held apart in them belonged originally together and tends to merge' (IM 80). 'The differentiation springs from an initial inner union between thinking and being itself' (IM 101). Of course, even though this needs to be explained, it is difficult because any explanation must proceed out of our present philosophical position, where thinking and being no longer have the same unity. We now proceed by way of concepts and logic.

But logic, that is, the science and doctrine of philosophical thinking, 'was able to arise as an exposition of the formal structure and rules of thought only after the division between being and thinking had been effected ... Consequently logic itself and its history can never throw adequate light on the essence and origin of this separation between being and thinking' (IM 102). In short, both the origin of being and thinking and the present philosophical understanding of their separation must be questioned. Further, this questioning must be of a sort which is no longer traditionally logical if it is to think these two. Necessarily, Heidegger's account is going to be tentative and changeable until he finds a new way to think and speak, for example, concerning the question of the differentiation of being and thinking which 'is a name for the fundamental attitude of the Western spirit' (IM 22).

The task before Heidegger is clear, even if there is no immediate prospect of a complete understanding or account. He begins to lay out the questions which must be answered concretely in an account of 'the nature of the original unity' and 'original separation' of being and thinking (IM 104). Again, the emphasis in the originary situation is on their togetherness, now lost. 'If the separation between being and thinking was an essential, necessary separation, it must have been rooted in an original bond between them. Our inquiry into the origin of the separation is first and foremost an inquiry into the essential bond between thinking and being' (IM 104). Accordingly, the story of being begins with Parmenides' and Heraclitus' accounts of being, thought by way of *binding together.* Parmenides, whom Heidegger understands to be both 'farsighted thinker and poet' (IM 81) (the two figures who experience being), elaborates being 'as the pure fullness of the permanent, gathered within it' (IM 82). Heidegger specifically cites Fragment 8, which says 'how it stands with being': 'for being present it *is* entirely, unique, unifying, united, gathering itself in itself from itself' (IM 82).

Heidegger argues against recent interpretations which stress the opposition of Parmenides and Heraclitus. In fact, Heidegger stresses their agreement by elaborating the element of gathering in their thought: whereas Parmenides speaks of being in terms of gathering, Heraclitus speaks in this way of Logos. Commenting on Heraclitus' first two fragments, Heidegger says, 'What is said here of *logos* corresponds to the actual meaning of the word "collection" [*Sammlung*]. But just as the German word means 1) collecting and 2) collectedness, so *logos* means here collectedness, the primal gathering principle ... It means: the original collecting collectedness which is in itself permanently dominant' (IM 108). Since, for Heraclitus, '*Logos* is the steady gathering, the intrinsic togetherness of the essent, i.e. being' (IM 110), at the beginning of Greek thinking we find primal, active unities. '*Logos* characterizes being in a new and yet old respect: that which is, which stands straight and distinct in itself, is at the same time gathered togetherness in itself and by itself, and maintains itself in such gatheredness ... *Eon,* beingness, is essentially *xynon,* collected presence ... *xynon* is ... the original unifying unity of what tends apart' (IM 110). Further, this 'gathering is never a mere driving-together and heaping-up. It maintains in a common bond the conflicting and that which tends apart. It does not let them fall into haphazard dispersion' (IM 113).

As this makes clear, if being is understood – originarily – as gathering and togetherness, apartness also is thought, for only what tends apart can or need be brought together. That is, Heidegger is showing that Heraclitus and Parmenides thought being and thinking in a way that involved (or posited) an actively occurring unity. It is usually held that Parmenides says, in Fragment 5, 'Thinking and being are the same.'

According to Heidegger, this is one of those traditional misinterpretations and translations which separate us both from the Greeks and from our subject matter (IM 115).[14] How are thinking and being the same? 'We know that this unity is never empty indifference; it is not sameness in the sense of mere equivalence. Unity is the belonging-together of antagonisms. This is original oneness ... Being and thinking in a contending sense are one, i.e. the same in the sense of belonging together' (IM 117).[15] Thus, Heidegger attempts 'to regain the basic and original truth of the maxim' by a different translation, which also means by way of a different interpretation: 'The maxim does not say: "thinking and being are the same." It says: "There is a reciprocal bond between apprehension and being"' (IM 122).

Again, Heidegger knows that this needs to be elaborated. But before further analysis and detail flesh out the story, more of the basic features need to be sketched. Along with the belonging together and apartness of being and thinking, Heidegger notes that the Greeks thought the togetherness and apartness of being and humans. Yet, the link between these two matters is not what we might suppose. It might appear that since thinking is a human activity, the question of thinking and being is identical to the question of humans and being. It is not that simple. When, according to Heidegger, Parmenides says that being and thinking belong together, he is telling us about how human beings belong together with being. 'Being dominates, but because and insofar as it dominates and appears, appearing and *with* it apprehension must *also* occur. But if man is to participate in this appearing and apprehension, he must himself be, he must belong to being. But then the essence and the mode of being-human can only be determined by the essence of being' (IM 117). That is, the story of being becomes the story of human being because humans are drawn into history, not by any power on our part, but by being itself. We do not begin to question our experience of homelessness from being by looking toward an earlier state where being and human being appear as already separate entities. Such a description is already a condition of homelessness; an originary belonging together must be sought in an even earlier phase where human being 'is determined by the essential belonging-together of being and apprehension' (IM 118).

To be understood, though, humans and apprehension (what Parmenides speaks of as *noein* and what we call thinking) must be thought differently than is usual in modern anthropologically oriented philosophy and science. Apprehension was not originally a power belonging to clearly defined human beings but a 'process in which man first enters into history as a being, an essent, i.e. (in the literal sense) comes into being' (IM 119). Thus, rather than beginning with being and humans as two opposites whose relationship is uncertain, Parmenides tells the story of the spinning out of humans and being: 'apprehension is not a function that man has as an attribute, but rather the other way around: apprehension is the happening that has man' (IM 119).

Even as the story of being was originally one of being's togetherness with human being, it was also one of human being's separation from being. The two belong together in a particular manner: being prevails, and apprehension happens along with it (IM 117). Parmenides' account of the appearance of human beings as both disoriented and related to being is the crucial definition of human-being, and it embodies an essential characterization of being. The separation between being and being-human comes to light in their togetherness. We can no longer discern the separateness through the pale and empty dichotomy of 'being and thinking,' which lost its roots hundreds of years ago, unless we go back to its beginnings. 'The mood and direction of the opposition between being and thinking are so unique because it is here that man comes face to face with being. This event masks the knowing emergence of man as the historical being' (IM 119).

Once again, we find that to be human is to be separated from being, even as that separation results from a belonging together. Originary being at home devolves into homelessness insofar as humans become human. Since we learn about this through the utterances which project something new, that is, through originary poetry, Heidegger consults Greek poetic thought. Parmenides and Heraclitus are poetic thinkers, where thinking has the priority; but being and human-being are also taken up in the thinking poetry of Greek tragedy. 'Sophocles' *Antigone* (lines 332–5) powerfully tells us of our experience of the uncanny. The first line anticipates the theme: There is much that is strange, but nothing that surpasses man in strangeness.' The poet's insight into the essence of human being is described here. In Heidegger's gloss, 'Man, in *one* word, is *deinotaton*, the strangest' (IM 125). 'We are taking the strange, the uncanny [*das Unheimliche*], as that which casts us out of the "homely," i.e. the customary, familiar, secure. The unhomely [*unheimische*] prevents us from making ourselves at home and therein it is overpowering. But man is the strangest of all, not only because he passes his life amid the strange understood in this sense but because he departs from his customary, familiar limits, because he is the violent one, who, tending toward the strange in the sense of the overpowering, surpasses the limit of the familiar [*das Heimische*]' (IM 127).

According to Heidegger, then, the Greek definition of humans does not see us as occasionally or accidentally involved in the uncanny; rather, Sophocles' lines say that to be the most homeless, the strangest of all, 'is the basic trait of the human essence, within which all of the other traits must find their place' (IM 127). It is because of this homelessness that Sophocles goes on to say about the human being, 'Everywhere journeying, inexperienced and without issue, he comes to nothingness' (IM 127). That is, humans are always in passage, or put another way, are always a passage because as no longer at home and not yet at home again, we are always in transition. We are 'cast out of every relation to the familiar and befallen by *ate*-, ruin, catastrophe' (IM 128).

The homelessness of humans reigns over them, even where they seem to experience power; indeed, it is precisely in such powers as thinking and saying that homelessness is strongest. But the un-canniness of language, for example, is concealed by its apparent familiarity. Misled by and toward the seemingly ordinary, humans are on the path of untruth, where we turn away from the essentially strange. And, in turning away from the normally concealed homelessness – now momentarily unconcealed in the words of the thinkers and poets – humans turn away from their essence and being. Even worse than ignoring our strangeness, humans do not even see it as uncanny. 'How far man is from being at home in his own essence is revealed by his opinion of himself as he who invented and could have invented language and understanding, building and poetry' (IM 131).

Since humans could never have invented the powers of language, building, forming, and understanding, which allow them to be human, the question becomes how we found our way to the overpowering (and thereby first found ourselves), then how we later lost our way (IM 132). For the moment, Heidegger indicates that we become homeless in regard to being and our own essence because we act as if we were our own guarantor – origin and source – of being at home. '[Human being] is without issue because he is always thrown back on the paths that he himself has laid out: he becomes mired in his paths, caught in the beaten track, and thus caught he encompasses the circle of his world, entangles himself in appearance, and so excludes himself from being. He turns round and round in his own circle' (IM 132). 'Yet all this concealed uncanniness belongs to the most extreme uncanniness: death. [This] strange and alien [*umheimlich*] thing that banishes us once and for all from everything in which we are at home is no particular event ... It is not only when he comes to die, but always and essentially that man is without issue in the face of death ... Thus his being-there is the happening of strangeness' (IM 133).

In his own terms, Parmenides says this too. We have seen that Heidegger interprets Parmenides as saying that *logos* means 'the togetherness of being [*physis*]'; it also comes to mean ingathering or human self-collection. 'It is *logos* as ingathering, as man's collecting-himself toward fitness, that first brings being-human into its essence, so thrusting it into homelessness, insofar as the home is dominated by the appearance of the ordinary, customary, and commonplace' (IM 142). We have, then, *logos* at a juncture, where on the one hand it points to *being* and its gathering and on the other to humans and theirs – and, later, historically, to the *logos* as a name for discourse and logic. But for now, it suffices to hear of *logos* in the gathering together of being and human being and to understand that the task of being human involves taking 'gathering *upon* oneself,' precisely in the midst of the upsurge of the uncanny (IM 146).

Radically, to be a human being is to be, essentially and unavoidably, the event of homelessness – homelessness from the familiar, from our own essence, and from being. So the story of the *unheimlich* and that of the question of being turn out to be the same story of homelessness, and one in which our own part must be faced and questioned. From what Heidegger has said it may seem that homelessness is a purely human condition or failing (even if unavoidable). That would be a mistaken impression. Homelessness is not the anthropomorphic history of humans and being seen from the viewpoint of humans. We are not homeless as we might be shoeless, having lost the latter gambling, perhaps. Rather, if we ask how it stands between humans and being, if we question how it is that in time humans and being are apart and yet belong together, then homelessness names the way of belonging, though apart. To question our experience of homelessness, rather than turn away from it, is to question its origin in the more than human – in being. 'The strangest (man) is what it is because, fundamentally, it cultivates and guards the familiar, only in order to break out of it and to let what overpowers break in. Being itself hurls man into this breaking away, which drives him beyond himself to venture forth toward being, to accomplish being, to stabilize it in the world, and so hold open the essent as a whole' (IM 137). All of this means that the story of homelessness is not reducable to an account of human accomplishments or failures. It is the story of being itself and the way being involves human being. Accordingly, this story of homelessness is both central to our question and must be taken up first, since as Parmenides, Heraclitus, and Sophocles tell us, before any homecoming could be even considered, to be on the right way we must face and endure homelessness. 'In his exile from home, the home is first disclosed as such. But in one with it and only thus, the alien, the overpowering, is disclosed as such. Through the event of homelessness the while of the essent is disclosed. In this disclosure unconcealment takes place. But this is nothing other than the happening of the unfamiliar' (IM 140).

Heidegger has begun to establish the main joints of the story of being: an originary past in which being and human being are established in the modes of being at home, then the long metaphysical tradition in which homelessness perdures, and finally attempted homecoming. Though he will later retell the story in greater detail, even at this point his basic articulation is not yet complete. He still needs to say something of what might come – and this includes his own attempted thinking and language which might hope to reinterpret and retranslate the history of philosophy and thereby the history of being. Of course, the emphasis in such a story of the future would be on homelessness overcome. Can a thinking questioning hope to be a homecoming? Heidegger is fully aware that what he can say in *An Introduction to Metaphysics* is not itself the achievement of what is necessary. Clearly, his thinking and language are still largely those of traditional metaphysics. This needs to be made explicit: he is beginning to be able to move toward a genuine questioning, but for the most part he relies on metaphysical concepts and patterns of language which are within the realm of homelessness. Here Heidegger's thinking is not yet the genuine questioning which he seeks, though it is attempting to move toward that questioning.

His position shows itself, for example, in the way thinking is presented. Where he develops the originary unity and separation of being and thinking, Heidegger treats thinking as representation (*Vorstellung*) because 'thinking sets itself off against being in such a way that being is placed before it and consequently stands opposed to it' (IM 98). Further, Heidegger understands thinking by way of the *power* which relates being and human being. Thus, in our tradition, thinking is one of the chief means we have for dealing with what is. Thinking, as representation, brings the object of thought before us, into our grasp. This is not mere metaphor or ornamental rhetoric. Representation as a means of power and control is central to what metaphysics means by thinking. This sort of thinking, most developed in philosophy and science, is the way we relate to what is: 'in representing we think of what is represented and think it through by dissecting it, by taking it apart and putting it together again' (IM 100).

Of course, thinking, too, has a history. Heidegger is concerned to tell of the changes that take place in our understanding of thinking from the beginning, where *noein* and *legein* (which Heidegger interprets as apprehend [*vernehmen*] and gather [*zusammen bringen; sammeln*], respectively) belong together through *logos*' development as statement and dominance over apprehension, to the point where understanding has the sense of judging representation (see, e.g., IM 161).[16] But Heidegger's intention is to do more than merely report an already delineated history; he intends to move to a better position on thinking, being, and human being. Not only is traditional thinking cast in aggressive terms, but so is Heidegger's. He says, 'If we wish to combat intellectualism seriously, we must know our adversary ... [in] a campaign'; 'In the seemingly unimportant distinction between being and thinking we must discern the fundamental position of the Western spirit, against which our central attack is directed' (IM 103, 99).

Heidegger goes on to indicate what alternative sort of thinking there might be – a new kind of thinking which attempts, from out of not being at home, a homecoming. 'It can be overcome only by a return to its *origins,* i.e. we must place its initial truth within its own limits and so put it on a new foundation' (IM 99). The thinking which the future requires, then, is a kind of thinking which returns to sources. 'The misinterpretations of thought and the abuse to which it leads can be overcome only by authentic thinking that goes back to the roots – and *by nothing else.* The renewal of such thinking requires a return to the question of the essential relation of thinking to being, and this means the unfolding of the question of being as such. To surpass the traditional logic does not mean elimination of thought and domination of sheer feeling; it means more radical, stricter thinking, a thinking that is part and parcel of being' (IM 103). This says a great deal. In the first place, it indicates that genuine thinking would be a kind of recovery of what has been lost, and that this recovery would aim to achieve a reunion with being. Here thinking would be a kind of remembering which would overcome the separation underlying the need to remember. This is not to say that such thinking would attempt to be the thinking of the past – that is impossible. And of course, to be authentic, this thinking which might overcome homelessness cannot pretend to an original state of being at home, nor can it shrink from going through the no longer being at home, which is precisely what it means to go 'through and beyond.' Rather, this thinking would be a new beginning which also hearkens back to the originary beginning. 'A beginning can never directly preserve its full momentum; the only possible way to preserve its force is to repeat, to draw once again [wieder-holen] more deeply than ever from its source. And it is only by repetitive thinking [denkende Wieder-holung] that we can deal appropriately with the beginning and breakdown of the truth' (IM 160; see also 32).[17]

Such new thinking, which Heidegger only begins to attempt here, would have the character of a homecoming, to be achieved only out of homelessness while returning to an originary home. And to unfold the question of being by moving through the history of being and human being, such thinking would be immersed in the story of homelessness and homecoming, even as it would play an active role in that story. Hence, Heidegger's project exhibits a problematic, even contradictory character. Though his authentic thinking proposes to be an alternative to traditional thinking, it is presented in language similar to that of aggressive representational thinking. Heidegger is aware of this difficulty and attempts to find another way to speak of authentic thinking. Even though he has not yet really succeeded in finding the appropriate language, it does at least come to him now and then. For example, where he interprets early Greek *logos* as gathering and togetherness and *noein* as taking a receptive attitude which accepts what shows itself (IM 118), there is a hint of a calm openness.

Still, the dominant tone is that of strife and power. The gathering is presented as a bond between the conflicting (IM 113); apprehension is also described in terms of interrogating a witness to see how things stand: 'When troops prepare to receive the enemy, it is in the hope of stopping him at the very least, of bringing him to stand. This negative bringing-to-stand is meant in *noein*' (IM 116).[18] At this point, Heidegger has only opened up the possibility of the language and thinking of homecoming. Remaining in the language and thinking of traditional metaphysics – in the homelessness where we, for all our power, are apart from being – Heidegger still tells the story from the strife-filled, uncanny position: '*Legein* and *noein*, to gather and apprehend, are a need and an act of violence *against* the overpowering, but at the same time only and always *for* it' (IM 148).

Though he does not yet have the means to go beyond not being at home and despite the fact that to be human is to be homeless, Heidegger makes a first move beyond the common and ordinary. He does so by taking upon himself the task of gathering human being back to its own essence – a project which proceeds, evidently, by way of gathering thinking (and thereby human being) back to being. Thus, *An Introduction to Metaphysics* is not a failure, because it does not yet tell the story of being as well as could be done. It persists in beginning to question, aware of its own place in the questioning. For it is in questioning that any hoped for homecoming will come about.

> Only where being discloses itself in questioning does history happen and with it the being of man, by virtue of which he ventures to set himself apart from the essent as such and contend with it.
>
> It is questioning contending that first brings man back to the essent that he himself is and must be.
>
> Only as a questioning, historical being does man come to himself, only as such is he a self. Man's selfhood means this: he must transform the being that discloses itself to him into history and bring himself to stand in it. (IM 121)

Since the question of being also turns out to be the question of human being which is drawn along, the relations between the two are of the greatest importance. For the thinker, no less than for the poet, both thinking and language are such relationships. This is why the language of Heidegger's thinking is central, especially in *An Introduction to Metaphysics,* which speaks along a borderline, with traditional metaphysical meanings, tones, and possibilities on one side and a yet undetermined set on the other. Since Heidegger is attempting, albeit with only little initial success, to pass from the first to the second sort of language and thinking, it is important to note the main ways in which he understands language suitable to his intended questioning. Three congruent ways of thinking the question of being present themselves in this book's language.

First, and normatively, the language of *journey* opens up the questioners' relationship with being and our task before it. That such movement is vital to Heidegger's thought is seen in his attention to verbal as opposed to substantive forms. Think of how *legein* indicates active gathering. Further, language itself moves and develops 'from dialects with their original local and historical roots' (IM 56). Even the origin which Heidegger wants to think is seen as active: 'The original means original only if it never loses the possibility of being what it is: origin as emergence (from the concealment of the essence)' (IM 122). Language shows movement; the movement involves being, human being, thinking, and language itself. *Legein* also means 'to say'; what is to be gathered and said is held in Heidegger's question, 'What sustains and guides the saga [*Saga*] of being?' (IM 60).

Where language allows us to think of our belonging to being as a journey to and from being, it is not surprising that language names sites and placements along the way. Secondly, then, the question of being and human being occurs in a language of *place*. Heidegger argues that, in contrast to modern philosophers, in their treatment of metaphysical concepts of space, the Greeks thought being and human being by way of place (*topos*). Here there is the possibility of thinking about 'that which withdraws, and in such a way precisely admits and "makes place" for something else' (IM 55). Of course, just as there are paths to beings and being, for the Greeks, the basic mode of being human is named in 'the foundation and scene of man's being-there, the point at which all these paths meet, the *polis* ... *Polis* means ... the place, the there, wherein and as which historical being-there is' (IM 128). But this scene of action is not sustained. 'Pre-eminent in the historical place, they become at the same time *apolis*, the city and place, lonely, strange, and alien' (IM 128).[19] Thus, Sophocles speaks of humans as strange insofar as we set out into the placeless (IM 129). But we are not merely placeless; even while placeless, we ourselves are understood by way of place. Unexpectedly, 'placelessness' and 'place' tell us of – lead us back to – our essence. Human being is called *Da-sein*, being-there, because Heidegger thinks about human being's belonging to being through the language of place. 'In accordance with the hidden message of the beginning, man should be understood, within the question of being, as *the* site which being requires in order to disclose itself. Man is the site of openness, the there. The essent juts into this there and is fulfilled. Hence we say that man's being is in the strict sense of the word "being-there." The perspective for the opening of being must be grounded originally in the essence of being-there as such a site for the disclosure of being' (IM 171).

The language of movement combines with that of place to name the goal of our journey. Heidegger asks the questions of being and human being 'to restore man's historical being-there ... to the domain of being, which it was originally incumbent on man to open up for himself' (IM 34). Further, this same language speaks of the journey to the home place. 'Our questioning brings us into the landscape we must inhabit as a basic prerequisite, if we are to ever win back our roots in history' (IM 32). Thus, language presents a geography of being wherein human being wanders. The saga of being and human being is articulated not only in the vocabulary and images of journey and place but specifically in terms of *home, homelessness,* and *homecoming.* Being itself is to be understood this way. The Greek experience of being, which they named *ousia* or *parousia* is misunderstood, according to Heidegger, if we translate it as 'sub-stance.' 'For *parousia* we have in German a corresponding term – *An-wesen* [presence], which also designates an estate or homestead, standing in itself and self-enclosed' (IM 50). Being, which endures as presence, is home. Further, or accordingly perhaps, the German verb for 'to be,' *sein,* has the inflected form '*wesan,* 'to dwell, to sojourn' (IM 59).

Though the language seems to say that being is the home place for humans and that humans are the site for the occurrence of being, this mutual being-at-home is not something within which we are already at rest. It is what we attempt to move toward in our questioning. Hence we return to the understanding of truth in movement and journey (see ET 30), but not in a simple linear movement that is either toward being or in errancy away from it. 'Truth not only shifts its abode; it changes its essence as well' (IM 156). Genuine questioning would be movement through a complex landscape of no-longer-home, homelessness, and not yet home. Before any homecoming might be achieved, Heidegger must start more fully from the place where we are. That is, before he will be able to think or say much more about the originary which lies in the past or the possibility of a new genuine response, which clearly lies in the future, he must elaborate the long history of being in-between. *This is our present metaphysical homelessness, the homelessness from being and our own essence, which is the uncanny story most in need of questioning.*

The History of Being: Metaphysics and the Essence of Human Being

Heidegger had articulated the basic features of the story of being by 1935, in works such as 'What is Metaphysics,' 'On the Essence of Truth,' and *An Introduction to Metaphysics.* Next, he elaborated the motif in a series of works composed in the same voice and mode of thinking between 1936 and the early 1940s. The seven most important considered here are the lecture courses on Nietzsche, given from 1936 to 1940; 'The Age of the World Picture,' from 1938; 'Metaphysics as History of Being,' 1941; 'Sketches for a History of Being as Metaphysics,' 1941; 'Recollection in Metaphysics,' 1941; parts of 'The Word of Nietzsche: "God Is Dead,"' 1936–40; and 'Overcoming Metaphysics,' 1936–46.

It should be emphasized that, in these works, Heidegger does not pretend to treat exhaustively the story of being. That proves to be a lifelong project. What he does do in these seven pieces is develop the story he has begun to tell. Our consideration of these works aims to establish that in them he does three things. He actually does elaborate the story of being: he fills it in by proceeding from out of our present situation of homelessness; he clearly articulates homelessness as the story of the history of being and the essence of human being. Of course, the tale is modified. Nonetheless, he works within the basic schema he has already worked out, emphasizing the story of metaphysics set within the triple temporal settings of originary thinking in the beginning, in metaphysics, and in genuine thinking yet to come. As we have seen, the age of metaphysical homelessness had already occurred by the time of the Greeks, when Sophocles told us that to be human is to be *unheimlich*. Though the entire story must be told and thought, Heidegger, in the seven works to be considered next, focuses especially on the homelessness of human being and being.

We began with an experience of the uncanny, but if we are to question genuinely, we must pass beyond the merely human. The task of articulating and reflecting on metaphysics, for example, is not an anthropological enterprise directed at interpreting a human achievement or failure. 'The history of being is neither the history of man and of humanity, nor the history of the human relation of beings to being. The history of being is being itself, and only being. However, since being claims human being for grounding its truth in beings, man is drawn into the history of being, but always only with regard to the manner in which he takes his essence from the relation of being to himself and, in accordance with this relation, loses his essence, neglects it, give it up, grounds it, or squanders it' (RM 82). The point cannot be overemphasized. Though we are involved in the story Heidegger attempts to tell and in the questions we need to ask, the story is being's. The saga concerns the history which unfolds, which is nothing other than being itself. Thus, though Heidegger may not have the language he needs to say all this properly, he clearly understands the history of being in a way which is no longer modern. From the modern point of view, the history of metaphysics is our own story because metaphysics is our own product. Not so for Heidegger.

To question our uncanniness, Heidegger questions metaphysics because 'metaphysics grounds an age, in that through a specific interpretation of what is and a specific comprehension of truth it gives to that age the basis upon which it is essentially formed' (AWP 115). This choice is not arbitrary, for the event of metaphysics is the advent of homelessness. Specifically, it is in metaphysics that there occurs the beginning of the fundamental distinctions and the separation of being from what becomes opposed to it. For Heidegger, 'the beginning of metaphysics is revealed as an event that consists in a determination of being, in the sense of the appearance of the division into whatness and thatness' (MHB 2–3; see also IM 79ff.). Metaphysics as the history of being begins with the separation of being and human being. The apartness and metaphysics dawn together. 'The history of being begins, and indeed necessarily, *with the forgetting of being* ... This strange remaining-away of being is due only to metaphysics as metaphysics. But what is metaphysics?' (WN 109). Since the next step would be to more adequately rethink metaphysics, the appropriate approach or vantage point would be crucial. 'If it is true that metaphysics accounts for its essence through this difference, obscure in origin, of the what and the that, and grounds its essence thereupon, it can never of itself come to knowledge of this distinction. It would have to be previously and as such approached by being which has entered this distinction. But being refuses this approach, and thus alone makes possible the essential beginning of metaphysics' (MHB 3).

That anything lies beyond the realm of metaphysics cannot be fathomed by our representational comprehension. Yet, we have not only forgotten being, according to Heidegger, but that and how we have slipped into forgetfulness itself. Hence, in these works, Heidegger focuses on the 'Oblivion of being [that] means: the self-concealing origin of being divided into whatness and thatness in favor of being which opens out beings as beings and remains unquestioned *as* being' (MHB 3–4).

The movement of thinking, then, turns from human activities toward being and, as an attempt at genuine thinking, tries to move backward through and in an opposite direction to the unfolding of being from origin. Being's movement away from origin moves only in one way. 'Being alone is'; that is, being, thought of as occurrence, 'itself is the sole happening' (RM 79). Further, though metaphysics and the history of being are not the same, the former is an event in and a part of the latter: 'metaphysics is the history of being as the progression out of the origin ... That history of being which is historically familiar as metaphysics has its essence in that a progression from the origin occurs' (RM 79).

Because of this movement, any recovery requires thinking that recalls or remembers. 'This progression allows the return to become a need, and allows recollection in the origin to become a needful necessity' (RM 79). Of course, no matter how much we need a homecoming, in thinking and to being, the past of being will never occur again, nor will our thinking ever again become the thinking which happened in the past. Any home which might come in a homecoming would be, not the primal home which no longer is and never again will be, but a future home which is not yet. Thus, Heidegger says that *aletheia* does not return to the origin (sHBM 55); later distinctions 'can never reach back to the original essential fullness of being, not even when it is thought in its Greek origin' (sHBM 56). The thinking called for needs to think the history of being without nostalgically attempting, or pretending, to be the thinking of the past, where there was no separation between being and humans. Instead, the *separation* must be elaborated and seen as far as possible in light of its origin. That is to say, metaphysics and its origin have yet to be discovered, much less genuinely questioned.

Homelessness characterizes metaphysics. But this is *not* a contrast to a primal scene of pure unity with a later condition of total separation. Rather, there are distinguishable epochs in which the relationships of belonging and separation vary. Each epoch has its own mode, in which, for example, being, the gods, human beings, truth, thinking, and language belong together and are separated. The history which Heidegger would eventually hope to tell would be the history of these complex, changing, phenomena.

Heidegger's present task, however, is more modest. It is to sketch the major aspects of the belonging and separation which prevail in the modern age, that is, in the time of homelessness. That modern philosophy is concerned with homelessness is not invented by Heidegger. This was already understood by Nietzsche in his penetrating critique of Western and, specifically, German metaphysics. As noted in the introduction, in his lectures Heidegger quotes Nietzsche's insight, '"German philosophy as a whole – Leibniz, Kant, Hegel, Schopenhauer, to name the great ones – is the most thoroughgoing kind of romanticism and homesickness that has ever existed: the longing for the best there ever was"' (N 35).[20] There is, then, an already experienced homesickness for being. But this is coupled with a homesickness for a specific cultural placement in the past, in which to be at home. Where Nietzsche speaks of the object of longing in *The Will to Power*, the home he speaks of is the Greek world. Homelessness has occurred between the early Greek world and ours, where being somehow has been lost or left behind. Nietzsche saw this.[21]

Heidegger, however, not only presents us with the part of the story which Nietzsche told but with what Nietzsche could not say, because it was too close to him. To do so requires finding a way to go forward, free from homesickness' backward longing. Heidegger undertakes the task by attempting to go beyond Nietzsche, saying that we not only are homesick for being, but have so profoundly forgotten being itself that we no longer understand that 'being' – represented as Will – is not our home. According to Heidegger, Nietzsche appears here as the most homeless of all homeless humans. He is at once the most aware of homelessness and homesickness and the most deeply erring in his movement toward the realm in which we are rooted.

In what way, though, does Heidegger better understand our homelessness? He begins by speaking of 'gods,' which immediately opens us to great confusion, since he changes what he thinks and says over the course of his career. This is because he mediates on the Western metaphysical tradition of religion and theology, as well as on the non-metaphysical positions of the early Greek thinkers and poets such as Hölderlin, and, of course, because the many divergent traditions (Judaism, Christianity, Islam, and others, not to forget atheism) wildly disagree – sometimes to the point of violence – about what is the case or what terms mean. This confusing maze of meanings will be partially clarified in the course of following how Heidegger unfolds his thinking (especially in chapters 2, 3, and 5). In the meanwhile, the most helpful roadmap for readers of a different or no religious perspective and/or those who are not Heidegger experts might be to keep three basic aspects in mind. These aspects hopefully are intelligible in themselves, independently of the names and beliefs assigned by various groups; thus, as a start to thinking this through, readers could begin by identifying the following three phenomena with whatever terms they already use. Overall, he thinks 1) the dimensions which are gathered together into a coherent world and that which is actually, historically sent or given or made; 2) the dynamic sending-disclosing itself, which also provides a trace back to the ultimate origin of the granting; and 3) the ultimate origin of the sending opening of our world. Though he gives various names to (and finds differing names in what others say for) the three basic aspects, they remain stable enough to be useful for now. Among the names specifically drawn from a 'sacred' or 'religious' vocabulary that we will see in the course of this book, for aspect 1, speaking about the dimensions that are gathered, he includes the 'divine' or 'divinities,' which he distinguishes from that which is sent as particular, usually referred to as 'gods,' or 'deity'/'deities'; for aspect 2, the sending-opening itself, he begins with Hölderlin's term, 'the holy,' or speaks in terms of messengers between the source and our world by referring to 'gods as heralds'; and for aspect 3, the ultimate origin, he also uses 'the holy' (which would indicate either that aspects 2 and 3 coincide or that 'the holy' has complexly multiple meanings) and the 'divine' or the 'godhead of the divine.' For now, the path of least confusion is probably for the reader to think about how she or he would name these three aspects and then simply start attending to how Heidegger begins to explain and criticize the ideas of god/gods as beings and of 'God' as 'Being' and then how he treats Hölderlin's term 'the holy.' To establish a point of departure we could pick up with Heidegger from the fact that many religious traditions believe that a particular god or gods (such as Zeus and Athena) interact with nature and human beings and that some of these traditions, such as many versions of Christianity, have developed metaphysical theologies. Heidegger explores and disagrees with these two views on the grounds that the former erroneously thinks of god/gods as entities (or even persons), that is, in terms of being (aspect 1), and the latter goes even further to mistakenly consider the 'Judeo-Christian-Muslim God' as the ultimate origin (aspect 3) specifically understood as the supreme entity, transcendental to the sensuous world, that is, as Being itself.

To begin an answer to this aspect of our homelessness, then, Heidegger notes that in the modern epoch we are no longer at home with the gods. He puts the matter dramatically: 'the gods have fled' (AWP 117).[22] This mode of presentation makes clear that the loss of the gods is not merely a matter of human consciousness. According to Heidegger, it is not the case that the gods are products of our imaginations or that they evaporate when we cease thinking of them. Still, we have our share in the process. For example, Christendom thinks God in a specific way, as an absolute cause of the world, which later becomes untenable. At the same time, to speak of departed gods is not an atheism, because though absent from our experience, gods nonetheless belong to our experience as absent. The way in which gods are for us is as in homelessness, separated but still belonging as separated. The modern age does not initiate the separation of humans and gods. Actually, he contends, it develops to an extreme what was already underway in medieval Christianity.[23] Further, the very event of human beings depends on separation from the gods. Genesis tells a version of the tale. So, too, does Heraclitus. 'According to Heraclitus what man is is first manifested (*edeixe*, shows itself) in *polemos*, in the separation of gods and men, in the irruption of being itself' (IM 118). Only such conflict which sets apart 'brings forth gods and men in their being' (IM 121). The homelessness that prevails between humans and the gods needs to be explored. Clearly no end is in sight; no end may even be possible.

At this point, Heidegger can only say that the question of the gods is tied up with the question of being which we have yet to learn to ask somehow originarily, 'a questionableness of being that will once again become capable of a god, as to whether the essence of the truth of being will lay claim more primally to the essence of man' (AWP 153). The larger story again emerges. The loss of the gods is an aspect of the loss of being. And this involves the unfolding of truth, thinking, and our own essence. The Greeks, according to Heidegger, thought the being of beings as the enduring and lasting: '*Being is presence as the showing itself of outward appearance. Being is the lasting of the actual being in such outward appearance*' (MHB 10). With this understanding Plato and Aristotle ground metaphysics. Eventually this Greek beginning unfolds through Roman and Christian metaphysics so that a being and being become understood, respectively, as *ens creatum*, that which is created, and as God, the personal Creator or highest cause (AWP 130).

Here we find a fundamental distinction between 'being and beings, which is not grounded and is at the same time hidden' (RM 81). However, this original distinction is not one we humans invent. 'The distinction is primally rather the presencing of being itself whose origination is appropriation [as *Ereignis* is rendered in the English translation]' (RM 82). In the beginning is appropriation. Appropriation is beginning. But being has been lost. There has been a double abandonment. As we might suppose, we have abandoned being. Human beings have turned away from being in their thought, language, and willing, all of which turn increasingly to beings and thence to mere beingness (RM 80; sHBM 68). As we will see, our reflection comes to be 'reflexion'; in the process, our understanding loses being and therefore has at its heart an uncanny element (sHBM 60; AWP 142). Modern metaphysical thinking completes the abandonment of being: 'The will has never had the origin as its own. It has always already intrinsically abandoned it by forgetting. The most profound oblivion is not-recollecting' (sHBM 3).

Since, even in the metaphysical tradition, 'will' denotes not merely a human faculty or power but being itself, there is more to the story. Behind our losing being is the history of being itself. That is, the most profound homelessness results from the abandonment of beings by being. Of course, this can scarcely be thought and said. At most, Heidegger can only indicate what we must learn to think. 'The surrender in which being abandons itself to the utmost deformation of essence of beingness (to "machination") is in a hidden way the self-suspension of the primal essence of appropriation in the origin which has not yet begun, not yet entered, its groundlessness. The progression of being to beingness is that history of being – called metaphysics – which remains just as essentially remote from the origin in its start as in its finish' (RM 80–1). At this stage of his thinking, Heidegger only tentatively sketches the history of metaphysics; he moves from attempting a direct engagement with being itself to focusing on how being might be recovered and on how it was lost. Not surprisingly, because a future homecoming to being is precisely what he is attempting, such a movement must turn toward the belonging together and separation of being, thinking, and truth.

Indeed, being and truth originally belong together. 'The actual essence of truth, in whose light a period of mankind experiences beings, participates in the history of being' (MHB 20). It turns out, however, that the relationship of truth and being is not simple, because being simultaneously discloses and hides itself. What we call truth is originally the unconcealment (*aletheia*) of being; at the same time, unconcealment is always accompanied by concealment (*letheia*). Before unconcealment can be thought, concealment must be seen and understood; yet, before Heidegger can say more of *aletheia,* he first has to try to trace out how *aletheia* and being have hidden themselves. Only in this way will any uncovering be possible. Thus, he interprets the story of the movement of being and truth by way of the transition from truth as Greek *aletheia,* through Christian faith (by which 'man is essentially installed in the attainment of salvation's certainty'), to modern scientific certainty (MHB 21). 'The origin, belonging to the history of being, of the dominance of truth as certainty is concealed in the *release* of its essence from the primal truth of being' (MHB 21).

The fundamental shift is from truth as the disclosure of being to truth as a relation based in some privileged beings. That is, truth comes to be seen in the providence of the divine or human intellect. Whether it involves the relation of intellect to beings or only intellect's consciousness of itself, the fundamental assumption is the same: truth derives from consciousness. Of course, truth is not just any sort of conscious apprehension but authoritative consciousness, that is, knowledge. Ultimately, truth is taken to mean *certainty* (MHB 20). 'As knowing beings, both realities, God and man, are metaphysically the bearers of truth and thus constitute the reality of knowledge and certainty' (MHB 21). Once truth appears as certainty, the ground and assurance of certainty come into question. For a medieval Christian, possessed of faith, God is the source and guarantor of such certainty. 'Before all, the creator god, and with him the institution of the offering and management of his gifts of grace (the church), is in the sole possession of eternal truth ... By himself, man can never become, and be, absolutely certain of this salvation' (MHB 21). Because the locus of truth is in faith for the Christian, the surest knowledge proceeds from theological interpretation of 'the divine word of revelation, which is set down in Scripture and proclaimed by the Church' (AWP 122).

Heidegger's story has taken us to a crucial joint. At the dawn of the modern epoch, truth is understood not only as correspondence but fundamentally as certainty; the certainty of *adequatio* of thought or statement to the way things are is grounded in God, who guarantees it and grants it to us. It is not difficult to see how this prepares for the modern conception of truth. We have already heard that the gods are gone. But if God no longer stands close by as origin and end of knowledge, our certainty would seem unfounded. On what could any surety be based? If truth is a matter of certainty, and if certainty operates in the realm of consciousness, then the medieval model, based on God as supreme consciousness, provides for its own replacement. 'The possibility is contained here of man's determining the essence of certainty by himself in accordance with the essence of certainty in general (self-assurance), and thus of bringing humanity to dominance within what is real' (MHB 21). Where truth is understood as certainty attained by human consciousness when it assiduously follows the rigorous methods of research protocols and logic-mathematics, we obtain the essence of modern science and technology (AWP 118). We ensure exact knowledge ourselves.

Deeply involved in all this is a changed understanding of being, thinking, and human essence. In the history of metaphysics, in which the Greeks thought being as presencing, Aristotle calls the actual which lies present of itself *hypokeimenon* and that which comes to be along with it, *symbebekota* (MHB 26–7). But a shift occurs in which being is no longer understood to be presenting as workness (*energeia*) but to be actuality (*actualitas*). What originally was seen as what presences itself (*hypokeimenon*) comes to be interpreted and translated – and thereby transformed – by *subiectum* and *substans*, 'which means the same thing: what is truly constant and real' (MHB 27). Much later, when the source of certainty is looked for, not in being as presenting or beings, but in divine or human being, 'the *subiectum* subsequently becomes the name which names the subject in the subject-object relationship, and also the subject in the subject-predicate relationship' (MHB 28).

The demand for certainty has always required an absolute foundation, 'a basis which no longer depends upon a relation to something else, but rather is absolved from the very beginning from this relation, and rests within itself' (MHB 26). When this demand is made at the beginning of modern metaphysics, where God no longer appears as the subject who can guarantee certainty, what is asked for is a being who can think in a way which can guarantee certainty (MHB 28). Descartes names this being and its thinking together *cogito* – I think. Descartes, in thinking being and beings and truth as certainty, thinks them as the objects of consciousness; and the *ego cogito*, as the constant which guarantees certainty. Because the requisite sureness derives from consciousness itself, the self 'proves to be that which underlies its own activity, i.e. proves to be the *subiectum*' (WN 100; see also 83). Because this means that the essence of consciousness is self-consciousness, everything is either a subject or an object for that subject. Humans simultaneously come into their own while 'entering into insurrection' against their place and the world's, as formerly understood. Now, the 'world changes into an object' set up before our consciousness (WN 100).

The relation of thinking to being and beings is understood in a new way: thinking now has to do with the subject's confrontation of the objects standing up before it. Humans can free themselves to a truth which they guarantee for themselves because the true is known within their own knowing (AWP 48). What Descartes calls *cogitans* and we translate by 'thinking' is, according to Heidegger, representing, which means laying hold of and setting before. 'To represent means here: of oneself to set something before oneself and to make secure what has been set in place, as something set in place' (AWP 149). As the representer who does all representing, human being becomes sure that it provides all certainty and truth; accordingly, it is 'made safe and secure, i.e., *is*' (AWP 150). Therein lies the strength and power of science, in the securing of the objectification of all that is (AWP 126). Representation is understood not only as certainty or knowledge but as power and the basis for technology. The connection becomes clear when we see that representation is apprehension and calculation. The original name 'to represent' (*vorstellen*) means, as just noted, to set something before oneself. This means that whatever is depends for its status on human being, and specifically as an object before human being (AWP 133).

Where being, beings, and ideas have become *perceptio*, something put in their place before consciousness, the world is understood as an object at our disposal, in fact, as an object already grasped and conquered: 'Representing is no longer a self-unconcealing for … but is a laying hold and grasping of … What presences does not hold sway, but rather assault rules' (AWP 133, 149). Such representation is also calculation, that is, the calculation in advance of what will be represented and the way it shall be represented. To be sure of an object, thinking aims to bring it predictably and manageably before thinking itself. This certainty of representation allows us to perform science as research (AWP 127). Eventually, Heidegger will need to think through representation for the entire modern epoch, as his 'Sketches for a History of Being as Metaphysics' makes clear in the notes on Descartes, Leibniz, Kant, Hegel, and Nietzsche. For example, representation as grounded in reflexion needs to be understood in light of the history of being and its relation to human being (sHBM 60; OM 97ff.).

In modern metaphysics, then, being and beings as objects, human being as subject, truth as certainty, and thinking as representation-reflection belong together. What belongs together is justified, that is, is made and shown to be right by and in the history of metaphysics. Specifically, the nexus returns us to the complex problem which appears at the advent of the modern age: how to justify our relation to beings and being. If, at the beginning, the relationship of human being with beings and their first cause was grounded in God, and if at the end of the modern age all relation to being devolves from the Will (metaphysically understood), then certainty as the subject's self-guaranteeing relationship with beings is the thread of justification which underlies the variations occurring over these three hundred years (OM 97).

At the beginning, the question of justification, that is, of justice (*iustitia*) is the religious one of human certainty and salvation. As God is lost, metaphysics increasingly emphasizes the subject as the source of rightness. This can be traced from medieval Christianity through Luther's theology, Descartes, Leibniz ('who first thinks clearly the volitional essence of the being of whatever is'), and Kant (who develops self-making-right in its legal emphasis), to the final metaphysics of subjectness, wherein Nietzsche sees justification in the will to power (WN 90ff.). From the Reformation through Nietzsche's thought (OM 97), 'Justification [*iustificatio*] is the accomplishing of *iustitia* (justice or rightness) and is thus justice [*Gerechtigkeit*] itself. Since the subject is forever subject, it makes itself certain of its own secureness. It justifies itself before the claim to justice that it itself has posited' (WN 89–90).

The history of metaphysics apparently becomes the story of human being: the relationships among being, beings, God, truth as certainty, thinking as reflexive-representation, and self-justification become more and more clearly understood by way of the human subject. Eventually, human being becomes the focus of its own story and the basis of metaphysical belonging and separation. Accordingly, thinking about what is, be it world or humans, becomes anthropology, that is, the explanation and evaluation of 'whatever is, in its entirety, from the standpoint of man and in relation to man' (AWP 133). The metaphysics of the modern age is apparently the history of human being coming to its fullness. The new ways in which beings, being, and human being belong together display an unprecedented autonomy: 'The essence of the modern age can be seen in the fact that man frees himself from the bonds of the Middle Ages in freeing himself to himself' (AWP 127). What is decisive here is not so much human being's relationship with beings and being, but that the relationship is understood to be self-constituted. We make, secure, and occupy our own position in regard to all that is (AWP 132 and 147ff.) The doctrine of humans displaces theological doctrines of gods and metaphysical doctrines of the being of beings. 'Philosophy in the age of completed metaphysics is anthropology' (OM 99).

It would seem that human being has freed itself to the point where it not only establishes a new house of its own, but in its modern mode of development is, far more radically, its own home. 'Because, in keeping with this freedom, self-liberating man himself posits what is obligatory, the latter can henceforth be variously defined' (AWP, 148). We can now specify our own wants and needs, as well as what will satisfy them; as autonomously self-securing we can not only provide, but be, our own home because all that belongs together is related as it is, and to us, by way of our own way of being. This is important: in modern metaphysics there is a new mode of belonging. For example, what is real and representation do belong-together, as is witnessed by Leibniz's thinking how they are the same: from their belonging-together stems the unity which 'constitutes the beingness of beings' (MHB 32ff.). And as already seen, 'subjectivity, object, and reflection belong together. Only when reflection as such is experienced, namely, as the supporting relation to beings, only then can being be determined as objectivity' (OM 97).

But if all this is not only apparently but actually so, how can this mode of the belonging-together of all that is, where the subject would be at home with itself, be the scene of homelessness as Heidegger earlier claimed? As he has told the story of modern metaphysics, is it finally uncanny? In what way?

In fact, it turns out that the very mode of belonging-together which characterizes the modern age contains within itself the deepest modes of separation and strangeness. In the unfolding of the subject as its own guarantor of the certainty (truth) of representation (thinking) – that is, of its relationship with beings – comes the increasing concealment of being itself. While superficially it appears, and even is, correct that human being becomes fully free and autonomous, actually we replace our originary home – being or God – with ourselves. That is, the gods are lost, and the world ('a name for what is, in its entirety'), as an object placed before us, becomes for the first time a picture (AWP 129, 130). Here, being itself becomes forgotten – which also means human being loses, or even squanders, its essence (RM 82). That is why Heidegger says the following, concerning the transformation of the being of being from the presencing of what is present to the object of representation: 'Where everything that is has become the object of representing, it first incurs in a certain manner a loss of being' (AWP 142).

Thus, at the consummation of the history of metaphysics, we find that our imparting value to objects is a compensation for this loss, even if only vaguely understood as such (AWP 142). What appears to be our creative power is the counterpart to a loss of being and a reaction to being's degradation. 'When the being of whatever is, is stamped as a value and its essence is thereby sealed off, then within this metaphysics – and that means continually within the truth of what is as such during this age – the very way to the experiencing of being itself is obliterated. Here, in speaking of such a way, we presuppose what we should perhaps not presuppose at all, that such a way to being has at some time existed and that a thinking on being has already thought being as being' (WN 103–4). This modest concluding disclaimer serves to distinguish the story of metaphysics from the story of the originary thinking which preceded it: the latter epoch's is a tale of homelessness, the former's one of being-at-home. The history of metaphysics is increasingly a history of homelessness because human being and being are further separated, despite all that newly belongs-together in the process of separation. Recall that the modern understanding of truth, thinking, human being, and being proceeded from a complex abandonment of being (as treated above). Here we can see more precisely what has happened to being.

'What is happening to being? *Nothing* is happening to being' (WN 104). That is, the outcome of metaphysics is, as Nietzsche understood, nihilism. Nihilism does not let being be what it is (WN 104). 'Now metaphysics not only does not think being itself, but this not-thinking of being clothes itself in the illusion that it does think being as a value, so that all questions concerning being become and remain superfluous' (WN 104–5). Thus, in its conclusion, metaphysics comes to nihilism. Just where we thought we were at home, there is a radical homelessness: 'Nihilism, "the most uncanny of all guests," is standing at the door' (WN 62).

The new belonging which occurs in modern metaphysics, as well as the separation, must be thought together. That which now belongs in a unity is as a whole separated from what earlier belonged in a unity. On the one hand, human being as subject, truth as certainty, thinking as representation-reflection, and the being of beings and God as objects all do belong together in the history of metaphysics. On the other hand, they unfold along lines which, step by step, come from early Greek understandings of human being, respectively, as 'the one who is looked upon by that which is' and as one who must gather (*legein*) and save (*su-sein*) what opens itself, truth as *aletheia*, thinking as opening to what presences by apprehending, and the being of beings as that which arises and opens itself as what presences (AWP 131).

Given this double dynamic, it would be presumptuous to say that the history of metaphysics is anything arbitrary. And to assume that such developments are an arbitrary product of human (mis-)understanding is to assume the modern position – that we are the creators of the meaning and history of being and beings. But Heidegger has contended all along that the history of metaphysics is no mere human product; rather, it is the history of being itself. 'Nihilism, thought in its essence, is ... the fundamental movement of the history of the West' (WN 62–3). Because metaphysics does not experience being, throughout its course, 'Nothing is befalling being itself and its truth' (WN 109). In the appearing of whatever is as such, the truth of being falls from meaning. It remains forgotten. Thus nihilism would be in its essence a history that runs its course along with being. 'According to this, metaphysics itself would not be merely a neglect of a question still to be pondered concerning being. Surely it would not be an error. Metaphysics, as the history of the truth of what is as such, would have come to pass from out of the destining of being itself. Metaphysics would be, in its essence, the mystery of being itself, a mystery that is unthought because withheld ... Metaphysics is an epoch of the history of being itself' (WN 110).

Nihilism, or metaphysics in its final phase, cannot know what is most crucial: 'It belongs to the uncanniness of this uncanny guest that it cannot name its own origin' (WN 63). Not only are we homeless, but we cannot specify the sense of this homelessness. Indeed, metaphysics itself has forgotten, does not understand, that it is homeless. Further, just as little as human being would be its own home (as metaphysics has come to suppose), so little is human being alone the source of the homelessness which holds sway in metaphysics. Precisely such interpretations and questions are what Heidegger means to present in his story of metaphysics. By telling us the history of metaphysics he hopes we will hear the story of homelessness and therein also hear the story of home. Metaphysics and being belong together, even as the former moves away from the latter: homelessness is a separation from and, yet, a belonging to home. That is, Heidegger holds that homecoming could only proceed from a questioning that engages the uncanny (WN 110).

Two points emerge concerning Heidegger's story of home and homelessness. First, he has only begun to sketch the events. Clearly, a fuller development of the transformations of being, human being, truth, thinking, and language from the early Greek to the contemporary epoch is necessary. And when he later understands more, he will return to this story. For now, he says what he can, and does no more than provide the outline of what has happened. Second, in *An Introduction to Metaphysics,* Heidegger emphasizes the Greek epoch, though he takes up later ones; in the subsequent set of works just considered, he emphasizes the long period of increasing homelessness after the Greeks. Yet, in these works too, he touches on the possibility of homecoming. Though unable to articulate very much about homecoming, Heidegger claims to have gone beyond homelessness, even if only barely and tentatively. He still tells us something of the future being at home of being, human being, truth, and thinking: since any homecoming would come out of and after our metaphysical homelessness, the story of being is also – and finally – the story of a home yet to be.

We have seen that the belonging-together which obtains in metaphysics is at a distance from what originally belongs together. Any becoming at home would have to involve a belonging-together in which being and human being would no longer be separated as they are now. Such a future event would be originary, even while not being the original belonging-together, which is long past. What is needed is opposite any 'flight into tradition,' with its 'self-deception and blindness in relation to the historical moment' (AWP 136). What is required is the sort of thinking and questioning which comes face to face with the painful and hidden, that is, with the homelessness in the midst of which we find ourselves. Insofar as Heidegger has seen that, in the history of metaphysics human being has come to eclipse being, he can say that the next phase would involve the withdrawal of our own obscuring influence. To ask about a return of, or to, being's truth is premature, unless we see that first our metaphysical posture as subjects grasping being and beings as objects in representational thinking must be overcome (AWP 154). 'Since thinking, on the edge of the time span of undecidedness in the history of being, gropes its way toward first recollection in being, it must at the same time go through the dominance of human being and leave it aside' (sHBM 67).

There are many possible junctures: being, truth, thinking, and human being historically come together and move apart in changing ways. To pass over from our present state to an epoch in which metaphysical barriers do not obscure being would be the task of a kind of thinking which Heidegger attempts to discover. Such thinking would be a re-collection because it attempts to gather together again, though newly, what first was together, but became separated. 'Recollection in the history of being thinks history as the arrival, always remote, of the perdurance of truth's essence. Being occurs primally in this essence. Recollection helps the remembrance of the truth of being by allowing the following to come to mind: The essence of truth is at the same time the truth of essence. Being and truth belong to each other just as they belong intertwining to a still concealed rootedness in the origin whose origination opening up remains that which comes' (RM 75). This arrival would be a homecoming, toward the looked-to event in which being, truth, thinking, and human being would be reunited. 'Recollection of the history of being entrusts historical humanity with the task of becoming aware that *the essence of man is released to the truth of being*' (RM 76). That is, it is *by way of recollection* that a homecoming would occur; further, this recollection is not merely a human creation but 'a bestowal which explicitly and uniquely gives the relation of being and man to awareness to be pondered' (RM 76).

Rather than understanding the story from the viewpoint of either human being alone or of being by itself, we have to look to the gathering of the two. That is why Heidegger does not speak of truth, thinking, or even language as purely human; nor are they purely being's. Rather, truth, thinking, and language occur in the *between* of being and human being. We need to learn to think these together. To ask, for example, about the essence of human being is also to question being: it is to question 'the manner and mode in which man is man, i.e., as himself; the manner of the coming to presence of selfhood, which is not at all synonymous with I-ness, but rather is determined out of the relation to being as such' (RM 37). Thus, the story of being would not be a story made up by Heidegger; it is being's own story. What he says, and before that, what is thought and questioned – by Heidegger and by us – needs to be attuned to 'the uniqueness of a saying of being' (RM 78).

According to Heidegger, this saying and the attendant recollection (which 'is a thinking ahead to the origin, and belongs to being itself' [RM 83]) have already begun to be granted, for instance (evidently), in what Heidegger has been given and been able to tell us about the history of being. That is why he locates the story on the threshold between the present metaphysical age and the epoch to come. Because of what he can say and ask concerning being and human being, we begin to see our homelessness and to see that it might be overcome. We see that we are not absolutely and hopelessly estranged from being. Nonetheless, no homecoming has yet been achieved, nor is any at hand. Heidegger is not so presumptuous as to claim that he has been given, much less accomplished, any such full experience of being. We have not yet learned the recollective thinking which would be part of a homecoming. Still, insofar as Heidegger at least begins to creatively question homelessness, that is, the history of being, we are granted an opening to reflection, 'even if this succeeds only in the form of an essential need which soundlessly and without consequences shakes everything true and real to the roots' (RM 83).

We are in a complex situation: a belonging together of being and human being persists throughout their historical separation in the metaphysical age. 'Reflection transports the man of the future into that "between" in which he belongs to being and yet remains a stranger amid that which is' (AWP 136) – an essential characteristic of homelessness and, therefore, of human being. While we are homeless, we yet belong to being.

Notice the language of these thoughts. We are 'between' homelessness and home; being and human being are separated but may gather together. This dramatic action occurs in the language of place and site, that is, in the language presenting home and its landscape. For Heidegger, 'place' and 'site' are also on the border between metaphysical homelessness and originary homecoming. When science and technology inquire into 'the essence of body and place' (AWP 117) they are grounded in the understanding of beings and being by way of position. That is, they are determined by metaphysical thinking. What is an object must have placement; it is placed in and by representation. And precisely when being becomes defined by Kant as 'merely position,' there occurs a definitive moment in the history of being, when being is no longer questioned (sHBM 65).

A transformation in the mode of belonging of human beings and being would involve a shift away from objects positioned before a subject toward a mutual belonging together. The formal relation holding sway in uncanniness would yield to a more homely situation. In fact, we find a correlate shift in language as Heidegger begins to think of a new rootedness or home (for instance, in the opening pages of 'Recollection in Metaphysics,' which speak of 'the wealth of the simple' [RM 75], and in his frequent use of examples such as houses, bed frames, and domestic items in the Nietzsche lectures). This non-metaphysical, homey language actually returns to the originary Greek: before the modern metaphysical treatment of being by way of relation and place (understood as formal position or location), Aristotle understood the Greek essence of being (*ousia*) to be 'presenting as dwelling of what is actual' (MBH 27; see also sHBM 68).

The question, then, becomes how to think the belonging together of being and human being – their placement. Human being itself is understood by Heidegger as the site of this reunion. Recall that we are somewhere between absolute homelessness and home: 'This open between is the openness-for-being (Da-sein), the word understood in the sense of the ecstatic realm of the revealing and concealing of being' (AWP 154). The task is to respect the limits of the thinkable and sayable, and that also means the unthinkable and unsayable: 'But these projects only bear witness to the dwelling in what is transmitted' (RM 78). Thus, when we face the *unheimlich* and question our human essence as homeless beings, we confront the possibility, as did the prodigal son, of neglecting and squandering that essence or of discovering and fulfilling it in a return home (RM 82). Just as homelessness is homelessness from our essence, and homecoming is a coming to being human, so too homelessness and homecoming are matters concerning being itself. In nihilism, being becomes homeless, that is, nothing befalls being so that 'being is not coming into the light of its own essence ... being itself remains wanting' (WN 110):

> It would lie in being's own essence, then, that being remain unthought because it withdraws. Being itself withdraws into its truth. It harbors itself safely within its truth and conceals itself in such harbouring ...
>
> At the same time, such withdrawal is preparatory to being's homecoming which is yet to come.

> In looking toward this self-concealing harboring of its own essence, perhaps we glimpse the essence of that mystery in the guise of which the truth of being is coming to presence. (WN 110)

To conclude, homelessness is not just a matter of human being or being, but of both as dynamically related; homecoming does not concern just human being or being as separated objects but the two as they come together in a way appropriate to their belonging-together. 'Recollection in the history of being continually entrusts the essence of man to being, not individual man, but man at home in his decisive character, in order that being may tower in the openedness of its own dignity and have a home in beings cared for by man's nature' (RM 76). If Heidegger has succeeded at all in raising the questions of homelessness, the history of being, and the essence of human being, then his story is not reducable to a historical report about these subjects but is an initial attempt at genuine thinking (MHB 1). And for us to reflect on what he says would require us to face homelessness and try to understand how it is more than a human matter, how it is the history of the separation and belonging-together of being, human being, truth, thinking, and language. But before these matters can be questioned, they must be experienced. Those of us who have not experienced them as he has may yet think them by way of the experience presented to us by his story – a story he would be retelling insofar as it is a saying of being.

Still, Heidegger himself does not have language adequate for the telling. If he is to make his way, he too needs help. Further, since he has glimpsed that homelessness may end in a homecoming, there is the question of how and to what extent the story of the homelessness of being and human being might also be a story of homecoming. What is needed involves human being's granting 'the word of response' to being so that it can shine forth and the origin, as the simple, granting its appropriation of truth (*Ereignis*) to us (RM 76). Insofar as this would be happening already, what Heidegger cannot think and say could be approached by way of a guide, that is, with the help of someone who has more fully experienced and spoken of homelessness and homecoming.

2 Poetic Wandering in the Foreign

While in the midst of thinking through our metaphysical homelessness, as described in chapter 1, Heidegger already realized the need for a guide, that is, for someone who had experienced these matters and who had language more adequate to what needed thought. To this end, he meditated intensively on the poetry of Friedrich Hölderlin – the first results of which he ventured to make public beginning in 1936. It is not at all accidental that Heidegger should choose Hölderlin as his poetic guide: Hölderlin, who wrote at the end of the eighteenth century, was a neighbouring Swabian especially concerned with home and homeland. Yet, as we will see, Heidegger was not attracted to Hölderlin because they both participated in the same 'spirit of the age' or because Heidegger found the poetry to his taste. Rather, beyond any connection understood by way of historicism or subjectivism, he realized that to find his way he required the company and tutelage of one who had gone the same way before him. It was because Hölderlin had thought deeply about and had seminally articulated the nature of home, homelessness, and homecoming – precisely the regions that Heidegger needed to learn to encounter and speak about – that he joined in fellowship with Hölderlin.

But even if Hölderlin paradigmatically poetizes home and homelessness, why should the story of the poet matter to a thinker? According to Heidegger, who begins to explain his understanding of these matters in his 1936 essay, 'Hölderlin and the Essence of Poetry,' the poet is important to a thinker attempting to make the thinker's way because the poet already knows, first hand, the very route to be covered (HEP 286, 290). Poetry may appear to be dreamlike or merely playful when compared with the daily reality in which we live, or with science. Yet, because the 'palpable and clamorous reality, in which we believe ourselves at home' is, in fact, an estrangement from what is essential, the genuinely poetic attempts to recover and hold what is lost in the everyday (HEP 286).

Poetizing the Holy's Opening for Dwelling

The authentic poet is one who does not live submerged in the seemingly homelike and apparently cosy realm of what is common and easy. The poet appears to be concerned with the 'unreal' precisely because of being already '"cast out" ... from everyday life and protected *against* it by the apparent harmlessness of his occupation' (HEP 286). Because removed, from the start, from the everyday and plunged into the *unheimlich*, the poet's dangerous journey, required of the poet as a poet, is unavoidably underway. Having accepted this condition and attempting to fulfil the poetic nature, the poet must resist the temptation to lapse into the comfortable. Caught between the home that was and the future home that is not yet, the poet might sleep through the uncanny time between, 'in this apparent emptiness. But he holds his ground in the Nothing of this night' (HEP 290). Hölderlin, then, does engage the homelessness which Heidegger, as he comes to understand himself in the 1930s, realizes he also must face and endure.

Though Heidegger can honestly say that he thinks metaphysical homelessness, he cannot claim to have the means to pass over into any homecoming, much less actually to have accomplished it. At best, he hopes and begins to prepare. Hölderlin, however, did move beyond our forgetfulness of our own nature and its basis, which reigns over and in our everyday busy-ness. Precisely in poetry, according to Heidegger, 'man is re-united on the foundation of his existence' (HEP 286). How is this so? How is the poet's experience related to our own, and the thinker's, experience and problem of homelessness? Further, how do poetry and poetic language play a part in the issue of human being and homelessness? Heidegger has chosen Hölderlin because the latter's poetry is essential; that is, it is not written to be self-indulgent or to relate idiosyncratic 'experience' or opinion. Not an arbitrary production, his writing is that to which he is called. In some strict sense, Hölderlin has poetizing as a vocation (HEP 271). Because it answers this call and because 'poetry creates its works in the realm and out of the "material" of language' (HEP 273), what Hölderlin says concerning the essence of poetry and language is to be taken seriously.

Where Hölderlin takes up the place, manner, and means of our living as human beings, he points to language. Language is the realm of the human. To be human is to have language; it is to be at home in language. According to Heidegger, Hölderlin does not mean by this, as we might suppose, that language is a human product or tool. Thought by way of 'home,' we do not create our own home: we neither make our linguistic home by ourselves nor manufacture a home by the linguistic instruments we produce and use. Rather, we are at home insofar as we become human within language. In Hölderlin's words, language has 'been given to man' (cited in HEP 273). Somehow, then, language is 'prior' to us and we inherit it. Of course, when we think about being human, we necessarily inquire as humans who already have language and can therefore question. Heidegger interprets Hölderlin as follows: 'We – mankind – are a conversation. The being of men is founded in language. But this only becomes actual in *conversation*' (HEP 277). Here are two insights. Human being occurs within language; in turn, language is only language insofar as it is conversation (HEP 277). Hölderlin specifies what conversation means in a line which runs, 'And have been able to hear from one another' (cited in HEP 277). Heidegger explains, 'being able to hear is not a mere consequence of speaking with one another, on the contrary it is rather presupposed in the latter process. But even the ability to hear is itself also adapted to the possibility of the word and makes use of it' (HEP 278).

That we can speak to and hear one another depends on a prior unity. Our hearing and speaking is coherent. That is, we *come together* in a *single conversation,* insofar as in that conversation 'there is always manifest that one and the same thing on which we agree, and on the basis of which we are united and so are essentially ourselves' (HEP 277, 278). In that conversation, that is, in language, what is human emerges and endures. Heidegger says, 'Language has the task of making manifest in its work the existent, and of preserving it as such' (HEP 275). What a striking thing to say! Language, according to Hölderlin, presents (and therefore may also conceal) what is (HEP 275). Heidegger elaborates, 'Since we have been a conversation – man has learnt much and named many of the heavenly ones. Since language really became actual as conversation, the gods have acquired names and a world has appeared. But again it should be noticed: the presence of the gods and the appearance of the world are not merely a consequence of the actualization of language, they are contemporaneous with it. And this to the extent that it is precisely in the naming of the gods, and in the transmutation of the world into world, that the real conversations, which we ourselves are, consists' (HEP 279).

Because things, gods, world, and our own human being are first given in language, language cannot be understood as a mere tool or expression subsequent to our pre-existent wishes and experiences. The poet primally recovers the essence of language: 'it is only language that affords the very possibility of standing in the openness of the existent. Only where there is language, is there world ... it affords a guarantee that man can *exist* historically' (HEP 276). Hölderlin, according to Heidegger, says that language is an event (*Ereignis*). It is the occurrence of opening and manifesting what is (HEP 276).

It might seem that poets are interested in language because they want to exploit its possibilities. Hölderlin, however, makes a more profound claim: poetry stands first, and everyday language follows only after poetry's initial opening. That is, 'Poetry is the inaugural naming of being and of the essence of all things ... Hence poetry never takes language as a raw material ready to hand, rather it is poetry which first makes language possible ... Therefore, in just the reverse manner, the essence of language must be understood through the essence of poetry' (HEP 283–4). Thus, what is opened opens in language, and language itself somehow originates in poetry. Correlative, not just any language manifests what is, for all too often careless, worn-out, or inappropriate language hides things. In contrast, poetic language is genuine conversation because it most clearly and purely opens a world.

Poetry establishes through what Hölderlin calls 'naming': 'This naming does not consist merely in something already known being supplied with a name; it is rather that when the poet speaks the essential word, the existent is by this naming nominated as what it is. So it becomes known *as* existent. Poetry is the establishing of being by means of the word' (HEP 281). Naming also ranges broadly. 'The poet names the gods and all things in that which they are' (HEP 281). The poets even name, and thereby make manifest, that which supports the existent: 'being must be opened out, so that the existent may appear.' Here we can see that the poet is not acting arbitrarily in poetizing, but doing a part in the service of the opening up of world. The poet's vocation is the laying down and giving of being and the essence of things (HEP 281). It happens that when the gods and the essence of things are named originally in poetry and first shine forth, human being can become what it is. That is, 'human existence is brought into a firm relation [with the gods and the essence of things] and is given a basis' (HEP 281). To say that human being becomes human is to say that human being comes into its essence as it comes together with the gods and things. Because it is given a basis in this coming together, human being too becomes established in poetry.

Though Hölderlin is making an exalted claim for the power of poetry, he is not claiming that the poets should be praised for exceptional individual creativity. Even though world, gods, things, and human beings are given in language and, indeed, by poetry (which makes manifesting language possible), this is not a story of subjective, artistic accomplishment. Recall that language itself is a gift. Poetry too is a gift, a gift which serves the giving. Though the poets name the gods, they do so only insofar as they are given the power to poetize, that is, the gift of nominating language. 'But the gods can acquire a name only by addressing and, as it were, claiming us. The word which names the gods is always a response to such a claim' (HEP 279). Even though having to speak in order that language genuinely manifest what is, the poet can only speak after having heard what is given to the poet. That is why Heidegger says that existence, which is opened for us by the poet and the gods, 'in so far as it is established (founded), is not a recompense, but a gift' (HEP 282–3).

Hölderlin is clear that world comes in language, language from poetry, and poetizing to the poets from the gods. The poets must courageously and patiently open themselves to the gods. Yet, openness can only prepare for what is given, or gives itself. According to Heidegger, 'The writing of poetry is the fundamental naming of the gods. But the poetic word only acquires its power of naming, when the gods themselves bring us to language' (HEP 287); or, as Hölderlin puts it, 'the ancient old father with calm hand shakes lightnings of benediction out of the rosy clouds' (cited in HEP, 284). That is, the poet stands exposed to the divine bolts insofar as the poet is a poet. The poet's task is to intercept the language of the gods, to absorb it, and to pass it on. Finally, the lightning flashes of the gods, even though passing through the being of the poets, are 'the divine gift to the people,' as Hölderlin puts it (cited in HEP 285). That is why Heidegger notes that the poet's art of receiving is at the same time a new act of giving (HEP 287).

According to Hölderlin, as interpreted by Heidegger, the poet, by receiving the power of language from the gods, established our world through poetry. The poet first opens up the essence of things, the gods, and human beings in their relations. Still, if Heidegger thinks through Hölderlin to think homelessness and home, we can ask what Hölderlin's story of the poet and language finally says about home? How is Hölderlin's story told in the language of home and homecoming? Actually, Hölderlin's poetizing concerning poetry, language, the gods, and the earth presents not only the story of the poets, but the essential features of human dwelling as well. He shows us how it is that the question of dwelling points to the nature of language, which also means to belonging. We have already seen how Hölderlin says that the way and site of human dwelling is in language. Specifically, we dwell in a world and, finally, in our own nature insofar as these are opened up by language. Our dwelling, then, is given to us. Of course, we have to take it up and inhabit it by opening ourselves to the genuine establishing of the poets, which they pass on from the gods. That is why our human sojourn on the earth is, perhaps, fundamentally 'poetic.' Hölderlin says,

> ... poetically, dwells
> Man on this earth? (cited in HEP 282)

In Heidegger's gloss, 'To "dwell poetically" means: to stand in the presence of the gods and to be involved in the proximity of the essence of things' (HEP 282).

Because the relations among human being, gods, earth, things, and being itself are established in poetic language, clearly poetic dwelling would be the site where essential belonging together occurs. In turn, by taking up the poetic sayings, a people speaks with its own voice and 'remembers that it belongs to the totality of all that exists' (HEP 287–8). Genuine poetry, then, and responsive human dwelling affirm our complex modes of belonging in the world: 'And who then is man? He who must affirm what he is ... But what must man affirm? That he belongs to the earth. This relation of belonging to consists in the fact that man is heir and learner in all things. But all these things are in conflict. That which keeps things apart in opposition and thus at the same time binds them together, is called by Hölderlin "intimacy." The affirmation of belonging to this intimacy occurs through the creation of a world and its ascent, and likewise through the destruction of a world and its decline' (HEP 224).

Since what becomes actual in history involves gathering together as well as scattering apart, our story would be one of both homecoming and homelessness. Though in opposite ways, each bears witness to our belonging to all that is (HEP 274–5). Thus genuine poems concerning this belonging dwelling are poems of home and witnesses to its successes and failures. In order that this belonging 'may be possible, language has been given to man' (HEP 275). In turn, as the heir, human being must respond by learning how to dwell, that is, by *learning to belong to the inti-*

macy of which Hölderlin speaks. Such belonging is specific and historical. When Hölderlin thinks dwelling by way of the world opened by the event of language, he thinks of the diverse 'populations' which inhabit locations within this site. Because 'intimacy' both binds together and keeps apart, the poet articulates the belonging in language, which acknowledges and bridges gaps: human beings are between earth and gods; the poet is between humans and the gods (as well as between humans and the earth).

The dynamic character of the intimacy requires that the language fundamental to the gods, the poet, and a historical people be constantly refreshed. Even though the sayings of a people may affirm a mode of belonging, 'often this voice grows dumb and weary' (HEP 288). Untended, genuine dwelling at home dissipates, until we find ourselves numbly and forgetfully back in the everyday – homeless. To counter such dissipation, the sayings of the gods must be passed on anew, as Hölderlin says:

> ... and truly
> Sayings are good, for they are a reminder
> Of the Highest, yet something is also needed
> To explain the holy sayings. (cited in HEP 288)

Heidegger takes it that part of his task is to explain this saying about sayings: 'In this way the essence of poetry is joined on to the laws of the signs of the gods and of the voice of the people, laws which tend towards and away from each other. The poet himself stands between the former – the gods, and the latter – the people. He is one who has been cast out – out into that *between*, between gods and men. But only and for the first time in this between is it decided, who man is and where he is settling his existence' (HEP 288–9). The between, where bidirectional intimacy occurs and is focused, provides (according to Heidegger and Hölderlin) the site where humans might become at home in and by way of poetry. In the between, we could come 'to rest; not indeed to the seeming rest of inactivity and emptiness of thought, but to that infinite state of rest in which all powers and relations are active (cf. the letter to Hölderlin's brother, dated 1st January, 1799. III, 368f.)' (HEP 286).

Through all this, Hölderlin has told us a great deal about the nature of home. Home is much more than a purely human fabrication, since – though we are responsible and active in establishing it – what we do is only a part of what is required. First of all, the gods give the poets language, and the latter pass it on, initiating the possibility of our participation. In this way, we receive and act within the between, in which humans, gods, earth, and things are held together and apart in what Hölderlin calls 'Intimacy?' Here, home – or being at home – would be a dynamic belonging, which we need to learn to accomplish in response to what we are given. Consequently, homelessness would be the passing away of belonging and the passing out of the between in which we might dwell. Homecoming would be the event of passage back to the belonging together of what is yet bound together even when held apart and in opposition.

Clearly, the poet is the necessary figure. The poet helps a people initially to become intimately at home. And when there is a danger of falling out of the between because of weariness or the dimming of the gods' gift of light, the poet holds back forgetfulness by remembering the way to belonging. Because, as Heidegger has already shown, we in the West are in an epoch of metaphysical homelessness (see chapter 1), and because Hölderlin, before Heidegger, endured the between into which he was thrown when he was cast out of comfortable, everyday life, Hölderlin is the poet who especially holds in memory and song what Heidegger needs to interpret and explain. The between in which we dwell (or fail to dwell), and which Hölderlin poetizes, is both spatial and temporal. In addition to being the site of the belonging together and being apart of humans, gods, earth, things, and the past, the between is the time of their belonging. To further complicate matters, we are between times. Hölderlin is essential to Heidegger because 'Hölderlin, in the act of establishing the essence of poetry, first determines a new time. It is the time of the gods that have fled *and* of the god that is coming. It is the time of *need* because it lies under a double lack and a double Not: the No-more of the gods that have fled and the not-yet of the god that is coming' (HEP 289).

The homelessness, which Heidegger must face, and the homecoming which he hopes to think are already experienced and spoken in the poet's story. In our time of need, the poet goes before us, showing the way; indeed, the poet established the way. In receiving the signs from the gods, having passed them along to us, 'the poet catches sight already of the completed message and in his word boldly presents what he has glimpsed, so as to tell in advance of the not-yet-fulfilled':

> ... the bold spirit, like an eagle
> Before the tempest, flies prophesying
> In the path of his advancing gods. (cited in HEP 287)

Because Hölderlin 'anticipates a historical time' and *dwelling* which we too look for, the question becomes whether we can understand what the poet holds out for us (HEP 290). Insofar as we seek to undergo homelessness to pass over to homecoming, we travel in a realm – a between – already opened to us through the work of the poet and the gift of language. Just as Hölderlin accepts and explains the bold sayings which are a reminder of the Highest, so Heidegger, in turn, needs to attempt to accept and interpret Hölderlin's sayings, especially those about the belonging that the poet remembers and re-establishes (HEP 288).

Hölderlin thinks the essence of human being out of human dwelling. His poetry names and thereby establishes this dwelling only insofar as it responds to the source which gives the opening in the first place. For Heidegger to think through our poetic dwelling on this earth, he must first hear what Hölderlin says. But since the story of the poet and dwelling is initially given to the poets themselves, what is attempted here is a listening to the primal saying itself. Heidegger interprets Hölderlin's poetry concerning this primal saying during the same period (from 1936 to 1941) as he attempts to articulate his own story of the history of being and the essence of humans (covered in chapter 1). Heidegger does this in three additional essays: 'Wie wenn am Feiertage' ('As If on a Holiday'), 1939; 'Andenken' ('Remembrance'), 1943; and 'Remembrance of the Poet,' 1943.[1]

Hölderlin tries to say how things stand between the poet and the people, and between them and the world. For example, he begins his poem 'As If on a Holiday' by describing a scene in which a farmer or peasant stands before the farmer's fields where fruit grows from the greening earth after a storm – the storm itself came from the heavens, that is, from the realm of the gods. In comparison, the poet too is brought up as a crop in the midst of the poet's fellows, on the earth, beneath heavens and gods (WWAF 51–2). Of course, it is on a holiday that this occurs, because a holiday is the special time when the gods are nearer and we can see that heaven and earth hold sway and secure a favourable abiding. While in today's usual sense a holiday means a day off from work with nothing special to do, Hölderlin thinks of it, originarily, as a *holy day* – a time when special attention is given to the holy. To raise crops successfully, the farmer works in accord with and in response to earth, heavens, and gods – to all that is given. So too does the poet. Thus, Hölderlin's story of the farmer is at the same time the story of the poet.

In poetizing this favour, Hölderlin says that nature brings up the poets (WWAF 52). Heidegger contends that this cannot be understood if we are careless about what nature is. To begin, it should not be understood according to prevalent ideas: nature is not simply one more being, to be distinguished, for example, from other beings such as artworks or humans (WWAF 56). Neither is it the sum of all beings, a kind of giant collection (WWAF 52); nor is it a god (WWAF 53); nor, finally, is it creation, as understood in Christian metaphysics (WWAF 59). According to Heidegger, the problem of properly interpreting Hölderlin's nature has to do with the Greek understanding of '*phusis*,' though apparently Hölderlin himself did not know the original Greek understanding (WWAF 56–7).[2]

This fundamental Greek word, '*phusis*,' which Hölderlin also says with *die Natur*, means a going forth or emergence. It names growth itself, the self-arising and self-disclosing (WWAF 56). Still, Heidegger does not want to go back to ancient Greek times (which would after all be impossible), nor to historically connect Hölderlin's understanding with that of the Greeks. But with Hölderlin, he does want to recover what *die Natur* names (which is also what '*phusis*' named). That is, what is to be brought forth in Hölderlin's poem and Heidegger's commentary is nothing antique, but the powerful emergence itself. How then does Hölderlin speak of the real characteristics of nature? In the first place, nature is the *omnipresencing*. It is the all and everywhere-present which presences in 'human works, in the historical destiny of peoples, in the stars and gods, also in stones, plants, and animals, also in rivers and storms' (WWAF 52).

This is to say that nature brings beings to appearance. The poet, then, speaks of epiphany. Here, what is appears as it is. Accordingly, nature is said to be *lighting:* it is the lighting up of the light by which beings become manifest. Things first shine in the light of this lighting (WWAF 56ff.). This lighting, *phusis*, is the going forth in the open within which anything can appear. This emergence does not come and go; it stays as the open. In short, nature is the emerging-enduring-lighting of the open. Hölderlin, according to Heidegger, also thinks omnipresencing, lighting nature as a gathering. In the lighting by which what is would be enabled to appear and become present is also gathered what is. What is gathered into the light is thereby brought into the possibility of its own nature and, at the same time, gathered together with all that is (WWAF 57). 'It allows the togetherness of all to appear in its gathering' (WWAF 60). Even further, in addition to giving the open to all that is gathered in it, nature gathers itself in its own emergence.

In one dimension, nature gathers, lights, and gives the open to all that is. But in another dimension, it holds itself back. Emerging occurs as one double action: in the pushing to the fore of what is and comes to appear, the source of the event itself does not come forward; precisely so that what is (and not itself) may be manifest, the source stays back as it puts forth what comes forth. The poet speaks of this complex dynamic by saying that nature both awakens and is in repose. It awakens to growth in giving the going forth of what is; it sleeps in that it holds itself back so that what is can appear in the open. This resting or withholding itself is a self-gathering. It gathers itself for self-disclosure, though it discloses itself precisely by its staying back to disclose what is. By withholding itself, nature preserves all that is in its opening and lighting (WWAF 57). Sleep and its proper time, Night, are preparations for wakening in day. Because of its double activity, the poet says that nature is both creative and self-renewing (WWAF 57).

This gathering in lighting's open specifies omnipresencing nature as the source of relations among what is. As the awakening, nature sets all opposition and belonging together into the open, where both opposition and belonging together are bound into a unity (WWAF 60). Another way of saying this is that nature mediates everything that is, bringing it into relation and into human perception or consciousness (WWAF 61). The omnipresencing is the mediation and the power of mediation which holds all things and all relations together (WWAF 67, 73). And nature itself, precisely because it mediates all that is, is itself immediate. Nothing comes between, or mediates between, the omnipresencing and what comes to presence. It requires nothing, neither god nor human being, between itself and what is (WWAF 61). Because the unmediated (the source which gives the open where all belongs) is close behind what is mediated (and therefore appears to us), the former is near, yet also far. As immediate, the source is very near; as not itself appearing (because only the mediated is given to us), the unmediated is unreachable or far (WWAF 61, 63).

In 'Homecoming/To the Kindred Ones,' Hölderlin speaks in another way of what he had named nature. Here he treats what he calls the serene (*Heitere*).[3] This poem tells us of a journey the poet makes in returning to the poet's native land. Approaching home, the poet experiences the joyous (*Freudige*). In 'Remembrance of the Poet,' the essay devoted to this elegy, Heidegger explains, as follows: 'How shall we name this calm mien with which all men and things give greeting to the seeker? We must name this inviting disposition of a home already approaching, with the phrase, which throws its light over the whole poem "Homecoming," the phrase "the joyous"' (RP 246). It is the joyous, which in Hölderlin has been made into poetry. Just as the poet (like the farmer) in 'As If on a Holiday' (or 'Holyday') was seen against fields, fruit, storm, sky, and gods, now the poet on this journey travels amidst mountains and valleys, breezes and clouds, earth and flowers, angels and gods, lake and heavens. In this gathering to which the poet is gathered in coming home, the joyous appears.

But the joyous itself is manifest because of something more original, the serene. Using what Heidegger has already said about the gathering of what is and its relationship in the space of the open, he elaborates on Hölderlin: 'The joyous is the serene. We call this also "the spatially-ordered" ... The spatially-ordered is, within its spatiality, freed, clarified and integrated. The serene, the spatially-ordered, is alone able to house everything in its proper place. The joyous has its being in the serene, which serenifies ... While the serenification makes everything clear, the serene allots each thing to that place of existence whereby in its nature it belongs, so that it may stand there in the brightness of the serene, like a still light, proportionate to its own being' (RP 247). Understood as the place where something becomes at home in its own nature and as a site for becoming at home in that to which it belongs, the serene gives home. Because it opens home to us, the serene gives the possibility of homecoming. In the serene, things are let into their natures, which is to say, they are kept safe. 'What remains safely preserved, is 'homely' in its essence' (RP 249). The serene, the highest above all else, 'is the streaming lighting itself. This pure lighting, which for each "space" and each "temporal space" houses (i.e., grants, here) a vacant place – this we call the serene. At one and the same time it is the clarity (*claritas*) in whose brightness everything clear remains, and the highness (*serenitas*) by whose strength everything high stands firm, and the joyfulness (*hilaritas*) in whose play every liberated thing hovers. The serene preserves and holds everything in tranquility and wholeness. The serene is fundamentally healing' (RP 251).[4]

The poet names this highest with yet another name: the serene is the *holy* (*das Heilige*) (RP 251). Hölderlin also speaks of the holy in 'As If on a Holiday.' There too he calls nature (understood as the lighting light – as is the serene) the holy (WWAF 59). With this name Hölderlin names the origin of all that is. As already noted, prior to all that appears there is 1) a source of the open in which what is appears; and 2) a source of relation, that is, a source of unity which holds all that is distinct and yet together (WWAF 53, 60). This source of belonging together is the holy.

Once having articulated the holy, the poet can specify not only what the open is and what occurs in the opening, but also that, and how, the holy grants the open. Hölderlin, in his poetry, says that *the holy is the opening of the open.* Because the open is the site within which what is comes forth and because what comes forth comes to appear in the lighting which occurs in the open, open and lighting are thought together (WWAF 56–7). Lighting and opening occur together. Here the poet speaks of *the event of disclosure of everything that is.* Hence the open is not just this or that place, nor is it any thing; rather, it is the 'place' which makes place and thing possible. The opening is the realm of all the more particular regions (WWAF 64). Further, because the open is the primal opening, it is not merely spatial (that is, it is the source of the spatial). It also opens time. Time, the possibility of historical existence, and that means human existence, is first given by the holy. In short, 'The openness of the opening accommodates itself to that which we call "a world"' (WWAF 64).

Hölderlin richly details what happens in this opening of the open. Most simply, a spatial-temporal *between* is opened, which is the site for the coming together of gods and mortals, heavens and earth, and the poet, too. For example, in 'As If on a Holiday,' Hölderlin says that the open opens for the ether (father of light), for the chasm (mother earth), and for the immortal gods and mortal humans who foregather in this between (WWAF 60–1). Dramatically, according to Hölderlin, this also is the scene in which the poet first appears – halfway between humans and the gods ('Andenken,' 103). The holyday which is the holiday in Hölderlin's poem is a wedding festival of humans and gods: it is the celebration of the marriage which occurs in and exhibits the between. The celebration, clearly an exceptional occasion, is the occasion for opening. Into this between, and out of this union of opposites, the poet is born. 'The day of the wedding feast, the wedding day, fixes the birthday of the poet, that is, the day, in whose light the open lights itself, so that the poet sees that coming, which his word must say: the holy' (A 103). Hölderlin calls the poet a 'half-god' because the poet is the fruit of mortals and gods, just as the grapes are the fruit of heavens and earth and the wine is the fruit of both and also of human work. Here, too, a historical people will have its birthday (A 106).

Because the holy opens the between as the place where mortals, divinities, earth, and heaven foregather, Hölderlin speaks of the opening as the building of a house for the guests invited in. The open, in opening the between, houses; it is spoken of as an inn (A 120). In this cordial place, what is can come into its own essential nature. The open is that in which alone the gods first come to be guests (visitors to humans),

humans can build a home, and the poet first comes to dwell (A 148). The opened between is where all have the possibility of becoming because it is there that gods and mortals alike are held in, or out into, life (WWAF 65, 71). Note, in speaking of the between as a housing, as a scene of gathering, the poet indicates not only how gods and humans can each become what they are, but that they can become themselves only when they are gathered together in one another's company (WWAF 69).

According to Heidegger, this is what Hölderlin says with the word 'love.' The love between gods and mortals indicates both their intimate relationship and their mutually necessary belonging together (WWAF 69). Further, the holy appears here, since it is the origin of the between. The holy, through the mediation of love, brings gods and humans together; through love they belong to its opening (WWAF 69). Here Hölderlin touches on the heart (*das Gemüt*) of all dwelling: for what is to be what it is, it must live in the open between, opened by the holy (A 85). Out of this heart comes the disposition and courage for the festival (A 126). Courage is needed because difference must both be allowed to endure and be overcome in intimacy. Gods and humans must bind themselves together, even as they remain different from one another, and through both movements come into their essence. Here difference appears in its difference (A 105; consider also the originary separation of gods and humans according to Heraclitus, treated in chapter 1). It is within the difference now opened up where all abides: dwelling is grounded in the appearance of difference itself (A 105).

Hölderlin presents the between as the opened space for gods, humans, earth, and heavens by speaking of an inn and of the scenes of gathering, whereas the wedding festival shows the between as temporal. The wedding day is a balanced point, held between other times. First, the celebration is specified to take place in March, the transitional time at the end of winter – a time between. The coming forth of spring mediates between (seasons). The poet also often speaks of the shift from night to day, for example, of night as the time of the fled gods and as still the mother of day, when the divine comes (e.g., A 110). Second, the day of celebration is an extraordinary day, not merely because the ordinary round of work ceases, though that is in no way incidental, but because of the holy event. In addition to love, deeds are celebrated because of the courage required to endure destiny and live historically (A 125–6).

Hölderlin says that in the between we have the origin of history, which is itself a gathering together.[5] The festival celebrates a double, but unified, occurrence: the coming to be of gods, humans, and the poet and the event of history (A 106–7). Radically, this between is situated between being (*Seyn*) and non-being (*Nichtseyn*), according to an essay of Hölderlin's ('Becoming in Disappearing'), a fact that emphasizes both the connection of his concern with Heidegger's and the poet's understanding of the holy's opening of the between as an event (cited in A 113). The between is the event whereby all that is comes forth. This is why Heidegger says that the holy occurs as the event (*Ereignis*) of greeting (*Gruß*). The holy greets and, in its greeting, the gods and humans, heavens and earth, poet and all things are enabled to come (back) to their own. The arrival of what is into its essential nature occurs in the originary greeting which the holy sends. Clearly, Hölderlin understands the greeting to be the hail (from the Middle English *heil*) which proceeds from the holy (*Heilige*). This greeting is the mediating of the holy.

The greeting displays the distance between the greeted and greeter, and overcomes that distance. Here distance is unfolded; and nearness, grounded (A 96). In such a greeting, which recognizes and sustains the greeted in its difference, the thing is let be as itself. The thing is greeted in its own essence and placed into its proper relation. This is the originary greeting which the holy sends (A 104). Such pure and simple greeting is also poetic, as we shall see (A 96). For Hölderlin, then, 'The festival is the event of the greeting, in which *the holy* greets and, in greeting, itself appears' (A 105).

Elsewhere, Hölderlin speaks of the same opening of the between and gathering, which the holy grants, in 'natural' terms. For instance, whereas in 'As If on a Holiday' we hear of a festival between heaven and gods, on the one hand, and earth and mortals, on the other, and of the poet born between, in 'Remembrance' Hölderlin speaks of a river and of the poet as a mariner travelling on it to the sea. Of course, the river itself runs between its origin in the waters of the high mountains and its end in the sea, between the deep waters of the earth and the rain of the heavens (A 98). Further, the rain gathers together what belongs together along its course: brooks and streams, trees and gardens, fields and fruit, mills and village, bread and wine, its banks and the ground, paths and people along the way (A 98ff.). And the poet's nature and energy appear in and through the streams as the river courses over the homey earth (A 97, 103, 145). That is why the poet speaks of the river passing as the silken ground on which women walk on spring holidays: on such days the open opens, and we are gathered to our own essence (A 102ff.).

In 'Homecoming/To the Kindred Ones' (or 'To the Kinsmen'), Hölderlin elaborates a scene in which the poet travels in a between. Here the poet is on the sea, beneath the sky and its clouds, which uncover themselves to the highest heaven. High into the sky are the Alps, with clouds between them; the clouds cover the lower valleys and ravines. Later the poet moves among the people of the poet's homeland (RP 243ff.). Clearly, the poet is gathered to something other than the poet's own self. The between opens to the holy (the highest of all), heavens, heralds/gods/angels, light, the poet, earth, and humans (RP 248, 252). This spatial and temporal between is presented here rather 'naturally' or 'ordinarily,' instead of in terms of the extraordinary holy festival. The serene – the holy – opens through its heralds, 'the angels of the house' and the 'angels of the year' (RP 248). Heidegger interprets,

> 'The house' is intended here to mean the space which for men houses that wherein alone they can be 'at home' and so fulfil their destiny. This space is given by the immaculate earth. The earth houses the peoples in its historical space. The earth serenifies 'the house.' And the earth, which thus serenifies is the first angel 'of the house.'
>
> 'The year' houses those times which we call the seasons. In that 'mingled' play of the fiery brightness and the frosty dark which the seasons offer, things blossom out and then close up again. The seasons of 'the year' give to man in the changing of the serene that time which has been meted out for his historical sojourn in the 'house.' 'The year' sends its greeting in the play of the light. The serenifying light is the first 'angel of the year.' (RP 248–9; see also WWAF 54)

Hölderlin says that the holy is the original opening and disclosure that grants the lightening opening wherein what is comes forth and is gathered into its own nature and with all that is. The holy, by its mediating greeting, gives the between where gods and mortals, heavens and earth come together. But this event, according to the poet, has *not* occurred once and for all in the past. It remains as opening, lightening, emerging, and coming forth. As granting itself, the holy is the *still coming*.

Essentially, the holy, whether called nature, omnipresencing, the serene, or by any other name, is the still-coming (WWAF 55; A 107, 114). As the presencing or emergence of what is, the holy comes (WWAF 67). That is, the holy is not a singular, initial event or place that once set things forth into being; rather, that anything at all now is, or may yet be, depends on the still and always original character of the holy. The holy remains origin, for that is what the holy *is* – not what it was but what it is insofar as it is the holy at all. It is the sending forth of all that is into emergence, but precisely in doing that, it itself stays back from the going forth (WWAF 55–6). Heidegger says that the holy, in its holding fast, remains the coming of all beginning (of what emerges) (WWAF 75). Further, in this remaining as origin, rather than passing out and away, origin continually comes to (be) itself (WWAF 60). According to this interpretation, the holy is a perpetual origin and thoroughly temporal in character: 'The remaining, as coming, is the un-forethought [not-yet-forethought, *unvordenkliche*] originality of origin' (WWAF 75).

Because of the character of temporal coming, Hölderlin says that nature is the oldest time and the youngest (WWAF 63). That is, as origin it precedes all else: the holy opens up the time periods and the historical (WWAF 76). It is the coming of time as the seasons of earth and growth; it is the coming of time as epochs of peoples and history (WWAF 51). And as the still coming, now and in the future, it is the youngest: 'Its remaining is the perpetuity of the continual' (WWAF 73). But to say that the origin as coming stays coming through past, present, and into future epochs is not to claim that it is beyond time or eternal in any transcendental, metaphysical sense. Rather, it is time, originarily. The holy and time are contemporaneous (WWAF 75–6). This leads Hölderlin to the point where he must elaborate the relation of the poet and the holy. The holy remains coming, but, according to Hölderlin, the remaining coming is kept coming through the word of song (WWAF 73). Though how the song belongs to both the holy and the poet needs to be explained, Hölderlin clearly says that the holy does not completely withdraw – at least not from the poet – but continues coming, even when it holds itself back (WWAF 55). In the holy's advancing to the poet, there is a 'condition' for homecoming, which still comes. The holy, as the still coming, still gives home – or the possibility of home – to the poet.

If the holy, understood as emerging nature or the serene, is the still-coming which grants the opening, if the holy sends a greeting to gather gods, humans, earth, heavens, and the poet in its between, how does this happen? How does the granting greeting come? What has it to do with the poet? Hölderlin signals an answer in his poems. As noted before, the event of the holy's coming is spoken of poetically in the language of lightning falling from thunderstorm and of daybreak, the transition time from darkness to day, wherein the lighting lights what is in the open. And to this, Hölderlin adds sound. He speaks of ringing (WWAF 58). What rings is the word. It is not immediately clear how the event of the opening should be connected with the word because, for Hölderlin, the daybreak of the open is silent. According to Heidegger's interpretation,

'The awakening of the lighting light however is the quietest of all happenings' (WWAF 58; see also 67). Yet, in this stillest occurrence of lighting, the word too occurs.

Not surprisingly, the word which clangs at the daybreak of the lighting opening is the genuine word of the poet (WWAF 58). The poet's words occur just then, not accidentally, but necessarily. Poetic words enable the opening. Hölderlin names such poetic words song. 'The word becomes.' As Heidegger explains, 'The thus arising word-work allows the belonging-together of gods and men to appear. The song gives testimony to the ground of their belonging-together; it attests to the holy' (WWAF 69).[6] Hölderlin is claiming that for the holy's opening to be effected, the poet is needed. 'And first there must be a poet, in order that a word of song may be' (WWAF 67). If the holy is the origin, which grants all coming to appear, the genuinely human word is nonetheless necessary for the articulation of the coming. For all the power and joy of the holy, it does not reach humans by itself, but needs the voice of the poetic singer because the occurrence of the gathering together comes about in and through song (RP 252; WWAF 66). For example, the specific time and place named in the wedding festival indicates that only the exceptional can initially open and light the between of our dwelling. The exceptional or unusual (*ungewöhnlich*) is opposite to the ordinary and commonplace in which we are apparently at home, but really uncomfortable and not at all at home (*unheimlich*). That is, the exceptional opens a way out of the *unheimlich* and opens the possibility of genuinely being at home (A 102–3). That is why Hölderlin speaks of opening and our coming into the between as a holiday. But the extra-ordinary opens itself up – and, finally, that means opening the open – only in the poeticizing commemorating celebration (A 103).

Still, the poet's work is not 'creative' in any modern sense of the word. The poet does not create what is in what the poet says, or even its meaning. Heidegger insists that the poetic, in addition to the already said/spoken holy, only opens the time-space of an appearing of the gods and directs into place this dwelling of historical humans on this earth (A 114). This is a complex claim. On the one hand, it is not the holy alone which opens: the holy opens when it is spoken out or uttered in the poetic. On the other hand, to talk about the already-said holy (which clearly does not just mean previously mentioned) is to recognize that in poetry the holy is already said. Heidegger is arguing that for the poetic saying to be possible, the holy must already be spoken. The holy must already have had its say. What it has to say is its greeting, which is said when it is sent on its way to the past.

The necessary word, then, is not only the poetic word – though it is that, it is also, and before all else, the word of the holy. The holy grants the opening between in its greeting, which is its coming (A 95). 'The serene is the origin of the greeting' (RP 253). Though the song of the holy only occurs (*ereignet sich*) in the songs of the poets (WWAF 6), the song (*der Gesang*) which opens is 'the word that only the holy can say' (WWAF 68; see also 72). Though the poet does truly necessary work in song, celebrating the holy word, because the song echoes the saying singing of origin itself, the originary greeting is not solely or primarily the poet's accomplishment. The poet can only greet insofar as the poet has already been greeted (A 99). Heidegger notes, 'Because the song only awakens with the awakening of the holy, so the mediated itself arises from the unmediated' (WWAF 72–3). For example, through the saying of the holy, the gods experience themselves and so bring themselves to appear in the dwelling place of humans on this earth (A 123).

The two ways of poetizing the holy come together: the visual imagery presents the holy as opening-lighting; the aural imagery presents it as singing-saying. Though the visual and aural modes would appear most obviously as dimensions of the same event if the lighting were thought as lightning accompanied by a thunderclap; instead here lighting is said to be the most silent and stillest event. That is because just as the opening itself is concealed or withdraws in order that what appears might come to the fore, so too what enables the sounded to be sounded does not call attention to itself by being loud but always still comes as that which – itself silent – lets come what is said to us through the poet's song. As to the latter mode, Heidegger says, 'The holy gives the word and itself comes in this word. The word is the event [*Ereignis*] of the holy' (WWAF 76).

Hölderlin's poetic saying elaborates how it is that the holy comes and that the poet sings. In the first place, being able to say is grounded in being able to hear. Thought of by way of its source, saying is originally a hearing. Of course, the belonging together of saying and hearing is what is called conversation (A 123–4). Here, we are thinking of the conversation between the holy and the poet. Before the poet can say the poet's poem, the poet must first hear the hail of the holy: poetic song originates in the silent greeting of the holy, which is the original word (A 124). To poetize, then, the poet must already have experienced origin. For this to have happened, the holy must have given itself to the poet. But the holy does not give itself directly to the poet. Recall that the holy, as the mediation of all that appears, is itself the unmediated. As we saw, that means that though it is the nearest of all, it is also far because it withdraws, or holds itself behind all that comes forth through its mediation. This spatially understood 'holding itself back behind that which emerges' is aurally understood as the silent. Again, that is why, though it speaks originally and echoes in all human words, the holy is the most silent. It speaks, but silently; it emerges by not appearing, so as to let what is appear.

The holy's saying comes to the poet when the poet hears the song through that which comes forth, that is, via world, god, and word. In 'As If on a Holiday,' Hölderlin says that song originates from the growth, that is, emergence, of nature, which is disclosed through heavens and earth and thereby directed out into song (WWAF 66). The light ray sent from the holy proceeds through a series of mediations: it comes from the holy through the gods to the poet (alternatively, it proceeds from nature through the earth and heavens to the poet); finally, as we will see later, it goes from the poet to the people (WWAF 68). That is why Hölderlin speaks of the opening which must occur: all must be opened, the homeland and the wind, the heart of mortals and the divinities (A 120). The relationship among these 'elements,' or dimensions, is complex. In order that a homeland be opened, the hearts of mortals must be opened. For that to happen, the heart of the poet must open. That happens when the gods, wind, and homeland too open to the poet. The wind is important here because it is the wind which pushes the lightning bearing storm clouds across the sky (the home of the heavenly ones), and it is wind which moves the mariners (the poets) from their homeland. The divine wind bears the greeting of origin (A 115).

In 'Homecoming,' Hölderlin also treats the poet's experience of the origin that holds itself back. Here the poet is said to discover 'the reserved' (RP 260). To write, the poet must make such a discovery; to write is to make it. And what is discovered is something other than the poet's own self and, finally, even than the messengers-heralds, angels, or gods who bring the message to the poet. What is discovered is the holy (RP 247). Heidegger says, 'For the gods are the serenifiers, who in the serenification announce the greeting which the serene sends. The serene is the origin of the greeting, i.e. of the angelic, wherein the innermost essence of the gods consists. By using this word "gods" sparingly and hesitatingly to apply the name, the poet has made more apparent the peculiar quality of the gods, as being the heralds through whom the serene sends greeting' (RP 253–4). The need of the poet to discover the lighting ray of the holy through the lightning flashes of the gods and heavens also explains the poet's need for companion poets – those who have, at the same time or beforehand, received the holy's greeting. In 'Remembrance,' Hölderlin says that the German poets need the fire of the heavens, which the Greeks long before had been given (A 86). This fire has the same origin as the lighting. Heidegger notes that the far-reaching inner light which reached Hölderlin required the latter to enter into poetic dialogue with Sophocles (RP 262). Of course, there is also a great danger here. The poet may mistake the gods or heavens for the source of the lighting rather than seeing the former as intermediaries. Then the poet forgets the origin, and poetry breaks off.

But when a genuine conversation among the holy, gods, heaven and earth, and the poet is sustained, we see that the poet can write because of the poet's already belonging to these. In 'As If on a Holiday' Hölderlin says that the poets divine the holy and that the poetic in essence belongs to the holy (WWAF 64). In a parallel manner, the poets remain or abide in their belonging to nature (WWAF 55). This belonging has a peculiar character because of the double movement of the holy. Since the holy always remains coming (in the past, present, and future) while withdrawing or holding itself back in favour of presencing all that is present, the poet's belonging will involve coming and staying back. The divinity thinks ahead into the distant, which itself does not withdraw, because it is the coming. However, because the coming itself, in its beginning, reposes and remains back, the presentiment of the coming is a fore-and-back thinking (WWAF 55).

Hölderlin and Heidegger understand the poet's belonging to the holy as such a for-and-back thinking. This belonging must be learned. And in learning how to belong to the coming origin, the poet learns to be at home (A 99). When saying that the poet prophesies the coming, Hölderlin does not, according to Heidegger, speak of prophesy in a Judeo-Christian sense (A 114). The coming the poet looks toward is held in the conversation already underway. In this conversation, a remembrance meets the remembered; in remembrance, the unity of the same thoughts, and thus of what belongs together, appears (A 127; see also 139). Hölderlin and Heidegger interpret the way the poet learns belonging, to be a thinking (*Denken*) which is a remembering (*Andenken*). This remembering thinking is also a loving, for it sustains and lets be the belonging together in which all that is and the holy too are what they are. In that this remembering thinking (a re-calling that which comes, accomplished through a holding back in favour of what emerges) is a conversation with the holy, gods, earth, and heavens; it is a questioning. Questioning is a thoughtful, that is, really hearing, listening to what is said. Remembrance is not merely a thinking back on what has come; it continues to ask concerning what continues to come. Questioning ponders (*bedenken*) (A 83).

Since the greeting lets appear the nobility of the essence of what is, and since the greeting of the holy is sent out to the poet, the poet joins the conversation by greeting, in turn, that which greets the poet. The poet's remembrance is this greeting (A 96). Specifically, the poet greets and thinks the gods, sons of the earth, earth, heavens, and all that we call world; finally, the poet greets and remembers the holy. That is to say, the poet reflects on becoming and learning to dwell at home in the originary remembrance (A 123, 149–50). Thus, the poet's opens out to dwelling. Clearly, in all that Hölderlin and Heidegger say concerning the saying of the holy and then the poet's belonging to the holy by the poet's gift, thinking, and remembrance, the poet joins the conversation by properly responding. At the dawn of the lighting opening, the poet must be wakeful, prepared for that which is coming (A 118). What is required is an openness which will let be both the immediate in its immediacy and the mediation in the 'mediating ray' (WWAF 71ff.). Here the poet would stay open and stay where the holy opens itself and, in readiness, lets the presencing always yet come (WWAF 55). Accordingly, Heidegger says that the poet has the heart for the coming because the poet wishes what is coming (A 126). 'Since, however, the joyous only draws near where it is met and welcomed by the composition of poetry, therefore the angels, heralds of the serene, appear only if there are any who are composing' (RP 249).

This specifies how the poet is needed by the holy. The saying of the holy, sent through the gods, earth, and heavens, is established only in the poetizing of the poet (A 83). Though the holy opens, its opening must be brought to appearance by the genuine poet who displays the belonging-together of gods, mortals, earth, and heavens, as noted at the beginning of this discussion (WWAF 55, 69). In a way, the poet grounds what is, because in the poet's genuine sayings provide a foundation for the holy's grounding-coming (A 126). 'The poet shows the open of the between, in which he himself first must dwell, in that his saying, exhibiting the source, follows it and thus is the abiding, which holds itself in the holy that must come into word(s)' (A 148). 'To name poetically means: to cause ... to appear in words' (RP 263). For these reasons, Hölderlin calls the poet a sign (A 123) – the one who points out the emerging and thus aids in its appearance (A 118).

Further, the poetic word preserves that which it manifests. The originary, which constantly keeps coming, needs a place to come to stay, to be held fast (WWAF 73). What the holy opens is made secure in poetry. For example, the opening itself and the between which is opened are exhibited in the commemorating composition. 'The showing brings the shown near and holds it distant' (A 147). This showing brings itself near only to what is shown. In the poetic establishing of gods, humans, earth, heavens, and between, the poet is also established. Specifically, it is through having a part in the conversation with the holy that the poet becomes who the poet is. Originally a conversation is given. In response to the holy's granted greeting, the poet poetizes: 'mortally thinking he composes the highest' (A 123). 'This remembering thinking of the good conversation speaks genuinely poetic language' (A 126). Because the poet's attentive response to the gift of the holy and composition belong to what the holy opens forth, when the opening is manifest and held in these compositions, the poet fulfils the poet's essence. The poet's own inmost being or nature is gathered in this belonging to the holy and to that which comes forth. Thus, as a result of that conversation the poet discovers both the poetic and the poet's own character.

In sum, the saying of the holy occurs. It grants the opening so that in the between, gods, humans, earth, heavens, and all that we call world can come to their own natures and into relationship with each other. The holy's gift of the opening greeting is sent to the poet, who experiences it, thoughtfully remembers what the poet has heard, and thereby learns to dwell in the holy's opening. The poet then composes the poet's own saying, and the writing becomes a sign, which establishes what appears by showing and holding it. Through these sayings, those who enter into such a relationship with the holy and the world become genuine poets. They come to be at home in the place where they properly dwell (in the holy's between) and come home to who they are, which allows them to pass on the greeting saying to their fellow humans. They thus found dwelling on the earth for humans (A 149).

The relationship of the holy's word with the poet's word and their relationship with the event of the opening of the between allow us a glimpse of the holy's essence, which is understood by Hölderlin and Heidegger as one of dwelling and home. The holy is thought in the language of place specifically as the abode and hearth. That is, the holy is the place wherein all dwells. In 'As If on a Holiday,' nature holds gods and mortals in life. As their containing and enabling home, it is that whereupon and by which they live (WWAF 65). Of course, thinking the holy this way emphasizes not only its enduring character but also its dynamic opening. The holy mediates. It mediates between all that comes to appear; it mediates in opening the between within which what is becomes manifest.

But if this is so, the holy is more than the home within which all comes to abide. More fundamentally, it is the originary centre and source of this dwelling. Accordingly, the poet calls it the 'pure' and 'eternal'; it is 'the pure heart' (WWAF 71ff.). It is pure because it is not mediated by anything else; it requires nothing between it and what is. To speak of the 'pure heart,' then, is to name the holy in its origin and to describe the sphere of the holy as a staying belonging (WWAF 73). All that is only is what it is insofar as it is *gathered into* the omnipresencing holy. Thus, the holy is the place and source of intimacy. And because, as the origin of time, it has been and remains the coming origin, the holy is the former and future intimacy. Recall that in 'Andenken' ('Remembrance') Hölderlin names the spring (the season of new coming) as the time of the festival of the wedding of the gods and humans. 'The holy is the Intimacy itself, is – "the heart"' (WWAF 73).

The poet develops the holy as intimate by speaking of the hail of the holy in familiar terms. For example, in 'As If on a Holiday,' nature smiles upon the peasant's fields and the place where we live. This 'smiling' is the effortless and friendly greeting of the holy to humans and earth, a greeting unconcerned with whether we realize either its magnitude or what really occurs. The originary is released in this smiling (WWAF 65). The interpretations of the holy as the place of abiding and as the inmost intimacy (or origin of belonging together) are unified in the image of the hearth: the heart of the home. As the abode of lighting opening, the holy illuminates and allows the shining forth of all that is present; as the hearth, it is the origin not only of a luminous glow of fire but also of warmth which draws mortals and gods near to it and around which they gather in their familiar belonging with each other, earth, and heavens (WWAF 56–7). 'The ember glows and enkindles in its glow all going forth into appearance' (WWAF 57). In 'Homecoming/To the Kindred Ones,' Hölderlin describes the homeland and the holy in the same way. Heidegger holds that Hölderlin, by using the old name *Suevien*, 'invokes the oldest, innermost essence ... of home' (RP 256–7): '*Suevien*, the mother, dwells near the hearth of the house. The hearth keeps watch over the ever-reserved glow of the fire, which when it bursts into flame, opens out the airs and light into the serene. Around the fire of the hearth is the workshop, where the secretly-determined is forged. "Hearth of the house," i.e. of the maternal earth, is the source of the serenification [the holy], whose light first pours out in streams over the earth' (RP 258).

But there is still another dimension to the holy. Though, as abode and hearth, the heart does gather and make manifest everything which becomes present and is the origin which provides place, it also displaces and hides.[7] The holy displaces (*entsetzen*) because by opening the between within which all first comes to be, it not only is the coming to/ of this opening, but before that is the preparatory *removal from* the ordinary and commonplace. For the holy's coming to come, it must first move us out of the places where we are estranged without knowing it. (Remember, in chapter 1 we saw that movement from the everyday into the uncanny, *unheimlich*, went before any homecoming.) In a passage of powerful and sustained movement, Heidegger says that the holy sets (*heraussetzen*) all discovery or experience out of its habit and habitation and thus removes from it its site and habitat. It dis-locates. It dis-locates so that it can re-locate. Thus dis-placing (*ent-setzend*), the holy is the awesome (*das Entsetzliche*) itself (WWAF 63).

Yet, this awesome displacement, which occurs in the holy's coming, remains concealed in the midst of the lighting beginning (WWAF 63). How could that be? Certainly, it does not make sense if we think of this event as dramatic and earth-shaking. Recall, however, that the holy's greeting comes mildly and quietly, albeit happily. The smiling hail which comes to pass in 'As If on a Holiday' is 'scarcely experienced' by humans, who, though they take this gift, also take it according to their own needs. Relaxed, the holy allows both its own releasement – out of the everyday, into the originary – and attendant (self-)covering over, deferring to the coming forward of the usefully common. It relinquishes humans to their misunderstanding of the holy (WWAF 65). (Earlier, we saw that Hölderlin says that nature appears to sleep. In this repose, nature gathers itself for self-disclosure. That is, a self-holding-back is inseparable from coming forth [WWAF 55]. Insofar as it remains the coming, the holy does not withdraw; but both the coming and holding-back shine forth out of the holy's gleam, as well as remaining hidden and secret within it.) In the generosity of the holy's lighting which lets what comes forth into presence appear, humans see and gather near to what becomes present, but not to the holy itself which is the origin of the presencing. The holy lets this be so in order that humans and all that becomes present may come together. In such self-concealing, the holy also displaces itself: it places itself (the unmediated) inconspicuously in back of the rest (the mediated), which it sets out and into place.

Into this dynamic of placement into abode and displacement, the holy draws the poet. It draws the poet in, to be educated in the site of homelessness and homecoming. For out of the holy's apparent sleep, day will come; out of concealment, emergence will happen. The poet must be prepared to have a part in all this. Such preparation begins, in terms of home, when the poet remains at the site of the concealed or lack and yet looks forward to home (A 128–9). In the double-dimensioned holy, the poet is greeted with a mystery: *the holy appears as the origin or home (inmost hearth and intimate heart) of home (the belonging together of earth, heavens, gods, and humans in the between – the site of gathering) and as the source of homelessness (displacement and concealment). To repeat, the holy is the origin of both homelessness and home.* Further, if the holy is the happening of homelessness and home, as the still and ever coming, which draws the poet into and along with its coming, *the holy would also have to be the source and event of homecoming. The event of the holy which the poet must experience and sing is the journey from originary home, through homelessness, to homecoming.*

Poetic Passage: Return to Origin

It turns out, then, that the story of the holy and that of the poet are the same. Experiencing and understanding the holy as origin of home, homelessness, and homecoming is nothing abstract; it is the journey that the poet must undertake to become the poet's own self. Finally, both the holy and Hölderlin articulate a poetic passage as a return to origin. It should be clear that Hölderlin's poems of homecoming do not merely record his individual comings and goings or idiosyncratic yearnings and 'life-experiences' (A 79, 86). What he says actually discloses to us the essence of what it is to become and be a poet, while bringing forth essential features of the holy itself. Were this not so, poetry would be interesting, perhaps, but scarcely central to Heidegger's questions. It must be kept in mind that Hölderlin thinks of the poets both as wanderers (as mariners on journeys by river or stream in 'As If on a Holiday' [or 'Holyday'], 'Homecoming,' and 'Andenken') and, in the very same works, as what fructifies our dwelling. For example, in 'Remembrance of the Poet,' the poets are said not only to travel on a river, but to be as a stream: the river makes a land (and poets) capable of cultivation; the poets, in turn, make a homeland arable (A 97, 79). This beginning of 'Remembrance of the Poet' corresponds to the opening of Hölderlin's 'As If on a Holiday,' which also begins with nature bestowing growth and crops and goes on to speak of the poet as the fruit of the wedding of gods and humans – a wedding that can only be celebrated insofar as the poet sings and establishes it (e.g., A 113). The poet's journey home, then, is seminal for the journey that is central for Heidegger and the rest of us.

In the poetic journey, as articulated by Hölderlin and explicated by

Heidegger, we can discern six phases: 1) an initial being at home (*zu Hauß, Heim, Heimat*) that is yet not a being at home: 'the poetic spirit is not at home / not at the beginning, not at the source. At the beginning, the Poetic spirit is not at home in its own house (*nemlich zu Hauß ist der Geist / nicht im Amfang, nicht an der Quell. Der Geist ist zum Beginn im eigenen Hause nicht zuhaus*)' (A 91); 2) homelessness or wandering in the foreign and unhomely (*ausfahrt in die Fremde, wandershaft in die Fremde, Unheimischsein*); 3) a turning point – back toward home – return home (*Heimkehr*); 4) the moment of homecoming or arrival (*Heimkunft*); 5) learning to become at home in the poet's proper domain (*Heimisch werden im Eignen, in seinem Entstehungsgrund*); and 6) abiding (*Bleiben, Bleiben-können, verweilen*) or dwelling (*zu Hauß sein*) in the nearness of the homeland (*die Nähe der Heimat*), near the primal source (*Nähe der Quelle*), near the origin (*Nähe zum Ursprung*) (A 91). Clearly, all of these meld together, especially the last two, which may continue simultaneously, though we can distinguish their meanings.

In the beginning, we find ourselves in the midst of home, familiar with our family, environment, and native land and gods. But while we are aware of home and open to it, we are not experienced in the holy itself. This is both because the holy holds itself back in concealment and because we seize on the beings about us (A 92). The holy is also lost in our experience because we lapse into the common and everyday. Where the poet attempts to grasp the un-mediated, it proves impossible: what the poet seeks cannot be had, except through beings, yet it simultaneously withdraws and conceals itself behind them. Without knowing it, the poet is oblivious to what is both nearest and held at a distance by the holy. In the beginning, then, the poetic nature is not really at home in the poet's own home (A 91). The poet, not really abiding in the origin of dwelling, still longs for home (A 92). Hölderlin says of this home which closes itself off from the poet, 'The home(land) [*Heimat*] gnaws on him' (A 89, 92).

How then to find what the poet longs for if what is at hand does not satisfy? The poet attempts to find a true home by wandering out into the foreign. In several poems Hölderlin couples what is natively given as the poet's own with something foreign which the poet seeks and needs to become the poet's own. For example, in 'Remembrance,' the poet has Germanic clarity of presentation and seeks Greek fire (the lighting fire of the holy) (A 86). In 'Homecoming,' the poet goes out to seek the clouds and mountains of the serene. In 'As If on a Holiday,' the poets travel the rivers to foreign lands (for instance, the East) and to the origin of human dwelling. In all of these instances, a passing out of the familiar and entering into the foreign is required for experiencing what is sought (A 93; RP 256). Thinking in the language of the poet's growth, Heidegger contends, 'All that should be fruit must go out into the fire. That is the law of the travel into the foreign to experience the heavenly fire. Nothing proper (of our own) on the homey earth is able to thrive without this ripening in the foreign, in which it almost can be scorched' (A 115). Because maturing in the foreign, the poet must journey out before returning to the poet's own (A 95). The poet must be a mariner.

The foreign provides the necessary distance and perspective for the poet to think on home (A 93). Of course, to discover what is lacking and longed for, the poet cannot moon over the home departed. On the outward journey, without lapsing into any nostalgic homesickness, the poet must leave off thinking of home and think instead on the foreign itself and what might be found there (A 142). The departed home must be let go of because in that place or condition the poet had forgotten, and been forgotten by, the essential origin (A 94). Accordingly, this departure (*Ausfahrt*) out over the sea into the foreign is called a gift: it is the giving of the possibility of discovering what is needed (A 86). That the 'bird of passage' might with waking eyes see what is proper to it and cultivate it, the wind, which bears the greeting of the holy, calls it out of the foreign to home (A 85). Thus, it is only while journeying in the foreign that the poet is awakened to homecoming and strengthened for a later abiding at home (A 95). Through this realization the poet learns of the need for the foreign and dangerous as well as of the homey (A 94–5). More precisely, the poet comes to understand that the foreign and the coming home belong together – and must be thought together (A 101). In this way, the outward journey has as its end; what the poet seeks – home and the poetic spirit – is given its place and its essence through belonging within wandering, a wandering by which the poet already begins the return home (A 137).

But only when coming to experience the source as source, that is, to experience the holy as origin, does the poet begin to understand that what the poet has discovered must be brought back and kept (safeguarded) in the homeland. Importantly, it is the holy itself that gives this experience, though the poet must be receptive and prepared for it. This experience marks another phase of the journey. It is the turning point, a home-turning that will end in a return home. 'But such a return is only possible for one who has previously, and perhaps for a long time now, borne on his shoulders as the wanderer the burden of the voyage, and has gone over into the source, so that he could there experience what the nature of the sought-for might be, and then be able to come back more experienced, as the seeker' (RP 258–9). The turning point occurs as the tipping of a balance. For example, at dawn night and day are balanced, then light tips over into an awakening (A 110). Further, the turning is most likely not a smooth continuation, since it requires a change in direction – a reversal – and likely a deliberate expenditure of energy. If we journey by foot across country, rather than by ship on the seas, only a leap suffices to pass from the side of the foreign, where we have been, over a stream, to the bank of the homey (A 111).

The action, which both passes between and binds together is the turning point. The poet, for example, experiences the belonging-together of the foreign and home and passes over from one to the other.[8] Thus, Heidegger says that the poet on this journey thinks back to (recollects) the foreign and thinks ahead to home (A 108). When capable of binding together what the poet had at home and what is necessary in the foreign, then the poet is ready to turn toward home.

At this point, the poet has to bring the poet's own self back out of the foreign to the homeland. The experience of the source is 'given up for the return home' (RP 255). The beginning of the homecoming occurs in Hölderlin's poems when the poet goes over to the poetic saying of the homey (for example, the homey stream); yet, homecoming itself only begins the turn home into one's own (A 128). That is, home is not reached in the journey abroad, nor in the turning around. Once the poet has experienced the source, the return home opens up what is properly the poet's own. What was seen in the outward voyage as ripening now appears in the homecoming as ready to be harvested. Among the mature fruits we find Hölderlin's definition of what comprises a genuine homecoming: homecoming is genuine when it is an arrival at what *is properly one's own* (*im Eigenen*). In such a homecoming, what is one's own would open up. This opening would be a freeing and welcoming into one's nature, place, and proper relationships. The essential return would be to such a self-opening home – the place of arrival and origin (*seinem Herkunftsort*) (A 94, 91).

Naturally, homecoming would seem to be a moment of arrival. It would be the event of reaching the home shore, familiar people, and the places to which one is long accustomed. The poet, after this successful outward journey and turn around toward home, does make such an arrival (A 118). But if homecoming were merely the achievement of one physical location as distinguished from another, the event would scarcely be central to any human transformation, much less to the holy. The occurrence of mere travel soon rings hollow, since nothing of merit is accomplished. That accounts for the apparently odd tone of Hölderlin's poem 'Homecoming,' which is ostensibly about Hölderlin's travels in 1801 to his home in Swabia. As Heidegger notes,

> The poem 'Homecoming' might have given a poetic description of a joyous return home. Yet the last stanza, attuned to the word 'care,' gives no hint of the joyfulness of someone returning home completely carefree ... Certainly the 'homecoming' which ... [is spoken of] is much more than a mere arrival on the shore of 'the land of one's birth.'
>
> At home the people and the things seem pleasantly familiar. But as yet they are not really so. Thus they are shut away from what is most their own. (RP 243–4)

As Heidegger's comment on Hölderlin's tone makes clear, such an essential achievement at one's proper place has not yet occurred in the poet's landing and setting foot on shore: the people at home are closed off from their own. Heidegger explains,

> And therefore home at once delivers this message to the new arrival:
>
> That which thou seekest is near, and already
> coming to meet thee.
>
> Even with his arrival, the returning one has not yet reached home. Thus home is 'difficult to win, the shut-away.' Therefore the newcomer will remain in search of it. Only what he seeks is already coming to meet him. It is near. But what is sought is not yet found, if 'find' means to receive what is found as one's own, to be able to dwell in it as a possession. (RP 244)

Recall that after leaving home the poet came to experience the source as source on the outward journey but was unable to experience the source directly (it never could be had directly). The poet found it indirectly in what it brought forth. Hölderlin says this in his poems by having the poet recognize the source and follow its flow down its streams to the sea, where the flowing manifests its full richness. The poet says that we are not the source of remembrance; though we must actively travel the streams to the sea, 'it is the sea which gives and takes remembrance' (A 142). Note, just as in the passage cited above, *home* addresses the poet, giving a crucial message to help with the poet's bearings. Part of the experience that arises from recognizing the source indirectly in its effluence is that the poet is now far from the source in a common-sense way (though, paradoxically, the poet has just come near it). Here, the poet seems to understand that the need for the source, which lies back in the poet's homeland, and which was there all along, though the poet did not until now understand it as source. In 'Remembrance of the Poet' Hölderlin says that once close enough to the foreign fire to be scorched, *the poet realizes the need for the foreign and the autochthonous origin which is no longer near.* This is the insight enabling the turn back home (A 94).

In 'Homecoming,' the poet sees that 'proximity to the most joyous (and that means also proximity to the source of all that is joyous) is not there "beneath the Alps" ... Then the Swabian homeland, far removed from the Alps, must be that very place of proximity to the source. Yes, that is how it is' (RP 256). Hölderlin's words provide a new, profound interpretation of home and homecoming. *Home is the real proximity to the source; homecoming is the return there,* where what is sought after 'is near.' This also explains what 'one's own' means: it is one's proper source, that is, the source of one's place and nature. It is at the source where the event of the opening of what is one's own occurs. Heidegger explains this discovery:

> It is in this proximity to the source that neighborhood to the Most joyous is founded. What is innermost and best in the homeland consists solely in being just this proximity to the source – and nothing else except that ... But now, if the innermost essence of the homeland consists in being the point of proximity to the most joyous, then what is homecoming?
>
> Homecoming is the return into the proximity of the source. (RP 258)

Still, in the arrival home, the poet has not yet achieved such a deep return to the proximity of the source. The poet has, however, come to understand that mere arrival is not a full homecoming, only a first step toward it. Clearly, just as the poet was not 'at home' with the source when at home as a youth and just as the poet's fellow citizens are not yet 'at home' in their daily lives, so for the poet, too, the unhomely can pervade 'home' just as much as it does the foreign (A 136). Put another way, the poet only begins the essential turn to home and homecoming once having arrived back at the poet's native home (A 117). Home, then, in keeping with what Hölderlin has repeatedly said of the holy, *remains the coming* (A 101; see also RP 244). The inner essence of home has long been prepared for by the poet and people; yet, it 'is still reserved,' as Hölderlin says in a draft for another poem (cited in RP 244). The holy opens itself;

but, Heidegger adds, 'in the dispensation of Providence, the essence is not yet completely handed over. It is still being held back … That then, which has already been given and is yet at the same time being withheld, is called the reserved … Why? Because they … are not yet ready for it – not yet ready to have the innermost essence of home' (RP 245). Though Hölderlin names what home is and specifies what homecoming would be, both he and Heidegger say that even in homecoming, understood as arrival back into one's native scene, genuine home (as proximity to the source) is not achieved. Somehow, *home is simultaneously already given and still withheld:* 'The essence of proximity seems to consist in bringing near the near, while keeping it at a distance. Proximity to the source is a mystery' (RP 259). Home is a mystery.

At this point, the poet arrives at a deeper understanding of home and is led to a further phase of homecoming. *It would seem that the holy, as the primal and ultimate source, would be the radically originary home. Hölderlin, however, says that because the holy can never be experienced directly – since it is the totally unmediated mediation of all that emerges – our proper place, our own home, is proximate to the source. Homecoming, then, would not be coming to be in the source itself but into proximity to the source. This is what the poet learned that enabled the poet to achieve the beginning of a homecoming.* If the poet comes to understand that what has been long sought is already at home, a home newly returned to, the poet also sees that it needs to be understood for what it is. This homecoming is not just an initial coming to or arriving at the place which may be home; it is a continuous *becoming at home* (*Heimischwerdens im Eigenen*), a returning to where the poet belongs – a prolonged passage to the nearness of the source (A 87). This becoming at home would be the *persisting learning* to become at home. Again, that is what Hölderlin and Heidegger mean by saying that home is the coming: it continues to come to the poet, who must continue to learn to become 'at home' near it (proximate to its coming).

But it is not enough just to say that home-becoming is a learning, without elaborating what such learning is. Clearly, it would have to be a learning of the own or proper (as already began in the poet's journey into the foreign, where the poet found the foreign fire and began to assimilate it with the poet's own clarity of presentation). Heidegger notes that the Greeks, too, had to learn their own: the fire so near the gods. At first they were not at home there either and had to go through the foreign. Such free use of what is our own is most difficult (A 87). This learning of one's own – here the poet's – requires *careful thought.* The poet must think what is and is not for the proper use of the poet's own essence and the source. For the poet, of course, this also means a thinking writing, because of the need to say the coming of the holy and the homecoming (A 113). At any rate, the poet now sees that the learning must occur through a kind of thinking which does not once and for all achieve and hold on to its 'answer,' that is, its proper place. Rather, if homecoming really is to be a continuous journey, then the learning-thinking adequate to it must retain all six dimensions of the whole: the initial 'being at home' (which in fact is 'not being at home'), the wandering into the foreign, the turning point(s) toward home, the return home as the moment of arrival, learning to become at home once back, and accomplishing home as abiding near the source (A 139).

Why? If having forgotten what had been learned while in the foreign, the poet would lose what enables homecoming, that which initiated the trip and could be combined with the poet's own (e.g., as the 'fire of the gods' balanced the poet's own coolness in Hölderlin's 'Remembrance of the Poet'). What occurred in the past –the journey into the foreign – must be kept coming (A 116). Therefore, the poet's trip into the foreign does not end with the return home – it needs to be preserved in thinking (A 83). Because the poet needs to think all the phases of the journey to hold the experience and understanding of the source, the poet's thinking moves to and fro, forward and back (A 101). Recall that the poet was homeless just to the extent of having forgotten the holy or the holy's not having come to the poet. For example, earlier in life the poet mistook the gods (really only beings) for the holy. There the holy as source was obscured. In such misunderstanding, 'the open of this between closes itself' (A 104). Similarly, the poet might forget who the poet is (needs to become) and the poet's own origin (A 93–4). It is precisely as this self-closing that home gnaws on the poet according to Hölderlin.

For these reasons, Hölderlin says that the thinking (*Denken*) approximate to the poet is remembrance (*Andenken*). *Remembrance is the poet's own, proper way of thinking home and homecoming.* In fact, the poet's journey in thought and the poet's comprehending return really take place in such remembrance. Heidegger says that in the remembrance of the mariners (poets) and lovers (the gods and humans), the originary essence of remembrance first comes to light. This remembrance is a making secure; in letting itself run over what a festival is (the theme which thinking itself holds on to) this thinking can hold itself fast in its own essence. The remembrance establishes the thinking in its essential ground.

Whether remembrance is actually originary remembrance depends on whether it holds origin fast in its essence (as understood at the end of the journey home) (A 143–4).

Because such remembrance not only enables us to learn origin but keeps it secure, it is the care-full thinking required of the poet. It must keep the foreign as foreign and the origin as origin, not letting either disappear in favour of the things that emerge or as a result of partial understanding (A 91–2). For example, the source needs to remain the source, reserving itself behind what comes forth. The poet must not force it into hiding by attempting to seize it directly to bring it into the foreground, thereby destroying the mystery. Accordingly, the poet must learn to let it be both near and far. That is why Heidegger says, 'But now if homecoming means becoming at home in proximity to the source, then must not the return home consist chiefly, and perhaps for a long time, in getting to know this mystery, or first of all in learning how to get to know it. But we never get to know a mystery by unveiling or analyzing it; we only get to know it by carefully guarding the mystery *as* mystery' (RP 259). Here we see the proper attitude of the poet to the source. In remembrance, the poet guards the mystery by coming near it and yet not being overly bold. This remembrance, or learning to be at home, is joyful: 'The original essence of joy is the process of becoming at home in proximity to the source' (RP 261). It is also thankful. Heidegger connects the poet's establishing remembering thought (*Gedanken*) with thanking (*ein Dank*) because its response greets and is grateful for the source's greeting (A 85). Hölderlin describes this quiet attitude by saying, 'many a man is shy [or, full of awe – *Scheue*] about going to the source' (A 129; see also 146).

There is more. To learn such becoming at home through remembrance is learning *abiding* (*Bleiben*) proximate to the source. Heidegger says that remembering is a greeting (the poet's greeting responds to the holy's) which is a return to one's own. The allowance or learning of such greeting is an abiding – again, back in the constellation of one's own homelessness (in the foreign) and an always-coming-home (to origin) (A 96–7, 138). The poet, then, thinks on what has been, and on what comes, by thinking over abiding (A 127). This abiding must be learned because the poet, though having arrived at home, has not yet learned to abide near the source. That is the poet's next task – in which remembrance is vital, since it is a means of staying near the source. Not only must the poet learn such staying (A 89, 117); so, too, must any historical people. We are all called to find what is ours, to learn its proper use, and to hold on to it (A 88, 117). Such abiding is the return to and keeping of one's proper origin, according to Heidegger, insofar as it is the way to homecoming which the poet achieves by holding the whole of home and homecoming fast in remembrance (A 118–19).

Abiding, then, is not something accomplished once and for all; it is the lasting task of the poet and people. Considered as the movement from arrival at home to becoming really at home, abiding is continuously learned and as such can be seen as a distinct phase of homecoming. However, insofar as learning abiding passes over to become and remain true abiding, it has yet another character: as a thoughtful, preserving way of living, learning abiding would become dwelling. In its final phase, therefore, *homecoming is dwelling in a place near to the source.* Because abiding as becoming at home, by way of remembering the whole of the journey into homelessness and home-turning, turns imperceptibly into dwelling near the source, Heidegger says, 'The abiding in one's own is the path to the source. It is the origin, in which originates all the dwelling of the sons of the earth. The abiding is a going into the nearness of the origin. Whoever dwells in this nearness, accomplishes the essence of abiding' (A 145). The poet's wandering far from home and eventual coming near to the holy provides the ground upon which dwelling near to the origin can be established (A 138). This dwelling keeps the way to the coming-near established and maintains the nature of the near-coming as the coming to the essence of origin (A 145–6). That is, the dwelling both stays (it is stable) and stays the coming (it is dynamic or active).

When dwelling near the origin, the poet is near to and far from the holy because of having let the origin stay discretely at the distance it requires and because of its having come nearest precisely when it can stay withdrawn, hidden behind that which emerges (A 92, 148). *Here the poet experiences origin as origin, the primal home* (*Urheimat*) (A 140). *It comes forward as the source of home so that the poet's proper home is where the origin outpours a home to the poet – in proximity to the origin.*

As noted before, the poet's homeland is the place close to the hearth and source which remains inmost (RP 258). Heidegger says, 'Proximity to the source is a proximity which reserves something ... but this proximity does not take the most joyous right away, it only causes it to appear in *just this character* of the stored-away. In the essence of proximity a clandestine process of reservation takes place. The fact that the proximity to the most joyous reserves the near, is the mystery of proximity' (RP 260). Because this home of home is the origin and the originary ground of the poet's essence, the poet's story tells both of the holy and the poet's own character (A 92). Therefore, Heidegger adds, 'The vocation of the poet is homecoming, by which the homeland is first made ready as the land of proximity to the most joyous, and in the process of guarding it to unfold it – that is the care of homecoming' (RP 266).

Though it is impossible to do such a thing as summarize what we have learned from the poet's story of the poetic passage to origin, it is important for us to hold on to what has been said if we are to continue to try to think about it. Of course, we can return again and again to the poet's words and to Heidegger's – that would be our best course and primary responsibility. Yet, we also need to hold in memory what we have heard, begun to understand, and needed in order to stay on our way into the issue of homelessness and homecoming. These phenomena have not receded into the past of the Western world, neither with Hölderlin's or Heidegger's death nor with any other event. Home and homecoming keep coming (A 84, 87). Similarly, what Hölderlin and Heidegger, respectively, accomplish in their remembering poetizing and thinking is not a backward movement or nostalgic longing for a personal experience which is no more (A 83, 86). Rather, remembrance is a greeting which goes forth to the call which hails it (A 96). Along with the poet and Heidegger, we must attempt to retain the full journey in memory, continuing to think the belonging in relation to both the foreign and to the poet's (and our own) proper source and place close to the source. At the very least, we need to keep before us what the poet's story has disclosed in regard to four aspects of the matter at hand: the nature of home, the poetic achievement, the prospect and task for the rest of us humans, and the necessary role of thinkers.

As to the first, the character of homecoming and home are manifest in several ways in Hölderlin's work as interpreted by Heidegger. The very form and language of the poet's story brings forward the difference between the first phases of the journey and the last ones. The beginning of the story covering the trip away from home, for example, with its treatment of fast movement across the sea, has a linear quality emphasizing direct movement and action. In contrast, the final phases treating the homecoming, while retaining an energetic sense of being underway as (be)coming, shift from the horizontal dynamic and images of crossing the water's surface to speak of a three-dimensional opening in order to unfold a 'habitable' sphere of abiding. In this tri-dimensionality (opened vertically to the holy), we find the open itself. Put another way, in the open between earth/sea and heavens we hear of the place for dwelling.

The inmost essence of this full-dimensioned dwelling place – home – is explored through what Hölderlin says about the poetic experience and understanding. He tells us that home is already given to us and yet still withheld. It is the reserved (RP 245). That home is the between, the opening in which we each have what is our own but where differences among what belong together are preserved. We also hear about origin itself: that it is origin, which, as coming, gives the essence and relation of all that emerges. Origin grants place. Or, in terms of what is named 'the holy,' to say that the holy grants place is to say that it houses in space and time (RP 251). The essence of home, which yet remains kept open for us, comes forth in this granting: 'What remains safely preserved, is "homely" in its essence. The heralds send greeting from out of the serene, which keeps everything in a state of homeliness. The granting of homeliness is the essence of home' (RP 249). These words speak of the primal home of home.

Reflecting these insights concerning home, the poet says that homecoming is both achieved and always still underway and that homecoming is the return to the proximity of the source. Specifically, we discover the need to learn to become 'at home' near the source, since homecoming really only begins with our arrival at home; the learning requires searching for the essential and getting to know and let be mystery. Such learning-abiding may become a dwelling near the source through constant remembering. Then, too, homecoming and home are not – linearly or directionally – separate phenomena, with one coming before and one after, one achieved and the other left behind. Finally, home is not only something we seek though our active homecoming; originally, home approaches us. That is, the holy, in keeping itself held back, also constantly comes to us as origin. It too has its arrival (A 106). *Homecoming is the occurrence of origin: it comes to us. Therefore, homecoming is the coming home of the origin to what it makes at home. Homecoming is the giving of origin itself.* In all that Hölderlin says here, and that Heidegger helps us interpret, we encounter a dual sense of home and homecoming. Our own, proper homecoming would be a dynamic coming to and dwelling near the source, which, as the essence-allocating source of all, itself continues to come to us as the primal 'home': the origin and granting of all home and homelessness.

Hölderlin's second set of insights is simultaneously simple and profound: *homecoming is a poetic achievement.* Though we seek home and though it must first come to us, the poet is a necessary intermediary between humans and the holy (whose greeting is brought by its messengers). '[The holy] is already approaching ... Yet what is now already approaching, still remains the sought-after. Since, however, the joyous only draws near where it is met and welcomed by the composition of poetry, therefore the angels, heralds of the serene, appear only if there are any who are composing' (RP 249). Because the holy gives itself in its saying through the poet, who must establish home by a saying, Hölderlin says that the origin is the poet's sole concern. As home, origin constantly and always gnaws on the poet (A 92). That is why Heidegger has chosen Hölderlin before all others as a guide in his own search for home. In regard to Hölderlin, Heidegger contends, 'All the poems of the poet who has entered into his poethood are poems of homecoming' (RP 233).

Even more dramatically, Hölderlin and Heidegger say that *the return home is accomplished in the writing remembrance of the poet.* Recall, the poet learns to abide in proximity to the source by learning remembrance. But this remembrance is nothing other than the bringing together in thinking of the fundamental phases and 'players' within homelessness, homecoming, and home. In remembrance, the gods and humans, earth and heavens, and the origin itself are brought and held together. Remembrance is a homecoming. Of course, remembrance is not a silent, interior psychological process of the poet; rather, it is the poet's remembering saying. That is, it is the poet's writing or composition (A 151).

Heidegger claims that all genuine poets (not just those casually so identified) manage a way for the ultimate source of home to appear in words (RP 263). Though the proper word is usually lacking for the highest, seeking it is the goal of the poets and their rarest and most essential achievement (that means gift, when it is given): 'To prepare joyously the fitting proximity to the Near for the greeting heralds, who bring greetings from the still-reserved discovery – that is what determines the vocation of the poet' (RP 264). According to Heidegger, *Hölderlin actually achieves such homecoming and establishing of home in poems* such as 'Homecoming' and 'Andenken,' as we hear in the conclusion of the essay, also titled 'Remembrance of the Poet,' where Heidegger says that the greeting of the holy comes to us through Hölderlin: 'Its abiding becomes established in the word of the poem "Andenken"' (A 150–1). 'The poet comes home, in the act of coming into proximity with the source. The poet comes into this proximity, in the act of telling of the mystery of proximity to the near. He tells of this, in the act of writing of the most joyous. The writing of poetry is not primarily a cause of joy to the poet, rather the writing of poetry *is* joy, is serenification, because it is in writing that the principal return home consists. The elegy "Homecoming" is not a poem about homecoming; rather the elegy itself, taken as the very poetry of which it is comprised, is the actual homecoming' (RP 261).

In addition, the poet comes home to the poet's own self in the writing of poetry. Here poets achieve their own essence, in their harmonious response to the call of the holy, where they must first come to dwell (A 148).[9] Hölderlin says that writing is the ripening of the poet; through it the poet becomes the mature fruit grown by nature (A 116). Of course, not all those who attempt poetry, or even begin the journey, succeed in becoming at home (A 134). In regard to the insight that the opening of the between in which we might dwell is both spatial and temporal, Hölderlin tells us that the poet's efforts toward homecoming are crucial because they take place at just that time when homelessness prevails. Immediately after Heidegger speaks of the poet's vocation, he adds, commenting on Hölderlin's poems, 'The time of the reserved discovery is the age when the god is lacking. The "failure" of the god is the reason for the lack of "holy names." Nevertheless, because the discovery in being reserved is at the same time near, the failing god sends greeting in the Near of the heavenly ... So for the poet's care there is only one possibility: without fear of the appearance of godlessness he must remain near the failure of the god, and wait long enough in the prepared proximity of the failure, until out of the proximity of the failing god the initial word is granted, which names the high one' (RP 264–5).

Thus, Hölderlin says that the genuine poet appears not just at a time that is important to the poet, but at a crucial time of homelessness between gods and humans. That is why poets are indispensable for Heidegger and all the rest of us. Though it would be an exaggeration and mistake to say that the poets write just for the sake of humans, the poets are vitally needed for our homecoming. Here, then, we have another dimension of what Hölderlin shows us – the prospect and tasks that lie before all of us who are neither poets nor thinkers (at least not in the deep sense that Heidegger is, even if we are earnest apprentices). The wholly human question is how we live now and might live on the earth, how we might endure the foreign and strange and achieve homecoming and dwelling, even as the poet did (A 88ff.).

In order for us to be on the way through homelessness, and to homecoming and dwelling at home, the open must have opened. That is, the between must already be granted by the holy and established by the poets. The latter are needed because we humans do not first of all or directly come to understand the mystery (proximity to the source): 'For the sake of this knowledge there must always be another who comes home for the first time and tells of the mystery' (RP 259; see also 268–9). As we have seen, the poet is such a one.[10] The poet helps first bring about a dwelling place for people. As to the ground that the poet establishes and holds fast in remembrance, 'on this ground, then, the sons of the earth shall dwell, if they poetically dwell upon this earth. The poetry of the poet is now the founding of abiding' (A 149). In short, 'Poetizing is remembering. Remembrance is establishing. The establishing dwelling of poets shows and dedicates the ground for the poetic dwelling of the sons of the earth' (A 151). Additionally, Hölderlin and Heidegger say that all of us must learn to dwell as the poet does – poetically, that is, in the establishing of the word, where we listen to the saying of the holy and respond with our own saying, which lets be and preserves that greeting opening (A 91, 95). Poetically we too need to find our dwelling place and learn to dwell as children of the earth, with the gods, on the earth, beneath the heavens (A 123).

But even if the holy grants the between and the poet articulates and establishes a place for us in proximity to the source, what the poet alone accomplishes is not enough, because, as we have seen, home is not accomplished once and for all, not in an individual's life, nor certainly for an entire historical people. Once the poet achieves homecoming in writing, it must be kept coming. *It is 'a homecoming which is continuously being enacted so long as its message sounds out a bell in the speech of … people'* (RP 261).[11] This is why Hölderlin says that the poet appears as a sign: the poet is sent from and to the origin, if only we can hear the poet, 'read' and follow what the poet points to. 'Then homecoming really consists solely in the people of a country becoming at home in the still-withheld essence of home; previous to that, even, it consists in the "dear ones" [poets] learning at home to become at home' (RP 245). That the work required beyond the poet's achievement – the understanding and continuation of homecoming – might be adequately provided by the way the rest of us listen, think, and act is not very likely. The poet most probably needs more help than most of us can give. That the people of any place need even further assistance is well understood by Hölderlin, and the way he deals with the issue entails a fourth set of insights. Here we cannot miss the reason why he is so important to Heidegger, as well as to the rest of us. *Hölderlin says that homecoming is also the task for the thinker – and this on behalf of all of us who would pass through homelessness.*

In chapter 1, we saw that Heidegger faced the metaphysical homelessness of our epoch, and, at the limit of his own resources of thinking and language, broke off his own saying to find and hear a guide, Hölderlin, whose sayings responded to the saying of the holy (as we have seen in chapter 2). *In turn, Hölderlin returns Heidegger to his own calling and task.* The poet says that there is a complex series of mediations needed to open home, or its possibility, to us. The holy sends its greeting, by way of the gods, to the poet, who, hearing, tells the people. But the poet's word, which carefully guards mystery, is fragile; further, the people are not always ready to respond to it. The poet's word, then, itself requires someone to hear and understand it, preserve it, and pass it on.

The poet addresses the poet's sayings 'to the others in the homeland, to become hearers, in order that for the first time they should learn to know the essence of the homeland' (RP 266–7). Heidegger, interpreting Hölderlin, specifies a succession of figures involved in homecoming, since 'those residing on the soil of the native land are not yet those who have come home to the peculiar essence of home' (RP 267). 'Thinking of this kind [the poet's] first produces the deliberating ones, who do not precipitate the reserved and ... guarded discovery. Out of these deliberating ones will come the slow ones of the long-enduring spirit, which itself learns again to preserve with the still coming failure of the god. The deliberating ones and the slow ones are for the first time the careful ones. Because they think of that which is written of in the poem, they are directed with the singer's care towards the mystery of the reserving proximity. Through this single turning towards the same object the careful hearers are related with the care of the speaker, "the others" are the "kindred" of the poet' (RP 267). Clearly, Heidegger (as he presents himself) is one who hears the poet, thinks the poet's discovery, and is therefore carefully directed to the mystery of the proximity of the source. Turned toward homelessness, homecoming, and home, Heidegger is kindred to the poet.

When the careful ones enter into kinship with the poet, 'then there is a homecoming. But the homecoming is the future of the historical being of [a] people' (RP 268). *Note, here Heidegger himself achieves a homecoming: he comes to realize that he is kin to the poet, and in this kinship he begins to come home to his essence as a careful one – as one who thinks homecoming and home.* 'For now there must be thinkers in advance, so that the word of the writer may be heard. It is the thought of the careful ones alone – directed to the written mystery of the reserving proximity – that is the "remembrance of the poet." In this remembrance there is a first beginning, which will in turn become a far-reaching kinship with the homecoming poet' (RP 268).

Indeed, as we will see in the rest of this book, as a homecoming thinker, Heidegger will develop a far-reaching, lifelong kinship with the homecoming poet. For now, though, it is clear that Heidegger begins to think of himself as having such a kinship. Though the address quoted just above is entitled 'Remembrance of the Poet' (see RP 232), Heidegger also speaks to us through the titles of his essays, which often simply 'say again' the names Hölderlin has given (for example, 'Homecoming/ To the Kindred Ones' and 'Andenken'), since Heidegger's close interpretations of these poems are themselves a remembrance and homecoming by a kindred one. Further, according to Heidegger,

> In hearkening to the spoken word and thinking about it so that it may be properly interpreted and retained, they ['the others'] are helping the poet. This help corresponds to the essence of the reserving proximity ... For just as the greeting heralds must help, in order that the serene may reach men in the serenification so too there must be among men a first, who poetically rejoices in the face of the greeting heralds, in order that he, alone and in advance, may first conceal the greeting in the word.
>
> But because the word, once it has been spoken, slips out of the protection of the care-worn poet, he cannot easily hold fast in all its truth to the spoken knowledge of the reserved discovery and of the reserving proximity. Therefore the poet turns to the others, so that their remembrance may help towards an understanding of the poetic word, with the result that in the process of understanding each may have a homecoming in the manner appropriate for him. (RP 268–9)

Hölderlin says,

> ... But alone he cannot easily maintain it,
> And the poet gladly joins with others,
> So that they may understand how to help. (cited in RP 269)

Even if, by turning to Hölderlin's poetry, Heidegger has found that he is kin to the poet, he must still learn how to help and in doing so find the homecoming appropriate for himself. At this point, he sees that the thinker's task, like the poet's, is remembrance. That is, if Heidegger is concerned with his own task of facing, enduring, understanding, and speaking about homelessness, he must not only travel through homelessness, as did Hölderlin before him; he must also hold it in remembering thinking, as the poet did in remembering poetizing. That is why Heidegger says, when beginning to think Hölderlin's poetry, 'As practice for "Remembering the Poet" let us listen to the elegy "Homecoming"' (RP 233). The remembrance of the poet and the thinker belong together; so, too, do their homelessness and homecoming.

Heidegger develops not only this similarity but also their differences. Whereas the poet achieves a homecoming in poetizing, the thinker, in remembering thinking, *stays in the unhomey – unheimlich* – even if passing through it. Heidegger says of the poet, and of himself, that the poet's questioning is a thinking toward 'becoming at home in one's essential place [*auf das Heimischwerden im eigenen Wesensort hinausdenkt*].' 'Yet the poetic questioning is another art than the thinking questioning, which ventures itself in the essentially question worthy, and in this brings itself to a different issue than the saying of the holy. The thinker thinks on the unhomey [*das Unheimische*] which for him is not a moment of passage, but is his "being at home" [*zu Hauß*]. The recollective questioning of the poet, in contrast, poetizes the homey [*Heimische*]' (A 129). Without doubt, Heidegger's concern with Hölderlin is not the product of idiosyncratic enthusiasm for him, nor of any nostalgic attraction to him as a neighbouring Swabian. Rather, their relationship arises out of the strictest 'necessity of thought,' as Heidegger himself tells us (RP 232). That is, both arise from what is granted to them in common. The end of Heidegger's thinking of Hölderlin's poetry is a return back to what is his own as a thinker in our needy time. Heidegger's proper home is seen to lie in our epoch's 'metaphysical homelessness and uncanniness [*das unheimlich*].' Further, as he has been all along on his journey with Hölderlin, he remains underway to his own homecoming – where such a homecoming would not leave the *unheimlich.*

For home and dwelling, it turns out that the story of the poet's return to the proximity to the source opens out so the poet sees that in the overarching event of homecoming the all-encompassing homeland or home – the between – is the gift of the origin. This story is also one of the holy's granting of home to gods and humans, on the earth and under the heavens. Further, because the opening of such a dwelling place requires thinking helpers, this same story also turns out to be one of the thinker. The holy grants home and homeliness, which establishes the poet, who, dwells in it. The poet, in turn, with the help of the thinker, establishes the dwelling place for humans and opens for us the chance to continue a historical response to what we hear through our mode of speaking and our actions. Since, within this placement and region, Hölderlin's 'poems appear like a shrine without a temple, where what has been made into poetry is preserved' and because the poet needs the thinker's assistance in mediating between the holy and a people, Heidegger sees his work as a building on to the dwelling opened by the holy and framed by the poet (RP 234).[12] Accordingly, Heidegger's own story and saying need to keep homecoming coming. In turn, our task now would be to see whether and how Heidegger works out his remembering thinking and saying over his lifetime, as a homecoming of his own, in kinship with the poets and in proximity to the source – and in the careful service of his fellow human beings. Perhaps for Heidegger, as he says of Hölderlin the poet, in learning his own vocation there is a coming that would also 'first release the homey to a coming' (A 99).

3 Turning toward the Overcoming of Homelessness

In chapter 1, we followed Heidegger as he faced up to homelessness as the problem, not only of our time, but of our entire metaphysical heritage. Before he could press further into his homelessness, much less attempt any sort of homecoming, he had to rest at the limit of his own resources. For all he had thought and said, a guide was needed for further progress over the impasse. In chapter 2, we listened to Heidegger's conversation with his poetic guide, Hölderlin. Hölderlin had passed over into the foreign and homelessness; he had experienced the holy Source. He had also returned home, and perhaps most importantly, had achieved a genuine homecoming in thinking and language by holding homelessness, homecoming, and home in his remembering writing. Here Heidegger found additional resources that he needed for his own journey: he found a paradigmatic guide and discovered his own role as a helper in the hearing and saying of the holy's greeting. That is, he found that his task involved a careful, helpful thinking and saying, understood as remembrance. Further, in regard to his own attempt to think and say the homelessness of being and human being, he came to take part in the way Hölderlin's language facilitated the journey.

In this third chapter, we will see how Heidegger combines the movements, resources, tasks, and possibilities of the first two 'series' of achievements. Naturally, there would be interaction between Heidegger's thinking and writing about metaphysical homelessness from 1929 to about 1943 and his meditative explications of Hölderlin from 1936 to 1943, with their respective subject matter and styles.[1] After all, one person is thinking and saying all this. Thus, Hölderlin's influence already begins to work in the 'metaphysical' writings seen in chapter 1. For example, the contribution of Hölderlin (presented in 'Hölderlin and the

Essence of Poetry,' 1936, and 'As If on a Holiday' [or 'Holyday'], 1939) clearly appears in 'Recollection in Metaphysics,' 1941 (which treats recollection (*die Erinnerung*), origin, origination, appropriation, and the saying of being). Nonetheless, just as clearly, the two sets of works are distinct, each with its own theme and style.

As is the third. In the third group of works, Heidegger *consolidates and focuses* his thinking in several ways. They bring together what so far is diffused in his technically philosophical, historical, and poetically inspired works. In this way, they remind us of the ray of light which, focused by the gods, struck the poet. In addition, they centrally hold together and present Heidegger's insights. That is, they articulate what he sees concerning metaphysics, poetic thinking and saying, the holy, and being. Finally, these works concentrate the energy of Heidegger's understanding for a future release into what he must do in order to travel further into homelessness and, perhaps, to achieve homecoming, especially insofar as they are the means by which he finds a way to articulate his own position more fully and to sound out alternative approaches he will take in years to come.

This gathering of thought, which enables him to move forward in homecoming, occurs first in a book-length project from the mid-1930s that he kept secret for a half-century (*Contributions to Philosophy* (*From Enowning*) [1936–8]), then continues in a series of books and articles generally made public from 1943 to 1949: parts of 'Overcoming Metaphysics' (1936–46), 'The Word of Nietzsche: "God Is Dead"' (1936–40, 1943), 'Postscript to "What Is Metaphysics"'? (1943), 'What Are Poets For?' (1946), 'Letter on Humanism' (1947), and 'The Turning' ('Die Kehre') (1949).

In this third set of writings, Heidegger exercises a new vocabulary, unfolds a distinct subject matter, and develops his own distinctive style (that does far more than meld what occurs in the first two sets of works). Here he finds a new 'voice' in and for the thinker's story of homelessness and homecoming. Evidently, in the course of elaborating his problematic and trying to work out a new way of thinking and saying by going alongside Hölderlin, Heidegger experienced an enormous burst of, let us call it, insight that enabled him to write in a way he could not before. Discretely for years, but then publicly in the 1940s, he developed this new resource for the journey. We can see the impact of the encounter with Hölderlin in the new vocabulary Heidegger employs, and his own achievement in applying it to a different subject matter. Given the power of words for Heidegger, it is critical to attend to how he more and more often thinks and speaks by way of, for example, 'enowning,' 'event,' or 'appropriation' (*Ereignis*), 'turn' (*Kehre*),' 'open,' (*Offen*) or 'between' (*Zwischen*), 'displacement,' 'home' (*Heim*), 'mystery' (*Geheimnis*), 'give,' 'grant,' 'lighting,' 'fire,' 'dwelling,' 'abiding' and 'abode,' 'proximity,' 'near'/'far,' 'to'/'fro,' 'coming,' 'absence' and 'failure' (of gods), 'difference,' 'heart,' 'gods,' 'earth,' 'heavens,' 'sons of earth,' 'fruit,' 'wine,' 'festival,' 'source' and 'origin,' 'remembrance' (*Andenken*), 'guard,' 'keep,' 'preserve,' 'silence,' 'shyness'/'awe,' 'thank,' 'hear,' 'listen,' and 'cor-respond.'[2]

Clearly, in his style of thinking and writing (and of speaking in lectures and seminars), Heidegger will now go forward, differently than before. Far more importantly, and not reducible to a mere difference of vocabulary, with the help of Hölderlin's language and thinking the theme opens freshly (new meanings, characteristics, and relations can be established and maintained) and Heidegger becomes skilful in the art of originary, remembering thinking and saying. He finds a way to go about thinking that is precise but not metaphysical. That enables him to get beyond the barrier of metaphysics in order to think it from both the inside and outside. At the same time, he does not need to break off in silence but can proceed rigorously.

Though Heidegger learns from his close meditation on poetic texts and his conversations with the poet and will use this deeper understanding (for example, in some of his reflections on Nietzsche's *Thus Spoke Zarathustra* and later with other poets), the movement of his thought is also notably discontinuous. *Contributions* appears as a *distinctive, dramatic struggle with what might be said non-metaphysically* (a struggle that Heidegger himself admits he often loses) such that he *simultaneously also continues writing in a relatively straightforward way* in this third set of works (CP 61). Here, Heidegger speaks more directly and on his own, for himself. After *Contributions,* these works present, for the most part discursively, what he sees and thinks at this gathering point. Stylistically, then, in this phase Heidegger gathers himself, his resources and difficulties, with the mystery that he seeks. With the new language Hölderlin provides for what must be thought, Heidegger's journey can begin again, but he must begin it himself because what such language can say must first be thought in the mode of originary understanding. Thus he moves from his dialogue with Hölderlin to undertake the necessary remembering thinking in the works to be considered in the present chapter.

Language and Thinking: Entering the Overcoming of Metaphysics

The new originary way of inceptual thinking and saying, as he came to call it, appears to have reached its first significant form as *Contributions*, planned perhaps as early as 1932 and composed mainly between 1936 and 1937, with a final section written in 1938, and only belatedly made public in 1989.[3] As we are seeing, Heidegger wrote polysemously, and almost restlessly. Indeed, *Contributions* is itself markedly multi-vocal. It continues to explore metaphysics (even as Heidegger also plays that line of thought out more fully in the works considered in chapter 1). It acknowledges and develops the singular importance of Hölderlin, 'who has already gone ahead of us' and has 'become now our necessity, in his most unique poetic experience and work,' thus continuing to express a respect, even reverence, for the poet as our critical guide, as we examined in chapter 2 (CP 247). Finally, it articulates a new, third way of speaking, to accomplish the task of finding a new, non-metaphysical way of thinking and saying in light of what Heidegger learned from Hölderlin, but without Heidegger's pretending to be a poet.

Contributions, then, initiates this third course by dramatically venturing along and trying out a previously uncharted trajectory. Here we can literally watch Heidegger struggle to shape his language and thoughts, often trying out variation upon variation as he seeks the requisite precision and rigor. It appears that Heidegger kept this work protected, even hidden, until he found acceptably suitable ways to unfold before others the radical thought that came to its initial articulation here. In *Contributions*, then, he does not work with a given, much less a fixed, language or set of ideas worked out beforehand. Instead, he is trying them out for the first time. 'But the pathway of this enthinking of be-ing does not yet have a firm line on the map. The territory first came to be through the pathway and is unknown and unreckonable at every stage on the way ... The territory that comes to be through and as the way of enthinking be-ing is the between' (CP 60).[4]

That the talk of pathway, line, map, territory, stages on the way, and ground is not isolated or accidental underscores the fact that *Contributions* continuously, deliberately, and explicitly develops through the language, structure, substantive saying and thinking, and attempted *performative enacting* of homelessness, home, and homecoming. As a central part of what it does in its several voices and trajectories of meaning, *Contributions* proceeds by unfolding the problems of our current historical situation and possible alternatives in the language and structure-figure of a journey out of and returning back into various modes of belonging and abiding.

Reflecting on the title and task of what he has attempted here, Heidegger strikingly notes that 'the "work" is the self-unfolding structure in turning-back' (CP 54). Congruently, in the first few pages of the 'Preview' of *Contributions*, Heidegger begins by saying – in terms not immediately clear, but worked out in the rest of the book and for years afterward – that in 'the age of crossing from metaphysics into be-ing-historical thinking,' he can venture only an attempt at a future thinking, since such thinking 'is underway, through which the domain of be-ing's essential swaying – completely hidden up to now – is gone through, is thus first lit up ... *Contributions to Philosophy* enacts a questioning along a pathway which is first traced out by the crossing to the other beginning, into which Western thinking is now entering. The pathway brings the crossing into the openness of history and establishes the crossing as perhaps a very long sojourn' (CP 3).

Heidegger also explicitly lays out a basic map of the required journey in the very first pages of *Contributions*. Though the 'time of re-building ... has not yet arrived ... in the meantime, in crossing to the other beginning, philosophy has achieved one crucial thing: projecting open, i.e., the grounding enopening of the free-play of the space-time of the truth of be-ing' (CP 4). And the other beginning of thinking is named thus because it must be the only other beginning according to the relation to the one and only first beginning. We are concerned with how 'thinking in the crossing accomplishes the grounding projecting-open of the truth of be-ing as historical mindedness' (CP 4): 'In the knowing awareness of thinking in the crossing, the first beginning remains decisively the first – and yet is overcome as beginning ... [since] reverence for the first beginning ... must coincide with the restlessness of turning away from this beginning to an other questioning and saying. The outline of these *Contributions* is designed to prepare for the crossing and is drawn from the still unmastered ground plan of the historicity of the crossing itself' (CP 5).

Thus, the project, even as an experiment that bursts forth, is in broad outline clear enough, though that says as much or little as saying that Odysseus' journey was to Troy and then back home and is passed on to us in a foreign tongue. Specifically, Heidegger's preparatory plan for the voyage indicates that *we need to travel from where we are, back through the first beginning,* to *an other* beginning. The description and the enactment quickly become complicated as they are, respectively, elaborated and carried out. Three pages after the passages just cited, Heidegger makes sure we understand that this is no smooth movement along a fixed road, but involves a 'leap,' 'enleaping,' a 'cleavage' (CP 7), and considerable other obstacles and dangers: 'The "between" of Da-sein overcomes ... not, as it were, by building a bridge between be-ing (beingness) and beings – as if they were two riverbanks needing to be bridged – but by simultaneously transforming be-ing and beings in their simultaneity. Rather than possessing an already established standpoint, the leap into the between first of all lets Da-sein spring forth' (CP 11). 'The relapses into the hardened ways and claims of metaphysics will continue to disturb and to block the clarity of the way [CP 9] ... Those who question ... establish the new and highest rank of inabiding in the midpoint of be-ing, in the essential sway of be-ing (enowning) as the midpoint ... For truth is the between [*das Zwischen*] for the essential swaying of be-ing and the beingness of beings' (CP 10).[5]

But this is to get ahead of ourselves, that is, ahead of *Contributions,* since an outline of an itinerary does not obviate the journey. Still, even if we do not know what this story means or how to go about it or along with it to recognize what Heidegger tells us and to hold it in mind, we can draw the provisional itinerary of *Contributions* – to be filled in later, since at this point most of these terms are much like *terra incognita* written on old maps next to a sketch of a mountain or a fantastic animal. At least seven of the major dimensions of the journey will be carefully elaborated by Heidegger:

1 A crossing over or leap
2 From where we are
3 Through the midpoint/between
4 Through the domain of be-ing's essential sway/openness of history
5 Through the turning/*Ereignis*
6 To the first beginning
7 To the other beginning.

We must, and can only, start 'from where we are' (CP 35). An analysis of today's problems leaves no doubt that our world desperately needs a new trajectory – which, Heidegger will argue, requires a return back to the beginning of our effective cultural history, to move, indirectly, forward into the future. We are so substantially uprooted from any tenable ground of what has been our historical placement that Heidegger speaks of the 'derangement of the West,' in the face of which we must be 'mindful of the darkening of the world and the destruction of the earth in the sense of *acceleration, calculation, and* the *claim of massiveness*' (CP 83). He adds, 'The struggle against destruction and uprooting is only the first step,' albeit a crucial one (CP 70).

At the level of our historical social existence, we are now uprooted by technological machinery that organizes and disciplines the planet. Heidegger points to what requires thinking:

> The machine, what is its ownmost, the service that it demands, the uprooting that it brings. 'Industry' (operations); industrial workers, torn from homeland and history, exploited for profit.
>
> Machine-training; machination and business. What recasting of man gets started here? (World-earth?) Machination and business. The large number, the gigantic, pure extension and growing leveling off and emptying. Falling necessarily victim to trash and to what is sham. (CP 274)

Yet, the 'growing uprootedness' that results from 'the bewitchment of technicity,' for all its seriousness, is not the greatest problem (CP 85, 87). Since it derives from the dominating representational-calculative mode of thinking that has become the arbiter of all meaning and the measure of all that is said or known to be: 'Thought in a fundamental manner, all of this means that beings as such are re-presentable and that only the representable *is*' (CP 76) – not at all an innocent situation, since it means that beings and representational epistemology have replaced or obscured being.

Because of the 'absence' of being, our historical position is dangerously hovering near an abyss, in that the uprooting which we thus far have considered is itself a *dimension* 'of that which Nietzsche recognized for the first time as nihilism' (CP 83). Herein, Heidegger contends, we find, as masked, the deeper ground: the abandonment of being (CP 83). Thus, while 'in its ordinary meaning the word machination is the name for a "bad" type of human activity and plotting for such an activity,' in the more fundamental 'context of the being-question, the word does not name a human comportment but the manner of the essential sway of being' (CP 88). The primal rootlessness is due to a disconnection from being. What is required is a 'leap to safety,' that is, a return from metaphysical modernity to a new rootedness (CP 61–2), where the question is one of radically 'rethinking being-historically (but not "ontologically")' (CP 71).

Would the attempt to return from rootlessness to a rootedness in which we can reside somehow amount to a coming back to what is familiar? Decidedly not! In *Contributions* Heidegger reworks much of what he said in *Being and Time,* including Dasein, but he does not really develop that earlier work's line of thought concerning the everyday and uncanny. That may be for several reasons: (*i*) it can be reasonably expected that we know what he says in *Being and Time* if we are reading *Contributions;* (*ii*) Heidegger himself notes that there are 'many things that are unaccomplished in *Being and Time*' (CP 61), and this may not be one of them (or not one of the most important of them); (*iii*) he may be going in a distinctly different or additional direction; and, of course (*iv*) he continues to retrieve and deconstruct metaphysical thinking in a series of works that continue for years (as we began to see in chapter 1) (CP 61). In any case, beyond the analysis of the everyday, *Contributions* stresses that our unique historical placement, need, and task of homecoming must start, not with wonder as it did for the Greeks in the first beginning, but now with startled dismay. 'Startled dismay means returning from the ease of comportment in what is familiar' because 'what has been familiar for so long proves to be estranging and confusing' (CP 11). In short, to try to remain in the familiar, assuming it would be where we are at home, is precisely the wrong thing to do: in the familiar, we are not only homeless but oblivious to the fact and what it means.

In the midst of the familiar, we are most homeless and even propelled into the requisite journey, despite ourselves. The first awareness of being underway may come when we become conscious of, and begin to think, that the familiar is strange and how it is so (estranging because it hides what now appears to be strange) and how in our encounter the strange (which will turn out to be that to which we most deeply belong) appears as modes of displacement. In our immersion in the swirl, even useless surplus, of objects about us we fail to question the familiar and thus fail to 'touch upon what is uncanny in this epoch' (CP 77). 'The bewitchment of technicity and its constantly self-surpassing progress' is at the base of 'the uncanniest indication of the disappearance of sites for decision' (CP 87).

Not only the ways of our contemporary world but words themselves hide the strangeness behind what is familiar. 'Every saying of be-ing is kept in words and namings which are understandable in the direction of everyday reference to beings and are thought exclusively in this direction, but which are misconstruable as the utterance of be-ing ... The word itself discloses something (familiar) and thus hides that which has to be brought into the open through thinking-saying' (CP 58). As a complementary insight, the fact that attending to that which must be thought would require many names is not an indication of a problem but may confirm the 'richness and strangeness' of what must be named (CP 16). Thinking and saying, then, must make their way through this complex interplay of the familiar and the strange.

Here we also have both a characterization of and a charge against philosophy: 'in philosophical knowing a transformation of the man who understands takes place with the very first step ... The thinking of philosophy remains strange because in philosophical knowing everything ... is always exposed to displacement' (CP 10–11). It is not so much that philosophy itself is strange but that it must persist in moving in the realm of the strange, because strangeness is an essential feature of what must be thought: 'philosophy must return to the beginning, in order to bring into the free-space of its mindfulness the cleavage and the beyond-itself, the estranging and always unfamiliar' (CP 29). Heidegger's strong claim is that we 'need to be displaced' and that the question of 'how is man to be displaced' from the familiar and into the strange cannot be hubristically answered under the assumption that it is something we can 'accomplish' by ourselves, but rather only by becoming open to seeing 'that this displacing comes over human beings' (CP 19).

In the passages of *Contributions* just considered, Heidegger has already said that it is be-ing that is strange and hidden behind the familiar. It also turns out that the familiar is familiar and the strange strange precisely because being hides itself. At the primary level, our rootlessness is hidden behind our technological mastery and metaphysical mode of thinking: 'the danger has power to the extreme, since everywhere there is uprooting and – what is even more disastrous – because the uprooting is already engaged in hiding itself' (CP 69). In the extraordinary sections 52–8 on the abandonment of being, *Contributions* explains, 'Abandonment of beings is strongest at that place where it is most decidedly hidden. That happens where beings have – and had to – become most ordinary' (CP 77). Similarly, the uncanny 'disappearance of sites for decision' which we experience – or more dangerously, do not experience – 'indicates the abandonment of being' (CP 87). The disclosure and hiddenness, the ordinary and strange, are in dizzying play. 'Where beings have necessarily to be the most familiar, be-ing is necessarily and *all the more* ordinary and most ordinary. And since [at the same time] now be-ing "is" in truth what is most *non*-ordinary, be-ing here has withdrawn completely and has abandoned beings. *Abandonment of beings by being* means that be-ing has withdrawn from beings and that beings have become initially … only beings … *Abandonment of being* means that be-ing abandons beings and leaves beings to themselves' (CP 77, 78; see also 163).

Not only are we rootless and estranged just when we are the most in the midst of familiar beings or objects, but ultimately we are in the uncanny because be-ing has withdrawn and hidden itself behind these beings. From the other, non-metaphysical beginning, 'one sees that, when being abandons beings, be-ing *shelters and conceals itself* in the manifestness of beings and is itself essentially determined as this self-withdrawing sheltering-concealing. Be-ing already abandons beings, while ἀλήθεια becomes the basic self-withholding character of beings' (CP 78). Here Heidegger locates the heart of our current homelessness: '*Forgottenness of being* is not aware of itself; it presumes to be at home with "beings" and with what is "actual" … For it only knows beings. But in the way of the presencing of beings, beings are abandoned by being. *Abandonment of being* is the ground of the forgottenness of being. But abandonment of beings by being sustains the illusion that beings are now ready to be handled and used, not needing anything else [CP 80] … The innermost ground of historical uprooting is one that is more essential, grounded upon what is ownmost to be-ing: that be-ing itself withdraws from beings and thereby still lets beings appear as "beings" and even as "more-beings"' (CP 81).

To recover from our homelessness, what is needed is a going back. According to Heidegger, for this going-back it is necessary:

1 to remember the abandonment of being in its long, hidden, and self-hiding history. It is not enough to point to what belongs to the present time.
2 to experience the abandonment of being equally as the distress that *towers over into the crossing* and animates the crossing as access to what is to come. (CP 78–9)

Beings, including human beings, need to be 'put back into be-ing'; hence the need for the leap that will open a site for the possibility: 'The echo of being wants to retrieve be-ing in its *full essential swaying* as enowning' (CP 81). That is, the needed coming back of being 'where uprooting is to be overcome by way of a new rooting' (CP 82) is the ground of a homecoming.

Though genuine thinking has a central role to play in overcoming the displacement – for instance, by trying to understand the abandonment of being and by becoming attuned to the resonance of the echo, insofar as the 'mastery of this uprooting' and 'distress' is due to our being 'dis-enowned by be-ing,' a change in direction from homelessness to home-coming could finally only come out of be-ing (CP 81–2, 78, 84). Be-ing, which in the course of its metaphysical history, plays itself out as with-drawing, hiding, and abandoning, would have to shift back – turn around – in some way. 'Now the *great turning around* by be-ing is neces-sary, that turning around in which beings are not grounded in terms of human being, but rather human being is grounded in terms of be-ing' (CP 129). Any turning toward home in which we might participate would have to be grounded in a turning by be-ing itself.

We have returned to the basic layout and trajectory of *Contributions:* from out of our current situation at the end of the metaphysical unfold-ing after the first beginning with the Greeks, we need to move away from metaphysical modernity toward what is other than modernity – which will turn out to be the nexus of, diversely, the first beginning, another beginning, and an originary realm (CP 60–3). It appears that there will be no simple direction, no clear pathway. 'For there are no bridges, and the leaps are not yet accomplished' (CP 23). From the initial, barely begun, opening of the other beginning that appears to be occurring, we catch a glimpse of how be-ing would have to turn, presumably bringing us along. This turning from the passage of the historical-metaphysical to the twinned first and other beginnings would be the initiation of the crossing, the initial opening of a site for the crossing-over from the first beginning to the other beginning that needs to occur.

With this complicated prospect in mind, could we – that is, we, as somehow included in the opening opened by be-ing – take a short cut and head toward a homecoming by attempting to go forward directly from where we are now to the other beginning? Why does Heidegger indicate, as we saw just above, that we must *go back* to the first beginning, for example, by remembering? Would not a turn to go straightforwardly from where we are as rootless to where we could again be rooted be the turn toward home? Apparently not. 'There is no direct way back [to be-ing]' (CP 52). Heidegger spends considerable effort in *Contributions* to explain that and why we cannot proceed directly to the originary abode we seek. He again enlists the bridge metaphor: 'There is no bridge from here to the other beginning' (CP 42; see also 23). In homey terms, we can think of this literally: there is no way to go from one end of a first deep valley to the next one if the mountains in between – that shape the valley – are too high to cross (leap over). We would need to go back to the common broad meadow that opens the way to both valleys and thence to the other valley. The same would be true of any dense forest path. Often, the long way – back and then out again – is the only way.

But of course, it is not finally a physical journey that Heidegger is speaking about. We cannot go directly from where we are, because the places, ways, or dimensions of which he is speaking do not exist as beings-objects or states of being or of beings. They are not yet fixed. Not only is there no fixed road but as yet no place to which a leap can be made, not even one for a leap to cross over. Rather, all these places, ways, and dimensions first and only come about in the journey. The only way anywhere is, as we shall see, the indirect way of the opening of a middle ground, as a between from which a springing forth might occur. So, we cannot go where we ultimately would go; we can only go where it is possible to go next, and then set out again from there. Eventually, since there is not and never will be direct, continuous passage from where we are to where we need to go – from the end of the first beginning back to its beginning and thence to another beginning – a bold move, an unpredictable and discontinuous move will be necessary.

We need to go back, then, from where we are, by way of a between that needs opening, through the long history of metaphysics to the beginning of the first beginning with the Greeks, and only from there set out anew toward the pathway of the other beginning that might eventually lead to a final shelter and inabiding (CP 78). We cannot turn directly from the present to the future but must follow the double turning opened by be-ing: the turn back into the past and then the possible turning from there to an alternative future. Even that is not the whole story: the 'crossing from the end of the first beginning to the other beginning ... is [only] at the same time the take-off for the leap, by which alone a beginning and specifically the other beginning ... can begin' (CP 162). 'The leap, the most daring move in proceeding from inceptual thinking, abandons and throws aside everything familiar' (CP 161). Perhaps here we get a better sense of the importance of 'to and fro,' of the 'near and far,' of which Heidegger often writes.

An instance of such an indirect movement can be found in the back and forth between the familiar and the strange already considered, where, in the dynamic of the hiding and disclosure of being and be-ing, there was both a *dis-placement from* the first dimension and a complementary *coming-into* the other from the first. As noted earlier, we must be displaced from the masking that occurs in the familiar and into the estrangement that must be faced and thought. As we work through – or into – the strange, we may come into a new mode of abiding. Closely related is 'displacing human being [out of itself and] into Dasein' (CP 260). Here occurs the possibility that 'humanness in the end takes over a task that moves humanness away and displaces it into that question-worthy matter, Da-sein' (CP 221). Since the displacement into Dasein simultaneously 'opens up above all the unsettledness of a being' this amounts to another mode where we are led out of the familiar and into the strange (CP 221). But there will be a resettling, if we manage a persisting 'inabiding' in Da-sein, that would come about through 'a renewed inceptual struggle with its sheltering-into what is created by historical man' (CP 221).

One dramatic type of historical accomplishment happens when the displacement out of human being and into Dasein is 'continued' as a further passage from Dasein into the establishment of a historical people. When a people becomes a people, that is when they come to what is their own and can cease circling around themselves and end their wandering beyond themselves – a new rootedness might occur. How might such an end to exile come – how such an abiding (CP 79, 380)? According to Heidegger, not out of a thinking-saying 'that belongs either to the purposeful activity of an individual or to the limited calculation of a community,' but only through a new mode of inceptual, historical-thinking, which would happen, if at all, only as part of the integration of historical humans and historical-being (CP 4). How to inceptually think historical-being and the possibility of a people? Through its displacement into Dasein, because Da-sein is the ground of history and thus nothing less than the 'domain of the decision' whether a 'genuinely historical be-ing of people is won or lost' (CP 21; see also 67). 'In what ways does a people become a people? ... Mindfulness about what belongs to "being a people" constitutes an essential passage-way ... [The] philosophy of a people is that which ... historically founds the people in its Da-sein, and which prevails upon a people to become guardians of the truth of be-ing' (CP 30; see also 21, 24, 29).

The character of the requisite originary thinking holds a significant clue: 'Reservedness determines the style of inceptual thinking in the other beginning' (CP 12). Since such 'reservedness and reticence in silence' is a site of opening for god, it also names Da-sein – which is nothing other than 'the historical "between" [*Zwischen*] of the counter of gods and man' (CP 280, 337). Thus, Heidegger can 'summarize': 'A people is only a people when it receives its history as apportioned in the finding of its god ... But how should a people find god ...? Da-sein: what is it other than *grounding* the being ... of the ones to come who belong to the last god? What is ownmost to a people is grounded in the historicity of those who belong to *themselves out of* belongingness to god' (CP 279).

Given who and where we are in our present placement in metaphysics, we cannot ourselves complete the transformation of human being into Da-sein and establish the relationships necessary to become a people. Still, the beginning of inceptual thinking gives us a way to see that it is unnecessary to remain isolated as modern 'subjects'; and its own mode of 'silent reticence' provides one way for us to prepare for others already with us – others who will help and guide us (CP 277). That is, according to Heidegger, originary thinking catches a glimpse that, because the turning is already underway, 'today there are already a few of those to come' who are within the grounding attunement to enowning and in relationship with the gods and thus can and do come to lead the way to the necessary relation to god (CP 280, 66–7, 277–8). 'Those who are to come ... come to stand before the hints of the *last god*' (CP 57) – though 'the last god is not the end but the other beginning of immeasurable possibilities for our history' (CP 57, 289; see also 293).

The ones to come include (among several types), 'those few individuals who, on the essential paths of grounding Dasein (poetry – thinking – deed – sacrifice), prepare in advance the sites and moments for the domains ... in which an originary gathering is prepared – a gathering in and as which what dares to be called a people becomes historical' (CP 66–7). Heidegger has already found, and again acknowledges here, that Hölderlin is such a one, indeed 'the poet most futural [and thereby historical] of those ones to come; ... he *traverses* and transforms what is the greatest' (CP 281; see also 90, 143, 342). Specifically, 'Hölderlin's word – a word which again names gods and man' – is essential to the 'grounding-attunements which appoint future man to the guardianship of gods' needfulness' (CP 298). And according to Heidegger, in reference to Hölderlin, 'attunement is meant in the sense of inabiding' (CP 24; see also 277–8).

Thus, far from being an individualistic activity as we understand it today, becoming a people involves a series of displacements and new relationships: displacement from human being into Da-sein and through Da-sein's grounding historicity into becoming a people, which also depends upon the guiding help of those to come, those such as the poet Hölderlin who prepare for a belonging to god and thus a new beginning. In these movements into Da-sein and toward becoming a people, 'man once again comes to *himself* and recovers self-being' (CP

23). Through the necessary displacements, then, human beings are displaced into Dasein and then come to their own essential character ('ownmost way of being'; CP 29), which would be first aspects of homecoming.

There is obviously more to this same fundamental understanding. Dasein is articulated as a site and moment for more than human being because it would be Da-sein only insofar as it is also the site for the moment when the truth of being occurs. As such, Dasein belongs to enowning: 'As the grounding that takes the strifing ... into what is opened up by the strife, Da-*sein* is awaited by humans and is carried in the inabiding which sustains the "t/here" [*Da*] and belongs to enowning' (CP 22). Playing out the relation, we can say that insofar as humans came to abide in Da-sein, they would come to abide in the opening of the truth of be-ing. In the extended development into becoming a people the same would hold: we have just seen that those who are to come (in order to help us become a people) themselves already belong to enowning and to gods; similarly, as noted, a people would care for and belong to the truth of be-ing, 'whose truth this people must ground, but once, in a unique site, in a unique moment' (CP 64). Thus, another dimension of homecoming: in addition to humans coming to their ownmost way of being in Dasein, such coming to themselves would also be a mode of belonging to enowning, 'if thanks to the displacing man comes to stand in enowning and has his abode in the truth of being' (CP 19).

Further, as the displacement of human being into Dasein, and even into becoming a historical people, inabiding in enowning does not involve humans alone (even counting those who come before), nor humans *as* alone. Not only in the passages treated above, but already on the first two pages of *Contributions*, Heidegger speaks of a 'release into the *intimacy* to the ... gods' and Da-sein, and in the pages that follow affirms the relationship: 'Situated creatively in this groundbreaking-attunement of Da-sein, man becomes' related to the gods, seeking to become attuned to 'the stillness of the passing of the last god' and the 'undecidability about the flight of gods or their arrival' (CP 3–4, 13, 9; see also 17). It is precisely by coming into relation with one another that both humans, displaced into Dasein, and the gods simultaneously come to their ownmost, all in belonging to enownment.

That is why Heidegger speaks of 'need' and does so in a kind of round-robin manner. Being, human beings / those who are to come / Da-sein, and god *all need one other.* Heidegger contends that a 'transformed thinking of being is announced' in connection with the understanding of Da-sein, since 'be-ing itself would need to ground the truth of its essential sway only in such transformation of man' (CP 310; see also 173, 185, 240, 310). In turn, Da-sein, of course, needs being and belongs to it, partly through god; god also needs being and needs Da-sein. Over its course, *Contributions* lays out the mutually constitutive interrelationships:

> Be-ing needs man in order to hold sway; and man belongs to be-ing so that he can accomplish his utmost destiny as Da-sein. (CP 177)

> Be-ing 'belongs' to man, so much so that man is needed by be-ing itself as the preserver of the site for the moment of the fleeing and arrival of gods. (CP 186)

> The recognition of the belongingness of man into be-ing through god, and admission by god that it needs be-ing. (CP 291)

> But gods *do need* be-ing ... 'Gods' need be-ing in order through be-ing – which does not belong to gods – nevertheless to belong to themselves. Being is needed by gods: it is their need ... But when be-ing is the needfulness of god, when be-ing itself finds its truth only in en-thinking, and when this thinking is philosophy (in the other beginning), then 'gods' need being-historical thinking, i.e. philosophy. (CP 308–9; see also 358)

> How few know that god awaits the grounding of truth of be-ing and thus awaits man's leaping-into Da-sein. (CP 293)

There is yet one more dimension to the mutual coming into ownness that needs at least to be mentioned: 'history (*Geschichte*) understood as the strifing of the strife of earth and world' (CP 66; see also 337). That is, in addition to Da-sein, the strife of earth and world provides time-space; in 'the tug of earth and world' there is a site for the moment of the unfolding of the truth of being 'in beings' (CP 21). Disclosure and hiddenness also obtain in this other dimension, in 'the preservation of earth and the projecting-open of world in the strife of earth and world' (CP 67). Here too, in developing the passage from beings to be-ing and to thinking about both the 'producing' and 'being-taken-back into the earth' of 'stone, plant, animal, human,' Heidegger speaks in the language of our guiding motif. The dynamic of both sheltering and projecting open 'occurs already in the midst of beings that are opened up – as rooted in the earth and rising in a world' (CP 50, 183).

To return to the core dynamic here, we should say that, in the displacements from the familiar into the strange and from human being into Dasein and (with the guidance of those to come) becoming a people, a coming into mutual relationship allows human being, Dasein, gods, earth, and world to belong together with enowning; and thus, in coming to abide in *Ereignis,* all simultaneously come into their ownmost. In telling us of all this through the vocabulary of and overall unfolding structure of homecoming, Heidegger explicitly focuses on and develops the realm and event that is named the between. 'The domain that is Da-sein is that "between" which first grounds itself and sets humans and god apart and together, owning one to the other' (CP 21). 'The territory that comes to be through and as the way of enthinking of be-ing is the between itself [*Zwischen*] that en-owns Da-sein to god; and in this enownment man and god first become "recognizable" to each other, belonging to the guardianship and needfulness of be-ing' (CP 60). Perhaps most seminally, or at least in an especially unified manner, Heidegger says, 'Every saying of being ... must name en-owning, that "between" [*Zwischen*] of the "inbetweenness" [*Inswischenschaft*] of god and Dasein, world and earth, and must lift the between-ground [*Zwischengrund*] as ab-ground [*Abgrund*] up into attuning work, always decisively *interpretive of the between* [*zwischendeutig*] ... The "between" [*das Zwischen*] which bursts open gathers what it removes into the open of its strifing and refusing belongingness, moves unto the ab-ground, out of which everything (god, man, world, earth) recoils in swaying into itself and thus leaves to be-ing the unique decidedness of en-ownment' (CP 341).[6]

Our task now is to continue to follow Heidegger in the decisive issue at hand: interpreting the between – the open itself, the mid-point of the crossing between the first and the other beginning. Importantly, we hear of *coming into* the between: beyond crossing from where we are or passing out of where we have been (that is, from homelessness), we are already turned toward a going into (that is, are realigned homeward). Displacement into Da-sein is a displacement into this middle because Da-sein itself is a between. As already said in passages cited above – though we did not highlight it then, as we do now – the between is the site of complex relationships, of *all* relationships. '*Dasein:* the "between" [*Zwischen*] which has the character of a mid-point that is open and thus sheltering, between the arrival and flight of gods and man, who is rooted in that "between"' (CP 23). 'Da-sein is the turning point in the turning of enowning, the self-opening midpoint of the mirroring of call and belongingness ... In this way Da-sein is the *between* [*das Zwischen*] between man (as history-grounding) and gods (in their history). The between [is] not one that first ensues from the relation of gods to humans, but rather that between which above all grounds the time-space for the relation, in that it itself leaps forth into the essential swaying of be-ing as enowning and, as self-opening midpoint, makes gods and humans decidable for one another' (CP 219). Again, the between is not the site for connecting fixed or given objects or beings, but the opening where humans and gods, earth and world, first can come into their own modes of being. It is between beings and be-ing. As we will shortly explore, it is between the first beginning and the other beginning. All these possibilities are possible, at base, because the between is the *open of enowning* (CP 20; see also 302).

If our current plight is the upshot of the abandonment of being and if we must first go back to the first beginning that is 'no longer,' before another beginning might unfold into a new way to the future and rootedness, the site for the crossing from one beginning to the other is the critical place in our placement. The character and possibility of the site, as Da-sein, as between, has only begun to be disclosed. Perhaps even more crucially, the nature of what happens at this site must be thought. We would be able to go to the other beginning only by turning to, returning to, the first beginning. The opening of this opening could not be a human accomplishment. Rather, it would seem, be-ing would have to take, or be, the initiative. But putting it that way makes it sound as if being were 'something' or to be thought of as having 'agency.' Since be-ing as enowning includes Dasein, here Heidegger is working to say that we need to set aside ideas of human control: any turning in/as the opening to another beginning would be as a change in the dynamic of disclosure-withdrawl (of what hitherto has been hidden behind beings).

If we at least have some glimmer of what it means to say that the between is the opening of enownment and that only be-ing can initiate the opening, Heidegger has brought us to where we might try to understand the *turning*. As enabling a return to the first beginning, as the between in which the crossing over might happen, being would occur as a turning, as 'enownment and its turning' (CP 23). Such turning would be a world-shattering, world-originating event. 'Be-ing holds sway as enowning. The essential sway has its center and breadth in the turning' (CP 22). Further, according to Heidegger, the event is the basis (principle of organization, perhaps) for *Contributions*' language and structure of complex movements: 'Enowning has its innermost occurrence and its widest reach in the turning [*die Kehre*]. The turning that holds sway in enowning is the sheltered ground of the entire series of turnings, circles, and spheres, which are of unclear origin, remain unquestioned, and are easily taken in themselves as the "last"' (CP 286). 'The turning's trajectories [*Kehrungsbahnen*] of enowning ... the turning between belongingness and the call, between abandonment by being and enbeckoning (the enquivering of the resonance of be-ing itself!)' happens in the between, as Da-sein or as time-space (CP 260). 'And within the turning: Enowning must need Da-sein and, needing it, must place it into the call and so bring it before the passing of the last god ... Turning holds sway between the call (to the one belonging) and the belonging (of the one who is called). Turning is counter-turning [*Wider-Kehre*]' (CP 287).

Insofar as Ereignis opens – 'as *enowning which is in itself turning* [*in sich kehriges Ereignis*]' – insofar as a between might be established where the necessary crossing over could begin, the open-between would be the place where we would need to belong in order to come to ourselves (CP 130). That is, it would be the site wherein would be enacted the relationships of human beings and gods, of beings and being, of earth and world, that would amount to the sheltering in which all dimensions would reside together.

We are, at best, in the beginning of the between, though certainly thankful to be so. We have only begun to hear, or hear that there is, a call. But we have not begun to respond – perhaps we are only beginning to realize that we must learn a new way to think and act. In short, our time is the time between call and belonging. Because 'the turning between belongingness and the call' will unfold in/as its own time, there is no rushing the turning or crossing (CP 260). 'Hesitating refusal' (no longer abandonment, but now the staying away of grounded 'self-sheltering concealing'), an 'originary' or 'outstanding manner of enopening ... is the resonance of the turning between "the call" and belongingness, en-*ownment*, be-ing itself' (CP 265).

Hence, our present homelessness in the abandonment of being is not 'a sinking and dying away' at the end of all possibility of a world; it is not the prelude to nothing or oblivion (CP 268). Rather, 'this abandonment is originarily remembering-expecting (belongingness to being and the call of be-ing' (CP 268). The between, then, is the site where the appropriate attunement is 'deep awe' (CP 12). It is *the* place to be by way of and 'in the echo of be-ing out of the distress of abandonment by being and only means further that enowning opens up neither from within the call nor from within a belongingness but only from within the "between" [*Zwischen*] that resonates both' (CP 269). Though only barely beginning a turn toward home, and just learning how to go about homecoming, we at least catch a hint of what might come about: since the truth of being is the between, since be-ing itself is – gives – the between, and since we might come to abide there, amazingly we have the prospect of becoming at home with a mode of be-ing, all abiding in a domain of enowning (CP 10, 19, 172, 241–2, 290).

But in our current placement, we need be mindful to focus, not on (being at) home, but on homecoming. 'If thanks to this displacing man comes to stand in enowning and has his abode in the truth of be-ing, then he is primarily still only ready for the leap into the deciding experience' (CP 19). The task is not to try to be elsewhere or do otherwise than learn to remain in the between, therein becoming attuned to and responding to the turning, the occasion for the crossing-over leap. And even insofar as a leap over to the other beginning might happen, that would not mean that the first beginning and its metaphysical unfolding could be abandoned. Just the opposite, it would be crucial to continue along both pathways, staying in the open, continuing to cross over and back: 'thinking in the crossing dare not succumb to the temptation of simply leaving behind that which it has grasped as the end ... of metaphysics ... On the contrary, in its essential impossibility metaphysics must first be played-forth into ... philosophy['s] other beginning' (CP 120, 122). We need to 'still bring along what *has been* of the hidden being-history, that detour [*Umweg*] though which beings – however it might appear – which metaphysics had to take in order *not* to reach being and so to come to an end that is strong enough for the distress for another beginning, which at the same time helps in returning to the originariness of the first beginning and transforms what is past into something that is not lost' (CP 306).

As noted at the beginning of our analysis, Heidegger says on the first page of *Contributions* that 'this pathway brings the crossing into the openness of history and establishes the crossing as perhaps a very long sojourn' (CP 3). It would seem that the proper role for humans is not to pine for a final being-at-home but to learn to dwell as underway – in and as homecoming. Though the project is not fundamentally a human one, but *Ereignis,*' we do need to participate properly. In the advent of the turning-opening the greatest possibility and responsibility for humans would be to respond appropriately to the call of be-ing. Our greatest vocation or calling would be to hear, to attend to, to answer the call of enowning (CP 23). Staying in the opening, we are called on, for example, to learn to think and say the opening. En-thinking, the truth of being, is essentially a projecting-open. What is ownmost to such a projecting-open is that, in enactment and unfolding, it must place itself into what it opens up (CP 39).

From the perspective of reading *Contributions* by way of the leitmotif of homecoming, several sections that are both breathtaking and almost unbearably dense appear just where one would expect a dramatic climax, according to classical (Aristotelian) conventions. In section 255 ('Turning in Enowning,' chapter 7, 'The Last God,' CP 286–8) and section 263 ('Every Projecting-Open is a Thrown One,' chapter 8, 'Being,' CP 318–20) Heidegger fuses enowning as turning and human being as returning.

In the disclosure of the turning that evidently came to him, Heidegger caught a glimpse of, and could begin to try to say, at least four dimensions of the phenomena. Here I try to put these four aspects into a clean order or 'narrative,' which is not something he did in *Contributions.*

1 Before – or at – the beginning of the first beginning, enowning unfolded an enowning throw, which opened out to, called to, human being for a response. The throw and response would have happened at the same time. The responding (exemplarily as inceptive, projecting-opening thinking) would have performed a double movement: a '*throwing free from*' and '*a returning to*' enowning's throwing: 'man throws himself free of a being unto a be-ing ... By throwing himself free of "a being," man first becomes man. For only in this way does he return to a being and *is* he the one who has returned' (CP 318). And 'this way' would only occur insofar as enowning's throw (*Zuwurf*) or call (*Zuruf*) is the basis for the projecting-open, in which the removing itself away from and returning to the enowning throw happen at the same time. Here human being would have been able to experience returnship (*Rückkehrschaft*) as the way in which this being dwelt, belonging to *Ereignis:* 'But the return! One must first know the manner of dwelling and the concomitant gift ... [and] which view of being man as the returner [*Zurückkehrer*] retains' (CP 319). Along with the critical elucidation of Da-sein's double response in section 263, with two amazing sentences in section 255 Heidegger articulates the complexly intimate belongings inherent in the double movements of enowning, Da-sein, and god: all three go 'back and forth,' 'to and fro': 'But how is this to be grasped more definitively: the *throwing oneself free* (moving away from)? ... Man as the receiving one ... [is] the one who already returns from the free-throw' (CP 319). 'The call is

befalling and staying-away in the mystery of enownment' (CP 287). 'The hints of the last god are at play in the turning as onset and staying-away of the arrival and flight of gods and their places of mastery' (CP 287).

2 That dynamic of call and response at the beginning did not hold, for even though 'man up to now is the one who in the free-throw has at once returned, who in this way has traversed for the first time the *differentiation* of a being and of be-ing,' this amazingly happened 'without [human being itself] being able to experience this differentiation and even to ground it' (CP 318–19). Not surprisingly, humans alone were 'not capable of mastering the relationship': as beings came to the fore and be-ing withdrew, human being forgot the achievement of an initial, and the possibility of a continuing, necessary response (mode of dwelling); returnship (*Rückkehrerschaft*) did not stay; the history of metaphysics unfolded toward today's forgetfulness and rootlessness in machination (CP 319).

3 Enowning, as the returning turning (*kehriges Ereignis*), still, and newly again, calls Da-sein forth and back (*vorrufende Rückruf*) (CP 130).[7] Again, we have a chance to respond to the enowning throw (*Zuwurf*) and call (*Zuruf*). We might return to our ownmost as belonging to the call through our response in returning to and preserving the throwing of enownment. In this moment, Da-sein needs to participate in the crossing to the other beginning toward which the turning opening opens: its task is to 'get hold of the counter-resonance of en-ownment, i.e., to shift into this counter-resonance and thus first of all to become itself: the preserver of the thrown projecting-open, the grounded founder of the ground' (CP 169).

4 Heeding the beckoning of the enowning throw would mean remaining related to beings and metaphysical history while experiencing a new belonging to what could unfold from the other beginning. This remaining or abiding in both would be a new mode of the double removing itself away from and returning to the enowning throw. Now, in the newly possible projecting-open that opens in the turning, there would be a moving away from beings and returning to be-ing, also involving – holding on to and not forgetting – the history of returning to being or beings, since out of the first beginning a moving away from be-ing and a returning to beings still plays out in our world. The retrieval of the new possibility in the new beginning cannot allow a forgetfullness, this time, of either alternative pathway. It is essential to retrieve and not to let that which is just again beginning to disclose

> itself slip once more into oblivion: 'But thrownness is attested to only in the basic occurrences of the hidden history of be-ing and indeed is for us especially in the distress of the abandonment of being and in the necessity of decision' (CP 169). Insofar as we might now better respond to enownment's call and throw as it turns back, we might experience a new mode of dwelling, continuously going away from and returning to, remaining in and as returnship (*Rückkehrerschaft*) to enowning's throwing. The calling and response would be to remain always underway in the to and fro, that is, in homecoming.

In answer to our question of the possibility of being or becoming 'at home with ourselves,' it appears that home is a domain of events wherein humans will be owned unto themselves only when they themselves reach into the open time-space in which an opening can take place (CP 36). That is, only in the between where we might – displaced over into Da-sein – come to belong in intimacy with the gods, with the strife of earth and world, with *Ereignis*. Just as we now belong where we are in the mode of rootlessness in the abandonment of being, futural rootedness would be a matter of a 'belongingness [that] has been awakened by the call' of enowning (CP 57). Here history occurs and a people might come to their own, which is to say an originary, dynamic network of relationships might come about among humans and Da-sein, gods, earth, and world (CP 279, 337).

The call from homelessness, in fact, begins (only seemingly paradoxically) as a call out from the familiar into the uncanny, a displacement into the strange, into the between (CP 19). 'Be-ing is the hearth-fire in the midst of the abode of gods – an abode which is simultaneously the estranging of man (the "between" [*das Zwischen*] in which he remains a (the) stranger precisely when he is at home with beings)' (CP 343). But as we have seen, *Ereignis is turning, is turning back; Da-sein is also a returning*. Thus, the call ends – or, better, becomes – a call to belonging, to enownment, to *Ereignis;* a call that we might answer only by remaining underway, attempting to cross over, by way of the dis-placements of the opening between. The call of enowning, in all its phases, is a call homeward – a call to the possibility of return – to which our proper response would be to begin and persist in homecoming.[8]

The next integration of Heidegger's work on metaphysical homelessness and the impact of Hölderlin, further developing the distinctive originary characteristics of the third set of writings, is strikingly seen in 'Postscript to "What Is Metaphysics."' In 'What Is Metaphysics' (1929),

Heidegger had spoken about the experience of dread or anxiety in which the uncanny (*unheimlich*) opens up beneath us. This dread reveals Nothing to us. However, in 1943, the same year as 'Remembrance' and 'Remembrance of the Poet,' Heidegger adds the 'Postscript to "What Is Metaphysics?"' In the latter work, after journeying with Hölderlin and realizing the shyness with which the poet and the poet's thinking helper must – which means they may – approach the holy source, he does not forget dread, the uncanny, and Nothing but recalls and adds to them (begins to preserve) what he has glimpsed in the poet's homecoming (pWM 349–61). Developing what he began to explain about *deep awe* and *dread* (for example, in section 6, 'Grounding Attunement') in *Contributions*, Heidegger now says, 'The clear courage for essential dread guarantees the most mysterious of all possibilities: the experience of being. For hard by essential dread, in the terror of the abyss, there dwells awe [*Scheu*]. Awe clears and enfolds that region of human being within which man endures, as at home, in the enduring' (pWM 355).

With dread, belongs awe. In the uncanny, a region of home opens; along with Nothing, being unfolds itself. Heidegger begins to focus with stereoscopic vision: never losing sight of the homelessness which must be faced and endured, he also sees the homier relationship of human beings and thinking with being. Importantly, Nothing is not thought now as no-thing, that is, scientifically and metaphysically in terms of beings. Instead, it is thought originarily – in light of the origin – as being. This approach retains 'the mysterious multiplicity of meanings' of Nothing and of being itself (pWM 353). Here is the note of a happier relation of humans to being: 'Man alone of all beings, when addressed by the voice of being, experiences the marvel of all marvels: that what-is is' (pWM 355). A path home begins to open in thinking the occurrence of Nothing and being.

Continuing from the realization, first privately articulated in *Contributions*, but now made public for the first time in 'Postscript to "What Is Metaphysics,"' Heidegger shows how this opening relationship which needs thinking also involves a new way of talking, conscious all the while that his efforts move between metaphysical and originary language: 'It is of the essence of such transitions that they are, within certain limits, compelled to speak the language of that which they help to overcome' (pWM 350). The required thinking must focus on just such obstacles, obstacles not just in its path but inherent to its own origins, character, and possibilities. Such obstacles, like homelessness itself, are not to be avoided. Meeting them 'will make our questioning more genuine. All questions that do justice to the subject are themselves bridges to their own answering' (pWM 351). 'Then we must necessarily ask what metaphysics is in its own ground. Such a question must think metaphysically and, at the same time, think in terms of the ground of metaphysics, i.e. no longer metaphysically' (pWM 351). Traditional metaphysical understanding and its way of thinking – with logic and calculation – must not be denigrated or abandoned. As the thinking which prevails in metaphysical homelessness, it must be retained and carefully thought through (recollected). Still, in order that metaphysics might be thought, the thinker, realizing that logical-calculative thought is but one mode of thinking, must learn to practise another as well (pWM 356–8). Thus, Heidegger says, 'Only, reflection must take everything back again in the calm mood of patient meditation,' then adds, 'The thinking whose thoughts not only do not calculate but are absolutely determined by what is "other" than what is [being], might be called essential thinking' (pWM 352, 357).

Only a long quotation will allow us to hear this essential thinking and Heidegger's originary way of saying it. This thinking

> expends itself in being for the truth of being ... This sacrifice is the expense of our human being for the preservation of the truth of being in respect of what-is. In sacrifice there is expressed that hidden *thanking* which alone does homage to the grace wherewith being has endowed the nature of man, in order that he may take over in his relationship to being the guardianship of being. Original thinking is the echo of being's favor wherein it clears a space for itself and causes the unique occurrence: that what-is is. This echo is man's answer to the Word of the soundless voice of being. The speechless answer of his thanking through sacrifice is the source of the human word, which is the prime cause of language as the enunciation of the Word in words. Were there not an occasional thanking in the heart of historical man he could never attain the thinking – assuring that there must be thinking [*Denken*] in all doubt [*Bedenken*] and memory [*Andenken*] – which originally thinks the thought of being. But how else could humanity attain to original thanking unless being's favor preserved for man, through his open relationship to this favor, the splendid poverty in which the freedom of sacrifice hides its own treasure? (pWM 358–9)

Obviously, Heidegger's originary thinking here not only thinks being, it also preserves Hölderlin's enunciation of the saying of the holy; it further develops, of course, words-thoughts such as 'echo,' 'clears a space' (i.e., opens a between), and 'sacrifice,' quarried from *Contributions* and polished.

The above clarification of the thinker's task in relationship with being, thought with the poet's experience always in mind, indicates both a practical agenda and manner or mood – which Heidegger will develop for years. For example, the thinker must be patient, and in thinking (which is an *art*), must look 'to the slow signs of the incalculable and [see] in this the unforeseeable coming of the ineluctable. Such thinking is mindful of the truth of being and thus helps the being of truth to make a place for itself in man's history' (pWM 359). It is precisely in this careful thinking of being's coming and what is necessary for it that the thinker, by way of essential thinking and saying, participates in the coming of being. Heidegger says, 'Obedient to the voice of being, thought seeks the word through which the truth of being may be expressed' (pWM 360). Then he adds, in a vocabulary which obviously echoes what Hölderlin said of the ever-coming, yet reserved source, 'Only when the language of historical man is born of the word does it ring true. But if it does ring true, then the testimony of the soundless voice of hidden springs lures it ever on. The thought of being guards the word and fulfils its function in such guardianship, namely care for the use of language' (pWM 360).

What Heidegger says and thinks (not only in the works already considered but in those to come) aims to prepare the way for being's coming. Accordingly, he says, 'Out of long-guarded speechlessness and the careful clarification of the field thus cleared, comes the utterance of the thinker' (pWM 360). As we see here and as we saw by the end of the Hölderlin essays, the thinker's character and task is closely related to the poet's; and the guarded origin of the poet's naming and the thinker's utterance are alike. Yet, differences lie behind the similarities: 'But since like is only like insofar as difference allows, and since poetry and thinking are most purely alike in their care of the word, the two things are at the same time at opposite poles in their essence. The thinker utters being. The poet names what is holy' (pWM 360). Heidegger, then, comes to see that his task is like the poet's in that it requires language and thinking not of clever invention, but which 'through paying attention to the voice of being, thinks beyond it into the attunement occasioned by this voice – an attunement which takes possession of the essential man that he may come to experience being in Nothing' (pWM 354–5). Just as the poet's remembering words respond to and establish the saying of the holy, the thinker's essential thinking and saying preserve and bring the word of being.

Yet, his proper task is his own, not the poet's. The thinker must think and speak of homelessness so that the thinker may come to homecoming. That means the thinker must become so attuned to being as to hear being's voice when the latter speaks within the homelessness of metaphysics. Thus, with the poet's help, the thinker also newly sees that 'The question "What Is Metaphysics?" remains a question. For those who persevere with this question the ... postscript is more of a foreword. The question "What Is Metaphysics?" asks a question that goes beyond metaphysics which has already entered into the overcoming of metaphysics' (pWM 349–50).

From 1936 to 1946, Heidegger made notes 'on the overcoming of metaphysics' (OM 84). I briefly noted a few sections of this work, descriptively titled 'Overcoming Metaphysics,' in chapter 1, when considering the themes of justice and subjectivity. Obviously, notes over a ten-year period are diverse. Those considered earlier developed themes in a way congruent with his other 'metaphysical' works of the 1930s and 1940s. However, for the most part, 'Overcoming Metaphysics' shows Heidegger's journey in its movement parallel to the poet's quest. Though this relationship is most obvious in the concluding sections (xxvii–xxviii), we can see the impact of the Hölderlin essays throughout many of the notes and the resulting difference from the works considered in chapter 1 (as a reference point, 'Hölderlin and the Essence of Poetry,' which appeared in 1936, the year Heidegger began these notes).

Recall the poet's journey out into and back from the foreign. Even after returning from homelessness, the poet had to keep that homelessness as an essential part of homecoming. The foreign was held in the understanding remembrance of the entire journey. In fact, only insofar as the poet entered, endured, and later kept the meaning of homelessness fresh in homecoming could the poet learn to dwell at home. As we saw in *Contributions*, our most proper response to the throw and call of enowning is to remain underway, and continue in homecoming (rather than pine for a final being at home). In the set of works derived from that source, then made public, Heidegger considers an overcoming which is similar to the poetic journey through remembering. That is, overcoming metaphysics does not mean that metaphysics is dealt with once and for all and then disposed of, as a problem neatly and finally solved. Rather, metaphysics would be overcome in that it is retained, even while its limitations and the confines of its specific meaning and possibilities are no longer the final limits of meaning and possibility. It is overcome in that it is incorporated in a 'perduring thinking' (OM 91).

Here, metaphysics would no longer hold us captive, as the homelessness from being. Still, this homelessness would not be a problem that is past (for example, because it ceased to enclose us or to be of concern). Just the opposite: homelessness from being continues. Any pretence that we can exclude homelessness from our concern is a sham. Indeed, no genuine homecoming would be possible if we ignored homelessness. Only when the separation is recognized as enduring can an overcoming of the separation occur. Then homelessness would be remembered and would be dealt with continually. Here Heidegger calls for the remembrance of being, including remembrance of the history of being and human being and their relationships (OM 84–4). Again, like the poet's insight into a historical people coming to dwell in the holy, Heidegger's interpretation of metaphysics holds that we must overcome the history of metaphysics, not to finally cut it loose from ourselves once and for all but to move through it to an originary relation to being and beings. The overcoming of metaphysics, then, is the *continuing journey* of the thinker, not an accomplishment. Heidegger says, 'we may not presume to stand outside of metaphysics because we surmise the ending of metaphysics. For metaphysics overcome in this way does not disappear. It returns transformed, and remains in dominance as the continuing difference of being and beings' (OM 85).

This way of thinking the overcoming of metaphysics clearly utilizes what Heidegger has learned from Hölderlin, picks up the early themes of the metaphysical oblivion of being (that is, homelessness), and develops what he struggled with in *Contributions* (see OM 85). As we saw in chapter 1, Heidegger had understood the story of being and human being with reference to the Greek past, the long metaphysical age, or ages, which include the present and the possibility of a future new relationship with being. Now, Heidegger reinterprets this same structure, along with the poet's journey from home, through wandering, to the experience of the source, and, after arriving home, the learning to dwell proximate to it. In the early Greek epoch, being and humans would have been together, and human beings would have been at home in that source. Then there is the long wandering of the metaphysical history of the West (of which, our era is a moment). In the necessary development and completion of metaphysics – that is, the history of being – the truth of beings (which has come to claim and dominate truth) declines (OM 85–6). Finally, when metaphysics runs to its final completion and collapse, that of which the thinker speaks (analogously to the poet) comes about: 'Only after this decline does the abrupt dwelling of the Origin take place for a long span of time' (OM 86).

Given the frame of the history of being as the history of original home, homelessness, and final originary homecoming and dwelling, because he avoids any solution inadequate to overcome what must be endured and understood, Heidegger focuses on our current epoch. He speaks of our current displacement in terms which not only correspond to Hölderlin's speaking of the holy, but which also think this metaphysical homelessness as analogous to the biblical descriptions of mortals, who, cast out of the garden, must labour and later attempt an exodus (and homecoming) through the desert. He speaks of 'The fact that man as *animal rationale,* here meant in the sense of the working being, must wander through the desert of the earth's desolation' (OM 85).[9]

To be metaphysically outcast is the fate of the West. This means 'that [metaphysics] lets mankind be suspended in the middle of beings as a fundamental trait of Western European history, *without* the being of beings ever being able to be experienced and questioned and structured in its truth *as the twofoldness* of both in terms of metaphysics and through metaphysics' (OM 90). However, such a fate is not to be shunned. It is necessary as a phase in the history of being 'because being itself can open out in its truth the difference of being and beings preserved in itself only when the difference explicitly takes place' (OM 91). This can occur, according to Heidegger, only through the oblivion of being and the dominance of beings over being (OM 91). But so far, the difference of being and beings (in which the truth of being simultaneously presents and hides itself) 'itself remains veiled' (OM 91; see also *Contributions,* e.g., 77–82, 306, 319).

In metaphysics, human beings are displaced from the truth of being even while they seem more than ever to have the truth of beings at their command. Strangely, it is just while we wander the ways of untruth that we increasingly live in the sphere of the correct.[10] The latter is the place of our homelessness. Heidegger says, 'But the correctness of the untrue which remains concealed *as such* is at the same time the most uncanny thing that can occur in the distortion of the being of truth. What is correct masters what is true and sets truth aside' (OM 100). Understood this way, what humans need is the truth of being in which the Origin would open and could be held in remembering thinking (OM 91–2).

Heidegger develops the character of our metaphysical drifting amidst beings and our own will to power and self-grounding age by picking up what he had more usually referred to as machination in *Contributions*, now calling our epoch technological – where 'technology' does not just denote machines as the special means of production, but connotes the historical character of all objectified beings, whether thought of as nature, culture, ideology, or politics (OM 93). He says, 'The name "technology" is understood here in such an essential way that its meaning coincides with the term "completed metaphysics"' (OM 93). In technology, Heidegger finds the planetary struggle which is oblivious to the difference of being and beings. That is, it holds the recollection of the abandonment of being. As he explains, 'The essence of the history of being of nihilism is the abandonment of being in that in it there occurs the self-release of being into machination' (OM 103). Note, it is not finally humans who create technology by developing machines to extract power over beings; rather, being allows, and lets itself into, technology. That is why Heidegger adds that technology is not to be lamented or seen as a 'decline' (OM 103). Like the poet's homelessness, this wandering away is yet a necessary part of the journey home. Though painful, the pathway must, in a properly understood sense, be overcome-incorporated.

Thought by way of technology, our metaphysical epoch is clearly no homey site. Heidegger elaborates the era in terms of the constant using up of things, all of which are mere raw material, including human material.[11] Even war and peace are absorbed into the sphere of manufacture and of consumption. So too are art and poetry (OM 104–8). This scene of consumption is not a place to dwell but the desert through which we drift when on the path of untruth, erring (*irren*, to go astray).[12] Thought in comparison with the home where we would dwell close by being, technology is a vacuum, a vacuum that is still expanding. In this vacuum it is being which is evacuated; in this vacuum, beings, 'the materials of what is real, are suspended. This emptiness has to be filled up. But since the emptiness of being can never be filled up by the fullness of beings,' we proceed aimlessly, although thoroughly organized in our frenzied business of producing (and therefore consuming) enough beings to fill our lack (OM 107). We live in this 'vacuum of the abandonment of being' (OM 107).

In this emptiness, because they are cut off from the truth of being, beings lose their own character. The phenomenon manifests itself everywhere in the homogenization of our lives and world. Here, because beings are seen in their use as a supply to satisfy our hunger for being (which they can never satisfy), they become a mere stopgap to appetite. What each essentially is no longer matters (just as biochemistry assures us that the external appearance of our 'food' – rather than minerals, vitamins, proteins, etc. – does not count. Before the needs of the human will in the vacuum, all beings become uniform. But this uniformity is a placelessness: it is as barren and without bearing or comfort as the desert in a sandstorm. Thus, Heidegger speaks of the uniformity as compared with our desired dwelling at the origin. He says this uniformity 'is as far removed from the simplicity of what is original, as deformation of essence [is] from essence, although the former belongs to the latter' (OM 101).

In contrast to the way being, human beings, and beings would gather as a world allowing for dwelling, with technology (as the duration of the abandonment of being) we find not so much a world as a scene where the 'earth appears as the unworld of erring' (OM 108–9). 'The "world" has become an unworld as a consequence of the abandonment of beings by being's truth. For "world" in the sense of the history of being means the nonobjective presencing of the truth of being for man in that man is essentially delivered over to being ... The world has become an unworld in that being does presence, but without really reigning. As what is real beings are real. There are effects everywhere, and nowhere is there a worlding of the world and yet, although forgotten, there is still being' (OM 104). Heidegger returns us, then, to being as overcome. In metaphysics, we experience being overcome by beings, though this has long been hidden from us while it has been happening (OM 84–5). Here, too, overcoming means absorbing: being has been absorbed by beings; and its truth, by correctness. In turn, because the oblivion of being must be incorporated, Heidegger thinks the overcoming of metaphysics as a preliminary sign of this coming primal occurrence (OM 91). Here, beings would no longer expropriate the unconcealment of being as being, that is, the truth of being. In the parting of human being and being from the metaphysical-technological domination of beings, the origination of truth would open up and radiate upon human being (OM 92). That is why Heidegger says, 'Overcoming is the delivering over of metaphysics to its truth' (OM 92).

Thus, the overcoming of metaphysics involves a change in which the truth of beings declines in favour of the recollected truth of being (OM 85–86). This decline is already underway, though until now it has been hidden from metaphysical human being. As beings and human being (represented as will) yield way to coming being, both being understood alone and beings understood alone are incorporated so that the two might first appear together in their difference. Neither is lost or drops away; instead, the twofold would remain as continuing difference of being and beings (OM 85, 91). And how will the overcoming come about? On the one hand, by the coming of the most original itself; on the other, in the remembrance of the thinker. This is like the coming of the holy in its greeting saying and the responding, remembering writing of the poet. The thinker would prepare for the coming of being's truth by attending in thinking to the overcoming of metaphysics: it is in the thinker's recollecting thinking that the overcoming would be established (though it would in no way be a thinker's creation).

As at the poet's dawn, we are between the age of metaphysics' darkness and the coming lighting. Metaphysics is passing away, though only at length and slowly. According to Heidegger, 'with Nietzsche's metaphysics, philosophy is completed ... Completed metaphysics ... gives the scaffolding for an order of the earth which will supposedly last for a long time' (OM 95). That means that metaphysical-representational thinking, long called 'philosophy,' which in itself never could understand metaphysics, will give way to recollective thinking which thinks both metaphysics and the coming Origin (OM 91). So, understanding the overcoming of metaphysics appears as a passage over from one phase or place in the journey of being and human being to another. With the transformed relation goes the necessary, attendant transformation in thinking. Therefore Heidegger says, 'But with the end of philosophy, thinking is not also at its end, but in transition to another beginning' (OM 96). What is beginning is the turning toward home.

Like the poet whose remembering saying was made possible by the holy's saying, the thinker (whose 'perduring thinking' still thinks overcoming) must be given 'something' even more primal than metaphysics (in which being is overcome) or than the preliminary sign of the overcoming of metaphysics (in which being's radical authority is overcome). Indeed, developing the insight in *Contributions* that enowning begins the turning, the turning back to the first beginning, here, for Heidegger, remembrance experiences and names what is more primal, and therefore more concealed, which begins to show itself: 'This is *Ereignis* itself' – translated in the English here as 'appropriation' (OM 91). (This significant shift – from rendering *Ereignis* as 'enowning,' as done in *Contributions,* to using 'appropriation' – begins to introduce a complex, indeed contested, set of alternatives. I let these stand, since, as explained in the preface, I use the available English translations, indicating the shifts but leaving final decisions to the readers.)

Note, it would be an illusion to take this phenomenon as a final occurrence leaving all other aspects and events over and done with. Rather, remembering thinking attempts to keep the whole (parting and coming back together) in mind. Here Heidegger does not pretend to say much about appropriation, but he does say that it has begun to become unconcealed. This opening – the origination of truth which answers to human being and calls us – must be glimpsed as best it can be, and an attempt must be made to think it non-metaphysically, which also means recollectively, without letting go of the metaphysical phase and the transformation from the one to the other. Again, an analogy with the poet. The thinker, too, before saying anything to us about overcoming our metaphysical homelessness, must experience what comes to the thinker, in order to help it to begin to come to the rest of us. 'No transformation comes without an anticipatory escort. But how does an escort draw near unless appropriation opens out, which, calling, needing, envisions human being, that is, sees and in this seeing brings mortals to the path of thinking, poetizing building' (OM 110).

Heidegger, then, thinks of us as homeless wanderers, as workers turned into mere labourers, as 'thinkers' who only reckon and calculate for use (understood metaphysically as consumption and mastery), but also as those who might at least have the possibility opened to pass beyond drifting and to build a home outside the scaffolding thrown up by a completed metaphysics (OM 95). Such building near to the origin would be done by means of recollective thinking and poetizing. Heidegger, attempting to realize his kinship with the poet, which includes his differences, speaks of a new possible use (now understood as the proper use of being and human being by being) which would be an adequate response to the opening appropriation.

He hints at the character of this response by calling our attention to the earth upon which we need to build our poetic and thoughtful dwelling. He says, 'The unnoticeable law of the earth preserves the earth in the sufficiency of the emerging and perishing of all things in the allotted sphere of the possible which everything follows, and yet nothing knows' (OM 109). Of course, neither birch tree nor colony of bees oversteps its possibility; they 'dwell' in it (OM 109). But the case is different with humans, who first live in homelessness and, by way of wilful technology (where being is metaphysically understood as Willing, in the tradition of German metaphysics with Hegel, Schopenhauer, Nietzsche, for example), drive the earth beyond the possible, that is, out of its essence and into desolation (OM 110). How might we build and live in this desolation of the earth which stems from metaphysics and in the midst of which we wander (OM 86)? Heidegger has glimpsed a possible mode of thoughtful building and abiding which would preserve the possibility opened in appropriation: 'Shepherds live invisibly and outside of the desert of the desolated earth ... It is one thing just to use the earth, another to receive the blessing of the earth and to become at home in the law of this reception in order to shepherd the mystery of being and watch over the inviolability of the possible' (OM 109).

With the transition in overcoming metaphysics, we are at a crucial turning point in our journey – similar to the poet's moment of turning-home. Here, Heidegger speaks of a transformation in thinking which can come about only insofar as appropriation newly discloses. Here, the thinker's homecoming (and following that, ours) in recollective thinking points to the prior turning home of being toward being and human being. That is, we are at a crucial point in the history of being – the historical point of the completion of metaphysics held paradigmatically in the work of Nietzsche. What must be thought is this 'distinctive Appropriating' of metaphysics, especially as 'it has entered its ending. The ending lasts longer than the previous history of metaphysics' (OM 85).

If appropriation calls the thinker to attend to the story of being and human being, and if the history of being (as metaphysics) is being transformed, what Nietzsche said in the completion of metaphysics is of the greatest importance. Therefore Heidegger listens carefully to Nietzsche. For example, in 1943 Heidegger gathered his meditations of 1936 to 1940 into 'The Word of Nietzsche: "God Is Dead."' Again, as with 'Overcoming Metaphysics,' some sections of 'The Word of Nietzsche' were considered in chapter 1, as part of Heidegger's treatment of the modern metaphysics of justice, subjectivity, and the will. A large part of this essay, however, clearly shows the imprint of Hölderlin, who was a major concern for Heidegger during the same years. Here we will treat those sections in which Heidegger gives a close reading of Nietzsche's texts (e.g., *Thus Spake Zarathustra* – a reading similar to the ones Heidegger devoted to Hölderlin. Simultaneously, we find a new language and way to think, derived from Hölderlin but used to interpret and tell the story of being. Though Heidegger reads Nietzsche in a manner now informed and influenced by Heidegger's reading of poetry, he reads Nietzsche as a thinker – that is, as one who utters being.

'The Word of Nietzsche' is concerned with a moment of turning: 'This pointing of the way will clarify a stage in Western metaphysics that is probably its final stage' (WN 53). Here we find a point similar to the turnabout in the poet's journey, yet the thinker's movement is different in that it involves, before a turning around, a turning-over. This overturning (*Umkehrung*) is Nietzsche's turning upside down of previous (Platonic) metaphysics in an inversion that precedes Heidegger's attempt at overcoming it. Using the alternative image of a stream for the thinker's as well as the poet's journey, Heidegger says, 'Through the overturning of metaphysics accomplished by Nietzsche, there remains for metaphysics nothing but a turning aside into its own inessentiality and disarray' (WN 53). That is, Nietzsche's turning-over affords no progress on the journey home but is the final turbulence of a stream so full of back currents, eddies, and sloughs that we no longer gainfully ride on it.

Thus, this essay, like 'Overcoming Metaphysics,' slips into a position between those metaphysical works taken up in chapter 1 and the poetic ones of chapter 2. In chapter 1, we heard Heidegger tell the story of the thinker taking up the history of being and the essence of human being, especially the epoch of homelessness. In chapter 2, we found the story of the poet and the holy, especially in regard to homelessness and homecoming. Here in 'The Word of Nietzsche,' Heidegger again takes up the story of being itself, but now in a mode that echoes his exploration of the poetic. At the beginning of the essay, Heidegger emphasizes the story of being, and its parallels with the holy, which Hölderlin described as the ever-coming. Heidegger says, 'In every phase of metaphysics, there has been visible at any particular time a portion of the way that the destining of being prepares as a path for itself over and beyond whatever is, in sudden epochs of truth' (WN 54). Being prepares its own path, which would also mean that it prepares certain paths for beings. As being clears its own path, it variously reveals and conceals its coming from human beings. In the course of the coming along its path, being may hold itself back or withdraw into the self-concealment of its own essence (WN 110).

Along with any story of being's coming, we will hear a story of preparatory thinking, because such thinking helps being come. Heidegger talks of being's path and our paths of preparatory thinking as part of a more comprehensive image. Recall that Hölderlin spoke of Nature as the ever-coming source which, along with its own fruits, grows and matures the poet. Further, the poet, like the farmer, aids in the cultivation of what emerges on its own. As Heidegger notes, this is the originary *physis*. In 'The Word of Nietzsche,' Heidegger thinks the character of preparatory thinking in the same way. The preparation of place by thinking is like what occurs between farmer and *physis*. Here is what Heidegger says of the thinking which, moving in its own ways, helps being come along its path:

> Sharing in thinking proves to be an unobtrusive sowing – a sowing that cannot be authenticated through the prestige or utility attaching to it – by sowers who may perhaps never see blade and fruit and may never know a harvest. They serve the sowing, and even before that they serve its preparation.
>
> Before the sowing comes the plowing. It is a matter of making the field capable of cultivation, the field that through the unavoidable predominance of the land of metaphysics has had to remain in the unknown. It is a matter of first having a presentiment of, then of finding, and then of cultivating, that field. (WN 55)

It appears that Heidegger has had his presentiment of the necessary field. This came in his experience, in his early thinking and writing on metaphysical homelessness and a possible homecoming, and in his discovery that Hölderlin already spoken from just such a home ground, barely established. The holy and the poet, and appropriation, already show the field, if only fleetingly. But Heidegger must find this place himself – the place where he would grow to what is his own and would help cultivate the coming of being. Hence, he immediately goes on to say,

> It is a matter of taking a first walk to that field. Many are the ways, still unknown, that lead there. Yet always to each thinker there is assigned but one way, his own, upon whose traces he must again and again go back and forth that finally he may hold to it as the one that is his own – although it never belongs to him – and may tell what can be experienced on that one way.
>
> Perhaps the title *Being and Time* is a road marker belonging to such a way. (WN 55–6)[13]

Clearly, Heidegger's characterization of thinking as way-making is important. Thinking is the way to and through homelessness; being already is on its way, the thinker must be too. For now, it may suffice to call attention to two features of such talk. First, the way and path of thinking are not images important for themselves; rather, they devolve from and belong to the more comprehensive figure which they follow. That is, the walk along a way is but a part of the more important growth and cultivation. Second, the way leads to a field, which when cultivated, becomes a place for growth, that is, a place which houses and nurtures. In short, preparatory thinking is understood by Heidegger as a way which belongs to growing and cultivation, but the latter is interpreted as the emergence of home – the granting site of our proper fruitfulness. That is why Heidegger speaks of this thinking as the homecoming of being and human being: 'For the reflection we are attempting here, it is a question of preparing for a simple and inconspicuous step in thought. What matters to preparatory thinking is to light up that space within which being itself might again be able to take man, with respect to his essence, into a primal relationship. To be preparatory is the essence of such thinking' (WN 55). The task, then, is to help prepare for a homecoming by thinking about our place of habitation. This can only begin where thinking begins to recognize its own nature as preparation and, in the midst of metaphysical science and technology with their calculative thinking, to persevere 'continually under the obligation of first finding its own abode' (WN 56).

Heidegger presents a modest, even humble, description of what he is doing and of what is necessary. Because we dare not pretend we are ready to cultivate the field, nor even that we have found and dwell near it, we can only try to find it. Still, we can do that. Further, since such a task is long, longer than the lifetime of those mortals who would undertake it toward being, we must help one another. The poets help the thinkers get underway, and the thinkers help safeguard and interpret the poets' words: 'it is important only that learners in thinking should share in learning and, at the same time, sharing in teaching after their manner, should remain on the way and be there at the right moment' (WN 56). Of course, all such human thinking and saying has as its purpose, helping being come. Thus, 'that thinking, which is essential and which is therefore everywhere and in every respect preparatory, proceeds in an unpretentious way. Here all sharing in thinking, clumsy and groping though it may be, is an essential help' (WN 55).

Heidegger's understanding of thinking as helping the growth and cultivation of a home place also involves light. Remember that Hölderlin spoke of sunlight in day and spring, of the lightning from the sky, and of the holy's ray, passed through the gods. Similarly, Heidegger speaks (as we saw just above) about thinking's lighting up the space wherein being might bring human being into a primal relationship (WN 55). In this figure, of course, thinking is reflection; the original lightening-opening proceeds from (is) being. That is, thinking belongs to the manifestation of being, to its unconcealment or truth.[14] The light is needed because, in metaphysics, being is hidden. Despite the continual reference of beings to being, Heidegger explains, 'yet the truth of being remains unthought, and not only is that truth denied to thinking as a possible experience, but Western thinking itself, and indeed in the form of metaphysics, expressly, but nevertheless unknowingly, veils the happening of that denial' (WN 56). The thinking which so far 'has remained unmindful of being itself' still 'remains thoughtless, and engenders only the semblance of reflection so long as it fails to think on the place of habitation proper to man's essence and to experience the place in the truth of being' (WN 104, 65–6).

Though this means that thinking must think toward the home of being and human being, it first must think and help achieve its homecoming. Before this is possible, because we are in the midst of a metaphysical homelessness that must be endured and travelled through as the untruth of being, thinking must start where we are now. Therefore, preparatory thinking, in preparing for the proper habitation of human essence in the truth of being, questions metaphysics. Accordingly, Heidegger dwells on Nietzsche. Nietzsche, just as Hölderlin, is not important because he somehow might be personally 'attractive' to Heidegger. Nietzsche is important as a thinker because his metaphysics, and that also means his representational thinking, holds what we must think: 'the thinking through of Nietzsche's metaphysics becomes a reflection on the situation and place of contemporary man' (WN 54). What Heidegger finds when he thinks about metaphysics as focused by Nietzsche is that over time our supposedly comfortable place in being has been turned upside down. According to Heidegger, Nietzsche interpreted God, both as the 'Christian God' and metaphysically, that is, as the metaphysical realm of the suprasensory (WN 61). After the late Greek interpretation of Platonic philosophy and in Christianity, according to Nietzsche, 'God is the name for the realm of Ideas and ideals' and has been considered 'to be the true and genuinely real world' (WN 61). But we no longer live in the house of God (WN 57).

Heidegger's interpretation of what Nietzsche did is both a cultural description and an assessment. Heidegger claims that, 'Through the overturning of metaphysics accomplished by Nietzsche, there remains for metaphysics but a turning aside into its own inessentiality and disarray. The suprasensory is transformed into an unstable product of the sensory. And with such a debasement of its antithesis, the sensory denies its own essence. The deposing of the suprasensory does away with the merely sensory and thus with the difference between the two … It culminates in meaninglessness' (WN 53–4). When Heidegger says that Nietzsche overturns metaphysics, he means that Nietzsche's metaphysical inversion upsets and allows the collapse of what was. This overturning

(*Umkehrung*) – and difference – which disposes of the sensory and suprasensory is *not* the subsequent overcoming (*Überwindung*) which Heidegger seeks and which involves an incorporation and passing beyond metaphysics.[15] For all Nietzsche's efforts, according to Heidegger, Nietzsche never overcame metaphysics: 'Yet, because the highest values hitherto ruled over the sensory from the height of the suprasensory, and because the structuring of this dominance was metaphysics, with the positing of the new principle of the revealing of all values there takes place the overturning of all metaphysics. Nietzsche holds this overturning of metaphysics to be the overcoming of metaphysics. But every overturning of this kind remains only a self-deluding entanglement in the Same that has become unknowable' (WN 75).

Because Nietzsche's counter-movement remains entangled in metaphysics in such a way that 'metaphysics is cut off from its essence and, as metaphysics, is never able to think its own essence,' we are not only homeless but unable to find our way at all (WN 61).[16] Previously, under Greek Platonic philosophy or Christianity, humans made their way even while homeless. True, there was no clear movement toward home but only a trek through the desert; still, there was not confused milling about. But with Nietzsche and the completion of metaphysics, we become radically disoriented. Thus, 'if God as the suprasensory ground and goal of all reality is dead (without effective power or bestowing no life), if the suprasensory world of the Ideas has suffered the loss of its obligatory and above all of its vitalizing and upbuilding power, then nothing more remains to which man can cling and by which he can orient himself' (WN 61).

Thought in the language of home and place, our homelessness occurs in a vacuum. At first we try to fill the vacancy ourselves, with our movements, activities, busyness and business, and creativity (previously, creativity was God's characteristic) (WN 64). 'That is, if God in the sense of the Christian god has disappeared from his authoritative position in the suprasensory world, then this authoritative place itself is still always preserved, even though as that which has become empty' (WN 69). But despite our efforts to exert our will to be masters in the era in which will 'unites itself to what it wills,' we cannot provide our own way, much less our own home (WN 78). Nietzsche recognizes this and would sweep away such futile efforts (forms of incomplete nihilism). Completed nihilism would 'do away even with the place of value itself' and thus be the 'overturning of the nature and manner of valuing' (WN 69–70). But in this process, Nothing spreads to fill the absence of God. Metaphysically this means that Nothing displaces, or replaces, being. Heidegger asks what is 'happening to being in the age of the domination, now beginning, of the unconditional will to power?' and finds that '*Nothing* is happening to being' (WN 102, 104). Being becomes debased to beings and to a value and is not acknowledged as being (WN 104). Heidegger elaborates, 'Nothing is befalling being itself and its truth, and indeed in such a way that the truth of what is as such passes for being, because the truth of being remains wanting' (WN 109). 'Being is not coming into the light of its own essence. In the appearing of whatever is as such, being itself remains wanting. The truth of being falls from memory. It remains forgotten' (WN 110). 'That is why in the passage just cited ("The Madman") there stands this question: "Are we not straying as through an infinite nothing?" The pronouncement "God is dead" contains the confirmation that this Nothing is spreading out. "Nothing" means here: absence of a suprasensory, obligatory world. Nihilism, "the most uncanny of all guests," is standing at the door' (WN 61–2).

Our metaphysical homelessness, then, is brought to a head and named by Nietzsche as nihilism. In nihilism we are most not-at-home. Here, we are so oblivious to our home (understood as the source from which all comes and to which we seek to return in the future), and even to our homelessness, that Heidegger says (intending to include Nietzsche), 'It belongs to the uncanniness of this uncanny guest that it cannot name its own origin' (WN 63). But the preparatory thinking which begins to move in the overcoming of metaphysics can at least start to experience the origin and history of nihilism and the overturning of metaphysics. Since, according to Heidegger's thinking, metaphysics shows itself as the history of being, where being is hidden by beings, metaphysics appears 'as the truth of what *is* as such in its entirety' (WN 54). In the 'Postscript to "What Is Metaphysics,"' written in the same year as 'The Word of Nietzsche' was delivered (1943), Heidegger says, 'In the is-ness of what-is metaphysics thinks the thought of being, but without being able to reflect on the truth of being with its particular mode of thought. Metaphysics moves everywhere in the realm of the unknown and unfathomable ground' (pWM 351). If nihilism is the happening of Nothing to being, and if metaphysics is the history of the uncovering and concealment of being, then the nihilistic oblivion of being is part of metaphysics. According to Heidegger, nihilism is not a particular doctrine, but a 'historical movement' which, in its essence, is 'the fundamental history of the West' (WN 62). That is why 'Nietzsche thinks nihilism as the "inner logic" of Western history' (WN 67). Heidegger elaborates this history in the language of place and placement: 'The realm for the essence and the coming-to-pass [*Ereignis*] of nihilism is metaphysics itself [thought as] the fundamental structure of that which is, as a whole, insofar as that whole is differentiated into a sensory and a suprasensory world and the former is supported and determined by the latter. Metaphysics is history's open space ... [for the] decay in the essence of the suprasensory [which we name] its disessentializing [*Verwesung*, deposing or perishing]' (WN 65). The ground of nihilism is in metaphysics, for the latter is the encompassing scene in which the drama of nihilism unfolds. Of course, metaphysics cannot see itself or nihilism, precisely because in it being is concealed. 'But if the essence of nihilism lies in history, so that the truth of being remains wanting in the appearing of whatever is as such, in its entirety, and if, accordingly, Nothing is befalling being and its truth, then metaphysics as the history of the truth of what is as such is, in its essence, nihilism' (WN 109).

Worst of all, metaphysics consummates nihilism, just where it imagines it is overcoming it. Nietzsche's metaphysics, as the will to value, 'clothes itself in the illusion that it does think being in the most exalted manner, in that it esteems being as a value so that all questions concerning being become and remain superfluous' (WN 104). But here, most deeply of all places, being is not thought of and let be as being (WN 104). Here is a radical concealment of being, a thoughtless barrier on its, and our, paths. Heidegger says, 'It not only strikes down that which is as such, in its being-in-itself, but it does away utterly with being. The latter can, where it is still needed, pass only for a value. The value-thinking of the metaphysics of the will to power is murderous in a most extreme sense, because it absolutely does not let being itself take its rise, i.e., come into the vitality of its essence. Thinking in terms of values precludes in advance that being itself will attain to a coming to presence in its truth' (WN 108).

Here we see the force and direction of the figural in Nietzsche's story, especially when compared with Hölderlin's. The poet spoke of the homecoming to the holy in images of growth, nurture, festival, health, and reception. Nietzsche speaks of our radical homelessness (which supposes itself to be the creative, wilful erection of its own home) in images of death and killing, disaster, violence, power and mastery. Of course, Nietzsche tells the metaphysical tale that Heidegger has just explicated as the story of the death of God. Nietzsche does not say there is no God, but something far worse: we have murdered God (WN 105). Nietzsche's use of images to tell this story contrasts sharply with Hölderlin's use of the 'same' figures: 'How were we able to drink of the sea? Who gave us the sponge to wipe away the entire horizon? What did we do when we unchained the earth from the sun?' (WN 106).

With Nietzsche, we find a world destroyed: nature is wrenched apart and consumed by the wilful 'I' of the modern subject; a metaphysical order is abolished; our human abode is cast loose from all mooring (WN 106–8). Whereas Hölderlin first saw the source as source in its effluence in the sea, Nietzsche sees us consuming it. Where Hölderlin found that the horizon appeared as night turned to day, with the dawn of the holy's ray marking the festival of the wedding of gods and human being, Nietzsche sees us erasing away the enveloping realms within whose structure we have lived. Where Hölderlin saw the sun and earth bound together by a light yielding growth, Nietzsche sees darkness fall. But for Heidegger, recalling the relation of these two, Hölderlin sees more than Nietzsche. Indeed, Hölderlin sees what comes *after* Nietzsche and nihilism. The comparison of images is all the more important, then, because in them Nietzsche specifies what now is occurring and what we must think through. Insofar as Nietzsche tells the story of nihilism, he elucidates a great deal, but insofar as he remains entangled in metaphysics and nihilism, his story also conceals much. Heidegger is clear in his assessment: 'in relation to being itself, then, even Nietzsche's own experience of nihilism, i.e., that it is the devaluation of the highest values, is after all a nihilistic one. The interpretation of the suprasensory world, the interpretation of God as the highest value, is not thought out from being itself' (WN 105).

Heidegger is claiming that his reflection has been enabled to go beyond Nietzsche's thinking to name the origin of nihilism, where nihilism in itself cannot do so (WN 54). Or, at least, it prepares to go beyond – to overcome – nihilism, and even metaphysics, by thinking from out of being's truth and destining (WN 109). In contrast to Nietzsche, who speaks of what is killed, demolished, and broken apart, Heidegger, like Hölderlin, speaks of what belongs together and what comes near. Heidegger says, 'What is given to thinking to think is not some deeply hidden underlying meaning, but rather something lying near, that which lies nearest, which, because it is only this, we have therefore constantly already passed over' (WN 111). What lies near? Metaphysics does, as the history of the relation of being, beings, and human being. 'Preparatory thinking therefore maintains itself necessarily within the realm of historical reflection. For this thinking, history is not the succession of eras, but a unique nearness of the same that, in incalculable modes of destining and out of changing immediacy, approaches and concerns thinking' (WN 57).

Since, of all events, nihilism may lie closest to us, so too does forgetfulness of being. But even in the oblivion of being, being is near. Indeed, because the whole of metaphysics, according to Heidegger, does not experience or think being as being, 'The history of being begins, and indeed necessarily, *with the forgetting of being*. It is not due then to metaphysics as the metaphysics of the will to power that being itself in its truth remains unthought. This strange remaining-away of being is due only to metaphysics as metaphysics. But what is metaphysics?' (WN 109). Though in nihilism Nothing overcomes being, it is not nihilism which has the power to cover over being. Though metaphysics (in which nihilism is grounded and within which it takes place) involves forgetting being, metaphysics cannot ignore being, much less cast being into oblivion. Rather, such occurrences can only occur when they proceed from being itself:[17]

> Thus nihilism would be in its essence a history that runs its course along with being itself ... According to this, metaphysics would not be merely a neglect of a question still to be pondered concerning being. Surely it would not be an error. Metaphysics, as the history of the truth of what is as such, would have come to pass from out of the destining of being itself. Metaphysics would be, in its essence, the mystery of being itself, a mystery that is unthought because withheld. Were it otherwise, a thinking that takes pains to hold to being in what is to be thought could not unceasingly ask, 'What is metaphysics?'
>
> Metaphysics is an epoch of the history of being itself. But, in its essence metaphysics is nihilism. The essence of nihilism belongs to that history as which being itself comes to presence. (WN 110)

Heidegger refers to – includes – his own preparatory thinking here. His questioning the essence of metaphysics is understood as proceeding from being, not as his own 'creation.' His questioning, according to him, is the response to being's call. Further, and this returns us to where we began to reflect on 'The Word of Nietzsche,' Heidegger is now telling the story of being's own occurring as the origin of nihilism, which also means, as being makes a path for itself, beings, and human beings. This same coming opens to its helpful, preparatory thinking, whether it appears nearby in the poet's words or far away, as in nihilism. In either case, the thinker moves on along the path, looking for being's closing and opening place (field). Heidegger adds,

> It would lie in being's own essence, then, that being remain unthought because it withdraws. Being itself withdraws into its truth. It harbors itself safely within its truth and conceals itself in such harboring.
>
> In looking toward this self-concealing harboring of its own essence, perhaps we glimpse the essence of that mystery in the guise of which the truth of being is coming to presence. (WN 110)

Because Heidegger's preparatory thinking must think homelessness (that is, metaphysics and nihilism) to prepare its way to a homecoming, he listens carefully to Nietzsche's madman who, as he speaks in *The Gay Science* and *Thus Spoke Zarathustra*, experiences the loss of God and the loss of home. The Madman asks, 'Whither is [the sun] moving now? Whither are we moving now? Away from all suns? Are we not plunging continually? Backward, sideward, forward, in all directions? Is there any down left? Are we not straying as through an infinite nothing? Do we not feel the breath of empty space? Has it not become colder? Is not night and more night coming on all the while?' (cited in WN 59; Nietzsche, *Gay Science*, sec. 125). The madman cries incessantly, 'I seek God! I seek God!' Why is he called a madman? And why does he cry out as he does? Both for the same reason: because, as Heidegger says, 'He is "de-ranged." For he is dis-lodged from the level of man hitherto ... Nonetheless, in this way he has only been drawn utterly into being the predetermined essence of man hitherto, the *animal rationale*. Thus, his displacement takes place in modern metaphysics. As god and his place are overturned, the displaced madman has no place because representational thinking can no longer think. It avoids being and avoids its own dread at the absence of being by self-deception, brave chatter about being' (WN 112).

But no longer capable of originary thinking, this kind of thinking, embodied by those standing in the marketplace, no longer seeks God. In contrast, and another reason why Heidegger dwells on him, the madman still 'seeks God, since he cries out after God. Has a thinking man perhaps here really cried out *de profundis?* And the ear of our thinking, does it still not hear the cry? It will refuse to hear it so long as it does not begin to think' (WN 112). Thus, if in our own homelessness, we have not yet experienced thought, and if such images pass too quickly to help, perhaps we should slow down and be more careful (WN 111). Heedful thinking may still be experienced by some, as perhaps by the madman.

Recall that the calling and searching for god was the vocation of the poet. Once again, then, holding on to the words of Nietzsche, and thereby onto metaphysics and nihilism (homelessness), Heidegger the thinker turns to the poet in this time without God.

Obviously Heidegger is engaged in a complex task, attempting to think and tell the story of homelessness in modern metaphysics. To do that he must think the history of modern metaphysics from within. Yet, to see the truth about metaphysics, which it cannot see for itself, he must also move beyond it by thinking originarily. Heidegger demonstrates this double stance in his 1946 essay, 'What Are Poets For?,' where he moves back and forth, and into and beyond metaphysics. His movement here is even more elaborate than before. We have seen that, concerning the story of homelessness, the poet is called by the holy and the gods, and the thinker by being. In 'What Are Poets For?' Heidegger moves more deeply into a thinking dialogue with poetry (which he began in the Hölderlin essays) but *also explicitly links the poet and the poetic concern with the gods to the history of being, which he has not done thus far.* This is a delicate connection because though poetry and thinking are akin, they are also different. Therefore Heidegger needs to insist on, and begin to explain, their relationship lest either loose its essence, as would happen if poetry were misused as a source for philosophy (WPF 96).

Attuned to their differences, he patiently attempts to become 'at home with the nature of poetry as well as with the nature of thinking' (WPF 98). Though he admits he has not the ability to bring the two into their full difference and accord, he furthers the dialogue between them. Above all, this sounds a new note: Heidegger explicitly develops his task as a thinker listening for being's call, together with the poet's listening to the saying of the holy. Both, in their different ways, participate in the history of the homelessness and homecoming of being. Heidegger says, 'But there would be, and there is, the sole necessity, by thinking our way soberly into what [Hölderlin's] poetry says, to come to learn what is unspoken. That is the course of the history of being. If we reach and enter that course, it will lead thinking into a dialogue with poetry, a dialogue that is of the history of being' (WPF 96). Of course, if thinking is to enter into conversation with poetry in order to help find its way through homelessness, it must begin in the midst of our present disorientation. Heidegger has already indicated a common point between poets and thinkers: the gods. To be sure, they understand 'god' differently. For example, Hölderlin's naming of the gods helps establish the message which they bear from the holy – for him gods are heralds. In contrast, as

'The Word of Nietzsche: "God Is Dead,"' makes clear, 'God' is interpreted philosophically as the metaphysically suprasensible. But both the poet and Nietzsche agree, the gods are fled in our age of homelessness.

Heidegger understands that Hölderlin's question, 'what are poets for in a destitute time?,' refers to our time, the time which is 'the end of the day of the gods' (WPF 91). Because the great gods, such as Heracles, Dionysus, and Christ, 'have left the world,' our era 'is defined by the god's failure to arrive, by the 'default of God' (WPF 91). This does not mean that now there are no gods, that no individual is in close relationship with the Christian God, much less that the divine (*die Göttliche*), as opposed to a particular god (*Gott*), wholly disappears. What it means has to do with home: when the gods are fled they are no longer publicly, vitally united with a historical people so that the two live out time together in mutual belonging, that is, in dwelling. As Heidegger puts it, 'The default of God means that no god any longer gathers men and things unto himself, visibly and unequivocally, and by such gathering disposes the world's history and man's sojourn in it' (WPF 91).

Poetically thought, the gods and their light depart from us. As Hölderlin puts it, 'the evening of the world's age has been declining toward its night. The world's night is spreading its darkness' (WPF 91). In this darkness we wander, homeless and lost. To consider our destitute time, Heidegger shifts from thinking with Hölderlin to thinking with Rainer Maria Rilke, who, in the course of his poetry, came to realize the destitution of our time. Rilke, who moves within the sphere of metaphysics and in the shadow of Nietzsche, inquires into our painful time as one that involves not only the lack of gods but a confession as to our own natures as well. Our 'time remains destitute not only because God is dead, but because mortals are hardly aware and capable even of their own mortality. Mortals have not yet come into ownership of their own nature' (WPF 96).

Once gods and humans fall apart from one another, they also lose their own essence. It is when bound together in love that immortals truly are immortal and mortals are mortals. That is, the joy of love and the pain of death come together; even as the living bond between gods and humans is celebrated, so is the rift between them (and for mortals, the gulf between life and death). But when the relationship fails and the gods flee, mortals lose their way and the essence of life and death become veiled (WPF 96). In such a time, though mortals exist, they need to learn love, death, and the mystery of pain (which simultaneously binds and separates). In our metaphysical state of subjectivity, we are so far removed from our nature as mortals that we will, perhaps above all else, to abolish our nature as mortal. Heidegger says, 'The self-assertion of technological objectification is the constant negation of death. By this negation death itself becomes something negative; it becomes the altogether inconstant and null' (WPF 125). But such a technological effort to deny our mortal character is precisely what endangers us: 'What has long since been threatening man with death, and indeed with the death of his own nature, is the unconditional character of mere willing' (WPF 116).

The denial of death, then, which proceeds from the concealment of its and our essence, is metaphysical. Rilke sees this. As he writes in a letter, 'Death is the *side of life* that is averted from us, unilluminated by us' (cited in WPF 124). Here death is thought in the sphere of beings. Heidegger comments, 'death and the realm of the dead belong to the whole of beings as its other side ... Within the widest orbit of the sphere of beings there are regions and places which, being averted from us, seem to be something negative' (WPF 124–5). But the interpretation of everything, including death and love, in the sphere of beings is a feature of metaphysical darkness. Rilke, then, along with our understanding of death, operates in the darkness of the concealment of being. Heidegger notes, 'The time is destitute because it lacks the unconcealedness of the nature of pain, death, and love. This destitution is itself destitute because that realm of being withdraws within which pain and death and love belong together. Concealedness exists inasmuch as the realm in which they belong together is the abyss of being' (WPF 97).

Rilke speaks of the relation between beings and being, understood metaphysically, by way of a planetary image. In his language of spheres and gravitational attraction, beings would come together and belong together – in the movement 'home' – by way of 'pure gravity.' For example, Rilke says in his *Book of Pilgrimage*, 'The ore is homesick. And it yearns to ... return to the open mountain's vein and on it the mountain will close again' (cited in WPF 114). Being draws all particular beings toward itself as the centre. Being holds all beings in this *draught* toward itself. Heidegger explains Rilke's understanding, 'this center of the attracting drawing withdraws at the same time from all beings. In this fashion the center gives over all beings to the venture as which they are ventured. In this gathering release, the metaphysical nature of the will, thought of in terms of being, conceals itself' (WPF 104).

Rilke uses the word *Bezug* to designate this pure draught. He does not use the word to connote mere reference or relation, as it usually does.

Rather, for Rilke, 'the drawing which, as the venture, draws and touches all beings and keeps them drawing toward itself is the *Bezug*, the draft, pure and simple' (WPF 105). Another basic word for Rilke, a word in which the language of metaphysics speaks clearly, is 'the open,' which designates 'the whole draft to which all beings, as ventured beings, are given over' (WPF 106). Rilke says 'open' because the word says that the draught flows openly, unrestricted; the open is open, or unrestricted, because it 'is the great whole of all that is unbounded' (WPF 106). Rilke thinks of the loss of our place through the metaphysically understood draught, *Bezug*, and open. In this destitute time, humans threaten their own nature by self-willing, and yet our nature 'resides in the relation of being to man, its draft upon him' (WPF 115). Rilke says that we set ourselves apart from the pure draught and are opposed to the open. As Heidegger notes, 'By building the world up technologically as an object, man deliberately and completely blocks his path, already obstructed, into the open' (WPF 116).

Correspondingly, what we seek as home is a security, where 'to be secure is to repose safely within the drawing of the whole draft' (WPF 120). For Rilke, this security in the open would need to be 'created' in a daring act by metaphysical willing because, according to Heidegger, 'to create means to fetch from the source. And to fetch from the source means to take up what springs forth and to bring what has so been received' (WPF 120). It is just this belonging to the open which is now threatened; in this loss our natures are also risked and endangered. Rilke holds that we must be converted to the open's draught by way of pure interiority – understood as metaphysical subjectivism, and called 'the heart' (WPF 129ff.).

In the course of his originary description of (and attempt at) homecoming out of metaphysical homelessness, Heidegger proceeds in part by explicating the manner in which Rilke spoke of metaphysical homelessness and, like Nietzsche, remained within metaphysics, even as he tried to find a homecoming. Rilke's poetry of homelessness and home for the heart in the draught of the open, for all its yearning for home and homecoming, yet remains metaphysical, that is, homeless. That is why it is so important to hear what he says. No mere rhetoric or vocabulary of home accomplishes a homecoming. Indeed, that is precisely the problem. Metaphysics thinks itself at home; it is oblivious to its deepest homelessness. According to Heidegger, though Nietzsche and Rilke both articulate metaphysical homelessness, they do not understand it for what it is. The next move, then, would be to understand them together and thereby from the metaphysical core: 'Only a more primal elucidation of the nature of subjectness will serve to show how, within the completion of modern metaphysics, there belongs to the being of beings a relation to such a being [the Angel of the *Elegies*], how the creature which is Rilke's Angel despite all difference of content, is *metaphysically the same* as the figure of Nietzsche's Zarathustra' (WPF 124).

Rilke's language of 'open,' *Bezug* ('draught'), and 'heart' 'is within the being that bears the stamp of metaphysics' (WPF 133). It may appear otherwise, for in his poetry he seems, as does Hölderlin, to speak of 'nature,' 'life,' 'animals,' 'flowers,' 'the heart,' and 'the gods.' But with these words, he in no way thinks or says what Hölderlin does. Just the opposite, Rilke uses them metaphysically. For example, in a letter Rilke describes the 'open' by way of subject and object: 'we stand *before it* [the world], by virtue of that peculiar turn and intensification which our consciousness has taken' (cited in WPF 108). Or, according to Heidegger, Rilke takes 'nature' in Leibniz's sense: it means the gathering power of the being of beings (WPF 100ff.). Yet again, the spherical aspect of the being of beings names the unifying trait of being from its unconcealing centre – which Heidegger understands originarily as presence (WPF 123–4; see also WN 87). In short, 'For Rilke's poetry, the being of beings is metaphysically defined as worldly presence; this presence remains referred to representation in consciousness, whether that consciousness has the character of the immanence of calculating representation, or that of the inward conversion to the open which is accessible through the heart' (WPF 132).

That Rilke's language is metaphysical, even when it does not look like the metaphysical language of the philosophers, is of the greatest significance for the relationship of thinkers and poets. Specifically, because of his poetic language, Rilke speaks and thinks differently than Heidegger. The latter engages the former to hear metaphysical poetry from the inside, but on his own, Heidegger speaks originarily, that is, differently. For example, 'What Rilke designates by [open] is not in any way defined by openness in the sense of the unconcealedness of beings that lets beings as such be present' (WPF 106). In originary terms, Rilke's open 'is precisely what is closed up, unlightened' (WPF 106). This discussion of Rilke's language also sheds light on the relationship between Heidegger and Hölderlin. Heidegger does not use Hölderlin's poetry as a source for philosophical ideas or as a mine for interesting words. One does not become or cease to be metaphysical merely by adopting a particular vocabulary. Clearly, Heidegger needs to elaborate these relationships.

Rilke's importance, then, lies in his poetizing our metaphysical homelessness and in his attempt to overcome it. His poetry, starting from the realm of particular beings, sings out of and into the abyss (*Abgrund*) of being, that is, in the absence of a ground for the world that appears when the gods flee (WPF 92, 98). Rilke's homelessness and longing sound in a letter of 1925: 'To our grandparents, a "house" or "well," a familiar steeple, even their own clothes, their cloak *still* meant infinitely more, were infinitely more intimate – almost everything a vessel in which they found something human already there, and added to its human store. Now there are intruding, from America, empty indifferent things, sham things, *dummies of life* ... A house, as the Americans understand it, an American apple or a winestock from over there, have *nothing* in common with the house, the fruit, the grape into which the hope and thoughtfulness of our forefathers had entered' (cited in WPF, 113).

This cry echoes that of Nietzsche's madman and asks, 'Is there to be no more home?' Before Heidegger attempts any answer he needs to let the question stand. Still, what appears as negative from the metaphysical viewpoint of beings as a whole is understood differently in originary thinking. According to Heidegger, thought as part of the coming of being in itself, even Rilke's painful song, for all its genuine distress, speaks of 'neither a decay or a downfall. As destiny (our destitute era) lies in being and lays claim to man' (WPF 142). Here the death of mortals and of God remains a question. But death may now be understood first metaphysically and then originarily as something that gathers us toward home, as the mountains claim their ore: 'as this gathering of positing, death is the laying-down, the law [*Ge-sitz*], just as the mountain chain [*Gebirg*] is the gathering of the mountains into the whole of its chain' (WPF 126).

Rilke's story, it turns out, is part of the story of homelessness. Metaphysical homelessness is the tale of the separation of being, beings, and human being, whether found in the writings of a philosopher like Nietzsche or told in a different way by the poet Rilke. Thus, in thinking through our destitute time, thinking must converse with poets like Rilke. We could say that we have two pairs of thinkers and poets. Nietzsche and Rilke think and poeticize, respectively, from within metaphysical homelessness (see, e.g., WPF 108, 134); Heidegger and Hölderlin think and poetize from out of homelessness into homecoming – or, at least, Heidegger is underway where Hölderlin already succeeded.

Heidegger would not need to claim that thinking converses with poetry only in destitute times but simply that it is especially important then. The death of the gods, to which Nietzsche and Rilke testify, is itself not the worst news for homeless humans. What is worse is that because metaphysics (even for all the insight of a Nietzsche or Rilke) attempts to overturn homelessness by the will to power or the heart; it does not still long for or seek the gods. Heidegger explains, 'The default of God forebears something even grimmer, however. Not only have the gods and the god fled, but the divine radiance has become extinguished in the world's history. The time of the world's night is the destitute time, because it becomes even more destitute. It has already grown so destitute, it can no longer discern the default of God as a default' (WPF 91).

Heidegger understands the divine (*die Göttliche*) to be higher than the gods (*die Götter*) because it sends the particular gods near to us (see WPF 141). When the divine itself darkens, its and our own natures slip into concealment. Thus, the holy itself of which Hölderlin speaks is hard to discern in Rilke's song, which also 'still keeps to the trace of the holy' (WPF 96). But it is just this trail that Heidegger, attending the poets, must follow. 'Meanwhile, even the trace of the holy has become unrecognizable. It remains undecided whether we still experience the holy [*die Heilige*] as the track leading to the godhead of the divine [*die Gottheit des Göttlichen*], or whether we now encounter no more than a trace of the holy. It remains unclear what the track leading to the trace might be. It remains in question how such a track might show itself to us' (WPF 97). The question of what poets are for in our destitute time finds a second answer in light of this question. The first answer was in terms of our homelessness: poets articulate our destitution for us. But now, Heidegger says that insofar as they are poets, they stay on the track of the holy. This is true of a metaphysical poet like Rilke as well as of an originary one like Hölderlin.

Holding himself in the draught of the open, Rilke ventures a song which is 'a breath for nothing. The singer's saying says the sound whole of worldly existence, which invisibly offers its space within the world's inner space of the heart' (WPF 140). Though such a song does not first or really listen to what is said by the holy, nonetheless, because such poets experience the unholy, they are underway on the track of the holy. They hail the globe of being, that is, the whole of beings. Heidegger elaborates,

> The unholy, as unholy, traces the sound for us. What is sound beckons to the holy, calling it. The holy binds the divine. The divine draws the god near.

> The more venturesome [poets] experience unshieldedness in the unholy. They bring to mortals the trace of the fugitive gods, the track into the dark of the world's night. As singers of soundness, the more venturesome ones are 'poets in a destitute time.' (WPF 141)

Because Hölderlin experiences the unholy more deeply than Rilke and even comes out of it, Heidegger begins and ends this essay in dialogue with Hölderlin. In Hölderlin's experience and poetry, for example, 'Dionysos the wine-god brings this trace down to the god-less amidst the darkness of the world's night. For in the vine and its fruit, the god of wine guards the being toward one another of earth and sky as the site of the wedding feast of man and gods. Only within reach of this site, if anywhere, can traces of the fugitive gods still remain for god-less men' (WPF 93). These words give us something quite different than Rilke's representational understanding of the earth, in which the real destitution (of nature as object for the radical subjectivity of the interior heart) is so obscured that it appears solely as a need to be met (WPF 93, 109ff.). According to Heidegger, Hölderlin deeply gathers into poetry the nature of poetry in a destitute time. Hölderlin shows that

> Poets are the mortals who, singing earnestly of the wine-god, sense the trace of the fugitive gods, stay of the god's tracks, and so trace for their kindred mortals the way toward the turning. The ether, however, in which alone the gods are gods, is their godhead. The element of this ether, that within which even the godhead itself is still present, is the holy. The element of the ether for the coming of the fugitive gods, the holy, is the track of the fugitive gods. But who has the power to sense, to trace such a track? Traces are often inconspicuous, and are always the legacy of a directive that is barely divined. To be a poet in a destitute time means: to attend, singing to the trace of the fugitive gods. This is why the poet in the time of the world's night utters the holy. This is why, in Hölderlin's language, the world's night is the holy night. (WPF 94)

The darker this night becomes, the more destitution prevails, 'in such a way that it withdraws its very nature and presence' (WPF 94). Hölderlin was let into such an obscuring darkness. But – and here Heidegger elaborates Hölderlin's poetry and its place in a remarkable way – the darkness which besets the poet is the darkness brought on by the withdrawal of being. Heidegger is surprisingly explicit: 'The poet thinks his way into the locality defined by that lightening of being which has reached its characteristic shape as the realm of Western metaphysics in its self-completion. Hölderlin's thinking poetry has had a share in giving its shape to this realm of poetic thinking. His composing dwells in this locality as intimately as no other poetic composition of his time. The locality to which Hölderlin came is a manifestness of being, a manifestness which itself belongs to the destiny of being and which, out of that destiny, is intended for the poet' (WPF 95). Heidegger does not say here that the holy is being, but he does say that Hölderlin undertook his homecoming poetizing in the manifestness of being – which also includes being's oblivion (WPF 95).

Hölderlin leads the way in the history of being. His works achieve a 'position in the course of the history of being' which Rilke's do not, and Hölderlin is far more experienced 'in the land of the saying of being' than we have yet become (WPF 98). Therefore, Heidegger says, 'Hölderlin is the pre-curser of poets in a destitute time' (WPF 142). Rilke, in his metaphysical way, and Hölderlin, more originarily, move in the history of being and, in their poetic sayings, foretell and safeguard the being to which they belong. Further, 'What occurs in the arrival gathers itself back into destiny,' that is, in the poet's foretelling saying, being gathers itself. Here, Heidegger makes another stunning explication (WPF 142). If being gathers itself in the poet's sayings, then, thought by way of homelessness and homecoming, being makes itself at home (albeit as hidden) in language. 'Being itself traverses this going over and is itself its dimension' and appears as more than 'even being itself, so far as we commonly conceive being in terms of particular beings' (WPF 131–2). Being, beings, and human beings come into their own and back into the nature of their truth in language (WPF 131). According to Heidegger,

> Being, as itself, spans its own province, which is masked off (*temnein, tempus*) by being's being present in the word. Language is the precinct (*templum*), that is, the house of being. The nature of language does not exhaust itself in signifying, nor is it merely something that has the character of a sign or cipher. It is because language is the home of being, that we reach what is by constantly going through this house. When we go to the well, when we go through the woods, we are always already going through the word 'well,' through the word 'woods,' even if we do not speak the words and do not think of anything relating to language. Thinking our way from the temple of being, we have an intimation of what they dare who are sometimes more daring than the being of beings. They dare the precinct of being. They dare language. All beings ... each in its own way, are *qua* beings in the precinct of

> language. This is why the return from the realm of objects and their representation into the innermost region of the heart's space can be accomplished, if anywhere, *only in this precinct.* (WPF 132)

In its context, what Heidegger says in this passage applies first to Rilke and therefore to the being of beings. But since it alludes, beyond that, to being coming into its own, it further tells about being's homecoming: *the homecoming would come about in language.* That is why language is not just the house of being, but the genuine house – the temple – of being. By putting it this way, Heidegger emphasizes the coming toward one another of being and the poet's words concerning the holy, the divine, and the gods. In the hallowed place of language, being would become, out of the unholy, 'the hale and whole' (WPF 117). In its hidden way, being already comes even in metaphysical language, for example, in Rilke's sayings. Humans who have language 'within the being that bears the stamp of metaphysics' may mistake 'language from the start and merely as something [we have] in hand, like a personal belonging.' Nonetheless, even with our representational, propositional assertions, we are not fully cut off from being (WPF 133). Still, the poets' genuine sayings beyond willing are more fully language, following 'something to be said, solely in order to say it.' What is to be said would then be what by nature belongs to the province of language. And that, thought metaphysically, is the sound wholeness of the open,' that is, particular beings as a whole (WPF 137–8). Rilke's genuine sayings would do this: he sings 'the healing whole in the midst of the unholy' (WPF 140). Presumably, Hölderlin's sayings say something else.

In 'What Are Poets For?,' Heidegger presents language as the home of being. Understood metaphysically, through Rilke's poetry, language is seen as the precinct wherein being (the whole) ventures particular beings and human being, and where it comes to itself (WPF 136). *It is a further task to understand more fully – originarily – the glimpse of unconcealment contained in Heidegger's saying. To do so, Heidegger himself would need to attend to the words of Hölderlin, wherein language might be shown, originarily, as the temple of being.* Apparently, in this essay Heidegger already speaks from an originary thinking and saying beyond metaphysics. Yet, insofar as he attempts to think, from within, metaphysical poetry with Rilke, to some degree he remains bound by metaphysical language and thinking (just as was the case in his effort to think metaphysical thinking with Nietzsche). The difficulty will remain. *It also partially accounts for the several voices in Heidegger's corpus, and often the combination of voices within individual works.*

Sometimes metaphysical language sounds out; sometimes (as when Heidegger is in concert with Hölderlin), we hear the originary; at other times, Heidegger, seeking his own voice, weaves these two together.

The Mutual Turning of Being and Human Being

What Heidegger says here, with the help of Rilke and Hölderlin, bespeaks a change in being. He has found that being is coming in language. Dynamically, it is changing because it is still coming into 'its own self and into the nature of its truth' (WPF 131). Thus, he says, 'When we think on this, we experience within being itself that there lies in it something "more" belonging to it' (WPF 132). It appears that a turn occurs here, a turn which *may* be a turn home – which also means it may not be so. Such turning always draws human beings along with/in it. Humans now live in an age of homelessness, separated from the gods who have departed. Any turning toward home for us would have to begin in the realm of the unholy within which we dwell. Unavoidably, our dangerous activity takes place in the abyss – where we now find ourselves without a ground. Heidegger points out that 'The word for abyss – *Abgrund* – originally means the soil and ground toward which, because it is undermost, a thing tends downward. ... The ground is the soil in which to strike root and to stand. The age for which the ground fails to come, hangs in the abyss. Assuming that a turn still remains open for this destitute time at all, it can come some day only if the world turns about fundamentally – and that now means, unequivocally: if it turns away from the abyss. In the age of the world's night, the abyss of the world must be experienced and endured. But for this it is necessary that there be those who reach into the abyss' (WPF 92).

As we have seen, those who venture where 'all ground breaks off – into the abyss' are the poets. That is why Hölderlin indicates that what saves only comes where there is danger, that is, poetic risking in language of beings and human being, and even of being itself. Out of this dangerous place we might end our homelessness. To come home would be for us to find a ground to again send down roots and to stand (here, Heidegger still thinks of home and growth together).[18] This would also be to come into our nature, which now is unavailable to us. Accordingly, Heidegger says, 'The salvation must come from where there is a turn with mortals in their nature' (WPF 118).

However, since our homelessness is a separation from the gods, any turn home would involve both humans and gods turning toward one another, into their relation and their own natures. Recall Hölderlin's poems of the wedding feast of gods and humans where it was said that the gods and mortals must turn together. Still, such a turning is neither haphazard nor accidental but a careful procedure. Heidegger, interpreting Hölderlin, explains, 'The turning [*die Wende*] of the age does not take place [*ereignit sich*] by some new god, or some old one renewed, bursting into the world from ambush at some time or another. Where would he turn [*kehren*] on his return [*Wiederkunft*] if men had not first prepared an abode for him? ... The gods who "were once there," "return" [*kehren*] only at the "right time" – that is, when there has been a turn [*wenden*] among men in the right place, in the right way' (WPF 92). If mortals must make a place ready for the gods, they first must be empowered to move out of the homelessness, even before the gods, as Hölderlin says in his poem, 'Mnemosyne,'

> ... The heavenly powers
> Cannot do all things. It is the mortals
> Who reach sooner into the abyss. So the turn is
> With these ... (cited in WPF 92)

And since mortals only turn when they begin to discover the way to their own nature, part of that nature is that they stay closer to the abyss and reach into it sooner by realizing that it is an abyss and by seeing and tracking what the abyss, in its darkness, covers (WPF 93). Those who first come to such understanding and way-making are the poets and the preparatory thinkers. They begin, in language, to prepare the abode for the gods. How are humans able to do this? What enables us is what we are close to, even when we hang in the abyss: being. Since all the while it conceals itself in its absence, being also touches mortals as presence (WPF 93). The thinker, by thinking being, first reaches into the abyss and prepares to turn out of it to prepare for the coming of the gods. The poet, by contrast, thinks what enables humans to prepare for the gods: as is proper to the poetic nature, the poet discovers traces of the divine and holy. Heidegger, commenting on Hölderlin's poetry, notes, 'How could there ever be for the god an abode fit for a god, if a divine radiance did not first begin to shine in everything that is?' (WPF 92).

If, before any reunion, gods and mortals must turn toward one another, and if there must also be a ground for their turning (thought of by the poet as the divine radiance and by the thinker as being), once again – as Heidegger already said in *Contributions* – it appears that any turning at all comes from the primal turning of being (or, for the poet, the holy). Understood from within metaphysics, Rilke, according to Heidegger, spoke of this turning. In metaphysical language, our opening ourselves to our belonging to the being of beings (the open) implies that 'the open itself must have turned toward us in a way that allows us to turn our unshieldedness toward it' (WPF 122). Still, we have not achieved anything resembling a homecoming. What Heidegger presents thus far consists of traces, glimpses, the barest beginnings of movement in a new direction. We are still homeless. Further, for all the turning which the poet and thinker observe in the being of beings, not all turning is a turning home. Heidegger speaks of the possibility of the gods returning in terms of a coming home, but the language of the prior, detectable turning of humans and the being of beings is much more neutral. In the – still metaphysical – venture of Rilke and our age, we have a 'situation in which matters may turn out one way or another' (WPF 103). Language holds this ambivalence in the medieval word *die Wage* (balance), which means risk, as well as the apparatus for balancing; this word, according to Heidegger, 'comes from *wägen, wegen*, to make a way, that is, to go, to be in motion' (WPF 103). It remains to be seen whether poet and thinker will be able to distinguish turns which become dead ends from those which might lead to an open way. Even of the latter, only a few might open to a homecoming.

In the way along these risky paths, Heidegger is between ways. That is, as we saw in chapter 1 and in this chapter, Heidegger's proper concern is with metaphysical homelessness and with those who genuinely speak from it, as do Nietzsche and Rilke. As we saw in chapter 2 and in this chapter, however, Heidegger has need of and allegiance to Hölderlin because he is attempting originary language and thinking. In this third series of works, then, where Heidegger moves in both metaphysical and an originary language and thinking, we see more clearly how he is beginning to discover the means to pursue his own task regarding homelessness and being. He is beginning to see the possibility of a homecoming, by way of language and remembrance which turns beyond – forward from and back beyond – metaphysics. Thinking, twinned with poetry, endures metaphysics and might enter into its overcoming, passing over to the site of the belonging toward one another of earth and sky, mortals and gods (WPF 93). What in needed is for Heidegger, from out of his attempted accord with poetry and now on his own as a thinker, to be able to think and say the turn from homelessness to homecoming.

Heidegger pursues his own originary thinking and thoughtful saying of language as the house of being in a letter to Jean Beaufret, then released in 1947 as 'Letter on Humanism.' But even the important fact that Heidegger develops his understanding of language and being less metaphysically and more originarily in this essay falls short of indicating its full importance. The larger point is that 'Letter on Humanism' attempts a distinctive approach to what needs to be thought. In Heidegger's own terms, the essay is poised between two paths and attempts its own (third) way into a primordial thinking. 'Letter on Humanism' constantly refers, first, to what Heidegger thought in *Being and Time;* second, to what he found Hölderlin to be saying; and thirdly, to what he himself yet needs to do. Positively, *Being and Time* was an effort to begin a homecoming for Dasein; but, according to Heidegger himself, though he thought being as broader than all beings, 'For all that, being [as *transcendens*] is thought on the basis of beings, a consequence of the approach – at first unavoidable – within a metaphysics that is still dominant' (LH 216). Further, many other metaphysical distinctions and oppositions (such as *existentia* and *essentia*) are not yet in question for Heidegger (LH 205). Thus, this early attempt was not wholly successful, as Heidegger admits:

> In the poverty of its first breakthrough, the thinking that tries to advance thought into the truth of being brings only a small part of that wholly other dimension to language. This language is still faulty insofar as it does not yet succeed in retaining the essential help of phenomenological seeing and in dispensing with the inappropriate concern with 'science' and 'research.' But in order to make the attempt at thinking recognizable and at the same time understandable for existing philosophy, it could at first be expressed only within the horizon of that existing philosophy and its use of current terms.
>
> In the meantime I have learned to see that these very terms were bound to lead immediately and inevitably into error. (LH 235)

Though Hölderlin himself passed beyond metaphysics to an originary poetry, Heidegger admits that he had not yet done so, because his early interpretations of Hölderlin still depended on *Being and Time* and thus also remained ensnared in metaphysics. Heidegger himself cites, as an example of the shortcoming, treatment of being as the unmediated-immediate: 'In the lecture on Hölderlin's elegy "Homecoming" (1943) this nearness "of" being, which the *Da* of Dasein is, is thought on the basis of *Being and Time*' (LH 217).

Hence, the turn of thinking taking place in 'Letter on Humanism' is a distinctive part of Heidegger's overall movement and uniquely develops the means of homecoming. In chapter 1 we saw how he began thinking the history of being as a double movement of metaphysical homelessness: being withdraws from human being; humans wander off into subjectivity over and against objects. There he realized that before any homecoming is possible, a turn home would be necessary – in which being and human being would mutually turn back toward one another. In the works so far considered in this chapter, Heidegger indicates that being may turn in its path, first to come to itself and then to open the site for human essence. Being's coming through, or to, its own domain occurs in language, as was metaphysically glimpsed in 'What Are Poets For?' Obviously, such an event needs to be understood by an adequately originary thinking because only out of such an experience of being's turn 'does the overcoming of homelessness begin from being, a homelessness in which not only man but the essence of man stumbles about' (LH 218).

In chapters 1 and in this chapter we have seen how Heidegger has begun to explore homelessness and, in the latter, to catch a glimpse of a turn toward home. From what he came to understand in the Hölderlin essays (treated in chapter 2), even if thought somewhat metaphysically, and from his meditations on the relation of essential thinking and poetry (also considered in chapter 2), he has an idea of what to look for as a turn, and in a turning. What is required next is to look for the turn as turn, that is, to see being as being. In fact, in this third series of works, the turn begins to occur for Heidegger – the turn that is the overcoming of metaphysics, and which, in its understanding of being, human being, thinking, and language, turns toward home. 'Letter on Humanism,' is part of this turn in thinking being's path homeward and thinking's abode. Of course, the turn merely begins in 'Letter on Humanism' and its congruent works. It would only be much later that any homecoming might come about. Still, the beginning of a turning is what is most necessary at this juncture in Heidegger's thinking, before any journey home, moment of arrival, or learning to become at home (all of which would need to remember homelessness) would be possible.

The kind of turning point Heidegger seeks, as discussed above, has been prepared for in the works of the 1920s, 1930s, and early 1940s, especially in the breakthrough of *Contributions.* In addition, Heidegger consolidates much of what he has thought concerning metaphysics since *Being and Time* and concerning poetic truth in 'Letter on Humanism.'

This allows him to hold and focus the accomplishment, as would be necessary within a turning already begun. Yet, just as clearly, he is still – necessarily and doubly – in the midst of the foreign. He is deep within homelessness; perhaps, with the Nietzsche and Rilke essays, deeper in metaphysics than ever before. And Heidegger is in the foreign precisely in his most recent affinity and dialogue with poetry because, for all the nearness of poetry and thought, they are also different. As what is 'complementary' but not his own, poetry is indeed foreign to the thinker – all the more so the more the poetry and thinking are genuine.

For the sake of analogy (only), recall Hölderlin's journey to find what he needed in the foreign. As a German poet with the ability to present clearly, he sought the Greek fire. Thought by way of Hölderlin's trip, Heidegger as a German might seek the Greek as the foreign. As one devoted to thinking he might seek language. As being is his own concern, he might also look for the holy. As a thinker, he might seek the companion poet. In any case, in order to come home to his own, Heidegger must, as he has, venture into frightening metaphysical homelessness and into a more comforting (and therefore even more dangerous) poetic journey which still leaves him homeless. Just as the poet only achieved his proper homecoming, farthest from the source, by first seeing the source as source in its effluence to the sea, so must Heidegger come into his own turning toward home in an experience – as he now understands it – of being as being. 'Yet being – what is being? It is it itself' (LH 210). Of course, such an experience or movement is possible because of what he first saw in the 1930s and began to articulate, for example, in *Contributions*, that enowning has turned, and how; because of that, we (Heidegger included) might turn toward the first and another beginning.

Insofar as this understanding continues to occur in the mid-1940s, 'Letter on Humanism' is a work that tells of Heidegger's pivotal insights. Though without elaborating, the essay seemingly does begin to articulate Heidegger's originary insights and interpretations of being itself, language, thinking, and human being. If these insights are genuinely originary, they would be a turning toward home, and not just another turn which becomes still more entangled in metaphysics. Like the poet experiencing the source, as the poet's home stream comes into the sea, Heidegger speaks of being itself when he travels along the path of metaphysical homelessness amidst beings (which have long concealed being). Beings now display being itself, which pushes them aside. Being is what arrives (*das Ankommende, l'avenant*) by coming into accord with human being. Thus, Heidegger speaks not just of thinking 'the advent of being' but of 'being as advent' (LH 241).

What does it mean to experience being as advent or coming – if we are careful not to assume that Heidegger means the same as Hölderlin? Heidegger elaborates the issue in three ways. Throughout the letter he speaks of being as a primordial element (*das Element*) – which enables (LH 196). It is what properly enables thinking to be thinking and beings to be beings. In that sense, as enabling something to occur, it is an advent of thinking or being. Primally, it is not only the advent, but advent understood as the enabling itself (*das Vermögen*) (LH 196). What does it mean to say that being is the self-enabling? Heidegger understands being's giving as dual. Being gives itself, granting its truth, or unconcealment. What Heidegger cautiously and imprecisely said in *Being and Time* (BT 212) is thought more precisely and thoroughly here: being gives, where the '"gives" names the essence of being that is giving, granting its truth. The self-giving into the open, along with the open region itself, is being itself' (LH 214). In addition to its pure gift of its own unconcealment, being also gives the essence of what is. It gives the essence of all beings, including that of human being, as well as of thinking and language. In the language of a loving event (echoing Hölderlin's wedding festival), Heidegger says, 'Being has fatefully embraced [something's] essence. To embrace a "thing" or "person" in its essence means to love it, to favor it. Thought in a more original way such favoring [*Mögen*] means to bestow essence as a gift. Such favoring is the proper essence of enabling, which not only can achieve this or that but also can let something essentially unfold in its provenance, that is, let it be. It is on the "strength" of such enabling by favoring that something is properly able to be. This enabling is what is properly "possible" [*Mögliche*], that whose essence resides in favoring' (LH 196).

As favouring, being is the home out of/in which all, and all relationships, proceed. Heidegger adds that being itself 'in its favoring presides over thinking and hence over the essence of humanity, and that means over its relation to being. To enable something here means to preserve it in its essential sway, to maintain it in its element' (LH 196–7). And being gives the relation of beings to being in a manner that also preserves the 'difference of both,' which metaphysics does not think (LH 202–3).

Because human being is given its manner of abiding in relation to and difference from being by being itself, human beings belong to being. This giving of being, when unconcealed, is understood as the truth of being thought by human being. Heidegger says, 'Belonging to being, because thrown by being into the preservation of its truth and claimed for such preservation, [recollecting thinking] thinks being' (LH 236). 'At the same time thinking is of being insofar as thinking, belonging to being, listens to being. As the belonging to being that listens, thinking is what it is according to its essential origin' (LH 196). In thinking, human being properly responds to its granting origin – to the advent of being; simultaneously, being is understood as that which appropriates humans. Just as being preserves what is in its essence, being gives to humans as part of their essence the helping to preserve being's truth and the letting be of the manner of being of things. That is why human thinking is a listening: it is a response that hears and holds on to what is given. The essence of human being, then, lies in being set out into a journey toward our home – to being itself – 'insofar as being appropriates man as ek-sisting for guardianship over the truth of being into this truth itself' (LH 224).

Heidegger again elaborates being in a way which echoes but – as in *Contributions* – goes beyond, *Being and Time*. Being gives humans their place from out of its unconcealment. In this realm, humans are not understood as masters of beings, as in the case of metaphysical willing, but as embraced by being: 'Man is rather "thrown" from being itself into the truth of being, so that existing in this fashion he might guard the truth of being, in order that beings might appear in the light of being as the beings they are' (LH 210, see also 217; compare with *Contributions*, where he said that enowning's throw and call calls forth a double response from Dasein: a throwing itself free and a returning to enowning). Now, in 'Letter on Humanism' Heidegger says that being gives human being, as well as claiming and calling us into the presence of its unconcealment (LH 209, 221). 'But in the claim upon man, in the attempt to make man ready for this claim, is there not implied a concern about man? Where else does "care" tend but in the direction of bringing man back to his essence' (LH 199). That is to say, being, as the enabling, granting, and appropriating, summons humans back into their essence and primordial origin. Being thus calls on human being to turn back home. How? In language. It is in language that being gives itself to us, by granting its nearness in language and hiding its farness there. That is why Heidegger simply says, 'Language is the lighting-concealing advent of being itself' (LH 206). Thought via these two ways of speaking (being calls us home and the nearness of being/home 'occurs essentially as language itself'), language is no longer understood metaphysically but originarily (LH 212). Heidegger can now newly interpret the thought of language as the house of being. Since being unconceals itself in language, language in its essence is 'the house of the truth of being' (LH 199), a home still denied to us in our metaphysical homelessness in the history of being. Heidegger explains, 'According to this essence language is the house of being which comes to pass from being and is pervaded by being. And so it is proper to think the essence of language from its correspondence to being and indeed as this correspondence, that is, as the home of man's essence' (LH 213).

Heidegger frequently speaks of the belonging of being and human being in terms of the open and light. Being gives: it gives itself into the open; the open opens as the site for the coming forth of beings and human being. He calls this *world* – where world does not mean physical beings, the planet earth, or the sum of entities, 'but the openness of being. Man is, and is man, insofar as he is the ek-sisting one. He stands out into the openness of being. Being itself ... is as this openness ... "World" is the lighting of being into which man stands out on the basis of his thrown existence' (LH 228–9, see also 204, 207, 211). Lighting and open belong together. Heidegger has spoken in this manner since *Being and Time*, as he constantly notes in this essay. But in the course of his increasingly originary thinking, he also comes to speak of the lighting-concealing coming of being – which is language – in terms of homecoming and home. That is, his thought which moves by way of home is his originary thought: language is the house of being. In its home human being dwells (LH 193).

'Thus language is at once the house of being and the home of human beings. Only because language is the home of the essence of man can historical mankind and human beings not be at home in language' (LH 239). Insofar as we understand language as the house of being and the home of humans, we can follow the unfolding of homelessness as the loss (withdrawal and forgetting) of the home, a turn toward home as the experience of this home as home, and homecoming as the journey back to where humans thoughtfully dwell in the house of being (LH 239). Speaking by way of our essential abode in being, Heidegger can – more than he could in the language of *Being and Time* – articulate what part human being plays in the overcoming of homelessness. He insists that thinking by way of home is not idiosyncratic or accidental but initially belongs to the subject matter itself. 'This dwelling is the essence of "being-in-the-world." The reference in *Being and Time* (p. 54) to "being-in" as "dwelling" is no etymological game. The same reference in the

1936 essay on Hölderlin's verse, "Full of merit, yet poetically man dwells on this earth," is no adornment of a thinking that rescues itself from science by way of poetry. The talk [in this work, the 'Letter on Humanism' itself] about the house of being is no transfer of the image "house" to being ... And yet thinking never creates the house of being' (LH 236–7).

According to Heidegger, humans come into their essence only when in the house of being, close to the being which claims us. He says of human being, 'Only from that claim "has" he found that wherein his essence dwells. Only from this dwelling "has" he "language" as the home that preserves the ecstatic for his essence' (LH 204). Even more strangely, 'In his essential unfolding within the history of being, man is the being whose being as ek-sistence consists in his dwelling in the nearness of being. Man is the neighbor of being' (LH 222). Clearly, then, we are at home when near to being and homeless when separated from it. The chance to return from our homelessness must first be given by being giving its truth and granting our essence by enabling our thinking, while we must respond by shepherding being's coming in our recollective thinking and saying. Heidegger notes,

> Homelessness so understood consists in the abandonment of being by beings. Homelessness is the symptom of oblivion of being. Because of it the truth of being remains unthought. The oblivion of being makes itself known indirectly through the fact that man always observes and handles only beings.
>
> Homelessness is coming to be the destiny of the world. Hence it is necessary to think that destiny in terms of the history of being. (LH 218–19)

But how do humans, even if able to overcome homelessness as the oblivion of being, become the neighbours of being? What are our responsibilities as neighbours? As noted, we are given the gift of neighbourliness by being, though it is up to us to accept it in our response. Further, we would preserve the neighbourliness, and thereby our own essence, by the way we dwell. That is to say, we dwell close to being and belong to it insofar as we guard the truth of being: 'Man is the shepherd of being' (LH 224). The figure elaborates the way that being, which gives itself to humans, also appropriates them: being gives itself and appropriates us 'for guardianship over the truth of being and into this truth itself' (LH 224). According to Heidegger, such understanding experiences the essence of human beings more primordially than does metaphysics (LH 224). In contrast to the latter and its humanism, originary thinking holds that, 'Man is not the lord of beings. Man is the shepherd of being. Man loses nothing in this "less"; rather, he gains in that he attains the truth of being. He gains the essential poverty of the shepherd, whose dignity consists in being called by being itself into the preservation of being's truth' (LH 221).

To become fully human we all need to learn this dwelling which guards being's truth. How do we hear and guard being's truth? Heidegger says that we do so in originary thinking, which is a site where Heidegger shows how being, human being, language, and things come together. The relation of being to the essence of human beings is granted by being and is guarded and brought back to being by thinking as the two turn toward one another and meet in a common 'place' (LH 193). Heidegger claims that such originary thinking would not merely discuss the turning of being and humans into language; rather, it would attempt to think the turn which actually occurs as 'the only gift that can come to thinking from being. But it is also the case that the matter of thinking is not achieved in the fact that the talk about the "truth of being" and the "history of being" is set in motion. Everything depends on this alone, that the truth of being come to language and that thinking attain to this language' (LH 223).

Heidegger is not so bold as to claim that this gift has been given to him as a place where he is at home. As a result, he more modestly attempts to think a (preliminary) turning toward the truth of being. Any turn would involve the experience of the essence of thinking itself, in its approach to being and language. Indeed, as noted earlier, thinking is enabled and given by being and belongs to being, not beings. Essentially, then, thinking is to be understood 'by and for the truth of being' (LH 194). Again, this develops something misunderstood in *Being and Time*. Human being, as standing out into the unconcealment of being, has in thinking an 'ecstatic relation to the lighting of being' (LH 207). Thinking is called away from the representation of beings, which also treats being by means of the concept of beings, and toward a 'meditation on being itself' by thinking the truth of being (LH 227).

The changed charge for thinking is to reflect on what is nearest. Heidegger explicates, 'Being is farther than all beings and is yet nearer to man than every being, be it a rock, a beast, a work of art, a machine, be it angel or God. Being is the nearest. Yet the near remains farthest from man' (LH 210). 'He at first fails to recognize the nearest and attaches himself to the next nearest. He even thinks that this is the nearest. But nearer than the nearest and at the same time for ordinary thinking farther than the farthest is nearness itself: the truth of being' (LH 211–12). This nearest comes out before us by pushing aside all the veiling beings, for which it made an opening in the first place. That is, it turns toward us precisely out of the homelessness in which it keeps itself. Clearly this calls for a turning response in our thinking: 'can thinking refuse to think being after the latter has lain hidden so long in oblivion but at the same time has made itself known in the present moment of world history by the uprooting of all beings?' (LH 232).

Accordingly, the thinking which responds and attends to the near, calls it back from the far. It recalls the near. That is why Heidegger says that thinking recollects. 'Thought in a more primordial way, there is the history of being to which thinking belongs as recollection of this history that unfolds of itself' (LH 215). The essence of originary thinking now appears: 'Such thinking is, insofar as it is, recollective of being and nothing else' (LH 236). Recollective thinking is different from representational thinking. Because it does not reduce being to a concept but does think the truth of being, the former is more rigorous – which also means less 'logical,' understood representationally – than conceptual thinking (LH 235). Unlike metaphysics, it can thoughtfully 'reach and gather together what in the fullest sense of being now is,' namely, homelessness and turning to a homecoming to the truth of being (LH 221). This insight brings Heidegger back to language, because it is in historical language that being is entrusted to recollective thinking (LH 239). By way of the image of language as the house of being, where being appears in that house, Heidegger interprets being, language, human being, and thinking together. 'Thinking builds upon the house of being, the house in which the jointure of being fatefully enjoins the essence of man in the truth of being' (LH 236).

Earlier, Heidegger said that being gives human being and our relation to being, yet that relationship must be safeguarded. The preservation is accomplished in thinking, where 'To accomplish means to unfold something into the fullness of its existence, to lead it forth into this fullness – *producere.* But what "is" above all is being. Thinking accomplishes the relation of being to the essence of man' (LH 193). Though thinking brings forth the relation between being and human being, it does not make or cause this relation. As was the case with the poet, humans cannot claim to *create* being, beings, or the relationship between them. Only where these are already given, though in need of coming into their own, can humans help unfold them (LH 193; see also 216). Being's giving is prior. Following the gift, humans can accept the given relation and witness it: to do so is to bring it into the unconcealment which is being's truth. As Heidegger notes, 'Thinking brings this relation to being solely as something handed over to it from being' (LH 193).

Heidegger says, in short, that being and its relationship with the essence of human being become manifest in thinking. If we ask how this occurs, an answer is to be found in the image of the site of the coming together of being and humans as they unfold together in their house – in language. 'In thinking, being comes to language' (LH 193). The poets and thinkers in their careful saying accomplish 'the manifestation of being insofar as they bring the manifestation to language and maintain it in language through their speech' (LH 193). Recall that Hölderlin held that the saying of the holy, which was given to mortals, also needed the sayings of the poets to establish it. Here Heidegger is making a similar claim in regard to being. It is in language that we have something to hold on to, so we can heed and attend to it (LH 239).

Heidegger's third way of speaking yields a fuller interpretation of the relation of being, thinking, and language. Being gives itself, and thinking responds. This mutual turning toward one another occurs in language. Heidegger elaborates,

> For thinking in its saying merely brings the unspoken word of being to language.
>
> The usage 'bring to language' employed here is now to be taken quite literally. Being comes, lighting itself, to language. It is perpetually underway to language. Such arriving in its turn beings ek-sisting [human] thought to language in a saying. Thus language itself is raised into the lighting of being. (LH 239)

Where thinking is a deed, it is not understood metaphysically, as the subject's production of objects and powerful connections, but originally, as part of the unfolding of the relation of being and beings. In this accomplishment, thinking, by holding itself (listening) in being's coming, also 'lets itself be claimed by being so that it can say the truth of being. Thinking accomplishes this letting' (LH 194; see also 199). Such thoughtful saying would be far from any wilful self-imposition; just the opposite, historical saying (*Saga*) which belongs to the matter of thinking (being), 'lets being-be' (LH 236; see also 241).

In its thoughtful saying, thinking comes to being and lets being come forward too. Accordingly, Heidegger says that thinking can help bring us out of the painful separation from being and conduct us 'into the realm of the upsurgence of the healing [*des Heilens*]' (LH 237). Both the nihilistic rage against being and the healing occur only in being. Heidegger says, 'To healing being first grants ascent into grace; to raging its compulsion to malignancy' (even nihilism proceeds from being to nothing) (LH 238). Thinking must think both the nihilating essence of nothing and wholesome being and help bring them to language, which is accomplished when some humans go before the rest of us in thinking our homelessness and the homecoming to being, that is, in bringing it into language. For example, 'Those who think and those who create with words are the guardians of this home' (LH 193). The thinkers and poets accomplish the manifestation of being not merely by bringing it into language but also by maintaining it there, carefully guarding it. They first learn dwelling themselves and then help us. That is why, as noted earlier, Heidegger says that in thinking, which brings being into language, thinking builds on the house of being and therefore helps prepare its own home (LH 236). Language is the house of being and the home of humans because, in it, being and human being mutually hold and heed one another: 'This abode first yields the experience of something we can hold on to. The truth of being offers a hold for all conduct. "Hold" in our language means protective heed. Being is the protective hold that holds man in his ek-sistent essence to the truth of such protective heed – in such a way that it houses ek-sistence in language' (LH 239).

If the thinker and the poet help accomplish the mutual abode of being and human being, then they both belong to the history of being. Except on a few occasions, until 'Letter on Humanism,' Heidegger has distinguished the thinker and poet by saying that the former thinks and says being and the latter the holy, even though their respective experiences and journeys are remarkably parallel. Here, however, he is much bolder than ever before in explicitly speaking of the relation of the poet and being. (In the Hölderlin essays, Heidegger made but one mention of Hölderlin and *being* [*Beon, Seyn,* be-ing]; otherwise he always spoke of the holy.[19] He later broached the connection in 'What Are Poets For?,' as seen earlier in this chapter; see also WPF 95, 98, 142).

Heidegger dealt with Hölderlin in 'Letter on Humanism' precisely because the poet is not a humanist in the traditional sense but an originary thinker of human destiny in relation to being, which Heidegger also attempts to be. Hence, he contrasts Hölderlin with the famous eighteenth-century German humanists Winckelmann, Goethe, and Schiller (LH 201, 219). Hölderlin is, in his own way, closer to Nietzsche because both wrestle with metaphysical homelessness: 'Nietzsche was the last to experience this homelessness. From within metaphysics he was unable to find any other way out than a reversal of metaphysics. But that is the height of futility. On the other hand, when Hölderlin composes 'Homecoming' he is concerned that his "countrymen" find their essence. He does not at all seek that essence in an egoism of this nation. He sees it rather in the context of a belongingness to the sending of the West' (LH 217–18). For just this reason, Heidegger shifted from the metaphysical concerns of the works treated in chapter 1 to Hölderlin's poetic journey, considered in chapter 2.

Hölderlin goes before Heidegger in thinking the 'essence of the homeland,' 'world-historically out of nearness to the source' (LH 217, 218). But Heidegger holds, this historical movement in regard to the nearness of the source is nothing other than the history of being. Hölderlin's concern with the German people is no patriotism or nationalism, but attention to the German people's homecoming and learning to abide, along with those of other nations, close to being: 'The homeland [*Heimat*] of this historical dwelling is nearness to being' (LH 218 [169]).[20] Here, as thinker, Heidegger says being, instead of source, as did the poet Hölderlin. Heidegger continues, 'As the destiny that sends truth, being remains concealed. But the world's destiny is heralded in poetry, without yet becoming manifest in the history of being. The world-historical thinking of Hölderlin that speaks out in the poem "Remembrance" is therefore essentially more primordial and thus more significant for the future than the mere cosmopolitanism of Goethe' (LH 219).

Note what is happening here. Heidegger is now speaking about Hölderlin and using his poetry in quite a different way than in the Hölderlin commentaries. Those commentaries were just that, explications staying close to what the poet himself saw and said. There Heidegger followed after, as an apprentice who would learn to travel the same way with the guidance of the poet who had gone before. In contrast, here Heidegger speaks as the helper of the poet, that is, as one who, having taken up and preserved the poet's saying, not only continues to do so but becomes bolder to (properly) help make manifest what the poet only heralded (LH 219). Responding to the poet's word, Heidegger begins to say what is needed to accomplish the manifestation of being in thoughtful language that is his own (LH 193, 239). In this movement, as a thinker, Heidegger goes beyond Hölderlin into the thinker's own homecoming to being. As noted, where Hölderlin named the holy, Heidegger now says being.

But Heidegger does not simply or directly identify the source and being with one another. He needs to take up the relation of the holy and being, which is also one of the poet and the thinker. He notes that Hölderlin's meditations on the mysterious relations of the West to the East in 'The Ister,' 'The Journey,' and 'Remembrance' think, now in Heidegger's own words, 'nearness to being.'

> In such nearness, a decision may be made as to whether and how god and the gods withhold their presence and the night remains, whether and how the day of the holy dawns, whether and how in the upsurgence of the holy an epiphany of God and the gods [*im Aufgang des Heiligen ein Erscheinen des Gottes und der Götter*] can begin anew. But the holy, which alone is the essential sphere of divinity [*der Gottheit*], which in turn alone affords a dimension for the gods and for God, comes to radiate only when being itself beforehand and after extensive preparation has been illuminated and is experienced in its truth. Only thus does the over-coming of homelessness begin from being, a homelessness in which not only man but the essence of man stumbles aimlessly about. (LH 218 [169])

A great deal is going on here! Heidegger is articulating the relationship of the realms which the poet names: the Christian God and the gods are manifest in the dimension given by divinity; in turn, divinity moves in the open of the holy. But unlike the poet, who broke off after speaking of the upsurgence of the holy and of our home as a dwelling in proximity to this source, Heidegger continues. He says that *the holy originates in being,* where the latter primordially gives itself and must first be experienced. *This really is a turning for Heidegger,* but as we saw in *Contributions,* a turning for human being that is possible only *insofar as being has already begun turning, opening a between for human being/Da-sein and the gods.* Like the poet, the thinker experiences turning when the source shows itself as source and the thinker so experiences it. But in this instance, Heidegger names the source of the source (the holy): being. Being *is the primordial origin, even of the holy.* So, being would be the home of the holy. And a homecoming to the source, with a subsequent dwelling near to it, would be only the beginning of a deeper homecoming, one which would recognize that home is not the holy, but that which enables the holy. (Of course, learning to dwell near being is another matter.)

This insight helps to explain two important issues concerning Heidegger's relation to the poet and the realm of the sacred: how Heidegger makes use of sacred themes non-sacredly and how, from the vantage point of a turning, he self-referentially interprets his own earlier 'metaphysical' and poetic essays. Heidegger often uses obviously religious language and themes in his own way, while denying that any secularization is occurring.[21] To cite an instance, while commenting in 'Letter on Humanism' on a phrase from *Being and Time* ('Man ek-sists'), he notes, 'But it would be the ultimate error if one wished to explain the sentence about man's ek-sistent essence as if it were the secularized transference to human beings of a thought that Christian theology expresses about God (*Deus ist suum esse* [God is his being])' (LH 207). He then goes on to attempt to explain this non-metaphysically. A little later he contends that the forgetting of being in favour of beings 'is what ensnarement [*Verfallen*, literally a 'falling' or 'lapsing'], means in *Being and Time*. This word does not signify the "Fall of Man" understood in a "moral-philosophical" and at the same time secularized manner; rather, it designates an essential relationship of man to being within being's relationship to the essence of man' (LH 212).

First, Heidegger is distinguishing his – admittedly, still provisional – thought from a secular humanism, which as part of metaphysics shifts from a Greek understanding, through a Christian one, to the modern secularized anthropomorphism. This increasing oblivion appears in the transfer of the Christian idea of God as Creator into creativity as the function of human will (as Heidegger pointed out, for example, in 'The Word of Nietzsche'). Heidegger wants to make clear that even the inadequate language of *Being and Time* does not move within this metaphysical degeneration. Yet, Heidegger does not speak in a sacred way. He is neither de-secularizing nor re-sacralizing, as might be the poet who leads us out of the unholy back into the holy. He is not a poet; his home is not in the holy. Yet as he has just said, being is the origin of the holy and the human falling from being is to be interpreted within the mutual relationship of being and human existence. His thinking is neither theistic nor atheistic because it does not move toward or from God; it moves toward being itself. Heidegger's distinct thinking of being, the holy, and human being would be originary. A turning-around occurs here: rather than continuing on the metaphysical path from (Greek) being, through (Christian) God, to (modern) beings, Heidegger leads us 'backward' – he recollects – from beings, through God to divinity, through divinity to the holy, beyond the holy to being itself. His originary thinking and language move against any secularization because they remember back to the holy and even back to what is more originary than the holy (see LH, 218, 230).

We can see, in an unusually explicit moment, the development of Heidegger's thought through its first movement concerning the 'metaphysical' subject and limitations (for example, in *Being and Time*) and related works through its second pulse (the Hölderlin essays) to the third dimension, where Heidegger's own originary thinking and saying emerge more fully. In 'Letter on Humanism,' he densely clarifies this triple thinking 'In the lecture on Hölderlin's elegy "Homecoming" (1943) this nearness "of" being, which the *Da* of Dasein is, is (1) thought on the basis of *Being and Time;* (2) it is perceived as spoken from the minstrel's poem; (3) from the experience of the oblivion of being it is called the "homeland"' (LH 217). Heidegger is not saying that *Being and Time* is a totally metaphysical work or that any metaphysical thinking and language destroy the interpretation of Hölderlin, though he admits the limitations of his thinking and language in this period. Rather, he is showing that there are three related but changing aspects. That is the reason for the sentence just quoted having three parts. 1) *Being and Time* is the beginning or basis of Heidegger's thoughtful journey; 2) in the Hölderlin essay, the poet and his saying take precedence, though nearness is thought from out of *Being and Time;* and 3) out of the thought of *Being and Time* and that about Hölderlin's poems, there emerges, even then, an originary thinking which – as Heidegger's own, but beyond *Being and Time* – understands the nearness and oblivion in the language of being itself. Even if Heidegger's understanding of Hölderlin's words on historical human existence and homeland are limited by his still partially metaphysical resources, they are beginning to open originarily in an overcoming of the metaphysical.

From the vantage point of 'Letter on Humanism,' Heidegger celebrates the transformation of philosophy into recollective thinking: 'But thinking is an *adventure* not only as a search and an inquiry into the thought. Thinking, in its essence as thinking of being, is claimed by being' – which is what arrives, as *advent* (LH 240–1). From this turn, neither the homelessness of the oblivion of being nor the poet's homecoming can be allowed to slip into forgetfulness; both must constantly be recollected in the thinking that now might turn toward home. Consequently, Heidegger remains a companion to the poet. The holy and being begin to be more deeply understood in their belonging because 'the thinking that thinks from the question concerning the truth of being questions more primordially than metaphysics can. Only from the truth of being can the essence of the holy be thought. Only from the essence of the holy is the essence of divinity to be thought. Only in the light of the essence of divinity can it be thought or said what the word "God" is to signify ... The dimension of the holy ... indeed remains closed as a dimension if the open region of being is not lighted and in its lighting is near man. Perhaps what is distinctive about this world-epoch consists in the closure of the dimension of the hale [*das Heilen*]. Perhaps that is the sole malignancy [*Unheil*]' (LH 230).

In this closure, for all the accomplishment of the beginning of a turn, the poetic and thoughtful dwelling which protects the holy and being has yet to be fully learned. We have barely experienced the essence of being, beings, human beings, language and thinking. At most – and this may be to claim too much – some poets and thinkers, perhaps including Heidegger, may have experienced a turn which is occurring. Even if Heidegger does glimpse home and the turn toward it, we still dwell in homelessness, according to Heidegger, 'without yet being able properly to experience and take over this dwelling' (LH 217).

Because Heidegger's thinking prepares to heed a turn which comes from being, his increasingly originary understanding of being, language, thinking, and human being should be interpreted as part of thinking's journey home, that is, toward being and its house – language. Since Heidegger is attempting his own, proper, homecoming to being out of metaphysical homelessness, albeit with the necessary help of the poet, it would not be surprising if his journey would parallel the poet's. 'Letter on Humanism,' which consolidates Heidegger's movement and anticipated quest, evidences this comparison. Recall the six phases of the poet's journey: 1) living (unthoughtfully) near the source in the poet's youthful home; 2) wandering off in search of the foreign and enduring homelessness; 3) experiencing the source as source – the turning point which enabled a turning toward home; 4) a homecoming which was (*i*) the journey home, and then (*ii*) the moment of arrival home (all the while with homelessness kept hold of in memory); 5) the becoming at home in which the poet had to learn to abide; 6) this continually learned abiding becoming a dwelling near the source. In 'Letter on Humanism,' Heidegger deals with these same phases and indicates where he is on the journey. He speaks of 1) the primordial abode of the early Greeks; 2) metaphysical homelessness; 3) a turn (the originary understanding of being, human being, thinking, and language as our home and/in the house of being just considered above); 4) homecoming (our task); 5) and 6), the dwelling we have yet to learn, much less practise faithfully, and to which we cannot pretend to before the turn occurs.

Since Heidegger insists that we face our homelessness rather than nostalgically yearn for what is lost, in 'Letter on Humanism' he thinks it not as a peripheral matter, but as his focal concern. The questions which Jean Beaufret posed and which Heidegger answers here centre around humanism; but, Heidegger contends, 'Every humanism is either grounded in a metaphysics or is itself made to be the ground of one ... Accordingly, every humanism remains metaphysical' (LH 202). If he is to consider humanism, Heidegger initially, or still, proceeds from within metaphysics, and that means from the situation of our homelessness. He says, 'Indeed every inquiry into being, even the one into the truth of being, must at first introduce its inquiry as a "metaphysical" one' (LH 202).

Earlier, in speaking of being itself, Heidegger said that being enabled thinking. Now he adds that in metaphysical-representational thinking, 'being, as the element of thinking, is abandoned by the technical interpretation of thinking ... [Judging thinking by the standard of "logic"] may be compared to the procedure of trying to evaluate the nature and powers of a fish by seeing how long it can live on dry land. For a long time now, all too long, thinking has been stranded on dry land' (LH 195). (Note that here Heidegger speaks in accord with Hölderlin, for whom the source, flowing in the homey streams, was intimately related to the sea; the poets were as mariners.) Thought another way, metaphysics mistakes the light which humans create or (as the suprasensible) the divine light for the lighting of being. In fact, 'This means that the truth of being as the lighting itself remains concealed for metaphysics' (LH 211). The darkness of metaphysics is that it does not think being but beings as a whole (LH 202). This is oblivion not only to being but to beings too, and to the difference of being and beings (LH 202–3).

A related darkness also veils humanism, which emerges out of late Greek culture, develops especially in Roman civilization, then endures through the 'so-called Renaissance,' through the nineteenth century (with Marx) to existentialism in our time (with Sartre) (LH 200ff.). In metaphysical humanism the essence of human being is cut loose from being itself because it is always related to something other than being. The ancient definition of 'man' as a rational animal contrasts humans with other beings; the Christian definition contrasts humans with an other-worldly god and hence sees our life in 'this world' as 'only a temporary passage to the beyond'; Marx finds our humanity in society and 'nature' (LH 200ff.). Correspondingly, action which might achieve homecoming is impossible because the genuine action of a thinking which responds to and accomplishes being is precluded by subjectivistic activity and technological doing – which we mistake for action, though it is indeed powerful (LH 193, 216–17). Language, too, 'under the dominance of the modern metaphysics of subjectivity almost irremediably falls out of its element' and denies us its essence, its belonging to being. 'Instead, language surrenders itself to our mere willing and trafficking as an instrument of domination over beings' (LH 199). When language becomes the mere speech of the rational animal there is the covering up of 'the essence of language in the history of being' (LH 213).

Throughout, humanism, which is a metaphysics of human being in contrast to other beings, forgets being and consequently the essence of human being, language, thinking, and action (though this is not merely a human failing) (LH 208). This concealment of being in humanism is homelessness. 'Homelessness is coming to be the destiny of the world. Hence it is necessary to think that destiny in terms of the history of being. What Marx recognized in an essential and significant sense, though derived from Hegel, as the estrangement [*Entfremdung*] of man has its roots in the homelessness of modern man. This homelessness is specifically evoked from the destining of being in the form of metaphysics and through metaphysics is simultaneously entrenched and covered up as such' (LH 219).

Out of this homelessness, and therefore in opposition to metaphysical humanism, Heidegger attempts a turn home – a journey already underway in *Being and Time* (LH 210). However, as we began to see above, Heidegger himself notes that much of what was thought there was unavoidably still thought metaphysically. Yet, according to Heidegger, it is too easy to suppose that 'the attempt in *Being and Time* ended in a blind alley' (LH 223). That is, there *was* a first breakthrough. And as we have seen, Heidegger has continued on his (this) way. He insists that *Being and Time* contained aspects which did point beyond metaphysics. For instance, one aspect of calling human being ek-sistence was to think it as standing out beyond comparison with beings, in the truth of being (LH 204ff., 210). At the very least, since one should judge only 'after he himself has tried to go the designated way, or even better, after he has gone a better way, that is, a way befitting the question,' Heidegger asks that we see the work as preparatory insofar as it begins to kindle what must be tended later on (LH 223). The originary language to think this comes only gradually – and is still coming. The task of overcoming homelessness remains: 'In the face of the essential homelessness of man, man's approaching destiny reveals itself to thought on the history of being in this, that man find his way into the truth of being and set out on this find' (LH 221).

Clearly, Heidegger has, by the time of 'Letter on Humanism,' been on the voyage out into homelessness for a long time. But has he also begun to turn toward the home of being and human being? He speaks in 'Letter on Humanism' of his increasingly originary language and thinking as entering such a turning. Of course, in the first place, we have everything that he originarily says concerning being itself, language, thinking, and human being (treated just above). This does seem to show an experience and understanding 'beyond' metaphysics. In addition, Heidegger himself points out the difference between the movement of this originary thinking and that of metaphysics. His thinking, he says, moves close to the near, as did the poet's when recognizing the source as source. Heidegger describes this movement as a 'descent' and a 'step back,' thereby distinguishing it from the movement of metaphysical thinking and associating it with Hölderlin's remembrance. Heidegger says, 'Thinking does not overcome metaphysics by climbing still higher, surmounting it, transcending it somehow or other; thinking overcomes metaphysics by climbing back down into the nearness of the nearest. The descent, particularly where man has strayed into subjectivity, is more arduous and more dangerous than the ascent' (LH 231).

He employs the traditional hierarchical image here for the metaphysics that has ruled in the history of being since Plato: being, the realm of the suprasensible, is up; beings, in the realm of the sensible, are down. Platonism and Christianity thought metaphysically, by moving upward from particular beings to transcendent being (which still was understood metaphysically as supra-sensible being); Hegel, too, thought according to this image (LH 228ff.). What appeared to be a rejection of the hierarchy in the nineteenth and twentieth centuries was, in fact, merely a change which depended on, and therefore still shared, this image. Marx apparently inverted Hegelianism and Christianity by comprehending beings as everything, that is, by metaphysically determining that every being is the material of labour (LH 220). Nietzsche also inverted Platonic metaphysics while still remaining entangled in its fundamental scheme (see 'The Word of Nietzsche' 60–1); Sartre seemingly reversed the traditional relation between existence and essence (LH 208). 'But,' Heidegger points out, 'the reversal of a metaphysical statement remains a metaphysical statement. With it [Sartre, for example,] steps with metaphysics in the oblivion of the truth of being' (LH 208). The same is true of the 'Marxian and Nietzschean inversions' (LH 215).

Moving beyond inversions and reversals that still move back and forth between beings and being understood metaphysically but fail to turn toward being itself, Heidegger characterizes originary thinking as descending, not from being to beings, but out of metaphysics itself. The image indicates a humbling, homecoming movement, as opposed to the self-important willing and valuing which characterizes metaphysics in its completion. Such a descent involves giving up ourselves as understood subjectively and our power in favour of simple, homey being itself. Setting aside the grandiose pretension of 'absolute knowledge,' originary 'thinking is on the descent to the poverty of its provisional essence': gathering to the simple saying of being (LH 242).

Heidegger says that this descent of thinking to the nearness of being is also a 'step back' because, even when we draw near to the nearness of being by the descent of thinking, it remains hard to see what is near. Recall that Hölderlin, in his journey, had to make a double step back: he had to step away from the source which was close in his youth to see it, then he had to step back again toward it, holding his whole journey in memory. The step back of which Heidegger speaks corresponds clearly to the first of these movements and prepares for the second. As he describes the thinking care for being, 'Because there is something simple to be thought in this thinking it seems quite difficult to the representational thought that has been transmitted as philosophy. But the difficulty is not a matter of indulging in a special sort of profundity and of building complicated concepts; rather, it is concealed in the step back that lets thinking enter into a question that experiences – and lets the habitual opining of philosophy fall away' (LH 222). The step back is a stepping out of representational and back to originary thought, which would enable a homecoming – a step back to being.

For Heidegger, the change from metaphysics to thinking's descent and step back to being would be a turn. The direction would turn from the metaphysical movement away from being to an originary thinking toward it. Heidegger goes even further, asserting that what he has managed to say originarily concerning being, language, thinking, and human being *participates* in this turning. Note, he does not claim to create it or to complete it but does say that his thinking belongs to it. His surprisingly bold remark appears near the end of 'Letter on Humanism,' just after his saying that being always remains underway to language and brings humans with it (who, in turn, help bring the word of being to language by their historical, thoughtful saying; LH 239): 'But just now an example of the inconspicuous deed of thinking manifested itself. For to the extent that we expressly think the usage "bring to language" which was granted to language, think only that and nothing further, to the extent that we retain this thought in the heedfulness of saying as what in the future continually has to be thought, we have brought something of the essential unfolding of being itself to language' (LH 240).

In the language of 'Letter on Humanism,' the claim that being unfolds into language joins Heidegger's writing with Hölderlin's. Earlier, Heidegger had said that Hölderlin actually achieved a homecoming to the source in his poetry, by way of his remembering, establishing poetizing. Heidegger now speaks of his thoughts as retained in the heedfulness of saying and thinking, that is, of his thinking as a remembering saying (LH 240). Understood in regard to Hölderlin, even if Heidegger experiences and says a glimpse of the turn of being and thinking toward one another, his nearness is still far and must be remembered and interpreted on the long journey home and later in learning to dwell near being. Still, freed from representational-logical thinking, we can *learn* how to experience originary thinking, 'and that means at the same time to carry it through' (LH 194).

In this light, we can better understand Heidegger's famous remarks in 'Letter on Humanism' about his turn – though at the time when the work was published, less than a handful of Heidegger's intimates had an inkling of the existence of *Contributions*, much less of what he had begun to say there of enowning's turning and his own then critical assessment of the limitations of *Being and Time*. The turn refers to 'the adequate execution and completion of this other thinking that abandons subjectivity' (LH 207). Apparently, the turn into originary thinking was not accomplished in *Being and Time* as it was published – without the third division of the first part ('Time and Being'). Heidegger explains, 'The section in question was held back because thinking failed in the adequate saying of the turning [*Kehre*] and did not succeed with the help of the language of metaphysics ... This turning is not a change of standpoint from *Being and Time*, but in it the thinking that was sought first arrives at the location of that dimension out of which *Being and Time* is experienced, that is to say, experienced from the fundamental experience of the oblivion of being' (LH 208).

Heidegger says that enowning's turning-opening is responded to in originary thinking's response – together the two simultaneously enable bringing the oblivion of being and being's turning into originary language. For this, originary thinking itself must first be given the turn by being and so arrive at the turning. From this turning point alone can the oblivion of being be understood. In the language of the journey, after setting out into homelessness but failing to adequately understand and say it (in the works covered in chapter 1) and after witnessing the poet's homelessness and homecoming in originary poetizing (in the writings treated in chapter 2), Heidegger begins to come into the experience of being and originary language, which enables the (at least tentative) saying of a turning – which, in turn, could lead to a homecoming and (for the first time) the remembering understanding of the essence of homelessness and of home. At this point, 'Letter on Humanism' makes clear that, like the poet, Heidegger travels into homelessness and arrives at a turning point. From this vantage, prior to turning toward home in the homeward journey, Heidegger can understand the original home of thinking, the home where thinkers dwelt before metaphysical homelessness. This is like the poet's understanding of his youthful home, occurring only when the poet had enough distance to see what was near all along. Heidegger's experience of the turn, which steps back from metaphysical representation (that is, philosophy) also gives him the requisite distance. So, he takes up the primal home.

The originary meditation on being itself can alone, Heidegger says, reach the 'primal mystery for all thinking' which is concealed in the sayings of the early age of thinking. For example, what Parmenides says (*esti gar einai*, 'for there is being') and 'the primordial essence of *logos*' are 'still unthought today' (LH 214–15, 227). The thinking and saying of the early thinkers was not yet philosophy and was therefore prior to the disciplines of 'logic,' 'physics,' and 'ethics,' 'yet their thinking was neither illogical nor immoral' (LH 232). The same is true of the early poets' 'sagas,' such as the tragedies of Sophocles (LH 232). Heidegger briefly indicates the depth of this primal Greek thinking, in contrast to humanism's concept of 'ethics,' by listening to 'a saying of Heraclitus which consists of only three words [and yet] says something so simply that from it the essence of the ethos immediately comes to light' (LH 233). Heidegger argues that the saying *ēthos anthrōpōi daimōn* (Fragment 11) is normally mistranslated by modern metaphysical thinking as 'a man's character is his daimon.' In contrast, Heidegger claims, thought originarily and in a Greek way, 'Ethos means abode, dwelling place. The word names the open region in which man dwells. The open region of his abode allows what pertains to man's essence, and what in thus arriving resides in nearness to him, to appear. The abode of man contains and preserves the advent of what belongs to man in his essence. According to Heraclitus' phrase this is *daimos*, the god. The fragment says: Man dwells, insofar as he is man, in the nearness of god' (LH 233).

It is not accidental that when Heidegger reaches the turning point that provides *a vantage* from which to see the primal home, he hears Heraclitus speak of our essential abode as the region which allows the arrival of what resides near our dwelling – such a saying is parallel to Hölderlin's articulation of homecoming as coming to dwell in the proximity to the source. Further, according to Heidegger, Heraclitus says that we dwell, as humans, near a god, whereas Hölderlin similarly says that gods and mortals come to dwell together at the wedding festival. At the point of thinking's turning toward home, Heidegger finds that Heraclitus and Hölderlin both speak of home and also say the same concerning the originary character of home and human being's dwelling. Heidegger goes on to elaborate his interpretation of Heraclitus' fragment by recounting a story which Aristotle tells (*De parte animalium*, I, 5, 645a17): 'The story is told of something Heraclitus said to some strangers who wanted to come visit him. Having arrived, they saw him warming himself at a stove. Surprised, they stood there in consternation – above all because he encouraged them, the astounded ones, and called for them to come in with the words, "For here too the gods are present"' (cited in LH 233). If we listen carefully to Heidegger's commentary on this story we hear not only an explication of how primordial thinking thought human being, gods, and being, but what will come to characterize Heidegger's thinking too. As we will see in the following chapters, Heidegger becomes as much like Heraclitus as like Hölderlin. That is, as Heidegger works out what Heraclitus experienced and said, the latter increasingly becomes a guide, showing a way to homecoming thinking, as does Hölderlin. This means that when we, as readers and thinkers, come to hear Heidegger talk about home and homecoming, we must see ourselves reflexively as like the foreign visitors.

For these reasons, it is important to hear Heidegger's comments at length as he speaks of Heraclitus' saying the simple that resides near and about the way it abides in nearness. His words tell of home, once primal, which also is the end of the thinker's (Heidegger's) own homecoming. Heidegger says,

> The group of foreign visitors [*der fremden Besucher*], in their importune curiosity about the thinker, are disappointed and perplexed by their first glimpse of his abode. They believe they should meet the thinker in circum-

stances which, contrary to the ordinary round of human life, everywhere bear traces of the exceptional and rare and so of the exciting. The group hopes that in their visit to the thinker they will find things that will provide material for entertaining conversation – at least for a while. The foreigners who wish to visit the thinker expect to catch sight of him perchance at that very moment when, sunk in profound meditation, he is thinking. The visitors want this 'experience' not in order to be overwhelmed by thinking but simply so they can say they saw and heard someone everybody says is a thinker.

Instead of this the sightseers find Heraclitus by a stove. That is surely a common and insignificant place [*alltäglicher und unscheinbaren Ort*]. True enough, bread is baked here. But Heraclitus is not even busy baking at the stove. He stands there merely to warm himself. In this altogether everyday place he betrays the whole poverty of his life. The vision of a shivering thinker offers little of interest. At this disappointing spectacle even the curious lose their desire to come any closer. What are they supposed to do here? Such an everyday and unexciting occurrence – somebody who is chilled warming himself at a stove – anyone can find any time at home. So why look up a thinker? The visitors are on the verge of going away again. Heraclitus reads the frustrated curiosity in their faces. He knows that for the crowd the failure of an expected sensation to materialize is enough to make those who have just arrived leave. He therefore encourages them. He invites them explicitly to come in with the words *Einai gar kai entautha theous*, 'Here too the gods are present.'

This phrase places the abode (*ēthos*) of the thinker and his deed in another light. Whether the visitors understood this phrase at once – or at all – and then saw everything differently in this other light the story doesn't say. But the story was told and has come down to us today because what it reports derives from and characterizes the atmosphere surrounding this thinker. *Kai entauatha*, 'even here,' at the stove, in that ordinary place [*an diesem gewöhnlichen Ort*] where every thing and every condition, each deed and thought is intimate and commonplace [*vertraut und geläufig*], that is, familiar [*geheuer*], 'even there' in the sphere of the familiar, *einai theous*, it is the case that 'the gods are present.'

Heraclitus himself says, *ethos anthropoi daimion*, 'The (familiar) abode is for man the open region for the presencing of god (the unfamiliar one).'

If the name 'ethics,' in keeping with the basic meaning of the word *ethos*, should now say that 'ethics' ponders the abode of man, then that thinking which thinks the truth of being as the primordial element of man, as one who eksists, is in itself the original ethics. (LH 233–5 [183–6])

Without doubt, Heidegger's commentary does speak for itself. Yet we too may stress several points. Here Heidegger thinks the primal Greek understanding of being as home and as the simple. That is an originary experience and understanding. Heidegger finds that Heraclitus shows his *foreign* visitors (*die Fremden*) being in the image of the hearth that warms; Hölderlin showed Heidegger the holy in precisely this same way; later we will see Heidegger also show us the same. The atmosphere surrounding the thinker is familiar. But it is radically different than the commonplace or ordinary which is *unheimlich* – the latter initiated the journey into homelessness and continues to pervade it; the former is what was close, as experienced in a turning point: the near and truly homey. The two are separated by the journey through homelessness and by the turning. Here Heidegger also says what thinking is and is not. It is a humble way of belonging and dwelling at home, which clarifies Heidegger's own attempts at originary thinking and his critics' misunderstanding of that effort. He produces no ethics and avoids humanism, precisely because humanistic – that is, metaphysical – thinking and ethics wander in homelessness, rather than ponder the abode of human being (*ethos*) as originary thinking does. Just as the sceptical visitors are welcomed in by Heraclitus' words, 'Here too the gods are present' (and as they are by Hölderlin's poetry about the wedding feast of mortals and gods), so we are invited with what interests us in our subjectivistic homelessness by Heidegger's saying, in effect, 'Here too human being finds a dwelling place and home becomes present.'

In brief, the deeds and abodes of Heraclitus and Hölderlin appear to be the same. And Heidegger's own thinking – in this turning to being – also comes to this same place. The story Heidegger retells, and upon which he comments, articulates the essence of home. In homelessness, home is far away; and yet, as understood at the turning point, home is near – though the journey from the turning point to home remains ahead and is a long one. *The story of Heraclitus keeps safe the essence of home that Heidegger must hold on to in thinking as he passes through the turning point and begins his actual homecoming. It also provides hints as to how we are to understand and follow Heidegger's thinking homecoming – it helps us see what to look for (anticipate).*

In 'Letter on Humanism,' Heidegger finds himself, at the juncture of the third and fourth phases of homecoming (according to the poet's articulation). 1) He has left his home (and has meditated on thinking's primal home from the vantage of his turning); 2) he has endured homelessness (in his early works and with the poet, as considered in chapters

1 and 2, and in the works taken up in this chapter, since homelessness must always be remembered in thinking); 3) he experienced the turn of being and thinking (as related in the essays treated in this chapter). It is far too early to pretend to the originary thinking and language necessary for stage 5, learning to become at home, and for stage 6, dwelling near the Source. What is proper next, then, is to turn from the turning point itself (stage 3) to homecoming (stage 4) – remembering that on the journey home all the movements, phases, and places of the journey thus far are to be recollected and held in thinking, which means increasingly pondered and, hopefully, ever more deeply understood. The task is not to 'check off' homecoming as a fleeting experience now 'accomplished' as we rush on to the next venture. Instead we need to attend to the joint between the turn toward home and homecoming, we need to let the phenomena of homecoming be.

Because we do not yet really encounter the mystery, we must persevere through homelessness and the lack of fully adequate originary language: 'But if man is to find his way once again into the nearness of being he must first learn to exist in the nameless' (LH 199). We do this by giving up our self-importance and talking and letting ourselves be claimed by being and its language. 'Only thus will the preciousness of its essence be once more bestowed upon the word, and upon man a home for dwelling in the truth of being' (LH 199, 207). By holding on to and heeding our homelessness we still seek the near; but, after the turn, it becomes possible to journey *toward* it, rather than simply out into the foreign. Accordingly, Heidegger says, 'Let us also in the days ahead remain as wanderers on the way *into* the neighborhood of being' (LH 224).[22]

What Heidegger says in 'Letter on Humanism' and elsewhere (e.g., *Contributions*) makes clear that we should not expect an easy or short journey home from this point – for all the importance of the turning of *Ereignis* and the possibility for responding-thinking which is occurring. On the one hand, homecoming, homelessness, and the turning itself must constantly be thought and more deeply experienced, lest the trip home fall into forgetfulness and become easy but superficial meandering, rather than genuine homecoming.[23] On the other hand, the turning has just begun, since even in the initial coming of originary language and thinking there is barely a glimpse of the *beginning* of the turning toward one another by being and human being. Receiving and learning originary language and thinking will be a long and difficult task, even as it is necessary for the turning and homecoming to continue to come – that is, for the nearness of being to human being to come nearer still.

Accordingly, Heidegger's thinking and saying are not radically different after the turning which occurs in the essays treated in this chapter. Still, we do see and hear a change from his early metaphysical language and thinking to what begins in *Contributions* and then continues to develop as originary language and thinking. We find a difference that does not imply abandoning altogether what he thought and said on the outward journey into the homelessness of metaphysics. This is clear in essays such as 'Overcoming Metaphysics,' 'The Word of Nietzsche,' 'What Are Poets For?,' and 'Letter on Humanism,' where the language characteristic of metaphysics and, for example, *Being and Time*, continues but is permeated, and increasingly displaced, by originary language. Heidegger's own comments on *Being and Time* are important in this regard because they acknowledge that *Being and Time* was limited by its metaphysical language, yet that it began to point to and open to originary language, in which he becomes more and more nearly at home.

Reviewing Heidegger's thinking journey thus far also shows us its future itinerary as a homecoming through homelessness. In chapter 1 we saw Heidegger think metaphysics, that is, the era of homelessness in the history of being, as well as the possibility of thinking this homelessness from a point of view outside of metaphysics. In the essays of chapter 2, he thought the poet's homecoming out of homelessness to a new, originary homecoming and learning to dwell near the holy. In the works covered by this chapter, Heidegger attempts to join the understanding gained through the first two 'alternatives' – metaphysical homelessness and originary homecoming – to find the thinking and saying required for his own way home. In these works he begins to experience originary language for himself and, by his thinking here, to 'risk a shock that could for the first time cause perplexity ... [and] awaken a reflection – if the world-historical movement [of being] did not itself already complete such a reflection – that thinks not only about man but also about the "nature" of man, not only about his nature but even more primordially about the dimension in which the essence of man, determined by being itself, is at home' (LH 225). This thinking turns toward home.

But since in the turn itself homecoming is just able to begin, and certainly not be completed, the turn opens out to the remaining journey. Heidegger acknowledges that, 'At best, thinking could perhaps point toward the truth of being, and indeed toward it as what is to be thought. It would thus be more easily weaned from mere supposing and opining and directed to the now rare handicraft of writing' (LH 223). Where his attempts at the handicraft of writing must try to go is at least tentatively clear from the point of view of the turning toward home. The journey back will be continuous with the journey thus far. Heidegger is embarked on but one journey, where the travel out into the foreign and strange (*unheimlich*) and the trip back home are discernable phases of one complex experience. Homelessness and homecoming are not accidentally joined or disjoined; homelessness belongs together with, and is part of, homecoming. In addition, there will be an obvious symmetry between homelessness and homecoming because the return home re-covers the same ground as the outward journey. After, and because of, the turning toward one another of being and human being, it is possible to better understand the landscape – and that includes home itself. Still, we expect a change. The understanding will be different because it is originary. Homecoming will not be a mere repetition of what already occurred but an originary recollection. For example, metaphysical homelessness, originary thinking and language, being and human being, homecoming and poetic dwelling will all be thought and said in a way which is thinking's (and Heidegger's) own way – neither the way of metaphysics (that is, philosophy) nor the way of poetry.

Foremost on the itinerary of homecoming, then, is a stepping back into and recollecting of homelessness, which remains, while moving toward being, a movement through (*i*) the primordial home; (*ii*) philosophy and metaphysical homelessness; and (*iii*) the thinking and home yet to come. Remaining wanderers across this three-dimensioned realm, we need to attempt to think the uprooting of all beings and how being shows itself here, since, as Heidegger says, 'The history of being is never past but ever stands before' (LH 194). A) Being directs thinking 'at the present moment of the world's destining into the primordial dimension of its historical abode' (LH 231). Farthest back, though still before us, is the thinking and saying of the early Greeks, and what they thought, because it 'is still unthought today' (LH 215). This is the land of original thinking, which came to an end (LH 195). B) Closer by in the long metaphysical present which stretches from the Greeks to today, and is not over yet, is the sphere of philosophy and the homelessness of contemporary human beings (LH 217). C) Finally, there is the realm of the recollective thinking which we need to learn and which belongs to the history of being, by recollecting the unfolding of that history (LH 215). Heidegger says that 'the thinking that is to come is no longer philosophy, because it thinks more originally that metaphysics – a name identical to philosophy' (LH 242).

These three movements which form the journey back through homelessness are unified in that they all think the truth of being, even though it unfolds its history in complex ways, including its various ways of obscuring itself. Heidegger makes the point another way where he says all thinking (including all homeless philosophy) 'remains where it is in order constantly to think the same' (LH 215). He explains, 'To bring to language ever and ever again this advent of being which remains, and in its remaining waits for man, is the sole matter of thinking. For this reason essential thinkers always say the same. But that does not mean the identical. Of course they say it only to him who undertakes to think back on them … To risk discord in order to say the same is the danger' (LH 241).[24] Because all essential thinking belongs to being – including that of metaphysical thinkers, where being's truth is deeply sheltered in being itself and thereby concealed – Heidegger says, 'All refutation in the field of essential thinking is foolish. Strife among thinkers is the "lover's quarrel" concerning the matter itself. It asserts them mutually toward a simple belonging to the same, from which they find what is fitting to them in the destiny of being' (LH 216).

In addition to the journey back through homelessness to thinking's primal and still coming home, thinking has a second major project. It must learn to think originarily, and that means it must articulate house and dwelling. We have seen that in 'Letter on Humanism,' Heidegger notes 1) that the reference in *Being and Time* to being-in as dwelling is no accident; 2) that the same reference in 'Hölderlin and the Essence of Poetry' is deliberate; and 3) that it is as deliberate as the talk in 'Letter on Humanism' about the house of being. Given what Heidegger consistently and explicitly says in all three strands of his thinking thus far (the metaphysical homelessness, the poet's homelessness and homecoming, and Heidegger's own attempt to find his way in light of the first two), the task that lies ahead is clear. He says, 'But one day we will, by thinking the essence of being in a way appropriate to the matter, more readily be able to think what "house" and "to dwell" are' (LH 237). Since Heidegger says that the house of being is language – the house which thinking never creates but builds upon – the appropriate way to think the essence of being is by trying to understand what it is to say that language is the house of being and the home of human being. This journey of thinking will also need to pass through the same three moments of the journey back: from the primal understanding of language, through its metaphysical obscurity, to its originary, essential character. The first realm is that of 'the world's primordial belongingness to being' (LH 198); in the second, language denies us its essence in that it appears as an instrument for our willing or as expression (e.g., LH 199); in the third sphere, thought and poetry liberate language 'into a more original essential framework,' that is, into its mystery (LH 194, 199). Of course, in thinking of language as home, the thinking again will come close to the poets.

A third dimension on the itinerary appears out of the second. If thinking is to think the essence of being and thereby appropriately think what house and dwelling are, and if, as we heard in the auspicious story about Heraclitus, being comes in the near or simple and familiar, then Heidegger would need to think home and dwelling in a more familiar way (than as representational language). House and dwelling would have to be thought by way of simple things and our familiar homes. This journey, as the other two, would pass from an original being at home where we once dwelt surrounded by familiar things and through the experience of the ordinary and commonplace as the *unheimlich* which obscures both being and the things themselves. Here thinking would need to understand the 'forgetting the truth of being in favor of the pressing throng of beings unthought in their essence,' which is what 'ensnarement [*verfallen*] already meant in *Being and Time*' (LH 212). But this is yet to come because 'What is strange is the thinking of being in its simplicity. Precisely this keeps us from it' (LH 240). The end of this thinking for Heidegger would be achieving his own understanding and saying of the familiar and home.

That Heidegger looks forward to these last-mentioned journeys home (where home, being, language, and thing are all simple) is apparent from the way he ends 'Letter on Humanism,' speaking reminiscently of Hölderlin's poem about the poet being grown by nature (the holy) just as the crops were nurtured by nature and the farmer. Of thinking and of his own coming path as a thinker, Heidegger notes, 'Thinking gathers language into simple saying. In this way language is the language of being, as clouds are the clouds of the sky. With its saying, thinking lays inconspicuous furrows in language. They are still more inconspicuous than the furrows that the farmer, slow of step, draws through the field' (LH 242).[25]

'Letter on Humanism' is obviously a central work: it collects Heidegger's previous movement and holds the turning toward one another of being and human being in thinking and language. Three major insights are given here, all of which need to be thought through: 1) homelessness and homecoming are characteristics of the relationship between being itself (which as advent enables, gives, and appropriates) and thinking (which delineates the relation); 2) language is the house of being and the home of humans; 3) Heraclitus tell us that the primordial home (the abode of the thinker) is to be found in the intimate and familiar (*geheuer*) (234 [186]).

The immediate task for Heidegger, however, is to let the turning come, rather than rushing precipitously toward what he barely glimpses. In this self-restraint, through which thinking would attempt to let itself and thereby being and human being into language, thinking must be careful not to try to say more than it can. To come to language, thinking must be quiet and listen to the saying of being – just as poetry must listen to the saying of the holy before it speaks its own word. Here what is needed is a 'proper silence' before being's silent saying. 'But who of us today would want to imagine that his [the thinker's] attempts to think are at home on the path of silence' (LH 223)? If, at best, we could move toward the truth of being, we would need 'to attend to the fittingness of thoughtful saying,' which 'does not imply, however, that we contemplate at every turn *what* is to be said of being and *how* it is to be said. It is equally essential to ponder *whether* what is to be said is to be said' (LH 241). The cohesion of this hopefully thoughtful and shy saying is thus triply determined 'by the law of the fittingness of thought on the history of being: rigor of meditation, carefulness of saying, frugality with words' (LH 241). The step at hand is to bring these characteristics to bear on thinking what is closest: the turning itself.

As we might expect from the story of the poet's homecoming, the moment of turning for a thinker also exhibits a burst of originary language and thinking. The exuberance of the experience manifests itself this way, of course, but since the turning originates not in any human doing but from being itself, the extraordinary character is part of the epiphany of being turning toward human beings. Heidegger says this turning in noticeably originary language in a brief essay based on a lecture given in 1949, 'The Turning' ('*Die Kehre*'). The language of this essay is unusual, to say the least. If we look at this or that originary word, we find that most have previously appeared, often in the Hölderlin essays, and of course, in the long unpublished, unknown *Contributions.* But before 'The Turning,' Heidegger has not publicly used originary language so exclusively and densely. The language almost stops us in our tracks: the first sentence says, 'The essence of enframing is that settling-upon gathered into itself which entraps the truth of its own coming to presence with oblivion' (Tu 36). There are two reasons why Heidegger begins to speak this way. First, the language marks the difference between the originary thinking (homecoming) which occurs after the turning and the still somewhat metaphysical thinking (homelessness) that went before it. Second, as Heidegger holds, the homecoming comes only in being's and our mutual turning into originary language. Necessarily, then, if it unfolds at all, thinking will increasingly move in originary language.

Homecoming is not inherently faster than homeless wandering; indeed, we might expect it to be a slower, more careful and deliberate journey, especially since, as it goes along, it must also recollect and gather together what went before and what remains coming. If we are to understand the story of homecoming, and follow Heidegger on his homecoming, let alone attempt to achieve our own, we too have to go by way of originary thinking and saying. In this language, Heidegger thinks and tells the story of homecoming, attempts to achieve his own homecoming, and heuristically aids us in our efforts. 'The Turning' focuses on the turning toward one another of being and human being which enables the latter's homecoming. That means, first of all, that before a turning can be a turn toward home, it is a turn away from homelessness. Heidegger reminds us that our homelessness is not primarily due to any shortcoming on our part (though we do bear responsibility for our increasing subjectivism, for example), but instead originates in being itself. Our uncanny lack of a place to be at home takes place within a displacement of being. Of all the dangers we face, we stand helpless before being's concealing itself; cut off from being, we remain homeless. Yet, more dangerous still is that this self-concealment itself 'remains veiled and disguised. This disguising is what is most dangerous in the danger' (Tu 37). The turning, then, begins with being's turning, with the unconcealment of the concealment of being. That is not to say concealment ceases, but that being lets its concealment show itself for what it is. Turning begins with being's coming to presence as concealment and unconcealment.

In our time, according to Heidegger, 'the danger is the epoch of being coming to presence as enframing' (Tu 43). 'Enframing' (*das Ge-stell*) names the way being comes to presence by concealing its coming. Its coming is held in oblivion because everything – that means all beings and all relations of beings – appears to us as a standing-reserve (Tu 36–7). By *enframing*, Heidegger names the way all beings are set in relationships as a supply to be used in contemporary technology.[26] He is not saying that enframing is avoidable. It is the way being now both gives itself to us and conceals itself from us. Our specific danger – the way being comes concealed (which may itself be veiled) – is this coming to presence of Enframing. Heidegger says, 'But where is the danger? What is the place for it? Inasmuch as the danger is being itself, it is both nowhere and everywhere. It *has* no place as something other that itself. It is itself the placeless dwelling place of all presencing. The danger is the epoch of being coming to presence as Enframing' (Tu 43).

So being is the primal home: the home of all dwelling. But being itself 'comes to pass' in a strange, unhomely way: 'what comes to presence is this, that being dismisses and puts away its truth into oblivion in such a way that being denies its own coming to presence' (Tu 43). It now happens that the concealment (for example, in Enframing) of being begins to shed its disguise so that it appears *as* concealment. This is the first turning of the oblivion of being out of oblivion. While being would still be in darkness rather than light, its darkness is seen for what it is. That is why Heidegger observes that, 'Perhaps we stand already in the shadow cast ahead by the advent of *this* turning' (Tu 41). Such an initial turning comes from being because its concealment is no longer merely concealment (even when disguised) but the way being comes. Heidegger elaborates this seemingly strange coming:

> But what happens there where the danger comes to pass as the danger and is thus for the first time unconcealedly danger?
>
> That we may hear the answer to this question, let us give heed to the beckoning sign that is preserved in some words of Hölderlin. At the beginning of the later version of his Hymn 'Patmos,' the poet says:
>
> But where the danger is, grows
> The saving power also. (Tu 42)

At this point, Heidegger makes a bold claim. He says that these words can be thought more fully than ever before in originary thought: 'If now we think these words still more essentially than the poet sang them, if we follow them in thought as far as they go, they say: Where the danger is as the danger, there the saving power is already thriving also. The latter does not appear incidentally. The saving power is not secondary to the danger. The selfsame danger is, when it is *as* the danger, the saving power. The danger is the saving power, inasmuch as it brings the saving power out of its –the danger's – concealed essence that is ever susceptible of turning' (Tu 42).

Being conceals and unconceals itself. It comes as danger and as saving power. It advances as and into homelessness; it can turn into the advent of homecoming. At the moment of advent it would be a turning. Being would save itself and human being from homelessness by beginning its own turn. Heidegger originarily thinks what being's saving means: 'It means to loose, to emancipate, to free, to spare and husband, to harbor protectingly, to take under one's care, to keep safe ... That which genuinely saves is that which keeps safe, safekeeping' (Tu 42). Obviously this is the language of homecoming, home, dwelling, and the growth and nurturing which take place in them. 'To save' means 'to bring and keep home.'[27]

Because the turning of being would begin with oblivion's turning to stand as oblivion and with its abiding as oblivion, being's own turning becomes its safe keeping out of oblivion and its coming as this safe keeping. The oblivion staying as oblivion comes to recollective thinking. Safe keeping can come to thinking too, as Heidegger explains: 'Thus rescued through this abiding from falling away out of remembrance, it is no longer oblivion. With such in-turning, the oblivion relating to being's safe-keeping is no longer the oblivion of being; but rather, turning in thus, it turns about into the safekeeping of being' (Tu 43). Here being appears not only as advent and the turning of oblivion into 'the safekeeping belonging to the presence of being,' but as that which grants a favour. Even in its self-concealment, this as-yet-ungranted favour was harboured by being. Now, according to Heidegger, 'in the coming to presence of the danger there comes to presence and dwells a favor [*wohnt eine Gunst*], namely, the favor of the turning about of the oblivion of being into the truth of being. In the coming to presence of the danger, where it *is* as the danger, is the turning about into the safekeeping, is this safekeeping itself, is the saving power of being' (Tu 44).

Being grants homecoming by first granting a turning, a turning which it held and safeguarded throughout homelessness. Heidegger puts it succinctly, albeit densely: 'As the danger [that is, as coming to presence as Enframing], being turns about into the oblivion of its coming to presence, turns away from this coming to presence, and in that way simultaneously turns counter to the truth of its coming to presence. In the danger there holds sway this turning about not yet thought on. In the coming to presence of the danger there *conceals* itself, therefore, the possibility of a turning in which the oblivion belonging to the coming to presence of being will so turn itself that, with *this* turning, the truth of the coming to presence of being will expressly turn in [*einkehrt*] – turn homeward – into whatever is' (Tu 41).

To lay out the distinct dimensions Heidegger specifies five aspects of the turning: 1) being turns *away* from its mode of coming to presence; and thus 2) turns *counter* to its unconcealment; 3) this same movement is a turning *about*, then, into the oblivion of its coming to presence; and this is so because 4) it is a turning *into* and *abiding* of oblivion (unconcealed and belonging to being as such and therefore no longer an oblivion of being but a turn *about* and *into* the safe keeping of being); and when oblivion becomes this safe keeping, 5) the unconcealment of the coming to presence of being will *turn in toward home* (Tu 41, 44–5).

In all this turning, Heidegger finds only being. No being or human being is cause or effect here because, necessarily, being itself adapts itself and its mode of coming to presence. Therefore Heidegger says, 'Sheerly, out of its own essence of concealedness, being brings itself to pass into its epoch' (Tu 44). To say that being turns homeward into whatever is, is not to say that being turns toward and enters into particular beings. Rather, it turns into that which genuinely is (*Das was eigentlich ist*), where, as Heidegger explains, 'What genuinely is, i.e., what expressly dwells and endures as present in the "is," is uniquely being. Only being "is," only in being and as being does that which the "is" names bring itself to pass; that which is, is being from out of its essence' (Tu 44). Being itself turns itself home. Its home is nowhere else and nothing else than itself. Being *is its own home, and being uniquely turns toward home to dwell and endure as present, that is, as itself, as home* (Tu 44). (Heidegger had first written, but not made public, that 'being was its own abode' some fifteen years before, in *Contributions*).

Heidegger speaks of being's homecoming not only in terms of place and enduring dwelling, but since this homecoming is the advent of unconcealment of place and dwelling, in terms of opening-lighting. He says, 'In this turning, the clearing belonging to the essence of being suddenly clears itself and lights up. This sudden self-lighting is the lightning flash. It brings itself into its own brightness ... [When] the truth of being flashes, the essence of being clears and lights itself up. Then the truth of the essence, the coming to presence, of being turns and enters in' (Tu 44). Thought this way, where being's turn to its own homecoming is also the lightning flash of its own essence, *being brings itself back into its own proper place,* as *lighting-clearing.* Heidegger develops this language: '"To flash" [*blitzen*], in terms of both its derivation and of what it designates, is "to glance" [*blicken*]. In the flashing glance and as that glance, the essence, the coming to presence, of being enters into its own emitting of light. Moving through the element of its own shining, the flashing glance retrieves that which it catches sight of and brings it back into the brightness of its own looking – and yet that glancing, in its giving of light, simultaneously keeps safe the concealed darkness of its origin as the unlighted. The in-turning [*Einkehr*] that is the lightning-flash of the truth of being is the entering, flashing glance – insight [*Einblick*]' (Tu

45). When the oblivion of being turns into being's safe keeping, and being thereby turns in to itself, there is not just turning-in (*Einkehr*) and entering (*Einblick*), but the flashing-in (*Einblitz*) of being's unconcealment into hiddenness. Because being's taking-place is nothing other than being's taking-lighting its own place, Heidegger says, following what language itself puts together, 'Disclosing coming-to-pass is bringing-to-sight that brings into its own [*Ereignis ist eignende Eräugnis*]' (Tu 45).[28]

This difficult language and thinking articulate a genuine reversal – turning. All that we might ordinarily and metaphysically say and think is turned around with this originary turning of being and language. Metaphysically, we might say that human beings gain insight into beings; originarily, Heidegger says being turns and as entering glance comes to pass (*Ereignet*) as being. He elaborates this turn, though the first paragraph of comment (following) is almost impenetrable:

> *Insight into that which is* – this designation now names the disclosing that brings into its own that is the coming-to-pass of the turning within being, of the turning of the denial of being's coming to presence into the disclosing coming-to-pass of being's safekeeping. Insight into that which is, is itself the disclosing that brings into its own, as which the truth of being relates itself and stands in relation to truthless being ... From the first and almost to the last it has seemed as though 'insight into that which is' means only a glance such as we men throw out from ourselves into what is. We ordinarily take 'that which is' to be whatever is in being. For the 'is' is asserted of what is in being. But now everything has turned about. Insight does not name any discerning examination [*Einsicht*] into what is in being that we conduct for ourselves; insight [*Ein-blick*] as in-flashing [*Einblitz*] is the disclosing coming-to-pass of the constellation of the turning within the coming to presence of being itself, and that within the epoch of Enframing. That which is, is in no way that which is in being. For the 'it is' and the 'is' are accorded to what is in being only inasmuch as what is in being is appealed to in respect to its being. In the 'is,' 'being' is uttered: that which 'is,' in the sense that it constitutes the being of what is in being, is being. (Tu 46)

Obviously, for all his accomplishment, at this point Heidegger can only try to say what is needed in a way that only a few could or would be interested in following. Much more remains to be done to achieve clarity in thought and saying – let alone the delineation of house and dwelling as simple and familiar, as was in fact better achieved in 'Letter on Humanism.' But, more positively, Heidegger has come to a thinking and saying turning in a double way. We turn back to being. Or, rather, *we hear the thinking story of being's turning back to its own,* that is, *of being's own turn toward a homecoming to itself.* It is not just that Heidegger says and thinks that being's turning is coming to pass; in addition, he says and thinks being *as the disclosing–coming to pass* of turning (*Ereignis der Kehre*) (see also *Contributions*). Being's turn toward a homecoming opens up the prospect for a turning about for human being, which also might turn into a homecoming. For that to happen, human being's turning would have to be understood originarily. We could no longer think of homecoming as a merely human activity, for example, as the coming to a place of our own technological, political, or artistic creation. It would have to be thought out of, and as belonging to, the turning and coming to pass of being itself. Heidegger explains this turned or reversed understanding:

> When insight comes disclosingly to pass, then men are the ones who are struck in their essence by the flashing of being. In insight, men are the ones who are caught sight of.
>
> Only when man, in the disclosing coming-to-pass of the insight by which he himself is beheld, renounces human self-will and projects himself toward that insight, away from himself, does he correspond in his essence to the claim of that insight. (Tu 47)

Being turns homeward by beginning a turning within technology. That is why in its essence technology must be understood as belonging to being. We have to pass beyond thinking of technology as a human product and begin to see it as a way in which 'being itself takes place so as to adapt itself' (Tu 38). Strange as it seems, the essence of technology is being itself. Accordingly, turning to think the nature of technology is turning toward being. But to turn toward what is essential in technology, human being must first turn away from the self-willing which masks its essence, and 'must first and above all find its way back into the full breadth of the space proper to its essence' (Tu 39). The turning toward home by being thus opens for humans a turning into our essence (our home). Further, since human being comes back to its essence by coming back to being, this movement would begin the homecoming of being and human being in language and thinking which, in turn, would precede a dwelling together. Heidegger explains, 'The essential space of man's essential being receives the dimension that unites it to something beyond itself solely from out of the conjoining relation that is the way in which the safe keeping of being itself is given to belong to the essence of man as the one who is needed and used by being. Unless man first establishes himself beforehand in the space proper to his essence and there takes up his dwelling, he will not be capable of anything essential within the destining now holding sway' (Tu 39–40).

From being's turning, Heidegger's thinking takes a turn toward human essence and its belonging to being.

> It is toward the great essence of man that we are thinking, inasmuch as man's essence belongs to the essence of being and is needed by being to keep safe the coming to presence of being into its truth.
>
> Therefore, what is necessary above all is this: that beforehand we ponder the *essence* of being as that which is worthy of thinking; that beforehand, in thinking this, we experience to what extent we are called upon first to trace a path for such experiencing and to prepare that path as a way into that which till now has been impassable. (Tu 48)

The home of human being would lie in being, and our homecoming would be a going into our proper belonging to being. We would turn toward this belonging and accomplish it by travelling the paths of thinking, which themselves move within the sphere of language.

According to Heidegger, we would begin to respond to being's turn by opening ourselves to the way it comes, even when it comes dangerously, concealed in enframing and technology. We begin to do so, not by affirming and promoting technology, nor through any other 'doing,' but by thinking its manner of holding sway (Tu 39). That means we really have to begin by reflecting on thinking itself, which Heidegger does by partly describing our thinking in terms of a homecoming to being and language (the house of being). He holds that we need to begin to ponder the following:

> *How must we think?* For thinking is a genuine activity, genuine taking a hand, if to take a hand means to lend a hand to the essence, the coming to presence, of being. This means: to prepare [build] for the coming to presence of being that abode in the midst of whatever is into which being brings itself and its essence to utterance in language. Language first gives to every purposeful deliberation its ways and its byways. Without language, there would be lacking to every doing every dimension in which it could bestir itself and be effective. In view of this, language is never primarily the expression of thinking, feeling, and willing. Language is the primal dimension within which man's essence is first able to correspond at all to being and its claim,

> and, in corresponding, to belong to being. *This primal corresponding,* expressly carried out, *is thinking.* Through thinking, we first learn to dwell in the realm in which there comes to pass the restorative surmounting of the sending of being, the surmounting of Enframing. (Tu 40–1)

Our task is to participate in homecoming by preparing to think being and our belonging to it. We prepare for such thinking and belonging by learning to think within language and *to follow its paths.* First, we need to learn how to enter genuinely into language. Only after such a turning, which overcomes homelessness and turns into the realm of language where we might meet with being, would we learn to dwell there too – we would learn the latter through thinking (Tu 40–1). Because our homecoming to our essence is a movement toward our belonging to being and being's turn, our essence includes awaiting being's coming. We should not, then, be anxious to know whether being is now turning. The coming to pass of turning is nothing we can speed up or encourage, because the 'essence [of man] is to be the one who attends upon the coming to presence of being in that in thinking he guards it. Only when man, as the shepherd of being, attends upon the truth of being can he expect an arrival of a destining of being and not sink to the level of a mere wanting to know' (Tu 42).

We guard being's coming in thinking because thinking which recollects and remembers, holds on to what comes, and because thoughtful saying preserves and even builds on to the place where being will occur – language. We guard being in thinking whenever we think the manner of something's enduring and thereby bring it back into its proper relationship with being (we thereby aid being's homecoming). Strikingly, we even, and especially, do this by coming home ourselves to our essences as the thinkers, that is, shepherds of being. To come to understand our own essence this way is to help in our own homecoming. In Heidegger's sense, it is to accomplish it – that is, it is to bring being's turning and coming, and ours, into language.

Here Heidegger maturely develops the mutual and simultaneous coming into their ownmost of humans and gods, earth and world, and the enowning that was first laid out in *Contributions*) (Tu 47; see also 45, 48, 49). Now, he is able to make a bold claim, that being needs human being:

> Because being, as the essence of technology, has adapted itself into enframing, and because man's coming to presence belongs to the coming to pres-

> ence of being – inasmuch as being's coming to presence needs the coming to presence of man, in order to remain *kept safe* as being in keeping with its own coming to presence in the midst of whatever is, and thus *as* being to endure as present – for this reason the coming to presence of technology cannot be led into the change of its destining without the cooperation of the coming to presence of man. Through this cooperation, however, technology will not be overcome [*überwunden*] by man. On the contrary, the coming to presence of technology will be surmounted [*verwunden*] in a way that restores it into its yet unconcealed truth. (Tu 38–9)[29]

When humans correspond to being which needs and uses us 'for the restorative surmounting of the essence of technology,' we come into our essence (Tu 39). Here a double gathering occurs: responding, humans are gathered to being's coming to pass (*Ereignis*) into its own; in this corresponding to being, human being 'is gathered into its own [*ge-eignet*].'

Because the turning out of homelessness by being and human being begins a homecoming, Heidegger briefly says what the home would be. As did Hölderlin, Heidegger thinks home in the language of dwelling, and correspondingly, homecoming as coming to dwelling (see, for example, Tu 44). Out of the experience of the turning, Heidegger says something new. He thinks the dwelling together of being and human being by way of originary language. Of course, the originary words used here are just beginning to be said and still need to be thought more adequately. From the often halting and tangled language in 'The Turning,' for instance, the reader can tell that Heidegger is far from fluent in the new tongue, though it is wonderful that he can speak it at all and even help us think with some of the words and saying.

Heidegger says that when being turns homeward by turning, 'oblivion as such turns in and abides' so that 'it is no longer oblivion' but safe keeping. 'The safekeeping of being comes to pass; world comes to pass. That world comes to pass as world, that the thing things, this is the distant advent of the coming to presence of being itself' (Tu 43).[30] Being's coming is named in 'world' and 'thing.' Clearly, neither 'world' nor 'thing' can be understood metaphysically, that is, respectively, as the whole sum of beings or as one being.[31] Heidegger says a bit more about them: 'we have thought the truth of being in the worlding of world as the mirror play of the fourfold of sky and earth, mortals and divinities [*Göttlichen*]' (Tu 45). Once more Heidegger sounds like Hölderlin, who also spoke of heavens and earth, mortals and gods (though, for Heidegger, divinities are 'higher' than gods; see, e.g., 'Letter on Humanism'). Heidegger adds that when we are gathered into our own, we 'within the safeguarded element of world, may, as the mortal, look out toward the divine.' 'Otherwise not; for the god also is – when he is – a being and stands as a being within being and its coming to presence, which brings itself disclosingly to pass out of the worlding of the world' (Tu 47).[32] This worlding of the world, which occurs where 'stillness stills' (Tu 49), may be 'the nearest of all nearing that nears, as it brings the truth of being near to man's essence, and so gives man to belong to the disclosing bringing-to-pass that is a bringing into its own' (Tu 49). But prior to that, in Enframing, where beings are ordered as the standing-reserve or stock, 'the truth of being remains denied as world' (Tu 48). In the denial of world there also is 'the injurious neglect of the thing' which we take to be a mere being which is part of the stock (Tu 45, 49).

But though here Heidegger does little more than name 'world,' 'thing,' and the somewhat more familiar 'heavens and earth, mortals and divinities,' he does thereby indicate what must be discovered – experienced and understood – in the homecoming of being and human being. While cryptic, what he manages to say in 'The Turning,' speaks of, and out of, the turning of being and human being and toward their mutual homecoming. Still, and unavoidably, all turning and homecoming come to pass from the oblivion of being, that is, from out of homelessness. He ends the essay with questions, because the turning points us to where we must travel in questioning thinking. 'So long as we do not, through thinking, experience what is, we can never belong to what will be. Will insight into that which is bring itself disclosingly to pass? Will we, as the ones caught sight of, be so brought home into the essential glance of being that we will no longer elude it? Will we arrive thereby within the essence of the nearness that, in thinging the thing, brings world near? Will we dwell as those at home in nearness, so that we will belong primally within the fourfold of sky and earth, mortals and divinities?' (Tu 49).

Turning turns into home-turning. The word Heidegger uses for the turning-in of being (*einkehrt*) is a verb which means to enter, stay at, alight, put up at an inn. The corresponding human turning home is heard in the figurative sense of the German word, where it means contemplation. The disclosing coming to pass of turning (*Ereignis der Kehre*) becomes the disclosing coming to pass of turning homeward (*Ereignis der Einkehr*); the latter, in turn, may become homecoming (*eingeholt*, which though meaning 'gathered home' also connotes 'hauled in,' as with a rope). That this essay uses the most strikingly originary (and difficult) language and thinking thus far deployed on Heidegger's journey is not accidental. While the other essays considered in this chapter herald the turning of being and prepare, or even initiate, that of human being, 'The Turning' actually says the turning and begins to enact what we need to do. (Perhaps 'Letter on Humanism' does too, as even earlier it appears that *Contributions* did, though in Heidegger's own judgment the earliest hints required years of further reflection before being made public). How could it be otherwise – even if this happens after years of further reflection following *Contributions* – than that the originary language of the essay would be difficult, since the work's thoughtful saying accomplishes, for the first time publicly, a turning?

Not surprisingly, it is at the moment of this turning that Heidegger has and articulates central insights. Precisely here, he initially comes to understand that homelessness in our epoch is Enframing. Though this has to be thought out, he comes to experience the essence of our homelessness (the specific oblivion to being which holds sway in our era) in the turning – where that experience is part of the turning, where it enables the turning. He also sees that turning is primarily being's turning (which grants ours): being comes as a turning home (*Einkehrt*). Finally, he says that the disclosing coming to pass of being's presence is homecoming (*Ereignis*) to its own, that is, into and as being itself. This is newly said by way of 'world' and 'thing,' and by 'earth and sky, mortals and divinities.'

If we are to respond to being's turn we need to think what comes to light in it. We would have to enter originary thinking and language and travel by way of it. Thinking would have to learn to move from the turning to think – remember – 1) the primal home (being coming to presence); 2) our homelessness (the blockage and oblivion which occur in metaphysics and Enframing); and 3) homecoming (the originary belonging to come which is hinted at, for example, in 'world' and 'thing'). Such a triple movement out of the turning of being would be our responsive turning toward a homecoming and the beginning of the homecoming journey itself.

4 Originary Homecoming: The Moment of Arrival

A Arriving at the Early Greek Beginning: A Not-Yet-Metaphysical Abode

Heidegger is engaged in a double undertaking: he is attempting to think and say, that is to help unfold, the story of being as it discloses and conceals itself; at the same time, his thinking and saying are his own journey, which attempts to move from the homelessness of our epoch to achieve a homecoming with – as he understands matters at this point – being. Out of the experience of the homelessness of the history of being, the poet's homecoming, and the effort to increasingly make originary language and thought his own (considered, respectively, in chapters 1 through 3), Heidegger has to pass from (what may be the beginning of) the turning toward one another of being and human being and the return from the strange place far from home back toward home. He must, now (at least rudimentarily), become able to think and speak originarily, make his way back through homelessness to the source of home, and in that neighbourhood learn to become at home, not as he (or we) once were in the past but as he (we) may be in the future.

Heidegger makes his own originary journey back to the primal Greek experience of what has come to be called being in a series of works presented between 1943 and 1952. These are 'Aletheia,' a 1943 lecture focusing on Heraclitus' Fragment B16; 'Logos,' a 1944 lecture course on Heraclitus' Fragment B50 (the course was entitled Logic); 'The Anaximander Fragment,' composed in 1946; *What Is Called Thinking?*, a 1951–2 lecture course; and 'Moira (Parmenides, Fragment VIII, 34–41),' an undelivered portion of that course. The relationship between these works and what Heidegger has already presented is fairly simple, but not tidy. After the works considered in our first three chapters, in the fourth series to which we now turn Heidegger picks up and further unfolds the drama of homelessness and homecoming, but with a fuller understanding and better resources than before. For instance, if we note the year 1943, we see that the first work considered in the present chapter ('Aletheia') was presented the same year as 'The Word of Nietzsche' (which was one of the last 'metaphysical' works considered in the first chapter), the Hölderlin essays 'Andenken' and 'Remembrance of the Poet' (considered in chapter 2), and the 'Postscript to "What Is Metaphysics,"' (of our third chapter, where Heidegger seeks his own originary thinking). Clearly, Heidegger's thinking is quite complex at this point, though, as I contend, there need be little confusion as to the direction and relation of his various simultaneous movements and voices.

Heidegger returns – or stays with – the subject which concerned him in his works on metaphysics and the history of being. As noted, in his return travels through the same territory, he does not meander or bulldoze further into homelessness. Rather, through his increasingly originary language and thinking, he makes his way – carefully and gradually – back to the neighbourhood where being and human being belong together. While underway, he travels further into originary language and thinking and uses what he has experienced with Hölderlin. What Heidegger says and the style of the saying make these features obvious. In addition, these essays make a 'step back' from the work we considered in chapter 3, in two senses. As we will see, Heidegger moves back to the originary Greek experience; less interestingly, the works effecting this return are presented before the final ones taken up in chapter 3 (that is, we need to go back a bit in time, from what Heidegger said in 1949 with 'The Turning' to 'Aletheia' of 1943 and 'Logos' of 1944). In fact, this poses no difficulty, because Heidegger's thinking and saying are not themselves to be understood in any narrowly chronological way.[1] We have seen that his originary thinking had begun in works treated in chapters 1 and 2 and that the originary thinking which was underway became refined and focused in the works treated in chapter 3, but was not 'created' there. So, returning to 1943–4 simply picks up Heidegger's originary thought (already underway) on the Greeks.

What matters here is both Heidegger's telling of the story and its mode of unfolding. Heidegger articulates something occurring independently of his own narrative: the history of being, which is unfolding with its own dynamic or 'logic.' Because his own thinking, corresponding to this history, is already underway, how and when he tells the story is crucial, but clearly not a matter of the mere sequence of events in the 'flow of time.'[2] The saga, which we are attempting to follow, articulates a dynamic of homelessness and homecoming that has its own way and order. Further, since the story of being and human being remains open, not at all over and done with, and because Heidegger is telling it in the midst of its course, his own story and telling go to and fro, for example, as he experiences the thoughtful journey back to the original Greek experience and from thence to his own situation – a complex pattern of movement already foretold in *Contributions.*

The upshot is that Heidegger's works bear witness to his journey in thinking. But his thinking is a journey back and forth between homelessness and homecoming, where even after the turn and throughout the homecoming (indeed, especially there), he must remain in the uncanny and continue to rethink homelessness. In thinking as casting back and retrieving, the story – *and even the development* – of his speaking and writing is obviously something other than the day-to-day sequence of discrete and unrepeatable psychological and biological processes, as ordered chronologically.[3] Heidegger himself is very clear on this difference between the movement of originary thinking and the sequence of empirical causality as understood by metaphysical science. Therefore, without any disparagement of historical-biographical scientific scholarship, it behoves us to undertake something else if we want to follow the story of homelessness and homecoming.

This alternative task, in fact, is undertaken by Heidegger. He generates a fourth set of works, distinct from the series of the first three already considered, in order to 'go back' to think again what he already has thought, but now to do so more originarily. We can see this return to the theme of the first set of works in, for instance, his taking up 'errancy' and 'injustice.' At the same time, these new works are linked to the second and third sets by their increasingly originary style, which does continue to change and deepen and which, though found with Hölderlin, becomes more and more Heidegger's own. While he speaks originarily as Hölderlin did, he increasingly speaks with his own thinker's voice.

This fourth set of works can be followed more easily if we attend to two major structural forms that run through all of them. First, Heidegger treats the unfolding of the history of being in large phases. In chapter 1 we saw that he distinguished an originary being-at-home, metaphysical homelessness, and a no-longer-metaphysical home which might come about. Discerning the past pre-metaphysical epoch, the long-lasting, still-present metaphysical one (which was subdivided into the high Greek, Christian medieval, modern, and contemporary), and the future (hopefully originary) era provided a framework for thought. In his Hölderlin essays, Heidegger found six phases of homecoming (an original home, homelessness in the foreign, turning, homecoming as moment of arrival, learning to become at home, and dwelling near the source). In the fourth series of essays, we can see that Heidegger thinks through a similar sequence.

Second, all along Heidegger has considered the relationship of being and human being (through their historical epochs) by means of his explorations with language and thinking. For example, in 'Letter on Humanism,' he presented being as *advent*, where the latter gave truth and granted what is ownmost, thereby enabling thinking and appropriating human beings for guardianship. Language was seen as the lightening-concealing advent of being and thinking as accomplishing the relation of the manifestation of being because it brings being's word to language. Accordingly, the essence of human being was taken to lie in our dwelling as the neighbour of being, where we are at home in language and build on to the house of being, there to guard and care for it. Heidegger's work on the Greeks also moves through these relationships, in an attempt to understand how the early Greeks experienced them. In following his presentation of these relationships it seems clearest to begin by taking up some contextual issues (especially with 'The Anaximander Fragment'), then considering 'Aletheia' and 'Logos' together, next going back through the same subject with 'The Anaximander Fragment,' and finally returning yet again with 'Moira' and the appropriate sections of *What Is Called Thinking?* While this order of presentation is chronological, its point really is to share in Heidegger's journey in thinking. Often his procedure consists of deliberately going *over and over* (and over) the same subject: his disclosure is inherently bound up with *repeated, yet different, passings.*[4]

As a result, following him is easier in such cases if we do not attempt to abstract what he says about language in all five works on the Greeks and then move on to what all five say about thinking, and so on. Instead, staying on the path requires passing and repassing through the same originary Greek understanding of (what we call) being, human existence, thinking, and language. Still, we can see that between 1943 and 1951–2, in 'Moira,' for example, Heidegger does also move toward a fuller originary interpretation of the being of beings (the duality). His thinking genuinely does *move into* the primally Greek. Heidegger shifts from saying and thinking the turning of being to retrieving the early Greek experience of being because in the way the being of beings unfolded we simultaneously encounter 1) the site of an *originary home;* and 2) the *foreign* element which we, as contemporary homeless thinkers, must make our own in order to achieve a homecoming. Both the being at home and the homelessness of the Greek world disclose something still vital for us.

In the first place, we find that Greek thinking and saying indicate and establish the originary home for the West.[5] Without taking 'culture' in a narrow or superficial sense, we could say that the West had its youthful home in the primal Greek epoch. Thinking (understood as the thinking of being) spent its formative days there (then 'grew up' to be philosophy, that is, metaphysics). Where did this occur? In the primal unfolding – home – of the being of beings. The history of the event of being is, as primordial home, the Greek epoch. But the Greek epoch is also what is most strange to contemporary philosophy, and so it is 'the foreign' to Heidegger himself: the early Greek unfolding of home is what Heidegger needs to find and make his own in order to arrive in a homecoming. Here it is helpful to think of Hölderlin, who is always Heidegger's guide, even as he needs to make his own way home as a thinker. The poet achieved his homecoming by seeking his 'foreign' element – the Greek 'fire.' Hölderlin learned not only from the Greek poets but from the lightning and fire of which Heraclitus speaks. Nor is it surprising that Heraclitus is a starting point for Heidegger too, as we already heard in 'Letter on Humanism,' where Heidegger spoke of Heraclitus in such a homey way. Here, in contrast, since Heidegger has *not yet achieved* a home, as Heraclitus did, he approaches Heraclitus' saying and thinking as the foreign to which Heidegger must wed himself.

In the five essays considered here, Heidegger thinks into this original, foreign Greek realm, *not* back into his own thinking (for example, λέγειν and νοεῖν are Greek, not Heideggerian). But because Heidegger does (at least begin to) make these thoughts his own, he passes through them to arrive at his own originary thinking (as we will see later on, at the end of this chapter and in those following). Thus, Heidegger's own journey home begins here, in the attempt to think – that means remember and recover – Greek thinking and saying. By journeying into the Greek, he moves toward what calls for thinking, which is what needs thought now.

In 'Aletheia,' 'Logos,' 'The Anaximander Fragment,' 'Moira,' and sections of *What Is Called Thinking?*, Heidegger thinks and tells the early unfolding of the history of being. As noted, in the works taken up in chapter 1 he thought about metaphysics by keeping in mind the past (an original home), the persisting present (metaphysical homelessness), and the future (an originary homecoming). In his Hölderlin essays he followed the poet's journey from youthful home, through homelessness, turning, arrival home, and learning to become at home, to dwelling near the source. In the works considered in this chapter, he tells the story of being again and similarly, though with the Greeks he focuses on the character of the primal Greek home.

Heidegger doubly emphasizes the historical character of the unfolding of being and, correspondingly, of his own story, by beginning with Heraclitus. Heidegger's own originary language and thinking partially spring from Hölderlin's, and both are influenced by Heraclitus and what came to him. In addition, Heidegger begins the 1943 lecture on Heraclitus ('Aletheia') by reminding us of Heraclitus' influence in the history of thinking, which moved through, and was transmitted by, Plato, Aristotle, Theophrastus, Sextus Empiricus, Diogenes Laertius, Plutarch, and the Church Fathers – Hippolytus, Clement of Alexandria, and Origen (Al 102). So, what has this historical 'fact' to do with us? In our epoch, a change is underway – or may be. Heidegger asks, in 1946, 'what entitles antiquity to address us, presumably the latest latecomers with respect to philosophy? ... Do we stand in the very twilight of the most monstrous transformation our planet has ever undergone, the twilight of that epoch in which earth itself hangs suspended? Do we confront the evening of a night which heralds another dawn? Are we to strike off on a journey to this historic region of earth's evening? Is the land of evening [*Abend-land*, the West] only now emerging?' (AF 16–17).

If we are to understand such an occurrence, we have to think back to the first dawn, that is, to the first lighting of being, which comes from being into the thinking and saying of the earliest Greeks, according to Heidegger. From there may 'lie concealed in the historical and chronological remoteness of the fragment[s] the historic proximity of something unsaid, something that will speak out in times to come' (AF 16). Our task is to hear this unspoken, to think this unthought something which comes from being. To do so we need to find the early Greeks, as Heidegger explains, 'What once occurred in the dawn of our sending would then come, as what once occurred at the last (ἔσχατον), that is, at the departure of the long-hidden sending of being. The being of beings is gathered (λέγεσθαι, λόγος) in the ultimacy of its sending. The essence of being hitherto disappears, its truth still veiled. The history of being is gathered in this departure. The gathering in this departure, as the gathering (λόγος) at the outermost point (ἔσχατον) of its essence hitherto, is the eschatology of being. As something fateful, being itself is inherently eschatological' (AF 18).

As a homecoming thinker attempting to come back home to being, Heidegger must think this eschatology, not theologically or philosophically (even as Hegel did), that is, metaphysically, but originarily, 'that is, from within the history of being' (AF 18).

Returning in remembering thinking can only proceed from our present homelessness. That is where we are now and where we must begin if we are not to counterfeit a homecoming. Heidegger says, 'If we think within the eschatology of being, then we must someday anticipate the former dawn in the dawn to come; today we must learn to ponder this former dawn through what is imminent' (AF 18). Thus, arriving at home in the Greeks must not only begin but also stay in homelessness. Our homelessness and any homecoming, as well as the original Greek being at home, belong to being itself, as Heidegger repeatedly says. Being always keeps coming; but it always conceals and safeguards itself too. When we think our homelessness, then, we need to think not only the hiddenness of being, but how being comes in its very withdrawal. Similarly, in order to think Greek being at home in being, we need to prepare to think both being's unconcealment and the way it conceals itself there. 'Every epoch of world history is an epoch of errancy' (AF 27).

The unfolding of being, according to Heidegger, and according to its own necessity, always lightens and darkens. We see something, hopefully vital, and yet not everything for which we might hope. That is why Heidegger repeatedly says, as we think homelessness and the Greek being at home, 'As it reveals itself in being, being withdraws' (AF 26). He goes on,

> In this way, by illuminating them, being sets beings adrift in errancy. Beings come to pass in that errancy by which they circumvent being and establish the realm of error (in the sense of a prince's realm or the realm of poetry). Error is the space in which history un-folds ... Man's inability to see himself corresponds to the self-concealing of the lighting of being.
>
> Without errancy there would be no history ... When we are historical we are neither a great nor a small distance from what is Greek. Rather, we are in errancy toward it ... The *epoche* of being belongs to being itself; we are thinking it in terms of the experience of the oblivion of being. (AF 26–7)

If this is so, we belong to being and within the history that is being's unfolding, even in homelessness. We forget being. But according to Heidegger and the Greeks, that forgetfulness needs to be understood originarily (as the oblivion of being) and not as a mere psychological lapse or failure. Today, we have even forgotten the essence of forgetting (Al 108). To forget being is to be within being's concealment; to forget such concealment is also to be within it, and is part of it. We belong to the lighting and the darkening of being. That is why, according to Heidegger, the Greeks speak of oblivion as a sending of concealment and identify 'the concealment into which man falls by reference to its relation to what is withdrawn from him by concealment' (Al 109).

Here we can better understand how Heidegger's movement toward what is Greek pre-eminently includes the Greek language and Heidegger's translation of the Greek sayings, both of which being, as he says, 'strange.' 'Yet,' for a homecoming 'it is more salutary for thinking to wander into the strange than to establish itself in the obvious' (Lo 76). His attempt to originarily think homelessness and home focuses on the strange, that is, on what is said and thought in Greek words. The task is to think our relation to what withdraws from us by concealment. For example, Homer says of Odysseus (who covers his head when the Phaeacian minstrel Demodocus sings, and who – thus hidden – weeps): 'Then he shed tears without all the others noticing it' (*Odyssey*, bk 8, 83ff., cited in Al 106). Heraclitus also speaks of this hiding in Fragment B16: 'How can one hide himself before that which never sets?' (cited in Al 104). Thus, Heidegger continues, 'Now, if this word λήθω [I remain concealed], speaks to us in the saying of a thinker, and if perhaps it concludes a thoughtful question, then we are bound to ponder the word and what it says as comprehensively and as persistently as we can today' (Al 109).

The Greek understanding of what withdraws from us by concealment holds a most important insight into our homelessness. We know that we are always aware of homelessness to some extent; this is true of all epochs. There is always some concealment of being behind beings, since the commonplace always rises up to surround and befog us. To be human at any time is to experience homelessness. That is to say the obvious: there never is a pure being at home, if we mean by that a total absence of concealment. But that is not what being at home or becoming at home really mean. Genuinely to be at home (as were the early Greeks) or to become at home (as may occur in the originary realm to come) is to become at home with concealment as well as unconcealment.

If, then, the Greek understanding does not hold that being at home precludes concealment, what does it show us about homelessness? It says that for all the concealment and withdrawal between being and human being, that is, for all the genuine homelessness, being and human being are never totally separated. *Even in homelessness, being and human being belong together. They remain together, as separated.* Heidegger explains this Greek understanding of concealment, as it is given, for example, in Homer's *Odyssey* (bk 8, 83ff. cited in Al 109): 'Every remaining-concealed includes a relation to the sort of thing from which the concealment has withdrawn, but toward which in many cases it remains directly inclined. The Greek names in the accusative that to which what has withdrawn into concealment remains related: ἐνθ' ἄλλους μὲν πάντας ἐλάνθανε' (Al 109).

If being and human being remain inclined toward one another even in homelessness, Heidegger arrives at a new understanding of what 'Greek' and 'originary home' mean. They stand *at* the origin of the inclination; they stand *as* the origin of that inclination which endures even through separation. Elaborating this striking insight into *concealment as homelessness,* Heidegger says, 'In our manner of speaking, "Greek" does not designate a particular people or nation, nor a cultural or anthropological group. What is Greek is the dawn of that sending in which being illuminates itself in beings and so propounds a certain essence of man; that essence unfolds historically as something fateful, preserved in being and dispensed by being, without ever being separated from being' (AF 25).

Our problem, then, is not that we do not belong to and with being at all; rather, it is that in our homelessness, to which we persistently belong, we do not yet belong the way we might. In Fragment B50 Heraclitus speaks of this belonging in terms of hearing. He says that we should listen attentively to that to which we belong. Such a proper hearing hears into and beyond the obvious, through beings to being. Heidegger notes, 'Mortals hear the thunder of the heavens, the rustling of woods, the gurgling of fountains, the ringing of plucked strings, the rumbling of motors, the noises of the city – only and only so far as they always already in some way belong to them and yet do not belong to them' (Lo 65–6). Our hearing becomes successful when it inclines to what comes to it. As Heidegger puts it, 'We have heard [*gehört*] when we *belong to* [*gehören*] the matter addressed' (Lo 66). In homelessness, we attempt a homecoming by listening to the call from home, by trying to hear that to which we belong in its concealment, whether that concealment deepens as being withdraws or lightens as being turns. This is what Heidegger understands Heraclitus to say: 'If there is to be proper hearing, mortals must have already heard the Λόλος, with an attention [*Gehör*] which implies nothing less than their belonging to the Λόλος' (Lo 67).

The belonging to being which unfolds from the originary Greek home and persists, concealed, in our present homelessness might be uncovered. One obstacle is our present metaphysical understanding of belonging. For example, in our modern epoch we think of subjectivity and objectivity and understand that they belong together. Precisely here, Heidegger asks,

> How does it happen that even when we do note that they belong together we still try to explain each from the standpoint of the other, or introduce some third element which is supposed to embrace both subject and object? Why is it that we stubbornly resist considering even once whether the belonging-together of subject and object does not arise from something that first imparts their nature to both the object and its objectivity, and the subject and its subjectivity, and hence is prior to the realm of their reciprocity. That our thinking finds it so toilsome to be in this bestowal, or even on the lookout for it, cannot be blamed on a narrowness of contemporary intellect or resistance to unsettling or disruptive views. Rather, we may surmise something else: that we know too much and believe too readily ever to feel at home in a questioning which is powerfully experienced. For that we need the ability to wonder at what is simple, and to take up that wonder as our abode. (Al 103–4)

The way home to what is prior, then, proceeds by a questioning journey. We must begin to be at home in this questioning-thinking before our homecoming can proceed. Our proper first step from this point is to wonder at what Greek thinking says. 'How can we arrive at such a beginning? Perhaps by abandoning ourselves to a wonder which is on the lookout for what we call lighting and concealing?' (Al 104).

Before we follow Heidegger in taking up what Heraclitus says on this subject and, correspondingly, how he goes about the journey into the originary Greek, we can at least catch a glimpse of how the Greek is both an originary home for being and Western human being and the foreign for modern humans. Insofar as Heidegger succeeds in passing over to think what the early Greeks think and say, he will pass over to become at home in an originary thinking which will remain 'utterly foreign' to modern philosophy (M 84). Of course, the genuine home here is not just the Greek thought or originary thinking in which we must learn to feel at home: prior to that is being itself. Put another way, our becoming at home in Greek and originary thinking and saying would be a dwelling in or near what these thinkings and sayings house.

We have come to the realm of what is to be thought by way of a dialogue with early thinkers (Al 105). As the journey home proceeds through the now foreign, originary home of the Greek, we can take comfort that in our own homecoming we do not need to go alone. The Greeks will help guide us. Heidegger begins to follow them by trying to hear and attend to the strange Greek thinking and saying; we can begin by trying to hear the strange interpretations and translations that Heidegger uses to make his way (Lo 66). Our homecoming depends on becoming able to correspond to the Greeks' thinking and saying, which means to the riddles of the early fragments (Lo 60). But, Heidegger says, these riddles are not characteristic of particular thinkers or their sayings; rather, the riddles remain in the 'very matter thought' (Lo 60). Again, we hear Heidegger say that our homecoming aims not at the Greeks but to what was given to them, that is, to That which unfolds and conceals itself.

Because the thoughtful words of the Greeks indicate not just what they 'express' but the source from which they speak, 'it is essential that we translate ourselves to the source of what comes to language in [them] ... We must therefore seek the opportunity which will let us cross over to that source' (AF 28). The task is to pass by way of the originary thinking and saying of such figures as Homer, Heraclitus, Parmenides, and Anaximander (earlier, in *An Introduction to Metaphysics,* Heidegger had thought with Sophocles) and through that to the prior, primal origin. At our present point, homecoming is a matter of crossing back from our current metaphysical thinking and saying through the 'Platonic-Aristotelian conceptual terms' to the earliest 'preconceptual words,' where the latter must be understood precisely 'as they are thought in Greek' (AF 30). The gulf between the metaphysical and the Greek must be overcome in order to think the relation of being, human being, language, and thinking. First the gulf would have to be acknowledged for us to cross over it. Heidegger is clear and firm on this point. We must learn to let stand the differences between us (see, e.g., Al 115): 'Thoughtful translation to what comes to speech in [these fragments] is a leap over an abyss [*Graben*]. The abyss does not consist merely of the chronological or historical distance of two-and-a-half millennia. It is wider and deeper. It is hard to leap, mainly because we stand right on its edge. We are so near the abyss that we do not have an adequate runway for such a broad jump; we easily fall short – if indeed the lack of a sufficiently solid base allows any leap at all' (AF 19). To leap this way we must let go of metaphysical-representational distinctions and concepts because Greek thinking is 'anything but a kind of primitive and anthropomorphic representation.' We must also 'consciously cast aside all inadequate presuppositions' about such things as the Greek view of what we now call nature, or its 'seemingly poetic' mode of speaking (AF 22). Shedding these assumptions prepares us to cross the 'gap between the language of our thinking and the language of Greek philosophy' (AF 23).

Because any leap must take place from where we stand, Heidegger looks toward the strange Greek sayings from the midst of our metaphysical interpretation of them. He begins in the only way possible to think toward what Heraclitus, Parmenides, and Anaximander say – by standing within historical language, partly oriented by Nietzsche's and Hermann Diels' understandings (which their translations hold).[6] These translations themselves belong to a phase in the history of being. So too will Heidegger's translation, if he manages to 'get to what is said in the saying, so that it might rescue the tradition from arbitrariness' (AF 18–19). By attending to what Heraclitus, Anaximander, and Parmenides say, Heidegger moves through the subject matter of thinking (the early unfolding of the history of being) several times. This is not so much a repetition as a deepening understanding of what is the same, which also respects the differences between these thinkers and their words.

As noted earlier, Heidegger, as Hölderlin before him, finds Heraclitus a helpful guide out of our present concealment and homelessness. Heidegger seeks to become at home in wonder by wondering about lighting and unconcealing, presencing and gathering together, and sheltering and keeping safe. A first clue for Heidegger is seen in his finding that Heraclitus says the 'hiding' and 'coming out' of what we need as 'belonging together.' In Heidegger's interpretation, for Heraclitus presencing in the lighting involves a simultaneous self-concealing. If lighting gives presencing, then (*i*) it does so by laying before; (*ii*) this laying gathers together; (*iii*) this gathering secures what is in its essence (presencing); and (*iv*) in this revealing-presencing, this gathering also abides in a self-concealing. Though Heidegger needs to think this out and elaborate it, he apparently hears the outlines of a primal unfolding in Heraclitus' sayings. In the first place, Heraclitus speaks of fire. Understood as the lighting, fire not only shines brilliantly, but opens the openness wherein everything comes to shining. Heidegger comments on the lighting (*die Lichtung*) (which endures insofar as it illuminates), 'What belongs to [the lighting], and how, and where it takes place, still remain to be considered. The word "light" means lustrous, beaming, brightening. Lighting bestows the shining, opens what shines to an appearance. The open is the realm of unconcealment and is governed by disclosure. What belongs to the latter, and whether and to what extent disclosing and lighting are the same, remain to be asked' (Al 103). At the very least, though, it appears that lighting illuminates and lays bare; since it also opens, it is the bestowal of presencing (Al 118).

Fire, in addition to being the lightning governance of presencing, also means the meditative (*das Sinnende*). Meditative fire lays everything into presencing. It accomplishes this because the laying is a gathering: things are gathered and laid out as gathered. The gathering gathers things into their essence, which means into their essential presencing (Al 117–18). But the lighting that gives the presencing of what is, in Greek thought, is sheltered in concealment. That is, the revealing-lighting flashes out of concealing darkness. Homer thinks this way, as briefly observed above: Odysseus remained concealed, weeping under his cloak. In doing so he shied away from the Phaeacians. He withdrew and kept to himself reserved; thus concealed and reserved, Odysseus was present (Al 107ff.). His own presencing as weeping occurred as remaining-concealed in the nearness of everything present.

Heraclitus thinks the same when he speaks of lighting and concealment and brings that to which we belong (which still conceals itself) at least a little way into language. Fragment B16 asks, 'How can one hide before the never-setting?' Obviously, hiding asks about concealment and unconcealment, but what has that to do with the 'never-setting'? Heraclitus' saying reminds us that Homer's saying concerning Odysseus speaks not, as we might suppose, about the subjective self but about 'the governance of presencing – a meaning of being ... still unthought': presencing as 'luminous self-concealing' in the nearness of what remains in coming' (Al 108–9). Unlike metaphysical thinking, which starts from and aims at subjectivity, according to Heidegger 'Heraclitus' question is not first and foremost a consideration of concealment and unconcealment with regard to the sort of men whom we, with our modern habits of representation, like to interpret as carriers – or even creators – of unconcealment. Heraclitus' question, expressed in modern terms, thinks the reverse. It ponders the relation of man to the never-setting and thinks human being from this relation' (Al 109). In Greek terms, Heidegger continues, setting occurs as a going into concealment (as when the sun goes into the sea and evening darkness) (Al 110). Yet, what is never-setting also means the ever-rising, which does not remain concealed. Heidegger says, 'it becomes clear that Heraclitus thinks the ever-rising, not something to which rising is qualitatively attributed, nor the totality affected by the rising. Rather, he thinks the rising, and only this. The ever and always-enduring rising is named in the thoughtfully spoken word φύσις. We must translate it with the unfamiliar but fitting term "upsurgence," corresponding to the more common "emergence"' (Al 112).[7]

Thus, in *physis* (alternatively transliterated as *phusis*, φυσις) 'we hear a primal word of Greek thought' (Al 111). If the 'never entering into concealment is the enduring rising out of self-concealing,' Heraclitus would be speaking of the primal giving – of presencing (Al 118). 'The event of lighting is the world. The meditatively gathering lighting which brings into the open is revealing; it abides in self-concealing. Self-concealing belongs to it as that which finds its essence in revealing, and which therefore cannot ever be a mere going into concealment, never a setting' (Al 118). Here world does not mean the sum of natural or cosmic things. Rather, Heraclitus would be telling us that 'lightning flashes' says the same as the 'worlding of the world' (Al 117), where meditative fire is understood as the 'heart, i.e. the lighting-sheltering expanse, of the world' (Al 118).[8]

Heidegger's interpretation of Heraclitus' saying that lighting bestows presencing and, in revealing, abides in self-concealing, is developed in the essay 'Logos,' presented a year after 'Aletheia' and elaborating the same basic characteristics. In 'Aletheia,' as we have just seen, lighting bestows presencing by (*i*) laying before, which is (*ii*) a gathering that (*iii*) secures and (*iv*) abides in self-concealing. In 'Logos,' Heidegger understands Heraclitus to say that γόλος gives presencing through (*i*) a laying that (*ii*) gathers by 1) selecting and 2) bringing together and, then, by 3) sheltering, 4) accommodating, and 5) safe keeping (which together correspond to (*iii*) securing, in 'Aletheia'); this gathering and securing are (*iv*) laid within both unconcealment and concealment (also as delineated in 'Aletheia'); this laying is (*v*) sending: the fateful (a newly articulated dimension).

In 'Aletheia' Heidegger attempted to think originarily, rather than metaphysically, by following the language of light-fire-lightning-sun; in 'Logos,' he attempts the same, but now thinks by way of the actions that belong to a harvest.[9] For Heraclitus, according to Heidegger, Λόγος (*Logos*) gives the presencing of what is present (Lo 70). It does this because Λόγος lays: 'To lay means to bring to lie. Thus, to lay is at the same time to place one thing beside another, to lay them together. To lay is to gather [*lesen*]' (Lo 61). For example, in the fall harvest, the gathering of grapes requires that workers assemble together at the site of the hillside vines and nearby vineyard. The gathering and the laying, in which harvesters, fruit, and buildings are placed together before us, are not accidentally or externally yoked together. 'Rather, gathering is already included in laying. Every gathering is already a laying. Every laying is of itself a gathering. Then what does "to lay" mean? Laying brings to lie, in that it lets things lie together before us' (Lo 62).

Thought non-representationally, this gathering is far more than merely collecting what is scattered into a tidy heap; rather, it is like the gathering that we know as reading. Literally, reading (*lesen*) is a gathering in which we are gathered (via our thoughtful reading) into a text that itself is both gathered and held together by its subject. The gathering here proceeds from a complex fore-gathering (*Vor-lese*) which determines what is to be done and included. In a harvest, depending on what is proper to the specific crop, there will be 1) a selection, which will pick and glean from what is available. Next, 2) there comes the assembly of the fruit, where what has been taken piece by piece from the field or vine or tree is brought together. Clearly this is not just a throwing together, but something careful (as would be a deliberate political assembly). It is careful because 3) the harvest becomes what is now brought together into a shelter so that it can be preserved. The sheltering (*das Bergen*) requires that the fruit be 4) accommodated in a suitable place and way, which allows 5) the safe keeping of the crop for a long time (Lo 61).

The figure helps say what the laying is that Logos accomplishes. Logos' laying is a gathering of the same kind as the harvest because Logos selects and sends everything according to a sorting (to which we will return). It lays out by bringing together in its own way: 'The λέγειν or laying now to be thought has in advance relinquished all claims – claims never known to it – to be that which for the first time brings whatever lies before us into its position [*Lage*]' (Lo 62). Such bringing together is a sheltering: 'Laying, as λέγειν, simply tries to let what of itself lies together here before us, *as* what lies before, into its protection, a protection in which it remains laid down' (Lo 62–3). Finally, since this protection is an accommodating and safe keeping, we hear more about the site itself: 'What lies together before us is stored, laid away, secured and deposited in unconcealment, and that means sheltered in unconcealment' (Lo 63).

Laying, then, is gathering, understood multidimensionally. Together, these aspects tell how laying is, and laying says the way in which Logos gives presence. 'The ... lying before for-itself of what is in this fashion deposited ... is nothing more and nothing less than the *presencing* of that which lies before us into unconcealment. *Legen* is to lay. Laying is the letting-lie-before – which is gathered into itself – of that which comes together into presence' (Lo 63). 'Because λέγειν, which lets things lie together before us, concerns itself solely with the safety of that which lies before us in unconcealment,' the 'gathering appropriate to such a laying is determined in advance by safekeeping' (Lo 63). Heidegger explains, 'Λόγος lays that which is present before and down into presencing, that is, it puts those things back. Presencing nevertheless suggests: *having come forward to endure in unconcealment.* Because the Λόγος lets lie before us what lies before us as such, it discloses what is present in its presencing ... All disclosure releases what is present from concealment. Disclosure needs concealment. The 'Α-Λήθεια rests in Λήθη, drawing from it and laying before us whatever remains deposited in Λήθη. Λόγος is *in itself and at the same time* a revealing and concealing. It is 'Αλήθεια. Unconcealment needs concealment, Λήθη, as a reservoir upon which disclosure can, as it were, draw. Λόγος, the laying that gathers, has in itself this revealing-concealing character' (Lo 70–1).

Through understanding the harvest, Heidegger moves toward becoming at home with what Heraclitus says in Λόγος, which itself names the primal giving of home. Logos gives home and assembles us into it. Logos lays home before us, gathering and sheltering: 'In this fashion Λόγος occurs essentially as the pure laying which gathers and assembles. Λόγος is the original assemblage of the primordial gathering from the primordial laying. 'Ο Λόγος is the laying that gathers [*die lesende Lege*], and only this' (Lo 66). Of course, in this originary understanding of Heraclitus' words and of home, Heidegger finds that Λόγος belongs with εὸν Ἕν, ἀλήθεια, Μοῖρα (*Moira,* fate), and lightning. Where Heraclitus says, 'the unique One,' the all One (Ἕν, Πάντα) and names what unifies, Heidegger holds that 'It unifies by assembling. It assembles in that, in gathering, it lets lie before us what lies before us as such and as a whole. The unique One unifies as the laying that gathers' (Lo 70). If so, the unique One can be thought by way of Λόγος, which would be 'the essence of unification.' At the same time, Λόγος 'suggests the way in which the Ἕν [One] essentially occurs as unifying' (Lo 71). That is, thought non-representationally, Logos and the unique One's unifying are not remotely mechanical binding.

> The Ἕν Πάντα lets lie together before us in one presencing things which are usually separated from, and opposed to, one another, such as day and night, winter and summer, peace and war, waking and sleeping, Dionysos and Hades. Such opposites, borne along the farthest distance between pres-

> ence and absence ... let the laying that gathers lie before us in its full bearing. Its laying is itself that which carries things along by bearing them out.
>
> Ἓν Πάντα says what the Λόγος is. Λόγος says how Ἓν Πάντα essentially occurs. Both are the same. (Lo 71)

Further, as we just have seen, aletheia and Logos are the same (τό αυτό). 'λέγειν lets ἀλήθεια, unconcealment as such, lie before us' (Lo 70–1).

Heraclitus speaks of fate as this same juncture: 'the unique One unifying all is alone the fateful' (B32). 'But,' Heidegger notes, 'if the ἐόν is the same as the λόγος, the result is' that the *only properly* fateful matter is the Logos (Lo 72). He explains, 'But how is Λόγος the fateful, how is it sending proper, that is, the assembly of that which sends everything into its own? The laying that gathers assembles in itself all sending by bringing things and letting them lie before us, keeping each absent and present being in its place and on its way; and by its assembly it secures everything in the totality. Thus each being can be joined and sent into its own' (Lo 72). Heraclitus says (Fragment B64]): 'But lightning steers (in presencing) the totality (of what is present).'[10] This Lightning 'brings all things forward to their designated, essential place,' that is, homeward. Accordingly, 'such instantaneous bringing is the laying that gathers, the Λόγος' (Lo 72). Here, in originary Greek saying and thinking, the primal home and the giving of home (homecoming) are disclosed, illuminating Heidegger's journey. *Homecoming appears as a gathering. Logos gives homecoming by assembling and securing us to our own home in the laying which gathers.*

Because Λόγος lays by gathering, it gathers together and to itself not only what is present (say, beings in general), but also mortals (as more than mere beings). Mortals are assembled together and to the gathering itself (as the harvesters were assembled for and in the harvesting). Heidegger says, 'Laying secures everything present in its presencing, from which whatever lingers awhile in presence can be appropriately collected and brought forward by mortal λέγειν' (Lo 70). First of all, Logos is laying. It 'more originally' meant 'laying down,' before it came to connote human saying and talking (Lo 60–1). It is not helpful to ask how this transformation came about, if that amounts to inquiring causally into the chronology of meanings; that would overlook the event which comes to light here, 'whose immensity still lies concealed in its long unnoticed simplicity' (Lo 63). Mortal saying, too, originally occurs as laying, Heidegger explains, 'The saying and talking of mortals comes to pass from early on as λέγειν, laying. Saying and talking occur essentially as the letting-lie-together-before of everything, which, laid in unconcealment, comes to presence. The original λέγειν, laying, unfolds itself early and in a manner ruling everything unconcealed as saying and talking' (Lo 63).

And if saying is a 'letting-lie-together-before which gathers and is gathered,' hearing too is a gathering (Lo 64). Hearing would be the gathering of oneself that assembles upon one's hearing what is said, that is, which lets lie before it what is laid there. 'Hearing is primarily gathered hearkening' (Lo 65). Proper hearing would heed what is essential – and that to which we already belong (Lo 65–6). If hearing heeds what is said, it hearkens back to the letting-lie-together-before, that is, to Logos' primordial laying. Heidegger attempts such 'proper inquiry,' which 'must be a dialogue in which the ways of hearing and points of view of ancient thinking are contemplated according to their essential origin, so that the call [*Geheiß*] under which past, present, and future thinking – each in its own way – all stand, might begin to announce itself' (M 86). The hearing which belongs to saying would be a way of thinking. Genuinely questioning listening would be a way of thinking. In Fragment 6, Parmenides says, for example, that thinking is also a gathering, a point to which Heidegger calls our attention (M 89).[11] Heidegger goes on to think what νοεῖν, which we translate with 'thinking' means in relation to λέγειν: 'Νοεῖν, whose belonging-together with ἐόν we should like to contemplate, is grounded in and comes to presence from λέγειν. In λέγειν the letting-lie-before of what is present in its presencing occurs. Only as thus lying-before can what is present as such admit the νοεῖν, the taking-heed of' (M 89).

But this originary occurrence of laying, and hence of saying as laying and hearing and of thinking as heeding, which Heidegger claims originally shone forth (and which he claims to have again seen as it now discloses itself), falls into oblivion almost immediately after opening to the Greeks. 'The original λέγειν, laying, conceals itself. Λέγειν as laying lets itself be overpowered by the predominant sense, but only in order to deposit the essence of saying and talking at the outset under the governance of laying proper' (Lo 63). That is, laying withdraws in favour of saying; in turn, saying as letting-lie-together-before everything which comes into presencing itself is veiled over by the metaphysical understanding of saying, hearing, and thinking as physiological-psychological processes and as expression and signification (here utterance is understood as the phonetic and semantic) (Lo 64–5; M 90). In these shifts the original laying is deeply hidden – it is forgotten.

What Logos fatefully assembled and joined together to send to its own becomes dis-jointed and wanders, as homeless. In Logos, then, or out of its giving, comes concealing and injustice; that is, what is present is not right (AF 41ff.). To think the presencing of what is present and what is out of joint, and thus gathered into disorder, Heidegger turns to Anaximander. Anaximander, as Heraclitus and Parmenides, thinks and says the giving presencing by gathering, where gathering originally is understood as joining (a fateful way of bringing together), sheltering, and safe keeping in reserve – in concealment.

How is the presencing of what is present inherently disorderly – displacing the originary and proper relation to our home? We think of what is present temporally as the 'now'; spatially, as what is 'here' as an object before a subject. The Greeks, however, think it by way of 'alongside,' 'in the sense of coming alongside in unconcealment,' where the 'open expanse [*Gegend*] of unconcealment, into which and within which whatever comes along lingers' (AF 34). So, presencing is originarily thought as lingering. Something is present for the Greeks insofar as it tarries in the sphere of unconcealment. 'Such a coming is proper arrival, the presencing of what is properly present' (AF 34). (Even here the absent is related to the present: as what withdraws from unconcealment, the absent is present, too, in its own way.) Altogether, Anaximander tells us, as Heidegger interprets and translates him, this occurs 'along the lines of usage; for they let order and thereby also reck belong to one another (in the surmounting) of disorder' (AF 57).

How is what is present joined so as to be out of joint? Anaximander neither says that what is present ceases to be present nor says that only part of what is present is out of joint only some of the time. 'The fragment says: what is present as such, being what it is, is out of joint. To presencing as such jointure must belong, thus creating the possibility of its being out of joint' (AF 41). Heidegger explains,

> According to the fragment the αὐτά (τὰ ἐόντα), those beings that linger awhile in presence, stand in disorder. As they linger awhile, they tarry. They hang on. For they advance hesitantly through their while, in hesitation from arrival to departure. They hang on; they cling to themselves. When what lingers awhile delays, it stubbornly follows the inclination to persist in hanging on, and indeed to insist on persisting; it aims at everlasting continuance and no longer bothers about δίκη, the order of the while.
>
> But in this way everything that lingers awhile strikes a haughty pose toward every other of its kind. None heeds the lingering presence of the others. Whatever lingers awhile is inconsiderate toward others. (AF 45–6)

Thus, by lingering, which is what that which is present essentially does, what is present is in disarray because of the length of the while it would perdure if it could and because it clamours in front of the other present beings and ignores its proper belonging together with them. It is guilty, as it were, of disorder (*Unfug*); it is reckless (*ruchlos*). These words indicate the negative judgment about this way of presencing.

In terms of homelessness, Anaximander says that what is present, by its insistence on lingering as present, frustrates itself. It would stay at home in unconcealment, in the open of the presencing of what is present; but, doing so, it is necessarily homeless – it does not conform to the passing order of the while in which it belongs nor to its place alongside the other present things to which it belongs. It no longer remains at home lingering alongside other things in the while of unconcealment (AF 41–6). But if we look at the saying again, we see that Anaximander says, 'they let order belong and thereby also reck, to one another (in the surmounting) of disorder' (AF 47). That is, somehow the dis-orderly, reck-less lingering is surmounted: what is present lets order and 'reck' prevail. Heidegger originarily interprets 'reck' (*Ruch*): 'The Middle High German word *ruoche* means solicitude or care. Care tends to something so that it may remain in its essence. This tuning-itself-toward, when thought of as what lingers awhile in relation to presencing is ... reck' (AF 46).

Heidegger claims that Anaximander's words provide a key to the Greek understanding of presencing, by naming the manner in which it occurs: 'If what is present grants order, it happens in this manner: as beings linger awhile, they give reck to one another. The surmounting of disorder properly occurs through the letting-belong of reck' (AF 47). 'This letting belong is the matter in which what lingers awhile lingers and so comes to presence as what is present' (AF 48). To some extent, things that are present turn toward each other and allow the rest to be themselves (rather than trying to expel the latter). In this way, what is present also allows order to belong. Because what 'lingers awhile keeps to its while,' 'within the open expanse of unconcealment each lingering being becomes present to every other being' (AF 43, 47). Anaximander's figure, in which the things that are present turn toward each other so as to allow a dynamically mutual belonging and order to come, can be translated into the language of our current inquiry as 'the presencing of what is present enables homecoming to come about.'

Anaximander names the giving of the homecoming-belonging of what is present – or, in his terms, the giving of this order – in a word to which Heidegger tries to come home in originary thought, τὸ χρεών, usage (*Brauch*), usually translated as 'necessity.' In Heidegger's interpretation, '"to use" accordingly suggests: to let something present come to presence as such; *frui*, to brook, to use, usage, means: to hand something over to its own essence and to keep it in hand, preserving it as something present' (AF 53). Here homecoming would be coming into a proper essence and being kept as present.

Usage gives. According to Heidegger, this saying brings us to being:

> In the translation of τὸ χρεών, usage is thought as essential presencing in being itself ... Usage now designates the manner in which being itself presences as the relation to what is present, approaching and becoming involved with what is present as present: τὸ χρεών.
>
> Usage delivers what is present to its presencing; i.e. to its lingering. Usage dispenses to what is present the portion of its while. (AF 53)

Usage gives the presence of what is present by gathering, as Heraclitus, too, noted: 'presencing as such is ruled by the lingering-with-one another of a concealed gathering' (cited in AF 40). The gathering which Heraclitus called 'collecting' or bringing together and a fateful assembly, Anaximander calls jointure. As we have just heard, 'presencing comes about in such a jointure' – between approach and withdrawal (AF 41). This gathering is above all for the sake of sheltering which occurs in *aletheia* – unconcealment.

Heidegger's project is to help the originary being at home which Heraclitus and Anaximander said and thought (which soon thereafter slipped back into concealment) newly come back into unconcealment. Heidegger discovers that what we metaphysically think as being and beings conceals something more primordial. Further, the belonging together and separation (being at home and homelessness) of being and beings, including human beings, would conceal the relation itself – the very manner of belonging which we need to recover for a homecoming to the originary. When Heidegger thinks through Parmenides, for example, he comes to understand that the latter specifies neither 'beings in themselves' nor 'being for itself' (see 'Moira,' *What Is Called Thinking?*). 'Rather, ἐόν, being, is thought here in its duality [*Zweifalt*, twofold] as being and beings, and is participially expressed ... This duality [twofold] is at least intimated by such nuances of phrasing as "the being of beings" and "beings in being." In its essence, however, what unfolds is obscured more than clarified through the "in" and the "of." These expressions are far from thinking the duality as such, or from seriously questioning its unfolding' (M 86).

> Since the gathering that reigns within being unites all beings, an inevitable and continually more stubborn semblance arises from the contemplation of this gathering, namely, the illusion that being (of beings) is not only identical with the totality of beings, but that, as identical, it is at the same time that which unifies and is even most in being [*das Seiendsten*]. *For representational thinking everything comes to be a being.*
>
> The 'duality' of being and beings, as something twofold, seems to melt away into nonexistence, albeit thinking, from its Greek beginnings onward, has moved within the unfolding of this duality, though without considering its situation or at all taking note of the unfolding of the twofold. What takes place at the beginning of Western thought is the unobserved decline of the duality. But the decline is not nothing. Indeed it imparts to Greek thinking the character of a beginning, in that the lighting of the being of beings, as a lighting, is concealed. The hiddenness of this decline of the duality reigns in essentially the same way as that into which the duality itself falls. Into what does it fall? Into oblivion, where lasting dominance conceals itself as Λήθη to which 'Αλήθεια belongs so immediately that the former can withdraw in its favor and can relinquish to it pure disclosure in the modes of Φύσις, Λόγος, and Ἕν as though this had no need of concealment.
>
> But the apparently futile lighting is riddled with darkness. In it the unfolding of the twofold remains as concealed as its decline for beginning thought. (M 87; see also 90–1)

That may be why Heraclitus says Lightning. 'Heraclitus thought the Λόγος as his guiding word, so as to think in this word the being of beings. But the lightning abruptly vanished. No one held on to its streak of light and the nearness of what it illuminated. We see this lightning only when we station ourselves in the storm of being' (Lo 78). Our task for a homecoming, like the poet Hölderlin's journey to the source as a mariner, is to embark on the stormy waters, into the wandering where being's lightning may strike close by. We do this by listening and thinking, which changes the world 'into the even darker depths of a riddle, depths which as they grow darker, offer the promise of a greater brightness': 'The riddle has long been propounded to us in the word "being." In this matter "being" remains only the provisional word. Let us see to it that our thinking does not merely run after it blindly. Let us first thoughtfully consider that "being" was originally called "presencing" – and "presencing": enduring-here-before in unconcealment' (Lo 78).

This is of the greatest importance. Insofar as Heidegger has begun to become at home in the Greek, *he finds that what he had taken to be home –*

being – is not in fact home. Just as the poet who set foot on native shore only to discover that it and the poet's own self were still strange, and that the poet therefore really had to begin a proper homecoming – learning to become at home – *so too Heidegger, after thinking toward being for all these years, at the moment of his arrival comes close enough to it to find that being remains strange: it conceals a more primal home to which his journey must now begin.* The homecoming to the Greeks, then, well underway here, is only the beginning of Heidegger's own homecoming. The Greek is like the poet's youthful home, for, according to Heidegger, the Greeks themselves, though they lived amidst the lighting-unconcealment (and thus could think and say as they did), nonetheless did not experience the full essence of this home and giving. For example, Heidegger asserts, 'If indeed Parmenides was saying something about 'Αλήθεια, he must have been thinking within the unfolding of the twofold. Does he mention 'Αλήθεια? Of course he does, right at the beginning of his "Didactic Poem." Even more: 'Αλήθεια is the goddess. Listening to what she says, Parmenides speaks his own thought – although he leaves unsaid what the essence of 'Αλήθεια might be rooted in' (M 93).

Heidegger indicates depths thus far unsuspected: being and beings conceal the duality, which (rather than the being of beings) originally was understood as the presencing of what is present; the duality, in turn, lies in unconcealment, which has its essence rooted in an unnamed place. Home seems far away indeed as Heidegger apparently comes nearer. Heraclitus speaks of the giving of the presencing of what is present as occurring between mortal and immortal laying-before and thus as having a 'more primordial origin'; Heidegger, seeking an originary homecoming, asks, 'Is there a path for mortal thinking to that place?' (Lo 75). If there is, it is in thinking through language, through the opening that can only be given, not forced or demanded. Here the journey would be out into the flashing storm, where 'the golden gleam of the lightning's invisible shining cannot be grasped, because it is not itself something grasping. Rather, it is the purely appropriating event [*das reine Ereignen*]. The invisible shining of the lighting stream from wholesome self-keeping in the self-restraining preservation of sending. Therefore the shining of the lightning is in itself at the same time a self-veiling – and is in that sense what is most obscure' (Al 123).

In these words, Heidegger's attempt to think unconcealment, the unconcealment of the most primordial giving, is a turning to think the safe keeping – that safe keeping which oblivion would have to turn into to turn home (see 'The Thing,' 171–4).[12] Homecoming is thus a wandering through the darkness of concealment; if the wandering comes to an open place where unconcealing-lightening occurs, we can only be grateful. As we have just seen, the Greeks, as Heidegger originarily interprets them, think what gives home and what home appropriately is: the language is homey, as in the instance of the harvesting of a crop (which also gathers it to Hölderlin's language). Laying-before is done by fore-gathering, selecting, bringing together, sheltering, accommodating in a proper storage place, and safe keeping in the concealment which is a reservoir (see AF 36, 39); the reservoir enables the giving. *Notice the full circle of enabling completed here.* This is the language of home. But before Heidegger reaches this place to dwell there, he can only catch glimpses of it and say it in snatches, as best he can. His writing reflects this state of affairs. For now, he is still on the journey to his own home by way of his journey into the Greek – and the latter has just begun. The task then is to keep underway in the 'storm' of which he speaks. That means, it is necessary to try to think the duality and its unfolding, which also means to question thinking and language.

The turn in thinking from what seemed to the sought-for home – being – turns, in the originary Greek belonging, toward the duality. Homecoming is underway in this very movement: 'the unconcealing of the concealed into unconcealment is the very presencing of what is present. We call this the being of beings' (Lo 64). Or, 'beings are spoken in such a way that their being is expressed. Being comes to language as the being of beings' (AF 22; see also 50). And it keeps coming. Though the history of being begins as the oblivion of being, in which being keeps to itself and thus hides its distinction from beings, this distinction may have 'left a trace which remains preserved in the language to which being comes' and would thus 'already [have] unveiled itself with the presencing of what is present' (AF 51). Language especially holds this duality in the early Greek words: φύσις, Λόγος, Μοῖρα, 'Αλήθεια, Ἕν, Τὸ Χρεών, lighting (see, e.g., AF 39, 55). What is needed is for the early words to speak of the duality in 'our contemporary recollection' (AF 51). Heidegger notes, 'Nevertheless such daring [the addressing of being] is not impossible, since being speaks always and everywhere throughout language. The difficulty lies not so much in finding in thought the word for being as in retaining purely in genuine thinking the word found' (AF 52).

Because the primal giving of the presencing of what is present, which lays before by gathering and safe keeping, comes to Heraclitus, Anaximander, and Parmenides each in his own way, Heidegger finds that many words name the same. Recall, for Heraclitus, according to Heidegger, φύσις, Λόγος, Ἕν, and *Lightning* said the same (which is not to say they are identical) (AF 55). So too Parmenides' Μοῖρα and Anaximander's Tὸ Χρεών think what 'is essential in presencing – all these name the same' – still later, the same is said yet again by ἰδέα for Plato and by ἐνέργεια for Aristotle (AF 56). They all try to say how the presencing of what is present unfolds in and as duality. That is, the twofold is the place of and sending of the presencing of what is present (M 100). Further, this duality points to the most primal. Parmenides, for example, 'names Μοῖρα, the apportionment, which allots by bestowing and so unfolds the twofold. The apportionment dispenses (provides and presents) through the duality. Apportionment is the dispensation of presencing, as the presencing of what is present, which is gathered in itself and therefore unfolds of itself ... Μοῖρα has dispensed the sending of being ... into the duality, and thus has bound it to totality and immobility, from which and in which the presencing of what is present comes to pass' (M 97). Yet, fateful sending 'altogether conceals both the duality as such and its unfolding' (M 97). Thus, for Parmenides, the same 'is no longer a predicate, but rather the subject which lies at the core, what supports, and maintains' (M 95). 'As such, το αυτό, the same, reigns. Specifically, it reigns as the unfolding of the twofold – an unfolding in the sense of disclosure' (M 95).

Heidegger claims the same (spoken in Λόγος, Μοῖρα, and χρεών) not only names the origin of the granting of the presencing of what is present through the duality but also metes out language and thinking, and thereby gathers mortals to itself. Λόγος as λέγειν lays out and lets lie before us so that νόημα prevails, that is, so that what is laid out before us is kept safe and held in its essence. This sends mortal λέγειν and νοειν on their way: our saying (λέγειν) is the letting lie of what is laid before us by Logos (Λόγος), and our thinking (νοεῖν) is the responding taking to heart of what is so laid (see *What Is Called Thinking?* 194–244). Thus, the same conceals 'the revealing bestowal of the belonging together of the duality and the thinking that comes forward into view within it' (M 95). That is, what we call thinking and what we call saying (language) are given to us and are actually ways in which we belong to the duality. When, for example, Parmenides says in Fragment 3 that 'thinking and being are the same' he means, explicates Heidegger, that thinking is the gathering which corresponds to the presencing of what is present and thus comes from and belongs to it (M 84). They are called the same because they belong together; of course, only what has difference, and is not identical, can belong together (M 88).

On the same way toward each other, the duality presences in taking-heed-of (νοεῖν, thinking) and taking heed of is on its way to the duality – 'already gathered in the duality by virtue of a prior λέγειν, a prior letting-lie-before' (M 88). Νοεῖν is 'grounded in and comes to presence in λέγειν (M 89). Only what has already been laid down can be taken to heart and there kept safe. In saying (laying) 'the letting-be-before of what is present in its presencing occurs' (M 89). Our mortal saying also lays down and lets lie what is given to us in Logos' laying – gathering. (Clearly, saying and thinking in this originary Greek understanding are quite different from – and are the origin of – thinking and saying as representationally understood, for example, by way of logic and logistics, rather than originary Logos. This change and unfolding will be taken up in the next section, where Heidegger follows the withdrawal of the originary into the metaphysical.) In thinking the laying that gathers, then, Heidegger finds that Λόγος gives 'the essence of saying [*die Saga*] as thought by the Greeks. Language would be saying. Language would be the gathering letting-lie-before of what is present in its presencing. In fact, the Greeks *dwelt* in this essential determination of language. But they never *thought* it – "Heraclitus included"' (Lo 77).

Here in its originary Greek occurrence, language is the house where the duality unfolds the presencing of what is present and in which mortals are at home. (Think too, as Hölderlin has told us, how the dwelling that occurs in the original, youthful home is not yet thoughtful, which is why a journey into the foreign remains necessary before a genuine homecoming – a learning to dwell at home – can come about.) Heidegger notes the curious state which results from the long-unnoticed laying out of saying as itself a laying: 'Human thought was never astonished by this event, nor did it discern in it a mystery which concealed an essential dispensation of being to man, a dispensation perhaps reserved for that historical moment which would not only devastate man from top to bottom but send his very essence reeling' (Lo 64). This is why Heidegger is here, trying to think and become at home in the originary Greek and, perhaps audaciously, 'to reach back into what must be thought even more primordially' (M 94).

What is discovered concerning saying also holds for thinking. Thinking is the thinking and preserving of being. 'Thinking does not originate: it is, when being presences' (AF 40). Parmenides says that 'You cannot find thinking apart from the duality' because, Heidegger explains, 'thinking belongs with ἐόν in the gathering that ἐόν calls for, and because thinking itself, resting in the λέγειν, completes the gathering called for, thus responding to its belonging to ἐόν as a belonging which ἐόν uses' (M 91). Thinking, then, houses the duality insofar as it sends the presencing of what is present into the safe keeping of thinking; thinking belongs to and would be at home in the duality (M 90). That is why we can come home to thinking, saying, and thereby to the duality only by discovering them in their belonging; 'only where [each] belongs and is at home can we find it' (M 90).

Homecoming would be such coming into the proper, originary belonging together of mortals, the duality, thinking, and saying. Again, we find that while homelessness is a separation within what (already) belongs together even when separated, homecoming lies in their coming back together. Hence, Heidegger says,

> In one respect thinking is outside the duality toward which it makes its way, required by and responding to it. In another respect, this very 'making its way toward ...' remains within the duality, which ... comes to presence from the revealing unfolding.
>
> But disclosure, while it bestows the lighting of presencing, at the same time needs a letting-lie-before and is a taking-up-into-perception if what is present is to appear and by this need binds thinking to its belonging-together with the duality. Therefore by no means is there somewhere and somehow something present outside the duality. (M 96)

'The duality' seems to name – at this moment of interpretation and understanding – the home of homes, that is, the realm and giving of all homecoming.

This insight would indicate the way for homecoming to proceed: 'The duality conceals within itself both νοεῖν and its thought (νόημα) as something said. What is taken up in thinking, however, is the presencing of what is present. The thoughtful saying that corresponds to the duality is the λέγειν, the letting-lie-before of presencing. It occurs, and occurs only on the thought-path of the thinker who has been called by *aletheia* (αλήθεια)' (M 98). *There is a double homecoming then:* 1) *in thinking and language* Heidegger accomplishes an originary homecoming to Greek thinking, where 2) the giving of the presencing of what is present, thinking (νοεῖν), and saying (λέγειν) belong – as at home – together. Thinking what is said and into language would be our way and means home, as given in the primal giving of all homecoming. Heidegger concludes 'The Anaximander Fragment,' 'But what if being in its essence needs to use the essence of man? If the essence of man consists in thinking the truth of being? Then thinking must poetize on the riddle of being. It brings the dawn of thought into the neighborhood of what is for thinking' (AF 38).[13]

Heidegger's interpretation of what unfolds in the Greek experience understands that what calls for thinking and saying gathers humans toward where they belong; humans, for their part, are needed and used when they think and poetize and thereby help gather the giving into language and the safe keeping of remembering thinking. To articulate and think this laying that gathers was the task of the early Greek poets and thinkers; they attempted to take to heart and let lie before us in saying the laying that gathers and safe-keeps. Heidegger contends that before thinkers and poets were distinguished and separated from each other, where the former became identified as philosophers and the latter as self-expressive creators according to the metaphysical categories that developed in the course of the history of being, early Greek thinkers poetized. He explains: 'However, thinking is poetizing, and indeed more than one kind of poetizing, more than poetry and song. Thinking of being is the original way of poetizing. Language first comes to language, i.e. into its essence, in thinking. Thinking says what the truth of being dictates; it is the original *dictare.* Thinking is primordial poetry, prior to all poesy, but also prior to the poetic of art, since art shapes its work within the realm of language. All poetizing, in this broader sense, and also in the narrower sense of the poetic, is in its ground a thinking. The poetizing essence of thinking preserves the sway of the truth of being' (AF 19).

Because thinking must see the lightning flash of the laying-giving and bring it into language, the Greeks thought of the seer and originary poet together. The seer stands in the midst of the unconcealment of the presencing of what is present and sees in the midst of the concealment that occurs. Thus, the seer sees in and into darkness and, since 'seeing is determined, not by the eye, but by the lighting of being,' is said to be blind. The seer sees where darkness seems to hold sway – in the 'sheer oppression' of what surrounds us: 'The seer is outside himself in the solitary region of the presencing of everything that in some way becomes present' (AF 35). This being outside, which is the seer's way of being within and outside the duality, is the way the seer is outside the seer's own self (M 96). Beside the seer's own self, the seer is called mad (AF 35). Heidegger thinks the originary presencing before the seer by way of the old German word *war* ('was'), which means protection:

> We must think of *wahren* as a securing which clears and gathers. Presencing preserves [*wahrt*] in unconcealment what is present both at the present

> time and not at the present time. The seer speaks from the preserve [*Wahr*] of what is present. He is the soothsayer [*Wahr-Sager*].
>
> Here we think of the preserve in the sense of that gathering which clears and shelters; it suggests itself as a long hidden fundamental trait of presencing, i.e. of being. One day we shall learn to think our exhausted word for truth [*Wahrheit*] in terms of the preserve; to experience truth as the preservation [*Wahris*] of being; and to understand that, as presencing, being belongs to this preservation. As protection of being, preservation belongs to the herdsman, who has so little to do with bucolic idylls and nature mysticism that he can be the herdsman of being only if he continues to hold the place of nothingness. (AF 36)

Reflexively, this passage names Heidegger's own task, to preserve the presencing of what is present by remembering and holding in thoughtful saying what the early Greeks began to preserve: 'thinking is the poetizing of the truth of being in the historic dialogue between thinkers.' Heidegger, for his part, speaks about the light on which the seer and he depend for their homecomings in homely, poetic words: 'The play of the calling, brightening, expanding light is not actually visible. It shines imperceptibly, like the morning light upon the quiet splendor of lilies in a field or roses in a garden' (M 96).

Since Heidegger increasingly – originarily – speaks of the presencing of what is present, rather than of the being and beings, he also begins to stop speaking of human being or beings. Instead, he emphasizes the originary belonging to the giving/coming of presencing of what is present which occurs by way of thinking and saying (which the word 'herdsman' names). That is why he has used the word *Da-sein* to name the openness within which we can hold what comes. Now, thinking from his own understanding (see *Being and Time*) and with the Greeks, he originarily recovers another name, 'mortals.'[14] 'Mortals' names we who are appropriated by the same (Lo 75). But to speak of mortals requires hearing what the Greeks also said of the immortals – the gods – and the laying and gathering standing above them both (Lo 74).

That is, by journeying in an attempt to be at home in the now foreign, originary Greek, mortals, by way of thinking and saying, belong to what they are separated from: the giving of the presencing of what is present. He also gathers mortals to the others whom we originarily belong together with, though from whom we are now separated: the gods. He attempts, then, to gather mortals and gods together in remembering thinking and to gather them together with the most primordial. Heraclitus' Fragment 53 speaks of mortals and immortals together. Heidegger speculates, as he admits, on its meaning: the enduring-lighting lets gods and mortals come to presence in unconcealment, each in its own way. The gods and mortals are exceptional in character amidst what is present, in that

> precisely they in their relation to the lighting can never remain concealed. Why is it that they cannot? Because their relation to the lighting is nothing other than the lighting itself, in that this relation gathers men and gods into the lighting and keeps them there ... But of what sort is the presencing of gods and men? They are not only illuminated in the lighting, but are also enlightened from and toward it. Thus they can, in *their* way, accomplish the lighting (bring it to the fullness of its essence) and thereby protect it. Gods and men are not only lighted by a light ... so that they can never hide themselves from it in darkness; they are luminous in their essence. They are alight [*er-lichtet*]; they are appropriated into the event of lighting, and therefore never concealed. On the contrary, they are re-vealed, thought in still another sense. Just as those who are far distant belong to the distance, so are the revealed ... entrusted to the lighting that keeps and shelters them. According to their essence, they are transposed [*ver-legt*] to the concealing of the mystery, gathered together, belonging to the Λόγος in ὁμολογεῖν (Fragment 50). (Al 119–20)

Clearly, the nature of mortals and immortals needs to be thought through,[15] as does their relation to the primal giving.[16] Heraclitus, as Heidegger explains him, names the giving of the presencing of what is present, 'lighting' or 'fire' (Πῦρ), which means the ever-enduring rising (Al 117). 'Life' is to be understood here, not as a biologically conceived animality, but according to the proper modes of rising into the openings which remain concealed: mortals, gods, and animals all rise and are hidden in their own ways (Al 116–17). At this point, Heidegger has found that their essence is gathered together with the very giving and preserving of gathering–safe-keeping itself. Thus, the last lines of 'Moira,' concluding the essays on Greek thinking, say, 'the essence of mortals calls upon them to heed a call which beckons them toward death. As the outermost possibility of *Dasein*, death is not the end of the possible but the highest keeping (the gathering sheltering) of the mystery of calling disclosure' (M 101).

If gods and mortals are gathered into shelter in the concealing mystery according to the Greek, then, originarily, That which gives the presencing of what is present, thinking, saying, mortals, and gods is thought in the language of place and home (Al 119–20 and just above). The giving gathering appears, in other words, as the granting of home. In the midst of the strangeness of our homelessness, Heidegger has wandered into the still strange thought of the Greeks; there he encounters and needs to think – originarily – 'realm,' 'origin,' and 'topos' (τόπος).

Heidegger finds that Heraclitus' saying concerning the never-setting, ever-rising itself 'takes place in the realm [*Bereich*] of disclosure, not that of concealment' (Al 111 [64]). The problem becomes how to 'think the realm of disclosure and disclosing itself, so as not to run the risk of chasing mere terms' (Al 111). In trying to do so, he discovers that 'the never in any case setting names the realm of all realms [*Bereich aller Berieche*] for early thinking. It is not, however, the highest genus which subordinates different species of realms to it. It is the abode wherein every possible "whether" of a belonging rests. Thus the realm ... is unique by virtue of the extent of its gathering reach. Everything that belongs in the event of a rightly experienced revealing grows upward and together (*concrescit*) in this realm' (Al 115). Heidegger means that representational thinking, which proceeds by way of its logical distinctions, categories, and relations, and which thus also thinks 'realm' (*Bereich*) as a containing category or concept (for example, as the universal or all encompassing), cannot fathom what 'realm' originarily means (see AF 24 [308]).[17] He at least hints here that the latter is understood as the site of dwelling and gathering, that is, by way of home. Thus, disclosure would be the abode of all belongings. Rather than limit us to a specific realm as we usually think of it, the early fragments hold and say 'something exceptional which shatters limits and concerns the realm of all realms' (Al 119; see also 121). We attempt to move toward this realm of all realms, but nonetheless are 'adrift in errancy' (where we were sent by being). Here error is the realm in which we move away from and toward the calling of mortals. Heidegger drops a hint here by adding in parentheses that realm is meant 'in the sense of a prince's realm or the realm of poetry' (AF 26). Here realm is the site where the lighting-giving of the presencing of what is present is accomplished in language or in the founding and preserving of a 'state.' History unfolds here – as the self-concealing and unconcealing of the laying that gathers.

'Origin' too would have to be thought originarily, for the entire question of homecoming is not merely about what 'origin' means, in the sense of how the Greek is our origin; rather, Heidegger attempts to understand what 'origin' itself names for the Greeks. The Anaximander fragment, for example, speaks of 'where things have their origin' (cited in AF 13), and as we have seen, Heidegger contends that 'things arise' from the giving of the presencing of what is present, which gathers and shelters in concealment (and unconcealment) (AF 20). If origin is primal giving, realm is the place of its giving, or origin's giving is and gives realm before all else. The scene where mortals, gods, and all that is present are gathered together and let lie in unconcealment is the originary place where we are (become) at home. The Greek word τόπος names this, though it has become forgotten. Our ordinary mortal opinion set on the false trails of particular 'places' misses this: 'It never perceives place, τόπος, as an abode, as what the twofold offers as a home to the presencing of what is present' (M 99–100). What we need to do is to try to think the τόπος of the unconcealing giving so that we might discover and begin to learn to dwell in the abode of the presencing of what is present which is given and to which we are gathered in homecoming. But in the meanwhile, we need to think, endure, and try to pass out of the place where we are still homeless.

Part of what Heidegger sees when he begins to become at home in the Greek is that it is in the strangeness of the Greek that the origin shows itself as what it is: the giving of the home to the presencing of what is present. This is still an experience of turning, after Heidegger's beginning to make the foreign his own, toward a homecoming to his own home. But the Greek, as origin of the West and of our thinking and saying, is nothing to be 'had' again. We must continue journeying in the unfolding of the 'sending of the duality,' that is, of history (M 98). Since mystery has its essential abode in what is near but remains foreign, mortals need to be gathered to the unfolding of the presencing of what is present which is nearby, and still coming. No further homecoming is possible before we open to, then gather and safe-keep in originary thinking and saying the concealing-disclosing unfolding of the presencing of what is present: that is, the homelessness of our epoch.

B Leaping from Metaphysical Representation to Originary Thinking

Not Leaving the Place from Which We Jump

Today, according to Heidegger, we are at the beginning of the last stage of metaphysics, wherein what is real and what can be understood is disclosed as the technological – ordered and utilized in logistical systems. 'The presentation and full articulation of all beings, dominated as they now are everywhere by the nature of the technical, may be called technology. The expression may serve as a term for the metaphysics of the atomic age' (OtlCM 52). 'We don't at all need to fathom what this means. Who would presume to actually fathom this? But today we can do something else. Each person can meditate for a little while on the uncanniness that conceals itself in this apparently harmless naming of the age' (PR 29). The uncanniness, he argues, is the concealment that is correlate with technology's disclosures: precisely the very power of the technological obscures any possibility of a mode of being gathered together with and responding to that to which we belong and within which we could become ourselves: 'In the global epoch of humanity, the atomic age ... the power of the principle ... displays itself in a strange manner ... "strange" [*unheimlich*] ... not in a sentimental sense, [but in] that the unique unleashing of the demand to render reasons [*Grundes*] threatens everything of humans' being-at-home and robs them of the roots of their subsistence [*alles Heimische des Menschen bedroht und ihm jeden Grund und Boden für eine Bodenständigkeit raubt*], the roots from out of which every great human age ... has so far grown' (PR 30). The implication is not that we simply need to investigate the relation of technology to knowledge, for instance, the relation of atomic power to physics, but that we need to question how technology is bound up at the deepest level with our current homelessness (QCT 14, 21).

How would a homecoming questioning proceed? Heidegger has learned from Hölderlin that one possible way to a no-longer-metaphysical home lies through a return to the not-yet-metaphysical Greeks. This insight opens the critical pathway along which he, and we, might make a thinking journey, parallel to the poet's poetizing one. Since his initial originary insights, articulated as the best way possible in *Contributions*, Heidegger has been saying that a leap is required – a leap out of our current metaphysical homelessness, from there to the early Greeks as no-longer-metaphysically understood, from there to an originary future.

As we have seen, being apparently has turned in a turn that first makes possible, and calls for, our response. In response, and while in dialogue with the early Greeks, Heidegger has begun to come to his own manner of thinking and saying and has thereby managed to begin to retrieve new meaning from the early Greek realm. That is, the thinking leap is underway. But in such a jump it is neither possible nor appropriate to leave behind the place from which we jump. 'The leap is always a leap from ... That from which the leap of thinking leaps is not abandoned in such a leap; rather, the realm from which one leaps first becomes surveyable when one makes the leap – surveyable in a different way than before. The leap of thinking does not leave behind it that from which it leaps; rather, it assimilates it in a more original fashion. According to this view, thinking in the leap becomes a recollective thinking, not of the bygone, but of what has-been. By this we mean the assembling of what does not pass away, but which comes to be essential, that is, lasts, inasmuch as it vouchsafes to recollective thinking new insights' (PR 60). As a transition from his reflections on the Greek works to those we are now taking up, Heidegger further notes that this thinking leap also remains within the bounds of the languages within which we live. If we allow the bounds to hold, and jump over to the other side, 'we may yet learn what can come to pass in translation. The truly fateful encounter with historic language is a silent event. But in it the sending of being speaks' (AF 57).[18] The initial jump as or toward a homecoming shows that what is especially needed is that we remain within our current situation, learning to become open to the homelessness of our own era.

Heidegger contends that now – after the turning and through the gift of the beginning of an originary language and thinking – we are indeed coming to the initial glimpses into the unconcealment of what long has been concealed, that our lives as human beings and even being itself have been hidden by the metaphysical disclosure of beings as objects and by our instrumental mastery over nature. That is, there is a major difference between the early works considered in chapter 1 and what Heidegger can see and say in the works considered in this chapter. In the former, metaphysics was in fact Heidegger's youthful 'home in homelessness,' not at all the same placement to which he has now come – in which he more fully develops his own seeing and speaking. In this chapter we can see Heidegger retrieve many of the themes he treated in the works covered in chapter 1, though now he no longer operates representationally (at least, not always or simply) but by way of recollective thinking that allows a significant reinterpretation of the unfolding of metaphysics. Hence, this chapter's essays and books do not merely repeat what was found earlier; rather, Heidegger goes over the matter anew, effecting much more fully the necessary leaping out of the metaphysical.

That is why all three sections of this chapter treat works that make such a leap from the metaphysical to the originary and that subsequently move to and fro across the history of metaphysics. The three sets of writings constituting the focus of this chapter are distinguished in that each emphasizes a different one of the three major divisions of the historical unfolding of being: the previous section dwelt on Heidegger's leap into and coming back from the not-yet-metaphysical Greek; the current section, on how the leap into the originary enables a recovery of the meaning of the long history of metaphysics itself; and the next section, on Heidegger's most mature no-longer-metaphysical thinking and saying. Thus, what characterizes the essays and books considered in the current section is not that they are entirely distinct from the other two clusters of writings (of this chapter) that undertake the jump but that here he not only leaps originarily, but also persists in the thinking of the metaphysical era and the deep homelessness of our current technological systems – powerfully analysing all forms of metaphysics and especially that of our era in a way he was unable to before the jump.

The leaps in thinking and saying that Heidegger makes – which also return to focus on the history of metaphysics, stressing its end in technology and homelessness – occur in portions of *What Is Called Thinking?* (1951–2) and 'Moira' (1951–2), in 'The Question Concerning Technology' (1949–55), in strands of 'The Thing' (1949–50), in 'Science and Reflection' (1953) and 'Conversation with Martin Heidegger' (printed as an appendix to 'Principles of Thinking,' in *The Piety of Thinking*) (1953), *The Question of Being* (1955), *What Is Philosophy* (1955), *The Principle of Reason* (1957), in parts of 'The Principle of Identity' (1957), 'The Onto-theo-logical Constitution of Metaphysics' (1957), 'The Principles of Thinking' (1958), 'The Problem of Non-objectifying Thinking and Speaking' (1964), 'The End of Philosophy and the Task of Thinking' (1964) , and sections of *Four Seminars* (1966–73). Several pertinent passages are also drawn from 'Metaphysics as History of Being' (1961) and 'Sketches for a History of Being as Metaphysics' (1961) that were primarily dealt with in chapter 1.

The leaps involve jumping over from one way of thinking and speaking to another (EP 55). We cannot avoid facing up to and questioning the confused, shattered locale in which we find ourselves placed, a realm of oblivion (QB 67, 103; WP 43). Since that is where we are in the era of technology, it is impossible not to think and speak in the old language of metaphysics. Because metaphysical language renders it impossible to think the central question of being, a homecoming depends on finding a second, originary language, one that might be adequate to the required leap out of the metaphysical and thus able to open world and dwelling (QB 73; PN-oTs 28). Heidegger begins to succeed at the task by first entering a not-yet-metaphysical language with the early Greeks and the more contemporary poets of his region, recovering the meaning of the proper old words, freshly reinterpreting them (QB 79, 103, 109). The new, originary language would be a response, reciprocating the initiating change or turning of being itself. Certainly the language could not be the same on both sides of the leap, that is, remain unaltered during or after the crossing over from the metaphysical to the not-yet-metaphysical and no-longer-metaphysical. Since metaphysical philosophy, thinking by way of univocal representational concepts, cannot be left entirely behind, even as it increasingly takes over as the only legitimate mode of thinking and saying, Heidegger needs to complement it with the originary (FS 8). Hence, attempting to recover the alternative mode, he says that we can listen to what is said if we 'rid [our]selves in time of a habit which I shall call "one-track thinking"' (WCT 26).

The writings considered here accomplish the complex leaps to and from the originary and the movements across the unfolding of metaphysics by means of just such a 'mixed mode' of thinking and saying – mixed both in the thinking's style of movement and in the way of saying. The leaps are directly seen (even if not easily comprehended as such or followed) in the way the works move non-linearly, even 'non-logically,' from where we are to the early Greek and back and forth between the early Greek and Heidegger's own originary thought, all the while recollectively thinking to and fro along the long history of metaphysics from Plato and Aristotle to Nietzsche and our homelessness in technology. The two modes of thinking, representational and originary, occur in two very different vocabularies that are found side by side, intertwined, and ruffling against one another. The contrast of these two modes is all the sharper for their juxtaposition within pages of each other – or even on the same page – and largely accounts for the heterogeneity and difficulty of this part of Heidegger's corpus.

Heidegger's double action of jumping from the metaphysical to the originary (to accomplish a two-track thinking) and then coming back to move originarily through the history of the metaphysics gives this set of works its special style – a discontinuous jumping that allows and leads to a recollection and reinterpretation of the history of the not-yet-metaphysical, the metaphysical, and the no-longer-metaphysical, with a sustained elaboration of the homelessness of our current technological world. A striking example occurs in *What Is Called Thinking?* and in the related essay 'Moira,' where Heidegger continues his translations from the early Greek, leaping out of ordinary metaphysical, technological understanding to an originary interpretation, not only juxtaposing the two modes of thinking but deftly transforming the one into the other – right before our eyes. For example, Heidegger first lays out the usual representational translation of one of Parmenides' core sayings: 'One should both say and think that being is' (cited in WCT 171, 178). He then reinterprets it originarily as saying, 'Useful is the letting-lie-before-us, so (the) taking-to-heart, too: beings in being [– the presencing of what is present]' (WCT 228).[19] Quite a contrast between these two versions. Though, as we will see, he works out the originary thinking and saying for each dimension of Parmenides' saying, here the leap and the contrasting content of representational and originary thinking and saying can be seen in his treatment of the very first word, χρή, as 'needful,' 'useful.' 'We may assume without fear of being arbitrary that the "using" mentioned here is spoken in a high, perhaps the highest, sense. We therefore translate χρή with "It is useful"' (WCT 187).

Noting that, in Parmenides' saying, '"needful" indeed is the correct translation of χρή,' Heidegger explains that the word 'needful' derives from 'hand' and 'handling': when I handle something, it is usually because I have a use for it, I am considering using or am about to use it (WCT 186–7; FS 63). Using is taken to be a human activity and often as connected with making or technology. Heidegger then immediately leaps from this representational meaning, which focuses on production, to an originary realm (with an eye to the way Hölderlin approaches similar matters): '"Using" does not mean the mere utilizing, using up, exploiting. Utilization is only the degenerate and debauched form of use. When we handle a thing, for example, our hand must fit itself to the thing. Use implies fitting response ... use is determined and defined by leaving the used thing in its essential nature ... only proper use brings the thing to its essential nature and keeps it there. So understood, use itself is the summons which demands that a thing be admitted to its own essence and nature, and that the use keep to it. To use something is to let it enter into its essential nature, to keep it safe in its essence' (WCT 187). Hence, Heidegger leaps right before our eyes, substantially retranslating 'use' across metaphysical and non-metaphysical regions.

The other major accomplishment of this set of works – remaining within the site of the leap, that is, within our current homelessness, but now originarily going back and forth through the history of metaphysics, reinterpreting it in light of what is seen – occurs in an integrated cluster of phenomena and words which we need to follow in some detail. Travelling from the early Greek, to the metaphysical, to the originary, Heidegger treats the clusters of topics and the leaps depicted in figure 2.

Each of these clusters and leaps needs to be followed in some detail. Two-track thinking and travelling back and forth across the metaphysi-

Figure 2. Heidegger's journey from the early Greek, to the metaphysical, to the originary.

Not-yet-metaphysical Early Greek	**Metaphysical** Plato → modern → today's logistics	**No-longer-metaphysical** Emerging originary
aletheia (ἀλήθεια)	– truth as correspondence	– unconcealment
legein (λέγειν)	– language as expression	– letting-lie-before
noein (νοεῖν)	– forming representational ideas/ logic/logistic	– recollective thinking/ taking to heart
eon (ἐόν) and	– *being* and	
emmenai (εμμεναι)	– beings (as objects/ standing reserve)	– the duality: the presencing of what is present
poiēsis: physis (φύσις)	– nature/creation	
and *techne*	– technology-enframing (*her-aus-fordern*)	– * (*her-vor-bringen*)
to auto (τὸ αὐτό)	– identity	– the same-belonging together and difference
logos (λόγος)	– being: the ground of beings principle/ground/cause	– being without ground; abyss and play; beings without Why

*In this set of works, this dimension is not elaborated; it will be covered in the next chapter.

cal, the not-yet-metaphysical, and the no-longer-metaphysical takes us to the following considerations.

TRUTH-ALETHEIA/DISCLOSURE

As we have seen, Heidegger has been exploring the interpretation of truth and *aletheia* (ἀλήθεια) for many years, from *Being and Time, Contributions,* and 'On the Essence of Truth,' through 'The Origin of the Work of Art,' to 'Letter on Humanism' and 'Aletheia.' What is different in the works considered here is that, in addition to continuing to refine the originary translation of *aletheia* (unifying it powerfully with reinterpretations of *legein* (λέγειν), *noein* (νοεῖν), and *eon* (ἐόν) *emmenai* (εμμεναι), Heidegger moves back and forth from the early Greek through the several metaphysical variations to forcefully bring the interpretation to bear on the concealments and disclosures of our technological era and its homelessness. Since we have already seen Heidegger's basic retrieval of *aletheia*-unconcealment, we need not belabour it here. Instead, while attending to what is new, we can focus on how he runs through the history of the unfolding meanings, gathering them with those of the other key words he reinterprets to forcefully explicate scientific-technological truth.

In our current metaphysical understanding of thinking as a subjective process, taken to work properly when it operates according to objective logic, and our understanding, correspondingly, of language as a paradigmatic set of statements made to represent aspects of the world, our conception of truth satisfies one version of the demands of both thinking and saying. We hold that to grasp and fix an object by means of a concept is to either implicitly assume or explicitly claim that the concept and object correspond. If they do, the thinking-grasping is considered correct, that is, true. Parallel, if we affirm this relationship in regard to language, a statement or claim will be true if what is asserted corresponds to the relation that obtains between idea and object. The core understanding is that truth is the correspondence of idea and what is thought or said. After the classical Greek developments of truth as correspondence, especially by Plato and Aristotle, in the Roman and medieval worlds the Latin *veritas* was transformed as *adequatio* (correct correspondence, which, though distinguished from faith, complexly informed doctrine), and from there to the modern *certitudo* (established by the subject, in consciousness) (MHB 19–25; sHBM 55, 69–70; FS 14; see also WCT 39–44).

The seminal appearance of truth as the correct provides the epistemological basis for the development of the metaphysical correlate, that is, for the scientific determination of reality, which still reigns – our doctrine today, you could say (SR 156–7). It would seem uncontroversial to note that in the most recent phase of the metaphysical era, it is not so much philosophy, but rather science as technological that has become the realm of revealing, that is, of the truth (QCT 12). Here, where the real has emerged in and through our understanding of the certain, the factual comes to reign (SR 162); further, through Descartes and those who followed, the consequences of this mode of unconcealment unfold in the dynamic of subject and object. The measure proceeds from 'the representing, cognizing subject, by this subject and for this subject ... Only what presents itself to our cognition, only what we en-counter such that it is posed and posited in its reasons, counts as something with secure standing, that means, as an object. Only what stands in this manner is something of which we can, with certainty, say "it is"' (PR 27). As Heidegger points out, 'This all leads to Max Planck's thesis about being: "The real is what is measurable"' (FS 53).

In the midst of the astonishing manifestation of so many objects, so well known and controlled by calculating subjects, we live in the realm of the correct. The correct dominates as the goal and measure, not only of knowledge, but of 'what is' and operates congruently with the 'current conception of technology, according to which it is a means and a human activity,' and therefore first of all 'instrumental and anthropological' (QCT 5). But originally, Heidegger tells us, theory meant 'the beholding that watches over truth' or 'reverent paying heed' (SR 164–5; FS, 54); next the Greek *theorein* and *eidos* became for Latin *contemplari/templum*, that which sunders and compartmentalizes (SR 165–6), then the German *Betrachtung/trachten*, to strive, to manipulate; *arbeiten*, to work. In our technological era, theory ends as observation, that is, as the entrapment of the real (SR 166–7). (This point will be developed below, with Heidegger's further exploration of the principles and grounds of our knowing and of what is considered real.)

In contrast, as we have seen (in first and third chapters, and in the first section of this chapter), Heidegger explores how *aletheia*-unconcealment is the originary meaning of what becomes truth. Here we can see how Heidegger uses *aletheia* to originarily think humans as belonging, especially via saying and thinking, to the presencing of what is present. From the vantage point of the jump, humans, rather than being autonomous or the initiating source of meaning, are needed and used for the safe keeping of the coming to presence of truth (QCT 32–3). Even more importantly, *aletheia* is a key to moving from what calls for thinking to disclosing giving and to wrestling with the hiddenness and unconcealment of our current technological age.

At the end of *What Is Called Thinking?*, and consistent with what Heidegger has already said in other works already considered, he elaborates the presencing of what is present in the language of *aletheia*. For the early Greeks, he explains, when something such as a mountain range is thought of as being present and abiding, it is understood that

> What is present has risen from unconcealment. It takes its origin from such a rise in its being present. Having risen from unconcealment, what is present also has entered into what was already unconcealed; the mountain range lies in the landscape. Its presence is the rising entry into what is unconcealed within unconcealment, even and especially when the mountain range keeps standing as it is, extending and jutting.
>
> But this rise from unconcealment, as the entry into what is unconcealed, does not specifically come to the fore in the presence of what is present. It is part of presence to hold back these traits, and thus to let come out only that which is present. Even, and in particular, that unconcealment in which this rise and entry takes place, remains concealed, in contrast to the uncon-

> cealed present things ... All lying-before-us is already constituted in presence ... Presence does demand unconcealment, and is a rising from unconcealment – though not generally but in such a way that presence is the entry into a duration of unconcealment. (WCT 236–7)

Heidegger, then, is working out how *aletheia* is 'more primal' (in that it is an 'origin' of what is present) in order to bring unconcealment closer to some disclosure. This is necessary, since with the metaphysical bringing forth of beings, the rise from unconcealment does not come to the fore, much less the unconcealed itself. Heidegger's task, of course, is to make explicit the historical play of the paired concealments and unconcealments: 'In the beginning of its history, being opens itself out as emerging [*physis*] and unconcealment [*aletheia*]. From there it reaches the formulation of presence and permanence in the sense of enduring [*ousia*]. Metaphysics proper begins with this' (EP 4; see also OtlCM, 64). Even a cursory review of the dynamic from the early Greek understanding of *aletheia*, through to the representation of truth in the language of correspondence and correctness, to an originary insight into disclosure and opening shows that we need to think the character simultaneously of language, thinking, being and beings, *poesis* and *techne*, identity, and logic.

LANGUAGE

In the traditional, representational understanding, language 'is a system of signs' for speaking and writing (WCT 191). As such a system of signs, it is one of the – perhaps *the only* – principal means by which we express ourselves and connect with each other and the world. It is through language that what is experienced, felt, willed, or thought internally is brought outward, that is, by terms and sentences. In short, from this point of view we take it that language is a tool that we employ, the sensuous means for presenting suprasensuous meaning. Heidegger, however, argues that in this view we unthinkingly operate at a second remove from what is. He contends that in the long-dominant view, language itself disappears because the originary way language gathers us together with the world is already lost in representational abstractions. Developing a phenomenology of what is immediately given in a lifeworld, Heidegger points out that 'When we hear directly what is spoken directly, we do not at first hear the words as terms, still less the terms as mere sound. In order to hear the pure resonance of a mere sound, we must first remove ourselves from the sphere where speech meets with understanding or lack of understanding. We must disregard all that, abstract from it … The supposedly purely sensual aspect of the word-sound, conceived as a mere resonance, is an abstraction' (WCT 129–30).

Given the prospect of a no-longer-metaphysical belonging with the world, Heidegger returns to retranslate the early Greek, now not only understanding how *legein* became language as expression but also reinterpreting it originarily. To continue with the earlier example, in *What Is Called Thinking?* Heidegger proceeds to leap out from our position within metaphysics, while still using what he finds in the leap to freshly rethink the historical unfolding that leads to today. From where we are at the end of metaphysics, Heidegger notes in regard to Parmenides' saying, which is usually translated as 'One should say and think that being is,' that it is certainly correct to say that *legein* (λέγειν) means 'to state' and *noein* (νοεῖν) means 'to think.' But he immediately and energetically leaps away from this position:

> Let us at last speak out and say what 'stating' means! Let us at last give thought to *why* and in what way the Greeks designate 'stating' with the word λέγειν. For λέγειν does in no way mean 'to speak.' The meaning of λέγειν does not necessarily refer to language and what happens in language. The verb λέγειν is the same word as the Latin *legere* and our own word *lay*. When someone lays before us a request, we do not mean that he produces papers on the desk before us, but that he speaks of the request. When someone tells of an event, he lays it out for us. When we exert ourselves, we lay to. To lay before, lay out, lay to – all this laying is the Greek λέγειν. To the Greeks, this word does not at any time mean something like 'stating,' as though the meaning came out of a blank, a void, but the other way around: the Greeks understand stating in the light of laying out, laying before, laying to, and *for this reason* call that 'laying' λέγειν.
>
> The meaning of the word λόγος is determined accordingly. (WCT 198–9)

Thus, language needs to be reinterpreted by way of the originary rereading of *legein:* 'Laying, λέγειν, concerns what lies there. To lay is to let lie before us. When we say something about something, we make it lie there before us, which means at the same time we make it appear. This making-to-appear and letting-lie-before-us is, in Greek thought, the essence of λέγειν and λόγος' (WCT 202).[20]

THINKING

In *What Is Called Thinking?* Heidegger originarily reconfigures the character of thinking in the same manner as he did language. Here, too, at first glance it seems that we understand thinking well enough, at least while scientific research into cognition works out the details. Thinking is representation. We form ideas through physiological and psychological processes that represent what is thought. The internal, subjective processes (of or in the subject) re-present the objects of thought. Heidegger asks, 'Is there anyone among us who does not know what it is to form an idea? When we form an idea of something – of a text if we are philologists, a work of art if we are art historians, a combustion process if we are chemists – we have a representational idea of those objects. Where do we have those ideas? We have them in our head. We have them in our consciousness. We have them in our soul. We have the ideas inside ourselves, these ideas of objects' (WCT 39; see also FS 31). Ideas are the means by which we grasp, hold on to (remember), and manipulate what we have experienced in some way. Epistemologically, what matters is that we form our ideas correctly, so that they conform – co-respond – to the object. To correctly evaluate and effectively use representations we must naturally use good judgment and avoid mistakes or arbitrary procedures by following rules. The rules of valid thinking are given by, or amount to, logic. Logic is the name for the traditional doctrine of thinking. Hence, as Heidegger notes, 'Instruction on what to understand by "thinking" is given by logic' (WCT 153).

In contrast, originarily understood as questioning, thinking is not representational, but recollective (*Besinnung);* rather than aiming to revive the past, recollection would be astonished at the coming of what is early (SR 180; QCT 22). Just as the *unheimlich* is not finally a nostalgic stimulus toward the past, but a site in which we are now and from which we move to the future, so too recollection is the way we go forward by properly going back. Hence, in strikingly originary language, Heidegger explains recollective thinking (*Andenken*) and the 'recollectively anticipatory leap' (*andenkend-vordenkender Satz*) as an event in time:

> To recollectively think-upon what has been is to fore-think into the unthought that is to be thought. To think is to recollectively fore-think [*Denken ist andenkendes Vordenken*]. It neither dwells on what has-been as a past represented by historiography, nor is it a representational thinking that stares with prophetical pretenses into a supposedly known future.

> Thinking as a recollective fore-thinking is the leaping of the leap. This leap [*Sprung*] is a movement [*Satz*] to which thinking submits.
>
> Implied in this is that thinking must ever anew and more originally [*ursprünglich*] make the leap [*den Sprung springen*]. (PR 94 [159])

To newly understand recollection requires non-representationally rethinking memory, which is further complicated, according to Heidegger, because thinking as understood in the epistemology of metaphysics obscures the originary sense of memory. As distinct from the metaphysical tradition with its representational, calculative thinking, which culminates in scientific knowing and technological logistics, Heidegger ventures after the sense of what is said and laid before us by jumping over to the originary, crossing over by trans-lation (SR 155, 176, 180; see also WCT 175–8). In representational thinking, memory is taken to be the ability to hold on to an idea or is taken to be the act of retaining a representation of something now past. While Heidegger does not do anything so silly as denying that memory is a mental capacity of humans, he does argue that it is neither first of all, nor finally, such a process. Rather, he contends, the primal experience of memory is of being gathered together with what is not otherwise present: 'Memory is the gathering of recollection, thinking back [*Gedächtnis ist die Versammlung des Andenkens*]. It safely guards and keeps concealed within it that to which at each given time thought must be given before all else'; 'Poetry wells up only from devoted thought thinking back, recollecting [*Alles Gedichtete entspringt aus der An-dacht des Andenkens*]' (WCT 11 [97]). Or, again, memory is 'the gathering of thinking that recalls ... The gathering of recalling thought is not based on a human capacity, such as the capacity to remember and retain' (WCT 150 [97]). To help recall what is named in a recollective thinking, Heidegger reflects on the Old English noun for thought, *thanc* or *thonc*, which, he points out, survives today in our English plural word 'thanks,' which also means 'a grateful thought.' Whereas we usually take a thought to mean 'an idea, a view or opinion, a notion,' Heidegger argues that the old word *thanc* holds the telling clue: 'The root or originary word says: the gathered, all-gathering thinking that recalls' (WCT 139). 'Both memory and thanks move and have their being in the *thanc*. "Memory" initially did not at all mean as in Gray's translation the power to recall. The word designates the whole disposition in the sense of a steadfast intimate concentration upon the things that essentially speak to us in every thoughtful meditation. Originarily, "memory" means as much as devotion: a constant concentrated abiding with something' (WCT 140).

The difference between the two understandings of thinking is dramatic, both in specific content and in what is taken for granted – even when argued for or 'proven.' The traditional, representational view of thinking operates within the separation of subject and object, in which the goal of thinking and memory is to overcome the gulf between the internal processes and an external object (or previous internal event). Here a representation can be correct because it can get what is initially apart to correspond; this assumes, even depends upon, the difference and separation of subject and object, of internal and external (thus, we could even say that all of metaphysics moves within difference; FS 24). Opposite, originary thinking can recollect because it assumes, depends upon, a belonging together that obtains even when thinking and what is given for thought are apart. 'The *thanc* means man's inmost mind, the heart, the heart's core, that innermost essence of man which reaches outward most fully and to the outermost limits, and so decisively that, rightly considered, the idea of an inner and an outer world does not arise ... The *thanc*, the heart's core, is the gathering of all that concerns us, all that we care for, all that touches us insofar as we are, as human beings' (WCT 144).

Thus, recalling thinking is a giving thanks for what is given for thought. What is given for thought is brought forth, and properly responded to, when it is left alone, as it is and where it belongs. That too is what it means to be grateful for what is given, what it means to be thankful. What is let be in this manner is neither exploited nor changed, but kept safe. Heidegger says,

> All thinking that recalls what can be recalled in thought already lives in that gathering which beforehand is in its keeping and keeps hidden all that remains to be thought.
>
> The nature of that which keeps safe and keeps hidden lies in preserving, in conserving. The 'keep' originarily means the custody, the guard.
>
> Memory, in the sense of human thinking that recalls, dwells where everything that gives food for thought is kept in safety ... Keeping is the fundamental nature and essence of memory ... Only that which keeps safely can preserve – preserve what is to-be-thought. The keeping preserves by giving harbor, and also protection from danger ... from, as in Gray's translation, oblivion. (WCT 150–1)

In its originary sense, then, thinking is *thanc* and memory, the gathering of recalling thought which brings forth and preserves.

Returning to Parmenides' saying with this originary insight, Heidegger puts recollective thinking and *noein* (νοεῖν) into dialogue with each other. In the encounter, Heidegger finds that in *noein,*

> what is perceived concerns us in such a way that we take it up specifically, and do something with it. But where do we take what is to be perceived? How do we take it up? We take it to heart. What is taken to heart, however, is left to be exactly as it is. This taking-to-heart does not make over what it takes. Taking to heart is: to keep at heart.
>
> Νοεῖν is taking something to heart. The noun to the verb νοεῖν, which is νόος, νόῦς, originally means almost exactly what we have explained earlier as the basic meaning of *thanc,* devotion, memory. (WCT 203)

Thus, with an initial leap into an originary understanding, Heidegger can reconnect with the early Greek to explore the resources of *noein,* so that counter to representational thinking, he can unfold how originary thinking is recalling, gathering, and taking to heart (WCT 208).

But Heidegger does not just jump out of representational concepts to explore the not-yet-metaphysical early Greek and to gather that with the beginnings of a no-longer-metaphysical originary thinking. He also uses the originary insights into what is disclosed here to remain responsible for continuing to think through the historical unfolding of metaphysics, which means the representational unfolding of *legein* and *noein.* Explicating at some length the early Greek conjunction of *legein* and *noein* as it is found in Parmenides' saying, Heidegger contends that out of this early understanding of the unity of *legein* and *noein,* Plato and Aristotle differentiate them and codify, at its beginning, the representational implementation of thinking and saying. From their seminal articulation at the decisive start of the history of metaphysics, this representational understanding shifts across Roman, medieval, modern, Enlightenment, and German idealist philosophy to today. Though here we cannot follow, much less unpack, all the subtle twists and turns that Heidegger discerns, we can at least note that in *What Is Called Thinking?* he traces the inversions that occur from the early Greek not-yet-metaphysical epoch through to the metaphysical era (which, Heidegger contends, begins with Plato, who fixes the character of logic in the *Sophist;* WCT 222). As one example of the trajectory, Heidegger sketches out the following:

> Thinking becomes the λέγειν of the λόγος in the sense of proposition … Thinking appears as what is rational. *Ratio* comes from the verb *reor. Reor* means to take something for something – νοεῖν; and this is at the same time to state something as something – λέγειν. *Ratio* becomes reason. Reason is the subject matter of logic. Kant's main work, *The Critique of Pure Reason*, deals with the critique of pure reason by way of logic and dialectic.
>
> But the original nature of λέγειν and νοεῖν disappears in ratio. As *ratio* assumes domination, all relations are turned around. For medieval and modern philosophy now explain the *Greek* essence of λέγειν and νοεῖν, λόγος and νόῦς terms of their own concept of *ratio*. That explanation, however, no longer enlightens – it obfuscates. (WCT 210–11; see also 61, 15a4–57)

Heidegger moves through the history of metaphysics, showing how decisive these turns are for subsequent translations and understandings. 'Without the λέγειν and its λόγος, Christianity would not have the doctrine of the Trinity, nor the theological interpretation of the concept of the second Person of the Trinity … there would have been no Age of Enlightenment … no dialectical materialism,' no modern technology (WCT 204). For Leibniz, as we will see below, reason and logic appear as the law of identity; after 'Kant's "transcendental logic," reaches the highest meaning possible in metaphysics through Hegel,' where 'logic as dialectic' designates the 'movement of th[e] organization of the Absolute' as '"*Logic* or *Speculative Philosophy*"' (WCT 238–9) – certainly the culmination of the process in which 'λέγειν of the λόγος develops into a διαλέγεσθαι' (WCT 156). In our current technological epoch, logic shifts from classical 'what logic' into 'relational logic' and logistics, which 'today is developing into the global system by which all ideas are organized' (WCT 163). While Heidegger works out these changes in detail in many works, here the point is that his originary insight not only allows leaping into the early Greek and his own thinking and saying but permits him to remain underway toward home by rethinking our long metaphysical homelessness, not trying to leave it behind.

BEING AND BEINGS: PRESENCING OF WHAT IS PRESENT

If this originary interpretation of saying and thinking is a vital step in our process of beginning a leap toward homecoming, even while remaining in homelessness, it is because this way of reflecting on thinking and memory begins to explore how, as gathering and recalling, they involve more than human capabilities. That would be because memory and thinking belong with and within what calls for thinking. What calls for thinking? The answer also is held in Parmenides' saying, which is one more reason it deserves to command our attention: in it we already find *legein* and *noein* lying before us, gathered together with each other, but both also with being. 'The conjunction of λέγειν and νοεῖν, however, is such that it does not rest upon itself. Letting-lie-before-us and taking-to-heart in themselves point toward something that touches and only thereby fully defines them' (WCT 210). What is it for which letting-lie-before-us and taking-to-heart are useful? Heidegger answers directly: 'What else but that to which λέγειν and νοεῖν refer? And that is identified in the word immediately following [in Parmenides' saying]. The word is ἐόν. 'Eόν is translated as "being"' (WCT 214; see also 215). Finally, then, originary recollection thinks and says nothing less than our relationship to being. Further, Heidegger explains, *eon* ('being') has *two different meanings* because it is a participle: *a verbal and a nominal meaning.* That is, it *denotes the act of being and something in being. This basic duality which the word designates is the paradigmatic duality and begins to disclose something long concealed:* 'In keeping with that dual nature, a being has its being in being, and being persists as the being of being' (WCT 221). Here, though it is done quietly, Heidegger is laying out a major change in what he says and thinks. 'When we say "being," it means "being of beings." When we say "beings," it means "beings in respect of being." We are always speaking *within* the duality. The duality is always a prior datum" (WCT 227; see also OtlCM 64). According to Heidegger, Western metaphysical thinking from Plato and Aristotle to Nietzsche is based on this duality of individual beings and being. The history of metaphysics is the history of the unfolding modulations of the relationships of being and being, which up until now has not been disclosed, much less thought out.

Apparently, Heidegger can now discern more deeply what he has been questioning all along, but that has necessarily been hidden over the course of metaphysics. Here Heidegger's own thinking and saying initially retrieve, that is begin, a homecoming to the passage through which we must pass, toward what calls on us: certainly not beings, but not being either; rather, the duality, 'The distinction – the duality of the two – must be given beforehand, in such a way that this duality does not as such receive specific attention. The same is true for all transcendence. When we pass from beings to being, our passage passes through the duality of the two. But the passage never first creates the duality. The duality is already in use' (WCT 228). Heidegger contends that in metaphysics, 'however, no further inquiry and thought is given to the duality itself, of beings and being, neither to the nature of the duality nor to that nature's origin' (WCT 224). Hence, it is the task of originary thinking, with originary language, to think and say the duality and the origin (and 'development') of metaphysics within that duality.

In fact, in *What Is Called Thinking?*, Heidegger goes on to try to originarily retrieve the meaning of the hitherto concealed duality. He does so as he did with related words such as *chre, legein,* and *noein.* Since he admittedly cannot do all that is necessary for uncovering what *eon* says, he can only continue 'in a questioning mode,' in which 'the word ἐόν indicates what is present, and *emmenai* [ἔμμεναι], *einai* [εἶναι] mean "to be present"' (WCT 233). Duality, being of beings, means, then, according to Heidegger's provisional translating, presencing of what is present – where what is present is that which 'has risen from unconcealment,' and thus is linked to *aletheia* (WCT 236).[21] 'And presence itself? Presence itself is precisely the presencing of what is present. Presence does demand unconcealment, and is a rising from unconcealment – though not generally but in such a way that presence is the entry into a duration of unconcealment. The Greeks experience such duration as a luminous appearance in the sense of illuminated, radiant self-manifestation' (WCT 237). But our ordinary perception 'pays no attention to the still light of the lighting that emanates from duality'; 'dazzled by changes of color' of the beings around us, for example, 'it never perceives place, τόπος, as an abode, as what the twofold offers as a home to the presencing of what is present' (M 99–100). As one of his deepest insights in this period, then, Heidegger finds and lays out before us that it is not just being, but the duality – the presencing of what is present – what calls for thinking.

With this jump to seeing the duality as he does, Heidegger simultaneously finds an important way to newly articulate not only the character of the primal dimensions themselves but – what emerges as even more important – the relationship among them. We cannot start to think the dynamic interrelation of being and beings by first thinking of humans or beings and then going toward being (as we might try with a modern humanism or naturalism); nor can we proceed by attempting to go from being to beings and humans. Rather 'there is thought at the same time that which belongs together from the beginning and thus inevitably must be thought together – the being of beings and its relatedness to the nature of man' (WCT 106): 'as soon as I thoughtfully say "man's nature," I have already said relatedness to being. Likewise, as soon as I say thoughtfully: being of beings, the relatedness to man's nature has been named. Each of the two members of the relation between man's nature and being already implies the relation itself. To speak to the heart of the matter: there is no such thing here as members of the relation, nor the relation itself. ... Every way of thinking takes its way already within the total relation of being and man's nature, or else it is not thinking at all' (WCT 79–80). Heidegger's originary thinking and saying, then, accomplish a major jump, one that arrives at an indissoluble complex – the duality now understood as the presencing of what is present, humans, thinking, and saying, in and as their simultaneous *belonging together*.

While this belonging together may be the most important aspect of what Heidegger leaps into, I will return to it later, focusing for now on his major insights into the relationships of reason, knowledge, technology, and nihilism within metaphysics. Even a sympathetic reading of Heidegger's *What Is Called Thinking?* has to acknowledge that though he manages to begin to leap into the originary, he neither sustains it nor comes into his own fullest voice in that series of lectures and book. He is still learning how and beginning to jump. But that is not to minimize the accomplishment – he does jump, and continues to do so in the other works of this set (such as 'The End of Philosophy,' 'The Question Concerning Technology,' 'Science and Reflection,' The Thing,' *The Question of Being*, and *What Is Philosophy*). In light of what he has now recovered from the early Greek and by travelling across the history of metaphysics, Heidegger is in a position to provide a further crucial account of how it is not paradoxical – but perhaps even unavoidable – that our experience of homelessness is deepest at the same time that our instrumental technology is more powerful than ever.

The Originary Interpretation of Technological Homelessness, Nihilism, and the Groundlessness of Being

*FROM POIĒSIS (*PHYSIS *AND* TECHNE*) TO CONTEMPORARY TECHNOLOGY*

Now that Heidegger has originarily rethought *aletheia*, and the congruent powerful belonging together of the presencing of what is present and thinking, as well as that of metaphysics and epistemology, he can go over the meaning of technology in our homeless epoch yet again, now more profoundly interpreting it in its manifold dimensions. There are multiple concealments and unconcealments here, it turns out. Beginning in the middle of things, Heidegger contrasts the two realms between which a leap is needed. He contends that the current mode of technological disclosure itself 'conceals that revealing which, as *poiēsis*, lets what presences come forth into appearance.' Technology, then, 'blocks *poiēsis*,' and, consequently, *techne* as originally experienced (QCT 27, 30).

Thus, there is a great problem with technology, a great danger. It has cut us off from the primal mode of the world's coming forth. Originally, Heidegger explains, *poiēsis* was a bringing forth (*her-vor-bringen*) out of concealedness, that is, a mode of revealing. In fact, there were two modes of *poiēsis*. *Physis* named that coming forth which happens on its own (which has been transformed into what we now think of as nature, or in the most recent vocabulary, self-organizing phenomena or *auto-poiēsis*) (QCT 34). With *physis* there was an experience of 'the bursting open belonging to bringing-forth in itself.' But *techne* was another mode of disclosure, that in which the human arts enabled the 'bursting open belonging to bringing-forth not in itself, but in another' (QCT 10). Humans participated in the second mode in a wide variety of ways, since *techne* included not only handicraft and art, but works of the mind, such as poetry and philosophy (QCT 13, 34). Here there is a strong connection between producing and knowing; as Heidegger notes, the Greek *technikon/techne* named a mode of knowing, an episteme, until Plato (QCT 12–13). The production of things, then, was understood in terms of a complex network of natural and human forces, of intertwined knowing and making where the dimensions belonged together: 'Both words [*techne* and *episteme*] are names for knowing in the widest sense. They mean to be entirely at home in something, to understand and be expert in it. Such opening provides an opening up' (QCT 13).

In the primal granting of bringing forth, philosophical principles, such as the four causes, remain 'veiled in darkness.' Of course, this revealing is subsequently analysed, for example, by Aristotle (WCT 6; QCT 7–9). Then *techne* yields to inspection, so that the metaphysical Greeks already have a representational interpretation of what happens with technology and also represent technology as a means to ends. Technology, in other words, appears metaphysically from the first as instrumental and is understood as being for the sake of human acts (QCT 4–5). According to Heidegger, the central notion of technology, 'ending in work,' stretches from Plato's ideas about the process of making and Aristotle's view of *energia* to the Roman *operatio*/action and the Christian adaptation by way of efficient cause to God (T 168–9; SR 161–2). Christianity, with the doctrine of creator and creation, sees the natural world as what was divinely made – in imitation of which, we make things too. Passing over to the modern world, from which God gradually was erased or receded, the real appears as (the sum of) humanly made or natural objects, a familiar realm which we manipulate with our tools, large and small (SR 174; WCT 13, 14). The modern, post-Cartesian sense of the presence of beings amounts to 'objectness, the objectness of the real,' which Heidegger famously explicates in terms of '*Gegenstand*,' literally that which stands-over-against, and which is recognized in opposition to and by the subject (SR 162, 163, 168–9, 176; PN-oTs 28). Being as presence becomes equivalent to being as object (PN-oTs 31). The ontology, needless to say, is correlate with, or even derives from, the epistemology developed from Descartes to Hegel to Husserl, specifically from its grounding in *subiectum* (sHBM 64; FS 17, 23, 49, 64–75).

Heidegger's analysis of the historical transition of metaphysics from the modern realm to the current technological era contains what are understandably considered his keenest descriptions and diagnoses of our contemporary situation. By explicating how we have passed over from a world that disclosed objects while concealing much else, he throws into bold relief another still-metaphysical aspect, formerly concealed, but now becoming revealed: beings as standing reserve (QCT 17, 19, 27; FS 61–3, 74). The very power of the current disclosure is also central to its eerie character, which is strange both from the point of view of the world of objects in which we have lived for hundreds of years and from that of the no-longer-metaphysical being at home that we seek.

In this latest, just begun, contemporary phase, there is again a simultaneous disclosure and concealment: the coming forth of beings as stock, that is, as something accumulated and standing in reserve, waiting to be used, which simultaneously includes the dissolution of objects' fixed, objective characteristics. In contemporary technology, what anything is, what its materiality and form are, has nothing particularly to do with any supposedly 'inherent' features, but only with the total set of relations that obtain in the systems within which beings function. Where each element is what it is in light of, and only in light of, all the other mutually determining elements in the system, the development of networks of systems is self-regulating; everywhere it is secured (QCT 16, 17). All of the elements of a system are given as delimited or ordered in a particular way – engineered we would say – as the modular, where each element is identical and interchangeable with others of the same type and suitable to its function in the network of elements (see FS 62). This way in which beings are ordered forth according to the systems' consistent rules, which we call logistics, allows the production of vast stockpiles of modular elements, which are disposable and replaceable in the course of turnover (see FS

63). Part of or belonging to a reservoir, all beings, all elements, are on call when and where the system requires them, to be distributed within our global networks of production and consumption (QCT 14–15).

Note, though it has been a topic all along, one of Heidegger's most radical points needs to be made explicit, especially since he is so often misread on this topic. He does say that contemporary systems technology is dangerous, that it conceals the originary understanding of coming forth. But he does not say that technology is simply or fully 'negative.' Rather, technology is a way in which *aletheia* happens, an occurrence that is itself strange and unsettling (QCT 11, 12, 21). In it a new dimension of beings is unconcealed and a new world-era begun. He calls this new realm of truth, of disclosure, enframing (*das Ge-stell*). But in contrast to the primal producing that brings forth (*her-vor-bringen*), enframing is a challenging revealing, a challenging forth (*herausfordern*) (QCT 16). The manner in which beings as standing reserve are related to each other as sub-elements of systems, according to Heidegger, not only sets them into a network of mutually related flows, but sets them against each other in a sphere of contested power.[22] Here a realm of not 'being at home' unfolds. In terms of our leitmotif, Heidegger says, 'Now is there still, in these times, something like an "at home," a dwelling, an abode? No, there are "dwelling machines," urban population centres, in short: the industrialized product, but no longer a *home*' (FS 74). That is, in coming to appear as together constituting systems of standing reserve, individual beings are not let be in their other dimensions – neither as what comes forth in *physis* or *techne*, nor as thought by the Romans with *res* or *ens* (later modulated in the middle ages, where *res* serves to 'designate every *ens qua ens*'), nor as the created, nor as objects with fixed, essential characteristics, the potential of which needs to be allowed to develop (T 174–6). The shafts of wheat no longer spontaneously burst forth in the self-production of the earth, nor are foods created by God for his creatures to eat, nor do human subjects produce commodities with properties that can be measured in terms of use. Rather, the field is challenged by technology to produce ever more wheat; the wheat in turn is challenged by fertilizers to become bigger ever more quickly, by pesticides to resist insects, by genetics to be modified according to whatever specifications are desired.

In contrast to what we are called on to think and to which we need appropriately respond, the calling forth in contemporary technology is understood not in the modern, humanistic terms of what subjects call for, but more in the manner of a post-humanist occurrence in which we humans ourselves are called into question – challenged – by the enframing within which we also stand (QCT 24). Just as objects disappear, replaced by the modular elements of systems with only relational meaning rather than objective or essential characteristics, so humans are no longer disclosed as subjects but now are themselves reduced to appearing as stock. We are gathered now into enframing-*Gestell* so that in more and more aspects of our lives we belong within the standing reserve (QCT 18–19). The unemployed can apply at departments of human resources; our hearts and kidneys are stock in a global system of surgical transplantation. In explaining our surprisingly quick fall from having the status of controlling, productive subjects, to what amounts to a post-humanistic realm, Heidegger pointedly identifies the twin engines that drive the new global machine: 'the two sole realities of this age: the development of *business* and *the armament* that this requires' – 'the collusion between industry and the military' (FS 52, 56). While we may still understand ourselves and 'act as the producer[s] of all "reality," the man who finds himself today caught in the increasingly constraining network of the socio-economic "imperatives" (which are, seen from the history of being, the precipitates of enframing) can that man himself produce the means of working a way out of the pressure of the "imperatives"?' (FS 74). No. We commonly admit that technology, the system of systems, is 'out of control.' Thought at a more originary level, humans accomplish, through technology, but do not control, the unconcealment itself (QCT 18, 24). This affirms a theme that has been constant in Heidegger's thought: disclosure and gift of world is nothing human (all our transformations in understanding are derived from the '"clearing" of being itself'; 'thoughts come to us mortals' (CMH 68; PT 53), though we are gathered into it and play a role through our thinking, saying, and making-action (as when, once, in the bringing forth of a Greek temple, *techne* was a catalyst through which a place was established and a world began to unfold; QCT 21). However, in the enframing, we are further than ever from encountering what is our own: we are banished from ourselves, homeless in some extreme way (QCT 27).

Thus, the now dominating ways of technological revealing – unlocking, transforming, storing, distributing, switching about – not only challenge nature, changing the meaning of rivers, bridges, windmills, and forests, but inaugurate a double kind of homelessness: 1) from the metaphysical world of objects with which we have become familiar over the centuries and in which we have become comfortable in our everyday lives (and where we have enjoyed, even expected, ever increasing control and benefit); and 2) from the possibility of a non-metaphysical mode of being that might be part of the originary homecoming we seek. Hence, though enframing is indeed a mode of disclosure, what came before is falling into deeper and deeper concealment and what might come after lies in deep shadow and is even in danger of never coming forth. Though Heidegger did not have the vocabulary or image of black holes, he uses strong words that clearly convey the dark centripetal character of this powerful era: 'unfree,' 'deliver over,' 'homage.' (QCT 4). In the enframing, Heidegger finds, we are unable to enter the primal truth (QCT 28). We are blocked today, barred from finding a way to the primal meaning of things or our lives (QCT 26, 29).

Because the oblivion of our scientific-technological homelessness is both ontological and epistemological, and because the latter has dominated the former in the modern metaphysical era to the extent that what is considered as real is limited to that which we judge to be correct, it is necessary to understand that in which science lies, in other words, nature grasped through certain knowledge, including theory (SR 156–8; T 170). Even if technology is a mode of disclosure which threatens to render us more homeless than ever, what about the power of the scientific knowledge behind technology? Can we actually be in such danger when scientific knowledge is greater than ever, when precise, tough-minded criteria for how to reason and how to understand what is real are well defined and scrupulously applied? Of course, as a hallmark of the modern era we take for granted that thinking and science amount to the same thing; or, for the 'historically inclined,' that thinking (supposedly) becomes such when it becomes scientific with the scientific revolution, especially in the mathematical physics of Kepler and Galileo, subsequently developed by Newton and Leibniz, by Bohr and Heisenberg (FS 49, 53–5). Since Heidegger's originary meditation on technology and its uncanniness is obviously so different from the tradition of representational thinking found in technology and the kind of knowledge found in science, the question needs to be pressed.

'What kind of thinking is scientific?' The objective kind. Science is objective thinking about objects, which are represented in objective language. As we have seen, in the metaphysical epoch thinking develops as representation, governed in various ways by the changing character of 'logic.' In the modern era, though dominated by an emphasis on the subject, our understanding of thinking continues to develop from the ancients in terms of atemporal 'logic' and the objectively independent, both differentiated from what is 'merely subjective,' and yet simultaneously identified with (or grounded in) subjective, psychological processes (parallel to language as subjective expression) (SR 174–5). Scientific knowing develops its power to the point that it is taken to be the only kind of knowing. Objectivity is to thinking as objects are to the real: all that counts. The objective becomes the defining feature, not so much remembered as an ideal as assumed to be regularly normative and operational in science, technology, and calculation (PN-oTs 29; SR 170). Hence, as we saw earlier in regard to technology, with science's reckoning and manipulating it sets upon the real, ordering it into place. Science 'encroaches uncannily' on the real, indeed so much so that 'it places everything outside its own nature,' which is terrifying because unsettling or dislocating (*heraussetzen*)' (SR 167; T 166).

FROM TO AUTO, THROUGH IDENTITY, TO THE SAME (BELONGING TOGETHER) IN DIFFERENCE

In thinking the history of metaphysics, Heidegger's sophisticated work of untangling the shifting relationships of thinking and saying follows how *logos* (λόγος) was first representationally transformed into logic (the law of thinking) and now is becoming logistics, a mode of thinking and acting in the epoch of science and technology that brings its own uncanniness. As he moves back and forth across the unfolding of metaphysics, Heidegger engages the intersection of epistemology, language, logic, and metaphysics. A striking case of reinterpreting the dramatic shift in their relation occurs when he jumps from the metaphysical meaning of identity to its no-longer-metaphysical correlate (an originary interpretive leap at which he is exceptionally successful). The metaphysical-representational conception of identity, for example as seminally laid down by Aristotle, runs through two and a half millennia of philosophy as one of its central tenets. Heidegger treats the powerful variations of it at length, with special attention to what happened with Leibniz. In the shortest version, he finds that rereading the metaphysical tradition of 'identity,' back to the origins in early Greek thinking and saying, discloses that the 'identical' and 'different' are not the primary keys to discerning and understanding the relationships that matter most. Instead, the originary sense of 'the same' names the dynamic in which what belongs together comes into their own only in the gathering into belonging. Though what is understood as identical or different is derived from 'the same,' what is the same is not reducible to the identical. Rather, what is the same is what maintains difference in mutually coming to what is ownmost to each in its way of abiding while belonging in the gathering.

In *What Is Called Thinking?* we can see all the basic features of this jumping over from identity toward *to auto* (the same). Heidegger makes the claim throughout the book that the concept or principle of identity obscures an understanding of the way in which what belongs together does so. To cite only a few instances, he says, 'What is stated poetically, and what is stated in thought, are never identical; but there are times when they are the same – those times when the gulf separating poesy and thinking is a clean and decisive cleft' (WCT 20). He also calls on us to read Nietzsche as we do Aristotle, in 'the same manner, be it noted, not the identical manner' (WCT 71). Or, 'Thus Plato's definition of the nature of thought is not identical with that of Leibniz, though it is the same. They belong together in that both reveal *one* basic nature, which appears in different ways' (WCT 165).

Heidegger posits this distinction and interprets it, again, by way of Parmenides, who also says in Fragment 8, 'For it is the same thing [*to auto*, τὸ αὐτό] to think and be' (cited in WCT 240). Heidegger retranslates *to auto:* while acknowledging that the traditional translation as 'the same' is correct, he reinterprets what that means, moving away from the representational understanding of 'same' as 'identical' toward the originary by exploring how what is the same is said to be both together and yet held apart. What is the same is different, yet close together. Originarily, he contends, the same means 'not apart from ... but rather only together with': the same 'means what belongs together' (WCT 241). Here we find yet another modulation of homecoming: the gathering together of what belongs together, even when apart. Gathering and belonging together emerge as primal, though Heidegger does not succeed in saying this as fully as he might or as he does in other originary works to be considered in the sections that follow. Nonetheless, here he names a set of originary relations: '... in giving thanks, the heart in thought recalls where it remains gathered and concentrated, because that is where it belongs' (WCT 145). That is, belonging occurs because what belongs together (as the same) is already gathered together. Further, Heidegger says that gathering is primal in that the presencing of what is present, humans, thinking, and saying all belong together as gathered, as gathering.

In 'The Principle of Identity' (which is, in fact, a two-track work, like *What Is Called Thinking?*), Heidegger continues to explore how thinking and being belong together – how they are the same – and how 'each thing is returned to itself,' or in another formulation, 'that every A is itself the same with itself' (PI 24–5). With the benefit of his jump into Greek not-yet-metaphysical and originary no-longer-metaphysical thinking, he can provide a more sophisticated explication than hitherto of the origin and historical unfolding from Parmenides through Plato and Aristotle, to the tradition of German idealism, with special emphasis on Leibniz's principle of reason, but also including Hegel on scientific language and the perdurance of being, and finally also Nietzsche (e.g., 'The Principle of Identity,' 'Onto-theo-logical Constitution of Metaphysics'). The importance of German speculative idealism is obvious: 'Sameness implies the relation 'with,' that is, a mediation, a connection, a synthesis: the unification into a unity. This is why throughout the history of Western thought identity appears as unity' (PI 25). In the terms of our motif under study, Heidegger says that German idealism finally 'established an abode for the essence, in itself synthetic, of identity' (PI 25).

'Considered the highest principle of thought' in the metaphysical epoch, the principle of identity, formally stated and in its 'usual formulation ... reads: A = A' (PI 23, 24). But as Heidegger traces out on the first page of the essay, if we go back behind this customary representation of identity as the expression of 'the equality of A and A,' we find the idea that 'that which is identical, in Latin '*idem*,' is in Greek τὸ αὐτό,' which translated, means 'the same' (PI 23). Thus we can see that, understood from the early Greek, the formula, A = A, which speaks of equality, 'doesn't define A as the same. The common formulation of the principle of identity thus conceals precisely what the principle is trying to say: A is A, that is, every A is itself the same' (PI 24). Of course, this principle is nothing 'merely' – exclusively – logical or epistemological, since to say what something is is an ontological issue. In the principle of identity, precise, conceptual language, logical thinking, and an understanding of being all come together, or better, belong together. Accordingly, we are brought by the principle to the being of beings: 'As a law of thought, the principle is valid only insofar as it is a principle of being that reads: To every being as such there belongs an identity, the unity with itself' (PI 26).

In addition, as in *What Is Called Thinking?*, Heidegger points out that the being of beings appears most authentically with thinkers such as Parmenides, and that 'there speaks το αυτό, that which is identical, in a way that is almost too powerful' (PI 27). From this not-yet-metaphysical vantage, where thinking, beings, and being – though different – are 'thought of as the same, we find what amounts to the opposite of the metaphysical. Rather than the metaphysical doctrine in which 'identity belongs to being,' for Parmenides 'being belongs to an identity' (PI 27). 'In the earliest period of thinking,' of course, identity means something different: thinking and being belong together in the same and by virtue of the same' (PI 27). Heidegger's recollective interpretation, then, finds 'sameness to mean a belonging together' (PI 28).

Humans would also belong together with thinking and being, not just because we are the ones who perform the thinking, but because our thinking, experienced and thought originarily out of the belonging together, is a responding to being, a mode of enacting our belonging with it. Answering to being – or its call, as he puts it in *What Is Called Thinking?* – 'man *is* essentially this relationship of responding to being, and he is only this' (PI 31). He continues his thought in terms of being at home: 'being is present and abides only as it concerns man through the claim it makes on him. For it is man, open toward being, who alone lets being arrive as presence' (PI 31).

Heidegger has taken us, in a few short pages, from identity to being, and beyond. His originary insights, and just as importantly, his way of moving though the subject, are quite distinct from the metaphysical, in which what is related has an independent, pre-given character and then is connected, so that the logical and ontological problem becomes one of explaining how the coordination works. In contrast, thought by way of the same, by way of belonging together, each comes to be what it is only in the dynamic gathering together that is the belonging together (WCT 79–80, 86, 89, 100, 106–7). He explicitly notes that in metaphysical representations 'we do not as yet enter the domain of the belonging together,' an entry that – as with all the works considered in this section – requires a 'leap, in the sense of a spring,' a spring away from the representational understanding of humans as rational animals or as subjects connected with objects, and away from being which 'since the beginning of Western thought, has been interpreted as the ground in which every being as such is grounded' (PI 32).

Just as the same was concealed in representational concepts of identity, so was genuine difference. 'The step back goes from what is unthought, from the difference as such, into what gives us thought. That [veiling of the difference as such] is the oblivion of the difference,' and needs to be 'thought in terms of unconcealment' (OtlCM 50). Thus, by way of this recollective rethinking of the same, difference is also allowed to emerge, rather than being set aside or concealed in other ways: 'But the same is not the merely identical. In the merely identical, the difference disappears. In the same the difference appears, and appears all the more pressingly' (OtlCM 45). Understanding representationally, 'we will at once be misled into conceiving of difference as a relation which our representation has added to being and beings. Thus difference is reduced to a distinction, something made up by our understanding' (OtlCM 62). In contrast, thinking by way of the same, as the gathering belonging of things with each other, we can understand how each thing can first come into its own via dynamic, mutually constitutive relations with other things, that is, how in the same, genuine 'identity' and differences emerge simultaneously, and unproblematically. Difference also matters enormously in understanding being, since a major issue is the difference between being and beings. Hence, understanding 'difference as difference' would allow both a non-metaphysical interpretation, distinct from, for example, Hegel's focus on absolute unity, and another way of elaborating or perhaps even of moving beyond the duality (OtlCM 47, 50; see also PI 25). Given all these ramifications it is not surprising that Heidegger can say that thinking amounts to distinguishing (PN-oTs 26).

Rethinking identity and difference also provides Heidegger a way to push even further than he did in recollectively moving from representational thinking and correctness to *noein* and taking to heart (above) – far enough to be so bold as to claim that, if successfully originary, 'the step back thus moves out of metaphysics and into the essential nature of metaphysics' (OtlCM 51). A critical insight occurs in seeing that 'more rigorously and clearly thought out, metaphysics is: onto-theo-logic' (OtlCM 59). That is, the inner belonging together of metaphysics and epistemology, ontology, and theology is manifest in their accomplishment: in the first place they cogently (clearly and distinctly) lay out the principles and rules of thinking – thinking's own ground – and then they connect this ground with beings. Heidegger reinterprets reason, logic, theology, ontology, and ground, demonstrating that 'ontology ... and theology are "Logics" inasmuch as they provide the ground of beings as such and account for them within the whole' (OtlCM 59). Though he does this in many of the works considered in this section, perhaps his most mature, multiple-levelled interpretation of the metaphysical tradition occurs in *The Principle of Reason* (*Der Satz vom Grund*), where he focuses on Leibniz's seminal formulation of the principle, *nihil est sine ratione*, '*nichts ist ohne Grund*,' nothing is without reason (principle or ground) (PR 3).

FROM LOGOS, THROUGH BEING AS GROUND, TO BEING WITHOUT GROUND AND AS ABYSS

What of this specific principle, or of principle generally in the history of metaphysics? While Heidegger carries out many deft analyses of the modern era, without doubt one of the most important and subtle moves occurs as he recollects back from 'principle' the multiple senses of *Grund*, which names principle (both metaphysically and epistemologically) and ground (again in both dimensions), as well as our earthly ground. In the language of homecoming by means of thinking and saying, it is not at all accidental that the word *Grund* proves to be pivotal. It is rich in metaphysical and epistemological connotations, yet also carries an originary power both in its religious-poetic aspects (as will be seen in Heidegger's handling) and in juxtaposition with our current displacements, as an immediate, practical directive toward recollectively thinking what language says: 'German words are firmly rooted locations ... Today nothing in us takes root any more' (PR 15). Interestingly, though as usual he contrasts metaphysical meaning with what was first said in the (early) Greek, here Heidegger concentrates on the later span from the Romans to modern idealism by contrasting the Latin and German ways of thinking and saying. (Though the usual English translation of *Abgrund* as 'abyss' may somewhat obscure the fact, when he develops ground (*Grund*) and abyss (*Abgrund*) here Heidegger is picking up what he introduced earlier in *Contributions to Philosophy*, as we saw in chapter 3.)

Heidegger shifts attention from 'principle' to *Grund:* 'Nothing of what the word *Grund-Satz* says is apparent in the meaning of the Latin word *principium.* Nevertheless we go ahead and indiscriminately use the terms *principium*, Principle, and "fundamental principle" in the same sense' (PR 15). In a parallel manner we speak of axioms as principles, for instance, where Leibniz says, 'Axioms are principles that are held by everyone as being obvious – and scrupulously viewed – as consisting of limit concepts' (cited in PR 15). Yet, though for us, 'axioms and Principles have the character of principles,' such was not the case for the Greeks, as can be seen by the way Euclid used *axiom* in his *Elementa* to indicate, instead, something such as 'insight' or 'to have an insight': 'What are equal to the same are equal to each other' (PR 15). Heidegger can now put into play his already developed interpretation of the 'same.' What Euclid meant was that there was insight into what belonged together, through complex patterns of identity and difference. In the analysis of the tangle of 'axiom,' 'principle,' and 'fundamental principle,' we find another manner in which they are 'interchangeable,' that is, able to be translated into each other because they are understood to be 'the same.' They belong together in yet another, now representational manner, which also needs to be unpacked and contrasted with an originary sense to be found, not in the Greek, but in German. (Even the intricacies of 'identity' and 'difference,' treated earlier, that are rethought by

Heidegger from representationally meaning 'being equal to itself' or 'selfsame with itself, for itself' back to the originary 'belonging-together of distinct things in the same' circle round to be reinterpreted based on the senses of *Grund*, as Heidegger says in explaining the power of the same: 'More clearly: the belonging together of distinct things on the basis {*Grund*} of the same' [PR 8].)

Heidegger's focus on Leibniz and his bold claim that '*the principle of reason is the fundamental principle of all fundamental principles*' is partially based on the recognition that it underlies the metaphysical, epistemological, theological, and scientific modes of understanding beings, and beyond that, the connection of all four of these dimensions in their shifting relationships with being itself (PR 8). Though here we do not need to trace the details of Heidegger's compounding interpretations, several aspects are directly important for our themes. Overall, this dimension of Heidegger's thinking pushes further in its understanding of the history of metaphysics by consistently developing the modern interpretation of thinking as the correct and indubitable, beings as objects in the realm of empirical causality, and beings as founded in being.

As we have seen above, Heidegger argues that an early form of metaphysical challenging occurs in the demand for reasons that is integral to the modern assumption that what is taken to be the real is grounded in thinking: 'Human understanding, whenever and wherever it is active, always and everywhere keeps on the lookout for the reason why whatever it encounters is and is the way it is. Understanding looks for reasons insofar as it requires a specification for reasons. The understanding demands that there be a foundation for its statements and assertions. Only founded statements are intelligible, and intelligent' (PR 3). In the first place then, Heidegger makes the strong statement that Leibniz's principle 'is the supreme fundamental principle of cognition, as well as of the objects of cognition because, according to the guiding thought of modern philosophy, something "is" only insofar as a founded cognition has secured it for itself as its object' (PR 27).

Further, because a crucial nexus of scientific and philosophical ideas concerning beings and logical-physical relationships occurs in the understanding of beings and causality – causality as a conceptual understanding that grounds beings (as we have just seen), as well as what might be supposed to be operational dynamics among beings – Heidegger develops another version of Leibniz's principle: '*Nihil est sine ratione seu nullus effectus sine causa.* "Nothing is without reason, or no effect is without a cause."' Heidegger comments, 'Leibniz obviously posits the principle of reason and the principle of causality as being equivalent' (PR 21). *A dramatic relationship among grounds, causality, and beings is thus disclosed: when being as a ground withdraws into concealment, beings not only come to the fore, but do so to such an extent that only beings appear; where there is nothing other than beings the demand for a ground, a 'because' to answer 'why?,' can be satisfied only by reference to beings.* Hence, we pass over into a state in which it would not even occur to us that the cause of changes in beings might lie anywhere else than in other beings.

From this conjunction, Heidegger opens to an analysis both of how reason-logic and causality-physics are connected as they are in the history of metaphysics and to a glimpse of how these dimensions might be deconstructed and gathered together afresh and originarily. In fact, he goes through several interpretations; here we can see how he uses traditional scholarly (representational) language to carry out the analysis (later in this section, we will return to the topic to see how he uses originary language in yet another reinterpretation). Heidegger engages the modern assumption, for example, as formulated by Leibniz, on the way to explicating the originary force of the inverse. But, he cautions, it may well be imprudent to move too quickly, for example, by making the seemingly obvious point that syllogism is distinct from the physical, that 'Reason and consequence are not equivalent to cause and effect' (PR 21).

In a subtler, indirect approach, again focusing on the German and Latin, Heidegger traces back from Leibniz's Latin to Cicero's, undoing the assumption which occurred in the meanwhile that *Grund* is an unproblematic translation of *ratio,* in the double sense of 'reason' and 'grounds' – which 'also characterizes what we call a cause' (PR 98). Using an instructive text from Cicero, Heidegger explains that the Latin saying of *ratio* did not mean reason or ground: '*Causam appello rationem efficiendi, eventum id quod est effectum.* Translated in the usual manner this reads: "When I speak of a cause, I mean the ground/reason of an effecting; by effect, I mean what comes about as a result"' (PR 99). But, Heidegger contends, the opposite of the customary view is true, in that '*eventus* is what comes about ... [with *ratio efficiendi*], *efficere* is a bringing-forth and a producing' that belongs to the sphere of *ratio* (PR 99). Led back to *ratio* as generative, we find that *ratio* belongs to the verb *reor* the broad sense of 'reckoning' or 'calculation,' as when we 'render an account' (PR 100). In 'The Thing,' Heidegger contends that the Old High German word *thing, dinc,* specifies 'a gathering to deliberate on a matter under discussion, a contested matter,' but that this is the best way to translate the Latin *res* and the Greek *eiro* (*rhetos, rhetra, rhema*). What so concerns somebody, as in a case at law, the Romans also called *causa:* 'in its authentic and original sense, this word in no way signifies "cause"; *causa* means the case and hence also that which is the case, in the sense that something comes to pass and becomes due. Only because cause, almost synonymously with *res*, means the case, can the word *causa* later come to mean cause, in the sense of the causality of an effect' (T 174–6). After Descartes, and with Leibniz, the reckoning of *ratio*, of course, 'is accomplished by a representing I that is defined as the subject that is certain of itself' – which would 'have been alien to the Romans,' as well as to the Greeks (PR 100).

Of course, in yet another dimension of the tradition, theology also addresses the ultimate cause, the *summa ratio* of what is and comes about: God (PR 100). 'What is to be posited as the *ultima ratio* of *Natura*, as the furthest, highest – and that means the first – existing reason for the nature of things, is what one usually calls God ... As the first existing cause of all beings, God is called reason' (PR 27; see also 28). But where cause is understood as *causa sui* we again arrive at onto-theo-logy – that is, into the essential nature of metaphysics: 'This is the right name for the god of philosophy. Man can neither pray nor sacrifice to this god. Before the *causa sui*, man can neither fall to his knees in awe nor can he play music and dance before this god' (OtlCM 72).

Hence, through the transition from Roman and Christian understandings of cause and *ratio* to the modern one, and as the founding power of the sending (*Geschick*) of being that is *ratio* or God falls away, we are led to the human reckoning and calculation that eventually come to characterize our contemporary science and technology. What Heidegger works out technically for principle, reason, and cause in *The Principle of Reason*, just as in 'The Question Concerning Technology,' shows the distance between our humanistic conceptions of the production and manipulation of beings and the earliest thinking about causality – where '*ratio*' and '*techne*' were understood fundamentally as modes of bringing something into appearance, 'letting it come forth into presencing' (QCT 7–9). Since the originary human responsibility was to start a thing on its way to arrival, technology was nothing merely instrumental as we understand it today, any more than grounding reason (QCT 9, 10).

Because what is taken to be real in the modern metaphysical era (beings above all else, and in varying ways, being, God, and Nature) is ultimately an epistemological matter, reason and its principles, its multiple modes or sub-logics of philosophy, theology, and science are also intimately entangled with being as the ground that grounds all beings: 'The being of beings is thus thought in advance as the grounding ground' (OtlCM 58). This specifically is the positive achievement of metaphysical ontology and theology, which 'account for being as the ground of beings' (OtlCM 59).

Yet, just as his careful distinguishing, and relating, of thinking, beings, and being (in the modes of logic-reason, causality–the physical, and being-God) arrives at the deepest appreciation of how metaphysics and representational conceptualization have grounded beings in being, Heidegger makes a radical move in *The Principle of Reason,* seemingly denying ground. He elaborates how Leibniz's principle in its strict version says '*Nihil sine ratione*' (PR 32). Spelled out, or as Heidegger says, in its complete formulation, Leibniz writes, '*id, quod dicere soleo, nihil existere nisi cujus reddi potest ratio existentiae sufficiens:* "(the Principle) that I usually say (in the form): Nothing exists whose sufficient reason for existing cannot be rendered"' (cited in PR 32). It should be obvious that and why Heidegger rejects the modern, humanistic or idealistic stance that reason might be sufficient to ground what exists, to provide the foundation for beings as they are present. He also goes further, as might be expected, shifting from speaking about reason to speaking about being and of the accord between them: 'to being there belongs something like ground/reason' (PR 50). It is not surprising that metaphysically, for example, in the highest thought of Hegel, it would come to be thought that 'the being of beings reveals itself as the ground that gives itself ground and accounts for itself' (OtlCM 57).

Just here and unexpectedly, Heidegger turns sharply away. Contending against such now-traditional metaphysical misinterpretation, he argues instead that Leibniz's principle, 'Nothing is without Reason,' never means that 'being has a reason' or that 'being is grounded'; rather, 'according to the principle of reason, only beings are ever grounded ... "Ground/reason belongs to being" is tantamount to saying: being *qua* being grounds. Consequently only beings ever have their grounds' (PR 51). 'The new tonality reveals the principle of reason as a principle of being ... Something like ground/reason belongs to the essence of being. Being and ground/reason belong together. Ground/reason receives its essence from its belonging together with being qua being ... Ground/reason and being ("are") the same – not equivalent – which already conveys the difference between the names "being" and "ground/reason." Being "is" in essence: ground/reason. Therefore it can never first have a ground/reason which would supposedly ground it. Accordingly, ground/reason is missing from being … Being "is" the abyss' (PR 51). Being is the abyss? Is it not true, then, that at the heart of Heidegger's thought we do find, as some suppose, nihilism, the very phenomena from which he supposedly would help us leap free? Little wonder that Heidegger has been dogged by suspicion and even explicit charges of nihilism since his early days – despite his regular protests that such a view is a misinterpretation.

It may be that the essence of metaphysics does unfold, in the end, as the essence of nihilism, a theme Heidegger also develops in the other works considered in this section by thinking in terms of homelessness and homecoming (QB 87). He points out that Hegel already comments on how this urge to be 'at home' occurs at the beginning of the modern era in Descartes; he traces how Nietzsche, in articulating the will to will, continues this line of reflection, saying that nihilism wants homelessness as such (EP 61; QB 37–8). The question of the essence of nihilism, then, is central, as is the understanding of its historical unfolding and phases (QB 39). Looking toward the end, the final phase of its completion would occur as it approaches 'fulfilment' (QB 41, 49). Here the gathering of the philosophy of history would occur in which philosophy would be in its final stage, that of metaphysics and the being of beings (EP 55). As we have seen, in the overall arc of the history of metaphysics, given the character of globally spreading technological systems, we are in considerable danger of becoming even more homeless than we have been in previous phases of the metaphysical epoch. Heidegger believes this so strongly that he speaks radically: 'Man stares at what the explosion of the atom bomb could bring with it. He does not see that the atom bomb and its explosion are the mere final emission of what has long since taken place, has already happened' – in the uniformity in which everything is neither far nor near, is, as it were, without distance, which also means that 'despite all conquest of distances the nearness of things remains absent' (T 166).

Heidegger, however, does not look back to a golden pre-technological era. He takes pains to point out how the *unheimlich* is unchanging: it does not sentimentally refer back to the past as is believed in the usual identifications of the *unheimlich* and the nostalgic; rather, it is fully operative in the present and the future as that which robs us of all ground and rootedness. He contends that the more we harness energy, 'the more impoverished becomes the human faculty for building and dwelling in the realm of what is essential. *There is an enigmatic interconnection between the demand to render reasons and the withdrawal of roots.* It is important to see the form of the movement occurring in this lofty play between rendering and withdrawal' (PR 30–1). The '"strange" [*unheimlich*] ... "demand to render reasons [*Grundes*]" threatens everything of humans' being-at-home and robs them of the roots of their subsistence [*alles Heimische des Menschen bedroht und ihm jeden Grund und Boden für eine Bodenständigkeit raubt*], the roots from out of which every great human age, every world-opening spirit, every molding of the human form has so far grown [*gewachsen*]' (PR 30 [60]). Or, projecting from roots toward the originary that might come, Heidegger contends that 'the human will to explain just does not reach' the simple unity of the 'worlding of the world' (which we will explore in the next section of this chapter), since 'as soon as human cognition here calls for an explanation,' it falls short. Because it sees what belongs together only in 'separate realities, which are to be grounded in and explained by one another,' 'causes and grounds remain unsuitable' for what needs to be thought (T 180). Hence, as famously depicted by Nietzsche, nihilism is the strangest of all guests. Here, at our doorstep; now, at the height of our scientific knowledge, technological power, and mastery over beings. Since humans, as well as all beings, apparently are in increasingly many ways enframed, perhaps we cross over a line with technology, perhaps we reach a zero point, a point of nothingness and nihilism (QB 35).

Heidegger explicitly engages nihilism in *The Question of Being,* a response to Ernst Jünger, who develops Nietzsche's insights (especially in his 1932 essay, 'The Worker'), and to whom Heidegger acknowledges a debt in relation to what he was able to think in 'The Question Concerning Technology' (QB 45). In fact, Heidegger attempts to 'see through' nihilism, as he puts it, by thinking back from nihilism to the metaphysics behind it (and from there, perhaps even to recover now-lost being), though, with his limitations at this point, he acknowledges that he is satisfied with thinking 'of the essence of nihilism only in that way that we first take the path which leads into a discussing of the essence of being' (QB 37, 71). Precisely, he discovers that it is necessary to think back from nihilistic phenomena to the essence of nihilism, which 'comes before and ahead of ... and gathers them'; then, from there to think back even further to the essence of metaphysics. Whence any possible legitimation of the real? Whence the bestowal of meaning? From the divine, humankind, or, perhaps, being itself (QB 69)?

As we saw above, in the history of modern metaphysics, the real is increasingly defined in terms of reason – the real 'is challenged to put in an appearance within the horizon of the concept' – and in terms of causation by other beings (QB 65). Technology would be the maximum instance of the latter, our production par excellence, grounded in the former (the best calculative conceptualizations of the cognizing subject). Obviously, our current age's productive capacity is a matter of machinery and human workers, where, as workers, we have a double role – a role that, congruent with its basis in the essence of metaphysics, is doubly representational. Work both represents what is encountered through the conceptual and also re-presents or makes again its own power (ideally even increasing it) (QB 5, 61). Hence the seminal power of Marx in articulating the character of our age: 'Marxism thinks on the basis of production: social production of society (society produces itself) and the self-production of the human being as a social-being. Thinking in this manner, Marxism is indeed the thought of today, where the self-production of man and society plainly prevails' (FS 75; see also 52). At the turn of the millennium, we work in the 'knowledge industry' and in 'research' to produce theoretical foundations and practical implications, thus continuing to answer the demand, the challenge for reasons and results (QB 59). Similarly, insofar as beings require a chain of causality, we initiate it as workers and refine its effective movement with our instrumental technology. That is why, as Jünger develops it, 'active nihilism' can deal with the activity of work, making 'the total work character of all really visible from the figure of the worker' (QB 41).

Thus, we operate increasingly as workers, producing epistemologically and ontically (QB 63). How is this possible? In what is our nature as reasoning workers grounded? Ontologically, in being – being as the highest work. Again, Heidegger has already prepared an initial inquiry into this dimension of the history of metaphysics, having investigated how the earliest Greek understanding of the effortless coming forth of *physis* was replaced by the idea of God as Creator, the supreme Producer of all that is: 'The name for such an ontic "making" is *CREATIO*. This is why the *Summum ens* becomes CREATOR and all *ENS* is *ENS CREATUM*' (FS 25, 26). God was also thought as being, the uncaused cause. In its other modes, too, being, as the ground of all beings, has been metaphysically taken to be the source of all production. As Nietzsche finally argued, ontological production, on a planetary scale, not only of beings but of all life, occurs because of being (*Seienden*) as will to power, where the 'unfolding of the will to power into the unconditioned will to will' also is 'a production of being [*Sein*]' (QB 43, 85). Heidegger condenses the terms, saying, '"Work," understood in this way is, however, identical with being [*Sein*] in the sense of the will to power' (QB 59, 63). Because work (as power) is both human and of being as the will to power, Jünger 'recognizes in "work" ... the total character of the reality of the real' (QB 59).

According to Heidegger's interpretation, then, the essence of nihilism and the essence of work are bound up together, and both derive from the essence of technology, which, as one of the epochs of the unfolding of metaphysics, stems from that unfolding. It is metaphysics which 'gathers being and nothingness into its essence, determines the essence of nihilism' (QB 85, 87). Thus, if, in our technological situation, we find ourselves at the brink of nihilism, it would seem that to escape it would be the same thing as to leap out of metaphysics. As Heidegger has put it since *Contributions to Philosophy*, we would need a 'crossing over.' Heidegger now explores nihilism precisely in terms of 'crossing' and 'line' by engaging Jünger's work. Heidegger rejects the seemingly obvious alternatives to nihilism (striving 'for restoration of what has been' or 'seek[ing] salvation in flight' into logistics and other dimensions of technology), arguing that 'we experience the dismaying necessity that instead of wanting to overcome nihilism we must first try to enter into its essence' (QB 47, 103). Hence his respect for Jünger, who, facing up to the situation, aims 'at helping to get out of the zone of complete nihilism without giving up the ground plan of the prospect which "The Worker," proceeding from Nietzsche's metaphysics opened up,' where 'will may be regarded as the only source of the "giving of meaning" which justifies everything' (QB 47, 49). Of course, Heidegger himself disagrees, arguing all along that we need to move beyond Jünger's position which remains, even 'dwells in' the 'metaphysics of will to power,' as do Hegel and Nietzsche (themselves no strangers to nothingness) (QB 43, 45, 53; FS 18). An important point of contact in difference occurs where Jünger speaks of nihilism in the same terms we arrived at above: 'nothingness,' 'zero point.' It would seem that the necessary crossing would be from nihilism over to being. That is, that there would be a line (across the '0' point) between nihilism (the negative field) and being (the positive), so that humans would have the task of passing from one to the other.

Heidegger, however, responding to Jünger, argues that such is not the case: 'the entire human "component realities" also do not stand somewhere on this side of the line in order to cross over it and to settle down on the other side next to being' (QB 83). Rather, humans are ourselves the zero point: 'Man ... helps to constitute the zone of being and that means at the same time of nothingness. Man does not only stand in the critical zone of the line. He himself, but not he for himself and particularly not through himself alone, is this zone and thus the line. In no case is the line, thought of as a symbol of the zone of complete nihilism, like something impassable lying before man' (QB 83). What could that mean? At the least, that we somehow are already, and unavoidably, related to nothingness. That humans are not 'free agents,' currently detached from, or even opposite, being, which would have to be the case if we were to separate from being and needing to, able to, cross over to it. Here Heidegger continues what he said in *What Is Called Thinking?* three years earlier (as we saw above); now, in one of the most important movements in his thinking, he elaborates the duality and the belonging of humans within the being of beings: beings cannot be understood apart from being, as would be the case for much metaphysical thinking, including the modern sciences which hold that 'except for being there is "nothing else"' (QB 95; see also WCT 79–80, 86, 89, 100, 106–7). Neither can being be understood apart from beings (because being is not something standing by itself, we need to abandon holding that it appears for itself), nor as coming before beings and causing them ('what is present [beings] is brought forth in the present [being] but is, however, not caused by it, in the sense of an efficient causation') (QB 53, 81, 83; FS 22). Neither beings nor being have an independent, prior 'existence' – which is, in fact, usually said of being as well as of beings, since metaphysically it is thought of as the first being, the most primary being. 'Being present ("being") as being present always is a being present for the essence of man, insofar as being present is a demand which at times summons the essence of man. The essence of man as such is in a state of hearing because it belongs in the summoning demand, belongs in its being present ... We should just as decidedly have to drop the singularizing and separating word "being" as to drop the name "man" ... In truth, we can not then even say any longer that "being" and "man" "be" the same in the sense that they belong together; for in so saying we still let both be for themselves' (QB 77). That neither being nor beings could come first or be understood as over against one another, whether literally as objects (*Gegenstand*) or any other way, has implications for what Heidegger has been saying for years about 'the turning.' As Heidegger has explored from *Contributions to Philosophy* through 'Letter on Humanism' and 'The Turning,' it has seemed sensible, indeed it was a major breakthrough at the time, to speak of being turning. All possible change and homecoming seemed to depend on the insight that 'being takes a new direction.' But 'we now ask more properly whether "being" is something for itself and whether it also and at times turns in the direction of man. Presumably the turning itself, but still obscurely, is that which we embarrassedly enough, and vaguely call "being." But does such turning-toward not also take place and, in a strange manner, under the dominance of nihilism, namely in such a way that "being" turns away and withdraws into the state of absence?' (QB 75). If neither being nor human being is separable, it would make no sense to speak of being as turning first. Here Heidegger tries to think what so far has been left unthought: 'Thus the talk of a turning-towards on the part of being is a makeshift and completely questionable because being depends on the turning-toward so that this turning can never approach "being" first' (QB. 77). Nor, given their mutual interrelationship, could we speak of humans turning first (even if we were to ignore the no-longer-metaphysical acknowledgement that humans do not have the epistemological or ontological power to do so). The turning would have to be undertaken, achieved, simultaneously by being and humans.

The relation of being and human being to nihilism in the history of metaphysics, then, is indeed a matter of turning, but the turning neither of humans nor of being (whether alone or at first). Rather, beings and humans, in reciprocal relationship, would turn together. But this turning would neither proceed from nor establish being or humans as something in or for themselves; just the opposite, *what we have taken being and being to be has to 'go away'*: 'If turning-towards belongs to "being" and in such a way that the latter is based in the former, then "being" is dissolved [*lost auf*] in this turning. It now becomes questionable what being which has reverted into [*zurück*] and been absorbed by [*aufgegangen*] its essence is henceforth to be thought of' (QB 81). 'Being present is grounded in the turning-towards which as such turns the essence of man into it so that the latter may dissipate [*verschwende*] itself for it' (QB 83).

It would be hard to overemphasize the radicality and importance of what he thinks here. But because these matters are obviously exceptionally difficult to think and say – and perhaps at the limit of what he can say at this time – Heidegger breaks off for now and focuses instead on at least working out an understanding of being and human being as together now at the line, at the edge of nihilism. It would appear that today, in the age of technology as the completion of metaphysics, being and humans would turn together either toward the 'zone of complete nihilism' or away from it, toward something positive. In complete nihilism, being would 'move off in a unique estrangement [*unheimlichkeit*]' (QB 67, 89). What the positive might be, however, is not clear; nor need it be, since the unconcealment of the essence of nihilism carries with it the complementary concealment of its other, which is naturally obscure at this point.

Earlier, Heidegger had said that humans are the zero point in the line at the edge of nihilism. Now that we better understand that humans are inseparable from being, we also see more about how being too must be understood as nothingness (as 'zero,' as the 'abyss'). At the least, the moving away from metaphysics is a moving away from the obsession with beings: 'The essence of the nothing consists in the turning away from beings' (FS 57). Further, Heidegger affirms the mutuality of humans and being, saying, 'the essence of man which remembers belongs to nothingness,' and the belonging together of 'the state of being present (existence) and nothingness which as absence of the state of being present "negates" without every destroying it. Insofar as nothingness "negates," it confirms itself rather as a distinguished state of being present and veils itself as such' (QB 83, 67). Thus, both humans and being may turn together, away from complete nihilism, and yet positively, into or as nothingness. The positive turning together of both being and humans would be the crossing of the line, out of nihilism and the end of metaphysics, toward homecoming: 'Presumably, overcoming is only attained when, instead of the appearance of negative nothingness, the essence of nothingness which was once related to "being" can arrive and be accepted by mortals' (QB 79). At this point, Heidegger at least has managed to raise the question of where the essence of nothingness comes from and has begun to investigate its place (QB 81). It seems that the answer lies in the direction of being as withdrawn, which would be why turning toward the essence of nothingness could be a turn to the positive, even as the latter remains hidden.

Beyond what Heidegger has already said of technology and production as the challenging forth of beings, there is a further intimate connection between nihilism and work (and worker). Heidegger points to a dramatic change, a retreat from metaphysics as generated since Descartes, in which humans have been understood as the source of meaning and where transcendence disappears. The change occurs where being, as the will to power, becomes identical with work and leads to the technology now unfolding (QB 63, 55–61). The simultaneous disclosure of being as the force appearing in technology and the disappearance of the subject, of course, lead Heidegger to argue that the unfolding of technology is nothing merely human. Here too we would begin to see, in a post-humanistic way, that our fate or what is sent is a matter neither of our will nor of our technological resources. It may be that the shock of finally seeing the new mode of veiling and revealing that occurs in the strangeness of technology might move us to questioning. Only just now, perhaps due to the rush to do more and more, to use more and more, are we disturbed and moved to question the world that unfolds through technology (QCT 14). Perhaps becoming conscious of the strangeness within which we live, we might also become responsible for what is appropriate to us within the danger that surrounds us.

In the midst of our technological homelessness, it would be in/because of the turning that occurs that the possibility would open for our proper response, in a recollective questioning, to the change that brings about the dramatic retreat from metaphysics concerned with beings as subjects and objects. In terms of his originary analysis of the 'same,' being can be understood as the same as the turning, a turning that pulls humans along, a turning in which being and humans turn together (QB 75, 77). Along the way, and unavoidably, humans would abide for a time in the turning, which would be neither an original being at home, nor the possible becoming at home again in the future, but a kind of homelessness on the way to homecoming (QB 75). Hitherto we have not thought this condition or possibility, because beings have come to fully occupy our consciousness – preoccupying us – as being has dissolved in the turning. Indeed, though if ~~being~~ itself has come to be thought as a being, and thus has largely become concealed, Heidegger contends that it nonetheless remains faintly in our memory) (QB 81, 83). Precisely because of the great danger that we, caught up in our apparent technological mastery of beings and in representational thinking and language, 'will never come to abide anywhere,' we need to attend to the importance of listening and responding to the call (WCT 129). Since 'as hearers, we abide in the sphere of what is spoken,' we need to come to hear the summons of what calls for thinking 'in its native realm' – a realm that 'is uninhabitable not because our spoken speech has never yet been at home in it, but rather because we are no longer at home with this telling word, because we no longer really live in it' (WCT 130, 118). Discerning this alternative, positive prospect, from out of the uncanny, Heidegger directs us to 'the call ... [which] is a reaching, even if it is neither heard nor answered. Calling offers an abode' (WCT 124). 'The call sets our nature free, so decisively that only the calling which calls us to think establishes the free scope of freedom in which free human nature may abide' (WCT 133). According to Heidegger, then, nihilism is neither inevitable nor that with which he would have us conclude.

Where to then? How? Philosophy would remain en route to the being of being, since our task of questioning and attempting to speak needs to correspond to that which addresses us (WP 53). Our response, a co-respondence, would be our attempt to answer that which is question-worthy: the call, that is, the unthought (WP, 69; EP, 64). Movement within the established track of metaphysics, no matter how brilliant, will not do. Originarily, astonished by nihilism at the door, by the *unheimlich* technological era in which we find ourselves at the end of metaphysics, *we find that at the abyss – where, itself without ground, 'being is the abyss'* (PR 51) – *no mere bridge will do.* A leap is required, or a fall, a free fall (PR 53). That is why, as we have seen, in the works being considered here, though Heidegger continues to maintain the traditional representational vocabulary and thoughts in the non-originary parts of his two-track works such as *What Is Called Thinking?*, 'The Principle of Identity,' and *The Principle of Reason,* he also enacts his leap insofar as he finds an originary thinking and saying.

In fact, Heidegger executes a series of leaps. The first, remarkable in itself, is the leap out of metaphysics, springing clear enough of beings to recover much concerning previously concealed being, with an originary sense of difference and an appreciation of the duality, the being of beings, which in a subsequent crossing-over (trans-lation) is understood as the presencing of what is present. The leap from technology and nihilism, then, continues the enactment already announced and begun in *Contributions to Philosophy,* now reopening the prospect of moving toward an overcoming, a crossing over or out of metaphysics (EP 60; QB 43, 71). Such an overcoming involves passing by beings and thus accepting the arrival of nothingness and, for a time, dwelling in it (QB 79, 83). Perhaps this is now the normal state of affairs (QB 47). Heidegger has arrived at the abyss by leaping from technology and nihilism at the end of metaphysics and landing where we can see that, though beings have their ground in being (even now as objects are disappearing, replaced by standing reserve), that which unfolds in/as the technological epoch – being – has itself no ground. Listening again to what Heidegger says in *The Principle of Reason,* we need to hear yet another tonality – as he continuously cautions us – also using what he has said about 'the same: belonging together':

> To the extent that being as such grounds, it remains groundless. 'Being' does not fall within the orbit of the principle of reason, rather only beings do.
>
> Being and ground/reason: the same. Being: the abyss. (PR 51)

There is much here that might panic or anger us insofar as we are dedicated to representational conceptualization or reason. From this mode of understanding, being would be said to be outside the purview of, the control of, reason. Yes, Heidegger is saying that ground/reason belongs together with being because ground/reason is what it is from out of that belonging: being provides ground/reason. Here being itself is affirmed as the primal source. Nonetheless, this frustrates reason, which demands that what is needs to be accounted for, that its principle be spelled out. Even if being is not a being, so that we must learn to think being's difference from 'what is,' do we not find here (set up) a limit, a barrier, an outlaw to the laws of logic and language?

In dealing with this issue, Heidegger makes yet another major leap – an unexpected and radical jump. What is not surprising about this surprise is that it happens with the assistance of poetry and religious saying, given that he has learned so much from Hölderlin and that the arts, as an originary dimension of *poiēsis*, 'foster the growth of the saving power' (QCT 35). We have seen how Heidegger's analysis of the principle of reason, especially as seminally articulated by Leibniz, but also as traced though the history of metaphysics, leads to a fresh understanding of what was hidden before, that insofar as being withdraws by grounding beings so that they increasingly come to the fore, it conceals itself as that ground. Now that we can glimpse being as ground, it also follows that being itself is without ground. Being is the same as abyss. But that does not entail nihilism. Rather, even as representational philosophy would be scandalized by finding that being lies beyond its grasp, the insight opens recollective thinking to thinking beyond being merely as that of beings. Unexpectedly, in the middle of *The Principle of Reason*, Heidegger introduces a text that does not seem to belong, that goes counter to all that seems to be unfolding. It is important to explicitly note how Heidegger's interpretation here can move to an understanding that was not possible earlier. From the vantage point of being underway with the leap, he reflects on the deficiency of his earlier attempt at the theme, admitting that despite seeing 'correctly' in his 1929 essay, 'On the Essence of Reasons,' that the principle of reason spoke of the ground of beings, that step ran awry, missing much that was closest at hand, but not seen (PR 45). The difference now, though the danger of going astray always remains, is that he can proceed by using the thinking and saying he has originarily recollected in the works considered earlier in this section concerning *aletheia*-unconcealment, two-track originary and representational saying and thinking, *poiēsis-physis-techne*, the duality of beings and being, the same as difference in belonging together (instead of identity), and ground-reason-cause.

The strict formulation of the principle of reason – 'Nothing is without rendering its reason – means that cognition drives to find the reasons for what is, for what is cognized (PR 35). It asks, 'Why does what is cognized exist, and why is it the way it is?' In contrast, a poetic text of Angelus Silesius says,

> The rose is without why: it blooms because it blooms.
> It pays no attention to itself, asks not whether it is seen. (cited in PR 35)

Why does Heidegger insert this poem in the heart of his explication, especially when he knows that what he says about being as abyss reawakens charges of nihilism, or at least the complaint that he is far from speaking consistently as a reasonable philosopher? In fact, Leibniz and Hegel both knew of the poet, the physician ordinarily named Johann Scheffler, and the poem from which these lines are drawn, 'The Cherubic Wanderer,' that appeared in 1657. Though both Leibniz (a young contemporary) and Hegel appreciated Silesius, they also dismissed him as 'mystic,' which Heidegger readily, even provocatively, points out so as to press the issue of reason and identity, to find another way of questioning the meaning of 'Why?,' thus showing that, in fact, there are important, and overlooked, interpretations corresponding to the two modes of thinking (representational and originary). In a straightforward manner, 'why' asks for the reason for things, seeking answers in the form of 'because ...' – answers that the principle of reason and the concepts of ground and causality rigorously pursue. It would appear that Silesius is speaking nonsensically in the first line ('The rose is without why: it blooms because it blooms'), contradicting himself in saying that the rose is without why at the same time that he goes on (however obscurely) to explain why it blooms ('because it blooms'). To the contrary, Heidegger argues, the poet not only avoids any such obvious contradiction, but he provides a powerful opening to a second, originary sense of 'why.' Whereas we usually understand that in asking for reasons, 'why' amounts to the same thing as 'because,' according to Heidegger's dissenting reading: 'The poet speaks clearly. "Why" and "because" mean different things. "Why" is the word for the question concerning grounds. The "because" contains the answer – yielding reference to grounds. The "why" seeks ground. The "because" conveys grounds' (PR 36). As we have seen, in his originary vocabulary, Heidegger is saying that 'why' and 'because' are the same;

they belong together, but they are not 'equivalent.' In something of a tour de force, Heidegger unpacks the potential meaning of this difference. The poet is not confused about what grounds are, because he is not in the least denying that the rose has grounds or a set of causes. He immediately acknowledges this and specifies the reason why: 'because it blooms.'

What would be the crucial difference, though, between asking for and conveying grounds, such that the 'why' and 'because,' even if not identical, say something illuminatingly distinct? Heidegger finds the answer in the second line: 'It pays no attention to itself, asks not whether it is seen.' Apparently the poet is pointing out that the rose does not consider itself in the sense of ferreting out its own grounds. That would not seem to say anything so trivial as that the rose does not question or answer about its foundations, because it is not a thinking being (even though that might be a tempting line of interpretation that could connect with Leibniz's belief that every living being is a cognizing-representing being) (PR 42). At the least, Heidegger contends, it would more profoundly provide for an exploration of how the difference between the rose and humans would lie in that the latter 'must pay attention to what grounds are determinative for them, and how they are so' (PR 37). Whereas, traditionally, to be human is to have our essence as reasoning beings, as those beings whose essential existence comes from seeking principles and grounds, 'we humans cannot come to be who we are without attending to the world that determines us [in the way we abide] – an attending in which we at the same time attend to ourselves' (PR 37). The difference, then, is a difference in what the rose and humans are, in the way they each are (PR 38).

Whereas humans are unavoidably bound up with the search to find why, the rose has no need of a why to be what it is. Thus, in addition to developing what Heidegger has said about how humans are challenged in technology, and how this challenge is rooted in the older demand for reasons/grounds, the verse contrasts that challenging demand and its attendant metaphysical homelessness with the non-alienation of the rose from the original sense of *poiēsis,* of which, as we saw, *techne* and *physis* were both part. Though the rose does have causes in the ordinary sense, in a second dimension it is a coming forth that just comes forth. 'It blooms because it blooms.' Heidegger underscores the point that the rose remains *physis:* 'Its blooming is a simple arising-on-its-own' (PR 38).

Yet, according to Heidegger, even naming and directing us toward an understanding of the 'difference between the ways according to which the rose and humans are what they are' does not fully reach what Angelus Silesius says. The verse names something more deeply still by leaving it unsaid: 'and everything depends on this,' according to Heidegger, that 'humans, in the concealed grounds of their essential being, first truly are when in their own way they are like the rose – without why' (PR 38). In contrast to the metaphysical understanding of the essential character of humans as rational beings, as the ones who either find and articulate the reasons/grounds or, in the more modern version, who with representational certainty actually provide the reasons/grounds, here the lost belonging together of *physis* and *techne* is evoked. By way of the posited belonging together of *physis* in the rose and *techne* in humans, the poet and Heidegger set out the possibility of recovering the lost belonging together of both in/as *poiēsis*. Given the depths of originary thinking that he finds here, it is not surprising that, in contrast to those philosophers who dismiss the poet as a muddled mystic who has no part or place in thinking, Heidegger asserts that what the poet says is genuinely originary, coming 'before thinking,' that is, more originary than metaphysics' subsequent abstractions: 'the entire fragment is so astonishingly clear and neatly constructed that one is inclined to get the idea that the most extreme sharpness and depth of thought belong to the genuine and great mystics' (PR 35–37).

The cumulative effect of Heidegger's interpretive moves is quiet but powerful. While acknowledging that beings are what are grounded, and for which reasons need to be presented, he brings forward what was concealed when beings, grounded in subjects and caused by other beings, came forward as all that is. Heidegger works with the poet to bring into disclosure, by putting together as the same, all that emerges without why, without ground: being, as the abyss, and the modes of coming into unconcealment (*poiēsis*, as *physis* in/as the rose, and *techne* and poetry via humans). The strategy is to inquire about the long-forgotten realm of the 'other' than beings by questioning their ground, which lies in being, by pushing from inquiring into beings toward the no-thing, the nothing that being is. 'Insofar as being essentially comes to be as ground/reason, it has no ground/reason. However, this is not because it founds itself, but because every foundation – even and especially self-founded ones – remain inappropriate to being as ground/reason. Every founding and even every appearance of foundability has inevitably degraded being to some sort of a being. Being qua being remains ground-less. Ground/reason stays from being, namely as the ground/reason that would first found being, it stays off and away. Being: the a-byss' (PR 111).

Playing with the multiple senses of *Satz* (while intertwining them with the plural meanings of *Grund*), Heidegger works out how, just as the dimensions of *Satz* as principle and sentence/proposition clearly go together (as is seen by elaborating the metaphysical relation of legitimizing foundation [*Grund*] to language and logic), so too *Satz*, as leap or vault (as one would say, 'with a sudden leap he was out the door') is related to *Grund* (first as principle/grounds, and, as we will see, as earth or soil) (PR 53). 'The principle of reason is a vault into the essence of being in the sense of a leap.' That is, according to Heidegger, 'We really ought not any longer say the principle of reason is a principle of being; rather, we should say that the principle of reason is a leap into being qua being, that is, qua ground/reason' (PR 53). He contends, then, that the principle (*Satz*) of reason has provided a leap (*Satz*) over beings, into being as such (PR 96).

Because it has enabled him to discern something of the source of beings, back before metaphysics (and thus before the view that all meaning derives from the human subject), Heidegger says that this gift has laid before us how it is that 'The principle of reason is an uttering [*Sagen*] of being' that, even more importantly, finally 'speaks of being' (PR 49). In this leap – *der Satz vom Grund* – Heidegger's recollective thinking actually accomplishes a minor homecoming to what is nearest as our subject matter, but absent in our technological age. He recovers an originary sense of ground itself, taking us (back) from the homelessness in metaphysical reason/ground to the figure of rootedness in the deep, in soil where we may grow and thrive. That is, yet another jump is to the originary meaning of ground. 'When we ask after the fundamental meaning [*Grundbedeutung*] of the word *Grund*,' we find, as its oldest meanings, 'the basis, the *fundus* upon which something rests, stands, and lies. We speak of foundation walls [*Grundmauern*]' (PR 92).[23] As is hinted at in these examples, from the viewpoint of the originary thinker who works parallel to the poets, the usual representational concepts of rules and principles associated with *Grund* are 'quite abstract, that is, ... taken out of and cut loose from the realm from which the word, in a more inaugural manner, speaks the meaning we mentioned previously. On the one hand *Grund* indicates the depth, for example, of the seabed [*Meeresgrund*], of the valley floor [*Talgrund*], of the meadowland [*Wiesengrund*], of a crevasse [*eine Senke*], of low-lying land and terrain [*tiefer liegendes Land und Boden*]; in a broader sense it means the earth, the surface of the earth [*Erde, Erdboden*]. And even today in the Allemanic-Swabian dialect *Grund* has the even more original meaning of '*humus*,' which is loam, the heavy, fertile soil [*gewachsene Grund, die schwere, fruchtbare Erdboden*]. For instance, a flower bed that has too little soil must be given more of it in order for there to be satisfactory growth' (PR 96 [162]).

At this point, Heidegger moves through another translation, again recovering, unfolding and folding together the originary, pregnant words from the heart of his theme, saying (letting-lie before us), thinking (taking-to-heart), *aletheia*/truth/unconcealment, emergence (*poiēsis*): 'On the whole, *Grund* means the more deeply lying, and, at the same time, supportive realm. Thus we speak "from the bottom of the heart [*Herzgrund*]." Already in the sixteenth century, "to get to the bottom [*auf dem Grund kommen*]" meant "to ascertain the truth," "ascertain what actually is," that from which something follows. The language of thinking speaks of an essential ground [*Grund*] in this regard, of the grounds for the emergence [*Enstehungsgrund*], of the motive [*Beweggrund*], of the premise of an argument [*Beweisgrund*]' (PR 96). Of course, even while attending to 'the relationship of *Grund* to essence, emergence, movement, and proof [*Beweis*],' we cannot miss the obvious: our motif is doubly developed here. As we have just heard, *Grund* is articulated directly in terms of homecoming: '*Grund* is the sort of thing from which we arise and that back to which we return.' And as Heidegger has also explicitly underscored, the rose (named as belonging together with *logos* and play), as *physis* – emerging on its own – has its originary ground in the earth. *Physis* and *techne* would come together when the rose would be nurtured by humans, for instance as cultivated in the garden, after our first 'laying a bed of soil [*Boden bilden*]' (PR 96, 107 [180]). Thus, Heidegger distinguishes the two modes of thinking *Grund:* 'Thinking carefully, we nonetheless must agree that what *Grund* means – namely depth and earth and footing – simply has nothing immediately to do with Reason and perception' (PR 98–99 [162]). (Of course, we can misinterpret this if we hear the emphasis on 'nothing to do with' and miss the quiet, determining word, 'immediately.' The two sorts of meaning do have to do with one another, of course, since they amount to the double sense of *Grund* that Heidegger has been teasing out all along (PR 99). From the originary soil of the first beginning grew the subsequent metaphysical bifurcation of *ratio* into reason and ground: the latter two 'are divergent, but nevertheless are held in one and the same root and stalk [*Stamm und Schatt*], which is why even in their divergence – and precisely in their divergence – they converge' (PR 103–104 [173]).

In this series of successful leaps, Heidegger unfolds the core questions and plays out the two-track answers to each. To 'What is it that calls for thinking?' he has added 'What is "ground/reason"?' and 'What is it that calls us to think the words that play out as "ground/ reason"?' (PR 86–87, 95). To think these questions, still more leaps are required. We might guess that the answer to these questions of 'What calls' might be 'being,' even as we understand that Heidegger *is trying to think and say the dissolution of being* – for example, into the duality, the presencing of what is present, as being – as far as can be done. Heidegger finds that in his leap from the homelessness of technology (within the power and spirit of modernity, and especially its 'supposed completion,' as 'the atomic age') toward a homecoming, he has entered the region of being itself (PR 43). We ask where the demand for reasons comes from (PR 39). From us humans? From reason itself? Yes, according to various traditions of metaphysics. But as we have seen, the answer is that it comes finally – originally – from the realm of being.

In trying to recollectively think these relationships by way of the principle of reason, Heidegger arrives at the question of the belonging together of being and ground, and, as he has done before, finds that the best way into what it means lies by way of the early Greeks. In this case, it is again through Heraclitus, who can provide an originary clue: 'because [his sayings are] not yet philosophy, the thinker is not yet thinking and speaking metaphysically; that is, he still is in harmony with being' (WP, 51–53). As Heraclitus speaks the word, 'Λόγος names the ground. 'λόγος is at once presencing and ground. Being and ground belong together in λόγος' (PR 107). Heidegger also gets to the same place by another route. Working to retrieve the originary meaning of what is said, he moves back from the various names for reason, back to the Latin, which came from the earlier Greek. *Ratio* derives, ultimately, from λόγος (PR 105). What we find through this arrival is a positive dynamic. 'Λόγος names this belonging-together of being and ground. It names them insofar as it, in one breath, says: "allowing to lie present as allowing to arise," "emerging on its own": "φύσις," "being," and, "allowing to lie present as presencing"' (PR 107).

Heidegger elaborates what Heraclitus tells us about the dynamic. As is well known, Heraclitus speaks about play. The play, too, as being and the rose, is without why. In the famous Fragment 52, Heraclitus says, 'the *Geschick* of being: a that child that plays, shifting the pawns: the royalty of a child. [The play] plays since it plays' (PR 113). For the moment passing over the question of what *Geschick* means, the question begins to appear as to whether 'we must think being and ground/reason, being qua abyss in terms of the nature of play and indeed of the play which engages us mortals who are who we are only insofar as we live in proximity to death ... the most elevated play in which humans are engaged in on earth, a play in which they are at stake' (PR 112).

The play could turn any way, could turn out in dramatically opposite ways. The tensed alternatives in the homelessness of metaphysics at its end in technology are that humans and being together might turn toward a negative, complete nihilism or toward the positive possibilities that might emerge from the concealing/unconcealing dynamic of enframing. Clearly, in the history of the unfolding sending Heidegger has laid out for us, 'When sending [*Geschick*] reigns in the mode of enframing, it is the supreme danger' (QCT 26). However, as we began to see above, where Heidegger moved from nihilism to recover the essence of nothingness as related to being, a positive turning might be made into nothingness and being. If, with nihilism, being withdraws into self-concealment, yet, 'turning away and withdrawal are not nothing' (QB 75, 89). That is, the withdrawal that conceals itself is a sheltering – in nothingness, concealing and sheltering occur (QB 80). As Heidegger puts it, in commenting on some lines by Hölderlin, in addition to the prospect of nihilism, 'in technology's essence there roots and thrives the saving power' (QCT 29). As we have seen, Heidegger has been shifting from the representational sense of *Grund* as reason to the homey, originary sense of *Grund* (earth as ground) and to *Boden* (soil) and *Bodenständigkeit* (the indigenous, or rooted). Not surprisingly, here Heidegger develops the positive alternative, in terms of a homecoming, to just this originary ground, to the deep, to the fertile soil (PR 30 [60]). He brings technology and poetry back together, and joins them both with the fruitful soil – *physis* – to recover a new, originary version of the primal *poiēsis:*

> Thus, where enframing reigns, there is *danger* in the highest sense.
> *But where danger is, grows*
> *The saving power also.*
> Let us think carefully about these words of Hölderlin ... To 'save' is to fetch something home to its essence, in order to bring the essence for the first time into its genuine appearing ... Rather, precisely the essence of technology must harbor in itself the growth of the saving power ... Where something grows, there it takes root, from thence it thrives. (QCT 28)

In fact, Heidegger takes us deeper into the question of what gives ground/reason, what gives thinking. Specifically, he uses the same language of the originary, fertile soil to discuss how we still need to recollectively think that from which we remain 'far removed': 'an insight into the particular epochs of the full *Geschick* of being and into the way in which the epochs suddenly spring up like sprouts' (PR 91; see also 37). Here Heidegger provisionally uses the word *Geschick* to indicate what needs thinking. Since his leaping and moving to and fro across the history of the representational legacy (ground, reason, principle, *ratio, causa, Ursache* (cause), 'condition for the possibility') is an investigation of the unfolding of being, we can understand why he would now say that *Geschick* (usually translated as 'sending' or more problematically as 'destiny') names the *Geschick* of being (PR 92): 'the name sending of being [*Seinsgeschick*] [indicates] the epochs of being' (FS 43). And as we just saw, translating αἰών in Heraclitus' Fragment 52, he also finds 'The *Geschick* of being: a child that plays.' But that really only raises the question, 'What is the *Geschick* of being?' (PR 113).

Being, as the abyss, for Heidegger neither involves nor leads to nihilism. Rather, it opens to a question about the most 'primal power,' the play without why, though that is not at all an adequate way to name what needs to be thought. We do not even know how to name what is pointed to, though we have seen Heidegger provisionally use *Geschick*, which he thinks in terms of what he has painfully worked to recover and the belonging together of what Heraclitus named as the same: 'being's more original name,' λόγος, φύσις/the emerging-on-its-own/self-concealing, κόσμος-αἰών/world-time (PR 112–113 [187–88]). This last word (αἰών), Heidegger notes, is especially difficult to translate. 'One says: "world-time [*welt-zeit*]." It is the world that worlds and temporalizes in that, as κόσμος [kosmos], it brings the jointure of being to a glowing sparkle ... We hear that unsaid we name "the *Geschick* of being" [*Seinsgeschick*]' (PR 113 [187]). The *Geschick* of being is 'nothing other than the proffering of the lighting and clearing that furnishes a domain for the appearing of beings in some configuration along with the contemporaneous withdrawal of the essential provenance of being as such' (PR 88). But as he has also held since *Contributions to Philosophy*, any leap from metaphysics to the originary has only become possible because of a second change that has happened since the first change that started metaphysics, when being withdrew in favour of beings. He now speaks of that second change, the turning, as that of *Geschick:* 'the *Geschick* of being has taken a turn, presumably in the sense that being as such has awakened and come to the fore' (PR 55). All along, in travelling back and forth across the epochs of being, Heidegger has been rehearsing the history of being as

Geschick, looking at its epochs and the manner in which beings have emerged even as being has withdrawn itself (PR 68–69, 71). In the case of humans, still the same through our various modes of appearance as creatures or subjects or otherwise, 'we are the ones bestowed [*mit ihr Beschnkung*] by and with the clearing and lighting of being in the *Geschick* of being' (PR 85, 86 [145]; see also 75, 94). We are 'en-dowed [*be-gabt*] by the *Geschick* with the wherewithal to think beings,' and thus historically are bestowed (*verbleibt*) with our essence as humans (PR 86–7 [147]; see also WCT 118).

Heidegger has clearly moved from the representational to the originary. He has leapt from beings to being. How to make another jump, deeper still into the question of *Geschick* (PR 86–7, 95): What is it that bestows temporal play-space and endows, as legacy, the essential nature of what emerges? What is that which bestows and endows? *Geschick?* As noted above, Heidegger knows he needs to question the province of *Geschick,* to recollect the realm of what gives and grants, of what sends. As we have seen, we already belong within *Geschick,* specifically in that our endowment from the *Geschick* includes letting 'our nature reach thought' (WCT 118). In *What Is Called Thinking?* Heidegger goes on to say that because what calls for thinking both gives itself and, by calling us into arrival and presencing, endows us with our nature, we need to be most thankful for the gift and devoted to preserving it. 'We receive many gifts, of many kinds. But the highest and really most lasting gift, given to us is always our essential nature, with which we are gifted in such a way that we are what we are only through it. That is why we owe thanks for this endowment, first and unceasingly. But the thing given to us, in the sense of this dowry, is thinking ... When we think what is most thought-provoking we think properly. When we, in thinking, are gathered and concentrated on the most thought-provoking, then we dwell where all recalling thought is gathered' (WCT 142–3).

Because what calls for thinking and response still calls us forth, we also need to ask, 'Where do we so dwell?' 'What so gives?' (QCT 19; see also *What Is Called Thinking* 124, 150–1, 191, 194, 199) – remaining careful not to be misled by grammatical 'implication' into substantiating or attributing agency to any 'what,' which is more helpfully thought of (by means of what Heidegger has said thus far) as the disclosing granting itself. The granting can be thought utilizing what Heidegger has recovered of the meaning of the same as belonging-together, where difference remains, not reduced away into the equivalence of conceptual identity. So thought, the question, 'What so grants?,' has yet another answer, given in

'The Onto-theo-logical Constitution of Metaphysics': 'That differentiation alone grants and holds apart the "between," in which the overwhelming [being] and the arrival [beings] are held toward one another, are borne away from and toward each other. The difference of being and beings, as the differentiation of overwhelming and arrival, is the perdurance of the two in unconcealing keeping in concealment' (OtlCM 65). Given the simultaneity at all times of concealments with correlate unconcealments, as we have already heard Heidegger explain, and since belonging together is not a matter of mere physical proximity but of each and all together coming into their own, what belongs together can be so even when apart, even when one of the 'elements' or one of the dimensions is absent, or abandoned, or lost (FS 48). Heidegger notes, using the key motif, 'For example, whoever spends time in some foreign place is denied the dwelling-relationship to a home. The relationship of dwelling in a home is lacking. But this lack of relationship is itself an essential facet of the relationship called "homesickness"' (PR 42). Heidegger is telling us that the site of the giving, the realm of home, is the same as – can be understood in terms of – belonging-together.

The quest to stay underway in homecoming operates by our originarily thinking through the homelessness that occurs in the metaphysical grounding, as it appears with reason, logic, logistics, our subjectivity, and technological control, and by our thinking homelessness in the perspective of a deeper home in/as belonging together with the granting. How to think further, to play along with being, to enter into its bright and dark realm of sending in which, as what grounds and thus has no ground, 'as the abyss, [being] plays the play that, as *Geschick*, passes being and ground/reason to us' (PR 113)? Heidegger needs to continue to reflect on the temporal play-space Heraclitus points out as the lighting-clearing for what emerges. Dramatically, toward the end of the essay, 'The End of Philosophy,' he elaborates what it would mean to understand *aletheia*, unconcealment, as the origin of what is present by combining the language of place and opening with that of gift and granting – to begin to move into a region 'prior to' the mutuality of being and thinking. Increasingly arriving into his own voice, Heidegger interprets *aletheia* via Parmenides' poem in Fragment 1, in even more originary language than he has hitherto. He says that opening, as 'a "primal phenomenon,"' may be thought as 'that within which alone pure space and ecstatic time and everything present and absent in them have the place which gathers and protects everything' (EP 65–6). Or, 'unconcealment is, so to speak, the element in which being and thinking and their belonging together exist'

(EP 69). All lighting and so much more so our seeing, and even darkness, can occur only 'if openness has already been granted' (EP 66).

And what is the granting? How does it come about? Heidegger contends that 'It is only such openness that grants to giving and receiving at all what is free' (EP 66). According to Heidegger, then, Parmenides names the 'heart of unconcealment' as 'the place of stillness which gathers in itself what grants unconcealment to begin with. That is the opening of what is open' (EP 68). *Aletheia* here appears as originary fecundity: 'We must think *aletheia*, unconcealment, as the opening which first grants being and thinking and their presencing too for each other' (EP 68). In the very last lines of 'The End of Philosophy' (where Heidegger continues the critical task that has engaged him 'ever since 1930 to shape the question of *Being and Time* in a more primal way),' he notes that the name for the task 'will change' and thus points to the direction our questioning must now take (EP 55):

> Is it the well-founded unconcealment itself, thought as the opening?
>
> Does the name for the task of thinking then read instead of *Being and Time:* opening and presence?
>
> But where does the opening come from and how is it given? What speaks in the 'It gives'?
>
> The task of thinking would then be the surrender of previous thinking to the determination of the matter of thinking. (EP 71–2; see also FS 64)

What more could be said of the gathering-granting opening: both play-space and world-time? Pushing even further, Heidegger teases out how all that is named in this complex might belong together: ground and home, sheltering and stillness, place and time. Leaping as far as he can at this stage, he articulates in yet another modulation a word he has thought before and for a long time (at least since *Contributions to Philosophy,* though interestingly he does not use the word in the essay just cited, 'The End of Philosophy'). To think recollectively beyond even *aletheia,* to the very 'concealment in which unconcealment (*aletheia*) is based' would have to be a thinking back to that which has been, which has not disappeared because it remains what is imperishable in all that is lasting [*im allem Währen*] which the event of being ever grants [*das Ereignis des ~~Seins~~ gewährt*]' (QB 91). Thus, he names the gathering-granting opening *Ereignis.* As he later says in the course of the seminar in Zähringen, as long as we altogether think of origin in ontic-causal terms, we can say, 'It is the event [*Ereignis*] of being as a condition for the arrival of beings: being lets beings presence' (FS 59). But *Ereignis* is even more inaugural than *Geschick:* 'There is no destinal epoch of enowning. Sending is from enowning [*Das Schicken ist aus dem Ereignis*]' (FS 61). *Ereignis,* then, would be a still more primordial enowning, the still-continuing emerging within which all, including humans, first comes forth and lingers, and to which all belongs, together. At this point Heidegger manages to say only a bit more, that this moment of first arrival is an arrival at *Ereignis,* which itself first arrives.

In 'The Principle of Identity,' Heidegger presses significantly beyond both *What Is Called Thinking?* and *The Question of Being,* exploring how it is that within *Ereignis,* as event of mutual appropriation, all (including humans) comes forth and how the belonging together of all rests in this mutual appropriation (PI 31–2). Though most of what Heidegger says in 'The Principle of Identity' and in the later *Four Seminars* belongs to another set of articulations and accordingly will be developed in the next section of this chapter, we can note here that he can at least begin to explain *Ereignis:* 'Man and being are appropriated to each other. They belong to each other. From this belonging to each other, which has not been thought out more closely, man and being first received those determinations of essence by which man and being are grasped metaphysically in philosophy' (PI 31–2).

At the limit of what he can say, even with non-representational originary words, in the effort to continue a homecoming to the most originary gathering-granting, to which we belong even though estranged, Heidegger turns to an example that continues to develop a positive sense of 'home' and, I believe, also to elaborate the still missing temporal aspect: the world-time correlate to the play-space just named with 'open' and 'place.' As he did when shifting the interpretation of *Grund* toward earth or soil (*Boden*), Heidegger evokes the simple meanings and experiences of the belonging of humans together with each other, and together with the gathering-granting. We are told that in the 1969 seminar in Le Thor Heidegger said, 'that through Hölderlin he came to understand how useless it is to coin new words; only [gradually] was the necessity of a return to the essential simplicity of language clear to him' (FS 51).[24]

Invoking Hebel's homey language at this point so as to remind us that *poiēsis* and *techne* go together (just as *poiēsis* and *physis* did, respectively, with Silenius' rose and the fertile soil), Heidegger describes positive gatherings that have occurred and that may again happen. Here Heidegger performs another originary interpretation, explicating *wesen* as a verb related to *währen*, that is, lasting or enduring (QCT 30; also consider *wara*, SR 164–5). In his poem 'Kanderer Street,' Hebel uses the old word *die Weserei* to name the city hall, the place that gathers the life of the community, enabling the village's mode of existing to come to presence (QCT 30). The city hall, as also house and state, are noted as having a manner of enduring (*Wesen*) in the way they hold sway (*wesen*); in other words, in Heidegger's interpretation, essence (*Wesen*) does 'not mean a generic type; rather ... the ways in which [they] hold sway, administer themselves, develop and decay – the way in which they have their way of being [*Wesen*]' (QCT 30). This is to claim that 'all essencing endures,' a point reinforced by Goethe's use of 'the mysterious word *fortgewären* [to grant permanently] in place of *fortwären* [to endure permanently]. He hears *wären* [to endure] and *gewären* [to grant] here in one unarticulated accord' (QCT 30–1). These words speak then, according to Heidegger, of what is granted and tell us that primally what grants endures, as a higher enduring (QCT 31, 34). In the face of, and in contrast to, the homelessness that threatens in enframing, Heidegger affirms that granting (*Ereignis*) persists and that humans belong within such granting, that we are needed and positively used therein.[25]

In an address, also titled 'The Principle of Reason' and published with the lecture course of the same name, Heidegger continues, explaining that, '"Whiling," "tarrying," "perpetuating" [*Weilen, währen, immerwähren*] is indeed the old sense of the word "being" [*sein*]. "The while" names the ground. But qua the Whereas, "whiling" also names "the abiding": being. "Whiling" names both: being and ground; it names the abiding, being as the ground/reason. Being and ground/reason – in whiling – the same. Both belong together' (PR 127 [207–8]).

In the leaps we have been watching it is disclosed that the homecoming might be to *aletheia*, to *Ereignis*, and that dwelling as abiding for a time, that is lingering, in a belonging with opening-gathering-granting, might be a mode of whiling. Heidegger is increasingly able to leap, as he jumps out of metaphysics and to the domain of *Geschick*, and into the region indicated by Heraclitus: the temporal play-space. Echoing what Heraclitus named with λόγος, as Heidegger best manages to originarily leap and show us, this is the realm of what calls for thinking, that which grants opening, *aletheia, Ereignis,* Whiling. Many other fresh, powerful words (such as 'using,' 'gathering,' 'belonging together') are brought forth to reflect upon what calls for thinking, but Heidegger is unable to carry such thinking and saying to completion here. Words break off. It is no false modesty, but only honesty that leads Heidegger to say, again and again (despite the many moments of success he does have, and given the unavoidability of remaining in the site from which he leaps – hence two-track thinking), that 'we are not yet thinking,' 'we still need to learn to think.' He intends what he says here to be more than a reference to his well-noted position that science is not yet thinking, because it is embedded in the representational, not the meditative, and because it cannot be self-reflective without becoming philosophical; finally, he is directly exhorting us to enact the thinking that remains to be done (WCT 3–4, 100; see also FS 56).

We must remain underway, in the pathways of active questioning: 'The paths of thinking that belong to the situating discussion have the peculiar character that when we are under way on them we are nearer to the site than when, in order to become ensconced there, we convince ourselves that we have reached the site; for the site is of a different nature than a station or a place in space. What we call the site – here the site of the principle of reason – is what assembles what comes to be essential of a matter' (PR 60). Remaining underway in the questioning movement is our proper placement on our journey. Indeed, it is the place wherein we need to learn to dwell: 'we are here taking a way of *questioning*, on which the problematic alone is accepted as the unique habitat and *locus* of thinking' (WCT 185; see also 147). Heidegger, then, explicitly says that we dwell in the remaining-underway, 'Traveling in the direction that is a way toward that which is worthy of questioning is not adventure but homecoming'; 'When we, in thinking, are gathered and concentrated on the most thought-provoking, then we dwell where all recalling thought is gathered' (SR 180; WCT 143). Staying underway, in the jumping and moving back and forth, is only the barest beginning. We are not close to any stage of settling in, but instead must constantly return to and go over again the sites where we have always been, but not yet built. At best, he holds, we can prepare for dwelling, not being so bold as to intend 'the erection of the house for God and of the dwelling places of mortals,' but instead being 'content with constructing the *road*' which would lead through metaphysics and nihilism to a next, originary phase (QB 103–5). Hence, once again, we find that we must tarry in the foreign, that dwelling at home is denied.

Heidegger clarifies how the reflection and saying that are managed thus far are not yet any arrival at, much less dwelling in, a final home. The point is made in the final pages of the essay 'Science and Reflection,' dense with the vocabulary of home. There he speaks of arrival and being at home in reflection but explains how the arrival and being at home are intelligible only in regard to the remaining underway – in questioning – in the homecoming journey. He says that 'reflection first brings us onto the way toward the place of our sojourning,' with the consequence that we 'actually arrive at the place where, without experiencing it and without having seen penetratingly into it, we have long been sojourning.' Even so, we cannot speak decisively about whether our historical sojourn (*Aufenthalt*) 'adds to and enlarges the dwelling proper to it [*sein wohnen an- und ausbaut*],' because our 'reflection remains more provisional' (SR 181 [61]). At best, it 'would have to be content only with preparing a readiness' (SR 181–2). Yet, this is no small landmark, for where, 'through special favor,' successful reflection occurs so that we can leap to the non-metaphysical and remain underway, we find the prospect that 'that which is worthy of questioning will someday again open the door that leads to what is essential in all things and in all sendings' (SR 182).

Heidegger is openly self-critical in regard to the still-preparatory character and limitations of his overall movement on the pathways of recollective thinking and the accomplishments we have been following, laying out how the direction of decades of work, for example on the ontological difference, had to be given up in the end, even while there was no other way to arrive where he has (FS 22, 46–7, 78). Or, as he admits in another context, 'The task of our thinking has been to trace being to its own from appropriation [*Ereignis*] by way of looking through true time without regard to the relation of being to beings. To think being without beings means: to think being without regard to metaphysics. Yet a regard for metaphysics still prevails in the intention to overcome metaphysics. Therefore, out task is to cease all overcoming, and leave metaphysics to itself' (TB 24; see also FS 64). Here we have yet another – dramatic – shift in the journey.

What would the new task, 'free' or released from metaphysics, amount to? How would it be carried out? Apparently, the further originary thinking moves beyond beings and even past the being of beings or the presencing of what is present, toward what would be initializing emergence, the more opaque matters become. It is no accident that the poet and the mystical thinker are taken to be obscure. Though to be sure, the poets and Heidegger too have severe limitations in what they can see and think, and in what they can say, the real difficulty they have in finding their 'way through the obscurity now gathering' or through 'the clouded perspective on the principle of reason' is not because of the principle itself, but the darkness of its ground (PR 43). This source, the primal home, is the most obscure of all.

At least Heidegger has journeyed to a point where he can show us that, for all the obscurity in which we find ourselves, perhaps the darkness that is given is not quite so complete as it might be – it is not as black as is that which looms and threatens from the direction of complete nihilism. Rather than pure darkness, we have been given not only the flash of lightning in our dark night ('Profound visions light up only in the dark'), but at least, and more positively, a fog: 'the province to which [*Grund*] belongs lies in a fog [*Nebel*]'; 'a fog ... arises from the region of what is most thought-provoking' (PR 43, 39; WCT 14). Fog obscures, but is frequently also permeated by, or bears, a saturated, diffused, and pervasive of light – wherein, we are told, being, human being, and even being are dissolving, are being absorbed (in *The Question of Being*, being was said to 'be dissolved {*auflosen*} in the turning and to be absorbed {*aufgehen*} into its essence'; humans were also said to 'dissipate {*verschwende*}' themselves to or for it; QB 81, 83).

There may be partial disclosures as a fog momentarily lifts or clears; in any case there is concealment. It is very dangerous, actually foolhardy, to even think of leaping in the midst of a fog, especially when one knows that the fog is gathered at the edge of an abyss. From our seemingly 'comfortable,' too often unthinking, situation, we should not underestimate the extent to which Heidegger finds himself in a wild place, still full of barely discerned forms and dynamics. Luckily, he is guided by a few 'old, venerable words' which reveal enough to allow him to get his bearings and which provide – are – something of an opening, a sheltering resting place for the moment in the midst of homelessness. These ancient and sturdy words grow slowly and endure a long time, as do trees. Cases in point are the words that have enabled Heidegger's crossing over to the first beginning; his moving to and fro across the primal bifurcation where, from the first beginning, metaphysics split off; and his remaining within the unfolding of the history of metaphysics so as to follow the subsequent branchings, for example of ratio into reason and ground or of *poiēsis* into *physis* and *techne* (including poetry and philosophy). Elaborating the figure, Heidegger tells us that 'The Old High German word for a bifurcated bough, a bifurcated tree trunk and the entire tree that has grown in this shape is *Zwiesel*. We often find such forked growths under the old, towering pines of the upper Black Forest' (PR 103–4). Yet, other words spring up (perhaps out of the lightning flash), and even disappear quickly, as do blossoms on a fruit tree or flowers (DL 44–7; WCT 42). 'The meaning-fulness of those words,' Heidegger tells us, citing Hölderlin's 'Bread and Wine,' 'originate like flowers' in the 'all-playing structure of never-resting transformation.' A fusion of *techne* and *physis*, this 'meaning-fullness ... is the garden of the jungle, in which growth and cultivation harmonize with one another out of an incomprehensible intimacy' (QB 105).

Remaining Underway

'Where are we now? At the entry of our thinking into that simplicity which we call in the strict sense of the term the event of appropriation' (PI 37). This is perhaps surprising given that we are deep within the increasing homelessness of the end of the metaphysical era. But clearly Heidegger is not just mechanically running through some chronological accounting of the changing meaning of words or philosophical ideas. Nihilism in the epoch of technology is not just another phase of a story that needs 'to be filled in.' Rather, only in nihilism, if we come to realize its radical power and think out its reign of extreme danger, do we receive the shock necessary to perhaps experience what has been lost and concealed, a shock that might open to jumping out of metaphysics. In the *Gestell* we have found that a double or triple blockage endangers us such that we may entirely lose our essence, our relation to the other dimensions of the world (QCT 2). In questioning technology and facing nihilism we find an estrangement both from the modern, 'classical' metaphysical world and from any deeper originary realm; or, it could be said, there is a triple displacement insofar as the original realm itself has two dimensions: what was laid out in the past (the first beginning) and what might lie in the future (another beginning) (QCT 26, 33).

As challenged by enframing, humans are profoundly homeless, not only by being long-removed from originary belonging with being, but by losing even what identity we have accumulated through more recent metaphysical epochs. For all practical purposes, we so much live in the modern metaphysical disclosure that we take it for granted. It is common sense, is it not, that we are subjects and live amidst the sum of objects, which we increasingly control? More technically, Heidegger shows, we have been living in the metaphysical unconcealment of beings for more than two millennia and have become increasingly at home in scientific knowledge and technology as they have developed through the modern epoch to ours. As Jünger says, 'we dwell in metaphysics' (QB 53) That is, we are exceptionally comfortable in our role as ground – both as agents with great causal power over beings and epistemologically as the guarantors of intelligibility, as the source of legitimacy and of decision about what is considered to be real. This metaphysical-representational constitution of the subject is who we are and is correlate to the sphere of beings as objects. But as shown, in the enframing challenging the homelessness of the modern era of representation crashes over us insofar as we experience the disappearance of the comfortable foundational subject-object complex and the disclosure of all beings, including humans, as stock, ordered and standing in reserve. Hoping to avoid separation from all that is familiar by holding on to, by going back to, a classical, modern metaphysical realm, in which the subject-object relationship provided a comfortable sense of mastery and a seemingly secure epistemological and ontological place, is not possible. Indeed, Heidegger warns that we might stay bound within the just-beginning era of enframing and that its sway will be expected to last a very long time. Thus, we are also in danger of remaining exiled, of being unable to remain at home as subjects within a world of objects (no matter how homeless that realm may be in respect to being), much less enacting an originary homecoming. We may not be able to come out of enframing and its deep homelessness.

Still, now that the threat of complete nihilism enables us to experience the loss of even metaphysics up to now, that trauma can open us to the real question of what is hidden in the dominating disclosures of metaphysics. The gift and experience of the shock of disclosure is necessary, and should be welcome, Heidegger holds, because we have never experienced the absence of being (see FS 2). The withdrawal of being in favour of the disclosure of beings has been so gradual and the presence of beings so overwhelming that any first lighting by being as occurred for a few of the early Greeks has been totally forgotten. Since we have not actually felt the loss of the originary – being or the duality – we have no clue of that in regard to which we are primally homeless. Not, of course, that it would it be possible to return to such a relationship, such an historical unfolding. But at least now we have a glimmer of understanding that belonging together with being was our primal, 'real' home and that the current mode of being at home in metaphysics (in that which is now unconcealed to us) is correlate to no longer being at home in the originary (that which is concealed – both as being withdraws into concealment and even as that concealment is concealed, as *aletheia* is self-concealing) (FS 78).

There is a genuine breakthrough, then, when Heidegger shows us, by moving from nihilism through an analysis of the modes of homelessness, that we are so alienated from being that up to now the possibility of an originary past or future has been almost completely hidden from us (not completely hidden insofar as at least a few poets such as Hölderlin or Angelus Silesius have been struck by a lightning flash). Explicating our radical homelessness today at the edge of complete nihilism reanimates, in thinking and language, the layers and layers of historically folded, unfolded, and refolded concealments and unconcealments. The play of hiddenness and disclosure moves back and forth – the unconcealment of technological homelessness has, as a correlate, the concealment that the modern metaphysical is not a home after all (even though we have become comfortable, seemingly 'at home' in it); the disclosure of the homelessness of all metaphysics, including the end in technology, is intimately complemented by the fuller oblivion of a past home in being or the duality, or the possibility of a future originary home.

Startled enough, we finally begin not only to question today's strangeness but also to imagine what a homecoming would be. What would be possible in the future in the face of ever increasing technological homelessness? As we have seen, Heidegger shows how the long, seemingly roundabout, pathway (with unavoidable impasses or dead ends [*Holzwege*]; FS 61) toward an originary reunion requires reopening and following the historical unfolding of metaphysics and the question of being, of the being of beings, and, as we now see, of how being as abyss opens, not to nihilism, but to a possible homecoming to what is named, though not understood, as disclosing-granting-giving-opening, *Ereignis*, Whiling. The threat of nihilism first gives us an experience enabling us to question 'in what respect the saving power does most profoundly take root and thence thrive even in that wherein the extreme danger lies, in the holding sway of enframing ... [For] in technology's essence roots and thrives the saving power' (QCT 29). Heidegger, as we well know by now, moves along (with) both trajectories:

> The essence of technology is in a lofty sense ambiguous. Such ambiguity points to the mystery of all revealing, i.e., of truth.
>
> On the one hand, enframing challenges forth into the frenziedness of ordering that blocks every view into the coming-to-pass of revealing and so radically endangers the relation to the essence of truth.
>
> On the other hand, enframing comes to pass for its part in the granting that lets man endure – as yet unexperienced, but perhaps more experienced in the future – that he may be the one who is needed and used for the safekeeping [*Wahrnis*] of the coming to presence of truth. Thus does the arising of the saving power appear. (QCT 33; see also FS 60)

So, from where we are, homeless, at end of metaphysics, in enframing, 'We do not as yet enter the domain of the belonging together'; for homecoming, 'we must enter into what we call the event of appropriation [*Ereignis*]' (PI 32, 36). We can do so, in fact, because the thinking that has begun to respond to being struck by nihilism has taken us toward being and beyond. Specifically, it takes us to seeing being as abyss, where 'this abyss is neither empty nothingness nor murky confusions, but rather,' as groundless, opens to at least partial disclosures of *aletheia*, gathering-granting and '*Ereignis*, the event of appropriation' (PI 39). At a threshold, and still within and mindful of the dangers of complete metaphysical homelessness, we still need to cross over to that which we glimpse through Heidegger's jumps. At least, through the leaps, we see that a homecoming arrival (to *Ereignis*) can be imagined. 'What we experience in the frame as the constellation of being and man through the modern world of technology is a prelude to what is called the event of appropriation. This event, however, does not necessarily persist in its prelude. For in the event of appropriation the possibility arises that it may overcome the mere dominance of the frame to turn it into a more original appropriating. Such a transformation of the frame into the event of appropriation, by virtue of that event, would bring the appropriate recovery – of the world of technology from its dominance back to servitude in the realm by which man reaches more truly into the event of appropriation' (PI 36–7).

What happens next? Now that we face up to our deep homelessness, what is needed is being able to say and think more adequately what has only been glimpsed, the gathering-granting-opening to which we belong even when apart from it, the unconcealment of that which gives, *Ereignis*, Whiling. Heidegger has begun to leap into an originary sphere, but he is not yet able to sustain remaining there. He needs, in his own way, as have the poets, to come more fully into his own originary thinking and saying – which he does in the works that manage an arrival.

C Moment of Arrival into His Own: The No-Longer-Metaphysical

Heidegger's thinking leap from a representational to an originary realm is already underway in works such as *What Is Called Thinking?*[26] 'A Dialogue on Language,' and *Identity and Difference.* This journey toward home continues toward a moment of arrival. In fact, the arrival home is not a single flashing moment; it is a slow, long-coming transition that remains continuous. Still, the moments of arrival are also clear: in them

Heidegger moves beyond metaphysical theme and style to an originary matter and saying. The dimensions of the arrival, then, can be seen in the originary thinking and saying of Heidegger's 'two-track works' (especially *What Is Called Thinking?*) where he crosses over to both think metaphysics from an originary position and to begin to move along an originary way; of the works where he clearly develops more fully the originary thinking and saying of the giving of being (e.g., sections of 'The Principle of Identity' in *Identity and Difference*, 'Time and Being'; and of the works where the primal appropriation is thought and said in a striking, fully originary way ('The Thing' and 'The Way to Language'). Because after *What Is Called Thinking?* he does pass beyond the thinking of being to arrive at *Ereignis*, the works accomplish *another phase in homecoming:* that is, in parts of 'The Principle of Identity,' 'Time and Being,' the 'Protocol to a Seminar on the Lecture "Time and Being,"' 'The Thing,' a section of 'A Dialogue on Language,' and 'The Way to Language,' *Heidegger achieves homecoming as a moment of arrival into what is his own home.*

Though the works considered here do move beyond those previously considered, all of them clearly belong together. In chapter 3 we saw Heidegger begin to articulate his own style and subject (out of and contrasted with his treatment of metaphysics and Hölderlin in the works of the first two chapters). Actually, the works of chapter 3, marking the turning, were the serious beginning of Heidegger's own way that led to and was deepened in the works (treated in the fourth chapter) in which he learns to think and speak originarily from the Greeks (as he earlier had from Hölderlin) and in which he does jump, first into and then from recollection, and thus arrive at home. The works to be taken up now effect *the landing* of that leap. That is, *he does arrive* at a no-longer-metaphysical home, which is his theme, by way of and with originary language (which he also thinks). In Heidegger's terms, of course, such an arrival and coming into his (our) own would be given in the unfolding of a granting.

Recall that the story of the journey home through metaphysical homelessness eventually tells of the movement from 1) beings to 2) being, 3) to the being of beings, 4) to the presencing of that which is present, and finally 5) to the granting of the duality and the gathering-in of mortals (see chapter 4-A and -B). Still, for all the distance of the move beyond metaphysics up until now, it barely touches the no-longer-metaphysical shore of home. Any arrival there will clearly be marked as no-longer-metaphysical by thinking of being without beings (TB 2). Heidegger says, 'To think being itself explicitly requires disregarding being to the extent that it is only grounded and interpreted in terms of beings and for beings as their ground, as in all metaphysics. To think being explicitly requires us to relinquish being as the ground of beings in favor of the giving that prevails in unconcealment, that is, in the favor of [there is given]' (TB 6). Here Heidegger is on the verge of passing over from metaphysics and wandering in homelessness to the no-longer-metaphysical giving of being, that is, to our arrival at an originary home. We need to become aware of such a movement to understand how 'Time and Being' reverses and completes *Being and Time*. The latter attempted to think being and time by ontologically rethinking temporality; the former now lets go of and passes beyond that initial attempt into a new thinking experience with the giving of being and time and from which they can now be better interpreted.

To originarily rethink being and time in terms of giving, of 'the giving that prevails in unconcealment,' requires thinking of being without doing so in terms of beings, and time in the same way – a very difficult task. To do so, Heidegger makes a powerful and dramatic move, though one fraught with problems, focusing on and radically reinterpreting giving (specifically the giving of being and of time) by exploring the pathway opened up by the wording/thought, '*Es gibt.*' We need remain focally clear that this cannot be understood 'word by word' to mean 'it' 'gives,' since the German is used to indicate that something is taking place but without implying any agent or subject, as when one says '*es regnet,*' 'it is raining,' 'it rains.' The great danger is that in exploring the word's region the grammatical trap is especially hard to avoid: it almost unavoidably happens, even to Heidegger himself, that one inquires into the '*es,*' the 'it' – *though there is no* 'it' – and thus wonders if the 'it' is being, time, or 'something' else when that idea is precisely what needs to be overcome or avoided. The alternate English translation, 'there is' or 'there is given,' is better, but also is too static. It helps us to keep in mind that Heidegger continually struggles with these problems, on another occasion providing the helpful directive that since the main strategy is to rethink being without beings we do not want to say '*x* is,' but to think by way of '*x* is given' or better yet '*x* or *y* gives,' yet without substantiating any 'it' that does the giving, instead meaning 'by virtue of the gift of *x* or *y*, there is given ...' (as we will see in covering his essay 'The Nature of Language' in the next chapter).

But to stay focused on the points at hand, we note that Heidegger is trying to indicate that when we say 'being' and 'time' we are not invoking or referring to some 'it.' That is, we are not reifying what is fundamentally dynamic and eventful as temporally holding sway or enduring.

Thus, to explore being and time along this new line of inquiry, he puts it that there already is the disclosure of being – there is ('*Es gibt*') being – and of time – there is ('*Es gibt*') time. As a result of this shift, we have a new kind of question.

> In this way, the manner must become clear how there is [given] ['*Es gibt*'] being and how there is [given] ['*Es gibt*'] time. In this giving, it becomes apparent how that giving is to be determined which, as a relation, first holds the two toward each other and brings them into being.
>
> Being, by which all beings as such are marked, being means presencing. Thought with regard to what presences, presencing shows itself as letting presence. But now we must try to think this letting-presence explicitly insofar as presencing is admitted. Letting shows its character in bringing into unconcealment. To let presence means: to unconceal, to bring to openness. In unconcealing prevails a giving, the giving that gives presencing, that is, being, in letting-presence. (TB 5)[27]

Thought as 'presencing, letting be present,' being belongs to time (TB 10). In presencing, time-space opens (TB 14). Time, then, is a 'giving and opening up' (TB 15). We might suppose that this tells us that what comes to humans comes solely from the giving of being and/or of time, from and as the presencing of what is present. Or, it might seem that since being is presencing, time would be the origin of the giving (TB 17). But that is not so, Heidegger argues, 'for time itself remains the gift that is granted ['*die Gabe eines Es gibt*,' 18] whose giving preserves the realm in which presence is extended' (TB 17). Further, thought with being and not beings in mind, 'Time *is* not. There is [given] time' (TB 16). 'Thus,' while being and time themselves are bound up in a giving that prevails, the origin of the granting 'continues to be undetermined, and we ourselves continue to be puzzled' (TB 5, 17).

Paired with the disclosure of the 'there is being' and 'there is time,' understood in terms of giving, there also occurs a closure or concealment such that what so far has only occasionally been seen and mentioned now needs to be thought more explicitly and fully. In the broadest sweep, what earlier had been understood as the history of being now comes into question. That is, if being itself is now disclosed as belonging to [the primal giving], then what we took to be the history of being also belongs to that same endowing. This changes the interpretation of the whole story of homecoming: it is *not simply* the story of the loss and attempted recovery of being; it now also appears as the story of the concealment and disclosure of the unfolding granting of being and its configuration. Heidegger says, 'The development of the abundance of transformations of being looks at first like a history in the way in which a city or a people have their history. What is history-like in the history of being is obviously determined by the way in which being takes place and by this alone. After what has just been explained, this means the way in which [there is given] being' (TB 8). Being comes to be thought in the West, but the giving withdraws behind what it sends and gives. Accordingly, by the history of being Heidegger means the sending of being, behind whose being-sent and coming the origin of the sending keeps itself concealed. Heidegger adds, 'To hold back is, in Greek, *epoche*. Hence we speak of the epochs of the sending of being. Epoch does not mean here a span of time in occurrence, but rather the fundamental characteristic of sending, the actual holding-back of itself in favor of the discernability of the gift, that is, of being ... The sequence of epochs in the destining of being is not accidental, nor can it be calculated as necessary ... The epochs overlap each other in their sequence so that the original sending of being as presence is more and more obscured in different ways' (TB 9). Just as, much earlier, Heidegger saw that homecoming was not merely a human matter, now he says that neither is it purely a matter concerning being. Insofar as homecoming is granted in the unfolding, he arrives still more deeply within home.

Importantly, Heidegger sees this arrival at the 'there is given,' not as one more step in metaphysics, but as a movement out of it. In the sending of the giving that takes place 'we can also note historically the abundance of transformation of presencing by pointing out that presencing shows itself as the *hen*, the unifying Unique One [Ἕν Πάντα], as the λόγος, the gathering that preserves the All, as *idea, ousia, energia, substantia, actualis, perceptio, monad*, as objectivity, as the being posited of self-positing in the sense of the will of reason, of love, of the spirit, of power, as the will to will in the eternal recurrence of the same' (TB 7). Thus, arrival at the giving that gives – which sends all these transformations of being – does not add one more to the list; rather, it steps out of metaphysics to the origin. For Heidegger, the crucial understanding is how being is a gift: 'As the gift of this [there is given], being belongs to giving. As a gift being is not expelled from giving ... There is [given] being as the unconcealing; as the gift of unconcealing it is retained in the giving' (TB 6). The remaining task, then, where being is a gift, is to think the hitherto obscured 'there is given,' itself. In the first part of this chapter, in the homecoming to the originary, Heidegger reflected on the ways the Greeks said the giving and granting – though he claims they did not think it as such because it was concealed (TB 8). That would mean that originary interpretation requires thinking past being, as presencing, and the human. Heidegger presses the point, saying 'Presence means: the constant abiding that approaches man, reaches him, is extended to him. But what is the source of this extending reach to which the present belongs as presencing?' (TB 13). The question is about that which admits being and time to their own manner of holding sway (TB 19). We follow the investigation, according to Heidegger, 'simply by thinking the [origin] in light of the kind of giving that belongs to it: giving as sending, giving as an opening up which reaches out ... In the sending of ... being, in the extending of time, there becomes manifest a dedication, a delivering over into what is their own, namely of being as presence and of time as the realm of the open' (TB 19; see also 24). This inquiry also seeks the granting of the relationship of being and human being to one another (our homecoming is not to a past event). That is, it moves toward that realm 'through which man and being reach each other in what is their ownmost, achieve their active manner of abiding by losing those qualities with which metaphysics has endowed them' (PI 37).

Here we have the story of the moment of arrival home. The movement and final leap out of metaphysics, 'which also lets metaphysical thinking go, is required in order to experience authentically the *belonging* together of man and being. This spring is the abruptness of the unbridged entry into that belonging which alone can grant a toward-each-other of man and being ... The spring is the abrupt entry into the realm from which man and being have already reached each other in their active nature, since both are mutually appropriated, extended as a gift, one to the other. Only the entry into the realm of this mutual appropriation determines and defines the experience of thinking' (PI 33). Heidegger is arriving home here and naming the opening of giving: 'What determines both, time and being [and human being too], in their own, that is, in their belonging together, we shall call: *Ereignis*, the event of appropriation. *Ereignis* will be translated as appropriation or event of appropriation. One should bear in mind, however, that "event" is not simply an occurrence, but that which makes any occurrence possible' (TB 19).

Ereignis is thought in a manner similar to the thinking of the Greek disclosing granting. The latter, whether named λόγος or lightning, or with some other word for the same, was interpreted via the harvest (that which gives, gathers, keeps in (un)concealment, and so on). Now *Ereignis* names the giving and gathering of being, time, and mortals, for example. Heidegger says, 'We now see: What lets the two matters belong together, what brings the two into their own and, even more, maintains and holds them in their belonging together – the way the two matters stand, the matter at stake – is appropriation. The matter at stake first appropriates being and time by the appropriating that is concealed in sending and in the gift of opening out. Accordingly, [the source of the giving of being and time] proves to be appropriation' (TB 19). Obviously, this is confused if we go on to interpret *Ereignis* metaphysically, for example if we represent it as the consequent linking of two present beings or categories (being and time), as itself another species of being, or even as the universal concept which now swallows being. Nor, as just noted, can we understand it in the usual sense of 'occurrence and happening' (TB 20). That, while perhaps correct from a representational point of view, would reconceal *Ereignis* from us (TB 19–21).

Thus, *Ereignis*, just now pointedly named (though used by Heidegger for a long time, as discussed below), still needs to be questioned anew, and now thought about in a manner which corresponds to it, 'as extending and sending which opens and preserves' (TB 20). To think appropriation properly, *we must cease thinking of being;* that is, we must stop thinking one by way of the other. That is why Heidegger says dramatically, that as gift, 'being vanishes in the appropriation' (TB 22). Appropriation itself is a giving which sends and, as sending source, also keeps itself back – keeps itself back in a self-withdrawing from unconcealment which preserves what is its own (TB 22–3). At this arrival, we do not yet understand much about *Ereignis*, much less dwell in its nearness. But Heidegger can say, at his arrival, that it is thought in no-longer-metaphysical terms (that is, it is not thought by way of beings or being): 'What remains to be said? Only this: Appropriation appropriates ... To all appearances this says nothing ... But what if we take what was said and adopt it unceasingly as the guide for our thinking?' (TB 24).

How does the story go on after the arrival at *Ereignis?* Well, as we have seen, there is a difference between the way Heidegger tells the story of homecoming (including homelessness) and the way he experienced his own homecoming. His writings do double work here. On the one hand, they are his journey into homelessness, through a turning into homecoming which now occurs as arrival home. On the other hand, these same works tell this story in a manner which goes back and forth. Not surprisingly, in fact necessarily, because his works must thoughtfully say and *hold* the entire journey, he often later goes back over it in thought.

He does so with the arrival home, recovering the first arrival just made in the initial, if only tentative or partial, leaps to originary thinking (as we have seen, for example in WCT). (Note, if we attempt to think homecoming, we are not interested in the chronology of Heidegger's personal insights or experiences; rather, the matter for thinking is the way itself, and what is given there.)

In short, what we have just now found in 'Time and Being' and parts of 'The Principle of Identity' goes over again, consolidates, and keeps the passage from being and the arrival into *Ereignis*. But twelve years before 'Time and Being' and even before *What Is Called Thinking?* was delivered to a class, Heidegger spoke of this homecoming-arriving. He did so in 'The Thing,' which dates from 1949–50, and which presents a theme in a strikingly original voice. *Here Heidegger no longer thinks homelessness and homecoming in terms of the relation of human being and being, by way of language and thinking; rather, in 'The Thing,' he says and thinks the appropriation of world, that is, how thing gathers and stays mortals, divinities, sky, and earth.* Later, in sections of 'A Dialogue on Language' (1953–4) and in 'The Way to Language' (1959), he reflects on saying and thinking as belonging to this gathering.

This arrival at a no-longer-metaphysical shore in the treatment of 'The Thing' was prepared for as, and accomplishes, a passage beyond the still-metaphysical gathering attributed to 'works' within enframing (*Gestell*). That is, 'thing' says non-metaphysically the theme which must be originarily thought. Heidegger's thinking concerning things is concerned all along with understanding *Ereignis*, how it comes and gives, and how we come to it. The same holds for what he says concerning saying. Things seem near to us. They seem to be everywhere around us, but we do not yet think them non-metaphysically, or in a way other than as beings representationally understood. Thus, Heidegger's arrival into a no-longer-metaphysical home puts him near things which must be understood. Or, put another way, 'The Thing' brings him near things.

He finds that a thing partakes in giving; for example, water or wine is given over to a jug, and the jug, in turn, pours out the liquid as a gift. What belongs to the jug, and what the jug belongs to, are gathered in this saying. Each thing may have its own giving and gathering. We already have thought of the harvest with its gathering: selecting, collecting, and assembling, sheltering, accommodating, and so on. With the jug also occurs its own gathering which receives and holds, keeps, and bears for dispensing. Heidegger elaborates the example:

> How does the jug's void hold? It holds by taking what is poured in. It holds in a twofold manner: taking and keeping. The word 'hold' is therefore ambiguous. Nevertheless, the taking of what is poured in and the keeping of what was poured belong together. But their unity is determined by the outpouring for which the jug is fitted as a jug. The twofold holding of the void rests on the outpouring. In the outpouring, the holding is authentically how it is. To pour from the jug is to give. The holding of the vessel occurs in the giving of the outpouring. Holding needs the void as that which holds. The nature of the holding void is gathered in the giving. But giving is richer than a mere pouring out. The giving, whereby the jug is a jug, gathers in the two-fold holding – in the outpouring. We call the gathering of the twofold holding into the outpouring, which, as a being together, first constitutes the full presence of giving: the poured gift. The jug's jug-character consists in the poured gift of the poured-out. Even the empty jug retains its nature by virtue of the poured gift, even though the empty jug does not admit of a giving out. (T 171–2)

The jug, as a specific thing, belongs to giving in its own way: the jug's taking, holding, and pouring out gather, and gather in, giving. This gathering giving is itself held in language by an ancient word which denotes what a gathering is, *dinc* – 'thing.' Heidegger notes, reflecting on the originary meaning, 'the Old High German word "thing" means a gathering, and specifically a gathering to deliberate on a matter under discussion, a contested matter. In consequence, the Old German words *thing* or *dinc* become the names for an affair or matter of pertinence' (T 174). Setting aside the metaphysical history of this word and its relatives, what matters is thinking the nature of the jug as gathering-giving and the source. What is needed is thinking thing as gathering-giving.

If we look again at what comes to the jug and how it pours out, we find something simple, but elaborate. In an amazing passage that deserves to be quoted in full so that we can take it in slowly and completely, the better to ponder it, Heidegger reflects as follows:

> The giving of the outpouring can be a drink. The outpouring gives water, it gives wine to drink.
>
> The spring stays on in the water of the gift. In the spring the rock dwells, and in the rock dwells the dark slumber of the earth, which receives the rain and the dew of the sky. In the water of the spring dwells the marriage of sky and earth. It stays in the wine given by the fruit of the vine, the fruit in which

> the earth's nourishment and the sky's sun are betrothed to one another. In the gift of water, in the gift of wine, sky and earth dwell. But the gift of the outpouring is what makes the jug a jug. In the jugness of the jug, sky and earth dwell.
>
> The gift of the pouring out is drink for mortals. It quenches their thirst. It refreshes their leisure. It enlivens their conviviality. But the jug's gift is at times also given for consecration. If the pouring is for consecration, then it does not still a thirst. It stills and elevates the celebration of the feast. The gift of the pouring now is neither given in an inn nor is the poured gift a drink for mortals. The outpouring is the libation poured out for the immortal gods. The gift of the outpouring as libation is the authentic gift. In giving the consecrated libation, the pouring jug occurs as the giving gift. The consecrated libation is what our word for a strong outpouring flow, 'gush,' really designates: gift and sacrifice. 'Gush,' Middle English *guschen, gosshen* – cf. German *Guss, giessen* – is the Greek *cheein,* the Indo-european *ghu.* It means to offer in sacrifice. To pour a gush, when it is achieved in its essence, thought through with sufficient generosity, and genuinely uttered, is to donate, to offer in sacrifice, and hence to give ... In the gift of the outpouring that is drink, mortals stay in their own way. In the gift of the outpouring that is a libation, the divinities stay in their own way, they who receive back the gift of giving as the gift of the donation. (T 172–3)

The jug, then, gathers earth and sky, mortals and divinities, in its giving.[28] Here Heidegger speaks in *a 'high originary' voice of his own* that still also echoes the Hölderlin essays and which, like Hölderlin, speaks of gathering in the image of celebrating the wedding of these four. This fourfold which thing gathers is called 'world' by Heidegger (T 179, 181). Thus, thing gives and gathers world. 'The Thing' tells of what belongs together in a no-longer-metaphysical way; in doing so (by thinking the belonging together not of being and human being, but the giving of the fourfold in thing), Heidegger comes home – he arrives at world, wherein as mortals we belong and are gathered (see sTB 42). It remains to be said how this gathering is a being at home with one another of the fourfold. Heidegger explains it as a dwelling together, staying together, and belonging together. We have already heard him say that the spring stays and rock dwells in the water of the gift. As a result, according to Heidegger,

> In the gift of the outpouring, mortals and divinities each dwell in their different ways. Earth and sky dwell in the gift of the outpouring. In the gift of

> the outpouring earth and sky, divinities and mortals dwell *together all at once.* These four, at one because of what they themselves are, belong together. Preceding everything that is present, they are enfolded into a simple fourfold.
>
> In the gift of the outpouring dwells the simple singlefoldness [*Einfalt*, 'onefoldedness'] of the four. (T 173)

The thing, as a giving gift, is home to the fourfold. In the thing the four are gathered and held: the thing stays sky and earth, divinities and mortals. 'Staying, the thing brings the four, in their remoteness, near to one another' and also safe-keeps them there (T 177). Staying is not any mere 'persisting of something that is here.' Rather,

> Staying appropriates. It brings the four into the light of their mutual belonging. From out of staying's simple onefoldness they are betrothed, entrusted to one another, they are unconcealed. The gift of the outpouring stays the onefold of the fourfold of the four ... What is gathered in the gift gathers itself in appropriatively staying the fourfold ... Appropriating the fourfold, it gathers the fourfold's stay, its while, into something that stays for a while: into this thing, that thing ...
>
> The jug's essential nature, its presencing, so experienced and thought of in these terms, is what we call *thing*. We are now thinking this word by way of the gathering-appropriating staying of the fourfold. (T 173–4)

It turns out, then, according to Heidegger, that mortals and divinities, earth and sky, dwell, belong, and are gathered into the thing's giving gift, and since that gift stays and appropriates the four into unconcealment, they are finally gathered, belong, and are at home in appropriation. In Heidegger's coming to appropriation – that is, in its being given – there is a homecoming. Though that is not yet dwelling, it is nonetheless *arrival*.

Before moving on to tell more about the gathering-appropriating-staying of the fourfold, we need to think the importance of language for the journey home. If Heidegger earlier (for example, in 'Letter on Humanism') had said that language was the house of being and the home of human being and if he has now arrived at the shore of *Ereignis*, where language, being, and human being are no longer the originary or final theme of homecoming, how does what was called language belong together with what is understood as *Ereignis* and world? Heidegger develops these dimensions of language in sections of 'A Dialogue on Language' and in 'The Way to Language.' Here 'language,' metaphysically understood, is gone. In its place we hear of 'saying.'[29]

Like a thing, saying is understood by Heidegger as granting, gathering, disclosing, and sheltering. It is also a granting. To begin, however, Heidegger says that the nature of language is found in what the word 'saying' – *die Sage* – says. Not surprisingly, what Heidegger finds is that 'to say' (*Sage*) originarily is not the same as in the ordinary meaning of the verb. Saying is not merely reporting, as in, 'he says that, etc.'; nor is it even primarily a human utterance or expression at all. Nor does *Sage*, as shifted into our 'saga,' mean an old poetic invention or fiction about once-believed in, but now discredited, gods and heroes (WL 123). In contrast, 'the word "saying" ... means: saying and what is said in it and what is to be said' (DL 47). That is, saying-*Sage* names not a human activity, but that which is given and the giving which take place in saying. Here 'say' means 'the same as "show" in the sense of: let appear and let shine' (DL 47). Heidegger explains, 'In keeping with the most ancient usage of the word we understand saying in terms of showing, pointing out, signaling ... The *essential being of language is saying as showing*' (WL 123).

Before all else, such saying opens the possibilities of human speaking and listening. Our human saying is given in and stays within saying itself – saying speaks (says) to us and brings about our dialogue with the giving and with each other (a point to be thought further, a little later on). Insofar as we hear what saying says/shows, we humans are enabled to speak; we do not first invent language and then use it as a tool of communication as representational thinking would have it (see chapter 4-B, above) because our speaking depends on our already being within saying, carefully listening to it. Here our 'speaking is of itself listening. Speaking is listening to the language which we speak. Thus, it is a listening not *while* but *before* we are speaking' (WL 123; see also 124). Our speaking properly responds to saying – just as our thinking properly responds to that which calls for and gives thinking.[30] In short: '"Say" means to show, to let appear, to let be seen and heard' (WL 122).

Saying's letting is a granting and what it shows and lets appear (including our hearing and speaking) is the gift which it yields. This also means that saying gives us our natures as those who have saying (that is, speaking, listening, writing, and the ability to remain silent too). Heidegger says, 'If speaking, as the listening to language, lets *saying* be said to it, this letting can obtain only so far – and so near – as our own nature has been admitted and entered into *saying*. We hear *saying* only because we belong within it. Saying grants the hearing, and thus the speaking, of language solely to those who belong within it. Such is the granting which abides in *saying*. It allows us to attain the ability to speak. The essence of language is present in *saying* as the source of such grant' (WL 124).

Accordingly, beyond the traditional, metaphysical understanding, which holds that 'language ... is the foundation of human being,' Heidegger now originarily sees that we should not assume that we are unproblematically and safely close to (within) language. Rather, we need to acknowledge that we are far away so that we can question the strangeness and begin to make our way toward language's dynamic, inaugural 'granting of all this to man,' which, as we heard earlier, is now recast as the continually unfolding home of human being (WL 111–13). We become and stay at home in our natures as sayers insofar as we already belong within saying, but we are granted admission to this belonging within only by saying itself. Thus, gathering us in, saying gives; it gives home. Further, though more difficult to follow, there is the granting which saying gives (to) itself, which Heidegger barely hints at by saying that saying abides and remains gathered 'to its own idiom,' which also means into silence and the unsaid (WL 119, 124–5). Though saying needs human speaking, 'Saying is itself the abode of rest which grants the quiet of mutual belonging to all that belongs within the structure of the being of language' (WL 125).

Thought as the home that gathers everything home into itself, saying does not come after pre-given beings as something added to them or connecting them. Rather, its granting first gives human speakers to each other as capable of dialogue with each other and with *Ereignis*, so that we can dwell in its neighbourhood. It first brings about the disclosure of all that belongs within it. Heidegger elaborates,

> all radiant appearance and all fading away is grounded in the showing *saying*. Saying sets all present beings free into their given presence, and brings what is absent into their absence. Saying pervades and structures the openness of that clearing which every appearance must seek out and every disappearance must leave behind, and in which every present or absent being must show, say, announce itself.
>
> Saying is the gathering that joins all appearance of the in itself manifold showing which everywhere lets all that is shown abide within itself. (WL 126; see also 121–2)

This is why showing names the way saying grants and gathers. Heidegger's understanding, then, of saying is like his interpretation of the Greek 'giving takes place' ('It Gives') which proceeds from the 'image' of the harvest where giving is gathering which is determined by sheltering and storing. Saying, the granting safe keeping, within which mortals and all beings belong and come to presencing, gathers and shelters (WL 135). Further, in its own self-granting, it keeps and guards its own essence by holding itself back in silence and concealment (WL 122).

In its showing-disclosing, saying also shows its own self-gatheredness into its essence. Because saying gathers what belongs-together into itself, and thereby gathers itself to the rest, saying is not only a granting unity, but a unifying unity, which Heidegger now calls 'the design' (*der Aufriß*) and relates to what is cut or torn (*der Riß*).[31] He adds,

> The name demands of us that we see the proper character of the being of language with greater clarity. The 'sign' in design [Latin *signum*] is related to *secare*, to cut – as in saw, sector, segment. To design is to cut a trace. Most of us know the word 'sign' only in its debased meaning – lines on a surface. But we make a design also when we cut a furrow into the soil to open it to seed and growth. The design is the whole of the traits of that drawing which structures and prevails throughout the open, unlocked freedom of language. The design is the drawing of the being of language, the structure of a show in which are joined the speakers and their speaking: what is spoken and what of it is unspoken in all that is given in the speaking. (WL 121)

This is an especially complex paragraph. First, Heidegger rethinks and refers to his earlier understanding of language by way of the Greeks. Recall that in *An Introduction to Metaphysics* Heidegger had reflected on how the chorus in Sophocles' *Antigone* spoke of our uncanny nature as of the strangest ones, that is, as of the beings who have the power of language and dare furrow open mother earth (IM 123ff.). Now the design of saying is thought, not in the language of the earlier homelessness, but as belonging to homecoming and human saying. Hearing and speaking are seen to belong to the design of saying (WL 122). In addition, this current thinking of the design refers to the drawing structuring which Heidegger has thought as *Fug*. In section A of this chapter, we heard Heidegger listen to the Greek understanding of joining and how things could be out of joint. That, in turn, was transformed into thinking the *Gestell* (framing) of our own epoch. Heidegger now goes on to open the originary manifestation of design, as the way of gathering and disclosing which moves in language and multiform saying and which, in some sense, saying holds to and moves within (it gathers and holds what presences and itself in this mode of structuring and prevailing; WL 121).[32]

Finally, the passage also evokes what Hölderlin said of the poet and language. In Heidegger's Hölderlin essays, he elaborated the comparison of the growth of the poet and that of the crop nurtured by a peasant farmer: poetry and *physis* alike give growth and upsurgence, the latter silently, the former in language. Now we see that both belong together in the disclosing design of *saying* (WL 134). Design, then, names the originary unifying of saying which draws by showing: it draws humans and what presences (and even itself) into opening and presencing. It draws by gathering together what belongs together; it draws home, within itself, all that it shows.

It really is saying, then, before all else, that grants, shows, gathers, and preserves what presences, including humans (since our human saying is a hearing-responding) and even itself, into opening and presencing. Heidegger explains the complex unity by saying that language is a monologue (in an originary sense, not in Novalis' sense, beyond which Heidegger passes in his present arrival home): 'This now says two things: it is language *alone* which speaks authentically; and, language speaks *lonesomely.* Yet only he can be lonesome who is not alone ... [where there is given] something in common which presents us the most binding bond *with it.* The 'some' in lonesome is the Gothic *sama,* the Greek *homo,* and the English *same.* "Lonesome" means: the same in what unites that which belongs together' (WL 134). Saying's saying-granting gathers us back together to the same (that is, to the there is giving) and tells of the gathering home of what belongs together even while separated. Saying, like thing, *gives us the unspoken* to which we and it belong as gifts. But we come here only if questioning. Saying now grants this question: 'Where does the showing saying spring from? The question asks too much, and asks prematurely' (WL 126). It asks for the source, when we have barely arrived home.

What especially needs to be thought is the belonging together of saying (and thing, too) with giving: saying gives and is given. As we have seen, thing gives and gathers the fourfold in a staying appropriation; saying as showing gives and gathers humans and what becomes present. Heidegger names what saying says and what he sees in his arrival at this point: '*The moving force in showing of saying is owning* [*Ereignis*]. It is what brings all present and absent beings each into their own, from where they show themselves in what they are, and where they abide according to their kind. This owning which brings them there, and which moves saying as showing in its showing we call appropriation … The yielding owning, the appropriation, confers more than any effectuation, making, or founding. What is yielding is appropriation itself – and nothing else. That appropriation, seen as it is shown by saying, cannot be represented either as an occurrence or a happening – it can only be experienced as the abiding gift yielded by saying' (WL 127). There is a mutual granting, then: saying shows, yields appropriation; appropriation gives in saying. 'Appropriation assembles the design of saying and unfolds it into the structure of manifold showing' (WL 128). That is, appropriation gives by gathering and holding (saying and mortals too) (WL 128–129; consider too the Greek λόγος and τὸ αὐτό). But appropriation must be disclosed – and it is given, as disclosed, in saying. Here saying itself is disclosed as the saying of appropriation, but also as the saying which keeps the saying of appropriation. Thus, Heidegger says, the 'showing of saying is appropriating' (WL 129). This complex interplay of gathering and holding is considered by Heidegger in several originary ways, all of which attempt to say or at least hint at the giving of language and thing which also gives world.

In 'A Dialogue on Language' the Japanese partner in dialogue gradually comes to hear the word in which saying says its own essence: '*Koto ba*' (DL 45). *Koto* means the happening (*Ereignis*) of the lighting message of the graciousness (*Iki*). *Iki* is the Japanese word which, according to the dialogue, means the 'breath' and 'pure delight of the beckoning stillness' (DL 44–45). That is, it is a graciousness understood by way of the Greek *charis*, which in Sophocles is 'called *tikousa* – that which brings forward and forth' (*hervorbringen*) and says the same as the German *dichten, tihton* (DL 45–7). Thus, it names the *Ereignis* which reigns over all which needs sheltering and keeping, holding it in coming forth (DL 45–6). Further, since *Koto* 'also names that which in the event gives delight, itself, that which uniquely in each unrepeatable moment comes to radiance in the fullness of its grace' it can be thought along with *Ba*, which 'means leaves, including and especially the leaves of a blossom – petals' (DL 45). Heard all together, *Koto ba* says the petals that stem and flourish from the *Ereignis* of the lighting message of the graciousness that brings forth and holds (DL 47, 53). Language – *saying* – then, blossoms from *Ereignis*.

Heidegger attempts to think the mutual giving which occurs in saying. That which endows mortals, art, poetry, and saying with their nature comes as a gathering force which is yet radiant and delightful (that is why it is said to be gracious) (DL 13–14). The gathering is mutual because the granting comes to us and we also respond and come in(to) it. As Heidegger has said on several occasions, we hear what calls for thinking, and we come to dwell in the gathering. In this mutual gathering, there is a two-way movement: we bear ourselves into that which bears itself (and our natures) toward us – as gift. Heidegger calls this mutual gathering – bearing, 'gesture.'

> Inquirer (I): Gesture is the gathering of a bearing.
> Japanese (J): No doubt you intentionally avoid saying: *our* bearing
> I: Because what truly bears, only bears itself *toward* us ...
> J: ... though we bear only our share to its encounter.
> I: While that which bears itself toward us has already
> borne our counterbearing into the gift it bears for us.
> J: Thus you call bearing or gesture: the gathering which
> originarily unites within itself what we bear to it and
> what it bears to us.
> I: However, with this formulation we still run the risk that
> we understand the gathering as a subsequent union ...
> J: ... instead of experiencing that all bearing, in giving
> and encounter, springs first and only from the gathering. (DL 18–19)

This is difficult material, largely because it attempts to say the primal gathering which occurs in saying and to think the giving (in) the originary gathering.

Heidegger makes another attempt to say the same in 'The Thing' where he considers the staying of the fourfold in thing. There he thinks the gathering in a way which also attempts to avoid representational thinking and language. About the complex four dimensions, which need to be considered at some length, he says,

> Earth and sky, divinities and mortals – being at one with one another of their own accord – belong together by way of the simpleness of the united fourfold. Each of the four mirrors in its own way the presence of the others. Each therewith reflects itself in its own way into its own, within the simpleness of the four. This mirroring does not portray a likeness. The mirroring, lightening each of the four, appropriates their own presencing into simple belonging to one another. Mirroring in this appropriating-lighting way, each of the four plays to each of the others. The appropriate mirroring sets each of the four free into its own, but it binds these free ones into the simplicity of their essential being toward one another.

> The mirroring that binds into freedom is the play that betroths each of the four to each through the enfolding clasp of their mutual appropriation. None of the four insists on its own separate particularity.
>
> This appropriating mirror-play of the simple onefold of earth and sky, divinities and mortals, we call world ...
>
> The fouring, the unity of the four, presences as the appropriating mirror-play of the betrothed, each to the other in simple oneness. The fouring presences as the worlding of the world. The mirror-play of the world is the round dance of appropriating. Therefore, the round dance does not encompass the four like a hoop. The round dance is the ring that joins while it plays as mirroring. Appropriating, it lightens the four into the radiance of their simple oneness. Radiantly, the ring joins the four, everywhere open to the riddle of their present. The gathered presence of the mirror-play of the world, joining in this way, is the ringing. In the ringing of the mirror-playing ring, the four nestle into their unifying presence, in which each one retains its own nature. So nestling, they join together, worlding, the world.
>
> Nestling, malleable, pliant, compliant, nimble – in old German these are called *ring* and *gering*. The mirror-play of the worlding world, as the ringing of the ring, wrests free the united four into their own compliancy, the circling compliancy of their presence. Out of the ringing mirror-play the thinging of the thing takes place. (T 179–80)

In this light movement, the gathering force of thing brings us to appropriating, just as saying did and as did the leap from being. Again and again, we arrive at the same, at the giving, saying, calling, bearing toward mutual encounter, and at the unspoken that withdraws into is own safe keeping.[33] Heidegger's task in his arriving has been to leave unimpaired the giving so that it would be let come. By avoiding conceptually-representationally grasping 'the giving,' Heidegger arrives at what the word *Ereignis* says, at appropriation itself, as the primal giving (see, e.g., DL 22). He says, 'What is yielding is appropriation itself – and nothing else ... There is nothing else from which the appropriation itself could be derived, even less in whose terms it could be explained. The appropriating event is not the outcome (result) of something else, but the giving yield whose giving reach alone is what gives us such things as a "there is [*es gibt*]," a "there is" of which even being itself stands in need to come into its own presence' (WL 127). This arrival at the shore of the primal is not the end of the journey of course. Speaking of the homecoming journey prior to that, Heidegger adds a note to the text to point out that 'it may seem incredible to many of my readers that I have used the word "appropriation" ["*Ereignis*"] in my manuscripts for more than twenty-five years to indicate what is here in my thoughts. The matter, while simple in itself, still remains difficult to think because thinking must first overcome the habit of yielding to the view that we are thinking here of "being" as appropriation. But appropriation is different in nature, because it is richer than any conceivable definition of being. Being, however, *in respect of its essential origin*, can be thought in terms of appropriation' (WL 129).[34] Just as appropriation is not a being added to other beings, neither is it somehow combined with divinities, mortals, sky, and heavens to make a fivefold. Rather, in language and thing, the four are appropriated to each other; appropriation is this granting appropriating. But if appropriation is neither being nor beings, and if the latter two (the duality) are to be seen via the more primal duality in its essential Origin – in appropriation – then before we attempt to think and dwell in and near appropriation, we need to reflect on the event of passage out of homelessness of being and beings and the arrival at home, at the Originary shore of *Ereignis.* That means Heidegger would need to explicitly think of language, thing, world, and *Ereignis* by way of homecoming. And he does.

In these works, Heidegger thinks the homecoming in language of the movement out of danger, through the strange, into the near, to an arrival at our 'own.' Hence, when he speaks of thinking as a 'step back,' he means not only a going back to originary thinking to retrieve what has been lost to representational thought, but also a transformation which steps back to the home shore. In this way, Heidegger's thinking moves back in the reverse direction from which it started. *Being and Time,* for example, struck out from the ordinary into the *unheimlich;* after the turn and journey home, the works currently under consideration complete the movement from the *unheimlich* to what is known for the first time as our own (see also sTB 27). Of course, this movement does not in itself 'win' or 'force' homecoming, because it steps back and removes itself (from thinking as subjectivism) that is, from the central place in a cosmos. This holding-ourselves-back helps allow an opening into which giving might come (sTB 30). Which arrival would matter most? Not ours, but that of what is to be thought and said. What now comes to thought is 'there is given,' *Ereignis.* In such an arrival, we are held in the midst of giving.

If we are to respond to and partake in this arriving-homecoming it is of the utmost importance to follow the thinking and language of this movement – since that is how we would do our part in arriving. Thus, as before, Heidegger says, 'Let me give a little hint as how to listen. The point is not to listen to a series of propositions, but rather to follow the movement of showing' (TB 2). The movement of Heidegger's thinking and saying is not arbitrary, because what comes to pass has its own order. Thus, the present arrival is possible only in its proper place, which is proper in that it fits into the taking place of giving. According to Heidegger, 'In the sending of being there is never a mere sequence of one thing after the other: now frame, then world and thing; rather, there is always a passing by and simultaneity of early and late' (epilogue, T 184–5). Because these works stand in such a time of passing, they are presented by Heidegger just when he also presents others which continue the excursions into framing and homelessness (see this chapter, section B).

The arrival home is a movement out of danger. One way the danger appears is in the framing which is both a coming (in its own way) and a concealment of the giving. The obstructing framing (*Gestalt*) must be passed through and beyond. As it was put in a seminar, 'Between the epochal formations of being and the transformation of being into appropriation stands framing. Framing is an in-between stage, so to speak. It offers a double aspect, one might say a Janus head. It can be understood as a kind of continuation of the will to will, thus as an extreme formation of being. At the same time, however, it is a first form of appropriation itself' (sTB 53). The framing that reigns in technology must be overcome (see this chapter, section B, and, for example; DL 17) by the thinking which first arrives at and 'explicitly enters appropriation in order to say it in terms of it' (TB 24). Naturally, in arrival, the homelessness and wandering are not immediately put behind.

From the danger of enframing, and from the coming and self-concealment of *Ereignis* too, in thinking and saying dangers emerge. Because thinking and saying are granted in and properly respond to *Ereignis*, 'language always speaks according to the mode in which the appropriation as such reveals itself or withdraws. For a thinking that pursues the appropriation can still only surmise it, and yet can experience it even now in the *nature* of modern technology, which we still call by the still strange-sounding name of framing [Ge-Stell]. Because framing challenges man, that is, provokes him to order and set up all that is present being as technical inventory, framing persists after the manner of appropriation, specifically by simultaneously obstructing appropriation, in that all ordering finds itself channeled into calculative thinking and therefore speaks the language of framing' (WL 131–2). Language and thinking are dangerous, then, and there is no guarantee that the danger will be overcome within originary language. Still, it is clear that the propositional statements of representational thinking are an obstacle (see, for example, this chapter, section B). As we have seen, because 'our task is unceasingly to overcome the obstacles that tend to render such (proper saying of *Ereignis*) inadequate,' we must cease listening to propositions (TB 2, 24; sTB 25).

Perhaps the danger is greatest just where the movement seems most likely. In 'A Dialogue on Language,' Heidegger and the Japanese note the inherent danger in dialogue, especially when it involves the interplay of several languages and ways of thinking: Japanese and German, representational and originary. What might come may be ignored or shuttled aside, forced into alien and inappropriate concepts, improperly used, and so on (see 'A Dialogue on Language' throughout, especially pp. 2, 4–5, 13–15, 18, 26, 43). Here, powerful, world-conquering Western metaphysics reigns as the danger. It is also in the space of this danger that 'the default of God and the divinities is absence'; it lies between the no-longer- and not-yet-veiled (re)arrival (epilogue, T 184).

Heidegger, thinking by way of a journey, says one cannot pass out of the danger, except as one moves into and through the strange. That is why he continuously holds himself in the homelessness of metaphysics. That is also why he enters the realm of the Greek and of the Japanese, though these are strange in a different way. They are both more alike because (possibly) originary and therefore less dangerous than metaphysics, but also more distracting and more likely to entrance us and keep us from our own proper home, and therefore perhaps most dangerous of all, as was Circe to Odysseus. For these reasons, Heidegger moves through an absence and presencing 'which at times reaches uncanny proportions,' and through a 'distant inkling' and 'strange stillness' (TB 7; DL 2, 18). For example, in his dialogue with a Japanese, their use of words is acknowledged to be strange. Heidegger says, 'I don't deny it. But it seems to me, that, in the field in which we are moving, we reach those things with which we are originarily familiar precisely if we do not shun passing through things strange to us' (DL 33). The great danger here is that what should be experienced as strange will be shrugged off as not even interesting, or as curious but not a matter of wonder. So, Heidegger works hard to keep the strange. If instead of hearing what he says and listens to as a quaint but unreliable sequence of propositions, 'we experience the way to language in the light of what happens with the way itself as we go on, then an intimation may come to us in virtue of which language will henceforth strike us as strange' (WL

111). What remains strange has a chance to 'unbind and deliver language into its own' (WL 113).

The strange, if allowed to be strange, is not far away, but very near. That is because we are homeless and also because giving withdraws itself into concealment so that in giving what is near it becomes far (though as still giving, it remains near, too). Heidegger holds that appropriation 'is itself the most inconspicuous of inconspicuous phenomena, the simplest of simplicities, the nearest of the near, and the farthest of the far in which we mortals spend our lives' (WL 128; see also PI 38). This is neither illogical nor weird. It is merely complex: even in homelessness there is a belonging together of what belongs together even while separated. Otherwise there would be no homelessness, only being apart (e.g., physical or psychological separation). In such a relation to appropriation no homecoming would be possible. Heidegger goes on to explain our current placement. 'It seems as if we were now in danger of directing our thinking, all too carelessly, toward something that is remote and general; while in fact what the term event of appropriation wishes to indicate really speaks to us directly from the very nearness of that neighborhood in which we already reside. For what could be closer to us than what brings us nearer to where we belong, to where we are belongers, to the event of appropriation?' (PI 37). Of course, the neighbourhood where we are now lies within the bounds of language, and nearby (neighbour to) both being, on the one side, and appropriation, on the other. We are between homelessness and homecoming.

In our arrival home we find mystery: appropriation which nears in language and thinking. Insofar as we successfully pass out of the danger and beyond the obstacles, we manoeuvre through the strange so as not to miss mystery. Mystery must be left as mystery, that is, as veiled and veiling (DL 50). To let mystery be is difficult for our thinking and saying; we must learn to let silence prevail if we would live near concealment. That is why the call which calls out of the still is far. It is veiled and we keep it at a distance through our overeagerness to have it (DL 16). In arrival, we attend to the mystery of language: 'That which must remain wholly unspoken is held back in the unsaid, abides in concealment as unshowable, is mystery' (WL 122).

But once let alone, as the far, *Ereignis* can come near, for example, in thinking and saying: '"Fore" – into that nearest nearness which we constantly rush ahead of, and which strikes us as so strange' (DL 12). Such language, which pervades 'A Dialogue on Language' and related essays, attempts to exhibit the movement of homecoming to *Ereignis* – which is originary and still-coming in the Greek, in the originary thinking Heidegger seeks, and in its simultaneous disclosure and self-withdrawal. As giving, *Ereignis* gives nearness, is 'nearing nearness,' 'nearhood' (*Nahheit*) (TB 15). *Ereignis* nears not only in saying, but in thinking. The staying appropriation of the fourfold in things is called 'nearing' by Heidegger. In fact, the essay 'The Thing' opens by reflecting on the difference between the representational abolition of distance and originary nearness. The former hides the latter (T 165–6). Nonetheless, in our neighbourhood, things are close by language. Heidegger inquires into our homecoming-arrival by asking about the near, and by trying to arrive at it, that is, to effect a homecoming in thinking right here and now).

As we saw earlier, the thing, for example the jug, gives. It gathers the fourfold in its gift, where all four dwell together in a staying appropriation (T 172ff.). Here world and jug near. Heidegger explains,

> We have sought the nature of nearness and found the nature of the jug as a thing. But in this discovery we also catch sight of the nature of nearness. The thing things. In thinging, it stays earth and sky, divinities and mortals. Staying, the thing brings the four, in their remoteness, near to one another. This bringing-near is nearing. Nearing is the presencing of nearness. Nearness brings near – draws neigh to one another – the far, and, indeed, *as* the far ... Bringing near in this way, nearness conceals its own self and remains, in its own way, nearest of all.
>
> The thing is not 'in' nearness, 'in' proximity, as if nearness were a container. Nearness is a work in bringing near, as the thinging of the thing. (T 177–8)

Because thing gathers the fourfold, 'Thinging is the nearing of the world. Nearing is the nature of nearness. As we preserve the thing *qua* thing we inhabit nearness' (T 181). *Here, Heidegger arrives at yet another dimension of home; he says that homecoming is nearing. In achieving a thinking and saying which lets thing and saying give and gather, nearing can occur. In the granting,* thing and saying bring us home. In thing and saying we are gathered where we belong – into the fourfold, which also means into nearness. This is our step back, our arrival home.

Specifically, *we arrive at what is properly our own, that is, at an originary homecoming.* In this arrival we leave the homelessness of being and beings for the giving, which had withdrawn, but which now comes forward into unconcealment (TB 8–9). Hence Heidegger speaks of the gathering we have entered and the arrival of nearness in terms of the originary homecoming which begins to pass out of the long night of metaphysical homelessness: 'Here we need not look far. All we need is the plain, sudden, unforgettable and hence forever new look into something which we – even though it is familiar to us – do not even try to know, let alone understand in a fitting manner. This unknown-familiar something, all this pointing of *saying* to what is quick and stirring within it, is to all present and absent beings as that first break of dawn with which the changing cycle of day and night first begins to be possible: it is the earliest and most ancient at once' (WL 127). That is, it is the first and oldest because it is the giving which always has given, and it is the coming dawn because it comes to give us our own originary belonging.

This arrival is no purely human matter. We do come to our own by being appropriated by giving, but that event is part of a world being gathered together. In the largest sweep, everything present comes to its own essence in the arrival of and at *Ereignis.* This is the marvellous prospect that presents itself at the passage that leaves the reign of framing. Heidegger says, wonderingly, 'What if appropriation – no one knows when or how – were to become an insight whose illuminating lightening flash enters into what is and what is taken to be? What if appropriation, by its entry, were to remove everything that is in present being from its subjectivism to a commandeering order and bring it back into its own' (WL 133)? Appropriation, disclosing itself, also brings about a transformation in being, beings, human beings, language, thinking, and so on. *Appropriation is a bringing into its own.*' We have already seen that being and time come into their own in the gathering of the appropriation's giving. Heidegger says, 'In the sending of the sending of being, in the extending of time, there becomes manifest a dedication, a delivering over into what is their own, namely of being as presence and of time as the realm of the open' (TB 19; see also WL 127). That movement has been our journey: 'The task of our thinking has been to trace being to its own from appropriation – by way of looking through true time without regard to the relation of being to beings' (TB 24).

In the journey through homelessness, Heidegger had thought the relation of human beings and being, where the two were held together in language and thinking. Now, in the arrival home, he sees that home is something else: saying, thing, and originary recollection gather in the fourfold which is given in the giving – in *Ereignis.* Succinctly put (in the summary of a seminar on 'Time and Being'): 'Thus, at the end of the lecture on Identity it is stated what appropriation appropriates, that is, brings into its own and retains in appropriation: namely, the belonging together of being and man. In this belonging together, what belongs together is no longer being and man, but rather – as appropriated – mortals in the fourfold of world' (sTB 42).

The appropriation of world is the appropriation of our originary home, for it is there that we are gathered and that we belong. In appropriation each of the four comes mutually into appropriation and 'into its own being' (T 179). Thus, to speak of each now becomes possible, and each, in its belonging, also speaks of the others. Heidegger says, in the highly originary language of homecoming,

> Thinging, the thing stays the united four, earth and sky, divinities and mortals, in the simple onefold of their self-unified fourfold.
>
> Earth is the building bearer, nourishing with its fruits, tending water and rock, plant and animal.
>
> When we say earth, we are already thinking of the other three along with it by way of the simple oneness of the four.
>
> The sky is the sun's path, the course of the moon, the glitter of the stars, the year's seasons, the light and dusk of day, the gloom and glow of night, the clemency and inclemency of the weather, the drifting clouds and blue depth of the ether.
>
> When we say sky, we are already thinking of the other three along with it by way of the simple oneness of the four.
>
> The divinities are the beckoning messengers of the godhead. Out of the hidden sway of the divinities the god emerges as what he is, which removes him from any comparison with beings that are present.
>
> When we speak of the divinities, we are already thinking of the other three along with them by way of the simple oneness of the four.
>
> The mortals are human beings. They are called mortals because they can die. To die means to be capable of death as death. Only man dies. The animal perishes. It has death neither ahead of itself nor behind it. Death is the shrine of Nothing, that is, of that which in every respect is never something that merely exists, but which nevertheless presences, even as the mystery of being itself. As the shrine of Nothing, death harbors within itself the presencing of being. As the shrine of Nothing, death is the shelter of being. We now call mortals mortals – not because their earthly life comes to an end, but because they are capable of death as death. Mortals are who they are, as mortals, present in the shelter of being. (T 178–9; see also 172–3)

In this moment of Heidegger's journey, he speaks of the primal homecoming in which the fourfold gathers together in appropriation. World is granted as home where the four can be at home with one another. Within this homeward gathering, mortals simultaneously are folded into the fourfold, where they belong, and arrive at their own essence as mortals.

Since the primal homecoming is no creation or achievement of humans, but comes as a bestowal, mortals receive homecoming, and that also means our own mode of abiding, as a gift. The giving requires that humans be open to and welcome the gift. Heidegger says, 'If man were not the constant receiver of the gift given by the "[there is the giving of] presence," if that which is extended in the gift did not reach man, then not only would being remain concealed in the absence of this gift, not only closed off, but man would remain excluded from the scope of: [there is the giving of] being. Man would not be man' (TB 12). *Thought at the moment of arrival, beyond man and being, mortals and world arrive together in mutual giving in appropriation.* This can happen because 'appropriating has the peculiar property of bringing man into his own' (TB 23).

> Thus, in appropriation there is the disclosing-granting to mortals [of] their abode within what is ownmost to them ... If we understand 'law' as the gathering that lays down that which causes all beings to be present in their own, in what is appropriate for them, then appropriation is the plainest and most gentle of all laws ... Appropriation, though, is not law in the sense of a norm which hangs over our heads somewhere, it is not an ordinance which orders and regulates a course of events.
>
> Appropriation is *the* law because it gathers mortals into the appropriateness of their nature and there holds them. (WL 128–9)

To become a mortal means to become capable of death, as we have heard Heidegger say. But this coming to our nature as mortal is a coming to saying and thinking. That is why the opening scene of 'A Dialogue on Language' has the partners reflecting on the site of the grave of a mutual friend (DL 1). In granting our nature, appropriation allows us the capacity to say, that is, to listen to saying and to respond in our own speech (WL 128–9). Heidegger explains, 'Appropriation, in beholding human nature, makes mortals appropriate for that which avows itself from everywhere to man in *saying*, which points toward the concealed. Man's, the listener's, being made appropriate for *saying*, has this distinguishing character, that it releases human nature into its own, but only in order that man as he who speaks, that is, he who says, may encounter and answer *saying*, in virtue of what is his property' (WL 129). To simplify concerning these nested arrivals, Heidegger says that language comes to its own as saying and we come to our own as mortals within saying, which admits our proper saying (that is, hearing and speaking). Earlier, in journeying through metaphysics, Heidegger had said that language was the house of being and the home of human being (see, e.g., 'Letter on Humanism,' 199, and above, this chapter, section B, and DL 5, 23, for different languages as different houses). In the arrival, he sees that to be who we are is to be within saying where we are also 'needed and used to speak language' (WL 134).

Insofar as we are admitted into our essence in saying, we dwell there as mortals. Our initial task there would be to become open to hearing from saying so that saying can say. We would then let our speaking speak out of this prior hearing: 'The message-bearer must come from the message. But he must also have gone toward it' (DL 51). In such a hermeneutic calling, to be mortal is to hold ourselves, as message-bearers, in the prevailing relation to the message. This thought recalls our originary essence. For example, Hölderlin and the Greeks thought of mortals (poets) as interpreters of the gods, where Hermes 'brings the message of sending; *hermeneuein* is that exposition which brings tidings because it can listen to a message ... All this makes it clear that hermeneutics means not just the interpretation, but, even before it, the bearing of the message and tidings' (DL 29). Mortals, then, bear witness, and correspond to the saying. We preserve the message (DL 32–3).

Before following our arrival into saying to where it eventually leads, we should note that coming into our own as mortals is also coming to thing and thinking. In *Ereignis*, things come to their own as things: no longer presencing as mere beings, they fit into their proper nature in the appropriating of world. For example, Heidegger says,

> Inconspicuously compliant is the thing: the jug and the bench, the footbridge and the plow. But tree and pond, too, brook and hill, are things each in its own way. Things, each thinging from time to time in its own way, are heron and roe, deer, horse, and bull. Things, each thinging and each staying in its own way, are mirror and clasp, book and picture, crown and cross.
>
> But things are also compliant and modest in number. (T 182)

In our arrival home, we arrive from objects to an openness to things, whereby we may be gathered into world.

Then, too, we arrive at originary thinking. We come into our own nature insofar as we are able, within originary thinking, to make our way to the home shore. Thinking is the path which leads – between future and origin – to where reflection would be at home, into the call of saying and thing (T 181). We are bound, as mortals, to think what is said (see 'A Dialogue on Language' throughout), that is, to respond to it so as to let it come (epilogue, T 184ff.; DL 22). This means that thinking may always go astray, even in and after the arrival home. *Accordingly, our arrival at our home in saying, and into things, by way of thinking, also arrives somewhere else – at the region where the nature of saying, thing, and thinking are at home, that is, in the belonging granted by the giving named* Ereignis.

For Heidegger, if we ask where mortals are at home, the answer is that we can become at home when we come into saying because saying grants us our capacity to speak and therefore to be human. 'We are, then, within language and with language before all else' (WL 112). He elaborates, 'If speaking, as the listening to language, lets *saying* be said to it, this letting can obtain only in so far – and so near – as our own nature has been admitted and entered into *saying*. We hear *saying* only because we belong within it. *Saying* grants the hearing, and thus the speaking of language solely to those who belong within it. Such is the granting that abides in *saying*. It allows us to attain the ability to speak. The essence of language is present in *saying* as the source of such a grant' (WL 124). Here Heidegger starts to say the nature of saying in the region where it comes into its own nature. Parallel to what he told us about appropriation, saying is not another autonomous or fixed phenomena co-existing with the fourfold. Rather, it has its essence as and in the gathering granting. Hence, in attempting to say how saying comes as appropriating, Heidegger journeys 'into the region where the essential being of saying is at home' (DL 49).

The illuminations multiply: now not only do we come home to language, but language comes to its own in appropriating; in addition, *the coming home which is disclosed here shows itself as a belonging. That is, our homecoming to saying is a coming into belonging, belonging not only with saying but also to* Ereignis. We can come home only because we belong there already, even while apart. That is why Heidegger says, 'We can be those listeners only insofar as we belong within saying. The way to speaking begins with the fact that we are allowed to listen and thus to belong *to saying*. This belonging contains the actual presence of the way to language. But in what manner is saying present, that it can let us listen and belong?' (WL 126). *Our homecoming now shows itself to be the coming to the granted belonging-within which is given saying's gathering.* (Recall τï αυτό as the same, that is, as belonging together without being identical.) Saying, in fact, not only gives us our place, but sets all beings free into presence:

'Saying is the gathering that joins all appearance of the in itself manifold showing which everywhere lets all that is shown abide with itself' (WL 126). That is, insofar as anything comes to rest in its own essence, it does so as given by saying. In remaining, or, better, in now being disclosed as, this granting, saying also comes to its own essence, 'the manner in which language has being, that is, abides, that is, remains gathered in what language grants to itself, to its own idiom, as language' (WL 119). Here, then, 'Saying is itself the abode of rest which grants the quiet of mutual belonging to all that belongs within the structure of the being of language' as saying (WL125).

But, as noted before, though not yet fully thought, saying is not simply the primal abode, because saying itself has its nature in appropriation, and rests there. It is difficult not to think this metaphysically and representationally, and thus in terms of a succession of beings or nested physical containers or categories. Nonetheless, Heidegger finds that saying belongs essentially and primally to appropriation. For example, he says, 'The origin of the word – that is, of human speaking in terms of *saying* – its origin which is in the nature of appropriation, is what constitutes the peculiar character of language' (WL 133). Or, as he elaborates it, 'Saying, which resides in appropriation, is *qua* showing the most appropriate mode of appropriating. This sounds like a statement. If we hear only this statement, it does not say to us what is to be thought out. Saying is the mode in which appropriation speaks: mode not so much in the sense of *modus* or fashion, but as the melodic mode, the song which says something in its singing. For appropriating *saying* brings to light all present beings in terms of their properties – it lauds, that is, allows them into their own, their nature' (WL 135). How does appropriation grant and gather? In the singing of saying. Heidegger says, 'In the event of appropriation vibrates the active nature of what speaks as language' (PI 39).

Of course, thing, as the staying appropriation of world, also leads us to appropriation. So, too, does thinking which aims at the essential abode (PI 39). Earlier, Heidegger had spoken of language as the house of being and the home of human being. There, language was understood as the site of our neighbourliness and kinship to being. Now, however, Heidegger goes on to say that we are in language as appropriation, and thus language has its essence in appropriation. This goes beyond the earlier understanding to arrive at the nature of saying. Heidegger reflects, 'Language has been called "the house of being." It is the keeper of being present, in that its coming to light remains entrusted to the appropriating show of saying. Language is the house of being because language, as saying, is the mode of appropriation' (WL 135). Heidegger takes a further step to consolidate all this, and to clarify our homecoming: 'Because showing of saying is appropriating, therefore the ability to listen to *saying* – our belonging to it – also lies in appropriation. In order to grasp this fact and all it implies, we would need to think through the nature of mortals with sufficient completeness in all its aspects and rapports, but first of all to think through appropriation as such' (WL 129). Heidegger, then, develops our *arrival at appropriation*, which we now need to think and hold in thought. *He names the origin of our homecoming into our own essence.* As we have heard above, by naming, 'Appropriation grants to mortals their abode within their nature ... It is itself the most inconspicuous of inconspicuous phenomena, the simplest of simplicities, the nearest of the near, and the farthest of the far in which we mortals spend our lives' (WL 128; see also PI 38).

Of the greatest importance, here, is understanding that we belong to appropriation and can arrive at it as we have through saying: 'our relation to language defines itself in terms of the mode in which we, who are needed in the usage of language, belong to the appropriation' (WL 136). After the long concealment and separation from that to which we belong, our homelessness begins to end in this phase of homecoming. Heidegger surveys our situation:

> We must experience simply this owning [*Eignen*] in which man and being are delivered [*ge-eignen*] over to each other, that is, we must enter into what we call the event of appropriation [*Ereignis*] ...
>
> Where are we now? At the entry of our thinking into that simplicity which we call in the strictest sense of the term the event of appropriation ...
>
> The event of appropriation is that realm, vibrating within itself, through which man and being reach each other in their nature, achieve their active nature by losing those qualities with which metaphysics has endowed them. (PI 36–7)

Clearly, Heidegger thinks as appropriated the passage from being, human being, beings, language, objects, and so on, and the arrival at the belonging together of mortals and the rest of the fourfold through thing and saying. Of course, at the moment of arrival which passes over to an originary home, appropriation is only glimpsed. Because it is barely glimpsed, more needs to be thought and said later, in the learning to become at home. But because it is glimpsed, something can be said even at arrival – a first, necessarily incomplete impression as it were, but not therefore a misleading one, because only the genuine giving of appropriation enables the homecoming in the first place.

Heidegger can say a good deal, in fact. Consider all he has already told us about the appropriating which prevails in saying and thing, that is, about the appropriation of world. In addition, he now fills in what earlier was hinted at but left empty, in the saying of, for example, 'What claims our existence,' what is worthy of thought, and that ancient something which conceals itself in *a-letheia* (DL 3, 13; TB 24). At the very least, appropriation names the primal, 'For that appropriating, holding, self-retaining, is the relation of all relations,' where relation is originarily understood 'in terms of the appropriation' (WL 135). But appropriation still holds itself back, even when it grants our arrival at its shore. Heidegger explains that appropriation preserves what is its own. In certain epochs it has had to keep itself by expropriating itself of itself, that is, by withdrawing what 'is most fully its own from boundless unconcealment' (TB 22–3). This expropriation may be thought by way of belonging. For instance, in the gathering of the fourfold each of the four yields its 'own separate particularity' and so 'each is expropriated, within their mutual appropriation, into its own being. This expropriative appropriation is the mirror-play of the four-fold' (T 179).

In Heidegger's story of homecoming, *appropriation and the expropriation which belongs to it grant and gather home all that belongs together: the appropriating is a gathering together of what belongs together even when held apart. In nearing appropriating we arrive home – where we belong in our own essence as mortals, not alone, but essentially appropriated into the fourfold of world – this also means we belong in language and to appropriation. Thus, Heidegger tells the story of our arrival home in a way that is powerfully his own, and he arrives home in thinking and saying the appropriating of world. In a double way, then, thinking and saying come into their own here, as originary.*

The homecoming has been a long and complex journey. Nonetheless, the phase of homecoming as arrival at the home shore is distinct. The arrival takes place as the arrival into originary thinking and saying because thinking is a path to homecoming which moves toward that arrival by going through saying. So the thinking changes when the saying changes. This is *not* a mere change in vocabulary. It is a change in saying and thinking appropriate to the transformation of the theme, that is, of where the representations of homelessness give way to saying as the granting of homecoming. As noted in passing, Heidegger throws off the old language of metaphysics in his arrival – though he still often uses the old words to explain where he has been and to emphasize differences. For example, he no longer uses the term 'hermeneutics' (DL 12); he gives up 'language' for 'saying,' 'human being' for 'mortals,' and 'being' for *Ereignis*. He passes over from treating language, human being, and being to engaging saying, mortals, and appropriation. That is why earlier in his journey Heidegger did 'not surrender the word 'being' immediately and resolutely to the exclusive use of the language of metaphysics' and did 'not at once give its own name to what' he was searching for: 'How is one to give a name to what he is still seeking for? To assign the naming word is, after all, what constitutes finding' (DL 20). The task takes a long time – Heidegger speaks of decades – if it comes at all (DL 8).

Heidegger is clear about what this shift actually amounts to: as we just saw above (and also in *Principle of Reason*), it requires giving up thinking being in order to pass over to the hitherto concealed giving (initially via the 'there is given,' '*Es gibt*') that holds sway. Consequently, we can begin to see that, 'As the gift of this [there is given], being belongs to giving. As gift, being is not expelled from giving. Being, presencing is transmuted' (TB 6). There has been a long history of the transformation of being – Heidegger even gives us a list (TB 7). But the transformation of 1) being and beings, 2) the duality, and 3) the presencing of what is present into appropriation is of a different sort, since the former three have their origin in the last, as we saw above. Appropriation is not a form of being (WL 129, note; see also TB 21–2). Originarily, 'as we think being itself and follow what is its own, being proves to be a gift of the sending of presence, the gift granted by the giving of time. The gift of presence is the property of appropriating. Being vanishes in appropriation' (TB 21–2).

Of course, the thinking occurs in Heidegger's saying. *That is why the works considered here seem especially strange and difficult. In them Heidegger is passing over from one way of thinking and speaking to another.* Unevenly, then finally more sustainedly, he arrives home in a highly originary saying and thinking. Naturally, what he *says*, and, even more so what he *does, here*, appears strange because *it achieves an arriving home which neither he nor anyone else has ever done before* (and how much stranger for the rest of us, who are not remotely close to his ability or experience). In the broadest sense, Heidegger's story of arrival comes in a change of language and thinking – where his changed originary saying gives up metaphysical language and his originary thinking gives up representational thinking. Thus, as he already began to in *What Is Called Thinking?* (see this chapter, section B, throughout), he attempts to give up propositional language. Though he still lectures, uses statements, and seems to declare things, he makes great efforts to overcome these ways of speaking, which he sees as obstacles. There are, of course, limits placed on such an attempt by the social character of thinking: Heidegger's saying surely is radical enough to put off and even misguide many thinkers. How far he can in practice push originary language and still remain in dialogue is a matter which never ceases to concern him. That is why he often speaks in both representational and originary language, helping us to translate from one to the other, for example in *What Is Called Thinking?* and 'A Dialogue on Language.'[35] Clearly, though, his originary thinking and saying exhibit a major change, and works such as 'The Thing' stand as 'dramatic' instances of his originary arrival.

The new prospect and project, as well as some of its puzzlements, are explicitly pondered by Heidegger, as he prepares for the change in our relation to language (WL 136). 'But if the matter at stake prohibits our speaking of it by way of a statement, then we must give up the declaratory sentence that is anticipated by the question(s) we have raised' (TB 20; see also 24 and sTB 25). Obviously, Heidegger is struggling to move beyond the statement form, to finally show and say what is needed – and he succeeds, as we can see, in the works now being considered, even if the showing and saying are admittedly only barely underway. As I argue elsewhere, Heidegger does what he says – we might consider his accomplishment a vast, multi-year set of *performative utterances and acts.*[36] His new saying and thinking can be found in several 'clusters,' for example, in those which utilize 'movement' as a mode of saying and a way of actually accomplishing a homecoming in a 'high' originary style. Reminiscent of Hölderlin, who spoke of festival and play, flowing source, movement up- and down-stream, and the region of light and growth, Heidegger also moves in a playful-festive swing, to and fro in the region and opening of the source which still comes forth into our current, familiar scene. In the language of our leitmotif, Heidegger achieves and celebrates homecoming (one that is even more festive than Hölderlin's celebration).

Even without a complete explication we can apprehend what Heidegger is up to by attending to several examples (from a few works) in which Heidegger speaks in the vocabulary of movement and being underway: thinking is a path and wondrous road-building; hints are bypaths; questioning circles around; translation wanders back and forth (DL 6, 21, 24, 26; WL 126; WCT 226, 233). These various movements go back and forth (DL 12) from where we are to where we have been and where we are going, to origin and future, to the near and far. Originary thinking returns to sites left behind and rests at way stations (consider, too, language as the home to which we add, and Heidegger's return to ancient words) (DL 21, 12). Heidegger clearly points out the intimate connection between 'way,' appropriation, and originary language:

> To clear a way, for instance across a snow-covered field, is in the Almannic-Swabian dialect still called *wëgen* even today. This verb, used transitively, means: to form a way and, forming it, to keep it ready. Way making understood in this sense no longer means to move something up or down a path that is already there. It means to bring the way ... forth first of all, and thus to *be* the way.
>
> Appropriation appropriates man to its own image. Showing as appropriating thus transposes and appropriation is the way making for *saying* to come into language.
>
> This way-making puts language (the essence of language) as language (saying) into language (into the sounded word). (WL 129–30)

Accordingly, an originary mode of movement is called for. We find this in Heidegger's dialogue with a Japanese partner as the two listen finally not to each other, but to what saying says in words (DL 52, 45). This movement too is back and forth, and includes all the nearing and going into the strange and far; it swings widely, to and fro, and lets drift (DL 27, 28, 30). Leaving behind wilful metaphysical-representational thought and its attendant linear-logical assertions, Heidegger often lets the conversation drift to the subject matter or to a listening thinking and saying that takes place in a shyly reverent and hesitant movement (for example, DL, first half of 10, 28). That is why what is said stops and starts, and breaks off to leave thoughts unsaid. Heidegger too is reverent. As opposed to stridently insistent statements and injunctions, hints beckon in differing directions (DL 24, 25).

Heidegger insists that if we are to follow what he says we must do much more than keep up with the logical sequences of propositions. We must learn to go along with the saying and strange movement of his thinking that attempts to delineate nothing less than the mutual gathering of the fourfold, including the mutual belonging together of mortals and appropriation (e.g., TB 2). As is befitting, such an arrival occurs as playful and festive – *not* in an *aesthetic* sense, but as the luminosity of the gesture which bears and gives understanding and belonging (DL 4). Here, Heidegger claims, there is 'a playful thinking that is more compelling than the rigor of science' (DL 29). Dimensions of time interplay and, originarily, 'mirroring in this appropriating-lightening way, each of the four plays to each of the others' (TB 15). Dynamically, 'the mirroring that binds into freedom is the play that betroths each of the four to each through the enfolding clasp of their mutual celebration' (consider also Hölderlin's wedding festival of gods and mortals) (T 179ff.). The nimble movement of the originary gathering of the fourfold 'is the round dance of appropriating,' which 'is the ring that joins while it plays as mirroring' (T 180).

The festive movement to and from, which Heidegger says and which he accomplishes in moving freely to the fourfold and appropriation, is movement within the *realm of the open*, in which *mutual arrival* occurs. Heidegger frequently speaks of region (for example, DL 3, *Gegend*), especially of the region where giving and calling take place. In this thought pattern the dialogue is the site of the gathering force of the undefined which comes to us (DL 13). In this region, the mutual arrival of what belongs together occurs – as appropriating. What Heidegger says of gesture, gathering, and mutual bearing can now be better understood: in this festive, mutual movement Heidegger names and comes to (and gives us) 'the gathering which originarily unites within itself what we bear to it and what it bears to us' (for instance, DL 18–19, 26, 51). This realm *is* the scene of homecoming. (Of course, this is not meant representationally, as a place for independent pre-givens to enter. Appropriation is 'pre-spatial'; that is, it opens place in the first place. It gives homecoming as arrival, as the giving of the essence of mortals who arrive, and as the giving of language and thinking as all are given in homecoming [see TB 16].)

Not surprisingly, this cherished realm is described in familiar terms: it is the locus of meetings of friends, colleagues, master, and disciples – the departed forebears belong here too, fondly remembered and still engaged as we think through their works (e.g., DL 1–10, 31). In the primal homecoming, the fourfold comes together in a homey manner: 'the four nestle into their unifying presence, in which each one retains its own nature. So nestling, they join together' (T 181). More energetically, Heidegger articulates this region and movement in the vocabulary of source. Of course, we think of Hölderlin's journey to the source; but here, Heidegger is making his own proper homecoming – though, even in its differences, it stays close to Hölderlin's. (Note that Heidegger says, 'We might perhaps prepare a little for the change in our relation to language. Perhaps this experience might awaken: all reflective thinking is poetic, and all poetry in turn is a kind of thinking. The two belong together by virtue of that *saying* which has already bespoken itself to what is unspoken because it is a thought of thanks'; WL 136.)

Heidegger's saying says the source, which has given itself and come to originary language. He speaks of the source of our tradition and thinking, the possibility of a still-concealed single source of different languages, and of 'a giving in which the sending source keeps itself back' in its giving the river (DL 16, 8, 24; TB 22, 24). This source would be the wellspring of reality (*Wesensquell*) which also gives saying and thinking (DL 8, 24 [115]). If the source is not to dry up, our thinking and saying must 'give heed to the trails that direct thinking back into the region of its source,' in order 'to guard the purity of the mystery's wellspring' (DL 37, 50). Thought as the source, the source gives thinking and saying. The latter then would be a stream which flows from the source, and upon which we can travel toward and even from the source in thinking. In contrast to the representational expression of pre-given things or ideas through sounds, what is originarily spoken 'wells up from the formerly spoken and so far still unspoken *saying*' (WL 124). What has passed is held as a reservoir; what is yet to come is kept in concealment. 'And *saying* itself? Is it separated from our speaking, something to which we must build a bridge? Or is *saying* the stream of stillness which in forming them joins its own two banks – the *saying* and our saying after it?' (DL 124–5). Because 'our customary notions of language hardly reach as far as that,' it is a real accomplishment and homecoming to experience and be able to say, as does the Japanese dialogue partner, that in saying's hint, 'I have come to be at home only now through our dialogue' (WL 125, see also 'Building Dwelling Thinking' 146–9; DL 47).

The source which keeps itself back as source, behind the stream it sends, also sends – waters – what flowers and grows. Hence, the Japanese word for language is *Koto ba* – the petals or blossoms that stem from *Ereignis* (DL 47). *Ereignis* holds sway and shelters what needs shelter; in this realm of appropriation is given flourishing and flowering (DL 47): 'Think of cherry blossoms or plum blossoms' (DL 45). In the play of appropriation, Heidegger is reminded of the veiled, mutual arrival and homecoming of Giving and mortals which takes place in *saying* and our saying: 'In ancient Japanese poetry, an unknown poet sings of the intermingling scent of cherry blossoms and plum blossoms on the same branch' (DL 53). For such a coming and flourishing, we must be patient. But even if the fruit has not yet ripened for a harvest and storing, the blossoms, according to Heidegger, bloom. Homecoming occurs; mortals (including Heidegger) begin to arrive home to the playful, familiar scene given by the source.

Obviously, in speaking this way, Heidegger does pass out of representational speech and over into an originary saying. Just as obviously, what he says is an arrival. It is tentative, not always sustained, certainly not matured and established (except perhaps in 'The Thing'). *It is a first arrival. But he does not yet dwell where he has arrived.*[37] In at least three senses it is still a long way home into our own manner of abiding, into saying, thing, and thinking, into the appropriation of world. First, because the moment of arrival is not yet dwelling, we still have to become at home where we have arrived; second, the arrival must be held and understood, which only happens slowly. Third, even in arrival we must hold in thinking and continue to travel through the uncanny homelessness we still endure. Unless we do so, the journey will collapse into an 'easy solution,' that is, into forfeiture of journeying. Then too, in all these arrivings, still and always underway, some dimensions are always concealed. Thus, Heidegger says, 'We are, then, within language and with language before all else. A way to language is not needed. Besides, the way to language is impossible if we indeed are already at that point to which the way is to take us. But are we at that point? Are we so fully within language that we experience its nature ...? Do we in fact already live close to language even without our doing? Or is the way to language as language the longest road our thinking can follow? Not just the longest, but a way lined with obstacles that come from language itself?' (WL 112).[38] 'In truth, however, our reflection finds that it has come only within sight of the *way to language* it is seeking; it is barely on its traces' (WL 125).

Still, for all the limitations and qualifications, we *have arrived* at the path of saying in the present set of works, which is why Heidegger goes on immediately to speak of the first break of a new dawn, which allows the long night to begin to change to day (WL 127). We are within language. Our placement neither confines nor frees us: it allows for both the entrapment which prevents homecoming and for the opening to the arrival and to future dwelling. The belonging to representational language is an obstacle to homecoming, a binding (like enframing – *Gestell*) which we must 'undo,' if we can. Heidegger says of the representational speaking into which language has woven us, and from which we must 'free ourselves,' that we are not to go out of it, but to find a place where we can stay.

> This web indicated by the formula (we try to speak about speech *qua* speech) designates the predetermined realm in which not only this lecture series but all linguistic science, all linguistic theory and philosophy of language, in fact any attempt to reflect on language, must live. A web com-

> presses, narrows, and obstructs the straight clear view inside its mesh. At the same time, however, the web of which the guiding formula speaks is the proper matter of language. Therefore, we may not disregard the web which seems to crowd everything into a hopeless tangle. Rather the formula is to urge our reflection to attempt, not to remove the web, of course, but to loosen it so that it allows us a view into the open togetherness of the relations named in the formula. Perhaps there is a bond running through the web, which, in a way that remains strange, unbinds and delivers language into its own. The point is to experience the unbinding bond within the web of language. (WL 112–13, see also 130)

In his arrival at saying, Heidegger *has* entered the web and arrived at what rests within it. In passing from the representational to originary saying and thinking, the web becomes a floral bower (as 'A Dialogue on Language,' 45–7, makes clear).

Still within language, now understood as originarily freeing rather than metaphysically threatening and constraining, we find not only disclosure but also safe keeping. We move toward home and catch sight of sayings, which is not to claim that we occupy home and fully see saying and appropriation. As Heidegger notes, 'We are not capable of seeing the nature of language in the round because we, who can only say something by saying it after *saying*, belong ourselves within *saying*' (WL 134). As we have seen, originarily, what *saying* says is bound up with what we can hear.

If we have come to accept our limitations, that is, to accept our own nature as mortals, and thereby get ourselves out of the way of the giving, we may be freed from the web of representation. It also turns out that in this moment of arrival – release – we would be freed from striving to overcome metaphysics. As we have heard, the very attempt, however necessary, to overcome metaphysics (and this would include framing as well as being) was yet, as strident overcoming, itself still entangled in metaphysics. Now Heidegger reiterates, 'our task is to cease all overcoming, and leave metaphysics to itself. If overcoming remains necessary, it concerns that thinking that explicitly enters appropriation in order to say it in terms of it about it. Our task is unceasingly to overcome the obstacles that tend to render such saying inadequate' (TB 24).

Accordingly, in this moment of arrival, metaphysical homelessness is 'let be' and overcoming 'left alone'; we can begin living as ourselves in our proper homeland – in appropriation. Here, Heidegger explains, 'A transformation of language is needed which we can neither compel nor invent. This transformation does not result from the procurement of newly formed words and phrases. It touches on our relation to language, which is determined by sending: whether and in what way the nature of language, as the arch-tidings of appropriation, will retain us in appropriation' (WL 135).

The question then becomes whether our arrival home can be held. We still have to learn to become at home, that is, sustain our belonging to the appropriated fourfold, and learn to dwell there. That is the next step. But even before that, the homecoming arrival must be retained in recollective thinking and memorializing saying. We need to begin to become at home in our homecoming-arrival. As a way to hold it in mind, homecoming here shows itself as the arrival home, where home means 1) our own essence (and the proper essence of all, each in its own homecoming); 2) saying, thinking, and thing, which each in its own way give worlds to us; and 3) the mutual appropriating of divinities and mortals, earth and sky. *Through these passages, we arrive, past being and beings thought separately, past even the duality thought in difference and belonging, at our belonging to appropriating-granting.* And so to a further radical possibility – the giving which is named *Ereignis.* Appropriation is often thought of as event or happening; but it would be more originary to take it as the gathering-giving of belonging-together (which also means the grant of what is proper to each in the belonging together). *In coming home to* Ereignis *as giving, we are given our belonging. We are gathered into it. Thus,* Ereignis *is the grant of homecoming. Boldly put,* Ereignis *comes home to us in its transforming turn, as homecoming. As homecoming,* Ereignis *is the home we come home to, that we arrive at insofar as enowning unfolds.*

Looking back through the homecoming journey, we find that Heidegger has had the same experience as Hölderlin: upon the long-awaited arrival home, home appears strange. The arrival home is really the beginning of the genuine homecoming. At this point we have yet to learn what it means, and requires, to become at home in our own nature in saying and thinking and with things, in the appropriating fourfold. But in managing to think and say even this much, Heidegger does begin to come to his own in a kind of return and thus confirms what Hölderlin says in the hymn 'The Rhine': 'For as you began, so you will remain' (DL 7). If so, what happens comes as a gift, as homecoming.

But insofar as 'origin always comes to meet us from the future,' that is, insofar as origin remains coming toward us, it stays strange (DL 10). It remains the goal of homecoming. Heidegger and the Japanese understand this,

> Inquirer: But it seems to me that, in the field in which we are moving, we reach those things with which we are not originarily familiar precisely if we do not shun passing through things strange to us.
> Japanese: In what sense do you understand 'originarily familiar'? You do not mean what we know first do you?
> Inquirer: No – but what before all else has been entrusted to our nature, and becomes known only at the last. (DL 33–4)

What comes last is the deeper and longer homecoming: learning to become at home. Where Heidegger tells how the leap to the mutual appropriation of mortals and the rest of the fourfold is a marvellous gift, he also wonders at it: 'What a curious leap, presumably yielding us the insight that we do not reside sufficiently as yet where in reality we already are' (PI 33; see also 37).

Hölderlin came to his own homecoming to the proximity of the source and to his nature as poet by way of his poetizing, which responded to the source's saying. Heidegger also arrives home, coming into his proper mode of abiding as that of an originary thinker and to the granting of world by thinking homelessness and homecoming – that is, the belonging together in estrangement and reunion of what belongs together even while apart. Of course, because to be mortal is to be ever underway, Heidegger still needs to tell the story of learning to become at home and perhaps even of dwelling there. Such a project presupposes an experience of the matter itself, of the deeper homecoming (see sTB 26). Though Heidegger has to accomplish this for himself, now that he has achieved his own arrival home he can at least further avail himself of the help of the poets who have gone home before him and who say, and echo the saying of, what he needs to hear in order to follow.

5 Learning to Become at Home in Saying

Poetic Remaining in Apartness and Beginning to Learn to Abide

Both Heidegger's story of homecoming itself and the story of his own movement within that saga have arrived at the same point. In the course of telling us that and how there is an initial entrance to a home for humans, he has had to develop his own thinking and saying, and thereby has begun to become at home himself. Though so far he has little more than arrived, this in itself is no small achievement. Yet, ever since the Hölderlin essays, discussed in chapter 2, Heidegger has understood that to arrive at one's native shore is not at all the same as being at home there. In fact, arrival after absence, no matter how longed for and relished, may be arrival into something still foreign and strange. As he discovered in trying to follow what Hölderlin tells us, the actual moment of arrival 'home' is only the beginning of the deepest movements of homecoming; next, one needs to learn to become at home, on the way to a possible dwelling near the source.

For all Heidegger's accomplishments, then, he still needs to do more, which, almost by definition, requires resources beyond his own if he is to understand where he is and how to begin to abide there. He finds the aid he needs, as he did before, through the poets. Obviously, it is the greatest help to the thinker to be able to listen to what has already been partially experienced and said about homecoming to language, thing, the fourfold, appropriation, and the movement beyond arriving to learning to become at home. But crucially, poetry is important only because of what non-arbitrarily comes in it, or rather through it. Heidegger contends that neither the poets nor thinkers 'create' the story they tell. It is not to be taken as merely a 'fiction' in today's sense of 'just something somebody makes up,' however marvellous or astonishingly 'imaginative.' Rather, he claims, the poets say what they hear: the story of saying itself. It is because genuine poetry is the setting into work of what has been given that poetizing is of the greatest importance for the thinker.

Hence, he again composes works which stand close to the poets' poems – by responsively echoing what the poets say (as we will see), even as the poets echo the saying that gives itself to them. We find, then, twinned with the poets' stories, Heidegger's journey into mortals' homelessness and the poetic becoming at home and beginning to dwell – near the source. Yet, since Heidegger is not a poet, his specific task with what has been given is to respond by thinking recollectively or meditatively. That is, he must be careful to stay on his own way. One of the major differences between the poet and thinker, Heidegger has told us, is that for the thinker homelessness and the strange are never put aside. A homecoming would be counterfeit if, at any point, we ignored homelessness and lapsed into tranquilized everydayness, oblivious to mystery and the uncanny.

Thus, in addition to learning from the poets how to become at home, Heidegger simultaneously uses them to stay in the strange – the two are inseparable. Even where some poets may at least project what it would be to become at home and dwell, as apparently was the case with Hölderlin (according to Heidegger's thinking about the matter in his Hölderlin essays), apparently it is otherwise with Rilke and George, whom Heidegger also takes up; this is important because the thinker must always remain underway through the strange, even when at home. There are at least three reasons why this is so for the thinker. First, we are still human, and to be mortal means to be always underway, away from everydayness toward mystery – that is, toward home. There is no such thing as progress 'once and for all,' as the poets remind us: we have to unendingly learn to live in language. We do not yet reside where we belong, in saying. Then, too, homelessness still reigns in our epoch. Despite any turn and possibility of an originary epoch, the homelessness of nihilism and enframing are far from over; the strange continues to pervade our living in our native land, even after our arduous homecoming journey and arrival. Thus, the character of homelessness, home, and homecoming remains in question and will remain so. Finally, to be recollective, thinking can never dismiss or set aside what has gone before or what is strange. Originary questioning does not break off but always finds the foreign and the familiar given together, just as the disclosed and concealed.

Though his movement parallels that of Hölderlin through the phases of the homecoming journey, Heidegger is certainly not mechanically following a set of steps laid out in the poetry he happens to like. Rather, in his own journey home, which comes about as he attempts to think and say homecoming itself, he finds that a new way of thinking and speaking increasingly comes to the fore and that, once initially 'familiar,' it needs cultivation. Hence, close by the works that accomplish and tell of his first moment of arrival home, we find another set, presented between 1950 and 1968, which speak about and continue to attempt to accomplish the requisite becoming at home. These essays are 'Language,' 1950; 'Poetically Man Dwells,' 1951; 'Language in the Poem,' 1953; 'Die Sprache Johann Peter Hebels,' 1955; 'Hebel – Friend of the House,' 1957; 'The Nature of Language,' 1958; 'Words,' 1958; 'Hölderlin's Erde und Himmel,' 1960; 'Sprache und Heimat,' 1960; and 'Das Gedicht,' 1968.

To briefly sketch how it is that the works to be treated next constitute a distinctive cluster may be clearest if we consider their theme and way of saying. In some ways these essays are like those on Hölderlin which we considered in chapter 2, for example, in that they intertwine with the poetic texts. In addition to telling the becoming at home, these works, because they are close to the poets', are concerned with the neighbourliness of poet and thinker. If chapter 2 told of the poet's homecoming and if this reunion with poets is part of the thinker's own homecoming as learning to become at home, then, *here*, both the poets and Heidegger are involved with an originary belonging. Heidegger and the poets he considers attempt a non-philosophical way home (though Rilke, in the shadow of Nietzsche's metaphysics, was about something else, as we saw when treating 'Wozu Dichter' in chapter 2). The neighbourliness of poet and thinker is especially laid out where originary thinking and originary poetizing attempt an originary homecoming.

Still, these new pieces also come out of Heidegger's *own* successful experience of an initial turning (see chapter 3) and journey back through homelessness to the Greek origin and thence to an initial homecoming in the no-longer-metaphysical (see chapter 4). That is, while he works hard to *take up the poets again* and to continue to learn how to stay near what they say, he does not go back to a past stage. Earlier, trying to follow Hölderlin, Heidegger had spoken of home and homecoming in terms of being, beings, and human being, because, at the time when he *completed* those essays, he had *not* experienced or been able to say what Hölderlin had been able to experience and say. Now, after Heidegger's passage through and out of metaphysics and with his own arrival at *Ereignis*, the fourfold, language, and thing, he speaks and thinks as he could not have before. Thus, while the works considered in this chapter are like those of chapter 2, here *Heidegger's own*, more fully originary voice and character of becoming at home come forth.

That Heidegger speaks here in yet another mode, with a voice related to, but distinct from any we have heard thus far, is easy to appreciate if we attend to the ways his language both echoes and differs from the poets'. Heidegger's mode genuinely listens and responds to the poetic texts. That does not mean merely that he takes the text seriously, but that the poet's economical, tight saying sets the tone. Heidegger's reflections become interwoven with the poetic texts and accommodate themselves to the appropriate rhythms. He proceeds slowly and carefully and subtly retraces and retrieves what he hears in the poets. His pace of speaking is noticeably slow and hesitant. Even where Heidegger speaks in extended sentences, each phrase and word appears to be meditative. The impression is that short, careful – even shy – thoughts dominate. It is often surprising to look at what you have read and find it may consist of a 'normal'-looking paragraph of words. This is because what is said is spoken and, if we properly listen, can be heard as 'high meditation.' Still, for all its shyness, his thinking and saying appear firm and move smoothly. If anything, we feel a strange, sure, and quiet *power* in these works. Everywhere they exude a self-restrained energy. Their hesitation and holding back are not like a vibrating drill slipping and bouncing on an overly hard surface, but like the farmer and team of horses ploughing a field and carefully turning at each end, or like a child in a swing.[1]

In light of Heidegger's arrival and of what he now understands, he cannot rush the hoped-for dwelling near the source. Even further patience is required, because he needs to learn how to hold himself in the journey and thereby also learn, with the help of the poets, to stay in the strange. Paradoxically perhaps, through such self-disciplined holding back, Heidegger does also draw nearer in this phase of his work to the native land to which he has just returned. This phase of homecoming is characterized not by the new, but by intimacy, where yet another dimension opens to be experienced, thought, and said. In this set of essays, then, we should not expect the discovery of a new theme or words. Rather, what has already been discovered will now be explored, so that, in a deeper way, we can learn to become more fully at home.

Heidegger remains journeying to the native home with several poets who themselves stay in homelessness – he again accompanies Hölderlin, the master traveller in these realms, but also joins Stefan George and especially Georg Trakl, the poet of apartness. The essays that accomplish this travelling in the most extended way span a decade and include 'Language' (1950), 'Poetically Man Dwells' (1951), 'Language in the Poem' (1953), 'The Nature of Language' (1958), 'Words' (1958), 'Hölderlin's Erde und Himmel' (1960), and 'Das Gedicht' (1968). To pick up the story where Heidegger left off, the journey is still going on, through the current lack of dwelling, by way of the strange, and toward a home of our own. Because homecoming is a journey through and out of the strange or foreign, Heidegger continues on his way by questioning this site, as the poets speak of and out of it. That is what it means to discuss poetry: 'We use the word "discuss" here to mean, first, to point out the proper place or site of something, to situate it, and second, to heed that place or site. The placing and the heeding are both preliminaries of discussion ... Our discussion, as befits a thinking way, ends in a question. That question asks for the location of the site' (LP 159).

What is to be thought here, then, is the site of poetry, which also means the site of homelessness and homecoming. Such sites are thought and questioned by way of, and together with, the gathering of what belongs together. Heidegger says, 'Originally the word "site" [*Ort*] suggests a place in which everything comes together, is concentrated. The site gathers unto itself, supremely and in the extreme. Its gathering power penetrates and pervades everything. The site, the gathering power, gathers in and preserves all it has gathered, not like an encapsulating shell but rather by penetrating with its light all it has gathered, and only thus releasing it into its own nature' (LP 159–60). If the site gathers this way, to it belong both the separation and dispersion which precede gathering and the essential rest and keeping which it yields. Gathering would be situated in the midst of the movement to and fro, forward and back. Heidegger acknowledges that such non-linear, 'non-progressive,' inquiry will appear arbitrary and odd, even wayward (*irrweg*), to scientific inquiry (LP 159). Indeed, this procedure *is* essentially wayward: it keeps us upon the way.

Poets of our time, and not just one or two, tell us that we are still homeless, for all our yearning. In a late poem, Hölderlin says, 'poetically man dwells' (cited in PMD 213). Yet as he and Heidegger both see, this does not describe our current daily accomplishment or situation, but our calling. 'Do *we* dwell poetically? Presumably we dwell altogether unpoetically' (PMD 227). In some obvious way, this is so 'because' of high costs, overpopulation, and the other symptoms of our still-metaphysical age: 'Our dwelling is harassed by the housing shortage. Even if that were not so, our dwelling today is harassed by work, made insecure by the hunt for gain and success, bewitched by the entertainment and recreation industry' (PMD 213). As we have seen, these obvious 'conditions' are themselves in need of exploration and understanding. They indicate the real subject matter of thinking. Thus, as he turns to poetry, Heidegger says, 'That we dwell unpoetically, and in what way, we can in any case learn only if we know the poetic. Whether, and when, we may come to a turning point in our unpoetic dwelling is something we may expect to happen only if we remain heedful of the poetic. How and to what extent our doings can share in this turn we alone can prove, if we take the poetic seriously' (PMD 228).

Why? Because it is the poet who speaks about both horizons of the turning point: of the homelessness before, as well as of the homecoming after. And the first must be said before the other, and even still said in the midst of homecomings. Hölderlin, of course, held on to his contemporary site. So did Paul Valéry, who, immediately after the First World War, wrote 'The Crisis of the Spirit' (1919), where he asks whether Europe can become what it really is. According to Heidegger, that amounts to asking whether the world will end finally or restart in the technological, industrial mastery of the entire planet (cited in HEH 176–7). Here, in our epoch, the possibility of the fourfold's gathering as home seems threatened. Apparently, it may even be already devastated and overthrown (*zerstört*) (HEH 176). The loss is articulated by Stephan George and in a more entrapped, minor way by Gottfried Benn (NL 77, 100–1). It pervades the poems of Georg Trakl, which speak of the West. For example, Trakl's 'A Winter Evening' says, in Heidegger's gloss of its second stanza, that 'While many are at home within the house and at the table, not a few wander homeless on darksome paths' (La 196). As we will see shortly, those who wander are not a few unlucky souls, but those who, outside of false complacency, travel in the reigning situation.

In our age we are ruled by technology and *Gestell* and are continually on a darkening, erring way (*ein Irr-weg*) (even when we may be moving, or at least attempting to move, out of *Gestell* to experience and think the fourfold). As mortals, we remain on such a way (HEH 153). Here and now, the unhomely (*das Unheimliche*) encircles the planet (HEH 178). In the stillness which rules, the unhomely goes on, in that the voice of the gathering fourfold is still not heard. The fourfold remains withheld. The voice of the poet is still needed. We mortals continue to be separated from the endowing of home and, thereby, from our own manner of being. Trakl speaks of 'the generation that has been removed from its kind of essential being,' which is 'why it is the "unsettled" kind' (cited in

LP 170). Heidegger comments, 'What curse has struck this humankind? The curse of the decomposing kind is that old human kinship has been struck apart by discord among sexes, tribes, and races. Each strives to escape from that discord ... the discord is the curse. Out of the turmoil of blind wildness it carries each kind into an irreconcilable split, and so casts it into unbridled isolation. The "fragmented kind," so cleft in two, can on its own no longer find its proper cast' (LP 170–1). Here Trakl names the site in which we find ourselves: we are in the strange. 'Something strange is the soul on the earth' (cited in LP 161). Normally we understand this metaphysically, by way of Plato's doctrines, Plotinus, and Platonic Christianity. '[This common] notion presents the earth to us as earthly in the sense of transitory. The soul, by contrast, is regarded as imperishable, supraterrestial ... If it appears within the sensible world, it does so only as a castaway. Here on earth the soul is miscast. It does not belong on earth. Here, the soul is something strange. The body is the soul's prison, if nothing worse' (LP 162).

Yet, we know that originary thinking does not understand earth, body, soul, or the strange in this metaphysical way. Insofar as Trakl's poetry is originary and not metaphysical, 'strange' would not speak of home as transcendental, nor of homelessness as something ended by bodily decay. That is why, according to Heidegger, the line 'Something strange is the soul on earth' speaks from within a poem entitled 'Springtime of the Soul.' 'And there is in the poem not one word about a supraterrestrial home of the immortal soul. The matter gives us food for thought' (LP 162). Usually 'strange' is taken to mean what is unfamiliar to us, or that with which we are uneasy. But thought originarily, 'the German "*fremd*," the Old High German "*fram*" – really means: forward to something else, underway toward ... onward to the encounter with what is kept in store for it. The strange goes forth, ahead. But it does not roam aimlessly, without any kind of determination. The strange element goes in its search toward the site where it may stay in its wandering. Almost unknown to itself, the 'strange 'is already following the call that calls it on the way into its own' (LP 163). Thus 'strange' names our site: we remain strange in our staying underway to the site where we are placed and the call that we have yet really to heed. 'Strange' bespeaks our homecoming to our own.

What Trakl says, then, melds with Heidegger's own discovery that homecoming is arrival into the giving-coming into its own for language, thing, and the fourfold. Here the poet as poet speaks out of the poet's own and says something helpful for the thinker's step back to what, waiting, holds itself back (the appropriating, self-concealing, giving) (HEH 156, 177). Focusing on the homecoming of mortals to language (saying) which grants the fourfold, and thereby our mortal nature, Heidegger finds the poet's words help teach what we need to learn. Strangeness names our site and we who make our mortal way are strangers to ourselves and language (saying).

Of Trakl's stranger, Heidegger says, 'This stranger unfolds human nature forward into the beginning of what is yet to be born. This unborn element in the nature of mortals, which is quieter and hence more stilling, is what the poet calls the unborn' (LP 175). The poet speaks of 'blue wild game' which must recall the stranger. Called on to retrieve, that is, to think of the stranger, 'the blue game is an animal whose animality presumably does not consist in its animal nature, but in that thoughtfully recalling look for which the poet calls. This animality is still far away and barely to be seen. The animality of the animal here intended thus vacillates in the indefinite. It has not yet been gathered up into its essential being. This animal – the thinking animal, *animal rationale*, man – is, as Nietzsche said, not yet determined ... This animal's animality has not yet been gathered up onto firm ground, that is to say, has not been gathered "home," into its own, the house of its veiled being ... This animal not yet determined in its nature is modern man' (LP 166–7). What is said here, of course, needs to be thought, and, before that, carefully heard from the poet. If this is successfully accomplished, we might be released to what gives home. We could come to our own nature as mortals in language, if language comes (and was let come) to its own nature: 'The dialogue of thinking with poetry aims to call forth the *nature* of language, so that mortals may learn again to live within language' (LP 161).

Before we hear the story of the originary thinking of this journey to what is ownmost to mortals and language, however, more needs to be said about the poet's and thinker's remaining in the strange, as wanderers – lest even the poetic homecoming appear, misleadingly, as too easily overcome. As noted, despite our problems with living accommodations and conditions, it might appear that we 'are at home' because more and more of us live in increasingly comfortable buildings. But reflection makes clear that to dwell is not merely to occupy a place more or less our own, that is, does not amount to being surrounded by useful objects (PMD 214; see also BT). That even when 'well-housed,' still-enframed humans are not yet thoughtfully underway home is understood by Trakl, where he points out the 'Wandering ones, more than a few,' who remain afoot, moving through the strange (cited in La 200). These 'more than a few' – including, to be sure, poets and thinkers – help bring about the possibility of dwelling for the others. Heidegger explains, 'Those "wayfarers" must first wander their way to house and table through the darkness of their courses; they must do so not only and not even primarily for themselves, but for the many, because the many think that if they only install themselves in houses and sit at tables, they are already bethinged, conditioned, by things and have arrived at dwelling' (La 200).

For mortals to learn dwelling, then, poets and thinkers must go first through the dark ways (see also the Hölderlin essays). The thinkers follow the wandering poets, trying to question the latter concerning dwelling (and its relation to the poetic) (PMD 214). Hence, Heidegger moves carefully, trying at all times to keep within hearing of the one who precedes him through these dark courses. 'The stranger's footfall goes away into dusk' (LP 164). The stranger wanders ahead of the majority of the age who, as already noted, are decomposed – cast out of their proper cast. Heidegger adds, '"He yonder," the stranger, is the other one to the others, to the decomposing kind [*verwesenden* – in German, poet is *der Dichter*, literally 'composer,' and here the contrasting term means 'decomposing' as decaying]. He is the one who has been called away from the others. The stranger is he who is apart' (LP 171). Therefore, our mortal learning to become at home hinges on thinking through the strange, which in turn depends on hearing the strangers – those who are apart. These strangers remain strange.

This remaining wandering through the strange to come home names the site of our homecoming; and, as we have heard, the strangers both belong within and follow the call that calls them to their own (LP 163). In following the call into the strange, we come close to home, but without abolishing apartness. A case is found where, insofar as the poet answers the poet's call, the poetic naming of things also calls.

> Calling brings closer what it calls. However this bringing closer does not fetch what is called only in order to set it down in closest proximity to what is present, to find a place for it there. The call does indeed call. Thus it brings the presence of what was previously uncalled into nearness. But the call, in calling it here, has already called out to what it calls. Where to? Into the distance in which what is called remains, still absent.
>
> The calling here calls into nearness. But even so the call does not wrest what it calls away from the remoteness, in which it is kept by the calling there. The calling calls into itself and therefore always here and there – here into presence, there into absence. (La 198–9)

This passage occurs where Heidegger is speaking of the gathering of thing, saying, and the fourfold. In the complex calling and echoing/recalling, mortals (with poets first among them) are called near and simultaneously allowed to stay in the distant. In this double dynamic, they are fetched to their proper site. Heidegger goes on, 'Whither is such a being directed which itself assumes the nature of the strange, that it must wander ahead? In what direction is a strange thing called? It is called to go under – to lose itself in the ghostly twilight of the blue, to incline with the decline of the ghostly year. While the decline must pass through the destructiveness of approaching winter, through November, to lose itself yet does not mean that it crumbles into a shambles and is annihilated. On the contrary, to lose oneself means literally to loosen one's bonds and slowly slip away. He who loses himself does of course disappear in the November destruction, but he does not slip into it. He slips through it' (LP 171). Such movement, Heidegger says, brings 'us to a gathering, that is to say, to a site. Of what kind is this site? What shall we name it? Surely the name must fit the poet's language. All that Georg Trakl's poetry says remains gathered and focused on the wandering stranger. He is, and is called, "he who is apart." Through him and around him Trakl's poetic saying is tuned to one unique song. And since this poet's poems are gathered into the song of *him* who is apart, we shall call the site of Trakl's poetic work *apartness*' (LP 172). We would suppose that Heidegger's own naming the site 'apartness' also fetches the site and thinking together. Trying to stay in apartness, the thinker must try to question the site, as the site of mortal homecoming.

As noted, Heidegger's originary thinking of Trakl's originary poetizing concerning the soul is distinct from the metaphysical interpretation of the soul as suprasensuous and, for example, body as merely sensuous and transitory. Similarly, the heavens are no longer thought as the realm transcendent to the earthly, that is, as metaphysical. For Trakl and Heidegger 'soul' names our mortal nature. As essentially strange on the earth, the soul is always underway, wandering toward the site where its essential sway draws it, and toward the site where what would be its ownmost is drawn (that is, where its coming way of being lies). Unlike the soul as metaphysically conceived, the originarily understood soul or mortal nature does not seek to escape the earth: in its strangeness on the earth the mortal's soul needs to belong to the earth, to become at home here. Heidegger explains, 'The earth is that very place which the soul's wandering could not reach so far. The soul only *seeks* the earth; it does not flee from it. This fulfils the soul's being: in her wandering to seek the earth so that she may poetically build and dwell upon it, and thus may be able to save the earth *as* earth' (LP 163).

Soul has its homecoming to its own mode of abiding insofar as it comes home and begins to dwell upon the earth – where the earth is also let into what is its ownmost by mortals. Mortals and earth are simultaneously saved in their mutual homecoming. Accordingly, Heidegger says, 'Trakl's work sings the song of the soul, "something strange on the earth," which is only just about to gain the earth by its wandering, the earth that is the stiller home of the homecoming generation' (LP 196). With these words, Trakl and Heidegger are speaking about beginning to learn to become at home – the fifth phase of homecoming according to Hölderlin (see chapter 2). It is just here, in wandering toward the earth, that the soul becomes, not earthly in the manner of animals, but earthly in its own distinctive way. The wandering is a wandering into the whiling of life and a wandering toward death. Becoming newly born into their nature as mortals involves bearing themselves toward death, bearing themselves as capable of dying (La 200).[2] In becoming capable of dying, the soul does not decay but comes into its own appropriate place, leaving 'behind the form of man which has decayed,' that is, metaphysical man (LP 17–68).

In our mortal becoming at home on the earth, the soul continues wandering and begins to enter 'into the farthest reaches of its essential being – its wandering nature' (LP 180). It does so when it enters and becomes at home in its proper site. Trakl calls this site pain. The sway of the site is guarded and kept by the earth: Trakl says, 'Mighty the power of silence in the rock.' As Heidegger interprets the phrase, 'The rock is the mountain sheltering pain. The stones gather within their stony shelter the soothing power, pain stilling us toward essential being' (LP 166). And what is pain? How is it the site of our wandering in apartness? In 'A Winter Evening' Trakl writes,

> Wanderer quietly steps within;
> Pain has turned the threshold to stone. (cited in La 195)

Understood metaphysically and subjectivistically, pain would be an internal sensation, a matter for medicine and, perhaps, psychology. But thought originarily, pain names the separation of what belongs together. In this separation what belongs together is held apart and thus has the possibility of coming back together. In the pulling and holding apart and in the gathering together, there occurs the opening of a site which persists in/as homecoming – here named 'pain.' Heidegger explains,

> Pain rends. It is the rift. But it does not tear apart into dispersive fragments. Pain indeed tears asunder, it separates, yet so that it draws everything to itself, gathers it to itself. Its rending, as a separating that gathers, is at the same time that drawing which, like the pen drawing of a plan or sketch, draws and joins together what is held apart in separation. Pain is the joining … in the rending that divides and gathers. Pain is the joining of the rift. The joining is the threshold. It settles the between, the middle of the two that are separated in it. Pain joins the rift of the difference. Pain is the dif-ference itself.
>
> Pain has turned the threshold to stone.
>
> The verse calls the dif-ference, but it neither thinks it specifically nor does it call its nature by this name. The verse calls the separation of the between, the gathering middle, in whose intimacy the bearing of things and the granting of world pervade one another.
>
> Then would the intimacy of the dif-ference for world and thing be pain? Certainly. (La 204–5)

Once again, we come back to the home at which we have arrived before. We now become a bit more at home. We will return later to take up the dif-ference of world and thing and the giving of home. For now, it suffices to see that in its wandering into its mortal manner of abiding on the earth as earth, the soul becomes at home in itself and on the earth, insofar as it enters and begins to dwell in what is named 'pain,' which is itself sheltered by the earth.

Trakl's 'Thunderstorm' says,

> O pain, thou flaming vision
> Of the great soul! (cited in LP 181)

Heidegger elaborates the connection between our essential wandering and pain: 'The soul's greatness takes its measure from its capacity to achieve the flaming vision by which the soul becomes at home in pain' (LP 180). The soul can become at home in pain because, as we have seen, pain rends apart, making an opening for a joining and gathering. And as flaming vision, pain rejoins what is beheld, which specifies its 'power to disclose and convey' (LP 181). 'Pain' thus names what is ownmost to what is alive, to what becomes capable of death, to what might become at home. Heidegger continues, 'Only a being that lives soulfully can fulfil the sending of its nature. By virtue of this power it is fit to join in that harmony of mutual bearing by which all living things belong together. In keeping with this relation of fitness, everything that lives is of it, that is to say, good. But the good is good painfully' (LP 181; see also 183).

This painful character belongs together with disclosure because 'the living can give sheltering concealment to their present fellow beings and thus reveal them in their given nature, let them truly be what they are' (LP 181). That is also why soul and rock are called together by the poet in saying 'pain': mortals and earth are inseparably disclosed together into what is their ownmost. Trakl says, 'And softly touches you an ancient stone' (cited in LP 182). Pain, concealed in earth and mortals, is the site for their homecoming – for their disclosure 'out of concealed primal earthliness,' into their proper manner of abiding and mutual belonging (LP 183). Such pain is in harmony with what Trakl calls the 'blue.' In Heidegger's interpretation,

> The nature of pain, its concealed relation to the blue, is put into words in the last stanza of a poem called 'Transfiguration':
>
> Blue flower,
> That softly sounds in withered stone.
>
> The words sing of the wellspring from which Trakl's poetry wells up. (LP 183–4)

The wandering of the soul into and through pain is a wandering 'toward the blue.' The soul moves with gaze fixed 'ahead into the blue of night which holds' an earlier stillness – all this in the site where we become at home (LP 188). This movement toward the blue is critical to the soul, which is why the wandering mortals, on the way to what is their ownmost, are called 'blue game' (LP 167).

In blueness, whether of flower or sky (twilight dusk and even night, called a 'corn flower sheaf') or mortal, the holy is gathered and disclosed. Heidegger explains, 'The holy shines out of blueness, even while veiling itself in the dark of that blueness. The holy withholds itself in its withholding withdrawal. Clarity sheltered in the dark is blueness' (LP 165). And, 'For the blue shines upon the soul's face by withdrawing into its own depth. Whenever it is present, the holy endures only by keeping within this withdrawal, and by turning vision toward the fitting' (LP 183). But for Trakl, according to Heidegger, 'Blue is not an image to indicate the sense of the holy. Blueness itself is the holy, in virtue of its gathering depth which shines forth only as it veils itself' (LP 166).

The poet's and thinker's words indicate an intensification of becoming at home: mortals and earth are gathered together, as are the blue heavens and the holy (note, here, not the divinities). All this gathering takes place in the site of apartness and homecoming: pain. It remains to keep placing ourselves in this site and to heed it, as the place where that to which we come is kept. Consider the scene articulated by the poets' and Heidegger's sayings: concretely we encounter earth, flower, cornflower, rock, stone, forest, hill, pond (that is, earth); twilight dusk, ghostly night, the wind of the holy, God's wind, black cloud, 'the nighting pond, the starry sky,' the moon's cool light (heavens), mortal animal (mortals), the blue-holy (the holy) (LP 168–9).[3] Not surprisingly, in this concrete saying we seem to hear the coming-gathering of earth, heavens, mortals and the holy.

Two further characteristics of this scene are striking. The home 'scene' articulated here – in and by which we ourselves can become more and more nearly at home – is noticeably religious in tone.[4] To name it 'religious' is not to assume that 'the religious' is the same as 'the holy' or 'the divine/divinities,' since only the latter two are named in versions of the fourfold. Intended as something of a 'neutral' descriptive term, not implying any denominational religion, but rather a reverential tone in regard to the sacred, the meanings of 'religious' need to be filled in by what is said in the poems and essays, so that hopefully its use may be a step in questioning the relation of divinities and the holy. Nor would stressing the blue-holy by describing the scene's overall tone as 'religious' indicate that the other three of the foursome are swallowed in the blue-holy atmosphere. Simply, the mood of the blue-holy does pervade the striking scene. We cannot ignore such a striking constellation of elements and meanings. Heidegger explicitly treats Trakl's religious language (of which more will be said later); Heidegger himself speaks this way (LP 192–3). As does Hölderlin. In commenting on Trakl's 'A Winter Evening,' Heidegger elaborates what bears on 'the human homestead': the ringing of the vesper bell, how 'the houses of the many and the tables of their daily meals have become house of God and altar,' the tree of graces which roots in earth and 'opens itself to heaven's blessing,' where 'its sound blossoming harbors the fruit that falls to us unearned – holy, saving, loving toward mortals' (La 196; LP 201). For Trakl, 'God's speaking is the speaking which assigns to man a stiller nature, and so calls on him to give up that repose by which man rises from what is authentic ruin up into earliness' (LP 196). This homecoming gathering is religiously said. Further, in such naming of things world is gathered.

It is crucial here not to think by way of representational concepts, metaphysical categories, and logical exclusions. In the articulated scene, the dark (as in 'the dark night of the world's essential sway under metaphysical rule') is specifically said not to be identical with decay or gloom. As noted, the blue conceals itself in the dark and comes from the dark, disclosing itself (see LP 165, 183). And not only the holy comes out of the world's dark, but all the fourfold – world itself – lightens into dawning (blueness). *Clearly, Heidegger is moving more deeply into – becoming more at home in – the saying and thinking of becoming at home in the gathering of the fourfold.* Originary becoming at home takes place in the apartness in which the poets and Heidegger move. That is why apartness cannot be understood metaphysically any more than pain can be understood anthropologically. Apartness is neither a psychological nor a physical state of human being. Apartness is spiritual, but it is not 'of the spirit' in the sense of the language of metaphysics (LP 179). Rather, it is the 'gathering power,' in which mortals are newly born in a to-and-fro movement to bear their essence. It 'carries mortal nature back to its stiller childhood' and shelters that coming nature formed 'in the earliness of another beginning.' The story of homecoming has become one of the gathering that carries mortals home, where the place and dynamic of the homecoming are named not only as 'belonging together' but also as 'apartness.' 'As a gathering, apartness is in the nature of a site' (LP 185).

Where has following the story of mortals' still-wandering in apartness brought us? Heidegger answers, 'To the place where everything has come together in another way, where everything is sheltered and preserved for another ascent' (LP 172). In this site is kept the homecoming we are attempting to achieve. Our staying wandering in the world's dark night, the world's lighting dawn, even saying and thing, belong to apartness. 'All these are gathered up into apartness, not afterward but such that apartness unfolds within their already established gathering' (LP 177).

In saying apartness, Trakl, Hölderlin, and Heidegger sound alike. This belonging together in the manner of saying is related to their belonging together as poets and thinkers. But their relationship, according to Heidegger, points to a prior substantive issue: 'Is apartness at all and intrinsically related to poetry? Even if such a relation exists, how is apartness to gather poetic saying to itself, to become its site, and to determine it from there?' (LP 186). Travelling through apartness, the stranger departs from the unfinished form of human being hitherto and moves toward what is essential for mortals. In the poet's words, the stranger goes under or dies. Close by him, following his footsteps, comes one who listens and sings his going in apartness. Heidegger explains, 'A friend listens after the stranger. In listening, he follows the departed and thus becomes himself a wanderer, a stranger. The friend's soul listens after the dead. The friend's face has "died away." It listens by singing of death. This is why the singing voice is "the birdvoice of the deathlike" ("The Wanderers"). It corresponds to the stranger's death, his going under to the blue of night' (LP 186–7).

The one who follows, singing after his friend, is the poet. Speaking of George and Hölderlin, Heidegger says, 'in the singing the song begins to be a song. The song's poet is the singer. Poetry is song' (NL 77). Like the ancients, Heidegger thinks of poetry and song, the advent of gods and mortals, as belonging together. 'Song is not the opposite of discourse, but rather the most intimate kinship with it; for song, too, is language' (NL 78). Specifically the poet celebrates what he sings: 'Pondering, framing, loving is saying: a quiet, exuberant bow, a jubilant homage, a eulogy, a praise: *language. Laudes* is the Latin name for songs. To recite song is: to sing. Singing is the gathering of saying in song' (W 48). And, 'Rhythm, *rhusmos,* does not mean flux and flowing, but rather form. Rhythm is what is at rest, what forms the movement of dance and song, and thus lets it rest within itself. Rhythm bestows rest' (W 149).

In these words we hear what the poet does, who travels in apartness. Following the poet's friend, the poet both becomes a stranger and bestows rest in singing, praising. The poet lets wandering in apartness be kept in apartness. Thus, Heidegger says,

> To sing means to praise and to guard the object of praise in song. The listening friend is one of the 'praising shepherds.' Yet the friend's soul ... can give echo to the song of the departed only when that apartness rings out toward him who follows, when the music of apartness resounds, 'when,' as it says in 'Evensong,' 'dark music haunts the soul' ... The friend's invitation to conversation (in 'To One Who Died Young') reflects the haunting music of the stranger's steps. The friend's saying is the singing journey down by the stream ... In such conversation the singing friend gazes upon the departed. By his gaze, in the converse look, he becomes brother to the stranger. Journeying with the stranger, the brother reaches the stiller abode in earliness. (LP 187)

That is, in this following-singing, the poet has a homecoming as poet and friend, and comes to where the poet must dwell and to the poet's essence as poetic friend. 'Listening after the departed, the friend sings his song and thus becomes his brother; only now, as the stranger's brother, does he also become the brother of the stranger's sister' (LP 188).

Here we see how poetry belongs to apartness: 'Apartness is the poem's site because the music of the stranger's ringing-radiant footfall inflames his follower's dark wandering into listening song' (La 188). Here, too, precisely in the poet's singing, the holy, earth, and mortals come together in apartness.

> Thus the nature of apartness is perfected. It is the perfect site of the poetic work only when, being both the gathering of the stiller childhood and the stranger's grave, it gathers to itself also those who follow him who died early, by listening after him and carrying the music of his path over into the sounds of the spoken language, so that they become men apart. Their song is poetry. How so? What is the poet's work?
>
> The poet's work means: to say after – to say again the music of the spirit of apartness that has been spoken to the poet. For the longest time – before it comes to be said, that is, spoken – the poet's work is only a listening. Apartness first gathers the listening into its music, so that this music may ring through the spoken saying in which it will resound. The lunar coolness of the ghostly night's holy blue rings and shines through all such gazing and saying. Its language becomes a saying – after, it becomes: poetry. Poetry's spoken words shelter the poetic statement as that which by its essential nature remains unspoken. In this manner, the saying-after ... becomes 'more pious,' that is to say, more pliable to the promptings of the path on which the stranger walks ahead. (LP 188)

Trakl's poetry has its own belonging (both the belonging together of the poems and their belonging to their subject matter) in that they stay wandering in apartness – which is precisely the site where the poet belongs. Only while wandering in apartness can he make his *own* 'return' home 'into the primal earliness' (LP 190). This placement empowers the poems and poet: 'In the moving radiance that shines from the site of the poem surges the billow which starts the poetic vision on its way to language' (LP 191). Trakl's language, speaking of what it leaves behind as well as where it arrives in its journey, and of the journeying itself, is the language of and out of homecoming. Heidegger comments,

> The language of the poetry whose site is in apartness answers to the homecoming of unborn mankind into the quiet beginning of its stiller nature.
>
> The language that this poetry speaks stems from this transition. Its path leads from the downfall of all that decays over to the descent into the twilight blue of the holy. The language that the work speaks stems from the

> passage across and through the ghostly night's nocturnal pond. This language sings the song of home-coming in apartness, the homecoming which from the lateness of decomposition comes to rest in the earliness of the stiller, and still impending, beginning. In this language there speaks the journey whose shining causes the radiant, ringing music of the departed stranger's ghostly years to come forth ... [Here] sings 'the beauty of a homecoming generation.' (LP 191)

The poetizing homecoming journey occurs in apartness. The homecoming is a homecoming to the wandering in apartness, to the staying there. But it also opens the promise of a dwelling, that is, of a becoming at home where one has arrived. Those wanderers who follow the stranger's path in apartness do so, Heidegger holds, 'in order that they may "dwell in its animate blue."' In his explication of Trakl's 'Autumn Soul,' Heidegger adds, 'An open region that holds the promise of a dwelling, and provides a dwelling, is what we call a "land" ... The location of the site that gathers Trakl's work into itself is the concealed nature of apartness and is called "Evening Land," the Occident' (LP 195). The evening land concealed in apartness is not going down, it stays and ... awaits those who will dwell in it. The land of descent is the transition into the beginning of the dawn concealed within it' (LP 194).

The poet's talk of going under is not talk of decay, then, but talk of a transformation of the sending of the West. (Recall, the world's light was said to be concealed in its dark night.) Thus, Heidegger says that Trakl's 'poetic work is historical in the highest sense. *His poetry sings of the sending which casts mankind in its still withheld nature – that is to say, saves mankind*' (LP 197). To sing of homecoming in such a manner is in no way backward-looking, though it surely would appear so in our technological age. Really, it is the clear insight of one 'who sees and senses other things than the reporters of the latest news' and for whom the 'future' remains 'without the advent of a sending which concerns man for once at the source of his being' (LP 196–7). Perhaps surprisingly, a prime site is newly disclosed. Earlier it appeared that apartness was the site and that in apartness occurred the homecoming of which Trakl and Heidegger speak. But it now appears that this apartness itself belongs to and is concealed in the homelessness and homecoming that is the sending of the *West* and our proper *homecoming*. Thus the apartness and homecoming which Trakl portrays are the same as the homelessness and homecoming which Heidegger has been thinking all along.

This insight moves us beyond the relation between poetry and apartness to one of thinking and apartness, and thence back to the relation of poetry and thinking. Heidegger is clear that we should distinguish the stranger of the poetry of apartness (called 'Elis') from the poet's own self (LP 174). Still, as we have seen, the poet too, insofar as listening to and following the stranger, becomes a wanderer and stranger, now friend and sibling to the stranger. And there are others who become strangers, thereby becoming at home in their own manner of abiding. For example, Heidegger notes that 'the name "blue game" names mortals who would think of the stranger and wander with him to the native home of human being' (LP 167). Though it may seem bold to say so, it is equally clear that Heidegger means to name the thinkers as well as the poets among those mortals who become wanderers. We have already heard how the same site of apartness is that of wandering and homecoming for both poet and thinker. Further, the thinker listens to the poet and echoes what the thinker hears in the poet's own saying.

What Heidegger tells us about the relation of poets and thinkers is not an abstract classification, but an indication of his own relationship with the poets, about his story of what is ownmost to homecoming, and about the story of his own homecoming. Heidegger's words are reflexive. Transitively, Heidegger himself is a friend who listens after the stranger, follows the stranger in apartness, becomes himself a wanderer and stranger, says and thereby guards the apartness and wandering. Heidegger is one of the 'listening shepherds,' whose own saying, too, becomes pious (as briefly noted earlier) as it says-after (echoes) the homelessness and homecoming that the poet hears and says. *In his own homecoming, which is underway here insofar as he does follow along, Heidegger becomes at home, as a fellow wanderer, in apartness and the promise of a dwelling in the sending of the West.* Insofar as Heidegger hears the poets, he can say-after, that is, find the words to say (which means accomplish) his own homecoming and beginning to become at home (see NL 86). Here his thinking *does* move in the neighbourhood of poetry, even more intimately than might be expected. It moves where the neighbours are brothers and sisters, where they say the same (see NL 91).

Here, too, Heidegger's powerful thinking and saying, like Trakl's, is no mere 'dreamy romanticism,' as critics such as Derrida contend (still bound to subjectivistic-'enframed' thinking, however sophisticatedly at the end of post-Nietzschean metaphysics and nihilism). The homecoming that concerns Heidegger and the poets is no nostalgic return to what once was, nor to a primal bliss with being. Rather, it is the painful wandering, that is, the journey through apartness to the dwelling in the home that is just beginning to become home. Thus, the words which end Heidegger's essay 'Language in the Poem' apply not just to Trakl, but to Heidegger himself and to our homecoming too: 'There follows the rising of the song into the pure echo of the music of the ghostly years, through which the stranger wanders, the years which the brother follows who begins dwelling in the land of evening' (LP 198).

Heidegger's originary thinking of becoming at home and beginning to dwell near the source of our nature has come a long way since his early Hölderlin essays. Still, because Hölderlin remains a poet who says homecoming, he needs to be thought, not just once, but continually throughout our journey. Hence, Heidegger stays neighbour to Hölderlin, still attempting to think what the poet says. And now that Heidegger is well into his own homecoming, he is more fully able to do so.

Hölderlin, Heidegger contends in his 1960 essay, 'Hölderlin's Erde und Himmel,' has achieved his homecoming and yet in his poetry continues to remember wandering and the ways of wandering. Hölderlin thinks, as would Trakl later, the ways toward earth as earth, which means toward earth as the place for mortals, related to heavens and god. The wanderer of Hölderlin's poems is the poet's own self, who first wanders, then arrives, and later still, after reaching home, recollects (*andenkt*) these wandering ways. The poet's ways do not end at a moment of arrival home, but rest in song as still calling us (HEH 164). *Andenken* remains underway, becoming at home. For our part, it remains to think the place and ways which the poet preserved and kept safe in the poet's journeys and poetic memory and the places and ways the poet dwelt after travelling, which are especially vital to our learning-abiding, that is, to becoming at home (HEH 159).

This accomplishment and recollection by Hölderlin would make him the great poet of homelessness, homecoming, dwelling, and the continual homecoming that is the learning to become at home and, perhaps eventually, dwelling near the source. His own successful homecoming could help take us beyond perennial wandering. The wanderer-poet can thus say,

> Sweet it is, then, under the lofty shade of trees
> and hills to dwell, where the path is
> paved to church. (cited in HEH 165)

Hölderlin remains important because he says the dwelling which must be learnt: without forgetting the journeying, he poetizes concerning the ground in which mortals can be rooted and which bears them (*der Boden, der tragende Grund – Abgrund*) (G 190).

Clearly, Hölderlin says the same as Trakl – recall for example Trakl's movement from apartness, apartness' gathering of mortals to earth and the region of the promise of dwelling, and the same pious manner of saying. To learn dwelling, Heidegger must still think by way of Hölderlin's poetry. Further, according to Heidegger, other poets who listen to their wandering and homecoming brothers also follow Hölderlin. Heidegger says that Hölderlin's poems, first published from the manuscripts in 1910 and 1914, 'hit us students like an earthquake,' and adds that Hölderlin's work inspired not only Heidegger himself, but Rilke and George (NL 79). Rilke (as we saw earlier with 'What Are Poets For?') goes one way, Stephan George goes another, more nearby to Heidegger's path. For example, George's poem, 'Words,' according to Heidegger, 'forces us to the unrest of thought' (W 141). Here the poet has learned to renounce the poet's own self as the supposed (subjectivistic) source of power and meaning. As a result, George moves forward on his own journey as a poet. Heidegger adds, 'To learn means: to become knowing. In Latin, knowing is *qui vidit*, one who has seen, has caught sight of something, and who never again loses sight of what he has caught sight of. To learn means to attain to such seeing. To this belongs our reaching it; namely on the way, on a journey. To put oneself on a journey, to experience, means to learn' (W 143).

The lesson also applies to our learning to be at home. We hope to journey to and experience home – to become at home. Accordingly, Heidegger inquires into how the poet has learned, on what journeys the insight occurs, and through what land the poet's travels lead. The answer, not surprisingly, is that the poet speaks of journeys in the poet's own land. The poet, in poems, says how these 'journeys attain to that place where his claim finds the required fulfilment. This happens at his country's strand. The strand bounds, it arrests, limits and circumscribes the poet's secure sojourn' (W 144–5). In poems the poet comes there, to the source of words, learning there that the poetry does not control them as names for objects (W 147). The poem bears witness to the arrival into mystery – including, before all, the mysterious relation of word and thing – to which we will return later. In short, still in the company of the poets Hölderlin, Trakl, and George, the thinker must cross the same country. Insofar as Heidegger as thinker is successful, he manages to journey and become at home by thinking and saying our belonging (within thinking and saying) to the fourfold world. This much he has learned: becoming at home and beginning to dwell there is neither passive nor inert.

Rather, it is as complex and subtle a journey as any phase thus far undertaken.

In the moment of arrival (treated in chapter 4), Heidegger discovered that our home is in the fourfold to which we belong. We are gathered into world by thing. Such gathering-giving also seems to occur in the sway of saying which appropriates. In taking up the poets again to learn to become at home and to dwell there, with Trakl Heidegger comes to see apartness as the site of becoming human on the earth and, especially with Hölderlin, to see more of what it is to dwell on the earth, under heaven, and with god. What is required is to undergo the experience and interpretation of home so that we are transformed from travellers and immigrants 'on the outside' as it were, to those who genuinely dwell there(in). The works treated in this chapter are 'intended to bring us face to face with a possibility of undergoing an experience ... To undergo an experience with something – be it a thing, a person, or a god – means that this something befalls us, strikes us, comes over us, overwhelms and transforms us' (NL 57). If 'experience means *eundo assequi*, to obtain something along the way, to attain something by going on a way,' what we hope to reach is the abiding at home, in the source of home (NL 66). After gaining arrival, this remains our calling. Of course, Heidegger has already spoken of the fourfold within which we are gathered in our homecoming. But we as yet are not intimate with and in this realm. We are just beginning to learn to think about becoming mortals, which also means about what is ownmost to earth, heavens, divinities, and our belonging to them. The poets can instruct us in such matters.

We become at home on the earth only by letting the earth be earth; and earth is let alone as earth only when it is let come into its own relation with the rest of the fourfold. Earth lies beneath the sky. Thus, we could become at home on earth and beneath the heavens (PMD 220–1, 223). Here we also find the divine, which is manifested by gods. The gods, in turn, according to Hölderlin, appear through the manifestation of the sky, by concealing themselves behind it – and by thus showing themselves as concealed and by staying that way (PMD 222–3). For Hölderlin, then, 'God's *manifestness* – not only he himself – is mysterious' (PMD 222). In Hölderlin's late poem, 'In Lovely Blueness,' he says,

> What is God? Unknown, yet
> Full of his qualities is the
> Face of the sky. For the lightnings
> Are the wrath of a god. The more something
> Is invisible, the more it yields to what's alien. (cited in PMD 225)

Heidegger comments, 'What remains alien to the god, the sight of the sky – this is what is familiar to man. And what is that? Everything that shimmers and blooms in the sky and thus under the sky and thus on earth, everything that sounds and is fragrant, rises and comes – but also everything that goes and stumbles, moans and falls silent, pales and darkens' (PMD 225). In the blue, or 'behind it,' the gods stay concealed even as they join themselves to and bring themselves into the foreign (HEH 19). In contrast to the immortal gods, humans are mortal in nature (HEH 156). Yet, unlike the animals of the earth, which perish, only mortals 'can experience death as death.' And only we speak. Thus, 'the essential relation between death and language flashes up before us, but remains still unthought' (NL 107).

It is precisely the relations within this fourfold and its relation to language that the poet says. In singing, the poet holds them for us to thoughtfully experience. But neither the poet nor we have any of this for our own sake. Rather, what it gives to us all belongs to the holy figure (*Bilde*) which we help delineate (*bilden*) (HEH 158). In Hölderlin's poem of the wanderer's ways that ends as, and remains as, a poem of dwelling ('Greece'), he meditates on the belonging together of the fourfold. Relation is a poor word for this belonging, because it suggests the connection of entities with prior existence and fixed features.[5] In contrast, thought originarily relation (*Verhältnis*) means the enjoining in which the four become themselves, the proportion of all and each in the whole figuration and interplay, the belonging of appropriation. Heidegger thinks heaven *and* earth, mortals *and* immortals. But the *and* only weakly says the relation. In fact, each of the four, and all together, belong in a richer relation (*in ein reicheres Verhältnis*) which is the belonging together of the fourfold (HEH 156, 162, 170, 175, 178).

The relation-belonging itself needs to be thought. But first, each of the four must be allowed to become itself if there is to be a fourfold gathering into which mortals can come as mortals and there become at home. With the Greeks, Hölderlin thought of Nature (*die Natur, physis*) in the language of particular home places (as *die heimatliche Natur*) and regions (*Gegend*), that is, as the giving given to both mortals and gods, in and out of which both could live (HEH 158, 161, 180). Mortal living, of course, takes place on earth, but the earth has many holy places too, where the gods manifest themselves and the poet would dwell and be given dwelling (by earth and gods). In such cases and places, earth is let become earth (HEH 161).

According to Heidegger, Hölderlin speaks of the four and their richer belonging in the language of voice and saying-sounding. The heavens and earth, god and humans/mortals (*here* he says '*der Gott,*' not the divine, and '*der Mensch*' and '*die Sterblichen*') are, each in its own way, voices (*Stimmen*) which say/sing/sound, ring out (*tönt*) the sending (*Geschick/ Geschik*) which sends; they are the voices of sending (HEH 163, 165).[6] In the gathering of the four is voiced the fate of the entire ever-coming (*unendliche*) belonging. None of the four comes without the others. Thus, together they move, making their own music, to which they dance (HEH 170). The sending of the four is gathered in the four voices, which say (that is give) themselves together. Here we become at home as God nears, as earth and heavens near, as we as mortals near (G 186). The fourfold voices the nearness.

The gathering fourfold which voices homecoming is also gathered and given by things. Things give world to us mortals. They bear upon us as things, according to Heidegger, as they bear world to us. He says,

> The snowfall brings men under the sky that is darkening into night. The tolling of the evening bell brings them, as mortals, before the divine. House and table join mortals to earth. The things that were named (in the poem), thus called, gather to themselves sky and earth, mortals and divinities. The four are united primarily in being toward one another, a fourfold. The things let the fourfold of the four stay with them. This gathering, assembling, letting-stay is the thinging of things. The unitary fourfold of sky and earth, mortals and divinities, which is stayed in the thinging of things, we call – the world ... Thinging, they unfold world, in which things abide and so are the abiding ones. By abiding, things carry out world. Our old language calls such carrying *bern, bären* – Old High German *beran* – to bear; hence the words *gebaren,* to carry, gestate, give birth, and *Gebärde,* bearing, gesture. Thinging, things are things. Thinging, they gesture – gestate – world ... Things be-thing – i.e. condition – mortals. This now means: things, each in its time, literally visit mortals with a world. (La 199–200)

Further, in a mutual dynamic, 'the world grants to things their presence. Things bear world. world grants things' (La 202). We become at home insofar as we belong with things, things that along with us, abide in the very world they gather together and into which we are gathered.

Within *Ereignis,* mortals begin to find their proper place. The poet is one who has travelled here, into this within, into the midst of the gathering fourfold. And what the poet finds in the midst helps us to understand the place and the giving that we would call home. According to the poets, mortals dwell in-between: between the alien and familiar, between the far and near, between the height and depth. For example, Hölderlin says that mortals, dwelling on this earth, also look up to the sky, that they may seek the divine. Heidegger comments, 'The upward glance passes aloft toward the sky, and yet it remains below on the earth. The upward glance spans the between of the sky and earth. This between is measured out for the dwelling of man. We now call the span thus meted out the dimension. The dimension does not arise from the fact that sky and earth are turned toward one another. Rather, their facing each other depends on the dimension. Nor is the dimension a stretch of space as ordinarily understood; for everything spatial, as something for which space is made, is already in need of the dimension, that is, that into which it is admitted' (PMD 220). Moving within our questioning, 'We fall upward, to a height. Its loftiness opens up a depth. The two span a realm in which we would like to become at home, so as to find a residence, a dwelling place for the life of man' (La 191–2). Thus, mortals become at home in the spanning of the between. Here we pass 'beyond' the fourfold to the giving of the fourfold. That is, we arrive at what the fourfold itself depends upon, and what it essentially is. The between, however, is not a 'fifth' to be added to the fourfold; rather, it is the giving-site which gathers the fourfold, which *is* the gathering of the fourfold.

Saying Gives a Place: The Taking Place of Dif-ference

The between where world gathers is not simply the difference of earth and heavens, or of mortals and the divine, but also of world itself and thing. Only when there is a difference can there also be a gathering. The poets already have named the difference 'pain' and 'site': a holding-apart allowing and keeping a gathering together always coming. The between comes to be understood as difference. We heard above how things bear and keep world and how world gives the coming and staying of things. World and things then do not lie next to one another as objects might be conceived to do; nor are they yoked together, as two pre-existent beings might be. Instead, they arrive together, in the spanning of the between or difference. Heidegger explains,

> They penetrate each other. Thus the two traverse a middle. In it, they are at one. Thus at one they are intimate. The middle of the two is intimacy – in Latin, *inter*. The corresponding German word is *unter*, the English *inter*. The intimacy of world and thing is not a fusion. Intimacy obtains only where the

> intimate – world and thing – divides itself cleanly and remains separated. In the midst of the two, in the between of world and thing, in their inter, division prevails: a dif-ference [*Der Unter-Schied*].
>
> The intimacy of world and thing is present in the separation of the between; it is present in the dif-ference. The word dif-ference is now removed from its usual and customary usage. What it now names is not a generic concept for various kinds of differences. It exits only as this simple difference. It is unique. Of itself, it holds apart the middle in and through which world and things are at one with each other. The intimacy of the difference is the unifying element, the carrying out that carries through. The dif-ference carries out world in its worlding, carries out things in their thinging. Thus carrying them out, it carries them toward one another. The dif-ference does not mediate after the fact by connecting world and things through a middle added to them. Being the middle, it first determines world and things in their presence, i.e., in their being toward one another, whose unity it carries out. (La 202)

If we hear what this says we advance in becoming at home. Arriving at the home shore, Heidegger said that we came home into the *Ereignis* of fourfold. It seemed then that we would be at home in the middle of the four. But now we see that saying so only begins to give an inkling of what it would be to abide in the fourfold. It is not just that as mortals we belong with the divine, earth, and sky. We start to understand *Ereignis* and thing and the site of our dwelling when we hear of and attend to the giving and holding of the *middle* that remains foreign so long as we do not explicitly heed it. Insofar as the middle bears home to and for us, we still, of course, can become at home in the world; but now we can begin to see that *we become at home in the giving dif-ference* – and seeing this is a movement of becoming at home there.

Accordingly, meditating on what Hölderlin says of heaven and earth, Heidegger dwells not only on the richer belonging of the fourfold, but also on the middle (*die Mitt*). In an untitled poem (subsequently, and unhelpfully, titled 'The Vatican'), Hölderlin says, 'truly/entire relation, including the middle [*wirklich Ganzem Verhältniß, samt der Mitt*]' (cited in HEH 163).

The middle, too, must be included because it maintains the belonging and is needed in our contemporary homeless, technological epoch (HEH 163, 78–9). Recall that Heidegger spoke of earth, heavens, God, and mortals as the voice of sending. What is sent here in the sending is the entire belonging, which in the singing gathers itself. Here sending and the middle are the same. 'It sends' is the middle for it middles – brings and holds together – the four in their belonging together, in their fateful coming (HEH 171, 179). Heidegger says, 'Destiny brings home [*holt ein*] the four to itself in its middle, takes them into its safe keeping, sets (originates) them into intimacy' (HEH 171). The middle is disclosed as the all-gathering beginning, origination, setting-out (*An-fang*). 'The middle is, as the great sounding sending (destiny), the great origin,' which always keeps coming, which remains arriving (HEH 171).

Of course, as should be clear by now, what is said here must be understood originarily. As the originary gathering, middle first gives and maintains the gathering of world and thing – into their own. Heidegger says, 'The difference for world and thing *disclosingly appropriates* things into bearing a world; it *disclosingly appropriates* world into the gathering of things' (La 202–3). It is in this appropriating that we find our proper place in the between, for here it is given. Heidegger explains difference as itself 'neither distinction nor relation,' but as what originally allows world and thing to be held apart and together, 'The dif-ference is at most, dimension for world and thing. But in this case "dimension" also no longer means a precinct already present independently in which this or that comes to settle. The dif-ference is *the* dimension, insofar as it measures out, apportions, world and thing, each to its own. Its allotment of them first opens up the separateness and towardness of world and thing. Such an opening up is the way in which the dif-ference spans the two. The dif-ference, as the middle for world and things, metes out the measure of their presence' (La 203). We can become at home in dif-ference because it grants us a home by measuring us. This measuring is the taking and placing of us according to our measure in relation to sky, earth, and the divine. Here the place for our dwelling is measured out. Heidegger thus says, 'The nature of the dimension is the meting out – which is lighted and so can be spanned – of the between: the upward to the sky as well as the downward to earth' (PMD 220).

We take part in the measuring, but we do not provide the measure (see PMD 223). In fact, for Hölderlin and Heidegger, it is by taking the measure that we span the between and come to dwell in it. Becoming at home involves our own learning to measure properly. Heidegger elaborates as follows:

> According to Hölderlin's words, man spans the dimension by measuring himself against the heavenly. Man does not undertake this spanning just now and then; rather, man is man at all only in such spanning. This is why

> he can indeed block this spanning, trim it, and disfigure it, but he can never evade it. Man, as man, has always measured himself with and against something heavenly ... The godhead ['*der Gottheit*'] is the 'measure' with which man measures out his dwelling, his stay on the earth beneath the sky. Only insofar as man takes the measure of his dwelling in this way is he able to *be* commensurately with his nature. Man's dwelling depends on an upward-looking measure-taking of the dimension, in which the sky belongs just as much as the earth ... Measure-taking gauges the between, which brings the two, heaven and earth, to one another. (PMD 221)

We must learn to take the proper measure, then, in order to become at home in apartness (LP 186). *Measure-taking is crucial for homecoming*, 'Because only this measure gauges the very nature of man. For man dwells only by spanning the "on the earth" and the "beneath the sky." This "on" and "beneath" belong together. Their interplay is the span that man traverses at every moment as he *is* as an earthly being ... Because man *is*, in his enduring the dimension, his being must now and again be measured out. That requires a measure which involves at once the whole dimension in one' (PMD 223–34; see also 226).

It turns out that our dwelling is nothing static at all. Dwelling is no lapse into dormancy but a becoming at home as a constant homecoming, achieved by our continued travel, which traverses the dif-ference, that is, which properly measures the between, spanning earth and sky, our mortal nature and the divine. Heidegger comes, with this insight, to a deeper understanding of what and where home is, and to see that our homecoming necessarily involves travelling into what the poets call apartness, rift, pain, the separating-gathering, middle, dif-ference. His story thus returns us by way of dif-ference to what the poets say. Said by way of the house wherein we would dwell, dif-ference appears as the opening through which we would pass daily, by way of which we would have access to our dwelling. So thought, dif-ference would have to be seen as enabling-gathering into home. That is why, according to Heidegger, Trakl says that those who wander in apartness come to dwell by way of the middle that metes out the measure for world and things. This dif-ference, which carries out their intimacy and allows homecoming from the dark courses, is spoken in 'A Winter Evening' in the lines that we first heard above:

> Wanderer quietly steps within;
> Pain has turned the threshold to stone. (cited in La 195)

As Heidegger interprets these lines, they

> name something that persists and that has already persisted. It is only in turning to stone that the threshold presences at all.
>
> The threshold is the ground-beam that bears the doorway as a whole. It sustains the middle in which the two, the outside and the inside, penetrate each other. The threshold bears the between. What goes out and goes in, in the between, is joined in the between's dependability. The dependability of the middle must never yield either way. The settling of the between needs something that can endure, and is in this sense hard. The threshold, as the settlement of the between, is hard because pain has petrified it. (La 204; see also W 153)

How that homecoming comes about needs to be thought next in this learning to become at home in the homecoming into dif-ference. How does the dif-ference come – gathering? Heidegger says, somewhat surprisingly, that dif-ference calls: it calls world and thing together. 'In stilling things and world into their own, the dif-ference calls world and thing into the middle of their intimacy. The dif-ference is the bidder. The dif-ference gathers the two out of itself as it calls them into the rift that is the dif-ference itself. This gathering is the pealing (of the vesper bell in "A Winter Evening") ... The calling, gathered together with itself, which gathers to itself in the calling, is the pealing as the peal' (La 207). What this means is not yet clear. Still, it becomes apparent that the relationships, already set out, among our travelling through and out of apartness into dwelling, the poets and poetizing (that is, singing saying), and the bidding of world and thing in and by dif-ference, all belong together. It remains to think, How is the dif-ference related to language and poetry (and to things)? How does the dif-ference call, much less call fourfold and thing together, that we might be called home there?

Heidegger, following the poets, says that language bids thing and world 'to come to the between of the difference' (La 206). That is, as Heidegger has said before, language itself speaks. Its speaking is a showing and a giving, and it is in this between that language opens the sphere wherein we would learn to dwell. He has already arrived at such understanding (see chapter 4), but now he needs to think it through in order that he may begin to become at home in it. He remains underway to language, guided by the poets. 'The way allows us to reach what concerns us, in that domain where we are already staying. Why then, one may ask, still find a way to it? Answer: because where we already are, we are in such a way that at the same time we are not there, because we ourselves have not yet properly reached what concerns our being, nor even approached it. The way that lets us reach where we already are, differing from all other ways, calls for an account that runs far ahead' (NL 93). This is doubly so. Heidegger has yet to become at home where he has only just arrived; here the poets escort him. Mortals are not yet at home in language, even though they already move within it; here poetry is the mode of language that escorts.

Insofar as we are mortal, it is because we have language, that is, insofar as we can listen and speak. By speaking we are close to language. In these terms, to be mortal is already to be granted a place within language, where language enables our speech. We could not question anything, much less answer, unless we already belonged within this 'prior grant' (NL 58, 71). Language gives us our nature, and in its saying, also gives its own: '"To say," related to the Old Norse, "*saga*," means to show: to make appear, set free, that is, to offer and extend what we call world, lighting and concealing it. This lighting and hiding proffer of the world is the essential being of saying' (NL 93). Saying then gives as follows: saga is a grant (*saga*, saying; *Zusage*, grant). Thought by way of grant, language is a gift and giving. Thus, the poet George speaks of word in terms of prize and treasure in 'The Word.' Heidegger notes, 'We may recall that "prize" means a small and graceful gift intended for one's guest; or perhaps a present in token of special favor, which the recipient will henceforth carry on his person. "Prize," then, has to do with favor and with guest' (NL 79).

For the poet, however, who would be a guest in a strange land and return home with a prize, it is not simply that the word is a prize. As we have already seen, language calls world. Thus, while word is truly a gift, it, in turn, gives a greater treasure still. Ironically (and beyond dominant contemporary understandings of self and language) where world is lacking, the poet does not want to enter. But, precisely that realm is where he is called, and where he will come home into a world. Yet, world is not the only treasure. Thing too is given by language – according to George and as interpreted by Heidegger. They say, 'Only where the word for the thing has been found is the thing a thing. Only thus *is* it. Accordingly, we must stress as follows: no thing *is* where the word, that is, the name is lacking' (NL 62).

Understood originarily, this says nothing about metaphysical-linguistic idealism or the creative power of poetry and language. Rather, the poet must renounce just such an anthropocentric, or humanistic view. George and Heidegger simply say that word lets thing come into disclosure and bestows a relation to the thing upon us. Heidegger says, 'Stated more explicitly, the poet has experienced that only the word makes a thing appear as the thing it is, and thus lets it be present' (NL 65). Word also discloses itself here, as granting presence: in its own nature (essential being) as the giving of presencing (being) there occurs the being (essential nature) of language (NL 70, 72, 81). Here the poet successfully enters into the relation of word to thing, where the word itself grants and is the relation 'which retains the thing within itself' (NL 66). Moreover, in saying and thinking these things, which sound strange, Heidegger himself is following after the poet, through the foreign (NL 58). For the poet and Heidegger, there occurs 'releasement into the nearness of what is withdrawn but at the same time held in reserve for an originary event' (NL 66).

In learning to deny himself and to let the mystery of the word reign George says – according to Heidegger's explication of his poem – 'from now on may the word be: the bethinging of the thing. This "may there be" lets be the relation of word and thing, what and how it really is' (W 152). This holding himself back also is a homecoming because 'renunciation is an owning of self. Here is the abode of renunciation' (W 152). As a result, 'the word is also that possession with which the poet is trusted and entrusted as poet in an extraordinary way. The poet experiences his poetic call to the word as the source, the bourn of being' (NL 66). The word for word would truly be a prize. Yet, it could never be taken home to the poet's land, because at the heart of saying's nature, it withdraws into the farness of mystery, where the word, saying, belongs (NL 87). That is, in this new placement, the poet becomes attuned to mystery and must now must answer to it (NL 79 88; W 148). In this transformed relation to language, where the poet now listens to it, rather than pretending to master or create it, the poet becomes committed to the mystery and becomes thereby a poet: 'He has allowed himself – that is, such saying as will still be possible for him in the future – to be brought face to face with the word's mystery, the be-thinging of the thing in the word' (W 151).

As noted, in bethinging, word bestows presence (W 146). That is, the word itself is the relation of word and thing 'by holding everything forth into being, and there upholding it' (NL 73). Heidegger also attempts to become attuned and responsive to what he hears – *and lays out one of the most helpful glosses concerning what he finds in and does with 'es gibt'* (which usually is translated as 'it gives' or 'there is that which gives'):

> If our thinking does justice to the matter, then we may never say of the word that it is, but rather that it gives – not in the sense that words are given by an

> it, but that the word itself gives. The word itself is the giver. What does it give? To go by the poetic experience and by the most ancient tradition of thinking, the word gives being. Our thinking, then, would have to seek the word, the giver which itself is never given, in this 'there is that which gives' ... We do not mean 'There is the word' – we mean 'by virtue of the gift of the word there is, the word gives ...' The whole spook [*Spuk*] about the 'givenness' of things, which many people justly fear, is blown away. But what is memorable remains, indeed it only now comes to radiant light. (NL 88)

As saga, saying, the word gives. Word moves all things and brings thing and world near to one another (NL 95). Further, if we listen, saying thus announces itself to the poets and speaks in their verses (NL 99). For example, in Hölderlin's poems, 'once again the word appears in the region [*Gegend*], the region that determines earth and sky to be world regions, as it makes earth and sky, the streaming of the deep and the might of the heights, encounter one another' (NL 100 [206]).

The dwelling place where we attempt to abide would be the nearness of the fourfold gathering together in dif-ference. In their nearing, we come home. Nearness brings about this belonging. 'But,' Heidegger asks, 'What does nearness mean?' (NL 101). He answers, 'The movement at the core of the world's four regions [*der Gegenden des Weltgeviertes*], which makes them reach one another and holds them in the nearness of their distance, is nearness itself. This movement is what paves the way for being face to face. We shall call nearness in respect of this its movement "nighness" ... The persisting nature of nearness is not the interstice, but the movement paving the way for the face-to-face of the regions of the world's fourfold. This movement is nearness in the nature of nighness' (NL 104 [211]). By thinking of all belonging as representational relation, for example, calculative thinking thinks nearness as mere lack of distance and thus refuses nearness and makes 'a desert of the encounter of the world's fourfold' (NL 105). Alternatively, thought originarily, nearness is appropriation.

Further, saying is a moving of the fourfold. That is why it is called a showing: it shows the four into their mutual belonging and disclosure/concealment (NL 93). But if nearing is this motion of the fourfold, then nearing and saying are the same (NL 94–5). Heidegger elaborates,

> Anticipating, we defined saying. To say means to show, to make appear, the lighting-concealing-releasing offer of world. Now, nearness manifests itself as the motion in which the world's regions [*Weltgegenden*] face each other. ... here arises the possibility of seeing how saying, as the being of language,

> swings back into the presence of nearness. Quiet consideration makes possible an insight into how nearness and saying, being of the persisting nature of language, are the Same ... Language, saying of the world's fourfold [*Weltgeviertes*] ... is, as world moving saying, the relation of all relations. It relates, maintains, proffers, and enriches the face-to-face encounter of the world's regions [*Weltgegenden*], holds and keeps them, in that it holds itself – saying – in reserve. (NL 107 [214–15])

If, in its saying moving of world, saying holds itself back, it is, as it were, both saying and – as reserved – stillness. It keeps itself still in its saying of fourfold and thing. It also brings the fourfold and thing into mutual repose. It stills them. Thus all the saying moving is also a still stilling. It is the ringing of stillness (La 206–7; NL 107–8; see also 'The Thing' on ringing). In this peal of stillness, dif-ference holds: 'Thus stilled, thing and world never escape from the dif-ference. Rather, they rescue it in the stilling, where the dif-ference is itself the stillness' (La 207).

Heidegger finds that saying, thing, and world belong together as the first grants and calls the latter two. As the granting calling, language comes into its own; world and thing come to their own as bid into dif-ference. We, too, can be-come at home in what is ownmost to us and in this granting gathering. This bidding is the 'primal calling' and the 'authentic building.' We see the essential sway of language where saying bids by calling 'thing-world and world-thing to come to the between of the dif-ference. What is so bidden is commanded to arrive from out of the dif-ference into the dif-ference. Here we are thinking of the old sense of command, which we recognize still in the phrase, "Commit thy way unto the Lord." The bidding of language commits the bidden thus to the bidding of the dif-ference' (La 206).

Look where we have come. We began by attempting to become at home in the fourfold. We saw that with thing, world was appropriated. Yet according to Heidegger and the poets, such phenomena were not yet our genuine home, because even fourfold and thing are appropriated within the site named, dif-ference – the dimension of the gathering middle in which we are measured and can come home and begin to dwell. Thus, Heidegger said, 'the dif-ference calls world and thing into the middle of their intimacy. The dif-ference is the bidder' (La 207). Thinking how this is so, he thought language's still giving, where this means that saying calls near and lets presence thing and world. But as calling-giving, dif-ference and saying belong together: 'Language speaks in that the command of the dif-ference calls world and things into the simple onefold of their intimacy' (La 207). Saying, stilling, and dif-ference, then, belong together because they are the same. Heidegger says, 'The carrying out of world and thing in the manner of stilling is the appropriative taking place of the dif-ference. Language, the peal of stillness, is, inasmuch as the dif-ference takes place. Language goes on as the taking place or occurring of the dif-ference for world and things' (La 207). At this point, *we see how we primally come home: we become at home in saying as the occurring of the dif-ference for world and things. It is here that we find our measuring-homecoming into the primal articulation and assembly of home.*

Saying gives homecoming insofar as we become at home in saying. In its granting, language gives itself and all that follows from its coming into its ownmost. As Heidegger puts it, 'the occurrence of appropriation acts as that saying in which language grants its essential nature to us' (NL 90). In giving itself in its saying, saying gives us our mode of abiding as speaking mortals. It grants us to ourselves. 'Language speaks,' which means that '"it is language that first brings man about, brings him into existence." Understood in this way, man would be bespoken by language' (La 192). He adds, 'the structure of human speech can only be the manner [*melos*] in which the speaking of language, the peal of the stillness of difference, appropriates mortals by the command of the dif-ference' (La 209). The coming of dif-ference is said to be a stillness in which world and thing are held in repose. The peal of such stillness is not first of all, or even merely, human (La 207). Indeed, Heidegger says that the fourfold articulates the silent saying: earth, heavens, mortals, and divinities (sometimes, as we have seen, also gods or even God) and mortals, as we have heard, are all voices which sound the ever-coming belonging (HEH 170).

If we focus for the moment on the mortal voice, we hear that in its saying, language enables humans to speak in 'their *own way* in sounds' (La 208). Nevertheless, insofar as human being is brought into its own in its appropriation to the nature of language, it is, as speaker, used by the peal of stillness. More directly, 'Such an appropriating takes place in that the very *nature*, the *presencing*, of language *needs and uses* the speaking of mortals in order to sound as the peal of stillness for the hearing mortals' (La 208). *Again, we come home to ourselves, to our fuller nature and use: to voice or speak the still saying* (which also enables us to share-hear it and to dwell). Again, our dwelling and saying are gathered together.

We enter into our own homecoming and learn to become at home in saying – as the speakers of language – to the degree that we respond appropriately to disclosing appropriation and insofar as we answer the call into difference. First we listen to saying, then we respond by speaking. Heidegger says,

> Mortals speak insofar as they listen. They need the bidding call of the stillness of the dif-ference even when they do not know that call. Their listening draws from the command of the dif-ference what it brings out as sounding word. This speaking that listens and accepts is responding.
>
> Nevertheless by receiving what it says from the command of the dif-ference, mortal speech has already, in its own way, followed the call. Response, as receptive listening, is at the same time a recognition that makes due acknowledgement. Mortals speak by responding to language in a twofold way, receiving and replying. (La 209; see also *What Is Called Thinking?*)

Where do we authentically listen and speak? Where are we attuned to what calls? Perhaps not only in poetry, but if anywhere, at least in the authentic hearing and saying which the poet does, and which we call poetry.

If that would be so, then our becoming at home approaches the belonging of dwelling and saying, which now would be seen as the belonging of dwelling to saying and poetry, too. Heidegger says, 'Poetry and dwelling not only do not exclude each other; on the contrary, poetry and dwelling belong together, each calling for the other' (PMD 227). Again, the poets say something to help the thinker become at home here, just as they already have in their poetizing. For example, in one of Hölderlin's last works, he speaks and shares what he has experienced: 'poetically man dwells.' To say this is not to claim that we already dwell poetically, as proper hearers and sayers of what calls us. Rather, it is to say that somehow, even in our current, long unpoetic homelessness, we can be unpoetic and homeless only insofar as our homecoming and dwelling is, in essence, poetic. Only what can come home and dwell there can ever be homeless. No drop of water was ever homeless. Heidegger says, then, that 'the poetic is the basic capacity for human dwelling' (PMD 228). This is to say that essentially our becoming at home, as well as our dwelling there, depends on poetic hearing and saying (PMD 214). How so? To say 'poetically man dwells,' according to Heidegger, means that 'poetry first causes dwelling to be dwelling. Poetry is what really lets us dwell. But through what do we attain to a dwelling place? Through building. Poetic creation, which lets us dwell, is a kind of building' (PMD 215).

Since we have seen that we become at home in language, as the saying of dif-ference, that is, as the calling together of world and thing wherein we can dwell, then poetry somehow would have to build, or build on, the constellation. Poetry, according to Heidegger, builds because it gathers together and assembles what belongs together as dwelling. That is, poetry gathers earth, sky, mortals, and the divine. The poets name things in their poems: this 'naming call bids things to come into … arrival': 'in the naming, the things named are called into their thinging' (La 199). In turn, the things, as we have already seen above, gather the fourfold together. Poetry names things, in that it calls them out of and into dif-ference. It brings them (home) into their place, where they can come to their own nature and belong together. Poetry calls forth dif-ference itself – the dimension of world and thing (La 203). Such calling could only occur if poetry builds by spanning the between, helping our homecoming-measuring in the midst of the fourfold. We saw earlier that we become at home insofar as we properly measure ourselves and the between in which is given our dwelling. Now Heidegger, interpreting Hölderlin, says that we so measure by poetizing: 'Man's taking measure in the dimension dealt out to him brings dwelling into its ground plan. Taking the measure of the dimension is the element within which human dwelling has its security, by which it securely endures. The taking of measure is what is poetic in dwelling. Poetry is a measuring … In poetry the taking of measure occurs [*ereignet sich*]. To write poetry is measure taking, understood in the strict sense of the word, by which man first receives the measure for the breadth of his being' (PMD 221–2).

In his own way, Trakl says the same. According to Heidegger, Trakl's stranger does this in apartness: 'in apartness, the stranger measures off the parting … He is underway on a path' (LP 186). The measuring would be the path of becoming at home, of Hölderlin's dwelling poetically. When travelled carefully, it remains mysterious because it lets the far (for example, the heavens and the divine) come near, and yet lets them stay apart in dif-ference, concealed according to their own proper measure (PMD 224, 226). Thus, 'poetry, as the authentic gauging of the dimension of dwelling, is the primal form of building … Poetry is the original admission of dwelling' (PMD 227). The measure of Heidegger's thinking and his story of homecoming has become exceedingly complex. Thinking has begun to become at home in language, where language, as the saying of the dif-ference which calls world and thing into belonging, thus gives mortals their dwelling place. At the same time, dwelling comes about through poetizing-building: 'Poetry is what first brings man onto the earth, making him belong to it, and thus brings him into dwelling' (PMD 218).

Language, as the still saying and authentic poetizing saying, gives home. By our listening speaking we respond to its beckoning and, in the 'gathered taking-in,' enter to begin dwelling (La 216, 223). Restraining and attuning ourselves to listen 'determines the manner in which mortals respond to the dif-ference. In this way mortals live in the speaking of language' (La 209–210). It is not enough just to see that 'language belongs to the closest neighborhood of man's being' (La 189). In addition, Heidegger's own thinking through *Ereignis* of world and thing, difference, saying, and poetizing, *is his manner of becoming at home.* Thus, he says, 'To discuss language, to place it, means to bring to its place not so much language as ourselves: our own gathering into appropriation' (La 190). *In sum, after all his homecoming as travelling and as moment of arrival, now there is a homecoming as thoughtfully becoming at home and beginning to dwell there.* 'To reflect on language thus demands that we enter into the speaking of language in order to take up our stay with language, i.e. within *its* speaking, not within our own' (La 190). Our homecoming 'leads through a landscape': 'the poet's land belongs within that landscape': so, too, 'word, language, belongs within the domain of this mysterious landscape' (NL 67). It is here that we would properly dwell.

Now we can more easily 'look about us in the country where thinking abides' (NL 75). In the story of our mortal homecoming we have found that we become at home by poetry's listening response to saying. Of course, with Heidegger, we are undergoing our own homecoming by way of thinking's response to the poet's sayings, and thus to saying itself. Authentic thinking would also help build our dwelling, insofar as it, too, is a listening to language's speaking. Heidegger insists that, for/in originary homecoming, 'the authentic attitude of thought is not ⌊finally⌋ a putting of questions ... rather, it is a listening to the [prior] grant, the promise of what is to be put in question' (NL 71; see also 75–6). 'What thinking can do here depends on whether and in what way it hears the granting saying' (NL 79). We begin by listening to poetry, in order that through its responding saying, along with the poets, we might hear saying itself tell us what is worthy of hearing-thinking. And 'to let ourselves be told what is worthy of thinking means – to think' (W 155).

Where all this is the case, we find that we are starting to abide in the gathering together of thinking and poetry, which already belong together (W 155). Heidegger says, 'Both poetry and thinking are distinctive saying in that they remain delivered over to the mystery of the word as that which is most worthy of their thinking, and thus ever structured in their kinship' (W 155–6). It would seem that since both poetry and thinking, as two authentic modes of saying, have their 'proper habitat' there. They dwell in the same neighbourhood (NL 81, 84). Thinking, of course, follows its own way home; yet, this necessarily follows the poet's saying and thinking. Heidegger adds, 'But what am I saying? Is there thinking, too, going on in a poem? Quite so – in a poem of such rank (as George's 'The Word') thinking is going on, and indeed thinking without science, without philosophy' (NL 61). There is still 'the danger that we will think too little, and reject the thought that the true experience with language can only be a thinking experience. All the more so because the lofty poetry of all great poetic work always vibrates within a realm of thinking ... thinking in turn goes its ways into the neighborhood of poetry. It is well, therefore, to give thought to the neighbor, to him who dwells in the same neighborhood. Poetry and thought, each needs the other in its neighborhood, each in its fashion when it comes to ultimates. In what region the neighborhood itself has its domain, each of them, thought and poetry, will define differently, but always so that they will find themselves within the same domain' (NL 69–70; see also 80–1). By way of explanation,

> A neighbor, as the word itself tells us, is someone who dwells near to and with someone else. This someone else thereby becomes himself the neighbor of the one. Neighborhood, then, is a relation resulting from the fact that the one settles face to face with the other. Accordingly, the phrase of the neighborhood of poetry and thinking means that the two dwell face to face with each other, that the one has settled facing the other, has drawn into the other's nearness ... Let us stay with the most urgent issue, which is, to seek out the neighborhood of poetry and thinking – which now means the encounter of the two facing each other.
>
> Fortunately we do not need either to search for this neighborhood or to seek it out. We are already abiding in it. We move within it. (NL 82)

Apparently, the neighbourhood would be a place where we would be at home. But we are not at home, because thus far we barely begin to abide there, that is, barely begin to see that this neighbourhood and neighbourliness must be understood (NL 81). We begin to abide there as already within the sphere and also in the manner of learning to abide, as still homecoming. To avoid passive residence, we need to think our way into this neighbourhood. *Even though the poet may poetically dwell, thinking still remains homecoming.* Heidegger's elaboration is worth citing at some length:

> What about the neighborhood of poetry and thinking? We stand confused between two wholly different kinds of saying. In the poet's song ... wonder appears in a fulfilled, singing saying; in our (thinking) reflection something memorable appears in a scarcely definable – but certainly not a singing – saying. How can this be a neighborhood, under which poetry and thinking live in close nearness? It would seem that the two diverge just as far as can be.
>
> But we should become familiar with the suggestion that the neighborhood of poetry and thinking is concealed within this farthest divergence of their saying. This divergence is their real face-to-face encounter.
>
> We must discard the view that the neighborhood of poetry and thinking is nothing more than a garrulous cloudy mixture of two kinds of saying in which each makes clumsy borrowings from the other. Here and there it may seem that way. But in truth, poetry and thinking are in virtue of their nature held apart by a delicate yet luminous difference, each held in its own darkness: two parallels, in Greek *para allelo*, by one another, against one another, transcending, surpassing one another each in its fashion. Poetry and thinking are not separated if separation is to mean cut off into a relational void. The parallels intersect in the infinite. There they intersect with a section that they themselves do not make. By this section, they are first cut, engraved into the design of their neighboring nature. That cut assigns poetry and thinking to their nearness to one another. The neighborhood of poetry and thinking is not the result of a process by which poetry and thinking – no one knows from where – first draw near to each other and thus establish a nearness, a neighborhood. The nearness that draws them near is itself the occurrence of appropriation by which poetry and thinking are directed into their proper nature.
>
> But if the nearness of poetry and thinking is one of saying, then our thinking arrives at the assumption that the occurrence of appropriation acts as that saying in which language grants its essential nature to us. (NL 89–90)

If thinking and poetry are drawn into neighbourliness by appropriating-saying, they come to meet in the dif-ference. Since what is held apart in dif-ference is also held apart for gathering, and since what is gathered is what already belongs together, even though separated – thinking and poetry would meet in the same, in the midst of what belongs together. Accordingly, Heidegger adds, 'Poetry and thinking meet each other in one and the same only when, and only as long as, they remain distinctly in the distinctiveness of their nature. The same never coincides with the equal, not even in the empty indifferent oneness of what is merely identical … The same, by contrast, is the belonging together of what differs, through a gathering by way of the difference. We can only say "the same" if we think difference. It is in the carrying out and settling of differences that the gathering nature of sameness comes to light. The same banishes all zeal always to level what is different into the equal or identical. The same gathers what is distinct into an original being-at-one' (PMD 218–19; see also NL 106). At one and the same time, then, neighbourhood is disclosed and concealed. This is unavoidable, for even as it discloses, saying-appropriating-dif-ference conceals itself. Becoming at home continues indefinitely as homecoming because the giving of home is never finished, once and for all. Homecoming never is over and done with. It is always still coming, remaining homecoming.

Again, we are already in the neighbourhood of thinking and poetry, within saying. As human, we have long been here. Even when estranged, we were still within language, though not originarily. We have heard the story of how the poets and Heidegger have arrived into saying. But to be human, to be poet or thinker, is not static but a becoming, ever on the way home. As noted, we still have to become at home here, in a thinking experience, where thinking is always underway, attempting coming home. Heidegger says, 'That means now and first: we must learn to heed that neighborhood itself in which poetry and thinking have their dwelling. But, strangely – the neighborhood itself remains invisible. The same thing happens in our daily lives. We live in a neighborhood, and yet we would be baffled if we had to say in what the neighborhood consists. But this perplexity is merely a particular case, though perhaps an exceptionally good one, of the old encompassing perplexity in which all our thinking and saying finds itself always and everywhere' (NL 83). We remain underway then. As long as we are underway we still question the neighbourhood or our becoming at home, and the neighbourhood itself is still coming, requiring a staying underway. 'The neighborhood in question pervades everywhere our stay on this earth and our journey in it' (NL 84). Heidegger explains, 'When we listen to the poet and, in our own fashion, consider what his renunciation says, we are already staying in the neighborhood of poetry and thinking; and yet again we are not, at least not so that we experience the neighborhood as such. We are not yet on our way to it. We must first turn, turn back to where we are in reality already staying. The abiding turn, back to where we already are, is infinitely harder than are hasty excursions to places where we are not yet and never will be' (NL 85).

At the juncture where we find ourselves, we remain homecoming by again turning home. The turn now is not from the foreign toward home, but from where we have arrived and already are seemingly at home (which is stranger than any foreign land) to our abiding there in the manner of still and always becoming at home there. We continue learning this becoming at home-homecoming. Heidegger adds,

> What is necessary here is not only that on our chosen way we stay within the neighborhood of poetry and thinking. We also must look about us in this neighborhood, so see whether and in what manner it shows us something (as it has the poets) that transforms our relation to language. But of the way which is to lead us to the source of this possibility, it was said that it leads us only to where we already are. The 'only' here does not mean a limitation, but rather points to this way's pure simplicity. The way allows us to reach what concerns us, in that domain where we are already staying. Why, then, one may ask, still find a way to it? Answer: because where we already are, we are in such a way that at the same time we are not there, because we ourselves have not yet properly recalled what concerns our being, nor even approached it. (NL 93)

To become at home in saying is to keep on homecoming. There was a becoming at home into saying by the poets because poetry measured the dif-ference in which we learn dwelling. Following the poets, Heidegger is learning (and we too insofar as we genuinely follow) to become at home by thinking into this same neighbourhood. And though 'the country where thinking abides' is 'everywhere open to the neighborhood of poetry,' what of thinking's own region, 'so called because it gives its realm and free reign to what thinking is given to think' (NL 75; see also 77)? 'Thinking,' Heidegger says, 'abides in that country, walking the ways of that country. Here the way is part of the country and belongs to it' (NL 75).

The way of thinking must be fit for becoming at home. Heidegger is clear about the manner in which thinking has its fit. Further, if we are to follow the thinker in his homecoming we need to understand how his thinking becomes fit. Questioning would be a listening to the attitude of thinking toward poetic abiding because attitude means the manner that is fit or unfit for that to which it belongs. We have already heard how thinking would learn from poetry by following it in becoming at home. That engagement is disclosed as a learning to dwell poetically in language which is appropriation of dif-ference, the gathering of world and thing. The proper attitude of the thinker is a listening. The listening is directed toward the poet, who says what is heard from saying's own stillness. In turn, the primal saying is not first of all anything human. Rather, what says and calls is helped by many voices and involves more than the human. For example, according to Hölderlin, the fourfold's gathering in belonging is a fourfold singing. The four each voice this nearing (as we saw above; see HEH 170).

Hölderlin explains, according to Heidegger, how saying, as saga and showing, moves into disclosure in two more specific ways: nature and poem say. We can think of heavens and earth (though not these two in any isolated way, since Hölderlin, following the Greeks, includes humans and gods by way of *physis*, or *die Natur*) (HEH 180). We can also think of the voice of the gods which says and is echoed in the poet's saying by way of poetry. Hölderlin understands as 'the long-established saga [*die alte Sage*], the self-showing of great beginning,' that is, the ever-coming presence of what comes (HEH 181). And as we have seen in detail, for Hölderlin, the poem sings the same. It was in poetizing the poet's song of the wedding feast of humans and gods, earth and heavens that Hölderlin told us these things. Heidegger thought through them once before in his Hölderlin essays ('Wie wenn am Feiertag,' 1939); now he thinks along with Hölderlin once again (in Hölderlin's 'Erde und Himmel,' 1960). Hölderlin's poetry remains a source that continues to disclose the place and attitude of becoming at home and beginning to abide.

There is, according to Heidegger, a focus on a central site, one place of gathering for the four. This place is the middle, where the four come together in their belonging, as gathered beginning. A beginning (*ein Anfang*) is the sending of all gathered near/toward catching/taking-ahold of the four (*An-fang*), according to Heidegger (HEH 171). This coming near and taking hold together is the primal coming where 'beginning remains and abides as arrival [*Anfang bleibt als Ankunft*]' (HEH 171). Here, more localized places of gathering are gathered in one focal site. For example, all holy places are gathered to one primal holy place (HEH 181). We hear of the coming of 'one secret place [*Ein heimlicher Ort*]' to which the poet would belong, in a poor, native-secret manner [*als der arme (und heimliche)*] (HEH 172). Here is the building of the ever-coming belonging (*Es ist der Bau des unendlichen Verhältnisses*) (HEH 172). The poet calls this site and coming: the wedding festival. In celebration the poet sings the fest of the ever-coming belonging as the wedding of humans and gods (*Erde und Himmel, Menschen und Göttern;* and *der Gott*) (HEH 173, 175).[7] But the betrothed are also the earth and heavens. Hölderlin says that the bride is the earth, to whom the song of the heavens comes (HEH 173). Thus, according to Heidegger, 'The wedding is the wholeness of the intimacy of: earth and heaven, humans and gods. It is the fest and holiday (cf. holy day) of without-end belonging' (HEH 173, 175).

The poet sings the wedding festival and says the movement of the wedding. Thus, his singing-celebrating names the site of the belonging, the gathering-belonging itself, and the manner of the gathering. The earth and heaven, humans and gods circle, ringing round (*ring*) and as gathering (*das Ge-ring*) gathering, ringing (*ge-ring*), joining-nestling into unified belonging (HEH 171, 173–4; see also T 180).[8] (Note, *gering* also means humble, modest, slight, and is to be thought with needy-poor place (*am armen Ort*), though what is precious and richer – homey – first comes here, HEH 174.) The wedding of heaven and earth, which gods and humans celebrate provides the occasion for the poet to sing the round-celebrating dance (*der Reigen*) of gods (HEH 174). The ringing movement of the gods moves to the echoing song of the poet (HEH 174, 175). In singing the wedding feast of the ever-coming belonging together of the fourfold, the poet sings and celebrates his own gathering into this belonging together. 'The circling-dancing' 'is the ever coming belonging together and belongs to the needy, hidden place in the native fields [*heimlichen Ort im heimischen Gefild*] of the poet' (HEH 175). This is also the West, as fateful coming; yet again it is own homecoming, out of the secreted, to what is required and native (HEH 176).

More immediately, Hölderlin's poem, in its singing, points out the disclosure of the place of this celebration and gathering together (G 191). The remote place where approach/nearing is still coming, even as it remains remote, comes in this soft poetic wherein the poet dwells, singing and thinking on (and in) the joining-movement. It is from his placement, that is from his poem, that he sings and toward which he comes home (G 179, 187–8).[9] Thus, the poet finally names the site of the gathering together of what belongs together. As the site of the naming, however, his poem is, as singing, the coming-site. His shy singing *says* becoming at home and *is* a becoming at home. Here Heidegger's shift from Trakl to Hölderlin is significant. Though apartness names separation and gathering, Trakl's apartness yields way, in thinking's journey with the poets, to Hölderlin's wedding festival. Out of wandering in apartness as a stranger the poet winds up – in Heidegger's thinking journey with the poets – as singing in the midst of the wedding celebration, singing in a manner which gathers together the fourfold. His singing is a saying that helps world come forth and fosters his own becoming at home in the gathering.

Of course, the poet's song is still an echo, a response to the still saying, which, as we have seen above (early in chapter 2), stays back and is soundless (stays still) and uses the poet's voice to aid disclosure of the fourfold which comes forth (G 191). Saying also stays the fourfold, and brings their movement to rest, thus stilling, even as movement, keeps coming.[10] So movement and saying belong together and gather in a double stilling, which the poet sings. In seeking to become at home, the poet helps us to see what dwelling would be. It would be a poetic abiding on the earth, beneath the heavens, as mortals before the divine. The poetic abiding has been stressed here, but the rest of the phrase says, 'on the earth.' The poet would help us out of our unpoetic wandering on the earth, where we now master the globe through technology, only if he helps us come home to *earth as earth.*

Heidegger first comes to understand our homelessness from the neighbourhood of poetry (he notes that the neighbourhood of poetry and thinking 'pervades everywhere our stay on this earth and our journey in it'). Once there, he can see that our calculative thinking, which moves in conquest of our planet and 'worldless cosmic space,' is 'about to abandon the earth as earth' (NL 84). The second insight, and issue, is central to our homecoming and attempt to belong, since 'if we lose the earth, of course, we also loose the roots' (NL 99). Just in the midst of this danger, the poets lead us back and help us to become rooted again. Trakl, for example, according to Heidegger, says how the soul wanders 'to seek the earth so that she may poetically build and dwell upon it, and thus may be able to save the earth *as* earth' (LP 163). Since the fourfold belongs together, our dwelling as mortals is needed to let the earth be earth, just as earth is needed for us to have a place and way to dwell. We need to become fit to one another. Thus, Heidegger says, 'Trakl's work sings the song of the soul, "something strange on the earth," which is only just about to gain the earth by its wandering, the earth that is the stiller home of the homecoming generation' (LP 196).

As noted earlier, Hölderlin says that the earth (along with the rest of the fourfold) voices what is coming and sent. How does it do so? In 'Greece,' Hölderlin says that when rain falls on the earth beating on it as on a drum, the earth sings out:

> the earth …
> follows great laws, and science
> and tenderness and the width of heaven later
> becoming manifest, sing clouds of song. (cited in HEH 155)

Here earth and heaven belong together. Only with both joined is the song (the heaven's rain on earth's skin) possible. We know that. Here the earth is held open to receive the gift of the heavens. The poet names the openness: 'science' and 'tenderness' span the width of heaven. We have seen how science or knowledge (*Wissenschaft*) connects heavens to earth and man. The 'law of science' is the joining of what comes to man in a way that it can disclose itself to man (even if, in the mode of disclosure, we too eagerly grasp it). In the past, we have measured our place as well as the heavens and earth by way of science. Science also indicates how and that we are able to perceive what discloses itself (see also chapters 1 and 4-B on the relation of metaphysical-scientific representation and sensation). We continue along this path. Thus, now we need to heed the other, complementary law, and listen especially to it so as to measure our belonging on the earth, under the heavens, in their relation. Hölderlin indicates this manner of abiding with the name: 'tenderness' (*zärtlichkeit*) (HEH 166–8).

Tenderness, according to Heidegger, is used by Hölderlin to indicate the native essence of the Greek: their art of showing, letting appear what shows itself purely and thereby presences. For the Greeks, what brings the splendour of the presencing to appearance is the athletic warlike-struggle of heroes (also consider Heraclitus and Pindar) and the power of reflection (*die Reflexionskraft*) (HEH 166). These two (athletic struggle and power of reflection) belong together in what Hölderlin names tenderness. They name the highest showing, as where, poetically dwelling (and for the Greeks all art is grounded in poetic song), man brings all appearing – earth, and heavens, and the holy – to a stand (HEH 162, 164). Clearly, as the bringing to disclosure, tenderness does not, as we might non-originarily suppose, mean anything sentimental for Hölderlin (HEH 160). Tenderness is essentially both joyful-reaching (*erfreuend-reichendes*) and simple-receiving (*einfach-empfangendes*). It too opens the earth to heaven. When the opening of heaven and earth reaches things and world thus comes forth, there is joy. The joy, received when it reaches out, comes as simplicity, in the simple. That is why the poet sings of joy in the simple and strives to stay simple in his reception of the joy which comes in the singing language-full coming of the disclosure of thing and world.

Here tenderness binds heaven and earth, the divine and mortal. For example, the poet uses tenderness in letting be disclosed the love proper to the immortals-gods (HEH 169). Or, in a related manner, kindness (*Freundlichkeit*), as a measuring, appears not as an anthropological trait or metaphysically subjective characteristic of humans as in Rilke's use of 'heart' (see 'What Are Poets For?' 129–30), but originarily as in Trakl's use of the word ('God spoke a gentle flame to his heart: O man!') (La 155). Specifically, 'In Lovely Blueness ...' Hölderlin says,

> ... As long as Kindness,
> The Pure, still stays with his heart, man
> Not unhappily measures himself
> Against the Godhead. (cited in PMD 228)

Heidegger comments,

> 'Kindness' – this word, if we take it literally, is Hölderlin's magnificent translation for the Greek word *charis.*[11] ... Hölderlin says in an idiom he liked to use: 'with his heart,' not 'in his heart.' That is, it has come to the dwelling being of man, come as the claim and appeal of the measure to the heart in such a way that the heart turns to give heed to the measure.
>
> As long as the arrival of tenderness endures, so long does man succeed in measuring himself not unhappily against the godhead. When this measuring appropriately comes to light, man creates poetry from the very nature of the poetic. When the poetic appropriately comes to light, then man dwells humanly on this earth, and then – as Hölderlin says in his last poem – 'the life of man' is a 'dwelling life.' (PMD 229)

What this last sentence says can be written and read two ways: 'Hölderlin *does* take the measure and help us become at home in his poetry' and '*it is in his poetry* that Hölderlin takes the measure and helps us become at home.' Either way, measuring helps let earth be earth.

In the poetic dwelling on the earth, the poet shows the thinker how to meditate on homecoming. The poet's whole attitude – and manner of thoughtful-singing, which means becoming at home – demands that 'we are to think of what is called man's existence by way of the nature of dwelling ... we are to think of the nature of poetry as a letting-dwell, as a – perhaps even *the* – distinctive kind of building.' Heidegger adds, 'If we search out the nature of poetry according to this viewpoint, then we arrive at the nature of dwelling' (PMD 215).

In Heidegger's own learning to become at home in dwelling, his attitude is disclosed. The manner or mode of his thinking-saying shows its fit to the saying of the fourfold. The sustained style of the words and works that meditate on poetry approaches the careful, sure, slow style of the poetry itself. Each word appears measured. Each word matters. For example, Heidegger pauses to think the 'and' which connects 'Earth and Heaven': the 'and' speaks the belonging together in richer relation, not in mere connection. Heidegger speaks with a delicate balance of sureness and humility. His presentation emanates power and depth. But it does not seem brash or cocky. Rather, it is calmly forceful, moving slowly but inevitably. Still, it appears open to surprise and wonder. The style seems to be like the movement of a deep river or a Buddhist monk. Then, too, there is the impression of reserve. Heidegger speaks in a way to indicate that he could say more than he does, that what he says is the product of long and careful meditation on the poetry, that he is humble before the poets' gifted saying and trying to listen intimately to what would be said if let be. Careful, alert listening. Heidegger thinks and speaks as an animal in the brush, focused on a distant sound, often moving toward it, then stopping, alert to the rest of its surroundings too. Thus, even while sure and bold, Heidegger is properly shy – in favour of what comes to him. He notes, 'the authentic attitude of thinking ... is a listening to the grant' (LP 191).

What Heidegger says of the poets increasingly applies to his own thinking and saying. As we saw earlier, he becomes a brother who follows the poets. His way of going, even while it remains a proper thinking, also becomes close to theirs. Like the poets,' his attitude intensely shows the belonging together of what appears as apart: the mood is one of the powerful gentleness that must be 'called to hunt down God, [the] shy reserve called to storm heaven' (LP 190). The mysteriously strange language 'answers to the home-coming of unborn mankind into the quiet beginning of its stiller nature' and thus 'stems from this transition,' from 'the passage across.' This language of home-coming 'comes to rest in the earliness of the stiller, and still impending beginning' (LP 191).

Heidegger's thinking and saying, in its shyness, reserve, sureness, forcefulness, humbleness, care, listening, and openness, could be called pious. He notes, concerning originary thinking which is a questioning, and before that a listening, that he has 'some time ago' (in 'The Question Concerning Technology,' 35) used this name, where '"poetry" is meant here in the ancient sense: obedient, or submissive, and in this case submitting to what thinking has to think about' (NL 72). For Heidegger, poetry becomes poetry in becoming pious. He says, 'Poetry's spoken words shelter the poetic statement as that which by its essential nature remains unspoken. In this manner, the saying-after, thus called upon to listen, becomes "more pious," that is to say, more pliable to the promptings of the path on which the stranger walks ahead, out of the dark childhood into the stiller, brighter sunshine' (LP 188). So, too, because it is a thinking that follows the poet in a brotherly manner, the thinking that moves from youthful home, through homelessness, to a continuing homecoming becomes more pious as it becomes at home.

At this point, the poet's and thinker's relationship to religious language may become clearer. Though this is a deep and complex matter, we can see several basic features. Heidegger, along with the poets, proceeds in an increasingly pious manner and, with them, listens to and enters into religious language more deeply.[12] His story of homelessness has always used language from the realm of the sacred, but it is here in the works that tell the story of homecoming and dwelling in the language of thing and world that the most reverent attitude and religious style come to the fore. As the poet, Heidegger speaks at many levels, often simultaneously, when he tells of homelessness and homecoming in a manner that does not leave earlier phases behind while travelling through later ones.

I believe that Heidegger also glosses himself when directly speaking of Trakl. Consider his words not only as an insight into the poet's saying, but reflexively, as telling us about the site of his own work (homecoming) and his own saying-thinking manner of journeying and beginning to dwell:

> Because the language of this poetry (which sings the song of home-coming) speaks from the journey of apartness, it will always speak also of what it leaves behind in parting, and of that to which the departure submits. This language is essentially ambiguous, in its own fashion ...
>
> The poetic work speaks out of an ambiguous ambiguousness. Yet this multiple ambiguousness of the poetic saying does not scatter in vague equivocations. The ambiguous tone of Trakl's poetry arises out of a gathering, that is, out of a unison which, meant for itself alone, always remains unsayable. The ambiguity of this poetic saying is not lax imprecision, but rather the rigor of him who leaves what is as it is, who has entered into 'righteous vision' and now submits to it.
>
> It is often hard for us to draw a clear line between the ambiguous saying characteristic of Trakl's poems – which in his work shows complete assurance – and the language of other poets whose equivocations stem from the vagueness of groping poetic uncertainty, because their language lacks authentic poetry and its site. The peerless rigor of Trakl's essentially ambiguous language is in a higher sense so unequivocal that it remains infinitely superior even to all the technical precision of concepts that are merely scientifically univocal. (LP 191–2)

Heidegger's terms have multiple meanings too. Most of the important ones have both an ordinary or metaphysical-representational sense and a new or originary one. Further, many have several originary meanings (for example, 'saying' severally means 'language's giving showing,' 'the poet's listening singing,' 'the old saga of *phusis* ever disclosing itself,' 'the thinker's saying-after,' 'stillness and reserve,' and so on). To barely begin a list of Heidegger's words that carry multiple meanings in the works following the poets, 'language,' 'saying,' 'showing,' 'voice,' 'speaks,' 'sing,' 'call,' 'need,' 'hear-listen,' 'still,' 'word,' 'thing,' 'world,' 'earth,' 'heavens,' 'the divine,' 'god,' 'mortals,' 'ring-circle,' 'gathering,' 'appropriation,' 'dif-ference,' 'dimension,' 'measure,' 'pain,' 'site,' 'apartness,' 'pious,' 'reserve,' and 'dwelling.' This language does not lack neighbourliness with authentic poetry and its site, yet it becomes at home in its own as authentic thinking in its proper site of homecoming. These words 'of Heidegger's' say after the poet and yet say on their own. In Heidegger's terms, they 'arise out of a gathering' – the gathering together of what belongs together. That is, they emerge out of, and as, a becoming at home.

Heidegger's words concerning the poet (and reflexively, his own language of multiple meaning that I claim tells us about his work) continue as follows:

> This same ambiguity of language that is determined by the site of Trakl's poetic work also inspires his frequent use of words from the world of biblical and ecclesiastical ideas. The passage from the old to the unborn generation leads through this region and its language. Whether Trakl's poems speak in a Christian fashion, to what extent and in what sense, in what way Trakl was a 'Christian,' what is meant here, and indeed generally, by 'Christian,' 'Christianity,' 'Christendom' and 'Christ-like': all this involves essential questions. But their discussion hangs in a void so long as the site of his poetic work is not thoroughly established. Besides, their discussion calls for a kind of thorough thinking to which neither the concept of a metaphysical nor those of a church-based theology are adequate …
>
> The rigorous unison of the many-voiced language in which Trakl's poetry speaks – and this means also: is silent – corresponds to apartness as the site of his work. Merely to keep this sight rightly in mind makes demands on our thinking. We hardly dare in closing to ask for the location of this site. (LP 193)

If we listen to what Heidegger says, we find we are called upon to resist straying off in speculation about Heidegger's 'religiosity.' Opposite, his religious language (his movement through this region) demands that we focus on the site of his thinking work. That is, it returns us to that very site: homecoming.

Heidegger newly comes out of homelessness, back to one's (his) own, native land, to try to become at home there, not as a child, but most fully in what is his ownmost. The thinker follows the poet in the journey to a *native home* and in learning abiding there. But Heidegger consistently contends, for Hölderlin and himself, words such as 'fatherland-mother country' or 'Nation' do not have the meanings these terms carry in contemporary politics (consider Hölderlin's 'The Ister').[13] Instead, they name, religiously, our home in the fourfold. Heidegger explains this while commenting on a letter Hölderlin wrote to his friend Böhlendorff upon returning back home from southern France. Concerning what Hölderlin names and ponders (*bedenkt*) as 'the return or turning around to native country [or, alternatively, patriotic reversal, *die vaterländische Umkehr*],' Heidegger says, 'The "native" [or, 'patriotic,' *Vaterländische*] means the relation of the territory [land, *Land*] to the father as the highest God, means this life-dispensing "belonging" wherein humans, insofar as they have a "sending," stand. Similarly, the "national" [*das Nationelle*] means the land of birth (*nasci, natura*), which, as beginning, establishes the abiding' (HEH 159).[14]

The native land, then, is the region of the earth which opens for and admits our dwelling, and upon which we begin to become at home, under the heavens and with the divine. This native home, as earth, is our beginning and comes to us. It comes in language, in our native language. *Here Heidegger presses us to the fullest becoming at home yet achieved. He articulates the inmost essence of language, that is, the intimate source of the gift of home and homecoming.* 'Even the simple fact that we Germans call the different manners of speaking in different sections of the country *Mundarten*, modes of the mouth, hardly ever receives a thought. These differences do not solely nor primarily grow out of the different movement patterns of the organs of speech. The landscape, and that means the earth, speaks in them, differently each time. But the mouth is not merely a kind of organ of the body understood as an organism – body and mouth are part of the earth's flow and growth in which we mortals flourish, and from which we receive the soundness of out roots. If we lose the earth, of course, we also lose the roots' (NL 98–9). The path through religious language leads to the same place, according to Heidegger: 'Language is the tongue. The second chapter of the Acts of the Apostles, which tells of the miracles of Pentecost, says so in verses 3 and 4 ... In the Revised Standard Version ... "And there appeared to them tongues as of fire, distributed and resting on each one of them. And they … began to speak in tongues …" Yet their speaking is not meant as a mere facility of the tongue, but as filled with the holy spirit, the *pneuma hagion*' (NL 97; see also L, 206).

Critically, then, in saying, earth and God move: the movement is nearest and occurs primally in regional saying – in dialect. The poet Hölderlin sees this fact. In 'Walk in the Country' he says:

> Therefore I even hope it may come to pass,
> When we begin what we wish for and our tongue opens,
> And the word has been found and the heart has opened,
> And from ecstatic brows springs a higher reflection,
> That the sky's blooms may blossom as do our own,
> And the luminous sky open to opened eyes. (cited in NL 99)

And in 'Germania,' Zeus' eagle says the following 'to the quietest daughter of God':

> And secretly, while you dreamed, at noon,
> Departing, I left a token of friendship,
> The flower of the mouth behind, and lonely you spoke.
> Yet you, the greatly blessed, with the rivers too
> Dispatched a wealth of golden words, and they well unceasing
> Into all regions now. (cited in NL 99)

Heidegger adds, 'Language is the flower of the mouth. In language the earth blossoms toward the bloom of the sky' (NL 99; also consider *Koto ba* in 'A Dialogue on Language'). And in Hölderlin's 'Bread and Wine':

> Such is man; when the wealth is there and no less than a god in
> Person tends him with gifts, blind he remains, unaware.
> First he must suffer; but now he names his most treasured possession,
> Now for it words like flowers leaping alive he must find. (cited in NL 99–100)

Such important saying requires explanation, so Heidegger comments, 'Once again the work appears in the region, the region that determines earth and sky to be world regions, as it makes earth and sky, the streaming of the deep and the might of the heights, encounter one another. Once again: "words like flowers"' (NL 100; see also G 187). '"Words, like flowers": that is not a "break in the vision" but the awakening of the largest view; nothing is "adduced" here, but on the contrary the word is given back into the keeping of the source of its being ... When the word is called the mouth's flower and its blossom, we hear the sound of language rising like the earth. From whence? From saying in which it comes to pass that world is made to appear' (NL 100–1; see also DL). Thus, gods and mortals, earth and humans gather together in saying. Saying is given primally as local saying; local, place-bound saying is the site where home is first given and where, at last, we might become at home. Thus, precisely in becoming at home where we least anticipate any discovery, a discovery comes. *Home is in dialect.*

It remains for the thinker to deepen his abiding at home, which means to remain underway, still coming home to that which is his own. So far he has begun to do so. To learn such abiding, he has thought the poets' sayings and followed them into the neighbourhood where they both belong – into saying. Ultimately, that native land is where language flowers as *Mundarten.* Having passed over long ago from homelessness in the region of calculative-representational saying and thinking (see, e.g., NL 91), the thinker would learn to dwell nearby the poet, in the neighbourhood of what still comes as the gathering of the fourfold, as nighness (NL 104). If thinking (and that means both Heidegger's story about thinking itself and the story of his own accomplishments and failures) is to keep homecoming, it finally has to learn to dwell in saying. *That is, thinking has to think – to listen, let come, and experience, with the help of the poet and poetry – the 'flower of the mouth,' dialect as home.*

Learning to Experience Dialect and Poetized World

How can Heidegger, along with the poets, continue to become at home, now in language understood as dialect that gathers world? How can Heidegger listen to, let come, and experience dialect and home? By thinking and saying along with a poet who poetizes in dialect, along with dialect poems which poetize home through dialect. So, Heidegger begins yet again. With a set of works focusing on dialectal poetry – 'Die Sprache Johann Peter Hebels' (1955), 'Hebel – Friend of the House' (1957), and 'Sprache und Heimat' (1960) – he re-examines what has just been considered; further, even within these three works, he often starts over and over again. Isn't this too much? We may well wish that he and we could just go on directly from where we are to the next point. But it is not possible. We know that. Still, persisting with him, finding the energy and focus to 'begin yet again,' is not so easy. I can at least help a bit by not going through each of these essays line by line, as the reader will finally have to do, to really hear and come to what Heidegger says.

We understand that Heidegger cannot proceed by making assertions, directly telling us what follows from saying that home is in language and that language originally and ultimately is dialect. We understand that he and we must stay in the strange, that originary thinking – that is, homecoming – is neither a linear process nor ever over and done with, but instead is always underway. Arriving at home (say, in dialect) (which would correspond to phase 4 in Hölderlin's homecoming movement, as discussed in chapter 2) still requires long learning to abide there (phase 5), before any dwelling near the source (phase 6) would be possible. At least, though, we have arrived at dialect. Heidegger, mindful of those of us trying to persevere with him, does far more than repeat what he has found and said before; he newly thinks matters through, even if partially along familiar pathways. Writer and reader alike still have much to do, beginning with what is closest at hand: trying to understand what holds saying and home together, so as to sustain (*aushält*) their essential relationship (*Bezug*) (SH 29).

Focusing on the immediate task – thinking by way of language as dialect – Heidegger also stays near the homelessness which yet dominates the very possibility, let alone any partial accomplishment, of homecoming. He remains clear that he resides in the technological, while just starting the complementary originary learning to dwell. What is needed is a strategy of exploring the neighbourhoods 'where we are in reality already staying,' by simultaneously continuing to attend to the universal, univocal language of science, technology, and metaphysics, and by remaining in ordinary, standard High German, while also passing over to poems which say as dialect. Accordingly, Heidegger changes the way he seeks poetic guidance, shifting from Trakl and Hölderlin to Hebel. The transition itself indicates what Heidegger is doing: Trakl is especially the poet of apartness (though, of course, Hölderlin and Hebel also articulate and dwell in that region); Hölderlin especially speaks the gathering union of the fourfold, the wedding that allows difference without separation; Hebel, as we will now see, unfolds the gathering that specifically happens only in dialect.

Heidegger hopes, then, to move from initially arriving at dialect to beginning to abide in it by seeing how Hebel and his contemporaries did so (above, we have already followed how Hölderlin and Trakl continued learning how to abide in their neighbourhoods of poetry and thinking) (NL 82). Not only are Hölderlin and Hebel, like Heidegger, strongly rooted in and oriented to the local while still sophisticatedly moving beyond it, but they are from, and stay bound to, the same territory. Indeed, Hölderlin, a guide throughout, but especially to the arrival home, is from Swabia; Hebel, of special help concerning learning to dwell in the sphere wherein we live, is Alemannic. Heidegger, trying to think and complete his own full passage, is from Meßkirch, located in the borderland between Swabia and Alemannia, and sharing roots with both areas. Thus, Hölderlin and Hebel are Heidegger's neighbours, not only because they inhabit the same regions of thinking and saying, but because those shared dimensions are grounded in the same landscape.[15]

Though its importance might be missed in a casual reading, Heidegger emphasizes the appropriateness of Hebel for questions and experiences of homecoming, by devoting the entire first page of 'Hebel – Friend of the House' (and a bit beyond) to Hebel's life, and then most of the next three pages to covering what he wrote (Heidegger spends the first of the three short pages of 'Die Sprache Johann Peter Hebels' in the same way). This is most unusual for Heidegger, who famously says almost nothing – usually, nothing at all – about the authors he explicates. In contrast to his usual austere 'distance' from the people whose thoughts he ponders, his opening is friendly: 'It is good to know the course of this poet's life, for this is what ordained that the latent poetic source within him should spring forth' (HFH 89). We hear of Hebel's childhood and his connections with the Wiese Valley, which runs 'up into the Black Forest to the Feldberg.' The stunning echo of Hebel's trajectory and concerns with Heidegger's makes the latter's unusually personalized reflection worth citing: 'More than half of Hebel's life was spent far from his homeland ... a nearness to the land of his birth and childhood unceasingly and irresistibly penetrated the Wiese Valley and beckoned to him. The sap and energy of his native earth and the robustly cheerful attitude of the people there who held him in affection remained alive in Hebel's heart and spirit. The sole dream of his life, to be able to live and work as a village pastor in Markgräflerland, remained, however, unfulfilled. Even so, the magic of his homeland held Hebel in its spell. Out of a longing for his homeland his *Alemannic Poems* took shape' (HFH 89–90; see also SJPH 75). Not only is he a poet born out of homelessness and toward homecoming, every bit as much as was Hölderlin, but, exceptionally, Hebel makes his way home in dialect, which itself is beginning to unfold for us as an inmost pathway toward home. No wonder Heidegger treats him with such a careful deference.

If we consciously limit our purpose, we find that out of Hebel's *Aleman-*

nic Poems (1803), *Little Treasury* (1811) (which was a selection of the 'loveliest pieces' from the *Baden Province Calendar,* with its poems, stories, and reflections that he had edited), and *Letters,* Heidegger develops subject matter in the same originary terms that he has already worked out to understand home and dwelling: encounters with the foreign, nature, and poetry as the primal bringing forth into appearance (*her-vor-bringen*) of the fourfold (that is, saying's giving of world by gathering heavens, earth, mortals, and divinities), and language as dialect (HFH 91–2).[16] Note that my focus here is deliberate and temporary, since Heidegger denies that we can find any separable 'content' in poetry. It is useful, however, for us to discern in general what the detailed explications discover and unfold. In fact, Heidegger himself speaks more broadly in these three essays, especially in 'Die Sprache Johan Peter Hebels' and 'Hebel – Friend of the House,' even while insisting on a careful, detailed reading, such as he carried out (or, at least made public) several years later in 'Sprache und Heimat,' to which we will turn shortly, as we consider Heidegger's experience of reading Hebel.[17]

After beginning the essay 'Hebel – Friend of the House' with some comments on Hebel's life, Heidegger goes on for a few pages, explaining that Hebel is 'not a mere poet of dialect and a region' but 'a poet of world-wide import' (HFH 90). That would be because he not only freshly delineates the tension between the scientific-technological and 'historically determined dwelling' in his own time but continues to powerfully address us today with this question-worthy issue. 'We are errant today in a world which is a house without a friend, that is, which lacks that house-friend who in equal manner and with equal force is inclined toward both the technologically constructed world-edifice *and* the world as the house for a more original dwelling. Missing is that friend of the house who is able to re-entrust the calculability and technology of nature to the open mystery of a newly experienced naturalness of nature' (HFH 98). Heidegger clarifies how the poet Hebel recognizes and accepts the realm of Enlightenment science and technology that surround him. He is interested in reflecting upon and passing on to people of his country what the 'Physicists and astronomers' of modern natural science, and foremost among these, the 'goodly Copernicus,' newly present 'in numbers, diagrams, and laws' (HFH 97). But Heidegger recognizes the limitations of this appreciation: 'at the same time he brings it as thus represented back into the *simple naturalness* [*die Natürlichkeit*] of nature' (HFH 97). According to Heidegger, through this bifocal openness Hebel fully 'wants to incline his readers to ponder what manifests itself in the processes and conditions of nature permeating our inhabited world' (HFH 97; see also 93–4). That is a motivation for Hebel coming up with, as he himself writes, 'the beautiful idea of making the calendar of the *Rhenisch House-Friend* into a welcome and beneficent publication' that 'should constantly illuminate and shed light on the daily life of human being' (HFH 91).

The poet, then, provides a way to remain in and reflect upon the strange as it appears in the challenge of technology. Since Hebel poetizes both sides of nature, that dealt with by Enlightenment science and the simple naturalness of nature to which he would return, Heidegger can – needs to – continue to ask, 'What is it, then, that we as well, and all the more so we of today, must appreciate as worthy of urgent questioning,' that which 'has meanwhile intensified into something immeasurable and opaque, sweeping our age away to we know not where?' (HFH 97). Despite an apparent similarity and lineage between Hebel's (illustrated calendar) and today's 'news magazine,' Heidegger contends that the latter has 'superceded the old calendar and even destroyed it' because the news magazine 'scatters, distances, thrusts the essential and inessential onto the same uniform level of the superficial,' whereas Hebel's calendar 'was once able to show the enduring in the inconspicuous and to sustain alertness through repeated readings and reflections' (HFH 91). Following Hebel, Heidegger argues that, now more than ever, we face the problem of 'the calculating of nature [that] is offered as the sole key to the mystery of the world,' of finding genuine builders 'who know that through atomic energy man does not live, but rather perishes at best,' and of losing ourselves in regard to such technology-science, even when its goals seem peaceful and exemplary (HFH 98).

Overall, though, continuing his meditation on today's groundlessness and alternatives with Hebel, Heidegger does not focus so much on technology in its global outreach as on language itself, which doubly involves the foreign. In the first place, the very way Heidegger proceeds through the differences among languages explores the strange from within. In the contexts of multiple spheres of language – 'global' languages of universal science and technology; almost worldwide political and commercial languages (to limit ourselves to what spreads from/as the West: formerly Greek, or Latin, or French, now English); 'official,' standard national languages (*Hochdeutsch*, Spanish, American English, etc.) – we come to the heart of language when we arrive at the most local languages: dialects. Specifically, Heidegger explores this last realm within the 'larger' ones by talking through Hebel's poetry in these essays. Heidegger's tactic is to use standard High German to stay in touch with his audience (including us), while exploring the effects of two dialects, Hebel's *Oberdeutsch* and a north German-Dutch *Niederdeutsch* (he also moves a bit by way of Greek, Latin, and another related German dialect). Heidegger explains this procedure by noting that the High German translation does not really manage to hear or say the dialect, whereas the second dialect (the Low German into which the poem has also been translated), even though from another place, carries more of the world brought forth by Hebel's writing. Yet, Heidegger is explicit about the fact that these dialects belong to, and bring, distinct realms within which only some might dwell – he in Oberdeutsch and not in Niederdeutsch; others in the latter but not the former: 'for most of you the Oberdeutsch dialect is strange, to me however the Niederdeutsch dialect in the inmost manner of its saying is inaccessible' (SH 29–30). Yet, Heidegger goes on, it is by going through the strangeness of each dialect (which, in turn, estranges one group or the other), and through the dialects' differences, that both sides might come to experience the proper character of the dialects.

A second dimension of the strange appears in the encompassing worldwide languages. He argues that even though humans settle all over and are more powerful than ever, and are close to a global language (*Welt Sprache*) and commerce, we are homeless (*heimatlos*) insofar as we are becoming language-less (*sprachlos*) – so much so that we appear to live in a realm well described by what Nietzsche said in a poem that seems to verbalize the bleak image of one of Breugel's winter paintings:

> The crows cry
> it will soon snow
> those who have no home. (cited in SH 28)

Why so barren just when our telecommunications 'cry' so piercingly around the planet? The language that reaches everywhere is the language of facts, of assertions about 'what is the case,' that pose as obvious and all there is, when they are, of course, the results of complex historical processes and contentious interpretations. It is the language of univocal scientific representations, which would eliminate all polysemous relationships; it is the worn-down language of commerce (*Verkehrssprache*), increasingly global in its reach to create and manipulate desire for consumption; it is propositional language. Heidegger holds that just such language is incapable of responding to, of letting be, of bringing to light, subtle and delicate aspects of the multifarious mystery of what is given

(SH 39). We find, opposite such a universal, univocal language, a local language – that is, dialect – and a mode of saying other than assertion – that is, poetry.

To explore dialect and poetry simultaneously, Heidegger turns to Hebel, who fuses the two dimensions. As distinct from even the precise terms of originary thinking (much less the concepts of philosophy and science), Hebel's poetry articulates a specific place, people, time, and set of events. Dialect maximizes particularity because it gives us the most localized sphere of experience. It *is* the 'smallest' language, as it were, the manner of using mouth and tongue to produce sounds whose meaning rings *only from and for* a limited, concrete time-place. 'Where else could the sound of this domain [*Bereiches*] speak more intimately and intensely than in dialect?' (SH 47).[18] 'Language is yet always a respective language, that is born out of the historical sending of a people and tribe ... Home is similarly specific and as such historically granted. Language, spoken out of its reigning and essential sway, is, at that given time, the language of one particular home [*Heimat*]. Language awakens in a native manner [*einheimisch*] and speaks in the being at home of the house of the parents [*Zuhaus der Elternhauses*]. Language is language as mother tongue [*Muttersprache*]' (SH 27). 'Language speaks here in a dialect, that is, notably from a region [*Bereich*], in whose landscape a tribe establishes its home and dwells [*bewohnt*]' (SH 29).

The communal dimension is emphasized by Heidegger as he explores how language and dialect are aspects of the historical endowment and unfolding of a particular people and place. Of course, dialect is actively spoken among a specific group, a phenomena taken up by Hebel where he regularly sets his poetry in the form of dialogues (as between the mother and child in 'The Man in the Moon,' SH 40) and made explicit by Heidegger in one of only two times in the essay where he introduces Greek, here reading 'mother tongue' as dialect and local idiom (*Mundart*) by way of the foreign word διαλέγειν, meaning unfolding a selection (*auserlesenes*), speaking with one another (*miteinanderhören*) (SH 28).

Heidegger also plays out the idea (which we saw at the end of the previous section of this chapter) that language is the blossom of the mouth, even that the earth pushes up and out through the body and mouth (NL 98–101), by playing with the meanings of the term 'stem' (*Stamm*). For example, he says that the people (*Volksstamm*, tribe) stem or descend from (*stammen*) the countryside where they have their rootedness (SH 29). (*Stammen* also says 'originate' or 'spring from,' as does *entstammen*, which allows Heidegger to emphasize the relation of earthly, watery, and mortal origins that continue to come to the originary.) The time-play-space (*Zeit-Spiel-Raum*) of language, dialect, and home is poetized in the same terms. The open realm from which we descend is inherited and handed down (*angestammten überlieften*) (SH 28). Hebel's Wiese Valley is the dynamic scene of summer ripeness, with plants and grains and vines and cherry trees pushing up. The poet fulsomely speaks of rootedness and groundedness: as just cited, he says that in dialect the essence of language roots (*wurzelt*), it springs up 'rootedly [*wurzelhaft*] from a region'; these poems 'are rooted in the indigenous [*im Bodenständigen gewurzelt sind*]' (SH 28, 29; SJPH 75). This grounding in the earth provides the counter to the grounding in reason which Heidegger explored with Leibniz in *The Principle of Reason* (chapter 4-B above). (Heidegger would also have in mind the echo between *bilden* as connoting both composing images and educating, thus linking the cultivation of members of a society and of plants. It also appears that with the idea of attuned origin and descent, Heidegger draws on the consonance between *Stamm* and *Stimm*. *Stimm* – voice and vote – moves both in the direction of tuning singing voices or instruments (*stimmen*) and voicing social positions and political (dis)agreements (*einstimmen, zustimmen, Überstimmung*).[19] Harmony occurs in multiple modes, by way of the bringing forth (*hervorbringen*) in poetry and music and political concurrence. There are further echoes, of course, in *Stimmung*, such an important word in *Being and Time*, which also names mood or atmosphere; and in *Das stimmt*, which means 'that is correct,' thus connecting back with the history of 'truth.'

We see that we have already arrived, with Hebel's dialectal writings and Heidegger's thinking thereafter, in the sphere of images. So, if we return to the difference between propositional language and poetry, Hebel allows Heidegger to more profoundly explore what the poetry does, and how it does it. Hebel's social goal of illuminating nature and the life of a home place cannot, in this interpretation, be accomplished by any series of statements, no matter how carefully the series is logically linked. That is one reason why it is so important that poetry is not propositional (SH 36, 41, 42, 50). Though Hebel was a minister, Heidegger notes that any poetic sermon from him that would aim to liberate people from ignorance – concerning, say, nature – would need to be done in a way that is free. As did Søren Kierkegaard, with his artistic mode of indirect communication, Hebel does not direct 'incontrovertible' assertions toward the reader; in that sense, he 'wishes neither to instruct nor educate' but to let something come forth to be seen, so as to 'let the reader have his way' (HFH 96). This happens through the public images formed (*Gebilde*). Indeed, Heidegger points out that poetic saying has the fundamental feature (*Grundzug*) of an image formed (*Gebild*), which would connote both figural organization and education (SH 42).[20] As he puts it in 'Hebel – Friend of the House' and then repeats in 'From the Experience of Thinking' (1947),

> Only image formed keeps the vision.
> Yet image formed rests in the poem.
> [*Erst Gebild wahrt (d.h. verwahrt) Gesicht.*
> *Doch Gebild ruht im Gedicht.*]

He goes on to explain that *Bilden* is from the Old High German verb *pilon* that means the 'pushing, pulsing, driving forth' (*stoßen, treiben, hervortreiben*) that originarily names the first bringing forth to appearance (*her-vor-bringen*) – not a returning to or re-presentation, but an initial generation, a new begetting (SH 42).

What are the images in the writing of Hebel that Heidegger is considering here? As we see, Hebel says the character of dialect and poetry (*Bilden, pilon,* pulsing out) in self-reflexive terms of fruitful pushing. But what is the master figura, the overall organizing principle? In 'Summer Evening' for example, the poet sings the image of the gathered home place in the language of the rhythms of its energetic dynamic and the need for rejuvenation in rest and calm. There is so much, so complexly interrelated that only a poem's non-linear, multiple intertextual references could begin to coherently lay out the differences of the dimensions and the balancing of their relationships: the heavens' vault appears in contrast to valley; the span of the summer day is given, and counter to it comes the evening; with and opposite to the sun, the moon appears too. Hence the poet begins by commanding our attention: '*O, leug doch,*' look (at what comes to light and is let stay). Look, look, yet again look at this lively place: the buzz of nature in summer, the sway of the heavenly arc above the valley with its fields and meadows and village, with the variety of human actions and inactions. Look, look, yet again look at the homeward turning of the weary sun, tired from its manifold day's work and at the time when the worn out working people fall asleep – the origin of heavenly and mortal fatigue rendered unhidden in the realm opened through the poem (SH 39).

That night's sleep would be much needed and well deserved as part of the overarching rhythm of the domain. The difference between this sleep and another, in which we all too commonly sleepwalk through life, parallels the difference between the way everyday life appears to Hebel and Heidegger here and the blank everydayness (*Alltäglichkeit*) analysed in *Being and Time* (there averageness and levelling down are also contrasted with the 'discovering of "world" and disclosing {that} comes about by clearing away coverings and obscurities'; BT sec. 27, p. 129). It is from indifferent, flattened existence that we need to be roused to alert reflection, awakened by the poet and the thinker to the world that is coming to appearance and to our place in it (SH 45–6). In regard to nature and the rest of the world around us, Hebel chides the householder, beginning the very 'first page of the *Little Treasury* with the following sentences':

> Everything's fine for the gentle reader when he's sitting home among familiar mountains and trees with his family and friends, or when he's having a beer in the local tavern, and he doesn't give it a single further thought. But when the sun rises early in its quiet majesty, he knows not whence it comes; and evenings, when it goes down, he knows not whither it goes and where it hides its light throughout the night and on which secret pathway it again finds its way to the mountains of dawn. Or when the moon goes around pale and thin one time, and round and full another, again he knows not how this comes about, and when he looks into a sky full of stars, and the one twinkles more beautifully and joyfully than the other, he believes they are all there for his sake. And yet he really doesn't know quite what they want. Good friend, it is not commendable to see something all one's days and never ask what it means. (cited in HFH 96)

Epiphany (*Erleuchtung*) and hierophany (to use Mircea Eliade's term) occur simultaneously insofar as poetry first says and brings forth a world, a newly charged realm where before only the ordinary existed. The echo that is the poem, as Heidegger started to say in *Contributions to Philosophy* (where it appeared as one of the six joinings that enact thinking), is not at all a re-presentation, but a continuation that passes along that which is never depleted but still comes (CP 75, 80, 86, 91, 98). In that early work, he argued how the echo, though coming from the concealment of technicity and the epoch of the greatest disenchantment about what is, is also the echo of the sway of being and thus a movement toward the re-enchantment of the world. Though it is only implicit in these essays now being considered, Heidegger believes that what Hebel says is also an echo, as is clear from Heidegger's use of the same terms in explaining what it means for Hebel to say that with the sayings in the *Little Treasury*, 'he will now preach a sermon.' According to Heidegger it is 'the house-friend, not the minister' who speaks, and even then, the poet's preaching (*Predigen*) needs to be understood in the language of the Latin *praedicare*. 'It means: to recite something to someone [*etwas vorsagen*], and thus to bring news, and so to make known or renowned [*rühmen*] and thus to let what is to be said appear in its shining. This "preaching" is the essence of poetic saying' (HFH 96).

Hebel's poetizing lets the originary force of the dialect as opening saying still come; as echo it brings the news that and how the originary force unfolds in this place, for this people. Here, dialect provides yet another contact with the origin, which yet has power as the source that still comes. In and through the poetic saying of what is most nearby, the open realm opens. Hence, the poetry of Hebel, by limiting itself to the specific, makes itself, not small, but concentrated, ready to spread widely. This thought too, as others in this cluster, is completed in the images of rootedness and flowering: as Hebel famously said and Heidegger frequently cites, 'We are plants which – whether we care to admit it to ourselves or not – must ascend with our roots in the earth, in order to bloom in the ether and bear fruit' (cited in HFH 100). The poems are also part of the cycle: ripened by Hebel, they are ready to burst forth in a process of further seeding as their words and thoughts are scattered by the winds or gathered together and then sown wider still by humans – especially once transformed from locally spoken dialect into standard written German.

The low-key references that Hebel and Heidegger make to Plato's sun, Hegel's *aufheben*, or Enlightenment science are there to emphasize the differences between the philosophical-scientific concepts and Hebel's images formed. The latter are not merely vivid ways of presenting the former, nor even part of the metaphysical mode of thinking and writing. Again, the poetic echo neither imitates nor returns. For instance, whereas the lesson of Plato's writing about the sun is the start of metaphysics, the sun and realm that appear for and through Hebel do not point to, nor do they depend on, any further, transcendental ultimate. This poetically articulated world is no-longer-metaphysical, because what is given in the language of dialectal poetry is itself let be, to reverberate.

And what does the image formed in Hebel's dialectal poetry bring forth? At a general level, in 'Hebel – Friend of the House,' Heidegger answers in the same terms he uses elsewhere. He tells us that Hebel discloses 'more original possibilities for dwelling' where 'to dwell' 'designates to us the manner in which man, upon the earth and beneath the sky, completes the passage from birth to death. The passage is *multiform* and rich in transformations. It nonetheless remains throughout the chief trait of dwelling, of the human sojourn between earth and sky, between birth and death, between joy and pain, between work and word' (HFH 93). 'If we call this manifold "between" the *world*, then the world is the house that mortals inhabit' (HFH 93). Pressing deeper, Heidegger explains that when we see the poet as the friend of the household of mortal dwellers, we come to understand that in Hebel's poetized words 'what we commonly see of the world, of human and divine things' – earth and sun, moon, planets, comets, stars, boys and girls, good fellows in taverns, family and friends – becomes transformed through poetic saying (*das dichterische Sagen*) (HFH 92). The poetizing opens a between where these elements gather into a world.

Similarly, in 'Sprache und Heimat,' Heidegger explains how Hebel's *Alemannic Poems* bring forth the composition of 'the earth and works of mortals upon it, under the heavens' (SH 45). In this essay he explains in even more detail how 'the homey place first comes to light in the formed image [*Gebild*],' working through what Hebel writes of sun, moon, earth, men and women, boys and girls, valley and mountains, fields and meadows, the village and church spire, and God, to explain how Hebel, like Hölderlin, does justice to 'the simple joints of the four-fold that comes to saying in the *Gebild* of poems,' and 'first lets the mortals dwell on the earth under the heavens before the gods' (SH 46, 38–47, 48, 50). As *her-vor-bringen*, the poetic saying is a way of building in language a place or a world even, where we can dwell. This theme, of course, is continuous with Heidegger's overall position, as articulated in 'Poetically Man Dwells' or 'Building Dwelling Thinking.' With dialect we are brought to a specific, historical world; with Hebel's poetic articulations, to a unified realm, a cosmos. Thus, by remaining in the strange – in the differences among the two dialects and standard High German – Heidegger learns what it is to become at home – at least in regard to the home that was Hebel's and that might still be for contemporary Germans insofar as dialect remains a force moving through today's language, even if in a hidden manner – and not only in what is spoken but in thinking and doing, for these too occur in the local idiom (SJPH 74).

As in Heidegger's originary analysis of the early Greek notions of *Fug* (ἀδικία as *Un-Fug*, disorder, in 'The Anaximander Fragment'; see above, chapter 4-A), Heidegger speaks of the most serious homelessness, the deepest breaking of relationships among the dimensions of what otherwise might be a world, in terms of 'being out of joint.' Heidegger contends that disjointedness is an intimate aspect of the technological age – a sharp contrast with the ordered world brought to appearance by the well-composed, 'original and essential tune and agreement [*stimmende*] of Hebel's poetic saying in dialect. The gathering together that the poet accomplishes in setting-into-work the belonging of heavens and earth, mortals and divinities, is a putting into proper jointure [*Fug*, *Bezug*].' Today, as we see by comparing our world with the poetic realm disclosed by Hebel, 'the inherited, handled down connection among language, mother tongue, dialect, and home are out of joint [*die angestammten überlieferten Bezüge zwischen Sprache, Muttersprache, Mundart und Heimat schon aus den Fugen*]' (SH 28). Our task is to get back into joint, to be no longer dislocated, which here includes understanding the relation between language *and* home, where the 'and' is the binding word holding language *and* home to(ward) one another and depending on (*aushölt*) their essential relation (SH 29). The remedy to being out-of-joint can be found in the image formed by poetic saying: *Gebild could counter Gestell.* Hebel's poetic saying would doubly help with coming back into joint, relocating things in the relations where they belong. On the one hand, the world he delineates is 'in order'; on the other, not only poetry overall, but especially his exceptionally well-crafted compositions, are exemplary. As Hebel himself noted in his 1802 introduction to the Subscription of the first edition of *Alemannic Poems*, his wish was 'that folk poetry composed [*verfaßt*] in folk dialect would let language come before us to shine forth in its full structure and texture [*Gefüge und Gewebe*]' (SH 30).

Weary of the homelessness of our age, as well perhaps at having to deal with the same questions and seemingly the same alternatives over and over, in every pulse of thinking, we may well wish to be rescued. Well intended and following Heidegger for a long time, we might hope that the issue has played itself out in poetizing thinking. Is it not the case that home is in dialect? Or, perhaps dialectal poetry? Is this not an answer? A solution for what is needed? No. Unavoidably, such an answer, that language and home already come to their own in dialect, is only superficial. The general insight that Heidegger confirms and further develops in reading Hebel may be true enough, and thus part of an alternative disclosure that would counter, or complement, the dominant language of today, but the general is not sufficient. Recall the connection Heidegger developed in *The Principle of Reason* (chapter 4-B, above) between ground in its several meanings and thinking and saying. What is grounded in abstract, univocal concepts, however powerful, is not grounded as rooted in the earth; insofar as the former is part of our homelessness, the latter is a necessary element in any homecoming. This applies not only to philosophical, scientific-technological language, but even to originary thinking's generalizations. These being reflexively applied by Heidegger to what he himself presents as abstract insights, he insists that here we have no solution, no rescue.

To think language and home, and their relation, we would have, he tells us, to encounter the threat ourselves and recognize it as such (SH 29). We have only begun to walk such a pathway, trying to become open to such a personal event so that we might experience it and think it through. To think and speak otherwise than indefinitely and thus groundlessly is precisely why Heidegger has turned to Hebel and dialectal poetry. So, he and we have to begin again, passing beyond the continued development of the general interpretation of strangeness and language (even as dialect) and eventually beyond the understanding of poetry that accomplishes the *her-vor-bringen* of thing and the fourfold as world.

We seem so close, yet so far, from what may help. We have the questions: Language? Home? Poetry? We have poems specifically picked out by Heidegger to guide us. What next? Heidegger weaves another layer through these Hebel essays in which he tries to help us toward what needs to be experienced. He gives a hint by way of a poem by Jos. v. Eichendorff, which treats the realm of language and home:

> We long to come home
> And don't know where it is. (cited in SH 31)

The clue is not found in the content of what is said here, Heidegger contends, but through a strategic interpretation holding that the song is dormant in what is dreamt and that it only begins to sing if we hit upon the magic word (SH 31). What might the magic word be? How to hit upon it?

By hearing dialectal words. Found in dialectal poems. That would not mean seeking general, abstract ideas, now expressed in dialect rather than in a standard, major language. It would mean experiencing dialectal utterances speaking for themselves. Or, dialect letting shine forth what it can disclose through the image formed by the poet's poetizing. As the first stanza of Hebel's 'Der Sommerabend' says,

> O, leug doch, wie isch d'Sunn, su müed,
> Leug, wie sie d'Heimat abezicht!

O leug, vie Strahl und Strahl verglimmt,
Und wie sie's Fazenetli nimmt,
E Wülkli, blau mit rot vermüscht,
Und wie sie an der Stirne wüscht. (cited in SH 32)

What to do with this? It seems that we can discern '*Sunn*' (sun), '*Heimat*' (home), '*Strahl*' (ray), and '*Stirne*' (star) easily enough. And reading out loud so as to hear the sounds, we might imaginatively guess '*mued*' to mean '*müde*' (tired), and so on. But this is grasping at straws in the dark. Knowing our limits and intending to keep on our way at this more proper, deeper level of engagement with the specific, historically bestowed words and place, we encounter the poem and an explication in several different kinds of language that need not be abstract or indefinite: careful standard High German and two dialects: Hebel's own dialect (Alemannic Oberdeutsch) and a north German way of speaking (Niederdeutsch). This way Hebel's southern-dialectal poem is also considered in two translations.

Heidegger insists that the point is not to listen for 'content,' or what might be stated in these dialectal words, but to try to *experience* something of what is brought forth. A dialect is primarily a spoken mode of local saying and thus speaks only as it does. In a most serious sense, dialect is the sound of the mouth, the mother's mouth and tongue. Here we find the hometown's historical sounding off. Where sound may matter most, the ear is more important than the eye – thus the particular importance of Hebel, whom Heidegger credits as the unparalleled genius able to purely echo the sound of dialect in written language (SJPH 75; HFH 99). Properly heard, Heidegger contends, the Oberdeutsch words, even without poetic craft, have their own strong rhythm (SH 28). The words swing and sing. He goes so far as to say that 'Dialect poetizes itself' (*die gleichsam von selber fortdichtet*) (SH 48). Our task is to hear through Hebel's poems, that is, to 'thoroughly and hearingly [*gehörig*] think after the sounds spoken therein,' first attempting to bring the singing of the poem to 'ear and heart' (SH 29, 30). This would indeed be remaining in and going through the strange – not only through language generally understood, but by way of particular languages hopelessly foreign to us, and we to them.

Heidegger persists with a snatch of the sound of the Alemannic dialect itself, as locally spoken and as composed in Hebel's poem, contrasting the two dimensions and showing a bit of the way they belong-work together. On the one hand, Heidegger says that through the proper metre that Hebel has so well chosen, 'Summer Evening' lets us hear the sounding of the melody of the Alemannic dialect, so that we may be able to hold our hearing open for the singing song of the poem, without immediately attending to or comprehending anything that might be called content (SH 34, 30). On the other hand, according to his reading, counter dynamics are deployed. In the very first line, Heidegger holds, the language shifts, with the comma after the initial '*O*' ('*O, leug doch ...*'), erasing the iambic flow as the reader pauses, so that the tone reverses itself. In a further tension, though the rhythm and metre work well with ('properly contain') the dialectal sound, from the beginning the dialect strains against the metre in a tension that is only heard, when the poem is spoken. The poem would, then, already and complexly move by way of the modes of saying, where the poetic articulation both defers to and interrupts the sounds from the mother's mouth and tongue. Little surprise that the world that emerges in the poetic saying swings, that is, is dynamic.

Trying to convey the lively world brought forth in these poems, Heidegger begins to hear and read 'Summer Evening' with other of the *Alemannic Poems:* 'The Man in the Moon,' 'The Evening Star,' 'The Wiese,' 'January,' 'Winter,' 'Little Boy of the Woods,' and 'The Habermus' (SH 37–48). At the poem's beginning, Heidegger explains, the first stanza brings into view the turning home of the tired woman sun (*Frausonne*), that is, 'her setting into the sheltering-shepherding stillness, whose placement remains full of secrets.' The place the sun sets is the same site where the moon rises: the home place (*Heimat*) (SH 43). The second stanza takes up the rhythm of the day's work in the time-play-space (*Zeit-Spiel-Raum*) (SH 43). We find out that the sun is especially tired because it has to travel unusually far across the summer sky, whereas in winter, with its shorter days, the sun is granted a longer rest. In the low-lying villages of the Black Forest, the winter sun rises late and sets early; exaggerated in winter, the longer stillness appears as the quiet restfulness in which life seems to sleep. 'Summer Evening,' however, shows the region of the work which the sun performs over house and field, mountain and valley, 'her blessing called for by all' – a realm whose 'manifold richness' is 'spread before our eyes' (stanzas 4–7). Ploughed fields sprout with growth as do fields of grain full of birds fluttering after kernels, vineyards dense with leaves on the slopes, and blossoms gloriously flourishing on wildflowers in the meadows as on the cherry trees in the gardens – all even further enlivened by the 'industrious to and fro of bees and bugs' (SH 44). The tired peasant woman sun is joined by villagers washing and bleaching and by the boys and girls, men and women, engaged in the harvest, who –

though this is the hardest day's labour of all – yet fill the valley with joyful, mutual calling to one another (SH 44–5).

Reversing the point of view, Hebel shifts from looking down at the earth beneath the sky to looking up and away to the wooded summit of the mountains, 'above which the red ball of the sun remains a while before setting.' The magic afterglow of the red sunset shimmers around the church spire for a long time (as the setting sun, so tired, stops to rest along the edge of the field path home), 'letting the middle of the home village [*Heimatdorf*], and thus the village itself, come into view' (SH 45). All ask God for a 'good night' – and they must ask, because it does not come forth out of itself as does the 'most joyous and highest summer blessing and caring of the sun' (SH 44 46). In Heidegger's terms, *physis* and God differ too, as does the mode of the giving. *O*, this realm is wonderful – agreeing on this, Hebel's poem and Heidegger's explication both swing around together, returning back to the first stanza. The home valley closes to rest beneath the 'hesitant rising of the moon behind the pine wood on the dominant mountain summit,' a time when the sun now comes close to the silent spirits at night (SH 46).[21]

For all the simple splendour brought forth for us to see in the sun's lingering a long time in setting, the relation of the sky and earth is not fully understood unless the night sky is also shown, with the full harvest moon rising and looking upon the earth as the sun goes down (SH 45). At the height of the harvest, the work may last into the night, when cut hay is raked into small piles to protect it from the dew, so that as the sun sets in the west, the moon rises in the east, thus continuing a heavenly watch over the work of humans before they can sleep (SH 46). Indeed, the moon is variously elaborated by Hebel. Heidegger, not known for his sense of humour, appreciates Hebel's intent in pulling the reader's leg. Amidst the astronomy of natural science, the moon, as phenomenon, is described in 'The Man in the Moon' as a kind of community security guard, arrived to do a shift (SH 45): 'The house-friend, like the highest-ranking official night watchman, the moon, is one who stays awake the whole night through. He watches over the right kind of rest for the dwellers; he watches out for what threatens and disturbs' (HFH 94).

What is the grave danger the moon stands guard for, ready to sound the alarm? What does it in fact espy in the village? 'In the conclusion of the reflection on the moon,' (*Reflections on the World-Edifice. The Moon.* I, 326ff., cited in HFH), Hebel answers, 'the moon watches how boys kiss girls.' Heidegger goes along, commenting, 'The house-friend watches how boys kiss girls. His observing is one of wonderment, not a curious gaping. The house-friend sees to it that lovers are provided with a soft radiance, a moon-like splendor which is neither merely earthly nor only heavenly, but both, yet both as primordially inseparable' (HFH 94–5). Shifting quietly from the humorous to the serious, Heidegger shows us how both the poet and the moon are alike, reflecting or echoing the soft radiance that comes from without while themselves remaining inconspicuous. The 'softly restrained shining' and 'soft, hardly noticeable light' are the same as the 'little golden kernel' that the poet places here, and the same as the 'peacefully sounding word' which 'remains in tune with that which allows us to dwell' – the poet echoes the attunement and allowance where only insofar as mankind (as the mortal one) 'inhabits the house of the world' does it 'stand in the calling [*Bestimmung*] to build a house for the celestial ones, and a dwelling-place for himself' (HFH 92, 93, 95, 96). Heidegger, then, brings us to see what Hebel himself discovered. The deeper answer to the question of who the friend of the house is, is that it is not the poet, nor the *Baden Province Calendar*, to which the poet gave the same name (HFH 90–1), but the moon. The poet echoes the moon, the poems letting us see the moon before us as house-friend.

The shared responsibility of the heavens for earth and mortals is seen in that the moon guards the villagers as did the sun, which Hebel described as ambling up the country road when evening draws about the home place, moving carefully, as a friendly mother keeping an eye on her playing children. Of course, after the moon's appearance and then disappearance, the sun would rise again. In 'The Habermus,' Hebel poetizes how, in the earliest morning, even before the sun rises, its rays appear over the mountain as the sun combs its golden braids. Hebel, Heidegger tells us, teases out the play between 'rays' and 'combs' and 'ridges' or 'crests,' since the dialectal words *strehl* and *strehelen* belong together with *Strahl* (ray) and mean the same as *Kamm* (both 'comb' and 'ridges' or 'crest') (*Kamm* in contemporary German can also be said with *Strähl*, which circles back to resonate with *Strahl*). Immediately, in an acrobatic move, Hebel says that after the sun has combed its golden hair, the rays become knitting needles. And what does the sun knit with shafts of light? Cloudbanks (*Gewölk*) from the dew of the sky (SH 48–9).

How beautiful. (Wouldn't we agree with Hebel, who says '*tolli Frau*'; and Heidegger, '*Toll*' [great, amazing]?) Hebel and Heidegger show us how plain language and homely life come to be understood as immeasurably rich, how from the ordinary the mysterious unfolds so that the former is part of the latter's excess. The world brought into the image formed opens as a wonderful home, manifold, yet simple. In the open realm which Hebel delineated – so it could first be understood by the people of his country, thus enabling them and the poet too to become thoughtful and to genuinely dwell there – the everyday shines forth as astonishing, in contrast to the indifferent everyday described in *Being and Time* (as seen in chapter 1). I do not think it an exaggeration to say that these pages of 'Sprache und Heimat' (especially 34–41, 43–6), where Heidegger lets Hebel's saying and world come into standard language we can follow, are a high point of Heidegger's homecoming thinking and writing.[22] In any case, the results of his detailed readings are what, in fact, enable him to make the general remarks noted above, and to reaffirm (toward the end of the essay) that it is in the harmonious realm, from out of which the poem is spoken, that the sun and moon, mountains and valley, peasants and villagers, are all first brought together to one another and only thus to each its own character in mutual relation to the others (SH 49).

As Heidegger pursues his own central project of homecoming by learning to think and say, for example, how the opening of dif-ference that would allow for the gathering of world would be given, he finds that Hebel's dialectal poetizing confirms and extends what Heidegger already understands about the gathering of the fourfold or dwelling as abiding in language's saying; and that a detailed reading of Hebel helps open up for us a way to experience language as dialect and thus learn to dwell at home. Hebel's writing also provides a way for Heidegger to take another step in unfolding key originary words and phenomena, such as *physis*, difference, the same, the open, time, and truth-*aletheia*.

We have seen the extent to which Hebel's Alemannic poetry provides Heidegger with a rich, concrete way to articulate *physis* as bringing forth a world that melds with historical human *her-vor-bringen*. Within the poem, difference operates. So too within the larger collection of poems. Even prior to the concretization of *physis* and making it possible, difference, as that which opens for giving, has come quietly, but appropriately, through the various languages of these essays: the standard High German and the Niederdeutsch and Oberdeutsch dialects (plus, as we have noted, a bit of Greek and Latin, as well as a comparison with *Oberswäbisch*) (SH 46). In fact, Heidegger makes a point of the differences, while focusing on them as a way of 'remaining in and coming through the strange,' as we have seen. Precisely in this almost unbridgeable difference, each comes to its own: 'freely, into the estrangement of each and out of the difference of both to comprehend the inmost' (*Um freilich im Fremden das Eigene Und aus dem Unterschied beiden das Wesenhafte zu vernehmen*) (SH 30).

With the open that comes into appearance as a result of the play of the various languages – the products of locality and dialect – we also find that the same is said. This happens, since the poem is the site for the coming forth of the multiple dimensions, not each for or from itself, but as all simultaneously coming to their own together. Emphasizing the sounding or ringing tone (*Klang*) of what is said, Heidegger explains that 'the same' (*das Selbe*) in which the dimensions are brought forth out of concealment is 'the harmony of the whole realm [*der Einklang jenes ganzen Bereiches*] out of which the poem speaks' (SH 49). Recognizing the originary concordance (that is, the source of the poetizing and of the place) will only occur if we remember that, for Heidegger, what is the same is not the uniform or identical but the different, dynamically gathered together. Thus, Hebel and Heidegger present the former's home valley in its full atmospheric range, not allowing it to slip into a simplified character that might nostalgically be yearned for by the homeless. The poetizing puts before us what belongs together in a concrete historical way. The poem stresses over and over that the mountain valley is a scene of hard work and deep fatigue. The sun–peasant woman, long day's work done, is worn out, needing even to rest on the way home; only when the sun finally sets can humans, through with their own exhausting day's work, go to sleep. Rest comes only at night, when the moon finally rises, or in winter – harsh in its own way – when the slow days and long nights provide some relief – requiring perhaps some mending of a harness by fire or candle light and the daily chores of caring for the animals and making sure there is enough fire wood, but not staying in the fields all day long (SH 36). Thus, through the singing ringing sound of dialect the open realm appears as the banging and buzzing, the calling and answering of the whole valley and all in it, over which the sun sets and the moon rises – that is, as the valley of the Wiese, come to be seen as what it is, the poet's and villagers' homeland (SH 40). Yet though fruitful and exemplary for its time and place, it is neither a golden age of paradise on earth nor a way of life that could come again.

Hebel's poetry also provides Heidegger fertile ground for developing his thinking on time. Of course, from *Being and Time* onward he has contested the chronological conception of the flow of time that runs from Aristotle to contemporary science and history, recovering the alternative that he also found in Aristotle and St Paul: *kairos*, *Augenblick*, the decisive moment. He finds that Hebel also contributes to what needs to be thought in this regard. The first line of the second stanza of 'Summer Evening' that starts with "*s isch wohl,*' continues '*sie het au übel zit.*' As a whole, the line says that the sun has a bad time in summer, since it must labour so long and becomes tired (SH 36–7). As Heidegger does with other key words, he explains that the full sense of time (*Zit, Zeit*) cannot be understood if reduced to our modern or contemporary meaning, in this case to clock time.[23] While the Alemannic confirms that time is not most profoundly or originarily a matter of mere measure and that clocks are not simply chronometers, he dutifully, and perhaps playfully, notes the irony that in the dialect a pocket watch is called 'little time' (*das Zitli, das Zeitlein*). Hebel's poems bring the meaning of time-*Zeit-Zit* to clarity. Clock time would be derived not so much from the unvarying movement of the sun's or moon's crossing the heavens as from the integrated cycles of heavens and earth and humans in which, as we have heard, times are different (spring ploughing and sowing differing from summer haying; time varies within the day, as in the evening, when the sun lingers, changing its pace by tarrying a long while before setting). Here what matters and provides the measure is the appropriateness of what happens, that is, the primary question is about the right time for what is done and what is let go.

In 'Die Wiese,' the river which runs from the Feldberg, near Freiburg, to Basel (that is, through both Hebel's and Heidegger's territory) appears as a young girl who – in the convention of river poems, which are cast in the figure of a wedding – is to be married to a young Swiss boy, the Rhine (SH 37).[24] The poet says that she has come fully to her own self, mature in that her 'virtues and faults' are set, well established. In the frank language of the rural world, Hebel writes that she is ready to take a man.

> Feldberg's daughter, listen, you have matured in virtue and faults, so
> it seems to me, you are ready for a man, that is, to take a man,
> how about it?

In the original Oberdeutsch dialectal version,

> *Feldbergs Tochter los, de bisch an Tuged und Fehler*
> *zitig, chunnt's mehr halber vor, zum Manne, wie wär's echt?*

As translated into Hochdeutsch,

> *Feldbergs Tochter, hör zu, du bist Tugend und Fehler reif, so kommt es mir fast vor, zum Manne – d.h. einen Mann zu nehmen, wie wärs wohl?* (cited in SH 37)

'*Zitig*' then, means appropriate for (*geeignet für*), able to, mature for (*reif für*). '*Zit*,' '*Zeit*' name what is ready, what has reached its time and is ripe and beginning to sprout; the good time, the right time, happens when many seeds have had time to mature, explode out into the world (SH 37).

Hebel's Oberdeutsch also allows Heidegger to continue along the trajectory in which he traces the shift from truth as *aletheia* for the early Greeks to its metaphysical interpretation as correspondence and correctness and then to his own originary recovery of truth as disclosure. He now can take yet another step. The second stanza of 'Summer Evening,' meditating on '*zi*' as just considered, begins with "*s ist wohr*,' which Heidegger translates into standard German as '*es ist wahr*' (it is true). As he has before, he warns the reader that while (given our standard assumptions and interpretations) 'it is true' may seem to mean 'it is correct' or 'it is what is the case' (*es triff zu*), that is not at all what the poet says, both because the poem is not a propositional statement and because the poet and poem have the task of 'letting come to the full light' what is to be seen. Thus the thrice-repeated '*leug*,' 'look,' thought with "*s isch wahr*,' not only bears back on what comes to light in the first stanza, but informs all that follows as well (SH 35).

In the seventh stanza, Hebel writes, '*Es isch e Sach*,' which, Heidegger explains, in dialect refers to something specific, especially in the sense that there is 'something about it' – namely, that it is not known through and through, that some mystery remains, something secret and therefore mysterious. This is multiply so for the realm articulated by Hebel's poems. For instance, of course it is the case that the sun sets. Clearly, though, the poem brings to view 'her going under into the sheltering-shepherding stillness, whose placement is full of secrets [*ihren Untergang in die bergend-hirtende Stille, deren Ortschaft geheimnissvoll bleibt*]' (SH 43). The stillness, it would seem, is also the sphere of the 'still spirits' (*stillen Geisten*) to which, Hebel tells us, the sun is close when setting (SH 47).

In what would appear to be the deepest interpretation of that which he has been thinking as *aletheia*, *legein*, *noein*, more profoundly brought together in the simultaneous occurrence of disclosure itself and the human letting what comes forth lie before us in ear and eye and taking it to heart, thinking through the *wohl* and *leug* together, Heidegger powerfully interprets "*s isch wohl*' as follows: '*what* [that which] *the look should see now shows itself openly* (*in the open*) [*offen zeigt sich, nämlich was das leuge erblicken soll*]' (SH 39). He has never before said so well the dynamic mutuality of what is given, the giving, and our *appropriate* response.

Not surprisingly, Heidegger reads 'what [that which] the look should see now shows itself openly [in the open]' in terms of unconcealment: it names the bringing to light that at which we should look. He goes on to explicate how Hebel's poem speaks of the 'open realm, within which the entire day's work of the sun comes forth into unhiddenness [*den offende Bereich, darin das ganze Tagwerk das Sonne ins Unverborgene hervorkommt*].' Indeed, he multiplies the resonances, making explicit that the poetic saying – *her-vor-bringen* – is nothing other than the play of concealment/disclosure. The *her* says 'from the hidden and self-hiding, self-sheltering [*aus dem Verborgenen und Sichverbergenden*]'; the '*vor*' says 'into the unhidden, into the open [*ins Unverbergenden, Offenbare*]' – thus *her-vor-bringen* says 'bring forth out of hiding, into open disclosure' (SH 42). Heidegger goes on to explain how the seventh stanza's lines, which bring to a close the telling of the sun's day's work, reveal the 'happiest and highest of the sun's summertime blessings coming to appearance' (SH 39). Thus the seventh verse begins with a variation (of the first line of the second verse), "*s isch weger wohr*,' which he glosses, saying that '*weger* is a root word for the intensification of [the standard German] *wahr*, that is, obvious. "*Weger*" and "wegerle" are characteristically Oberdeutsch words and, among the old folks, are still used in Oberswäbisch. *Weger wohr* [then], names the entirely disclosedly obvious' (SH 39). The everyday life of the valley is full of secrets and wonderful when disclosed. Oh, look at the realm holding sway that is brought to our view that we should see: 'we come nearer the essential sway's region [*Wesensbereich*] if we experience what poetically inheres in dialect as what, for us, without our being focused on or conscious of it, is always already envisioned, and therefore itself can be called that which is seen' (SH 50). Now, we would not just live in the home place, but could learn to see it as rising from the marvellous and magical and thus experience it as re-enchanted.

A Parting of Ways

Since Hebel's dialectal poetry was a means for him and the people of his country to learn to dwell at home, the continuing power of that accomplishment in language and history enables Heidegger too to move further in his homecoming. Through reflection on the dialect's concrete, specific saying, he comes to a deeper, originary understanding of how we can dwell in language: 'Poetic saying first originates the shelter and caring shepherding, the place of the blessing [*Huld*] for a native place which can be a resting point in the earthly remaining underway of the dwelling humans' (SH 50). 'Language is, by virtue of its poetic essence, the most concealed and therefore the widest reaching, most intensely (definitive) granting *her-vor-bringen* of home' (SH 50). Hence, Heidegger's last words in 'Sprache und Heimat' affirm how definite it is that we should no longer speak of the relation of the two in terms of 'and'; rather, we are given, '*language* [dialect] *as home* [*Sprache als Heimat*].'

While these essays provide a clear, even helpful, final articulation of what the poets accomplish, showing how through them we may learn to dwell as part of the fourfold world, how language – as dialect – bestows and installs home, I cannot help but find that in them we begin to experience a parting of the ways after an intense engagement with dialect: Hebel and his beautiful past world resonate in one direction, and Heidegger with both his own present originary language and future possible dwelling at home moves in another. The parting of ways is unavoidable, as are the problems and possibilities over time. Heidegger could not be clearer in refusing a return to the past: 'To be sure, we of today can no longer return to the world experienced by Hebel a hundred and fifty years ago, neither to its intact rusticity, nor to its limited knowledge of nature' (HFH 98). Now, however, we can appropriately think through how it is that what is poetic in human dwelling depends on the poet. Such a response would direct us toward the future, since we would look ahead to where the poet beckons. Hebel, for example, brings us forward to language, to language that shelters us. So, there is no impulse to become a nineteenth-century Alemannic peasant, just as there is none to become an early Greek (despite all the misunderstandings about what Heidegger says and is doing).

Rather, insofar as we hear and understand what Hebel does – he brings his world to language, so while language continues to shelter that world and its dwelling inhabitants and to let appear what otherwise would remain concealed, so that he does learn to abide in his language and homeland and to help the people of his country do so, we come to see that Heidegger – and we too – can learn to enter into language thoughtfully, letting it be in order that we can come to dwell therein. The point of hearing Hebel, then, besides appreciating what he has accomplished and what occurred in his time, is to face the tasks that still remain and that are nearest to us: he went through the experience of his and his time's homelessness and achieved a homecoming; we can too. So, along with Heidegger, we part from Hebel and his dialectal saying.

Heidegger and the rest of us are now on our own – even with the poetic guides nearby and on call, we still need to try to complete the homecoming ourselves. Nor is even our basic companionship stable. We have already begun to feel Heidegger slipping away, to his own, where we cannot really or finally go: just now he moved deeper into his own local dialect; next – as we will see in the following chapter – he goes back home, at ease with his lifelong neighbours in Meßkirch and Todtnauberg.

Of course, as we prepare to hear the last of what Hebel says, what is most his own as the person he becomes – as 'a poet who realized with increasing clarity that his nature was that of the house-friend, and who took up that nature ever more decisively' (HFH 92) – we too need to become more fully ready to deal with our own situation, moving from the shared homelessness of our age to our own pathway, as Hebel did – as does Heidegger. The sober realization that we cannot follow Heidegger, either in his Oberdeutsch or into the heart of his village, Meßkirch, really should be no surprise, nor should it prevent us from honestly acknowledging that all along the same was more true than we would admit, while as eager companions we 'followed' Heidegger's Greek, or Latin, or, for that matter, his standard High German, though in some cases it was easier for us to believe we were closer than we perhaps were. Still, we have learned as best we could. And with all that Heidegger has written, we could still learn for a long time, even as, parting with Hebel and his lively world, we still enjoy the company and thoughtful words of Heidegger as he heads on the final pathway, most deeply and quietly into his own genuine home.

He does this in a handful of intimate, homey works, written about, and often delivered in, Freiburg, Meßkirch, and Todtnauberg. So, for a bit longer we can linger together with Heidegger as we listen, *overhearing* what he says in his hometowns. Focally speaking very locally (to his neighbours, occasionally including close colleagues), he also lets us come along by allowing what he says to be printed and distributed (for the most part in standard German), thereby – as he said of Hebel – finally reaching widely, and perhaps most powerfully, because most simply.

6 Staying Near the Source

Focus on Things, Places-Regions, Dwelling

Though there are many German languages, Hebel is the great guide to at least two types – dialect and standard written language. As we have seen, Heidegger chose Hebel as a guide because the long-exiled poet was dedicated to thinking home, because he was of the same countryside and shared a neighbourly dialect, and because he remains, Heidegger holds, the master teacher of the German language. The magisterial teaching is accomplished through his poetry, which both 'display[s] dialect [*Dialekt*] itself in its proper poetic character and bring[s] first the idiom [*Mundart*] to the fullness, breadth, and clarity of its own unspoken language' (SH 47). Heidegger boldly says that 'Hebel's meditations and stories [of the *Little Treasury*] speak in the simplest, the clearest, and at the same time the most enchanting and thoughtful German language ever written. The language of Hebel's *Little Treasury* remains the standard of learning for those preparing to speak or write that language in an exemplary way' (SH 99).

In what lies the mystery of Hebel's language? Not in any pretentious will to have a style, nor in any intention to write in the most popular manner possible. According to Heidegger, the mystery of the language of the *Little Treasury* lies in the fact that Hebel could embody the language of the Alemannic dialect in the conventional written language, so that in this manner he allows the written language to resonate as pure echo of the riches of the dialect (SJPH 75; HFH 99). Patiently, Heidegger has attended to Hebel's Alemannic dialect and standard German and has learned lessons from Hebel's masterful way of moving back and forth between these distinct modes of saying in order to help his general audience profit from the original power of the source dialect that continues to emerge in the usual language they can understand. Now, in Heidegger's 'final' works about home and homecoming, which include originary essays about dwelling and place, as well as his 'homey' works on Freiburg, Meßkirch, and Todtnauberg, he tries to do the same.

In fact, he speaks and writes in at least four languages: metaphysical-representational philosophical German, and his own distinctive originary German (both of which carry on separate dimensions of Greek and Latin), the German of his academic, professional life (Hochdeutsch), and his regional dialects (to which he passes over when in dialogue with Hebel and with his neighbours in Freiburg-Zähringen, in Meßkirch, and in Todtnauberg). As we know, we cannot follow his dialect but do have access to his other three languages; thus far, we have especially been following how he has laboured and significantly succeeded during his homecoming journey in moving beyond metaphysics to attain his own originary voice. What he sets into work for the first time in history also moves beyond ordinary German and becomes an originary bringing forth that occurs with the saying and thinking of *Ereignis, es gibt,* dif-ference, *einräumen,* and the like. Though that originary language partly stems from retrieving words and thoughts from the not-yet-metaphysical Greek or Old High German or the works of already originary poets and mystics, it also stays rooted in dialect, as with his Hebel reflections. As we will see, in the end Heidegger increasingly turns back yet again, now shifting from his originary accomplishment to dialect and to ordinary German, clearly following Hebel's pathway. But, first, there is much that needs to be said originarily.

Heidegger's thinking and saying has arrived at the point where he can use the fecund originary words to focus explicitly on dwelling, space, and things, while continuing to always remain underway. Thus, he cannot proceed at this point by 'arriving at' or positing an ultimate answer to what being at home might be. Even if he has come to a point of experiencing enough to begin to learn to dwell near the source, or perhaps even to start dwelling there (Hölderlin's phases 5 and 6, respectively), any such accomplishment would have to be by way of continuing to move along the entire trajectory of homelessness and homecoming. Heidegger's persistence in following the 'mandate' and staying in the strange, and moving to and fro is witnessed by the way he returns to pick up and modify what he thought earlier. In a kind of dialogue with himself, he often reworks what he has said previously, either adding appendices or epilogues to subsequent editions or sometimes writing entirely new essays.

In the case at hand, Heidegger continues to think dwelling, building, things, regions, space, and local place in the 1950s and 1960s by retrieving some major strands from 'The Origin of the Work of Art' (1935–6), that is, from the time of, or even a bit before, the revolutionary *Contributions to Philosophy*, and by weaving these together with new, related material. The insights are published as an addendum to 'The Origin' (added in 1956, as a result of Heidegger's continuing to think the subject matter for twenty years), in portions of 'Conversation on a Country Path' (1959, a dialogue from notes first written down in 1944–5), 'The Thing' (1949–50) – which we have considered, in part, in chapter 4-B in regard to other dimensions – and in two new essays, 'Building Dwelling Thinking' (1951, the culmination of what Heidegger says in the high originary mode concerning this topic) and 'Art and Space' (1969, among his last works, and one which exhibits his shift to a much simpler, relaxed language).

The addendum to 'The Origin,' according to Heidegger, 'explains some of the leading words' and is intended to resolve the clash between saying 'fixing in place of truth' and 'letting happen of the advent of truth,' by understanding 'fixing in place' not in terms of willing (as would be the case metaphysically and representationally) but as 'setting into work,' where '"to place," and "to set," is to "lay" ... drawn from the Greek sense of *thesis*, which means a setting up in the unconcealed' (as happens, for example, in 'letting a statue be set up'), and where being fixed means to be 'admitted into the boundary [*pera*]' or brought into the outline (as when 'by its contour in the Greek light the mountain stands in its towering and repose') (OWA, xxiv; aOWA 82–3). Attention, then, is brought to concrete things, to place and placement. The cumulative lesson, running from these early reflections on Greek temples and mountains, through to pondering Greek and German poetry with Hölderlin's *Hymns* to Greek-German rivers, and to Hebel's Alemannic mountains, valley, and village is that natural and humanly made things need to again become thought-provoking and to remain wonderful for us in what they set free by their *energia*, that is, by what they placed or laid out by their 'repose in the fullness of motion' (aOWA 83).

Our immediate task would be to wonder at things such as mountain and temple, the earth as ground of our dwelling. The project requires that we continue to move through the uncanny, but reflection does not have to 'start from scratch,' as it were, because our 'attentive dwelling within the sphere of things' already tells us 'much about things and our dwelling on earth' (OWA 25, 42). What seems natural to us is probably something familiar in a long tradition that has forgotten the unfamiliar source from which it arose. And yet this unfamiliar source once struck us as strange and caused us to think and wonder (OWA 12; see also 14, 54). Following Heidegger's path rethinking what we understand, or thought we did, is complicated, not so much because he (and we) need to go back to recover and rework what was thought over twenty years, but *because he already says much of this in another voice, in the very same works.* Here we are attending to what he says about things, dwelling, and placement that are complementary to, and interlaced with, what he said and what we have already considered in his two-track thinking that explicitly works out the differences between metaphysical-representational concepts and originary thinking (chapter 4-B) and in that of focally developing his own high originary mode of saying (chapter 4-C). We have seen that 'The Origin' and 'The Thing' move in both of these ways. Yet they do more. By generating multiple modes of thinking and saying within the same work, and by finally weaving major strands together ('irregularly,' but with clear principles of organization) in the course of the whole corpus, Heidegger produces and elaborates, yet harmonizes, polyphonic voicings.

To briefly clarify what he is doing, we can follow three basic kinds of language in the early 'Origin of the Work of Art': the relatively straightforward description or explicit presentation of representational conceptualization, basic originary thinking, and the 'proto'-development of the more extreme high originary language. A few examples should suffice. In the first two quotations below Heidegger combines both the straightforward representational and the originary (writing in the two-track mode); in the third, he begins with a burst of the proto–high-originary language, then shifts to an explanation in terms of the two-track difference:

- 'Truth happens in the temple's standing where it is. This does not mean that something is correctly represented and rendered here, but that what is as a whole is brought into unconcealedness and held therein. To hold [*halten*] originally means to tend, keep, take care [*büten*]. Truth happens in Van Gogh's painting. This does not mean that something is correctly portrayed, but rather that in the revelation of the equipmental being of the shoes, that which is as a whole – world and earth in their counterplay – attains to unconcealedness' (OWA 56).
- 'In the midst of beings as a whole an open place occurs. There is a clearing, a lighting. Thought out in reference to what is, to beings,

this clearing is in a greater degree than are beings. This open center is therefore not surrounded by what is; rather, the lighting center itself encircles all that is, like the Nothing that we scarcely know' (OWA 53).

- 'The *world worlds,* and is more fully in being than the tangible and perceptible realm in which we believe ourselves to be at home in being. World is never an object that stands before us and can be seen' (OWA 44).

What 'A Dialogue on Language' (which also has several sorts of thinking and saying, as we saw in chapter 4-B and -C) does for language, 'The Thing' – also a mixed work – does for that which it names. Though theme of the essay cannot be fully worked out and presented here, it has three streams of language and substance that flow into what becomes the whole essay.[1] One kind of language is straightforward talk about phenomena, such as those of our contemporary situation (we will see more of this sort of language in the first set of homey works, for example, in 'Memorial Address'). Another sort consists of the two-track saying and thinking that we have already followed in chapter 4-B; a third is the high originary. We have the following as examples of the three levels of language:

- *The straightforward* – 'All distances in time and place are shrinking. Man now reaches overnight, by plane, places which formerly took weeks and months of travel. He now receives instant information, by radio, of events which he formerly learned about only years later, if at all' (T 165).
- *The two track* – 'The jug remains a vessel whether we represent it in our minds or not ... Clearly the jug stands as a vessel only because it has been brought to a stand ... It is, to be sure, no longer considered only an object of a mere act of representation, but in return it is an object which a process of making has set up before and against us ... We shall not reach the thing in itself until our thinking has first reached the thing as a thing ... released from the making process, the self-supporting jug has to gather itself for the task of containing ... The emptiness, the void, is what does the vessel's holding. The empty space, this nothing of the jug, is what the jug is as the holding vessel' (T 167–9).
- *The high originary* – 'In the gift of water, in the gift of wine, sky and earth dwell. But the gift of the outpouring is what makes the jug a jug. In the jugness of the jug, sky and earth dwell ... The gift of the out-

> pouring is a gift because it stays earth and sky, divinities and mortals … Staying appropriates' (T 172–3).

The point of this brief anatomy of 'The Origin' or 'The Thing' is that in recovering the meaning of 'at home,' 'dwelling,' 'thing,' or 'placement' in the works we are now considering, Heidegger assumes and develops the differences between representational and originary thinking, even that of his own originary achievement, and then goes on to concentrate and develop thing and place to more deeply understand, and come to, building and dwelling. 'The Origin' lays down key thoughts that unfold fairly smoothly in 'The Thing.' The basic note, of course, which rings in 'The Origin' is *the truth as coming into unconcealment* that *happens*, for example, as *a bringing into work*. In this early essay we already hear of gathering and dimensions that later form as the fourfold and world (again, here I am not concerned with the complex story of the development of Heidegger's changing technical definitions and understanding of earth and world). In order not to repeat what Heidegger has already told us, and that we have considered above (especially in chapter 4-B and -C), we can hold key elements and relationships in mind by a short version: Things such as artworks gather together so as to constitute a world. For example, a temple-work fits paths and relations of (*i*) birth, death, and the shape of sending of human being together with (*ii*) the figure of the presence of the god; (*iii*) the heavens, the light of the day, the breadth of the sky, the darkness of the night; and (*iv*) the earth: the intimacy of simple belonging to one another and the source in its originarity – that on which and in which mankind bases its dwelling. Such fitting and gathering occur as the strife between earth (self-secluding and concealment) and world (self-disclosing and unconcealment) (OWA 41–2, 47–9). All together, 'The temple-work, standing-there, opens up a world and at the same time sets this world back again on earth, which itself only thus emerges as native ground' (OWA 42). 'The *world worlds*, and is more fully in being than the tangible and perceptible reality in which we believe ourselves to be at home' (OWA 44). Here, with the way he thinks thing, earth, and world Heidegger moves into the strange – into the midst of which we ordinarily would seem to be 'not at home.'

The setting into work and gathering can happen because 'in the midst of beings as a whole an open place occurs.' There is a clearing, a lightening, in which the happening of truth can establish itself in a variety of ways: by 'setting itself into work' as art, as 'an act that founds a political state,' 'as the nearness of that which is not simply a being,' as 'the essential sacrifice,' or in 'the thinker's questioning' (OWA 62). The work allows 'truth's being fixed in place' in the language of its coming to be, which depends on its being created and being held – that is, preserved – by those who 'respond to the truth happening in the work. Preserving the work, as knowing, is a sober standing-within the extra-ordinary awesomeness of the truth that is happening in the work'; that is, 'this knowledge ... makes its home in the work's truth' (OWA 67–8).[2] In the setting of truth into work, then, we have the fundamental tension: estrangement and the opening of a way toward home. In the clearing lightening in which truth happens in the work, 'the immediate circle of beings' (where 'that which is, is familiar, reliably ordinary' and where 'we believe we are at home'), is disclosed 'at bottom' (*im Grunde*) as not at all ordinary, but 'extra-ordinary, uncanny' (OWA 54 [43).

The passing out of the familiar and into the strange would be the work of both creators and preservers, who belong together, who together bring forth the 'creative preserving of truth in the work,' where art 'is the becoming and happening of the truth' (OWA 71). To each mode of creative founding (bestowing, grounding, and beginning) there corresponds, in addition, a mode of preserving, because the preservers are critical to a homecoming to the event of truth: 'a work is in actual effect as a work only when we remove ourselves from our commonplace routine and move into what is disclosed by the work, so as to bring our own nature itself to take a stand in the truth of what is' (OWA 74–5). As he sketches it out, the creative founding (*die Stiftung der Wahrheit*) and the preserving (*der Bewahrung*) have a triple sense: bestowing (endowing) (*Schenken*), grounding (*Gründen*), and beginning (*Anfangen*). 'The creative founding is a overflow, an endowing, a bestowing' (OWA 75 [62]).[3] This founding preserving that is the artwork 'is the spring that leaps to the truth of what is'; such a leap, Heidegger tells us, 'is what the word origin [*Ursprung*, literally, primal leap] means' (OWA 78). Hence, from the start of his radical rethinking of matters, along with *Contributions to Philosophy*, here we find a first leap out of the tranquilizing everyday, a leap that stays in the strange and yet would pass over to an originary beginning, and which, focusing on the inmost dimensions of home, would think homelessness and homecoming by way of things.

My claim, in the largest sense, is that at the point in his homecoming he has reached by the 1950s and 1960s, he might be moving from learning to become at home to an initial beginning to dwell near home – perhaps, at least in his best moments or in some dimensions. But he does so precisely by remaining underway in homecoming through the homelessness in the strange, which he accomplishes by returning along a coherent arc that runs from 'The Origin' through to 'Conversation,' 'The Thing,' and 'Building Dwelling Thinking,' and to 'Art and Space.' In addition to what has just been presented, I would note two further pointers in this direction. First, Heidegger ends 'The Origin' by breaking off on the topic of dwelling near origins, citing Hölderlin on the final state of his homecoming journey:

> Reluctantly
> that which dwells near its origin departs
> ('The Journey,' vers. 18–19, cited in OWA 78)

Since it is presumptuous to think he (or we) are close to any thinking and saying that actually accomplishes 'dwelling near origin,' and well aware of the concealment that surrounds what is self-sheltering, we still have perplexing questions – and, luckily, some helpful pointers. 'What about nearness? How can we come to know its nature? Nearness, it seems, cannot be encountered directly. We succeed in reaching it rather by attending to what is near. Near to us are what we usually call things. But what is a thing?' (T 166). Here the other directive would come to the fore that helps us to learn to think dwelling in the language of thing and place. An unintended clue to this is found in the slippage from the German text to the translator's version of Hölderlin's verses 18–19 (just cited) which omits the final word of this Hölderlin poem – the word with which Heidegger also ends his essay, *der Ort* (place).

> *Schwer verläßt*
> *was nahe dem Ursprung wohnet, den Ort.*

That which has slipped back into oblivion in the English translation is precisely what is most needed. A few pages earlier Heidegger explicitly focuses on what remains to be thought – the complement to place – thing: 'We can now return to our opening question: how do matters stand with the work's thingly features that are to guarantee its immediate reality. They stand so that now we no longer raise this question about the work's thingly element ... [but] take the work ... as an object that is simply there' (OWA 68–9). Reading backward in a recovery, reflecting from where Heidegger no longer interprets things in the direction taken by *Being and Time* – as he substantially had, when composing 'The Origin' – we can now see the essay as opening the originary thread he continued to successfully develop. His next words in the essay – 'To determine the thing's thingness ... anticipating a meaningful and weighty interpretation of the thingly character of things' – point toward the continuing problematic and questioning of the later essay 'The Thing': 'The thingness of the thing remains concealed, forgotten ... In truth, ... the thing as thing remains proscribed, nil, and in that sense annihilated ... Not only are things no longer admitted as things, but have never yet at all been able to appear to thinking as things ... What then is the thing as thing, that its essential nature has never yet been able to appear?' (T 170–1).

Given 'that [this] annihilation is so weird [*unheimlich*],' it is no accident that Heidegger has laboured to think the issue from several directions (T 170 [42]). Since we have followed his various approaches, we have substantial preparation to follow how he moves from 'The Origin' to the development of thinking and dwelling that occurs in 'The Thing' and 'Building Dwelling Thinking.' Since one of the principal modes of dwelling is by way of poetizing and since language and poetry are high on the list of the arts (things) that gather a world, Heidegger has substantially elaborated the phenomena in his conversations with the poets (ranging from 'Language' and 'Poetically Man Dwells' to 'Sprache und Heimat' on dialect, as we saw in chapter 5). Parallel, and precisely on the topic, in the course of developing his own originary language, Heidegger has also explicitly explained the details of the way things gather world. Not to belabour what he has already said, we can recall that the trajectory from his early originary saying ('the *world worlds*' in 'The Origin,' 44) culminates in the extravagantly ringing, singing of the high originary strand of 'The Thing' (initially considered above, in section C):

> The thing things. Thing gathers.
>
> Thing: we are now thinking this word by way of the gathering-appropriating-staying of the fourfold.
>
> The thing things. In thinging, it stays earth and sky, divinities and mortals. Staying, the thing brings the four, in their remoteness, near to one another. This bringing-near is nearing. Nearing is the presencing of nearness.
>
> The mirroring, lightening each of the four, appropriates their own presencing into simple belonging to one another ...
>
> The mirroring that binds into freedom with play that betroths each of the four to each through the enfolding clasp of their mutual appropriation

> ... Each is expropriated, within their mutual appropriation, into its own being. This expropriative appropriating is the mirror-play of the fourfold ...
>
> This appropriating mirror-play of the single onefold of earth and sky, divinities and mortals, we call the world. The world presences by worlding ...
>
> The fouring presences the worlding of world. The mirror play of world is the round dance of appropriating ... Out of the ringing mirror-play the thinging of the thing takes place ...
>
> The thing things world. (T 174, 177, 180–4)

What more might Heidegger say? The better question might be, not about what more, but about what differently? Certainly, after listening to and originarily explicating (in terms of thing and the fourfold gathering of world) Hebel's powerful but quiet poetizing of his homeland, Heidegger realizes that he needs to focus on the concrete and the historical if he would develop his own reflective questioning of things and world. As the poets *poetize dwelling*, he on his own path needs to *think dwelling*, particularly the means by which we *build* those things in which we dwell, build those things through which dwelling can occur. Hence he needs to concern himself with precisely what another essay title says: 'Building Dwelling Thinking.'

In one respect, 'Building Dwelling Thinking' continues to use the now familiar fourfold gathering to think dwelling and building and their relationship with each other. There is little by way of new formulations of the core dimensions or words – thing, mortals, divinities, earth, sky, world – beyond what he gives in his other works. However, there is a deepened focus on building and dwelling that, importantly, develops as Heidegger works out details of how gathering occurs. By becoming more specific, he can unfold the greater complexity and intricacy of what gathering itself means and of the relationships among building, dwelling, and thinking, as each separately, and all together, are more completely disclosed as diverse modes of gathering that yet belong intimately to one another.

It is helpful at the outset to notice the basic format of the essay 'Building Dwelling Thinking' proceeding by way of movements that tell us how building arises from and depends upon the more primal dwelling; at the same time, the essay's overall movement shows that the differences in the direction of the ways of thinking the subject matter (either beginning with building to pass over or back to dwelling, or, starting from dwelling to unfold building from out of it) are complemented by what appears as the same in both dimensions: both building and dwelling mean 'remaining' or 'staying' in a place (BDT 146, 148–9). The essay opens with a first question, 'What is it to dwell?' and proceeds by pondering a cluster of phenomena upon which Heidegger now needs to concentrate: dwelling, building, the domain to (within) which they belong, particular things such as bridges and highways that are buildings but not dwellings, as well as buildings such as houses in which dwelling may or may not occur (BDT 146–7). It also begins by reaffirming our current condition in the technological age: we are 'at home' on the highway or factory or in the power plant, but do not have our shelter and dwelling there.[4] What would warrant Heidegger making such claims about 'the measure of the nature of dwelling and building' (BDT 146)?

Insofar as language 'tells us about the nature of a thing,' direction toward an answer could be found in the originary retrieval of what building (*bauen*) and dwelling (*wohnen*) mean. According to Heidegger, building (*bauen*) immediately connects us with dwelling and the meaning of the various ways we might dwell in the course of our lives. 'The Old English and High German word for building, *buan*, means to dwell. This signifies: to remain, to stay in a place' (BDT 146). The original meaning, however, according to Heidegger, has been lost, though we find a trace of it 'preserved in the German word *Nachbar*, neighbor. The neighbor is in Old English the *neahgebur; neah*, near and *gebur*, dweller ... he who dwells nearby.' Heidegger finds another clue in that the original sense of the word *bauen* also says 'our word *bin* in the versions: ich *bin*, I am, *du bist*, you are.' *Bauen*, then, says that 'the way in which you are and I am, the manner in which we humans are on the earth, is *Bauen*, dwelling.' Thus Heidegger begins to explicate this dwelling in terms of the fourfold ('To be a human being means to be on the earth as a mortal. It means to dwell'), but adds, '*bauen* however *also* means at the same time to cherish and protect, to preserve and care for, specifically to till the soil, to cultivate the vine,' to 'tend the growth that ripens into its fruit of its own accord.' As 'preserving and nurturing,' such building 'is not making anything,' in contrast to 'shipbuilding and temple-building,' which 'as constructing, do make their own works,' as occurs in 'the raising up of edifices' (T 147). Apparently, in our 'habitual,' 'everyday experience' (with its increasing uncanniness and the dominance of beings, about which we have heard in the story of the history of the forgetting of being), objects and our activities come to 'claim the name of *bauen*, building, and with it the fact of building, exclusively, for themselves. The real sense of *bauen*, namely dwelling, falls into oblivion' (BDT 147–80). The fundamental dynamic discerned here by Heidegger is that it is not the case that our creative activity of building brings forth dwelling as a new mode of life on earth, but the opposite: 'We do not dwell because we have built, but we build and have built because we dwell, that is, because we are dwellers' (BDT 148).

We are led back, then, to inquire into the nature of dwelling which we can do by listening to 'the Old Saxon *wuon*, the Gothic *wunian*,' which Heidegger tells us, 'like the old word *bauen*, means to remain, to stay in a place,' but is also used to 'say more distinctly how this remaining is experienced' (BDT 149). Here Heidegger makes a subtle but significant 'advance' in precision and scope, moving surely across a web of analogous meanings: *wunian*, meaning to be or remain at peace; peace, *Friede*, meaning the free, *das Frye* – with *fry* meaning to preserve from harm and danger, safeguarded, spared. 'Real sparing is something positive and takes place when we leave something beforehand in its own nature, when we return it specifically to its being ... To dwell, to be set at peace, means to remain at peace within the free, the preserve, the free sphere that safeguards each thing in its nature. *The fundamental character of dwelling is this sparing and preserving*' (BDT 149). At this point in the essay Heidegger does two things, one of which – justifiably – is usually noticed and focused upon, though the other may be the more powerful insight.

Heidegger immediately reflects on the ways 'human being consists in dwelling' as integrated by the gathering and belonging of the fourfold. Though I mentioned above that the essay adds little to what Heidegger has to say about the originary dimension, in the following several pages he does, in fact, fill in what many of us hold on to as scarce concrete details to relate and puzzle out, details worthy of comparison with what Hebel poetizes. Heidegger explicates how the poet famously speaks of earth as 'serving bearer, blossoming and fruiting, spreading out in rock and waters, rising up into plant and animal,' and of sky as the 'vaulting path of the sun, the course of the changing moon, the wandering glitter of the stars, the year's seasons and their changes, the light and dark of day, the gloom and glow of night, the clemency and inclemency of the weather, the drifting clouds and blue depth of the ether.' He tells us that 'the divinities are the beckoning messengers of the godhead,' that 'out of the holy sway of the godhead, the god appears in his presence or withdraws into his concealment,' and that mortals are so called because they can die, which 'means to be capable of death *as* death' (BDT 150). Throughout these dense paragraphs, Heidegger repeats a kind of mantra: these four dimensions so belong to each other that to speak of one is to think of all four, even though 'we give no thought to the single oneness of the four' (BDT 149–50).

Yet, what follows is often glossed over – even as we seek ever more information about the fourfold – so, for example, we overlook the fact that sky means 'the sun and moon [on] their journey' and 'the stars [on] their course,' or neglect to follow Heidegger's attention to the unthought 'simple oneness of the four we call *the fourfold*' (when, for example, he reflects on the jug, since 'In the gift of the outpouring dwells the simple singlefoldedness of the four [*Im Geschenk des Guesses weilt die Einfalt der Vier*]' (BDT 150; T 173 [46]). Crucial though such attention is, what may be overlooked is the quiet but detailed explication of *gathering as preserving*, which Heidegger clearly announces as the 'topic' for the remaining two pages of the first part of 'Building Dwelling Thinking': 'Mortals are in the fourfold by dwelling. But the basic character of dwelling is to spare, to preserve [*schonen*]. Mortals dwell in the way they preserve the fourfold in its essential being, its presencing. Accordingly, the preserving that dwells is fourfold' (BDT 150). The importance of these four modes of preserving is underscored by Heidegger's use of the four words in returning to the phenomena in the second half of the essay (BDT 158–9; see also 150–1). The sparing and preserving happen in four ways: as saving, receiving, awaiting, and initiating (each of which is further described, yielding four more facets). Heidegger presents the modes of dwelling with unusual precision, both correlating each mode with a particular dimension of the fourfold and, in sum, saying much about the gathering of what belongs together. Mortals are said to 'dwell in that they save the earth' which means in the end 'to set something free into its own presencing' (also consider *Friede* and *Frye*); in the case of the earth, this entails stepping back from seeking to master and subjugate it (as deep ecologists appreciate, finding support in Heidegger). Mortals *receive* the sky as sky, *leaving* sun, moon, and stars to their rhythms, and the patterns of day and night and of the seasons to their own courses, as well as to what comes as blessing or problem. Even though our buildings and technologies can alter our environment and patterns of activity, is it because the sky is far enough beyond our power and control that we yet can and need to receive it (in contrast to the fact that we have a more engaged, active responsibility for the earth over which we have busily exercised dominion for as long as history or even myth tells)? Mortals dwell 'in that they await divinities as divinities,' seeking 'intimations of their coming' and ciphering properly 'signs of their absence,' in any case not mistakenly –

anthropologically – thinking that gods might be made by us. The waiting occurs in the homelessness of what has been withdrawn; and, enigmatically, Heidegger adds, 'In hope they hold up to the divinities what is unhoped for.' Finally, in regard to themselves, 'mortals dwell in that they initiate their own nature,' that is, use and practice their capacity for death. This would be neither a darkening of dwelling nor a drive toward an 'empty Nothing,' but preparation 'so that there may be a good death.'

Though compacted, a great deal is unfolded by Heidegger here, and he considers it important enough to use the same wording twice more, even in such a brief essay. We will shortly return to the second version (which varies a bit) but can now note that the third version, describing how buildings preserve the fourfold, somewhat surprisingly employs wording identical to that for mortals: 'The edifices guard the fourfold. They are things that in their own way preserve the fourfold. To preserve the fourfold, to save the earth, to receive the sky, to await the divinities, to escort mortals – this fourfold preserving is the simple nature, the preserving of dwelling' (BDT 158–9). Heidegger also makes a significant addition here as to the concrete historical ways dwelling, as gathering of world occurs, with the point emphasized both explicitly by what he says and by the level of repeated detail. Coming to better understand *dwelling as preserving* has direct and clear implications for what home would be and for what it would mean to become at home, that is, what we would be called to do in and as homecoming. 'In saving the earth, in receiving the sky, in awaiting the divinities, in initiating mortals, dwelling occurs in the fourfold preservation of the fourfold. To spare and preserve means: to take under our care, to look after the fourfold in its preserving. What we take under our care must be kept safe' (BDT 151).

If we know more about how sparing and preserving (*schonen*) are the ways we remain and stay in place, that is, build and dwell, we come to the next question. Concretely, historically, *where* does this occur? Heidegger directly continues, 'But if dwelling preserves the fourfold, where does it keep the fourfold's nature? How do mortals make their dwelling in such a preserving? Mortals would never be capable of it if dwelling were merely a staying on earth under the sky, before divinities, among mortals. Rather, dwelling itself is always a staying with things. Dwelling, as preserving, keeps the fourfold in that which mortals stay: in things' (BDT 151). In short, rather than presenting more about the fourfold gathering generally and abstractly, Heidegger has tried to be as specific as he could be, elaborating the gathering into world in which we participate in terms of the four modes of preserving. Thereby, quietly, he has brought us to the central aspect so far set aside: to things. Arriving at this point, Heidegger concludes the first section of 'Building Dwelling Thinking' by bringing the question of things and building to the fore. 'Staying with things, however, is not something attached to this fourfold preserving as a fifth something. On the contrary: staying with things is the one way in which the fourfold stay within the fourfold is accomplished at any time in simple unity. Dwelling preserves the fourfold by bringing the presencing of the fourfold into things. But things themselves secure the fourfold *only when* they themselves *as* things are let be in their presencing. How is this done? In this way, that mortals nurse and nurture things that grow, and specifically construct things that do not grow. Cultivating and construction are building in the narrower sense. *Dwelling*, insofar as it keeps or secures the fourfold in things, is, as their keeping, a *building*' (BDT 151).

Heidegger passes to the next section of 'Building Dwelling Thinking,' with a second question: 'How does building belong to dwelling?' He responds by limiting his inquiry to building as constructing things, and by working out what a bridge does even more concretely than before (for six pages). Not surprisingly, his main thrust is to describe and analyse how the bridge is a thing that gathers the fourfold into world (BDT 152–8). As he had earlier elaborated how the four dimensions are related in regard to mortals' dwelling by sparing and preserving, now he proceeds the same way for the thing, with bridge. Many of the relationships seen previously (save, set free, receive, leave, await, hold up, initiate) apply again. The bridge 'brings stream and bank and land into each other's neighborhood,' guiding and attending the stream through meadows, its piers resting upright and so bearing the arches that the latter 'leave the stream's waters to run their course,' holding the stream's 'flow up to the sky,' now taking it 'under the vaulted gateway and then setting it free once more' (BDT 152).

Letting the stream run its course in the way it gathers earth and sky to each other, the bridge 'at the same time grants their way to mortals so they may come and go from shore to shore,' and escorts mortals in this daily coming and going 'on the way to the last bridge [death]' as they 'bring themselves before the haleness of the divinities,' whether the latter's presence is 'as in the figure of the saint of the bridge' or 'obstructed or even pushed wholly aside' (BDT 152–3). Here, in an exceptionally poetic description, Heidegger concretely explains his insight:

> The bridge gathers to itself in its *own* way earth and sky, divinities and mortals.

> Gathering or assembly, by an ancient word of our language, is called 'thing.' (BDT 153)

Again, we arrive at the same place as did the entire first part of the essay – at the thing.

At this point Heidegger makes a second major move in thinking dwelling and thing, parallel in importance to developing dwelling as preserving, by exploring *how* the full, manifold dynamic of the fourfold gathering actually works. This involves his most substantial analysis of thing, space, and place, issues carried over and further elaborated in 'Art and Space' some fifteen years later. In 'Building Dwelling Thinking' Heidegger works out a complex answer involving at least a half dozen phases or relationships and perhaps a dozen major phenomena and originary words (BDT 153–60). Though he intricately goes over and over the composite and flow more than eighteen times in 'Building Dwelling Thinking,' a clear master figure emerges – it is a process akin to building a model bridge out of match sticks, where you don't use the same sort of pieces or combinations each time you glue a section together but somehow get the whole in the end:

Things (including buildings) are originary *places*
→ which admit and allow *sites*
→ wherein the fourfold can gather
→ providing *spaces*
→ that are representationally conceived.

We have repeatedly heard that things gather the four into fourfold world (BDT 153). For that to happen as a concrete, historical occurrence, there must be a way for the four to gather, that is, somewhere where this can come about. In contrast to representational science and philosophy that (in the classical Newtonian tradition) think of bridges and houses as objects which are situated in space considered to be absolute (pre-existing), homogeneous, and isotropic, originary thinking explores how the fourfold and the onefold of the four need to enter a site (since building first depends on dwelling). That is, room must be made for the fourfold to gather: the fourfold needs be admitted and installed into a site. It is this site for and of the four that subsequently allows the constitution of space (*Raum*) in the ordinary sense of space in which objects are located and as a set of positions, intervals, mere distances (*spatium, extensio*) to be occupied and traversed, or as abstracted and three dimensionally represented to be conceptually manipulated

(BDT 154–5, 157–8). In short, out of the occurrence of the gathering of the four into world, historical events and relationships come about that allow the founding and joining of what we conceive of and functionally operationalize as space. Of course, as we have also often heard, it is within the fourfold gathering, among things, that embodied mortals would have their stay, that is, would dwell (BDT 156).

But how is such a site, a site for the gathering, given? By things, insofar as things are gatherings and assemblies. The *way* things gather is such that they gather the four in a manner that provides a site. This is possible insofar as place is first given, where the advent of place makes room. Here is a remarkable insight and claim, more striking even than this nested set of relationships: for things to gather the four in such a way as happens, not only must there be place, but the things must themselves be places (BDT 154). 'To be sure, the bridge is a thing of its *own* kind; for it gathers the fourfold in *such* a way that it allows a *site* for it. But only something *that is itself* a place can make space for a site … That for which room is made is always granted and hence is joined, that is, gathered, by virtue of a place, that is, by such a thing as a bridge. *Accordingly*, spaces receive their being from places and not from 'space' … Things which, as places, allow a site we now in anticipation call buildings … These things are places that allow a site for the fourfold, a site that in each case provides for a space' (BDT 154).[5]

Heidegger has unfolded at least four new interpretations in these seven dense pages: that things are places; the dynamic sequence, thing/place → allowing a site for the fourfold to gather → permitting and providing space; the originary event that occurs when or as things open, allow, admit, install, gather; buildings now characterized as the constructing and preservation of things/places.

It is crucial to appreciate the 'world-event' Heidegger describes here. He is dealing with and against the situation in which the originary has fallen into oblivion. The primal scene does not begin with fixed, pregiven objects in a containing pre-given space which are then arranged into a desired or intended design. Such subsequent organization and the spaces objects take up, Heidegger contends, depend on the originary event in which aspects of earth and sky, for example, are first brought forth. In the case of the bridge, 'It does not just connect banks that are already there. The banks emerge as banks only as the bridge crosses the stream. The bridge designedly causes them to lie across from each other. One side is set off against the other by the bridge' (BDT 152). The gathering that things facilitate and achieve is newly eventful. 'The location is not already there before the bridge is. Before the bridge stands, there are of course many spots along the stream that can be occupied by something. One of them proves to be a place, and does so *because of the bridge.* Thus the bridge does not first come to a place to stand in it; rather, a place comes into existence only by virtue of the bridge' (BDT 154). From things as places that bring forth earth and sky, and gather them with mortals and divinities, Heidegger can now return to the issue of what building is, as constructing, and how it belongs to dwelling. Things do not occur spontaneously but are made. Indeed, building is doubly a production in that it both brings forth things (erecting houses, for example) and, in thus establishing them as places that hold and make room, 'brings the fourfold hither into' the thing (BDT 159). Understood as proceeding out of our capacity for dwelling and as 'already [having] responded to the summons of the fourfold,' building – bringing forth by constructing – 'is a distinctive letting dwell' (BDT 159). To be genuine and successful, building produces responsibly, that is, 'it corresponds to the character of things' so that, as we saw above, it can set them freshly into their own, to leave them to themselves. Here Heidegger has much more fully developed what he began to say in 'The Origin' about creating and preserving belonging together. Not only are the creators of works complemented by those who thoughtfully consider them or thoughtfully dwell among them, but the construction, the bringing forth itself, is a preserving that lets stay and spares things, the open site, and the fourfold in its belonging together.

Obviously, the coincidence between that which stays (mortals for a while, and things for longer or shorter spans) and that which provides a site for gathering and tarrying (things, places, buildings – mortals' constructions) is a powerful constellation. But clearly Heidegger is not claiming that human construction establishes entire epochal edifices of historical worlds already belonging with the gathering of the fourfold, hence the insistence that building proceeds from and because we are already capable of dwelling. More needs to be said about the granting of things, of places. How is it that places come to be granted? Or, in a longer version, how and where is granted the place/thing that gives the site for the gathering of the fourfold within which mortals dwell and by virtue of which they can build things in a manner that preserves those things and the fourfold, letting them be (each in its own and all in their belonging together)? Heidegger makes a bold advance in answering this deeper question in his late 'Art and Space' (1969). He does so by maintaining that the world-eventful opening far exceeds, but includes, the human.[6] The key to how places might be granted, he contends, is found in the old word *räumen*, which means to clear away. Places and things could be brought forth only if there were first a clearing out. Thought along a long pathway from the clearing as disclosed, for example in 'The Origin,' almost thirty-five years earlier, what then was considered with a forest clearing in mind now reappears as 'a freeing from the wilderness.' This sort of clearing out is named by *roden*, which, according to Heidegger, says what *räumen* means (AS 5).

The primordial clearing away would operate in two ways. It would bring forth the free, that is, establish 'the openness for man's settling and dwelling' (AS 5). This clearing away would also be 'the release of places toward which the fate of dwelling man turns in the *preserve* of the home or in the brokenness of homelessness, or in complete indifference to the two' (AS 5). Then, too, clearing is the release of places where gods appear or have disappeared, or where 'the appearance of the godly tarries long' (AS 5). That is, as we heard in 'Building Dwelling Thinking,' whether disclosed or concealed, abiding or fleeting, mortals and gods are brought forth at the sites opened by places which, we now are told, are themselves brought forth from an originary clearing away. The entire course of all the homelessness and homecoming through differentiated worlds would apparently be within such clearing away, or perhaps, would be a dimension of such opening and release.

There is yet another term that Heidegger uses in this context – region (*die Gegend*) – that is unusually complex and fluid, even for Heidegger. That is, it does not seem to have a stable meaning and is hard to fit into what he is saying. Allowing for the fact that he is not using representational concepts – so we should neither expect nor seek univocal meanings in a linear chain – the key words nonetheless would have their own way of being precise; for example, as I have been arguing, as part of a figura, a *Gebild*. 'Region,' however, seems to be exceptionally unstable, or perhaps unusually plural in meaning and performance. Suppose we take the clear overall set of relationships among the key terms here:

Einräumen →
grants →
thing/place (*Ort*) →
which admits →
site →
where the fourfold can gather →
and which provides space (*Raum*)

What Heidegger says would seem to have 'region' in two placements in the figure: after place, perhaps with site, and also before place, as perhaps a primal (articulation of) opening, as is *einräumen.* On the one hand, the meaning seems simple enough, as Heidegger presents it, several times: 'Place always opens a region,' and 'sculpture would be the embodiment of place. Places in preserving and opening a region' (AS 6–7). If place opens region 'in which it gathers things in their belonging together,' it would seem that this use of 'region' is close to that of the 'site,' wherein the fourfold gather together into world. Even where Heidegger complicates what he says, the same appears to hold: he adds, 'Gathering [*Versammlen*] comes to play in the place in the sense of the releasing sheltering of things in their region' (AS, 6). Things in their region would be intelligible if thought of as 'in their site' or 'in the world where things gather the fourfold.'

On the other hand, woven into the same three-page section of 'Art and Space' are wordings that make it sound as if region is 'prior' to place: 'And the region? The older form of the word runs *Gegnet.* It names the free expanse' (AS 6). Here, with *Gegnet* translated as 'that-which-regions,' region echoes 'that which calls for thinking' and as 'free expanse,' a dimension more originary than even place. This second, alternative meaning would appear to be continuous, as Heidegger speaks of 'locality as the interplay of places. We would have then to take heed that and how this play receives its reference to the belonging together of things from the region's free expanse' (AS 6). If region, free expanse, provides the directive, it would seem to be 'prior,' not 'subsequent,' to place and thing.

We can find some help for our interpretation in a dialogue, 'Conversation on a Country Path' (1944–5), in which Heidegger presents his most sustained treatment of *Gegend* and *Gegnet.*[7] We especially need to recognize two limitations so that we proceed modestly: first, even acknowledging that the dialogue form is not Heidegger's forte, compared with 'Dialogue on Language,' 'Conversation' is neither as powerful nor as successful, and, indeed, is rather overdone if not pretentious in sections. Second, the dialogue dates from some seven years before 'Building Dwelling Thinking' and fifteen years before 'Art and Space,' so is not an instance of his most mature thinking. Nonetheless, 'Conversation' is congruent with the later work and does 'fill in' enough of what region means to provide several major insights.

In the dialogue on a country path (*Feldweggespräch*), in which a scientist, scholar, and teacher discuss thinking, Heidegger initially focuses on the subject of region for most of three pages (CCP 64–6) and then makes significant additional points concerning region on nine more (CCP 69, 75–7, 79, 83–6). In the dialogue, the three participants manage to move from the realm of 'transcendental-horizontal-re-presenting,' in which objects appear to us, to consider 'what lets the horizon be what it is' (CCP 63–4). The teacher says that 'What is evident of the horizon ... is but the side facing us of an openness [*ein Offenes*] which surrounds us,' which directly leads the scientist to the question, 'But what is this openness as such?' (CCP 64 [7]). The teacher answers, 'It strikes me as something like a *region* [*eine Gegend*], an enchanted region where everything belonging there returns to that in which it rests.' (CCP 65 [38]).[8] Setting aside for a moment what looks to be a direct, dramatic description of region as the home to which all returns at the end of homecoming, we find that as the speakers proceed, trying to understand 'openness as a region,' they immediately accumulate a dense complex of assumptions and implications: as noted, the opening region would be that which lets horizon be, 'that which alone permits all sheltering,' 'gathering all,' and as that 'in which everything returns to itself' (CCP 65; see also 72–3, 83). Clearly, such 'a region for everything is not one region among many, but *the* region of all regions [*die Gegend aller Gegenden*]': 'what is in question is *the* region' (CCP 65 [38]). It could be that the ambivalence with which we began this discussion is resolved if 'one region among many' refers to region as site and if 'the region of regions' names the primal opening – *einräumen*.

At this juncture in 'Conversation,' a key (later reconsidered in 'Art and Space') is found in the old form of the word '*Gegnet*,' which means 'open expanse [*freie Weite*]' (CCP 66 [39]). As dynamically interpreted, the core would be 'the reign of its essential sway, its regioning [*das Walten ihres Wesens, das Gegnende*],' since *Wesen* can and should be taken as meaning holding sway (not 'essence') (CCP 65 [39]).[9] This is initially explicated in a way that yet again reinforces the primal character of region:

> Teacher: The region gathers, just as if nothing were happening [*nichts ereigne*], each to each and each to all into an abiding [*in das Verweilen*], while resting [*Beruhen*] in itself. Resting is a gathering and a re-sheltering [*das versammelnde Zurückbergen*] for an extended resting in an abiding [*weiten Beruhen in der Weile*]. (CCP 66 [39–40])

From the many strands woven into this sentence, we can first follow the thread of the core dynamic of openness, opening (whose original power is emphasized by Heidegger). *Gegnet,* that-which-regions, 'opens itself, so that in it openness is halted and held, letting everything merge in its own resting' (CCP 66 [40]).[10] *Gegnet* is 'openness itself [*Das Offende selbst*]'; or even more heavily stressed, '*Gegnet* is the opening of openness' (CCP 66 [40], 68 [42)], 69 [43]). With *Gegnet,* then, we find named the 'ur-opening' in which we can discern the nexus of several dimensions of what obtains. It gathers everything that belongs together, first each and all to itself and from there all to one another and each to its own, 'Because *Gegnet* regions all, gathering everything together and letting everything return to itself, to rest in its own identity [*Weil die Gegnet, alles gegnend, alles zueinander versammelt und zu sich selbst in das eigene Beruhen im Selben zurückkehren läßt*]' (CCP 86 [66]). The gathering is a multidimensional letting. As noted at the beginning of our discussion of 'Conversation,' *Gegnet* is the opening that lets the horizon come forth as horizon, permits all to shelter, and lets everything come back home to its ownness, which is, at one and the same time, in/as their belonging together. *To the already potent figure of homecoming in 'return to itself,' Heidegger adds the long-anticipated, long-held-off final possibility of completion: opening gathers and returns everything 'to rest in its own abiding' – to rest, to stay at home in itself and that to which it belongs* (both *Gegnet* itself and everything [*alles*]) (CCP 66).

Here Heidegger also quietly but surely moves us beyond what might be taken to be our current concern – space, place, openness – and even beyond naming home as *Gegnet,* to a wonderful unfolding of space-time. In the three short but powerful quotations immediately above, we have just heard that the open – region – lets all into an abiding (*in das Verweilend; Weile*), even more that *Gegnet,* opening, so opens itself 'that in it openness is halted and held' (CCP 69 [39–40]). *The 'spatial' is 'temporal' in all dimensions. Quite a homecoming and home!* The double-faceted character is stressed repeatedly in the dialogue, and in such a way as to insist upon the interplay, even a unity and convertibility of 'space' and 'time.' In the sentence immediately following the first major quotation above, we hear, 'So the region itself is at once an expanse and an abiding [*die Weite und die Weile*]' (CCP 66 [39]). It abides into the expanse of resting. It expands into the abiding of what freely turned toward itself' (CCP 66 [39–40]). Gegnet *would be the abiding expanse* (*die verweilende Weite*) (CCP 85 [64]) *which lets all come forward, and then return, the originary source that is home and the homecoming all together.* In *Gegnet,* then, we hear gathering, returning, re-sheltering, resting, abiding, all from and in the 'abiding expanse' (*die verweilende Weite; die Weile der Weite; Sie weitet in die Weile des frei*) (CCP 66 [40], 67 [41], 77 [42]).

As a mature articulation, far from but spun out of B*eing and Time*, Heidegger now says *whiling and expansive opening*. This brings forward yet another way to think the discontinuous opening and closing of worlds, the epochal shifts of what is hidden and what is disclosed. Not only all/everything – all dimensions of world and all things – but the historical sending of the metaphysical-representational and the originary would issue from/as *Gegnet as abiding expanse, the expanse of the abiding* (CCP 64, 72–3). 'The historical rests in *Gegnet* and in what occurs as *Gegnet*. It rests in what, coming to pass in man, regions [*vergegnet*] him into his nature' (CCP 79 [56–7]).

At this point 'Conversation' allows a way to think many key words – open, region, thing, place, gather, world, space, and the face of the horizon – congruently with 'Building Dwelling Thinking,' 'Art and Space,' and the related essays. (I have set aside the way 'Conversation' complements these works in Heidegger's thinking of granting increasingly in terms of letting, since in the final section of this chapter I take up that issue in *Gelassenheit*, that is, releasement.) Indeed, 'Conversation' lays out regioning in relation to things and human dwelling in the same way as do 'Building Dwelling Thinking' and 'Art and Space,' while adding further nuances and the 'unity' of the simple or onefold.[11] Specifically, 'Conversation' thinks regioning in a double manner – in things and mankind (CCP 75).

As we have seen, *Gegnet* as open expanse lets things into an abiding and to rest in their properly own (e.g., CCP 67). Since the regioning opening is the opening that yields and surrounds epochal shifts, the occurrence of horizon within which objects appear to us as and by way of representation is the same as the enduring presencing of beings as objects. Originarily, though, 'the things which appear in *Gegnet* no longer have the character of objects,' but rather that of things properly speaking (CCP 67). *In the opening, then, as expanse, things come forth; in the opening, as the whiling, things stay. Gegnet* 'also lets things endure in the abiding expanse [*Die Gegnet veweilt nun aber auch das Ding in die Weile der Weite*]' (CCP 75 [52]). The question becomes how to name and think regioning in regard to things. Since as/in letting (*lassen*) a thing abides (*weilen*) in itself, the dialogue indicates that it could be called *Bedingnis*, which perhaps can be best translated as specifying (rather than conditioning or determining).[12] Heidegger says that insofar as *Gegnet* 'specifies the thing as thing,' 'it is best called the specifying [or the conditioning] [*Sie bedingt das Ding zum Ding. Sie heißt daher am ehesten die Bedingnis*]' (CCP 77 [54]). The daunting task of thinking what *Bedingnis* means still faced Heidegger in 1944–5, and as we have seen, he patiently works on the issue during the 1950s and 1960s in essays such as 'The Thing,' 'Building Dwelling Thinking,' and 'Art and Space.' We again need to remember what we now know – that thinking things means leaving aside representations, in this case (because they are both powerful and ingrained in our thought patterns) the hard-to-avoid concepts of cause and effect and transcendental-horizontal relations. It becomes necessary to originarily think the 'relation' of *Gegnet* and thing 'only as regioning [*Vergegnis*]' (CCP 76–7 [52–3]).

But with the impact of *Gegnet* we also pass from thing to humans. That is, Heidegger has introduced, with thinking, the question of the relation of humans to thing, and thus the additional issue of the region for humans (CCP 77). *He contends that region regions thing as Bedingnis, whereas region regions humans as Vergegnis.* The latter is more obviously a variation on *Gegnet*, the basic name of opening itself. Though we will return to the relation of thinking to opening expanse (the free) and to letting, when we consider *Gelassenheit* in the next section of this chapter, we can at least see by now that originary thinking would be an opening, a letting oneself become open, to what is given for thinking, so that this would be the reciprocating response to what first opens and gives itself to (and calls for) thinking. Thinking, then would be 'to release oneself into the openness of *Gegnet* [*auf das Offene der Gegnet sich einlassen*]' (CCP 72 [48]; see also 77–82). But, as Heidegger insists, it is not humans who bring about the opening and responding; rather, 'prior to everything' *Gegnet* already 'appropriates what is ownmost to man for its own regioning [*Sie vereignet das Wesen des Menschen ihrem eigenen Gegnen*]' (CCP 83 [62]). Humans originarily belong with *Gegnet*, as appropriated (*ge-eignet*) (CCP 73 [49–50]). Thus, since regioning first brings forth the way thinking charts its course, we can also say that 'the nature of thinking' is specified (*bestimmt*) 'through *Gegnet* which as regioning first brings forth this nature' (CCP 74 [51]). Regioning, appropriating humans, is 'the prior, of which we really can not think ... because the nature of thinking begins there. Thus man's nature is released to that-which-regions in what is prior to thought [*Im Unvordenklichen also ist das Wesen des Menschen der Gegnet gelassen*]' (CCP 83 [61]).

Gegnet, then, unfolds this double movement of opening, regioning: *Gegnet* is the regioning of humans in releasement; *Gegnet* is the determining of things, whereby they endure in the abiding expanse (CCP 75 [51–

2]; see also 77 [53–4]). Opening is the opening of humans and things, respectively, as *Vergegnis* and *Bedingnis.* Accordingly, the task of homecoming thinking is to learn to open to the opening, that is, to the letting that is 'determining [for things] and regioning with respect to man' (*auf Bedingnis und Vergegnis*) (CCP 77 [54]) As the abiding expanse, the expanse of abiding that lets humans come to their own in conjunction with things that also do so and stay or rest in themselves, *Gegnet*-opening says the same as *einräumen* in 'Art and Space.' The latter, we have seen, is the granting (letting) of the tarrying of things and the dwelling of mortals among them.

By adding regioning-opening to *einräumen,* Heidegger clarifies that and how two simultaneous (spatial-temporal) levels of meaning operate. Thought spatially or temporally, at the most comprehensive or primordial level, the region – regioning, the opening expanse, as *einräumen* (as well as *Ereignis* or *es gibt*) – is prior to everything insofar as the first granting-letting of openness, gathering, sheltering, coming to one's own, and abiding occur and hold. At the concrete level of things and humans – and of the many regions within world that would correspond to what Heidegger also calls 'sites' – since 'human nature remains appropriated to that ... from whence we are called,' there is a return to the first origin of opening and thus to things and to humans gathering with everything else to which they belong, and thereby back to themselves. Such a return, in which 'everything belonging there returns to that in which it rests,' is clearly a homecoming – we could scarcely miss it, so saturated is the naming and thinking of the dynamic throughout the entire dialogue with the formed images and vocabulary of home and homecoming.

Of course, in one of its dimensions, region – as opening expanse, *Gegnet* – always names a clearing away, as does *räumen* understood via *roden.* Here Heidegger names a primal phenomenon that belongs in the family of *Ereignis* or *es gibt.* He immediately says as much in the next paragraph: 'In clearing-away a happening [*ein Geschehen*] at once speaks and conceals itself' (AS 5). 'How does the clearing-away happen? Is it not making-room [*Einräumen*] and this again in a twofold manner as granting and arranging [*zulassen und Einrichtung*]' (AS 6 [9]). This is a pregnant pair: granting does name again what Heidegger has originarily come to as giving, but now with a kind of renaming, since here granting is said in a way that shifts the connotation toward *letting.* On the one hand, granting also picks up the first of a set of critical terms – admit and install – that were rather cryptic in their appearance in 'Building Dwelling Thinking' (there he had said, 'Place makes room for the fourfold in a double sense. The place *admits* the fourfold and it *installs* the fourfold' [BDT 158]). On the other hand, arranging would couple with the second term – install – and would speak to the fact that what is admitted does not come as chaos, but as arranged into a cosmos, as set into some particular constellation (we will see this again with Heidegger's idea of *Bedingnis*). Making room (*einräumen*) would, for our sphere of dwelling, building, thing, and place, be the name for originary granting. In both 'Building Dwelling Thinking' and 'Art and Space' Heidegger specifies that the double sense of making room is admitting and installing, which run across the 'phases' of the unfolding: '*einräumen* – making room – admits' place, 'grant[ing] the appearance of things' (which are places); place, in turn, 'makes room for the fourfold,' '*admits* ... and *installs* the fourfold' and the realm of things 'present to which human dwelling sees itself consigned' (BDT 158; AS 5–6).

As noted, Heidegger is subtly shifting the connotation of granting in these sections, the importance of which may oddly correlate with its quietness. Always sensitive (since the reception of *Being and Time*) to the misunderstanding and the charge that anthropocentrism or covert metaphysical wilfulness lurks behind his dynamic terms (now *Ereignis, es gibt, Gegnet*, etc.), Heidegger is speaking in ways that emphasize the nuance of letting in granting. While grant can mean to actively exert effort to bring something about, it can also mean to allow, to not prevent, to let be. That would not imply a passivity, for as Heidegger stresses over and over 'letting be' would involve deliberate self-restraint, respect for that which would be let go, released into its own, freed. This alert allowance, and self-withholding, is emphasized by the words Heidegger chooses to use (rather than by any 'self-explanation' that would only mis-focus attention yet again). When he says 'a place is granted' he writes *eine Stätte verstatten*. In addition to the echoes of abode, room, and workroom in *Stätte* (even home in the poetic *bleibende Stätte*), *verstatten* conveys granting in the sense of permitting and allowing. He regularly uses *gestattet* (grant) here also, which means to allow, to not interfere with (BDT 154 [29]). Not only would these words be carefully chosen by Heidegger, but they themselves carry overtones of special deliberation and elevated importance. Specifically, *Stätte* is a term associated with the monumental, implying a place of lasting cultural or spiritual significance, a place that may be hallowed and ceremonial; *verstatten* signifies wholehearted support or permission, given after serious reflection or consideration.

Another master word Heidegger relies upon heavily here is *Schonen* (preservation) (we have already been introduced to the complex: preserve, spare, save, care for, protect, or conserve – multiple emphases recognized by the translator of 'Building Dwelling Thinking,' who renders the word with the double 'spare and preserve'). *Schonen* is also resonant with the connotation of 'letting be' held in other verbs – *belassen, wohnenlassen, zulassen* – and opens to the key word *Gelassenheit* (to be considered in the next section) (BDT 149, 158–60 [23, 33–4]; AS 6 [9]). In regard to 'spare' and 'preserve' Heidegger also writes '*bewahrt und geschont*' (spare and preserve), where *bewahren* (preserve, guard) means to keep in a safe place (the stem *wahren* means to watch out, guard, be prepared for action); this complex of meaning connects with Heidegger's use of *hüten*, meaning watch, guard, take care of, tend, or keep (BDT 149 [23]).

Though his thinking is very intricate, *Heidegger stresses more and more emphatically the primal granting as a 'letting,' and, intimately intertwined with granting, is preserving, sparing, caring* (as we saw when sparing meant, for mortals and buildings, saving the earth, setting it free into its own). Letting be and saving occur together and say the same as what receiving the sky meant ('leave to,' 'initiate into its own') (BDT 150–1, 158). The force of such granting, gathered with dwelling and the primal enowning, is concentrated in sentences that do not otherwise stand out, that is, that speak discretely, but clearly, to those would hear and think them: 'dwelling occurs as the fourfold preservation of the fourfold [*ereignet sich das Wohnen als das vierfältige Schonen des Gevierts*]' (BDT 151 [25]). To return to the way enspacing unfolds (*einräumen*), in addition to granting-admitting (as letting), it also arranges (AS 6). Or, in the earlier version of 'Building Dwelling Thinking,' it installs the fourfold (BDT 158). In 'Art and Space,' Heidegger says little more about this second mode, adding only that 'making room prepares for things the possibility to belong to their relevant whither, and, out of this, to each other' (AS 6). But, a bit of reflection leads us to see that admitting alone is not sufficient for the concrete historical building, emplacement, and gathering of fourfold necessary for a world to emerge. Though admitted to a group, one still needs to be installed – to be assigned to a legitimate and specific place, role, and set of responsibilities and rights, say as a teacher, as differentiated from a pastor, carpenter, or poet. Though admitted as part of a city, the places for public assembly or worship yet need be set in the right relation to topography and other buildings and institutions, which also means into the secular and sacred routines, to be arranged in the physical and social setting. Again, Heidegger implicitly covers this initial belonging to the relevant 'whats' by working out the series: mortals and buildings were to receive the sky, allow sun, moon, and stars, seasons, and day-night to their proper courses; to await divinities, open to intimations whether of their presence or absence, not replacing them with anything we have made; and to initiate or escort mortals to their own nature and capacity for death (BDT 151).

Of course, a great theme of these essays is the gathering of the four that lets each of the four be, while allowing all four to belong together in/as the fourfold – opening, clearing-away, would seem to be an instance, perhaps the paradigmatic one, of making room for the 'possibility to belong to the relevant [own] whither, and out of that, to each other' (AS 6). From considering the ongoing enspacing (*einräumen*), 'Art and Space' goes on to work out the implications for understanding place and to work back across the phases laid out in 'Building Dwelling Thinking' and treated above. It also again arrives at and emphasizes what may be the two major insights of the essays, laid out in four economical lines, only a paragraph apart: first, the still somewhat startling discovery that '*things themselves are places and do not merely belong to a place*'; and second, *coming to understand 'preserving [as] the gathering of things in their belonging together*' (AS 6).

Heidegger has come a long way toward delineating the character and complex modes of where and how the gathering of the fourfold might occur, of where and how place might be granted, of where and how we might build and dwell, that is to say, of where and how we might be homeless, home-coming, or at home. Of course, the 'temporal' character of world, things, and dwelling is not overlooked by Heidegger. *Einräumen*, enspacing, is temporal-spatial, the latest version of the space-time radically thought in *Contributions to Philosophy* some thirty-five years earlier and persistently explored since then. In 'The Thing,' Heidegger thinks staying and appropriating together:

> Staying appropriates [*Verweilen ereignet*].
>
> What is gathered in the gift gathers itself in appropriately staying the fourfold [*Das im Geschenk Versammelte sammelt sich selbst darin, des Geviert ereignend zu verweilen*].
>
> Appropriating the fourfold [*das Geviert ereignend*]: it gathers the fourfold's stay, its while, into something that stays for a while: into this thing, that thing.
>
> We are now thinking of this word [thing] by way of the gathering-appropriating-staying of the fourfold [*aus dem Dingen als dem versammelnd-ereignenden Verweilen des Gevierts*]. (T 173–4 [46]; see also 181)

In 'Building Dwelling Thinking' and 'Art and Space' Heidegger continues to articulate the relation of staying and the fourfold – mortals linger for a while, things (places) stay – though the use of *Ereignis-ereignen* generally falls off as he develops ways to say place-time-thing all together by way of region as abiding expanse and expanse of abiding. He also maintains his practice of using cognate nouns and verbs (especially gerunds), here to articulate aspects of both places and events: keep and keeping (and with both dimensions integrated); region and regioning; opening, dwelling, and building. Or, *eine Stätte verstatten* (to grant a place) echoes *stattfinden* (to take place, happen, occur). As we saw, Heidegger says that building and dwelling mean remaining and staying (*bleiben* and *aufhalten*), where the latter have the sense of hold up, stop, delay, as well as sustain, keep up, hold open, keep open, and where the related *sich aufhalten* says stay, stop, reside, and *Aufenthalt* means stay, residence, seat, domicile, stop. *We might say that being and time have dissolved into the more originary abiding expanse and the expanse of abiding within which things are let tarry. All such keeping, holding open, and staying and remaining that are concentrated in things and place are devolved from einräumen and belong together as place-occurrence.*

In one of the great sentences of 'Art and Space,' Heidegger writes 'Places, in preserving and opening a region, hold something free gathered around them which grants the tarrying of things under consideration and a dwelling for man in the midst of things (AS 7 [11]). We know that it is *einräumen* that so grants. In granting the tarrying of things there occurs a great fusion, *ein Verweilen gewährt*, the gracious granting, giving, allowing of tarrying – which we can see describes the sway of things, since things, as places, both gather and persist, staying open, holding open, and allowing the site for the gathering of the four (AS 7 [11]).[13] Hence the accuracy of the second part of the sentence, which assembles the character of thing, building, and dwelling: the granting of 'a dwelling for man in the midst of things' (AS 7 [11]). And, we can add, the primal opening, holding, and giving occurs in things, in regard to which humans have a critical productive and preserving role, as with the jug. 'The emptiness, the void, is what does the vessel's holding ... How does the jug's void hold? It holds by taking what is poured in. It holds by keeping and retaining what it took in. The void holds in a twofold manner: taking and keeping ... The twofold holding of the void rests on the outpouring ... To pour from the jug is to give. The holding of the vessel occurs in the giving of the outpouring ... The jug's jug character consists in the poured gift of the pouring out' (T 169, 172–3).[14] In thinking the openings that open so as to allow the giving to occur, Heidegger has arrived at the juncture of the stay of things, dwelling, and mortals. He says that to think of those who live in a human manner, that is, who dwell, 'already [is to] name the stay within the fourfold among things ... with the things themselves' (BDT 156).

A striking feature of these essays is that for all their close focus on dwelling, place and space, thing, and building, they do not arrive at any simple, much less final, formulation or summary phrase (for example, 'things gather and preserve dwelling'). While coherent, the essays actually *multiply* aspects, phases, and nuances. Indeed, one could say that variations, specifications, and differences proliferate. More and more words and characteristics are given for the major dimensions and their relationships: place, site, space, region; grant, give, let; free, open; whiling, tarrying, staying; divinities, beckoning messengers, godhead, god.

Crucially for his homecoming, in these essays, Heidegger has immersed himself in things, such as buildings, but has successfully avoided letting beings take over – the great danger and oblivion of the entire span of metaphysical eras. He has managed to arrive at and easily use an originary thinking and saying of things no longer tinged with the language and assumptions of beings, nor obliterated by the tranquilized everydayness described in *Being and Time.* Heidegger has taken us to the point where – without the oblivion that occurs when beings totally dominate, without being as metaphysically understood, without nihilistic technology, that is, without the most extreme homelessness – there is a homecoming to thinking and saying our dwelling place and the building of ways and places to linger as mortals. It is therefore no small matter that he can say, in 'Building Dwelling Thinking,' that 'mortals do not leave behind their belonging to the fourfold ... we come back to ourselves from things without ever abandoning our stay among things' (BDT 157). That speaks of a passage beyond homelessness to a homecoming, if not a dwelling, near the source.

Heidegger is, in fact, able to go on without anxiety about always learning to abide or even about dwelling near the source (the penultimate and ultimate phases named by Hölderlin), since by the end of 'Building Dwelling Thinking' *he has come to be able to remain in homelessness, stay fully engaged with the strange, re-entering our current precarious point, without being tormented by it.* He comes to a peaceful understanding that he and we are in homelessness, yet therein still gather together with the fourfold and in a mode of dwelling – indeed we would do so by learning to wonder at what shows itself as, and by means of, the uncanny. In the mode of remaining underway, we can experience homecoming while in homelessness by responsibly building, thinking, and poetizing. Heidegger says, calmly, 'The real dwelling plight lies in this, that mortals must ever search anew for the nature of dwelling, that they *must ever learn to dwell.* What if man's homelessness consisted in this, that man still does not even think of the real plight of dwelling as the plight? Yet as soon as man *gives thought* to his homelessness, it is a misery no longer. Rightly considered and kept well in mind, it is the sole summons that *calls* mortals into their dwelling' (BDT 161).

In the essays considered here, 'The Origin,' 'Conversation,' 'The Thing,' 'Building Dwelling Thinking,' and 'Art and Space,' Heidegger has moved from a relatively abstract or general (albeit not conceptual or representational) consideration of the gathering of the fourfold to a more concrete unfolding of particular things, such as bridges and farmhouses, to a more detailed analysis of gathering as preserving, saving, receiving, awaiting, and initiating. As noted, without neglecting the simple oneness of the fourfold, which gives directives to our building, and indeed even begins to remedy the fact that we seldom if ever give thought to that simple oneness, Heidegger nonetheless allows plenitude to out, in a multiplicity of complex differences (BDT 149–50, 158).

After learning from Hebel, Heidegger knows that this attention to detail, to difference, to the concrete, to the splendour of the simple is even more necessary. As he said in his dialogue with the poet, what is required is to attempt to experience what is said in the poetry (not to produce or follow a summary of its 'content'). From Hebel, Heidegger has also learned the value of standard language, a lesson we can see him practicing in these essays. Though he does not abandon his hard-won originary mode of thinking and saying, he does 'tone it down,' getting away from the 'hyper' language of the 1950s, such as 'world worlding,' 'thing thinging,' 'the ringing of the mirror playing ring,' 'the mirror play of the worlding world as the ringing of the ring' – all on one page! – and 'This expropriative appropriating is the mirror-play of the fourfold [*Dieses enteignende Vereignen* {mutual appropriation} *ist das Spiegel-Spiel des Geviert*].' In 'Art and Space,' he moves to a still powerful, but quieter, more precise and subtle language: the granting of tarrying and place, sparing, preserving and letting dwell, dwelling occurring as preservation (*ein Verweilen gewährt, eine Stätte verstatten; schonen, wohenenlassen, ereignet sich das Wohnen als das Schonen*), as variously seen above.

Just as the essays considered above focus on dwelling, building, place, and thing by recovering the trail from the early work of the 1930s ('The

Origin'), to achieve the high originary thinking of the 1950s ('The Thing,' 'Building Dwelling Thinking'), and to arrive at the simpler saying of the late 'Art and Space' at the end of the 1960s, so too Heidegger consistently speaks in a non-technical and unpretentious way to his neighbours and their guests about homey places and things in yet another and final set of works that also arc across time. In fact, in these modest addresses and occasional pieces Heidegger temporarily moves doubly to and fro: on the one hand, his thinking about his own home places unfolds across a span of time from his early reflection, 'Why Do I Stay in the Provinces?,' to the last things he did; on the other, he not only says a great deal at and from out of the closing of his life but does so by recollecting scenes from his childhood and the town where he grew up, as well as home events and sites drawn from the course of his life. Considered in the language of Hölderlin's six-phased figure, these essays and occasional pieces move from Heidegger's youthful being at home to venturing into the uncanny, turning along with the turning occurring as/in there is giving, identifying, and arriving at the place that is his own, beginning to learn to abide, and, finally, if not actually dwelling near the source, at least continuing in efforts to be capable of dwelling. As we will see, in these homey works, what he needs to say and the mode in which to say it merge into yet another voice, which speaks in a distinct cluster of essays: 'Why Do I Stay in the Provinces?' (1933–4), 'Conversation' (1944–5), 'Pathway' (1947–8), 'Johann Peter Hebel: Zähringer Rede' (1954), 'Das "Kuinzige"' (1954), 'Vom Geheimnis des Glockenturms' (1954), 'Memorial Address' ('Gelassenheit') (1955), 'Ein Wort des Dankes' (also appearing with the title 'Dank an die Heimatstadt Meßkirch') (1959), 'Dank bei der Verleihung des staatlichen Hebelgedenkpreises' (1960), '700 Years of Meßkirch' (1961), 'Über Abrahim a Santa Clara' (1964), 'Verlust der Heimat' (1966), 'Festansprache beim Heimatfest in Todtnauberg' (1966), 'Ansprache am 26 September 1969 in Meßkirch,' and 'Statt einer Rede' (1973).

What, in the end, does Heidegger have to say? What, in the end, does he do? What about Heidegger himself and homecoming? As Hebel thoughtfully poetized his Alemannic valley, Heidegger now poetically thinks his hometowns of Freiburg, Meßkirch, and Todtnauberg. But he does so neither in the rather unsuccessful verse of the experimental 'Out of the Experience of Thinking,' nor in the swinging, ringing high originary voice that became his own after so much effort, after so many attempts to think along the same lofty trail. Rather, many of these short homey compositions occur in the simplest, clearest language he ever manages and chooses to use. Truly he has learned from Hebel what he said he would: to convey the experience of local place and personal belonging in straightforward, High German, which also allows what he says to become public, accessible to a wider, non-academic audience. Of course, Heidegger is no 'stay at home,' limited (as he might have been) by a rudimentary vocabulary or provincial range of experience, no more than were others of his region and guides, Hölderlin, Hebel, and Abrahim a Santa Clara, who were sophisticated and imaginatively-intellectually venturesome, with broad-ranging experiences that moved deeply into the foreign, over to the Greek and then home again (Hölderlin), or to the most current sciences of their time (Hebel and Abrahim a Santa Clara), or to administrative responsibilities and then back (Abrahim a Santa Clara and Hebel). (Though it will not become fully clear until we hear what Heidegger says in his 'Home Festival Address' at Todtnauberg, the importance of successful administrative work for place and thing can be glimpsed initially in his comment that the best of all ways to translate the Roman *res* is with the sense of the Old German word *thing* or *dinc*, which is still preserved in English and which we continue to use when we say: '"He knows how to handle things," he knows how to go about dealing with affairs' (T 175). What Heidegger needs to say about home places, things, and people and the tone in which to say it together resolve in what appears to be something most natural and easy but is, in fact, the hard-won product of years of labour. Zen-like in concentration, his sparse thinking and saying finally allow an appropriate setting-into-work of the heart of what needs to be seen in homecoming: the splendour of the simple.

The Homey Works

Striving to learn from Hebel how to masterfully remain focused in the local yet reach widely by using standard High German in works that can be broadly distributed, Heidegger responds to the opportunity which presents itself in the many celebrations for which he returns to Meßkirch, where he grew up. Here, from out of and still within his own Swabian homeland, he can put what he has learned about homelessness and home into a form both appropriate for non-specialists and yet rewarding for those who wish to not only continue thinking with him but to continue onward on their own. Heidegger acknowledges the importance of the diffusion of these homey works as he expresses his gratitude 'to everyone for the small book which you, together with Herr Dr Klostermann, make accessible to a wider circle of readers' (DM 711).

What does he have to say to his Meßkirch neighbours and the guests from around the world who will follow his words through publications (or even the occasional sound recording)? Heidegger clearly unfolds simple but strong thoughts about homelessness, home, and homecoming in 'Memorial Address' ('Gelassenheit,' 1955, which is certainly one of the best short, straightforward essays he ever wrote), in 'Ein Wort des Dankes,' delivered at a commemoration of Heidegger's seventieth birthday), and in '700 Years of Meßkirch' (which was a celebration address at the centennial festival). These essays use a consistent voice to present coherent subject matter: in these talks he speaks in an explicitly 'teacherly' mode, occasionally by way of a kind of poetic musing, but more usually in direct and simple 'plain talk.' Not surprisingly, though, while complementary enough to be seen as a family of works, these essays still have significant differences.

Of course, on the occasion of celebrating major milestones in Meßkirch's history or his own life, when he returns to his hometown as a distinguished guest and speaker, it is natural, if not inevitable, that there be a focus on home and homecoming. Yet, what that means cannot be taken for granted, nor allowed to be treated superficially. Just the opposite: what is so obvious as to be banal needs to be shown to be question-worthy, and the audience must be drawn into the way of questioning. 'But what should we think about now, so that this moment of reflection, this evening can merge in its own way with our celebration of our homeland? First we should turn to homeland itself. Yet, there has been too much said and written about it. The theme "homeland" has become boring, not just accidentally, but for profound reasons. Asking about the reasons for this might be worth some time' (700YM 233).

Why is the motif boring? Because everything that can be said has been said. The history of the town has been recorded, discussed, and published; everyone has been brought up to date on the current situation (700YM 233). But, as Heidegger has insisted before, recollective thinking, which he practises and teaches both generally and in these circumstances, does not focus upon the past, nor does it let itself fall into nostalgia. So, Heidegger's task is to prevent the occasion from lapsing into merely looking back to what has gone on in Meßkirch, or in his own life. Rather, attention needs to be drawn 'to what is still to come,' which would mean to the future, as that future now bears on the present and as what will concern us even more than it does now (DM 713). As he nicely puts the same point in another essay, walking the path of recollective thinking (*Andenken*) does not mean going to the past (*züruckgeht*) but toward what still comes (*Gewesene*) to us, so that meditation thinks ahead and forward to what concerns one's hometown, country, or the whole globe (WD 32).

Anticipating his audience's scepticism concerning what might be said about tomorrow, or what might seem to be a claim on his part to be 'prophetic,' Heidegger makes a two-dimensional move, while assuring his listeners that they can – and must – come along for the thinking: he points us toward what is near and to the way we might think about the future (which, as what is near, will turn out to be the same thing). 'Yet anyone can follow the path of meditative thinking in his own manner and within his own limits. Why? Because man is a thinking, that is, a meditating being. This meditative thinking need by no means be "highflown." It is enough if we dwell on what lies close and meditate on what is closest; upon that which concerns us, each one of us, here and now; here, on this patch of home ground; now, in the present hour of history' (MA 47). If what is closest, right now, in the question before us, is the future of the hometown, we need to inquire into what we assume the future to be and what we believe we can know about the future and perhaps into our assumptions about the way we could try to control it.

> If 'future' means for us mainly the period of time following today in the coming years and decades, we will never be able to describe how this period of time will be filled, especially not if we try to calculate how in the coming period the economic situation of the city might appear, how agriculture and farming will change, which directions schools and education will take, what form and efficacy the Christian faith and the churches will contain. If we want to ponder over tomorrow in this way, we will take the future only as the extension of today in which everything remains uncertain.
>
> But what if we understand the future as that which is coming towards us today? In this case the future is not at all what follows upon today, but is that which projects into today. 'Today' does not mean a self-sufficient period of time, enclosed in all directions. Today has its origin in what has happened and is at the time disposed to what comes towards it. (700YM 233–4)

Though what Heidegger means by the second, unusual interpretation of the future may not be immediately clear, what is obvious is that he is laying out, side by side, two different – perhaps, alternative – dimensions of the world and of what understanding would mean. Without bringing his high originary language and elaborate 'logic' to bear on distinguishing the metaphysical-representational from the originary, Heidegger says the same plainly. In short, what we may think we already know very well from reading Heidegger is recast in ordinary language:

> There are, then, two kinds of thinking, each justified and needed in its own way: calculative thinking and meditative thinking. ... Whenever we plan, research, and organize, we always reckon with conditions that are given. We take them into account with the calculated intention of their serving specific purposes. Thus we can count on definite results. This calculation is the mark of all thinking that plans and investigates ... Calculative thinking never stops, never collects itself. Calculative thinking is not meditative thinking, not thinking which contemplates the meaning that reigns in everything that is ... [Recollective thinking] requires a greater effort. It demands more practice. It is in need of even more delicate care than any other genuine craft. But it also must be able to bide its time, to await as does the farmer, whether the seed will come up and ripen. (MA 46–7)

For simplicity's sake, it seems fair to say that the two modes of thinking correspond to two different world realms: calculation goes with the metaphysical-technological, and meditative thinking belongs with the originary. What of the future of Meßkirch (or of any and all habitations), then, as two possible ways of bearing toward us and being understood? Apparently there are – would be –two futures. To take the technological first, if we meditatively consider the future as

> what comes toward us, meets and determines us constantly – we do not pay attention to it, we are not able to say precisely what this coming towards-us is. But everywhere there are many different signs. Among them, for example, are radio and television antennas which we see in rows upon the roofs of the houses in cities and towns. To what do these signs point? They point out that the men there, where they externally seem 'to live,' are no longer at home. By the day and hour men become increasingly drawn away into strange, exciting, captivating and at times entertaining and educative realms. But these offer no permanent, dependable place of rest; realms constantly change from the New to the Newest. Limited but yet drawn forth through all of this, man is, at the same time, on the move. He moves from

> feeling at home to feeling alien. [*Er zieht um aus dem Heimischen ins Unheimische*]. The threat looms that what was once called homeland or hometown will fall apart and disintegrate. The power of alienation appears to be overpowering man so that he can no longer stand against it. (700YM 234 [575])

Or, 'briefly characterizing the mysterious [*geheimnisvollen*] state' of our age, Heidegger contrasts the difference between the cosmos opened up when we, radically, have just shot rockets to the moon (threatening, he holds, our life patterns with destruction) with an ancient poetess' reflection on the play of stars, moon, and earth (WD 32–3). The worldwide impact of space exploration and control, of course, takes us far beyond Meßkirch to global concerns, not only as a result of technology generally, but of military struggles bringing us to the edge of nuclear destruction. The address presented during the Cold War from a European site between two heavily armed antagonists need not explicitly point out that rockets capable of going to the moon are but one version of nuclear missiles, aimed in all directions, threatening our lives and cities far more than did the bombs that reduced noble Dresden to rubble and killed its inhabitants 'through a brutally calculated violent act' – events all too fresh in his audience's memories (VH 636).

The era of technology determines the world today, Heidegger reminds his listeners, through its intense and increasing pursuit of the new, its global reach, its systematic homogeneity, all running over the top of traditional settlement forms and ways of life.

> It is not a coincidence that we speak of the age of technology. Technology's history is subject to a puzzling race which constantly drives every aspect of modern technology beyond itself to something else. Not long ago, the modern period was called the 'atomic age.' This name is already old, replaced by the 'space age.' Overnight another title may turn up ... We see everywhere and in every moment in the most diverse forms what determines the world today. It is modern technology, dominating with a sameness of form the entire earth, even the extra-terrestrial precincts of the universe. The often-mentioned underdeveloped peoples are being given the gift of performance in, success with, and use of modern technology; the question is whether through technology that which is most their own, most their inheritance, is not being taken and transformed into alienation. Perhaps 'foreign aid' is basically nothing more than the race of the (apparently) highly devel-

> oped peoples and states toward the goal of dominating as quickly and decisively as possible world business, thereby gaining a means to power in the struggle of the great powers for the domination of the earth. The form of this domination will be determined through the absolute, technical state. (700YM 235)

Nor is it the case, as we might suppose, that technology itself is a matter of what we do by way of our scientific and instrumental power. 'Everyone knows the signs of technical production. We are astounded at them. And yet no one knows what really is being demanded of man today in a growing degree by such limitless business and production. What so overpowers man cannot lie purely in the power of man. Consequently, it remains puzzling and disquieting. Precisely this alien element is dominant in alienation, and through alienation comes towards man and determines his future. Tomorrow is not only the next morning after today, it already controls today' (700YM 235).

What might happen? Explosively, there could be horrific technological warfare in which much of the world would be destroyed. Or, quietly, the attractions, usefulness, and comforts of technological devices might become so obvious, so spellbinding, that we would forget that there was, or is, or may yet be, an other-than-technological world, which would amount to our becoming oblivious to what has been or might again become home. 'Meßkirch tomorrow? It will become woven into the network of the age of technology. A question not only for this city, not only for our country, not only for Europe, but for mankind on this earth is whether under the domination of modern technology along with the changes in the world worked by it there can be, in any sense at all, a homeland. Perhaps men will move off into homelessness. Perhaps the relationship to homeland, the attraction to homeland will disappear from the existence of modern man' (700YM 235–6).

Against what is, from a meditative perspective, the bleakest prospect, the complete and comfortable oblivion of the loss of our originary home, even the painful experience of unremitting homelessness has its merits. 'Perhaps, however, in the midst of the penetration of the alien, a new relationship to homeland is preparing itself. Perhaps even a festival like ours can work in this preparation, and through it win some significance for tomorrow. Many will doubt this, will doubt it precisely because the power of alienation and the weird seems to enchain every attraction to homeland. But in reality the situation is completely different' (700YM

236). The way the painful has saving power in regard to home has been, in fact, experienced by all of us. The task, according to Heidegger, is to make the hidden, or the implicit, explicit:

> Our language calls the attraction to home 'homesickness' [*Heimweh*]. Here the homeland is so forceful, more forceful than anywhere else. It seems as if for today's man, because he is at home everywhere and nowhere, 'homesickness' has died out. Although there are arguments for this possibility, we must guard ourselves before the assertion that modern man no longer recognizes homeland and homesickness. The attraction of the homeland is still alive – most alive where we may expect it the least, alive in a strange way we hardly notice.
>
> Let us think about this slowly. Homesickness is alive where man is constantly in the flood into the alien, which entertains him, bewitches him, fills his time, shortens his time, because time for him is always too long [*zu lang*]. Man can no longer do anything by himself. What does this say? Something very strange – that for today's man, who has time for nothing any more, his free time is too long ... In this 'he is bored' [*es ist einem landweilig*], nothing reaches him, for everything becomes boring. Everything is worth so much and so little because a deep boredom [*tiefe Langeweile*] penetrates our existence ... We want to spend a few moments thinking about how and whether in the alienation of the modern technological world there is at the same time homeland ... Apparently this deep boredom – in the form of a search for spending time – is the hidden, unadmired, deflected yet still unavoidable attraction to our homeland: our hidden homesickness [*das verborgene Heimweh*]. Our language speaks more thoughtfully than we guess. Our language says, when a person is homesick, that time hangs heavy [*wenn einer Heimweh hat: 'er hat lange Zeit'*]. This 'heavy' time, which is ours, is nothing more than the long while in which nothing speaks to us, in which at the same time, we seek something to speak to us in a way which would lay claim to us so completely that time would never remain empty, so that there would be no need for 'passing time.' 'In a little while' means 'in a short time'; a long time means boredom. Apparently the alienation of the technological world and the deep boredom as the hidden attraction to a desired homeland [homesickness] belong together. (700YM 236 [579–80])

So, we are still connected with, and need, more than the technological world, a dimension that cannot be fulfilled by representational and calculative means (700YM 237; see also FHT 646–7). Heidegger has quietly and commonsensically awakened his audience out of the long-while, out of the boredom, by way of the issue of home with which he started, to the future prospect of homecoming, that is, to the *possibility* that home might yet come to us in (from) the future. But, how might there be any positive prospect for a future home, given the full, obliterating power of technological homelessness as seems little disputed, and is just beginning? It does not seem that it could derive merely from the thread of experience of yet belonging in absence (as with homelessness) that has run through many of our lives. The answer, Heidegger believes, has at least two intertwining aspects. The first is that humans, as long as we are human, continue to have some measure of the power for recollective thinking – which Heidegger attempts to awaken and to exercise on this and all occasions. 'I would like to say at this moment: there can be no decline [*Untergang*] of humans on this earth because the original and initial fullness of their will and ability is yet preserved and saved' (WD 33). Secondly, and more powerfully, he contends, is the fact that the cosmos that unfolds, whether technological or originary, is not initially or ultimately of our doing. If these two aspects are as Heidegger describes them, the possibility of an adequate human response would not be without further resistance, nor would the originary easily disappear – though certainly it still might, perhaps even more fully and inexorably.

For his part, Heidegger lays out for his listeners the basic dynamic that operates – and differs – in each of the two major 'scenarios' (the possibilities of the unfolding of the technological and of the originary) and the two ways to think, within which we are caught in an 'ambivalent' historical situation. What are the alternative ways of thought, and where do they lead? It might seem that one would need to come to the fore, and the other move to the periphery, if not disappear altogether. That is precisely what has been happening as the technological increasingly obliterates the originary and as calculation obscures all mediation as it is increasingly taken to be the only valid mode of thinking and the only conceivable measure (as we heard in the examination of the *Principle of Reason*). In contrast to this exclusionary drive, however, there is an inclusionary alternative: recollective thinking, by its very character, needs to retrieve, hold, and reinterpret all modes of thought, including the representational. Or, in our terms, an originary homecoming requires that we remain in and with the strange – which is one more reason why we hear Heidegger patiently going over again, in ordinary terms, what we have heard before in more technical language. Thus, for an originary homecoming to our own nature and to the world we need both modes of thinking, both dimensions of the world. We need listen again to what Heidegger said before, now with an emphasis on the consequence of recollectively thinking the difference: 'There are, then, two kinds of thinking, *each justified and needed in its own way:* calculative thinking and meditative thinking' (MA 46).

Without prematurely trying to anticipate the critical outcome – which would be impossible in any case – as a kind of roadmap here, it will turn out that, in contrast to the prospect of homelessness, Heidegger develops two positive variations in which homecoming might come about. To just note them, for now, as landmarks of a sort that might help us keep our orientation, we may say that, on the one hand, the *originary sources,* precisely insofar as they are originary, *might continue to come forth.* If so, they could be recovered, protected, and held. On the other hand, *a new relation to homeland might come about,* perhaps discontinuous with what has been or with what we might expect.

To begin with the first prospect, the possible retrieval of the source, Heidegger works out how, if home is the source from which we come and to which we yet belong, even when apart, and if it might be possible to stay in contact with the origin's force, for example through commemorative events or recollective thinking and saying, then the hometown centennials and birthday festivals are precisely *the* times for such to happen – or for the best effort to be made to facilitate or be ready for the prospect. The distant force would need draw near, the slumbering power, awaken. 'How can we set ourselves on guard against the penetration of this alienation? Only in as much as we awaken, do we stir up the springs of feeling at home again and prepare the right course for its flow and influence' (700YM 234). And the best condition for this would be when the natural and human already maintain some mutual dynamic – as in a rural village set amidst forest and fields or in poetry that fuses images of both realms.

> Homeland is most possible and effective where the powers of nature around us and the remnants of historical tradition remain together, where an origin and an ancient, nourished style of human existence hold sway [*bestimmen*]. Today for this decisive task perhaps only the rural counties and small towns are competent – if they recognize anew their unusual qualities, if they know how to draw the boundaries [*ihre außergewöhnliche Bestimmung*] between themselves and life in the large cites and the gigantic areas of modern industrial complexes – if they present themselves not as models and criteria but as a holding on to what is eminently their own, as the guard of

> feeling at home. For this two things are necessary. First, we must recognize alienation, recognize where it is active and determinative [*bestimmt*]; secondly, that we do not let decay and decline the still essentially unpretentious powers of the homeland.
>
> To become equal to both these demands – this centennial could be a good 'occasion' for this, the right festival for it. (700YM 234 [576])

Key, of course, is how such 'holding' could be accomplished. It could be in events, words, or images in memory, of course, but also in what is pledged and continued. It would involve resistances, saying 'no' and so acting; it would also require initiatives, affirming 'yes' and carrying out what is necessary as a consequence. As noted, such caring and preserving could occur when the group's memory is drawn back over the course of the history of the community as a whole, over the course of the lives of individuals living in that community. Setting aside the demands of the technological, the festival opens just such a quiet realm for reflection, allowing the prospect for accomplishing a bit of what needs to be done: 'Over against the alien which comes towards us we must balance off what comes to us from our origin. So we bring to the noisy and the frantic, stillness and restraint.' This is why, Heidegger tells his audience, 'the central point of our village's jubilee' is the 'exhibition of the paintings of the Master of Meßkirch,' which provides an 'occasion before those works to find peace and recollection again, that is, in the homeland.' 'At the same time, the performance of the recently-discovered orchestral Mass by Conradin Kreutzer also is a calling back of gifts of the homeland fortuitously used' (as was, Heidegger adds in a personal note, Archbishop Gröber's gift of a philosophical book on Aristotle, given to him when then a high-school student). The continuity of community, held and renewed through things long remembered and newly rediscovered, becomes a rich resource (700YM 238).

In addition, Heidegger contends that there is a second positive possibility for homecoming, one that would lie in the generation of new modes of belonging. 'Perhaps, however, in the midst of the preparation of the alien, a new relationship to homeland is preparing itself. Perhaps even a festival like ours can work in this preparation, and through it win some significance for tomorrow' (700YM 236). 'But once meditative thinking awakens, it must be at work unceasingly and on every last occasion – hence, also here and now at this commemoration. For here we are considering what is threatened especially in the atomic age: the autochthony of the works of man' (MA 53). A bold claim, or hope, that would, at the very least, involve persistently exploring for opportunities to let meditation flourish, for it to discover and help (trans)plant seeds for a new rootedness. 'What could the ground and foundation be for the new autochthony? Perhaps the answer we are looking for lies at hand; so near that we all too easily overlook it. For the way to what is near is always the longest and thus the hardest for humans. This way is the way of meditative thinking. Meditative thinking demands of us not to cling one-sidedly to a single idea, nor to run down a one-track course of ideas. Meditative thinking demands of us that we engage ourselves with what at first sight does not go together at all' (MA 53).

Since there is no danger at the moment that calculative thinking or the technological realm will diminish, our immediate task would be to learn how to better think meditatively about both the technological and the originary – which is why Heidegger is addressing us in these works. We have just heard that meditative thinking requires that we think multiple meanings, even apparently incompatible phenomena, at the same time.

> Let us give it a trial. For all of us, the arrangements, devices, and machinery of technology are to a greater or lesser extent indispensable. It would be foolish to attack technology blindly. It would be shortsighted to condemn it as the work of the devil. We depend on technological devices; they even challenge us to ever greater advances. But suddenly we find ourselves so firmly shackled to these technical devices that we fall into bondage to them.
>
> Still we can act otherwise. We can use technical devices, and yet with proper use also keep ourselves so free of them, that we may let go of them at any time. We can use technical devices as they ought to be used, and also let them alone as something which does not affect our inner and real core. We can affirm the unavoidable use of technical devices, and also deny them the right to dominate us, and so warp, confuse, and lay waste our nature.
>
> But will not saying both yes and no this way to technical devices make our relation to technology ambivalent and insecure? On the contrary! Our relation to technology will become wonderfully simple and relaxed. We let technical devices enter our daily life, and at the same time leave them outside, that is, let them alone, as things which are nothing absolute but remain dependent upon something higher. I would call this comportment toward technology which expresses 'yes' and at the same time 'no,' by an old word, *releasement toward things* [*Die Gelassenheit zu den Dingen*].
>
> Having this comportment we no longer view things only in a technical way. It gives us clear vision and we notice that while the production and use

of machines demands of us another relation to things, it is not a meaningless relation. Farming and agriculture, for example, now have turned into a motorized food industry. Thus here, evidently, as elsewhere, a profound change is taking place in man's relation to nature and to the world. But the meaning that reigns in this change remains obscure. (MA 54–5)

In our multiply faceted, apparently ambivalent, situation, we are in the midst of the technological, which certainly is disclosed and yet uncannily hidden, but we are also, at least to some extent, still in the originary, though less obviously, and it is fading as the other-than-technological withdraws. Without using or elaborating his technical originary vocabulary of disclosure and concealment, Heidegger plainly says the same to his Meßkirch audience:

There is then in all technical processes a meaning, not invented or made by us, which lays claim to what man does and leaves undone. We do not know the significance of the uncanny increasing dominance of atomic technology. The meaning of pervading technology hides itself. But if we explicitly and continuously heed the fact that such hidden meaning touches us everywhere in the world of technology, we stand at once within the realm of that which hides itself from us, and hides itself just in approaching us. That which shows itself and at the same time withdraws is the essential trait of what we call the mystery. I call the comportment which enables us to keep open the meaning hidden in technology, *openness to the mystery*.

Releasement toward things and openness to the mystery belong together. They grant us the possibility of dwelling in the world in a totally different way. They promise us a new ground and foundation upon which we can stand and endure in the world of technology without being imperiled by it.

Releasement toward things and openness to mystery give us a vision of a new autochthony which someday even might be fit to recapture the old and now rapidly disappearing autochthony in a changed form. (MA 55)

Neither of the two possible positive alternatives – preserving existing experiences of home and discovering a new rootedness – is close to being assured. What to do now thus remains the pressing question. At the least, we need to persist in meditative thinking directed toward the originary.

But for the time being – we do not know for how long – man finds himself in a perilous situation. Why? Just because a third world war might break out

> unexpectedly and bring about the complete annihilation of humanity and the destruction of the earth? No. In this dawning atomic age a far greater danger threatens – precisely when the danger of a third world war has been removed. A strange assertion! Strange indeed, but only as long as we do not meditate.
>
> In what sense is the statement just made valid? This assertion is valid in the sense that the approaching tide of technological revolution in the atomic age could so captivate, bewitch, dazzle, and beguile man that calculative thinking may someday come to be accepted and practiced *as the only* way of thinking.
>
> What great danger then might move upon us? Then there might go hand in hand with the greatest ingenuity in calculative planning and inventing indifference toward meditative thinking, total thoughtlessness. And then? Then man would have denied and thrown away his own special nature – that he is a meditative being. Therefore, the issue is the saving of man's essential nature. Therefore, the issue is keeping meditative thinking alive.
>
> Yet releasement toward things and openness to the mystery never happen of themselves. They do not befall us accidentally. They both flourish only through persistent, courageous thinking.
>
> Perhaps today's memorial celebration will prompt us toward this ... If releasement toward things and openness to the mystery awaken within us, then we should arrive at a path that will lead to a new ground and foundation. In that ground the creativity which produces lasting works could strike new roots. (MA 56–7)

Since, as noted above, there is more than enough evidence that homelessness may be all that lies in our future (and we will find ever more to support such a prospect in the homey essays as we go along), we can continue to follow, and understand why, Heidegger here *emphasizes* the two positive alternatives for homecoming – tries them out for his audience, teaching and exploring the ways the town is in precisely this position and has just these possibilities.

There is much to be recollected in a homecoming, so too in the homeland celebrations, so too in Heidegger's final homey works. It is not only the civil events, strictly speaking, that provide appropriate circumstances for the community to gather together of an evening, to hear a speaker or attend a concert or engage in neighbourly conversation. Now that he has accomplished so much, so too are the commemorations of the way of a lifetime that occur in Heidegger's maturity and old age. For we are close by the end of Heidegger's personal journey, focusing on many of the last things he wrote and presented. This circumstance is explicitly recognized in the events and works before us – though, as Heidegger himself appropriately notes, perhaps with too little attention to what is opened in the meditations, in that well-meant complements also cover over the yawning question, the possible chasm into which we and he might yet fall. At the 1969 Meßkirch celebration of Heidegger's eightieth birthday, both the Japanese guest, Tsujimura, and Professor Fink set what appears to be the scene. Tsujimura concludes his address by saying 'This evening is a celebration. Our old, great thinker has come home.' Fink adds a traditional saying, 'Evening brings everything home, the child to mother, goats to the pen, the wine to lips' (Az80, 19, 21). But this event is not let be as cosy as it sounds; Heidegger himself intends that it remain the scene of rigorous, open questioning. Back to Meßkirch? Yes, certainly. Old? Of course. But at home? That remains *the* question. Heidegger pushes through this same phrasing and thought in the opening words of his address at the 700 Years of Meßkirch Festival: 'The evening, whether it is the evening of a day or of a life, the evening is the time and hour of reflection ... But what should we think about now, so that this moment of reflection, this evening can merge in its own way with our celebration of our homeland? First we should turn to homeland itself' (700YM 233).

Two ways to come home? More than merely resisting technological homelessness, the alternatives, as we have heard, might counter it, replacing the busy with the calm, the noisy with the quiet. 'One thing interacts with another, if only we try to pay attention to what works in stillness' – conserving and holding on to the enduring significance of places, things, people, and events, but releasement to things and openness to mystery leading to a new grounding (700YM 238). What has Heidegger to contribute? What can he teach the people of this countryside and guests?

Certainly, to recollect about the place and about its people is one and the same thing, for the belonging together of place and people is central to constituting homeland. The commemorative celebrations are the especially appropriate times for such memorial thinking. Heidegger elaborates how when visiting our hometown or gathering there to welcome those who return, 'memory is drawn back anew upon what has happened' – just as when visiting the cemetery 'we think back upon the time of our youth, we think about powers and forces which restore the healing, the fruitful and the lasting, sometimes even the significant' (700YM 237–8). Simultaneously listening to his country neighbour Hebel and saying what is Heidegger's own about place and thing, he ends 'Art and Space' with such a potent image, citing Goethe: 'it is … enough already if [what is true] hovers about and evokes harmony, if it floats through the air like the solemn and friendly sound of a bell' (AS 8). This image of powerful delicacy also resonates with what Heidegger finds in Hölderlin. In speaking of Hölderlin's poetry as 'like a shrine without a temple' (RP 234) (mentioned but not developed toward the end of chapter 2) Heidegger says, 'the poems are like a bell that hangs in the open air and is already becoming out of tune through a light fall of snow which is covering it.' He then goes on to cite lines from Hölderlin's 'Entwurf zu Kolomb':

> Sent out of tune
> By Little things, as by snow,
> Was the bell, with which
> The hour is rung
> for the evening meal. (cited in RP 234)

From the image formed (*Gebild*) by Goethe and that of the bell stilled in the snow we can see the trajectory of Heidegger's thought, from releasement to things and from openness to mystery – a movement that arcs to the 'The Mystery of the Bell Tower,' the English title of the next essay to be considered. In his 'Vom Geheimnis des Glockenturms' (1954), Heidegger, recalling childhood memories, muses on early Christmas morning.[15] The simple experience is tenderly pictured: mood and feelings, people and place, things and their powers. Deep in the night (3:30 AM), the child bell-ringers gather in the sacristan's house for an exceptional occasion. Full of anticipation for the event, likely not just over the last days of Advent, but through much of the year, the youngsters now inhale the sweet scent of evergreen boughs there from Christmas Eve and eye the table of milk-coffee and cakes that Heidegger's mother (the 'sacristan mother') has set out for them. But it is not really the food that attracts, we are told; it is the magic of the extraordinary moment.

Time to kindle the lanterns in the corridor, to stomp through the snow to the bell tower, to wake the sleeping town – not fully appreciated by the villagers at that time of night. Heidegger recounts the bells and their names and characteristics. The large bells, rung from the bell chamber itself, are a cause of anticipation, even concern, because of their make-up and the difficulty in ringing them properly. The peculiarity lies in that the clapper is secured to the huge bells and released only when they are in full swing. The effect is dramatic, of course. No gradual 'buhm,' 'buhm' working its way up to full sound; rather, silence (only the swish of the bells' movement to and fro), then at full swing, release and the full, deep tone: 'BHUHMM.' Only a skilled hand can measure when to let the bells sound out, only an expert ear can measure if the ringing happens correctly. At the end, the same procedure happens in reverse: full swinging and sounding; stop: ___ (full silence). Small wonder that the bell-ringers are anxious about getting it right.

But there are many other bells. When the big bell sounds on Christmas morning at 4 AM, it is joined by the smallest bell, '*Dreie*' (three-er) usually rung at three in the afternoon by the sacristan's boys (Martin and his brother Fritz), who at that moment are hard at play and loath to interrupt the games in the castle garden or on the bridge. To minimize the interference, they often move their play to the bells' space, that is, to the bell chamber or to the highest beams of the church tower where birds make their nests. These same small bells are rung at the time of funerals by the sacristan himself, Heidegger's father. In addition to the bells that sound the quarter hours (normally followed, when time, by the enumeration of the hours themselves), there are '*Alve*,' '*Kinde*' (rung for Sunday school and the rosary), the daily '*Elfe*' (eleven) (usually rung by the sacristan), the noon bell ('*Zwölfe*,' twelve), the '*Klanei*,' and '*die Große*.' There are bells for the angelus (saying office), for the day before holidays and at last evening vigils. The little mass bell on its thin rope is used by the sacristan to give the sign to the altar boys to ring the silver bell at the moment of consecration (though on Holy Thursday, Good Friday, and Saturday of Holy Week the bells are silent and the *Ratschen* – ratcheter – is used instead).

Heidegger's reflection on the rhythms when he and his brother rang the bells, instead of, or with, their father, or when the sacristan himself did the job (when the boys were in school at three in the afternoon or serving mass, or when the occasion was a funeral) not only recalls the ambivalence they had to the chore – with a pun articulating the link between ringing and suffering ('*gelitten*' [suffering], he tells us, is Schwabian for '*geläutet*' [ringing]) – but the social structure, where the sacristan's boys, for all their work and experience, would not be among the bell-ringing boys with whose Christmas anticipations the recollection began. These ringers were 'other boys.' As in Hebel's world, so too in Heidegger's, in its own distinctive way. The places, things, and activities that constitute village life play out over a plurality of times: Heidegger includes daily rhythms and the larger arcs of the seasons of heavens and earth, the course of human lifetimes and sacred cycles, all differentiated yet bound together. For example, at Easter there already is a pre-spring character to the landscape, across which the peals roll, even a shift toward summer. The interplay of all these dimensions occurs in a complex rhythm that is both orchestrated by the bells' sounding across the countryside and that sets the patterns into the bell's distinctive characters and uses. This is, indeed, openness to mystery and releasement to things and to a local way of life in its abiding rhythms.

Heidegger's only really extended commentary, beyond nuanced description of the space-time realm, comes at the end of the last paragraph of the reflection on 'the mysterious fugue' (*Fuge;* compare *der Fuge* as jointure, joining, as we saw in Heidegger's reflections on early Greek thinking) of church holidays, vigil days, the course of seasons, morning, noon, and evening hours so assembled every day that a ringing constantly traces through young hearts, dreams, prayers, and games. This mysterious fugue shelters one of the most enchanted wholesome and continuous secrets of the tower to keep it always changing and never repeated until the last ringing in/of the mountain of *be-ing* (*Seyn*) (GG 10).

A civic commemoration of a specific death, that of the famous Meßkirch composer Conrad Kreutzer a century before, was the occasion in 1949 for Heidegger to compose the other equally poetic reflection on his childhood Meßkirch, 'Pathway' ('Der Feldweg') – in language that echoes Hebel's description of his Wiesental. Heidegger musingly describes how as the church bells sound out the village's rhythms, so the pathway traces them over the landscape, moving out of and back, embracing village and landscape, seasons and the course of life. Running out from the park gate toward Ehnried, the pathway runs across the fields until, 'at the wayside crucifix it turns to the woods,' then through the barren moor country. 'The same fields and meadows accompany the pathway through each season and with an ever-changing nearness.' Counterpart to the tower's bells, at Christmas the pathway 'disappears in snow drifts behind the hill,' while in Easter's sun the pathway 'shines bright between rising crags and waking meadows.' As to each day, 'whether the Alps above the forests are sinking away into the evening twilight, whether the lark climbs into the summer morning there where the pathway swings over the rolling hill, whether the east wind approaches in storm from over where mother's home lies, whether a woodsman as night nears drags his bundle of brushwood to the hearth, whether a harvesting wagon sways homeward in the pathway's tracks, whether children are gathering the first flowers at meadow's edge, whether fog for days moves its gloom and burden over the fields – always and everywhere the message of the same rests on the pathway' (P 88–9).

Along the path in his youthful spring, Heidegger often sat on a 'roughly hewn bench' sheltered by a 'tall oak,' awkwardly trying to 'decipher' 'one or another of the great thinkers' writings,' and he found relief, when at his limit, by adjourning to traverse the trail's quiet unfolding. Back and forth from village to countryside, the youthful thinker moved just as did the farmers: 'The path remains as close to the step of the thinker as to that of the farmer walking out to the mowing in the early morning' (P 88). Past the great oak and in the forest, Heidegger's father, not only sacristan at St Martin's Church, but also a cooper, 'would look through the woods and sunny clearings for the cord allocated to him and his workshop. There he laboured, thoughtful when pausing from his efforts at the sound of the tower clock and bells.' Mother was even more present, her 'eye and hand ... surrounded their world. It was as if her unspoken care protected every being' (P 89). She watched over their play, as already mentioned in 'Vom Geheimnis des Glockenturms,' which also drew naturally and unselfconsciously from the woods: 'out of the oak's bark the boys carved their boats: equipped with rudder and tiller they floated in Metten brook or in the school fountain. The worldwide journeys of those games reached their destination easily and found their way to shore again. The dream element in such voyages remained hidden in a then hardly perceptible luster which lay over everything' (P 89).

Heidegger told us in '700 Years of Messkrich' (234), as we noted, that place and thing are most efficacious for homecoming when nature and the humanly made occur together. So here Heidegger elaborates not what mason or carpenter set into work in their towers, bridges, and benches but the natural things that speak to us, too. Thus, as the youths played and grew, 'the hardness and smell of oak wood began to speak more distinctly of the slowness and constancy in the tree's growth. The oak itself spoke: Only in such growth is grounded what lasts and fructifies. Growing means this: to open oneself up to the breadth of heaven and at the same time to sink roots into the darkness of earth. Whatever is genuine thrives only if man does justice to both – ready for the appeal of highest heaven, and cared for in the protection of sustaining earth. Again and again the oak says this to the pathway passing securely by. The pathway collects whatever has its being along the way; to all who pass this way it gives what is theirs' (P 89).

Heidegger's simple language lays out the gathering accomplished by the pathway with little 'to-do.' He rhetorically reinforces the dynamic character of the place and events through his choice of verbs that implicitly say that much of what happens is not human doing. It is not that Heidegger is anthropomorphizing the local things; rather, he is trying to find a way of saying the power that unfolds through these things (a way of saying the same as 'thing gathers the fourfold into world' without using his high originary – technical – vocabulary and at the same time providing specific, concrete historical instances of such gathering). Hence, Heidegger says, 'the old linden trees in the schloss garden gaze after [the pathway] from behind the wall'; 'along its edge the pathway greets' that tall oak and bench and 'escorts feet along the winding path'; 'with the years, the oak along the way frequently recalls the early games and choices' (P 88). Just as much as the poet's poem, these natural things say, if we can but hear the message. According to Heidegger, the message is simple, constant, and clear:

> Always and everywhere the message of the same rests on the pathway:
>
> The simple [*das Einfache*] preserves the puzzle of what remains and what is just. Spontaneously it enters men and needs a lengthy growth. With the unpretentiousness of the ever-same it hides its blessing. The breadth [*die Weite*] of all growing things which rest along the pathway bestows world. In what remains unsaid in their speech is – as Eckardt, the old master of letters and life, says – God, only God. (P 89 [39])

Hearing the message – and, perhaps, even ordering ourselves according to it – also depends upon our being able to become open to the origin by first recognizing that we do not produce it, giving up the anthropocentric view of the constitution of meaning – in which we have 'become detached and pathless' (P 89–90). Yet, insofar as we can hear it, the pathway and its message tell us of the gathered coherence over the entire course of a local space-time, that is, a local world. 'Along its path winter's storm encounters harvest's day, the agile excitation of Spring and the detached dying of Autumn meet, the child's game and the elder's wisdom gaze at each other. And in a unique harmony, whose echo the pathway carries with it silently here and there, everything is sparked serene' (P 90). All this quietly said, Heidegger brings us back to where we are by following the path's curve from away to back home:

> From Ehnried the way turns back to the park gate. Over a final hill its narrow ribbon runs through moorland until it reaches the town wall. It shines

> dimly in the starlight. Behind the schloss the tower of Saint Martin's church rises. Slowly, almost hesitantly, eleven strokes of the hour sound in the night. The old bell, on whose ropes boys' hands have been rubbed hot, shakes under the blows of the hour's hammer whose dark-droll face no one forgets.
>
> With the last stroke the stillness becomes yet more still. It reaches out even to those who have been sacrificed before their time in two world wars. The simple has become simpler. The ever-same surprises and frees. The message of the pathway is now quite clear ...
>
> Everything speaks abandonment [*Verzicht*] unto the same. Abandonment does not take. Abandonment gives. It gives the inexhaustible power of the simple. The message makes us at home after a long origin here. (P 90–1)[16]

These scenes of the Meßkirch of his youth also bespeak the earliest, seemingly unproblematic phase of the human journey. Here we have the image of origin in the sense not only of the source still powerfully flowing into a historical place and way of life, but also of (to again use Hölderlin's phases) the initial condition of being (still) at home, innocent of homelessness to come. 'Those [childhood] trips of play still knew nothing of wanderings when all shores stay distant' (P 89). Recollection of adulthood, of homelessness, yet remains to be undertaken. Not surprisingly, as Heidegger shifts to reflect and speak about these later phases and conditions, his voice changes. The relaxed, almost sweet, mode cannot continue. Adulthood and homelessness need to be said in a different way. In the remaining homey works we find that Heidegger assumes what can be termed a more 'teacherly' tone, sometimes in an elevated version appropriate for a formal address (as we already have heard in 'Dankansprache am 26 September 1969 in Meßkirch,' and '700 Years of Meßkirch'), sometimes with the mature, direct, and simple saying of what he has to teach, as we have already heard in 'Memorial Address,' sometimes in the manner of a friend or neighbour who happens to be a professor. This overall set of writings, many first delivered as talks, cover the three major scenes of Heidegger's adult life within a sublocality of Swabia (where, after all, he spent his whole life, since he was away from the region only from 1923 to 1928, when he taught at Marburg, living in rented rooms). So, we have homey works, not only from and about Meßkirch, but also Freiburg and Todtnauberg.

Freiburg, of course, was 'home base' for Heidegger. There he lived his life as a faculty member of the philosophy department and as a husband

and father. From second-hand sources we know that Heidegger had a house built there as soon as he was appointed to what had been Husserl's chair at Albert Ludwig University of Freiburg. Heidegger's wife, Elfride, evidently provided the direction to the architect Fetter, with Heidegger himself commenting only on the details of his study and the placement of some of the rooms – visitors to his study have commented on the stacks of manuscripts, and the ever present photo of Heidegger's mother, on the desk. The two-story house, Rötebuckweg 47, built at the very edge of the Freiburg suburb of Zähringer, initially had only a small brook and then fields behind it. Somewhat rural in appearance, though of contemporary suburban construction, it had a biblical inscription (from Proverbs 4:23, chosen and translated by Heidegger) painted on the wooden beam above the front door: 'Shelter your heart with all vigilance; for from it flow the springs of life.'[17] Next to the bell the card reads 'Visits after 5 PM.'[18] Of his life as a faculty member and about significant places at the university or in the city, Heidegger has said little, which is entirely consistent with his personal-professional custom of avoiding biographical details, emphasizing that the thoughts which come to – are given to – thinkers should remain at the forefront and not be pushed aside by the subjectivity of the modern age, much less by any cult of personality. That insistence that thoughts come to the thinker – that they are given and not any credit to the individual's creativity – is in the background of an account he presents of the scene so often re-enacted when guests came to have a word with him. The following low-key comments are made at the beginning of one of his many presentations of variations on his Hebel lecture, this one in Zähringer, on 5 September 1954.[19]

Heidegger begins his talk by describing how, when he lifts his gaze from the work table in his home study and lets it run out over the Fillibach (the brook), across the meadows and ploughed fields, then up the steep slope, it comes to rest on the tower of Zähringer Castle (reminding us in its sweep of the scene in the Wiesental described by Hebel and then Heidegger) (JPHZ 491). Heidegger recounts that, whereas visitors from all over the world, on entering the study, invariably comment immediately 'on the beautiful view' and the tranquility of the landscape, he always corrects them, explaining that it is the other way around. 'Here it is not a matter of a view out to a beautiful region [*Gegend*]'; rather, here 'entering the study, secret forces are at work on the work of thinking: [they are] the waking land, the quiet of the wooded mountain, the rooted power of the neighbourly people' (JPHZ 491).[20] Here, he goes on, 'only the simple and necessary blessing of a new hourly beginning of the day's work remains' (JPHZ 491). Though we passed over it just now, Heidegger also quietly but firmly insists on the belonging together of his work and that of his farming neighbours, and of both to the landscape in which they are communally gathered – of which he will say more in this set of homey works. When his gaze runs from the study to the castle ruins and back (along a trajectory also echoing that of the pathway in Meßkirch), then 'right before his eyes it is always clear how [his] work also only belongs together with the daily work of Zähringers below the castle and the production of its farmers in the field' (JPHZ 491).

Since this talk was given to residents of Zähringer and Freiburg, as well as guests from Bern, Heidegger allows himself a slippage into dialect – a striking signal that here he is at home in a way parallel to what he has been telling us by way of Hebel, and in contrast to all the other subsets of his corpus we have considered thus far. Weaving sentences in dialect in with the standard German, Heidegger asks how Hebel with his *Alemannic Poems* could be gifted or sent to us, if we do not 'open our ears and offer ready hearts' (JPHZ 491–2) (*'Wo denn so einer tagus tagi mit den andere Lüte uner der Zähringer Burg si Arbet tuet, do isch es ei tue, as er mit debi isch, wenn's e Zähringer Fescht mit so fründlige Gäscht us Bern git, wie am hütige Tag,' 'Ich saaget mir: do loßt en andere dra, der's besser cha – und das isch dr. Johann Peter Hebel'*). If we manage, we find that Hebel's 'saying speaks to both: it speaks to the soul of the guest, it speaks from the soul of the host, and this in a way [just] as directly as, for both, the Zähringer Castle remains a substantial sign of a common historical origin and sending' (JPHZ 492). The simple sentences let play together things and places (work table and poems; brook, fields, and castle; or Zähringer, Freiburg, Bern, and Hebel's Alemannic landscape); they speak of hosts opening to guests (Heidegger to his visitors, the Zähringers and Freiburgers to those from Bern and to Heidegger himself invited to give his talk).

At home, Heidegger not only receives visitors in his capacity as thinker and writer but, as a family man, also welcomes relatives and guests of the household. We hear of this in a letter, pointedly titled 'Verlust der Heimat' ('Loss of Home') that he sends on behalf of the whole family in 1966 to a cousin of his wife Elfride. The eightieth-birthday greeting to cousin Gerta Grabe is bittersweet, not avoiding the central pain of a world lost – a rich and happy home in Dresden, a husband destroyed there along with the city. Heidegger blends praise for 'the fullness of [her] life,' many appreciated roles (not just cousin, but mother, grandmother, great grandmother, and wife), and virtues, with fond memories of her and Elfride's common youth, Elfride at Gerta's wedding, and especially the hospitality (*Gastlichkeit*) she and her deceased (*heimgegangen*) husband provided, as when Heidegger visited Dresden to give a lecture in 1931, so that because of their openness, he did 'not come into strange country' (*nicht in die Fremde*) (VH 634–5).

Heidegger elaborates how he appreciated the hospitality of his hosts and the charms of their city. Gerta and her husband, Achim, escorted Heidegger on excursions in the area and to a wonderful meal at the house of her parents, whose festive table (reminding him of the earlier wedding dinner) was in a style that was simple, yet with an especially nice atmosphere, enhanced by her father's cigars and a certain lifestyle, also apparent in her aunt Anna. He observes that such a way of life, rare nowadays, cannot just be created from one day to another, but instead 'can only grow in a long and carefully tended tradition [again echoing what he said of Meßkirch and the oak along the pathway] in the midst of a common spirit [*eines gemeinsamen Geistes*] as was then offered by the unique city of Dresden' (VH 634–5). On the Elbe, Dresden was at the time one of the most beautiful and refined (*die schönste und vornehmste*) of the rising great modern cities.

Against such a lovely image, fondly evoked and shared, Heidegger non-nostalgically places the multiple losses. Beyond the destruction of Dresden and the sudden death of her husband in the bombings, there lies the passage of her son, Gottfried, through the Heidegger household in Freiburg, in rags on his way back from a French prison camp, and after that the further calamity of the division of East and West Germany, during which her daughter-in-law, Eva, amazingly managed to get the whole family over to the West. Even with a new placement there is no way around facing the loss of the former landscape, city, home, and entire way of life. Recounting all these catastrophes, Heidegger is explicit about the pain: 'darkness and suffering came into you life: loss of your beloved husband, loss of your beloved homeland, and restless migration [*Verlust des geliebten Mannes, Verlust der Heimat und ruhelose Wanderschaft*]' (VH 636).

Heidegger hopes that in her newly adopted area of the Black Forest, with its gentle foothills and beautiful villages, she has found to some extent a landscape to substitute for the one she would remember from her youth, with the mountain chains (*Erzgebirge*), where her mother's family dwelt – already known to him before his own visit, from Elfride's narratives (*Erzählungen*) – (VH 635). He concludes the letter by noting that though mortal works and hopes can do little, still 'if in mortal endeavors, a good spirit speaks through love and trust, affection and gratitude, care and devotion, then through such a spirit, as if by itself, the most beautiful gift [das schönste Geschenk] fashions itself.' This is what the whole Heidegger family offers (*einmütig*) to Gerta on her eightieth birthday, hoping that therein a corresponding home (*Aufenthalt*) may be granted (*gewährt*). In addition to those noble sentiments, Heidegger closes by adding a familial touch, noting that they welcome her and expect to see her in Freiburg, 'in a quiet corner on our terrace in the summer morning's sun with a good book or her knitting' (VH 637).

As Heidegger regularly says, the post-war years are full of difficulty, ranging from the severe housing and food shortages to the personal trauma of death and displacement: 'Many Germans have lost their homeland, have had to leave their villages and towns, have been driven from their native soil. Countless others whose homeland was saved, yet wandered off. They have been caught up in the turmoil of the big cities, and have resettled in the wastelands of industrial districts. They are strangers now in their former homeland. And those who *have* stayed on in their homeland? Often they are still more homeless than those who have been driven from their homeland' (MA 48; see also BDT 145–6). These historical personal losses are the concrete cases in point for Heidegger and his audience, the manifestations in everyday life of the reign of metaphysical-technological homelessness. Though he does not say it, in Freiburg he is going through his own attempts to recover from traumatic displacement. However generally understated (and often tense or even thickheaded), what he says makes clear that he is more than glad to come back to his home university and to resume the dimension of his scholarly and teacherly identity. As (to note just one example) in his 30 September 1951 letter to the Minister of Culture and Education, four days after being granted normal, full emeritus status, he specifies, that it 'returns me to an adequate relation to my home university [*Heimatuniversität*].'[21] At the same time, his personal library is twice saved. First, he and Elfride successfully protested against it being confiscated by the provisional city administration as directed by the French military government. Next they averted the threat that it would be taken to 'restock the library at the University of Mainz.' In the end, Heidegger manages to remain in the Freiburg house, rather than being evicted as a result of a more complete requisition by the provisional city administration (though the Heideggers had to share it with other families for some time, making for cramped quarters).[22] Once they regained the residence, they stayed in it until the couple moved, to accommodate old age, into a smaller house they built at the back of the lot – Elfride again overseeing the project. This house they referred to as Fillibach, after the brook.

Recovering himself in a new homeland, the mature Heidegger found his positive relationship with his hometown of Meßkirch important for reconstituting participation within the series of nested spheres there: his own life from childhood to returning as an honorary citizen, the town's 700 years of continuity, then the region's major cultural formations over the course of the last three hundred years. In addition to the three homey Meßkirch works already considered ('Memorial Address,' '700 Years of Meßkirch,' 'Dankansprache'), there are at least four more in the set well worth considering: 'Ein Wort des Dankes'; 'Dank bei der Verleihung des Staatlichen Hebelgedenkpreises' (comments Heidegger made on receiving the Hebel Prize in 1960); a significant and oddly ignored piece, 'Über Abrahim a Santa Clara,' from 1964; and a short presentation at the new Meßkirch high school, 'Statt einer Rede,' from 1973.

Of the many gifts of which he speaks, Meßkirch formally granting him the status of free citizen of the city (*Ehrenbürger*) in September 1959 (on the occasion of the city's celebration of his seventieth birthday) is an unusually explicit and full homecoming (WD 26–7). Such celebrations amount to performatives in which the gathering that accomplishes homecoming occurs, in which the opening which opens to and from homecoming opens. Home as region: *Gegen,* as regioning-opening expanse – *Gegnet* happens here. As Heidegger notes (with surprisingly little emphasis on such a choice word-sound, and surprisingly not as a direct point repeatedly made over all the years), such celebration is free, and thus simultaneously serious and festive (just as thinking itself, as at Meßkirch, as in Hölderlin's hymns): 'in thinking the insight into what is *set free,* that is *celebrated* [*was ist freigegeben, d.h. gefeiert*]' (700YM 238).

In the Meßkirch celebrations there are openings to the free span of people and events for centuries, openings to the many dimensions of the hometown's power that yet springs forth. The citizens and guests are gathered back together to remember and newly respond to their forebears: to the Master of Messkrich and his paintings, to Conradin Kreutzer and his musical compositions, to – broadening the surrounding region only a bit – Hebel. As Heidegger has said on other occasions, focusing on Hebel, the poetry, far from being obsolete, is as fresh and young today as it was one hundred and fifty years ago: indeed, 'in this man the slumbering poetic source sprang forth,' in large part because he belonged so profoundly to his homey, native landscape (*heimatlichen Landschaft*) and because, precisely through that local rootedness, belonged to a world-wide sending (JPHZ 492; DHP 565). Thus, Hebel's poetry continues to locate and inhabit that realm out of which all poetry and thinking come forth. On another occasion (Heidegger's receiving the prestigious prize on the 200th anniversary of Hebel's birth), the audience and theme allow Heidegger to move between Hebel's dialectal writing and the standard German of Heidegger's presentation, further enabling him to speak in a way that makes a double point about homecoming. First, for the learned guests and for the locals who know the dialect, he can powerfully claim that spoken in the second verse of the first strophe of *Alemannic Poems* is a word 'into which everything is gathered that can be said about Hebel':

> *Gang, wo de witt, suech no so ein!*
> *Sel isch verbei, de findsch mer kein.* (cited in DHP 567)

Subsequently, he shows (rather than tells) the wider audience *reading* the published talk that even amidst what we share in good spirit around the world, there is some understanding that is local. Obviously, both the finitude of the home region and the interplay of locality and breadth sounds loudly in the 'silence' that befalls most of us reading these lines. While Hebel scholars from all over the world, as well as the locals still using dialect can follow the insights and perhaps nod their heads in reflective agreement – Heidegger invited some of his Todtnauberg farmer friends to the event – most of us (belonging to neither group) hear almost nothing at all of what lies at the heart of the local here (though we may well be glad to be allowed to participate, and hear what we can of the bulk of the talk that reaches out more broadly).

Similarly, Heidegger brings others from Meßkirch into the light for their strong local connection and wide range. As we have found, Heidegger often thanks his early mentor, the 'fatherly friend' from Meßkirch, Konrad Gröber, later Archbishop of Freiburg, who, as pastor in Constance, gave the then seventeen-year-old high-school student his first copy of Brentano's *Aristotle's Manifold Meanings of Being*, which decisively sent the youth on his way to the question of being (700YM 238). Heidegger wants to stress to his audience, whether townspeople, students, or guests, that it is precisely the living tradition, passed on by example, teaching, and appropriate response, that maintains the spirit of place and the power of the homeland. Thus, what matters is not the relatively dead formal curriculum but the living exemplar of the master teacher or crafts person, of someone who is knowledgeable and admirable (AsSC 47). Hence the celebration of the other Meßkirch inhabitants just mentioned and the freshening of what they give us, so that our recollective thinking keeps the source coming.

On the occasion of an address to a Meßkirch school reunion in 1964, he invites his audience of classmates and others of the region into reflection with the old saying, 'Not everyone has straw in the head, who was born under a straw [thatched] roof.' With his wry insider's appreciation of the rural, Heidegger bids us listen to an earlier figure from the area, one who preceded even Hebel as pastor, teacher, and poetically-rhetorically gifted native son (and, I am arguing, he here identifies yet another 'fore-figure' for himself). Heidegger explains that Johann Ulric Merge, born about a kilometre away in 1644, the son of a local wine bartender, came from Kreenheinstatten to attend Latin school in Ingolstadt (as Heidegger went from Meßkirch to a short-lived stay with the Jesuits at Lake Constance). From there, Merge went to Salzburg with the Benedictines, and thence to Vienna, where he took the cloister name Abrahim a Santa Clara and at eighteen years of age entered the Franciscan order (Augustinian-Barefooted Friars). After his ordination in 1666, he began his teaching and preaching and, having meanwhile completed his work to be a doctor of theology and barely thirty-three, was appointed court preacher to Kaiser Leopold. The most powerful rhetorician of his day and the most read author, Heidegger tells us, Abraham a Santa Clara was also successful in the order's and in secular work, assuming the duties of Prior in his cloister in 1680 and ten years later becoming Provincial of the Franciscan order (as was Hebel, he was a successful administrator, 'gaining experience and insights with two trips to Rome,' and similarly spent his career away from his childhood home and native area) (AaSC 46–7).

So? What of his relevance today? His was a turbulent time as is that of Heidegger's audience. Born into the era of the Thirty Years War, which was followed by a continuing series of disasters, Abrahim a Santa Clara lived amidst as much homelessness as can be imagined. Heidegger stresses that his was a world of constant war, with its hunger and misery, a time of 'strange armies migrating through the land, of the plague, of the Turks at the walls of Vienna.' He found the world swinging between war and what could have been considered peace in a way that led to a juxtaposition, all at once, all in one place, of 'the nightmare of death and the lust to live.' What Abrahim a Santa Clara found '*bei uns*' and spoke about is all too familiar to Heidegger's audience – thus, just as do Hebel's, Abrahim a Santa Clara's words have force for us today (AaSC 48–9).

Just as Heidegger addresses his classmates and neighbours in our age at the beginning of a new pulse of scientific-technical disclosures, Abrahim a Santa Clara was part of the new creative period known as the baroque: the sphere of Bach and Händel, of the great baroque architecture of churches at Ottobeuren, Weingarten, Weißenau, Steinhausen, and Birnau, of Leibniz (whose patron, Leopold I, was also was Abrahim a Santa Clara's), and of the new modern physics – which today we call 'classical in distinction from atomic and nuclear physics.' Keeping interested in and appreciative of this new science (as was Hebel, later, of the Enlightenment's; as is Heidegger, in his way, of the science of subatomic systems and systems in general), Abrahim a Santa Clara said that 'a man without science is as a heaven without stars, as a nut without a kernel' (AaSC 48–9). (Note that Heidegger uses this quotation, and further deploys Abrahim a Santa Clara's words, to quietly play on the theme of the double-dimensioned worlds and two-track thinking: the representational-technical kernel of contemporary nuclear physics is contrasted with the originary kernel of the homely nut – the word for the former is *kernphysik*, and Abrahim a Santa Clara's quoted words for the latter are '*wie eine nuß ohne kern*' [AaSC 48–9].)

Abrahim a Santa Clara, who 'spoke and wrote' (Heidegger repeatedly emphasizes both) from 'a rich, global, far-reaching experience' and knowledge also operated from an inner freedom and courage when appropriate – no small accomplishment in the high-pressure realm of the royal court (AaSC 49). He consistently deployed his considerable rhetorical skills to educational ends. Abrahim a Santa Clara was a sharp critic of worldly vanities, many of which of course the royal court amply exhibited. Heidegger relates how on one occasion Abrahim a Santa Clara aimed pointed remarks at immodesty of dress. After a sermon reprimanding the court for the current women's fashion in terms that were so strongly worded that all Vienna was abuzz, the next Sunday a large crowd came to hear him make what was assumed to be a mandatory apology to his powerful listeners. In that first sermon Abrahim a Santa Clara had denounced, in his words, dresses that 'left half the studs [*Buckel*, buttons] open.' Now, with an expectant audience before him, he said, 'I have in course of my last sermon said that women who would follow the mode of male dress, don't deserve to be stuck with a manure fork. I take it back – They do' (AaSC 49).

Heidegger also tells us that one of Abrahim a Santa Clara's favourite themes was money, and so, too, a theme with which to use his rhetorical skills to draw his audience into thinking along. Heidegger relates how in a sermon Abrahim a Santa Clara asked, 'What had holy and blessed [*heilig und selig*] Gregory the Great XIX made? Money, the money? What had Charlemagne the Great XIX made? Money, the money?' The listeners naturally would think, of course not, holiness and blessedness do not let themselves be acquired by means of money. But then the preacher unexpectedly reverses the emphasis, saying 'Yes, Money' – the money which Martinus and Elisabeth and countless other holy and blessed (blissful, beatific) made, the money they donated to the poor. Heidegger notes that money is just as much an interest today, and assuming that his classmates and neighbours would agree, passes on what Abrahim a Santa Clara said about it, which would still hold good (AaSC 52–3): 'To make straight what is crooked; to make pliable what is coarse; to make beautiful what is bad; to make young what is old; to make hot what is cold; to make heavy what is light; to make deep what is shallow; to make tall what is low; to make dear what is hated, that is much and overmuch. And all this money can do' (AaSC 53).

In addition to the rhetorical skills that moved his hearers, his word play was also so notable that we are likely to misunderstand what is going on. Heidegger contends that what might be taken today, or by any superficial reader, to be instances of hyperbolic style are often those of the elaborate baroque style of Abraham a Santa Clara's day, or are actually examples of his sophisticated, polymorphous rhetorical strategy; even the title of one of his writings (typeset as an early version of concrete poetry) appears to be as elaborate and figured 'as the architecture of the pulpit of a Baroque church' (AaSC 50). Especially notable, according to Heidegger, is that Abrahim a Santa Clara 'thinks in images,' through which he lets us see directly what he wants to say (AaSC 50–1). His linguistic images (*Sprachgestalten*) and patterned language (as Hebel's *Gebilde*), his play with key words, and his listening to language to intimate multiple meanings are all means to render the images memorable and to stimulate thinking (again, clearly Heidegger's focus should also be taken as reflexive, describing what he works to learn and how his work should be interpreted). For example, where Abrahim a Santa Clara says that mankind is a '5 foot long nothing' it might seem as if this is a nonsensical contradiction, since nothing has no dimension, neither five nor any other number of feet. But, Heidegger explicates, here the contradiction tells the truth: the earthly measure of greatness (the more the better, as with power or money) goes together precisely with the 'lack of nothingness in terms of genuine significance' (AaSC 52). There is too little time to consider Heidegger's comments on Abrahim a Santa

Clara's treatment of death and nothing, but since the cemetery is a theme Heidegger constantly develops in these late, homey works (for example, in 'Memorial Address' and 'Festansprache'), we can note that he combines the comic and serious, comparing larks (*Lerchen*) in a field (*Acker*) to Christians in the cemetery (*Gottesacker*) (AaSC 52–3); or, as if to go with what Hebel and Heidegger gather from Nietzsche and others about mortals as plants, Abrahim a Santa Clara utilizes the homonym of rhyming words to say that 'man is a flower: today on the lapel, tomorrow before the broom [*Der Mensch ist eine Blum, sagst du, die heut vorm Busen, morgen vorm Besen*]' (AaSC 55).

It may be that Abrahim a Santa Clara is at his most highly poetic and potent best when treating the works of nature (again, as Heidegger told us earlier, the best chance to recover the source is when the cultural and natural remain together; 700YM 234). Heidegger suggests that perhaps Abrahim a Santa Clara's 'most astonishing and beautiful image is that of swans and snow.' Abrahim a Santa Clara says, 'Come here you silver white swans, who with your wings, put the snow on the offensive (bring the snow to defiance), paddle around on the water' (AaSC 57). Elsewhere he tells us, 'Don't you know, that human life would be like snow and clover, not at all lasting forever.' Heidegger thus explains: as snow dissolves in water, so might the snow white swans. But, they do not, for the swans, displaying their feathers of pure white, carry the snow over, across the water. The image formed, then, is that of the imperishable in the perishable or transitory.

At the same time, the images formed are themselves transitory, whether constructed of words or brick. Abrahim a Santa Clara pushes us toward the proper humility that comes from recognizing that we can neither hold on to nor ultimately depend upon that which we build, softening the lesson with his engaging play on the multiple meanings of words – *ich verlasse gen dasjenige, auf das sich niemand verlassen kann* – which Heidegger glosses for us: 'I leave behind all that upon which no one can depend, which means "to forsake or leave behind" in the sense of give up or abandon and "to let go" in the sense of build on something [*"verlassen" in der Bedeutung von preisgeben und "ich verlassen" in Sinn von: auf etwas bauen*]' (AaSC 54).

Abrahim a Santa Clara, from his time of war and death, from the scene of fashion, wealth, and power, from the age of new science and knowledge, remains timely. Thus, Heidegger still commends him and what he teaches to the Meßkirch community, as well as to us. The enduring lessons of the community and culture to be held and assertively kept alive are passed on by the teacher Heidegger: to die to the things of this world and to have the courage to follow the other measure that one finds – which requires a thinking that benefits from leaning to listen to language and to compose its forces into vivid images as a way to think (for example, the relation of the imperishable and the perishable [*das Bild für das unvergängliche in Vergänglichsten*]) (AaSC 54–5, 57).[23] Nor to be lost sight of is the cultured and personal model of Abrahim a Santa Clara himself. Fully rounded as a living person, learned and keen witted, a dedicated preacher and teacher, a gifted administrator in a turbulent time (with substantial efforts even in the secular sphere), he also found a way to follow his sending. For all of us trying to learn what those who have gone before still have to say today, Heidegger commends Abrahim a Santa Clara as 'a teacher for our lives and a master of language' (AaSC 57).

Obviously, one of the major contributions Heidegger can make to Meßkirch's potential for overcoming homelessness is by helping the inhabitants to reflect on, and thus recover, the still coming source of wisdom from the home region. This exercises his own talent and calling, as thinker and teacher, and also helps provide what is critically needed in the community. His common task with his neighbours, then, is recollecting and holding on to what is educationally valuable in Meßkirch today. What else will help education in Meßkirch? In his 1973 address at the dedication of Meßkirch's new high school, 'Statt einer Rede,' Heidegger can not conceal the ambiguity he finds in the new building, and uses the occasion to try to connect the audience with the thinking which comes in their own tradition and which they again need to engage.

He notes that the new school building now stands fully furnished to the standards of the industrial age. While the statement is correct and good in its way, we cannot help hearing – knowing Heidegger, as did his townspeople – that this is not fully a complement (SR 733). Heidegger asks where the high school stands, and he answers – with a shock to most of us – 'It stands close to a broad road, a road that used to be a narrow fieldpath and continues to be today and tomorrow in a hidden manner. This fieldpath, for one student, who for many years and often was underway on it, became a path of thinking that sought to follow and think after [*nach-zudenken*] the model of the great thinkers' (SeR 733). The *Feldweg* is paved! Trying to absorb that – though it is not news to the residents of Meßkirch or Heidegger's intimates – and wondering whether or to what extent it is true, what it means, while trying to keep up with what he has gone on to say, is no easy task. He says no more here about the technological displacement of traditional ways of life, of places in our hometowns and lands, much less of a cruel blow to what is intimately valued. Feeling like one of Abrahim a Santa Clara's listeners, who followed what was said and filled in the thought with the answer, 'Money? No, of course not, not money,' we may think, 'The Pathway? No, not *the* pathway.' But Heidegger has already gone on; in fact he had already gone on after identifying the location and its place in his life. It is not just that Heidegger proceeds non-nostalgically about this little lane in Meßkirch that begins at the end of Abrahim a Santa Clara Street and that is usually called *Bichtlinger Sträßle*, since after all a great many roadways in the world started out being paths and as paved have turned out to be useful. Quietly, positively, he affirms and explains that today and tomorrow the pathway continues to be, though concealed, *a* pathway.[24]

Heidegger develops this prospect by using the occasion to link the field path with what Kant spoke of as 'The Field of Thinking,' which was the sphere of his four great questions. Stretching a bit to bring Kant in as a member of the regional fold, Heidegger notes that Kant's mother's forebears were originally Schwabian, having migrated from Tübingen to Königsberg by way of Nürnberg. At any rate, Heidegger presses on, still standing by the paved-over path of the field path, still using it as a way of thinking toward Kant's Field of Thinking, whose questions – especially, 'What is man?' – are not only critical for the modern age, but even more pressing today, since in our technological-industrial society we are led to an especially disconcerting question, 'Does man produce himself?' (SeR 734–5).

Because this issue has been 'answered in the affirmative' in the last several centuries (so much so that it has become our strange assumption, though we do not recognize it as strange), we have the task of retrieving the question as a question. To do so, Heidegger tries to open us to think the 'other than the human' by asking whether it is possible that the being-there of humankind is defined by a sending it does not command, but to which it must join (*zu fügen*) and to which order itself in what it does and does not do (SeR 734). If we manage to begin to think these pressing questions about who or what contemporary humans are – a task which needs to take precedence, he contends, over all ordinary tasks and demands – then wherever we are, in whatever place of education, we are on a pathway, not physically, as on the one of his youth, but nonetheless still 'on the path as a way through the Field of Thinking and its guiding, decisive questions' (SeR 734). Every high school, indeed all schools, every place of learning and the whole educational establishment and sphere, Heidegger contends, is (on) a field path (SeR 735).

How have we come – after trying so hard to think from out of enowning, from what would have to be a turning from the homelessness of the Western world and our technological age, our age on the edge of nihilism – toward a still-coming source, toward home? How have we come to be listening to Heidegger, only three years before his death, and in what turns out to be the last significant public address he delivered, speaking to the students and citizens of Meßkirch in their new high school? Of course, this has happened because it is the way Heidegger has gone himself, ever the teacher, and because he has let us come along. We should not forget, moreover, that the formal civic celebrations, invitations, and honours the town gave Heidegger were not conferred upon one who had become a stranger. Just the opposite, Heidegger never really broke with his hometown, since he continued to visit regularly all his life. Indeed, he developed an independent adult relationship with the place and its inhabitants because he spent at least two long periods there each year, before the good weather in spring and after the bad weather reached the cabin higher up at Todtnauberg in the fall. At those times he worked intensively in the family home where he was born, now occupied by his brother Fritz – the two of them, we are told, developed a mutual, mature brotherly spirit. Heidegger, then, returns to, and brings us to, his homeland to hear the most intimate things about the nearest of what is near in order to learn about what yet comes today and can continue to come tomorrow.[25]

In these homey works Heidegger pursues questions about the character of homelessness in order to open up an understanding of what would constitute home and a homecoming, continuing what he has already thought in essays such as 'The Thing,' 'Building Dwelling Thinking,' 'Art and Space,' and 'Memorial Address,' concerning two simultaneously operative levels: home and homecoming understood in the language of origin, of *originary source,* and in the language of *specific sayings, things, and places,* as concretely and historically gathering the fourfold into world. In the course of his overall corpus, he has found many names for *the origin which would be our home, that is, the source from which all is given and that to which, still coming, we are recalled and need to return.* As the words and what speaks in them play with one another, folding and unfolding in a game of hide and seek, none are so much left behind as accumulated, even while new facets of what speaks in them are disclosed (the presencing of what is present, the duality, *Ereignis,* what calls for thinking, *es gibt,* there is giving, granting, whiling – more and more often said as a letting, opening, abiding expanse). Thus, by the time of the homey works we see that the appropriate response is not only meditative thinking (*Andenken*), but a releasement toward things and openness to the mystery that hides and reveals itself. We find a movement back to the originary, to its concealing and unconcealing (*heim* in *geheimnis*, *lethe* in *aletheia)*, that most importantly is a remembering and holding on to what comes and goes, striving not to forget – as might happen over the course of epochal shifts (as indeed, historically, being had been forgotten in the overwhelming disclosure of beings). The presencing of what is present becomes whiling (*Verweilen*), and, especially in 'Art and Space' and 'Memorial Address,' space is seen to arise from place as an opening opened by the open; the free opening is recovered as *einräumen* and then as *Gegnet* and *gegnen*, in which, as we have seen, place and time are given in their belonging together as the abiding expanse, the expanse of abiding.

In addition, of course, another distinctive feature of these homey works is the way they focus, through what they say and in the very phenomena they describe, on the concrete particular, on things, which turn out to be places. That is, while he is direct in saying that things gather within the opening opened in the originary regioning, clearing opening (*einräumen*, *Gegnet*) that lets things tarry, Heidegger is equally clear that and how *particular things also gather the fourfold of earth and heavens, mortals, and divinities into actual historical worlds.* He lays out how things gather so that mortals can settle and dwell among them, through compact descriptions of the temple and jug and farmhouse, by wonderfully recovering for us how Hebel's poetry delineates his Wiesental homeland, by quietly celebrating Meßkirch with his own hometown neighbours and guests in, for example, 'Vom Geheimnis des Glockenturms' and 'Pathway.'

As we saw above, Heidegger lays out the relatively clear understanding of the intricate relationships among the facets of space and place; to summarize, '*einräumen* grants a place which admits a site where fourfold can gather into world, a dimension of which thence can be abstracted and constituted as space.' But, as we also saw, a complication occurs, in that Heidegger also uses the same word, region (*Gegend*), to name both the primal opening in which places are granted and the sites admitted by places, that is, by specific things. In short, there also is an at least initially perplexing situation insofar as region, *Gegend* (*understood by way of Gegnet*), *seems to mean both primal einräumen and the sites admitted by 'thing' or 'place.'* I argued above that this tension could not, indeed need not, be resolved, since Heidegger is not thinking representationally, or in a linear logical manner, nor speaking of a sequence of cause and effect, but thinking figurally and polysemously (as he has been all along, especially with the figures of home, homelessness, homecoming). Thus, even if we follow the mnemonic of thinking of *Gegnet* as *the* region of all regions (*Gegend des Gegends), Gegend* unavoidably bespeaks (at least) two domains, since, as dynamic, region (*Gegend*) always needs to be thought of by way of *gegnen, Gegnet* and it has its still-coming origin in the latter. In this complex of meanings, none of which can be allowed to go away by recollective thinking, *Gegend* and *Gegnet* name, as the same, as belonging together, originary source and the sites admitted by particular, concrete things.

But even this is not enough. Though *Gegend* and *Gegnet* are introduced in 'Memorial Address' and 'Art and Space,' and the material relevant to the two substantial dimensions is developed a bit in his works on poetry and language (as we saw above), a surplus of meaning appears in the two works which significantly take up the words and phenomena ('Conversation on a Country Path' and 'Memorial Address'), beyond what elaborates either the originary 'opening free, expanse' or specific 'sites' admitted by things-places.[26] What Heidegger fully says involves more than even these two domains. He develops a third meaning for home and homecoming by using region (*Gegend,* via *gegnen*) to specify something like the scope, scale, or span wherein humans actually dwell. Region and regioning are delineated as local. Region names, not 'the whole world' (as we say in English), but 'world' as in home – region, landscape, and settlement. Were the word not so loaded with associations from his earlier *Being and Time* (which cannot possibly be treated here), I might be tempted to say that 'region' connotes the 'finite.' Better to stick with 'the delimited' or, in ordinary terms, the 'local.' In the same way that Heidegger had spoken of what is evident of a horizon as being 'the side facing us of an openness surrounding us,' we could think of region in this third sense as naming the domain of the open facing us as scope, scale, or span (CCP 64).

Though he does not explicitly sort out this third dimension, it is not in the least unusual for Heidegger not to do so. In his increasingly quiet manner, though he is delineating a dimension decisive for our dwelling, he unfolds the subject matter almost imperceptibly, yet this third domain permeates what he says, especially in these final, homey essays. There are several sorts of evidence for this claim: not only is there the substance of what is said made explicit in the excess meaning, but, once the third domain is recognized, it also becomes clear that it resolves anomalies and that it has been operating all along (even if we have been aware of it only implicitly). It is to especially elaborate this third dimension, I contend, that Heidegger spends so much time developing the *local* and *neighbourhood.* If we interpret region (*Gegend*) as locality, we can also make sense of the 'other' name that he insists upon in 'Building Dwelling Thinking' and 'Art and Space' that otherwise does not seem to fit with the rest of what he says, that recasts the terms in yet another way, destabilizing what we think he is saying. There he says that locality is an assembly of places (*Örtlichkeit-Versammlung des Orts*): here locality would name neither the originary source as *einräumen*, nor a singular, particular thing or place; rather, in addition to the first two senses, as an assembly or gathering of a complex of individual places into a sphere in which we can dwell, it designates a third sphere – as Heidegger precisely says, a locality. To be clear, saying that Heidegger thinks about home in three different, though congruent, ways by finding that region (*Gegend, Gegnet*) names three domains, does not at all imply that he develops a three-dimensional metaphysics or an ontology of three separate realms; rather, it is to say that he works out home and homecoming polysemously. What is given is given in (at least) three dimensions of meaning.

Heidegger speaks in the same 'localized' way about the 'scope' or 'span' of the temporal realm. The opening expanse opens for a while. Things while. Heidegger posits no continuous flow of time (our metaphysical-representational heritage since Aristotle), no steady march of progress (inherited from Hegel) – quite the opposite. The whilings are discontinuous and more than various. There are different whilings for different mortals; that is, there are different spans for the while of a single person, of a family, of a community. The while for which things tarry also varies widely, for example, the while allotted to a raindrop is not that of a deer, or a town hall, or a mountain. There are the various whilings of the way of life in a place, as in rural, traditional Meßkirch, or in Dresden in its emergent modern refinement, or Freiburg in the technological era.

Finally, what Heidegger says about language also develops this third meaning of region, regional. Between the scope of unqualified 'saying' and any individual's 'word,' we have dialect. We do not find homecoming and home in or as universal, global language, whether the univocal language of science-technology or that of communications and mass consumption, nor even in widely spread languages such as French, Spanish, or English (not to mention Arabic or Mandarin). Nor does he lay out what matters in the idiosyncratic language of any one person (even if a creative genius), or even one household. Rather, homecoming and home happen, paradigmatically, in dialect, that is, in the communal, neighbourly language of local place. The mother tongue and its home places are of a middle scope, which itself is variable. Heidegger names many such languages and language domains, sites of belonging and homecoming, not privileging or stabilizing any set of categories. In the examples he draws from his own region, there is no attempt to neatly align the instances or set boundaries, not in a given case, never once and for all. Just the opposite, we are given *flexible, overlapping, non-comprehensive ways of thinking and living* the relationships and kinships of people and dialects in the *same region or family of regions:* Swabia as a whole, upper and lower Swabia, the Black Forest, Alemannia, (Hebel's) lower Markgräflerland and the Wiesental, Thüringen, and Heuberg. In addition, there is no claim to exclusivity of one region or any grander, much less universal, projection (for example, to nation or continent or hemisphere), but instead the *affirmation of differences-identities as regional* and of the *plurality of those valuable homelands,* as each its own: 'during the last two centuries great poets and thinkers have been brought forth from the Swabian land. Thinking about it further makes clear at once that Central Germany is likewise such a land, and so are East Prussia, Silesia, and Bohemia' (MA 47).

Looked at in yet another, but complementary, way, to think of region as specifying the spatial-temporal-dialect domain for dwelling, is to think of what is appropriately scaled (and required) for human dwelling. His homey audiences certainly understand that we need to be able to speak of the places where humans might actually live (another facet of the originary question of proper measure). Here scale can be taken in the architect's sense: the relation or proportion of the elements of a building to a human body, as in the way a door might be in scale (that is, human scale) if it is eight feet in height, but not if it is twenty feet tall; or a building or plaza is said to be scaled if composed of human-body–size or smaller discernable sub-elements, or modules: exposed materials (such as brick or wooden-board siding) or articulated forms, such as windows, banding, or ornaments. Embodied and social, we live in the sites, the worlds, described as neighbourhoods, communities, and regional landscapes.

In addition to being rigorously grounded in meditative thinking, Heidegger's careful descriptions of home places that begin to unfold historical lifeworlds show us this third domain in a completely commonsensical way. Recall what he has said about Hebel's homeland, the landscape and life in the Wiesental valley and village; about Messkrich, its countryside and settlement; about cousin Gerta's Dresden and its surrounding areas. Nestled within these hometowns and native languages, people live out their lives. The critical relationship is between understanding human dwelling and interpreting region: the confluence of *Gegend, gegnen,* and *Gegnet* as locality, whiling, and dialect is played out in the way Heidegger uses these homey works to provide exceptional attention to the personal lives of people. What he does here really is extraordinary. At the simplest level, the personalization of these essays contrasts strikingly with his storied refusal of such concerns (we are told that, 'famously,' his entire biographical comment on Aristotle was 'he was born, lived, and died'). Of course, usually and professionally, he liked to deflect his listeners and readers from the modern subjective view of meaning and to preserve what is said from the cult of personality and fame. Beyond that heuristic, the same dramatic difference is found when we compare what Heidegger says in the homey works with what he has refrained from saying previously, even of the great guides, such as Hölderlin, whom we would take as exemplars. Now Heidegger changes what he says in two ways. First, as noted above, he goes on at length about Hebel's abilities, explaining that it does us good to know something about the life course of the poet because it joins (*fügte*) together what he originally brings to life (JPHZ 492). He provides extended, vivid – even humorous – tableaus from the phases of Abrahim a Santa Clara's life; he dwells on experiences and feelings memorable to cousin Gerta and their related families; he muses on the aura of his own childhood (and on his brother, mother, and father).[27]

Secondly, as also discussed above, he explicitly points out the importance (in contrast to what is written or to a formal curriculum) of the living model. He honours Abrahim a Santa Clara's guide, the young Benedictine priest Otto Aicher, echoing what he repeatedly says of his own fatherly friend Archbishop Gröber (AaSC 46; 700YM 238). Such personalization operates at many levels for Heidegger in the homey works, where he uniquely marks the final phase of homecoming as learning to dwell near the local neighbourhood and neighbours (and perhaps actually abiding there) by speaking with special care about actual regional people and of localized personal relationships. In recollective thinking he evokes and would have us celebrate and keep in memory the continuity of family, of community; as a teacher, he not only explicitly teaches these things, but rhetorically plays on the senses of *Bild* and *Bildung* as image formed, education, and cultural formation, both generally and as originarily accomplished by Abrahim a Santa Clara and Hebel (and Heidegger himself) in figural thinking, including the use of vivid images and images formed by words (*Sprachgebilde, das Gebild*) and by the force of dialect as used by local rural inhabitants. He weaves space, time, and language together in this third domain of description and meaning: in the sphere of *Gegend* as regional, which is that of dialect, we find most of what Heidegger has to say of persons and of their whiling. In this realm, home and homecoming are thought and said as local and neighbourly.

Altogether, quietly but spectacularly, Heidegger unfolds the triple meaning of home and homecoming. Especially through the details of the 'Conversation on a Country Path' and 'Memorial Address,' where he speaks of releasement to things and openness to the mystery, he moves from using region (*Gegend*) in its usual sense of spatial area to finally naming the 'whither' '*Gegnet*.' To say and think this word he explores by way of *einräumen* the mutual unfolding into each other of 'region' (*Gegend*) (as 'domain' or 'realm') and 'regioning' (*Gegnet, gegnen*). With region as *Gegen, Gegnet*, and *gegend*, it is clear that he has arrived at a word that in itself already wonderfully names all three domains: 1) the opening, abiding expanse, or expanse of abiding; 2) the region-locality-neighbourhood within which we live out the transitory span of mortal whiling; and 3) the sites admitted by specific things and places. Here Heidegger is close to the limit of what he can say, especially in his 'professional philosophical' or originary language, although in his 'final' voice in the homey works he manages to say the same less and less technically and for a wider audience. Because he can develop his deepest originary thoughts while working in the most ordinary language derived from his home place and appropriate to his audiences there, it is just in those places – in Freiburg but especially in Meßkirch and Todtnauberg – where we find him speaking subtly of the meaning of home (there seems neither point nor any chance of trying to recover or hold on to a local world or dialect at the internationally situated Albert Ludwig's University of Freiburg or in Freiburg itself, despite such efforts as a local newspaper's weekly column devoted to dialect). By focusing on region as the localized, Heidegger could speak of several domains all at the same time, to be heard differently by different listeners.

The key words addressed to the home audiences – *Gegen, Gegnet* – take us back to giving and receiving, which also enables Heidegger to articulate more about the gathering together of what belongs together. *Gegend, Gegnet* hold for us keys not only to understanding that all is given as a gift, but the manner in which that giving occurs. In the first part of this chapter we saw how setting-into-work, opening, and granting, all appeared more and more as letting, so now we can understand how what is granted not only comes in the mode of a letting but how that letting is localized (as we have just seen, 'spatially,' *Gegnet, Gegend* means opening as/in dialect, as/in home place or region) and transitory ('temporally,' the letting occurs over a while, as the slow, deliberate growth of the oak, or as the farmer, crafts person, and thinker must be patient until things are 'ripe,' or as the lightning comes and goes in a flash). Hence the gift/giving – localized and temporary – is a mystery, that is, the simultaneously hiding and disclosing. What is given as gift is unavoidably 'partial' and variable. Heidegger does not say 'all' or 'always'; he does not give us, or speak of what is given to us, as any transcendental beyond to regionally abiding. He also sets into the homey essays our appropriate response, if we would be open to receive the giving. We respond properly to the gift, to the locality of opening expanse, to the allocation of the duration of the whiling, to the abiding of things, when, in recollective thinking, for example, we retrieve and then hold on to and preserve the meaning of what is disclosed to us (thus helping the source to still come). We respond properly when, in our releasement from objects and systems toward things, we help the opening wherein a new, originary rootedness may occur, disclosing a new mode of belonging and homecoming in the present, to which the future comes (without being oriented to the past).

But if such as Heidegger lays out is so, there are profound implications. If all is a gift and if the giving is a letting, such that all that is granted is ephemeral – granted locally, for a while – then everything is a 'guest.' We too. We are let come into the regional opening that is given and that gives; we are invited into the play where things (that are themselves let tarry) specify (*bedingt, bestimmt*), gathering the fourfold into world. We abide in social-spatial-temporal domains, of modest and loosely bound scope, scale, and span, within situated languages (dialects). In all cases, in all places, and at all times, worlds and we are called forth, bid come; in all places and at all times, an opening opens for world and us, the abiding expanse provides a place and while to abide – but only in a region, only for a while. Because we are mortals, any dwelling at home would necessarily be transitory. How much more so, then, would be any homecoming, any learning to dwell?

Heidegger's homey works, in addition to what he explicitly discusses, implicitly say the same by newly emphasizing giving and guests. We have been following how, in these works – where he comes home to Meßkirch, Freiburg, and Todtnauberg, to abide with his neighbours and family – he comes by way of something worthwhile (still timely) that he tells his friends and neighbours and that he allows us to overhear through the publication of his work. Both the centripetal and centrifugal dynamics are critical, allowing Heidegger, just as Hebel and Abrahim a Santa Clara, to reach widely, precisely because of being strongly local.

Whether or not we have noticed, throughout the homey works, Heidegger introduces us to a growing company of guests. The Freiburgers and Zähringers have guests from Bern, just as Heidegger is their guest speaker. Heidegger welcomes guests to his study on Rötebuck Way. At the awarding of the Hebel prize, we have found, he asked that some of his farmer friends from Todtnauberg be present, a request that was granted. At Meßkirch events, not only is Martin Heidegger the honoured guest, but so too are his professional colleagues (for example, Fink and Tsujimura), who are made welcome. Indeed, the Meßkirch events are a festival of hosting and guests, of Heidegger and (to run through the array of salutations) of fellow free citizens, of other local people, of classmates, of school children, of the dead who are remembered or even invited back through their paintings, musical compositions, or writings. Not to mention the bell-ringing children welcomed on Christmas morning by the sacristan mother's table of milkcoffee and cakes or the welcoming way the place, pathway, trees, and gates facilitated the lives of those who move in the place's welcome. The bells and clocks also issue an invitation and a welcome as they give rhythm, making the inhabitants at home in their daily and seasonal rounds. The departed (*heimzugangen*) are guests in God's acre (the cemetery). In the letter to cousin Gerta, Heidegger celebrates how he was a guest of her family; in turn, the Heideggers hosted her war-weary son when he was coming home from France; she and her family were welcomed to the Black Forest; and then (on the occasion of a birthday gift being appropriate) she is bid a happy stay on the Heidegger family's terrace. Without repeating the points made above, we may also observe that Abraham a Santa Clara and Heidegger are gifted with kind mentors who welcome them into a religious or philosophical community and help set them on their pathways in life.

As Heidegger speaks to his Meßkirch neighbours over the fifteen-year course of these talks, and as he gathers them and himself with notable former townspeople from the seventeenth, nineteenth, and twentieth centuries, he is laying out – setting into a series of works – the span of the – his – Swabian homeland. It reaches from the kernel of Meßkirch itself, across the Black Forest and in complex ways to the comings and goings of its inhabitants to and fro in the wider world; it reaches over hundreds of years, potently to today; it centres on dialect, though to avoid provincialism and to gain the 'far-reaching expanse' central to critical understanding, it needs to be open to multiple languages (as the examples of Abraham a Santa Clara and Hebel have shown the students and guests of Meßkirch, not only through Abraham a Santa Clara's and Hebel's great writings, but in the way they masterfully intertwine those many languages, whether Latin, High German, or dialect).

Here, perhaps, we can appreciate the rich understanding that Heidegger would evoke with the figure of the plant he so frequently cites from Hölderlin:

> Johann Peter Hebel once wrote: 'We are plants which – whether we like to admit it to ourselves or not – must with our roots rise out of the earth in order to bloom in the ether and to bear fruit' (*Works*, ed. Altwegg III, 314).
>
> The poet means to say: For a truly joyous and salutary human work to flourish, man must be able to mount from the depth of his home ground up into the ether. Ether here means the free air of the high heavens, the open realm of the spirit. (MA 47–8)

Obviously, Heidegger has been exploring how autochthony – rootedness in native soil and tradition – is vital to successful growth and development. But if we only hear that dimension we miss the rest, that what is locally rooted is thereby capable and called on to strive to reach the ether. The image articulates how humans, between the sky and the earth, would be gathered together with them into a world. The figure allows Heidegger to speak of words or saying as blossoms. Recall that the Japanese word for language is *Koto ba,* the petals that flower from the flourishing of the graciousness that brings forth, and that Heidegger, pondering Hebel, elaborates dialect in the image of the earth rising through the body and mouth, so that the plant accomplishes and is the transformation of local nurture to flowers, fruit, and seeds that seminally spread – are broadcast – across the world (DL 45–7; NL 99–101). As we have heard, Heidegger assertively stresses how what Hebel and others have to say can be of worldwide import (neither parochial nor globalized in trivial media chatter) because it has genuinely sprung from the local; sheltered in the deep earth, it is enabled to freely rise into the open.

Both directions of the dynamic are necessary. Hence, in 'Pathway,' Heidegger tells us that 'again and again the oak says this to the pathway passing securely by ...'; that is, not only does the 'grounded' field path complement the towering oak, but the oak repeats the dual thrust in itself. Simultaneously, it is firmly rooted, delving down into the earth, and it rises, reaching upward. 'The oak itself spoke: Only in such growth is grounded what lasts and fructifies. Growing means this: to open oneself up to the breadth of heaven and at the same time to sink roots into the darkness of earth. Whatever is genuine thrives only if man does justice to both – ready for the appeal of highest heaven, and cared for in the protection of sustaining earth' (P 89). The image formed unifies temporal, as well as spatial, differences, not only the ether above and the soil below, but so, too, the slow growing and long-lasting oak and the ephemeral blossoms of a cherry tree. As the youthful Heidegger brothers grew up around the oaks of the forest and the oakwood of their father's workshop, they came to appreciate the 'slowness and constancy in the tree's growth,' the same slowness of ripening which the thinker, just as the farmer, must patiently await (P 89). Abrahim a Santa Clara also plays on the image, in contrasting the perishable dimensions of this world with the imperishable (as is a flower, mankind is in the button hole today and before the broom tomorrow; AaSC 55).

In the image of the fruit that is borne, two sorts of 'harvest' come forth out of the ordinary (which may or may not appear as the uncanny). In or from our surroundings and relationships with others develops the tranquilization of the everyday, the eclipse of being by beings, and the displacements of technological development. Yet, if the strange is let be, the wondrous may also emerge for recollective thinking. In its originary upsurge, then, the rooted is 'the green fuse that drives the flower' to the wide beyond, to the abiding expanse and the expanse of abiding. From the sheltered and secure, it exfoliates to the open. Hence, in these homey works Heidegger explores how from out of the simple the ordinary shows itself as wondrous. He finds support for this investigation even in Nietzsche, who says,

> 'The philosopher is a rare plant,' that is, which needs its own proper soil, whose secret growth and sustaining powers no chemical soil science can ever find out. A rare plant needs a rare soil. And if something trivial is true about it, then the rareness of our local (native) soil is characterized by the fact that this soil, the earth and heaven above it, have nothing unusual, nothing striking, nothing extra-ordinary [*'Der Philosoph ist eine seltene Planze'; d.h. sie braucht ihren eigenen Boden ... dessen geheime Wachstums- und Erhaltungskräfte keine chemische Bodenkunde jemals ausfindig machen wird. Eine seltene Pflanze braucht einen seltenen Boden. Und wenn etwas oder nur ein Geringes daran*

ist, dann ist das Seltene unseres hiesigen Bodens dadurch gekennzeichnet, daß dieser Boden, die Erde und der Himmel über ihm nichts Auffallendes haben, nichts Ungewöhnliches, nichts vorragendes]. (WD 33)

At this point, with the unity of the rooted and the free, Heidegger has come to and gives to us the giving and the gift; the opening of region as local place, as realm of dialect, as passing while; and indigenous and neighbourly hosts and their guests. Heidegger has come to, and brought us to, seeing home and homecoming in the opening abiding expanse that historically lets things and people gather together and in the concrete gathering around specific things, places, and actions as in Meßkirch over the last three hundred years. And he has managed to return and hold on to, not just the Meßkirch of his youth, but that of today and tomorrow. Of course, he is no longer really a regular resident of Meßkirch, since as professor and family man he lives and teaches in Freiburg. More to the point, he tells us that he thinks and thrives most fully in yet another place, his ski hut in Todtnauberg, located some twenty kilometres south of Freiburg. Here we have arrived at the third of Heidegger's adult home places. In Todtnauberg, though still 'the professor,' he finally also becomes one of the neighbours, one of the people who live nearby one another in an ordinary, regular but rich way. Heidegger explicitly thinks and celebrates this homiest of all homey themes from the first to the last, across the full span of his time and region, as we can see with special clarity by crossing between two 'book-end' homey works, his early 'Schöpferische Landschaft: Warum bleiben wir in der Provinz?,' of 1933–4 (literally, 'Creative Landscape: Why Do We Remain in the Provinces?,' but translated as 'Why Do I Stay in the Provinces?'), and the late 'Festansprache,' from 1966.[28]

The essay, 'Why Do I Stay in the Provinces?' (which could be read not as the refusal to enter a wider, more cosmopolitan realm, but as following Abrahim a Santa Clara in turning away from the superficially worldly), begins with a look at the hut and its setting. 'On the steep slope of a wide mountain valley in the Black Forest, at an elevation of 1150 meters, there stands a small ski hut. The floor plan measures six meters by seven. The low-hanging roof covers three rooms: the kitchen which is also the living room, a bedroom and a study. Scattered at wide intervals throughout the narrow base of the valley and on the equally steep slope opposite, lie the farmhouses with their large over-roofs. Higher up the slope the meadows and pasture lands lead to the woods with its dark fir-trees, old and towering. Over everything there stands a clear summer sky, and in its radiant expanse two hawks glide around in circles' (WISP 27).

Yet, Heidegger notes, this is how the landscape looks to the outside observer, such as a guest or summer vacationer. That is not how he experiences it, for this is the place where he engages in his thinking and writing. This place is his *work-world.*

> Strictly speaking I myself never observe the landscape. I experience its hourly changes, day and night, in the great comings and going of the seasons. The gravity of the mountains and the hardness of their primeval rock, the slow and deliberate growth of the fir-trees, the brilliant, simple splendor of the meadows in bloom, the rush of the mountain brook in the long autumn night, the stern simplicity of the flatlands covered with snow – all of this moves and flows through and penetrates daily existence up there, and not in forced moments of 'aesthetic' immersion or artificial empathy, but only when one's existence stands in its work. It is the work alone that opens up space for the reality that is in these mountains. The course of the work remains embedded in what happens in the region.
>
> On a deep winter's night when a wild, pounding snowstorm rages around the cabin and veils and covers everything, that is the perfect time for philosophy. Then its question can only be tough and rigorous. The struggle to mold something into language is like the resistance of the towering firs against the storm. (WISP 27–8)

This rooted placement and mode of interaction with the land and locals contrasts, in Heidegger's account, not only with the busy life of the urban-dwelling but with the public appearance and fame of his own life of lectures and conference trips, with even his 'teaching work down here in Freiburg. But as soon as I go back up there, even in the first few hours of being at the cabin [*Hüttendasein*], the whole world of previous questions forces itself upon me in the very form in which I had left it. I simply am transported into the work's own rhythm, and in a fundamental sense I am not at all in command of its hidden law' (WISP 28 [11]).

Such life is a matter of solitude, which 'has the peculiar and original power not of isolating us but of projecting our whole existence out into the vast nearness of their enduring presence [*Wesen*] of all things' (WISP 28). Nearby (though perhaps flickering out) there still remains the use of dialect, and a slowly-growing, irreplaceable continuity maintained though the inhabitants. Heidegger savours how 'the memory of the peasant has its simple and sure fidelity which never forgets. Recently an old peasant woman up there was approaching death. She liked to chat with me frequently, and she told me many old stories of the village. In her robust language, full of images, she still preserved many old words and various sayings which have become unintelligible to the youth today and hence are lost to the spoken language' (WISP 28–9). He finds that nearby people and things speak to him (as did the pathway and trees of Meßkirch) and help him keep the orientation on his way, on the unsure open way. Heidegger tells us that he benefits so much from, even depends upon, solidarity with this place and its people that when he was considering his second invitation to teach at the University of Berlin he was not ready to move forward to a decision without the touchstone: 'I left Freiburg and withdrew to the cabin. I listened to what the mountains and the forest and the farmlands were saying, and I went to see an old friend of mine, a 75-year old farmer' for advice (WISP 29).

Heidegger, however, is guarded in 'Why Do I Stay in the Provinces?,' saying little about the place and people, not only out of respect, but because outside interference and appropriation – including his own, as well as that of intellectuals, the culture industry, tourists, and vacationers (with their self-flattering, false familiarity, and the attendant self-deception) – destroy what is powerful enough to be the initial.

> The world of the city runs the risk of falling into a destructive error. A very loud and very active and very fashionable obtrusiveness often passes itself off as concern for the world and existence of the peasant. But this goes exactly contrary to the one and only thing that now needs to be done, namely to keep one's distance from the life of the peasant, to leave their existence more than ever to its own law, to keep hands off lest it be dragged into the literati's dishonest chatter about 'folk-character' and 'rootedness in the soil.' The peasant doesn't need and doesn't want this citified officiousness. What he needs and wants is quiet reserve with regard to his way of being. And independence. But nowadays many people from the city, the kind who 'know their way around' and not least of all the skiers, often behave in the village or at a farmer's house in the same way they 'have fun' at their recreation centers in the city. Such goings-on destroy more in one evening than centuries of scholarly teaching about folk-character and folklore could ever hope to promote. (WISP 29)

Just as the power of the place and its dialect might be preserved if left alone, from the vantage point achieved in 'Memorial Address' it now appears that the response to what is given there could be one of releasement, a saying 'yes' to the way of life but a 'no' to making it the self-conscious focus of attention, much less to exploiting it. What would be needed is 'letting it be.' If so, both of the possible positive modes of homecoming (preserving the originary source and opening to the new) might be operative here. As to the first mode, if holding on to and preserving are needed even more than recovery, the enduring character of the rural lifeworld comes to the fore. More than ever the pressing questions would become: Does the rural place sustain itself through the self-guarding way of life of the rural inhabitants and the deferential retrievals of a few such as Heidegger? Do the relationships of people and place and the ways these intimately shape Heidegger's work (as he himself tells us) hold? It would seem so, if we listen across the span of thirty years. In 'Why Do I Stay in the Provinces?,' Heidegger makes a strong claim about his thinking and writing in the Todtnauberg cabin: 'And this philosophical work does not take its course like the aloof studies of some eccentric. It belongs right in the midst of the peasant's work. When the young farm boy drags his heavy sled up the slope and guides it, piled high with beech logs, down the dangerous descent to his house, when the herdsman, lost in thought and slow of step, drives his cattle up the slope, when the farmer in his shed gets the countless shingles ready for his roof, my work is of the same sort. It is intimately rooted in and related to the life of the peasants' (WISP 27–8). Over the course of the next decades, Heidegger continually insists that his own proper work is of a piece with that of his neighbours, and in the same way, in common with their's, is grounded in the home landscape, way of life, and dialect. Heidegger would apparently describe himself in terms given by Hebel in his poem 'Wälderbublein,' where Heidegger finds the name *Ein Wälder*, a little boy of the woods, that is, someone raised in the Black Forest who owes his origin to 'house and field, mountain and wood' of the countryside (SH 48).

In *What Is Called Thinking?* (1951–2), Heidegger explicitly compares the work of the thinker and carpenter (which his father also was), both taking care and being thoughtful in responding to what is given and what might be brought forth.

> We are trying to learn thinking. Perhaps thinking, too, is just something like building a cabinet. At any rate, it is a craft, a 'handicraft.' 'Craft' literally means the strength and skill in our hands ... Every motion of the hand in every one of its works carries itself through the element of thinking, every bearing of the hand bears itself in that element. All the work of the hand is rooted in thinking. Therefore, thinking itself is man's simplest, and for that

> reason hardest, handiwork, if it would be accomplished at its proper time. (WCT 16–17)
>
> We chose the cabinetmaker's craft as our example, assuming it would not occur to anybody that this choice indicated any expectation that the state of our planet could in the foreseeable future, or indeed ever, be changed back into a rustic idyll. The cabinetmaker's craft was proposed as an example (to raise the question of) the relatedness to wood … relatedness to such things as the shapes slumbering within wood. (WCT 23)

In the Zähringer talk on Johann Peter Hebel, Heidegger explained to guests visiting his Freiburg study that the wonderful view out to the fields and mountains was not really the operative force; rather, the efficacious was to be found in what came from that realm into his work (1954). At the end of the arc of time and experience reached in his 'Festival Address in Todtnauberg' (1966), Heidegger continues to affirm what he had asserted early on, that 'The inner relationship of my own work to the Black Forest and its people comes from a centuries-long and irreplaceable rootedness in the Alemannian-Swabian soil' (WISP 28). The claim, then, is not only that the thinker's craft belongs together with the skills of all the other members of the community, but that all derive power and continuity specifically from the landscape where they are grounded and sheltered. Heidegger, it seems, has found a way to follow his path and come to his own – as thinker, writer, teacher – yet be able to live in multiple communities in such a way as to leave to others their distinct characters too. Heidegger (just as Hebel and Hölderlin) speaks of this simultaneous conjunction of all and each coming to their own through a common gathering together in a landscape at the same time that he speaks of the homeland's span in time and place.

But for all this congruence, the three sites of Heidegger's life and their respective lifeworlds are not at all identical. Nor has his life's course from one to the other been without valanced differences. Now that the story of Heidegger and of homecoming has arrived at Todtnauberg, we find both a continuous attitude or perspective traced out from 'Why Do I Stay in the Provinces?' to 'Festansprache,' more than thirty years later, and a constant contrast between the experience of and in the 'above' of Todtnauberg and the 'below' of Freiburg. 'Why Do I Stay in the Provinces?,' as just noted, is written from the perspective of Freiburg, and looks up toward the Black Forest hut from down below; we get his final position from the other end, which is Todtnauberg centric. His biographers tell us how he wrote in letters that 'his real abode, his home in fact, was the mountain hut in Todtnauberg, to which he was invariably drawn as soon as the term ended.' He always looked 'forward a lot to the strong mountain air – this soft light stuff down (below) ruins one in the long run. Eight days lumbering – then again writing.' It seems that he would have spent the whole winter up at the hut if he could, staying on to write: 'I have no desire to spend my time with university professors. The local country folk are far more agreeable – and indeed more interesting.' *Being and Time* and many subsequent works were written up at the hut, the spirit of which is vividly given when he writes, 'It's late night already – the storm is sweeping over the hill, the beams are creaking in the cabin, life lies pure, simple and great before the soul ... Sometimes I no longer understand that down there one can play such strange roles.'[29]

At the end, apparently, Heidegger finds he has achieved a personal homecoming and, as we will see, posits a way by which, together, local inhabitants and those of us from outside might achieve both kinds of positive homecoming: the preservation of the source that yet comes in the local and the releasement and openness that would allow a new rootedness to be established. What goes on in Todtnauberg that is so special? Perhaps the chance to retrieve and keep lost idioms and to experience that still robust way of life and speaking? Perhaps an openness to strangers, a possibility of insiders coming to accept outsiders as belonging? The giving of and openness to gifts? The giving of region, its locality, dialect, intertwined natural and communal rhythms; the giving and receiving of the belonging together – that constitute home and homecoming?

There is a double official occasion for the summer-time *Heimatfest* in Todtnauberg, and as Heidegger himself explains, good reason for him to find great satisfaction in being asked to deliver the celebration speech. The official occasions for the event are to commemorate the historical consolidation of the settlement Todtnauberg and the Rütte (an open area nearby) and that 700 years earlier the great mountain mining works were founded on the Todtnauberg, where the ore vein ended above the back section of the Rütte. Obviously enthusiastic about his being asked to speak at the Todtnauberg Fest, Heidegger takes the occasion to treat the theme of becoming and being at home at two levels: he festively meditates on the place and its inhabitants and tells the personal story of how he and his family came to be accepted in the community, how he came to be at home there through the gradual acknowledgment over forty-five years by just these Todtnaubergers (FHT 641). Heidegger takes the long way around to tell the story of how the cabin came to be, weaving a significant number of locals into the narrative and taking the opportunity to elaborate on each of them in turn, as well as on their forebears and their families' extensions.

The tale starts, not on the Rütte clearing (where his cabin is actually located), but in the nearby village of Todtnauberg. Heidegger recounts how he and his wife, Elfride, had wanted to build a small cabin, as a place to compose himself so as to concentrate for his work and to have a place for the family to be near nature (FHT 642).[30] In 1920 and again in 1921 Heidegger and Elfride had stayed for a short vacation with the former mayor, Eduard Mühl, the father of the currently ninety-one-year old Johann Mühl, who, Heidegger says, 'still stays, lingering among us' (*das heute noch unter uns weilenden*) (FHT 641). The senior Eduard Mühl was so renowned for his festival addresses that he was known as 'Festival Eduard' and, Heidegger concedes, would have been much better at giving the festival address than Heidegger himself.[31] Though Heidegger had never himself been present to hear any of the famous speeches, in the long winter evenings on the mountainside, Mühl had told the Heideggers many lively stories about his younger years, wandering as a 'brush seller in Switzerland,' acting, as was common, as the one who carried news from place to place – a living newsletter. He was the one who bound the community together by the endlessly changing storytelling of the village. Festival Eduard's second, much younger wife's home had been in (*stammte von*) 'Bureton,' and her now deceased father, carpenter Rotzinger, was the master teacher of carpenter Pius Schweitzer in the Rütte. It was this Pius Schweitzer whom, in 1922, the Heideggers had been instructed to seek out. They had been told in the village that Pius Schweitzer's house in the Rütte would be easy to find because his roof bore a little clock tower (the little bell, Heidegger notes, is still there, and rings through the high valley when someone has died and is being carried down to the village to be buried). A true master, known and respected not only for his exactness but also for his careful hand work, Pius Schweitzer also built Heidegger's cabin.

The widow of Master Pius Schweitzer, who died all too early, is Josephine, whom Heidegger acknowledges as well known for going to town to church wearing her *tracht* (the traditional regional dress) with a beautiful gold cap and '*dem langen Bendel de Rukke nabe*' (FHT 643). Still living, at ninety-one, she is well cared for by her daughter Pauline. In addition to Pius Schweitzer, another master carpenter worked on the hut, Oswald Kaiser. His careful entryway window, Heidegger can testify, remains true to the millimetre, almost half a century later. A quiet man, Kaiser made coffins for many Todtnaubergers, and when his time came, it went to his grandson Oskar to try to ensure that, after the grandfather's death, all in the house would continue as before.

To back up a bit, we note that Heidegger admiringly explains that even before Pius Schweitzer built the cabin, the latter already used his natural sense of proportion and simple beauty in choosing the site. The plot was a piece of abandoned land that belonged to Pius Klingele, known as 'Black Pius' who lived in the back part of the cloister. 'Black Pius' was a lively, easily agitated man – a hothead, and therein, Heidegger says, warming to the occasion, lies a lusty tale to be told, one that centres around the fast, sharp tongue of Sophie, a farm wife from Schneiderhof. Her husband, (the) Schneiderbauer, was a bull and goat breeder in the Rütte. On one occasion the excitable 'Black Pius' Schweitzer – whose cow, as a matter of course in village transactions, had been bred to one of Schneiderbauer's bulls – came to complain about the inferior calf that had come into the world as a result. He angrily laid out his complaint, placing blame on Schneiderbauer, claiming that he was guilty and should bear responsibility for the deformed calf. During his disparaging remarks about the quality of the insemination, Sophie politely interrupted him to say, '*Jetz hör doch uf mit dim dumme G'schwätz, 's nächstmol machsch 's du's ebe selber*' – in effect, 'next time, do it yourself' (FHT 643).

So, on a south-facing slope, deep inside the valley, the cabin came to be built and was regularly used across the seasons, sometimes by the entire family, sometimes by Heidegger alone.[32] Cabin life took place within the round of the landscape's rhythms. In the summertime harvest, during both the haying and second mowing (*im Heuet und Öhmdet*), the Rütte came close to the cabin, into direct neighbourliness, for example when Schneiderbauer with his sons and the Schweitzers started work already at four in the morning. Not surprisingly, Heidegger found that the rhythmic whoosh of the scythes through the grass gave a much more beautiful sound than the mowing machine.

But, of course, it is one thing to construct a cabin and occupy it, and quite another to become a genuine neighbour. Heidegger is explicit: 'I certainly lived with my family in the Rütte for the 45 years of the cabin. But having a cabin in the Rütte does not of itself bequeath the right, as one from the Rütte could claim, to be called "one from" [*aus*] the Rütte: that is, one who *belongs to* the Rütte peoples. Such a belonging one is not able to accomplish by oneself. It can only be granted [*zugesprechen*] by the right adjudication and this only by the Rütteners themselves' (FHT

641). Gratefully, Heidegger goes on, 'and so it happened to me, even if never in the form of a special dedication. It happened imperceptibly, of itself and with the passage of time' (FHT 641). (There is an interesting but subtle difference between this gradual, informal becoming situated in Todtnauberg, as just described, and how, already a native son of Meßkirch, he was later formally granted status as a free citizen there.) Heidegger admits to his audience (of now friends) that acceptance did not come so easily. In a comment sharpened by describing the quick-tongued Sophie Schneiderhof as having a good eye for human character, Heidegger concedes that 'initially she was mistrustful and not at all pleased about the strangers [*die fremden Leut'*] there over on the Gierwald, up above the back side of the Rütte' (FHT 641). There was, of course, the normal activity which absorbed Heidegger and the cabin, including visits to and from neighbours. For example, Heidegger relates how Brender Adolf, a bright mind, not overly fond of working, often (in the tradition of the village) told great stories to the Heidegger family when on summer Sundays he would stop by on his way home, a flower tucked behind his ear, after crossing over to Stübenwasen and Feldberg to visit his son (in fact, in his younger years he had taken care of the cabin). Heidegger tells how heartened he was when, on one of the Sunday stop-bys, Brender Adolf, 'laughing mischievously,' said, '"You are one of those who eats bread." That is to say, a regular guy who can't do it all and also makes mistakes "like me"; at the same time he also was saying, "You also belong to us" – to us where each one, as well as one may, does his job [*si Sach schafft*]. And, steadily, others said the same thing, so that powerfully something entirely simple and unpretentious came to appearance' (*ganz Einfache und Unscheinbare zum Vorschein*), that is, all the community members recognized 'the others,' the Heideggers (FTH 644).

This slow acceptance – as the slow growth of the oak Heidegger regularly mentions, is the culmination of what had begun over thirty years before this Todtnauberg festival, as Heidegger recognized and acknowledged at the time. For example, in 'Schöpferische Landschaft: Warum bleiben wir in der Provinz?,' in addition to admiringly describing the dying peasant woman's 'simple and sure fidelity which never forgets' the local heritage (in distinction from the fleeting celebrity of today's popular and even academic worlds), about which we have just heard, Heidegger goes on to celebrate and appreciate the great value of what she granted: 'Very often in the past year (1933) when I lived alone in the cabin for weeks on end, this peasant woman with her 83 years would still come climbing up the slope to visit me. She wanted to look in from time to time, as she put it, to see whether I was still there or whether "someone" had stolen me off unawares. She spent the night before her death in conversation with her family. Just an hour and a half before the end she sent her greetings to the "Professor." Such a memory is worth incomparably more that the most astute report by any international news about my alleged philosophy' (WISP 28–9). The mutuality of respect is witnessed in the note passed on by Petzet that the peasant women from the Rütte – and they alone were invited – came each year to Heidegger's cabin to celebrate his birthday with coffee and cake, an occasion on which he would recite some of Hebel's Alemannic Poems.[33]

What is the upshot of all these related events and of the arc of continuity and final incorporation into the community? Certainly nothing dramatic. On the contrary, here we find an imperceptible unfolding against the background of the ordinary. The former comes about in the quiet 'being accepted and being let be' (FHT 644). The latter, occurring in all the doings over the years, as well as in the Todtnauberg *Heimfest* itself, are understood by all to be forceful – both Heidegger's report and the villagers' stories make clear that the place is full of purposeful work and constitutive social interactions. And, not to be overlooked, the village is a site where people from the outside (such as the farm couple from Schneiderhof) are integrated into the community (as, similarly, Hebel, born in Basel, was accepted into the Wiesental home of his mother, after his father died). Even such a small, intensely localized place is not radically exclusionary: rather appropriate behaviour and time are factors that need to be taken into account, lest we make superficial 'judgments' about the osmosis that leads to inclusion.[34] These factors better help us understand Heidegger's initial characterization of social interactions at Todtnauberg (in 'Why Do I Stay in the Provinces?'), which could be mistaken as a paean to dullness but is not really, because what the locals do and do not say contrasts with the superficial chatter of the merely everyday, of tourists, and of the media, whose 'frantic abolition of all distances brings no nearness; for nearness does not consist of shortness of distance' (T 165): 'But in the evening during a work-break, when I sit with the peasants by the fire or at the table in the "Lord's Corner," we mostly say nothing at all. We smoke our pipes in silence. Now and again someone might say that the woodcutting in the forest is finishing up, that a marten broke into the hen-house last night, that one of the cows will probably calf in the morning, that someone's uncle suffered a stroke, that the weather will soon "turn"' (WISP 28). Here we have normal social life and common work, which leads Heidegger to say both that what he tells us here is nothing special and that it remains decisive for their being with and for one another.

The power of the ordinary falls into oblivion in the homelessness of the merely everyday: in the greyness of the latter we 'have ears only for the noise of media ... the simple seems monotonous to the distracted. The monotonous brings weariness. The annoyed find only the uniform. The simple has fled. Its quiet power exhausted' (P 90). But even though the 'number of those who still recognize the simple as their hard-earned possession is quickly diminishing,' this need not be so, both because the source still comes and because it can still be heard and responded to as long as there are some who yet can experience what matters. That 'the simple preserves the enigma of what abides and is great' is affirmed by Heidegger's own testimony as he already tries in that early essay, amidst the homelessness he so vividly evokes, to explain positively what he finds and values at the cabin: 'People in the city often wonder whether one gets lonely up in the mountains among the peasants for such long and monotonous periods of time. But it isn't loneliness, it is solitude' (P 70; see also WISP 28).[35]

While perhaps what is given and gathers in a great poem, artwork, or philosophical work comes rarely, and though we are unable to anticipate when, where, or through whom it might appear, being at home in the source that still flows is not reserved for rare genius (whether or not we consider Heidegger to be one). Quite the contrary. In-between the extremes of the exceptional genius and the 'they' in the merely everyday of boredom (as diagnosed in *Being and Time*), all of us, as long as we are human, retain the capacity to recollectively think every day. Heidegger explicitly stresses this point in 'Memorial Address.' (As we have heard, he says, 'Yet anyone can follow the path of meditative thinking in his own manner and within his own limits. Why? Because man is a thinking, that is, a meditating being. This meditative thinking need by no means be "highflown." It is enough if we dwell on what lies close and meditate on what is closest; upon that which concerns us, each one of us, here and now; here, on this patch of home ground; now, in the present hour of history' [MA 47].) Heidegger consistently contends that all are capable of meditative reflection. To cite just a few further examples, we may note that in addition to claiming that his work belongs with that of the farmer and carpenter, Heidegger insists that they too are thoughtful: when Heidegger sought that advice about whether to go to Berlin, his farmer friend 'thoughtfully put his faithful hand on my shoulder'; in 'Der Feldweg' Heidegger tells us that his carpenter father 'labored (in the workshop), thoughtful when pausing from his efforts at the sound of the tower clock and bells' (WISP 29; P 89). All the inhabitants can be acknowledged as having the possibility of being thoughtful in their own ways as a result of their work and lives being grounded in and responding to the same landscape.

Insofar as people thoughtfully have what is their own as carpenter, farmer, or thinking-writer, they remain in touch with the powerful source, and belong together so as to find satisfaction in their native landscape and community. They can avoid falling into the unreflective, so as to experience instead the still-coming origin. For example, 'The call of the pathway awakens a sense which loves the free and open and, at the propitious place, leaps over sadness and into final serenity [*Kuinzige*].' This serenity resists the senselessness of the merely utilitarian, as we can still hear in the Upper Swabian word, *das Kuinzige*, which first meant 'not useful' (*kein nutzend*) and then, in a way similar to what Heidegger found in the originary sense of *chre*, 'it is useful,' it came to have the sense of free, almost detached, playfulness.[36] 'In the pathway's seasonally changing breeze thrives this wise serenity whose mien often seems melancholy. This serene wisdom is at once "playful and sad, ironic and shy." Someone who doesn't have it already can never acquire it. Those who have it get it from the pathway' (P 71). Later, Heidegger further glosses the word for us, indicating that such rising-above is easily misinterpreted but is not at all arrogance; rather, it 'includes a homely care [*heimlatliche Zuneigung*] and liking of people and things and true care for them'; 'it includes a thoughtfulness, a melancholy for the real or substantial [*Wesenhafte*] which appears in the ephemeral, which dissolves contradictions into a higher unity and still remains active' (K 487). *Kuinzig* names 'a serene melancholy which says what it knows in veiled expressions.'[37] So, when work is done or a work-break is taken, as when Heidegger gathers in the evening with neighbours, at that moment he is not in his dimension of the famous philosopher-teacher of the wider world, but is one of them who happens to think and write, rather than cut hay, breed cattle, or join door to frame. In the hushed gathering, everyone comes together, as Bender Adolf says, as those who each produce what he or she should – and thus form community.

For this acceptance as a member of the community Heidegger is most grateful. Thus his thinking about all these occurrences, out of itself, becomes a thanks, not only for and to the place but for all his acquaintances and friends, for all the people in the village (FHT 644). But what is this place? The village, the hut, the Rütte? As a matter of denotation and orientation, as noted above, the Rütte is a clearing from the forest to allow for farming; in this case, as the location of Heidegger's cabin, it is the clearing from the Gier Forest (Gierwald) on the nearby mountain (Todtnauberg), near the village also named Todtnauberg (as a unifying geographical aid, recall that when opening the celebration which in part commemorates the founding of the great mine works 700 years before, Heidegger describes how the mountain's great ore vein ends in the Gierwald, at a point above the back part of the Rütte) (FHT 641). Usually, Heidegger points out, we do not think any further than this when using the name *Rütte*. But what do we learn from the Rütte if we meditatively think what it says, what it lays before us? The name *Rütte* is the same word, Heidegger explains, as 'the Alemannic *Rütti*, as the Swabian *Reute*, and the Thüringer *Roda*. *roden, reuten*, means to render fertile, to free the earth for land and soil, whereupon all can grow that mankind needs; it means to earn free space wherein man can settle and dwell' (FHT 647). (Note, *roden* is the same word Heidegger uses to explicate *Räumen* into *einräumen* in 'Art and Space' [AS 5]. That is, *roden* binds what he said when developing *einräumen* as a high originary term for the primal opening granting and what he says here in dialect and ordinary language.) Thus, if we now become more thoughtful, the place name *Rütte* can remind us that mankind constantly needs to keep open space for itself, where things from beyond can address it and specify (*bestimmen*) it (FHT 647).

The force of dialectal words depends both on the intensity and continuity of their use. How localized, how fragile they are for even the native population is stressed by Heidegger and can be directly appreciated by us as we strain to catch some fragment of their meaning for ourselves. A sure sign of the danger facing the village is the disappearance of the local dialect. Earlier it was different, not in that the dialectal words remained regularly used and easily intelligible, but because they were socially defended and expectations were made clear (in part by refusing to cede to any dominating outside or more widely spread language the privilege of prestige or of providing the norm). Heidegger makes the point by relating an incident in which the parish priest visited 'Old Balbi,' a small person with large coal-black eyes who still lived in the centre of the village at the beginning of the twentieth century. Once when the priest came by to look after her, she was agitatedly looking about, obviously searching for something. 'For what?,' he asked. She answered, 'The key to *Almäri*.' Not recognizing the word, he asked, 'What is that?'

She aggressively retorted, 'You would be a student, and not know what an *Almäri* is?' Heidegger gently notes that perhaps many of his listeners (and readers too) do not know this any more. The *Almäri*, in fact, is something entirely everyday, namely, '*Der Chuchikaschte*' (FHT 649).

The point, then, is not that dialect, or any language, continues to come forth without interruption or with anything like a process to be taken for granted; rather, no matter how strong, words need to be preserved. They need to be cared for and exercised. Local people need to do that, among themselves, and perhaps with a few guests – and often against likely overwhelming outside forces and technologies (ranging from marauding armies, to hoards of tourists, to the homogenization of a global mass media). The teacher, Heidegger, is also the pupil, wanting to hear and learn from the locals, his teachers in dialect – and its guardians, who need to be assertive in order to make sure that dialect words remain forceful and well-used. The continuity is, and needs to remain, powerful. Heidegger points out and explains the importance of the custom of beginning this very festival each time with the Todtnaubergers gathering together in the cemetery: those who rest in peace there still belong to the village and still speak, speak their own language, and we can only answer them with a thanks for everything that they mean to us and our lifetimes (FHT 644–5). The courage and deliberation necessary to preserve the communal heritage and the mother tongue would be the same 'inner freedom and courage' which Heidegger recognized and valued when speaking about Abrahim a Santa Clara and that Heidegger evoked when he told his audience in Meßkirch that releasement and openness flourish only through persistent, courageous, meditative thinking (FHT 649; AaSC 49; MA 56–7).

In the thankful and learning mood of the festival address, and amidst the celebration of the complete community, living and dead, Heidegger wants to catch sight of a way sign, 'from whence' would be granted (*zugesprochen*) the correct measures and boundaries (*Ziele*, scopes, as in the scope of region) to specify (*bestimmen*) a human character (FHT 645). He finds that all such is already known by anyone whose thinking and saying is as close to the Black Forest world and its people as 'he' is to the land lower down, the Markgräflerland, and its residents. He means J.P. Hebel, who, while a pastor there, lived (*war daheim*) in Hausen, a village on the Grenze, on the border between the back- and fore-Wiesen Valley. As both Heidegger's audience and we well know, but as he reminds us yet again, making the recollection explicit and complete, it was out of longing for this home place that Hebel produced his *Alemannic Poems*, that are in dialect, written in the mother tongue – while his *Calendar History* (*Kalendergeschichten*) speaks to readers in standard German (HFT 645). Heidegger then cites eight verses from the last of the *Alemannic Poems,* titled 'The Way Sign' ('*Der Wegweiser*'), to focus on the closing line, '*und 's sinn no Sachen ehne dra,*' which he translates as he thinks about it: the keyword, *ehne,* says 'on the other side,' and '*ehne dra,*' 'on the other side, over there.' Heidegger explains that in Hebel's poetry, 'matters [*Sache*] on the other side, over there' mean what is beyond the grave and death. (In addition to what Heidegger says in this address, when receiving the Hebel Prize he elaborates the same last line of the last of the poet's *Alemannic Poems* by way of '*Der Sommerabend,*' in which *e Sach* says that something is enchanting or wondrous because it is mysterious, as would be things insofar as none can stand by itself; thus a door is opened into the mystery from which they come forth and shine toward us – as would be the grave [DHP 565–6].) Also in daily life, there are things from the other side, over there. These are not apprehended with our senses, but nonetheless real (*wirklich*) and active for daily life. Such things will never be reached, Heidegger asserts, through our complicated machines.

What is on the other side? Among the many things are the 'reciprocal recognition (acknowledgment) and letting pass, trust and fidelity, helpfulness, but also cheerfulness and sorrow, the calm heart and joyful courage [*Anerkennen und Geltenlassen, das Vertrauen und die Treue, die Hilfsbereitschaft, aber auch die Heiterkeit und die Trauer, das ruhige Herz und der frohe Mut*]' (FHT 646–7). These intimate relationships are very much the same as cousin Greta's love and trust, affection and gratitude, care and devotion that Heidegger found (mixed in with her sorrows) and praised (VH 636). All such dispositions seem congruent with what he has been calling serenity – *Kuinzige.* All such interpersonal virtues are over there, beyond the graspable, not letting themselves be won by money or human power (again echoing Abrahim a Santa Clara); yet, they are 'nearer and weightier than all things that we think lie closest to us' (FHT 647). These matters from the other side, over there, specify our mode, if we would become fully human (FHT 646–7).

Bringing the point home to the place where he and his audience are gathered together, Heidegger notes that Todtnaubergers daily hear the word *ehne,* 'on the other side,' with the name *Ennerbach,* 'on the other side of the stream,' 'the stream beyond the stream.' The name *Ennerbach* now refers simply to a part of town, he says, and we no longer think beyond that. However, if we become recollectively thoughtful, this place-name can forever remind us that there are in the lives of humans things (given) already from the other side, over there, that we shall not forget (FHT 647). We may even say, in a symbolic sense, that every Todtnauberger, whether native or guest (*Einheimischer oder Gast*), whether having a house in Hangloch, on the Büreton, in the village, or in the Rütte, needs to constantly dwell on the other side, which is to say, must let the Todtnauberger's own self be specified by the things from over there. And, Heidegger goes on, just as it is with the name *Ennerbach*, so it also stands with the name *Rütte*. In the home festival in Todtnauberg, the name *Ennerbach*, just as *Rütte*, can put us into a thoughtful mood, not only for the present moment, but for the future of the town. Heidegger poses the same question regarding the future of Todtnauberg as he does of Meßkirch, but now arrives at a dramatically different answer. Yes, in the rapidly changing world, the inhabitants of Todtnauberg (just as those of Meßkirch) face tasks unknown in the past. However, here Heidegger boldly presses in an entirely new direction (one that, most likely, despite all the clues, we begin to understand only in hindsight, when rereading him) – he contends and proposes that one such task be to rescue and accept into the midst of the village the stunned, tired people of the great cities and industrial districts and to prepare a place for them to stay (*Auftenhalt*) 'where they suddenly can hear silence, where they can find rest in this silence, where they can experience what is a forest and an alpine meadow, what is a rocky slope and a lively flowing creek, what is a high sky and a sparkling starry night, what the following things mean – to dwell in such a landscape where humans still speak the strange expressive mother tongue' (FHT 648).[38]

Such opening up would only be possible if the indigenous Todtnaubergers can offer a gift in the correct understated manner to the guests, because the Todtnaubergers themselves must shelter their uniqueness and protect it from the urban manner of living and speaking. That is why the indigenous villagers require a special sense of tact and inner security which knows wherein everything finds its limits (another instance where 'small towns and rural counties recognize their unusual qualities and know how to draw (specify) the boundaries' (*ihre außergewöhnliche Bestimmung*), so as not to deny its proper way of life (FHT 648; 700YM 234 [576]).

A substantial reciprocity, then, is required. For it is equally necessary that the indigenous inhabitants and the guests respectfully recognize the other; this itself is possible only if everyday and everywhere the meaning of things from the other side remains alive in language and custom (T

648). Here Heidegger makes the most audacious move in the homey works – with perhaps the most radical things he has ever said: he risks all that matters most, the good will and home that have been granted him by the Todtnaubergers. No doubt the Heideggers were nicer than the inconsiderate city people and rude tourists bemoaned in 'Why Do I Stay in the Provinces?' but as Heidegger himself tells us, he and the family were still seen as strange and suspicious. Now he pushes to, maybe even beyond, the limit for a guest recently accepted, by commending to his rural hosts that they open their doors to the very strangers from the cities that he once castigated as deplorable and dangerous, and whom many of the villagers and those out on the Rütte would likely still believe to be that way today. Will not his Todtnauberger hosts shake their heads and say, 'I told you so; that Heidegger is a stranger and a strange one. We no sooner accept him as having the same views as we do than he turns around and tells us to open the doors for many others who are far, far worse than he and his family – such as even he despised when he came here.' Who would have guessed Heidegger would say such a thing in a place so small, in a situation so delicate and that he so treasures? True, we should not exaggerate to the point of thinking of the area as exclusionary, since we have heard how people leave and return (as with Pius Schweitzer) and, more importantly, are accepted from the outside (as were the Schneiderhofs); still, this is a sphere in which the locals perceive even two nearby sites, the village and the Rütte, to be so distinct that their subsequent union is consequential enough to be commemorated in just this festival (in which other small places, such as Hangloch and Büreton, are also noted in their particularity – difference, indeed, even if belonging together as the same).

The full force of 'Festansprache' becomes clear, then, only on reading it as a story of pushing to the maximum what Heidegger has learned and said about gift and giving as regioning, that is, about how all things, and especially mortals, are guests within the fragility of locality and the temporality of what lingers – guests who need to be appropriately thankful by responding, in turn, as hosts to yet other guests. Returning his words to the Todtnauberg community (*Gemeinde*, which connotes both people and place), Heidegger concludes his 'Festival Address' by saying that every thoughtful and insightful person will concede that, in our technological age, it is ever more difficult to find the measure (the specification of even a proximate scope) for allowing Todtnauberg to remain Todtnauberg. He tells us that this is why he links his thanks for his inconspicuous and yet beautiful and fruitful decades-long belonging to Todtnauberg, which has been granted (*gewährte*) to him by the Todtnaubergers, with his suggestion and desire that Todtnauberg may now and in the future never forget the mysterious phrase 'and that there are things from the beyond, the other side. If you keep to this word, you can at any time draw from it courage towards yourself, as well as the freedom regarding those who come to you as guests' (FHT 649).

How can we adequately hear what Heidegger says in 'Festansprache,' the words of which may be his most thoughtful, grateful, and joyous – his most serene? If we can hold in mind what he has said over more than the last thirty years and what he has just now commended from Hebel, we would hear the multiple meanings of our leitmotif. The poet's key words – 'on the other side, over there' – spoken from the situation of the homecoming in Todtnauberg, says that we need to experience and deal with, on the other side, over there, the homelessness of the metropolitan, technological-industrial world. It says, from the condition of homelessness in which we all find ourselves, that we need to recover and shelter what is on the other side, over there: the source that still comes, albeit weakly, in dialect, in region, in local ways of life – that is, the possibility of homecoming. Similarly, it says that from our current uncanny homelessness we need to release and open ourselves to what is on the other side, over there – to the possibility of homecoming that might come through saying 'yes' to technology and 'yes' to the others from the urban areas who seek refuge and relief, while saying 'no' to the potentially lethal dimensions of those same guests and the paraphernalia of global tourism and technology that would inevitably accompany them.

In another polysemous cluster, unfolding what Heidegger has said of region, of opening, we can hear the name *Rütte* echoing at least a treble meaning. The Rütte is, of course, the area opened on the side of the Todtnauberg, under the Gierwald, that has enabled farming and nurtured the region's life; it is the site of Heidegger's cabin and inspiration for his work; and, now united with the village of Todtnauberg, it is the place into which Heidegger has been accepted as a neighbour. In these three dimensions, it is the scene of his personal homecoming – it is in this community, with his neighbours and their shared historical concerns, even more than in Meßkirch, that Heidegger comes to his deepest, final adult home, as do the other native inhabitants (*Einheimische*); it is to Todtnauberg that he hands himself over in the end. By way of *roden, Rütte* also says *Gegnet* (opening, abiding expanse, expanse of abiding), *einräumen (primal giving-gathering), es gibt,* there is giving, what calls for thinking, the duality, the presence of what is present, *Ereignis,* granting and letting, whiling; that is, it names, as best as might be done, the ever-coming source. *Rütte* also names the specific regional things that gather the fourfold into world – local things such as the cabin, village stories, and dialect words that tarry, and among which we can settle and dwell.

Given the multifaceted force of the place to which he has come to belong and the power of what he has been able to think in his journey, it becomes clearer to us that no matter how apparent Heidegger's satisfaction that the locals affirm his place there, what he finds and says is not merely a matter of his own homecoming; rather, what is given is the very dynamic in which he and the villagers are gathered into the same life-world – together they are from out of the Rütte and Todtnauberg. Thus, when Heidegger hears Brender Adolf, and then 'steadily, others' say 'You are one of those who eats bread' and interprets this to mean, 'That is to say, a regular guy ... "like me"'; it means more than that he is accepted among the Todtnaubergers (as we understand from the first part of Heidegger's gloss on the event: 'at the same time (Brender Adolf) was also saying, "You belong to us"'). By now we have learned to try to hear all that is said, not just what is expected and obvious. Though we may not really hear it at first, Heidegger is reporting that, in addition to his being admitted by the locals, what is said amounts to a fully reciprocal understanding of home and homecoming. Read more carefully, he is saying that '*every person acknowledges each of the others,' which would entail that the validation comes from and to individuals* '*on both sides*' *and, critically,* '*wherever and whenever such happens to someone, it comes as a gift* [*Jeder anerkennt den anderen in seinem Eigenen und läßt ihn gelten. Wo immer und wann immer solches einem Menschen geschieht, wird es ein Geschenk*]' (FHT 644).

More profoundly, then, when Brender Adolf and the other Todtnaubergers say that the community consists of each and all who 'do what they are supposed to' (*si Sach schafft*), they bear out what Heidegger says repeatedly from his side, verifying that in the gathering together that is the giving of home, differences are preserved, or even achieved, by way of the simple unity in which no one stands alone and wherein all recognize each other in their own ways and let each be who they are. In accepting Heidegger as one of them, where each 'plays their part,' the locals also corroborate the profound continuity that plays across the community: thinking is a responsive craft and is patient as are carpentry and farming; and the other way around, carpentry and farming are thoughtful. Together, all are nourished and are neighbours because they are rooted and sheltered in the same home ground, in the same given and giving local landscape and dialect; all flourish only if they properly bide their time. Beyond Heidegger's personal homecoming (which is important) it is the village's thoughtful and poetic dwelling in this story-shaped, abiding place that is the 'something' which 'entirely simple and unpretentious came to appearance' (*ganz Einfache und Unscheinbare zum Vorschein*) (FHT 644).

Deeply grateful to be accepted, to be granted a homecoming, in that very homecoming (carrying along within it the entirety of his journey) Heidegger comes to understand more fully what he began to ponder earlier: homecoming is that wherein each is let into – is granted – what is their own in the gathering of what belongs together even when apart, which includes the uncanny or foreign and the homey, what is nearest and what is on the other side, over there. Further, homecoming requires staying underway in the double dynamic in which things of the Rütte open free space for humans to settle and dwell, while they as mortals reciprocally need to open a space where things far beyond themselves can address and specify them. It may seem strange – uncanny – that now that he has been granted a homecoming, Heidegger risks this long-sought gift by commending that the villagers open to other needy but dangerous strangers. This is because he courageously follows what stems from that originary gift and what he found in his own releasement: the local source should be let flow, as a further giving to yet other guests, 'downstream' as it were. But he can also see and say how, before the broadcast of the local can happen, the still-coming source might and must be preserved or even newly grounded – which only happens by first becoming rooted in native soil and thence enabled to bear blossoms and fruit to be offered to the wider world.

Appropriately, then, and not selfishly, Heidegger gives grateful thanks for and celebrates the greatest of gifts. Immediately after greeting his hosts (the local officials and those native to the place [*Einheimische*]) and the guests, his first words suggest a small alteration in the text of the festival program proposed by the mayor. He does not say why at first, but after the speech is completed and his audience and we have reflected upon it, we comprehend that he speaks as the guest given the gift of acceptance, as one who thinks and writes in the community just as others farm or build, as one who has been welcomed, made at home – and who, through this becoming-at-home, arrives at a place from whence thoughts could come and from within which he has been able to think and say all that has been given him from *Being and Time* to the end: things such as bell, snow, pathway, cabin, venerable words, and poems that gather the fourfold into a world, tarrying that we might dwell among them; the region named Rütte-Todtnauberg; the opening, abiding expanse – *Gegnet: einräumen.*[39] Perhaps now, by the time of 'Festansprache,' we can understand the richness of what he says so simply. He proposes to strike out from the subtitle of the 'Festival Address,' 'Professor Dr Martin Heidegger, Freiburg' and substitute for it *e Ma us der Rütt*, 'one from the Rütte' (FHT 649).

And what of us? That, of course, is the question, our question. What have we to recover, and how could we? What new relationship with a place and its people could we participate in, through what releasement and openness?

Afterword

There is much to be learned from Heidegger's lifelong homecoming, but not in the form of discrete ideas that we can apply bit by bit. Thus, this afterword is itself somewhat misleading, in that it attempts to indicate how what we have read and pondered bears on the four problems outlined in the preface:

1 The existential problems of each individual person – how to live, how to face life's challenges
2 Massive refugee displacement, forced emigration-immigration around the world
3 Technologies consuming and controlling life itself
4 Ecological disasters on a global scale – the destruction of our home of homes.

Certainly we have found that we need to become open to what is otherwise than we assume; that there are no answers, only better and better questions; that, finally, we come to our limits and face mystery. Along with his own insights, Heidegger passes along previous travellers' stories that remain critical for us on our journeys today, not least because some of the paths that have been and can be taken toward knowledge and power actually lead us even further away from home. Thus, what Heidegger shows is how to go about homecoming, or at least how a given approach leads to dead ends here and there, another to delays and detours or an alternative to somewhat more reliable passageways.

The force of what Heidegger says lies not in his illuminating commentaries on the places where others before him came to be home or the place where he may have (if he did) come to be at home, since those times and places are no more, are no longer retrievable (nor should they be) – and would not, in any case, be home for us. Or, should we say, *homes* for us, because we are highly diverse, with many distinctive capacities and shortcomings, many different possible worlds that may yet be gathered together to one wherein we all might come to our own.

A first set of guiding 'directives' bears on what we need individually, each of us. At the very least, we often seek help when facing the most basic questions: What can or should I do, here and now? Where might I seek to go or with whom might I attempt to be to achieve some happiness, satisfaction, or peace?

Suppose we start from Heidegger's articulation of homecoming as a gathering of what belongs together even when apart, such that each, simultaneously with others, is let come into its own (that is, let be into a region of the 'proper' or 'appropriate' that is never fixed, but dynamically and historically open).[1] Here we immediately become aware of a kind of paradox: by ourselves we cannot accomplish what is needed, yet we must nonetheless strive to our utmost to do all that we can. There are many reasons why acting alone is unavoidably inadequate. It is not so much that none of us has adequate power but that what we seek is constituted by multiple dimensions gathered together, of which we are but one (thus, we cannot, in principle, provide all that is required) and that such a constellation is finally given as a gift, if it comes at all (it is not anything we can 'make' for ourselves or force others to provide).

Yet, Dennis Skocz says, in commenting on 'journeying and locality (dwelling)' via Heidegger's *Hölderlin's Hymn 'The Ister,'* we 'must make our own journey, find our own way home, and take up our own abode.'[2] To do so, we need to start over – and over and over – from where we are. We cannot accumulate achievements, moving forward with steady progress, because we make mistakes, forget what we know, and find that, because of changed circumstances, what worked before is no longer effective. Indeed, as we go along things may well become harder, more complex, or more delicate, as happens when the complex spheres of love, politics, or nature unfold.

To begin, we have to take our bearings by trying to understand where we are – who we are – which, as one of the anonymous readers of this manuscript pointed out, requires 'truly coming to terms with one's situation.' Ignorance or self-deception at the start will set courses that are useless, since if followed they lead to places not at all a home. There are other facets to doing our part, since what we must do is called for by the gathering dynamic itself, which means by the other dimensions that need us because we have to provide that of which we alone are capable of providing: setting these dimensions to work in things, bringing into language what was hitherto concealed, and recollectively thinking (as Heidegger says about how Da-sein/mortals are the site of disclosure).

Here we pass over to three of the problems upon which Heidegger's treatment of homecoming bears. Ecological issues come immediately to the fore, especially as we cannot otherwise be called to change our behaviour to contribute to what the heavens and earth need for their own 'well-being,' much less become ourselves better able to dwell upon the earth.

Heidegger's impact is most established in the area of environmentalism, as his thoughts concerning care, shepherding, sheltering, dwelling poetically, and letting-be have stimulated deep ecology and many other environmental positions sensitive to the fact that our home on the earth is not something we establish by mastery, but comes as a gift to which we need respond with wonder, thanks, and guardianship.[3] Here we can appreciate a point that also could have been made in response to the first problem (about individuals): the issue of guardianship does not so much concern particular choices as a disposition or attitude that opens to what might come, to what might be given.[4] In terms of disposition, Heidegger counsels us to an alternative, originary manner of opening, distinctly humble and shy before the dimensions that once awed us – even as he acknowledges the rightful importance and place of calculative thinking and shows, in his analysis of technology from Sophocles' time to our era of systems, that our human ability to change what comes from *physus* is a central part of our character. Now that the deference of primal hunters, who once sought to propitiate the spirits of the great beasts they killed for food or to appease the forces of nature and sacred places, is long gone – yielded to the assumption that humans are the measure of all that matters and the end of all we meaningfully do – the question becomes how we might, today, appropriately recover the 'same' primal orientation.

Though representational concepts and scientific technology have brought us to a position of astonishing mastery over nature and its resources, there are multiple indications that not all is well. Beyond Heidegger's generative analysis and what many others tell us, environmental disasters unmistakably force us to face what has occurred on our watch: the destitution of once abundant resources, the extermination of entire species, and the destruction of multiple lifeworlds, rise in pollution, and exacerbated climate change.

To answer such environmental 'calls for action,' homecoming has shown us both what we need to do and what, before that, we need to cease doing. Though we cannot accomplish a homecoming by ourselves, we can almost thwart it – in the same way that we can refuse a gift, frustrating its offering. In building and increasingly living in almost fully artificial environments, where we have the lighting to extinguish the difference between the day and night, and the heat and cooling to eliminate the difference between winter and summer, we move toward obliterating the experience of the rhythms of the heavens and the response of the earth and what would sleep and wake upon it. Agriculturally, with the expenditure of great amounts of energy we render the seasons 'obsolete' by making all flowers, fruits, and vegetables available at all times of the year; we irrigate the deserts and farm what were rainforests. Nor do we shirk from engaging whatever means we can find to artificially produce births, turn back aging, and hold death at bay.

Despite frequent misunderstandings, the alternative path Heidegger lays out, on which we would let go of our urge to control, opening to what might come forth, is not passive. Rather it is fully alert, as ready as is possible for the decisive moment (*kairos*) when we must act non-arbitrarily (which means in 'fear and trembling,' for finally there is no justifying ground), using all our capacities for recollective thinking, originary saying, acting, and making-building so as to more sensitively discern and more subtly attend to what gives itself to us. An environmental case in point involves autopoiesis, complexity theory, and developmental systems theory which, with their phenomenological orientation and appreciation of how the human participates in the emergence of the 'web of life' without basis for exceptional domination, are beginning to develop a holistic understanding of the dynamism of the unfolding of the 'natural' world and life, along lines congruent with Heidegger's explication of *physus*.[5] We already come closer to being at home on the earth and within the rhythms of natural processes insofar as we attend to and nurture the mutual inter-determination of organisms and environments at every scale. A good beginning has been made by environmental strategies seeking to learn enough from non-linear self-organizing systems to develop appropriate and sustainable strategies and policies.[6]

Such an ethos of care appears in the way we build, for example, with the structures designed by Pritzker Prize winner Glenn Murcutt, which touch the earth lightly, or the green skyscrapers of Ken Yeang.[7] In addition, as we have seen in chapter 5, Heidegger's delineation of the source of place in regioning-*Gegnet-eräumen* is especially important (though significantly under-researched), for instance, as it correlates with the development of biocultural regionalism as a promising mode of environmental-social-economic development. Finally, an exceptionally clear instance of the necessary change from the attitude of calculatively dominating nature to one of becoming open is found in the Netherlands' new paradigm of accommodation and *genius loci*, with its changed understanding, attitude, and goals for the seas (or, more generally, water, liquidity, dynamics, flow, and technology itself).[8] Obviously, learning about becoming at home to dwell under the heavens and on earth also involves changing relationships among ourselves, that is, among the diverse human beings (many of whom are regularly ignored) in our community, region, and other worlds.

We see that the second problem – displacement – is already inherently involved in these ecological issues, since waves of emigration and immigration result from natural disasters and human activity. The former – floods, earthquakes, droughts, and famines – displace millions every year (and evidently will only increase with global warming). But the environmental chaos is often caused or exacerbated by human actions. Further, many large-scale environmental changes are inherently political, and not just in the sense of decisions having to do with refugees crossing borders and needing services. The political thrust of colonial regimes has often been to subjugate and forcibly move whole populations, as when plantations became production machines in the modern epoch or where forests are denuded in South America and Southeast Asia, destroying complex climatic-vegetative-animal-human lifeworlds, or in wars over territory, itself desirable for its resources (or strategic geopolitical placement or for whatever other 'reason').

Heidegger's journey through cultural and individual homelessness shows that at least four sorts of response are critical for a homecoming among the displaced. Primarily – what the displaced themselves are called to do – those rendered homeless themselves need to make three of these four responses: (*i*) face and deal with their situation, whether by experiencing some beauty or other value there, creating something worthwhile, or adjusting attitudes;[9] (*ii*) open to the new; and (*iii*) hold on to and preserve their inheritance. As we saw in regard to the first problem (concerning each individual person) we need an honest assessment of the situation. There indeed may be weeping and sorrow at the loss of the home place, whether realistically accepted as a difficult but temporary separation or even as a permanent 'exile' (perhaps fearfully grasped as not even the final stop while the displaced are being flung away from home). As Heidegger notes, in homesickness, whether as a result of short or as a result of permanent separation from a place, we experience the strength and vital importance of the connection in regard to who we are or would become. If not felt, it would hopefully be because one was already positively oriented to what is to come, for which the displacement is the occasion or means. Yet, if it is imposed, separating you from what you would hold on to if free, there is likely scant comfort in Heidegger's recounting that 'there is a time to let go' (of which more below) or his explaining that we must give up the comfortable (average everydayness) to enter the foreign and strange as a requisite first step in homecoming. Indeed, his words may feel cruelly cynical. Who wants to learn that forced displacement 'is is an opportunity for growth,' even if that is the most that can be made of it?

Indeed, there is scant consolation. Displacement *is* hard. As Heidegger described the scene in Abrahim a Santa Clara's day, marauding armies constantly crossed back and forth across the rural areas, and the intrigues of court life played themselves out in the city; and in the aftermath of the horror and destruction of World War II, in Heidegger's Germany there was massive dislocation, a housing shortage, and the new fear of living under the threat of the atomic bomb. Even the realms displaying paradigmatically coherent homes were harsh: the peasant world described by Hebel, though it has its beauties, is exhausting, even to the sun; the shoes painted by van Gogh bespeak wearying labour in the course of working on the earth; the world of the Greek temple, now in ruins, has vanished forever.

In all these situations we see the value of kindred travellers, those who have gone before and can help show us the way. Today, many of us believe that these friends, named 'poets' by Heidegger, especially include writers of many kinds and some of the teams that give us cinema. Here we find a great resource for discovering ways of dealing with homelessness (including those operative in post-colonialism and postmodern globalization) or the problems and pains even of freely chosen moves. The substantial and perceptive (and rapidly increasing number of) newsletters, plays, novels, films, songs (and perhaps some television programs) of exile and diaspora generated around the world explore the loss and attempted recovery, or transformation, of shifting identities.[10] These works subtly delineate inner felt experiences (which is especially valuable, given the feelings of isolation and loneliness that are part of the phenomena), unpredictable incidents, as well as likely ones, and possible 'moves' that would alleviate or worsen the distress, additionally inviting those who share the situations to reflect on these phenomena, perhaps even engage in serious dialogue.

Beyond bearing on individual trajectories, these works may provide common ground, perhaps joining audiences from diverse realms as they find themselves fellow travellers, job seekers or migrant workers, prisoners or hostages, exiles, or members of a military unit on duty at a difficult posting. Or, some may find themselves along with others far from the home they shared, the coherent sphere, either travelling together or, having newly arrived, seeking out uncles or cousins in a common enclave. Here the dislocated might find a fecund sphere and with it the obligation to hold safe the customs, language, and music that make them who they are. Consequently, the rest of us are called on to support the continuation of 'poetic' reflection, and with it the human capacity for saying and recollection that is seriously threatened by the drive for the merely utilitarian, a thrust that not only excludes contemplation, but, by focusing on doing, increasingly also excludes the genuinely political, by assuming that the doing amounts to nothing more than the production of 'stuff.'

How are we to find the right balance between safeguarding the heritage that still comes to us and making room for the new, so as not to merely live nostalgically in a severed past? It is important to remember that in moving beyond our entrapment within the sphere of beings Heidegger makes clear that a homecoming is not primarily, or even especially, a physical affair. Rather, homecoming is accomplished in (thoughtful) language, as happened for Hölderlin. This is not to say that home is something otherworldly or transcendental to our specific historical placement, but that the site and possible arrival are a matter of meaning, not spatial location – remember, in the story of the poet's journey even after arriving home the poet just begins to learn to dwell near the source.

In saying this, we are reminded that the literature and film of dislocation are also of interest to many of us outside the domains (of the dislocated) that are set-into-work. And far beyond satisfying any simple curiosity, such works can provide keys to our own broader understanding of the world beyond our immediate experience, evoking meditation on things humanly shared and on differences. That the media can open us to others' worlds, bringing to the fore the fourth sort of response, which we deferred discussing earlier – what those not displaced must do. Those who are not homeless need to (*iv*) learn to offer what is needed (by the dislocated) from others. That is, along with the displaced there are hosts, who also have capacities and responsibilities. While those who are homeless need to take into account the limits of their capability – which they nonetheless depend upon, as a necessary gift – those of us called upon to open ourselves as hosts and to give what is needed must learn to do so, first of all by becoming aware of the relation that necessarily obtains for there to be a gathering together into/as homecoming, of our own situation as 'homed' and of our obligations as such.

How likely is it that we do so now, even for those from other cities and regions of the same country, let alone those from other countries, seeking work, or a place to live, or acceptance in public spaces? Do we make welcome strangers – strangers who would live here, with us – by offering what they need? Do we open to how this would change us? As Heidegger said, thoughtfully and brashly at the end of his life and in the midst of celebrating his acceptance into Todtnauberg, we should so open. Those with resources need to accept and to prepare a place and to stay for those in need, which would only be possible insofar as the hosts are capable of offering such a gift. Such an opening requires that the hosts possess an inner security, as happens only if they shelter their historical uniqueness, knowing how to protect their boundaries and differences (especially since ruin may well be borne within the sphere of those in need) (FHT 648). For this to happen we at home (and for our own homecoming) must, in turn, take up the same three tasks treated above: dealing with our situation (as hosts), opening to the new (with multiplicity side by side or hybridity), and gathering, safe keeping, and treasuring our own set of customs, beliefs, and artistic inheritance (remembering that even remote mountain villages are not as unchanging as they may appear to be).

In regard to the complex of problems concerning environmental-social decisions impacting entire mixed communities (often pitting one against another) and dealing with the homelessness of dislocated people, it is critical to remember how strongly Heidegger emphasizes the generative force of the plural, the multiple, the differences that gather together without losing their uniqueness. Beyond the dynamic of the fourfold itself, in the case of relationships among specific lifeworlds, what he said in the works of chapter 5 is worth repeating: we can and need to implement flexible, multiple, non-comprehensive ways of thinking and living the relationships among regions and historically, culturally, and linguistically distinct peoples, allowing each to open to the others.[11]

The problems of the environment and displacement merge and further involve issues of the scientific-technological drive to control life itself, our fourth area of problems where Heidegger's homecoming provides guidance. As we have seen, plural lifeworlds – often side by side, with mortals in each gathered in a complex dance with atmosphere and climate, soil and vegetation, rain, stream, and lake (or ocean), bacteria, fish, birds, and animals – are historically entangled with the need to choose among them, order and rank them, impose conditions that limit or free their possibilities. The historical confluences of natural and social phenomena raise the question of the character of 'the living,' of 'life,' since these formations already implement not only the understanding of the continuity and differences between 'animals' and humans, but the vital determination of who shall live at all, and then (for those ceded the right to live) of how and where – a question of identity and place, that is, of home.

Such issues arise from the political spheres of environmental control and exploitation or from the political manipulation of displacement. (At one time such power was exercised by the sovereign, now by governments and even by corporations, as well as by powerful individuals and families.) Yet, more subtly, such political decisions and practices derive from a largely unthought source – particular historical interpretations of the character of life itself. And this is so in many aspects. The political facet treats the question of what/who has life, of what/who has life that is to be respected (with what rights). We can also appreciate, as a questioning pathway, the investigations carried out by Hanna Arendt and Georgio Agamben, who, proceeding from the Greeks to today, rethink with a Heideggerian inflection the tangle involving bare life (*bios*) and political life (*zoē*), then law.[12]

At the geographical and social scales, inseparable problems of cultural displacement and ecological integrity push beyond debates about conservation, preservation, or renovation, as the issue of sustainability comes forward as the question of sustaining entire lifeworlds (which include controlling the essential biological patrimonies of those worlds). No individual or subgroup of humans or animals is truly independent in the world. What really exists across the globe are interlocking ecosystems or eco-communities. In any given climatic and geological realm there are mixed communities of bacteria, plants, animals, and people, where none can be as it is, nor live as it does, apart from the dynamic patterns they all generate and sustain together. Thus, we cannot respect or change a particular kind of living being without also respecting or changing the entire complex environment. Practically, as well as theoretically, one either nurtures or harms entire eco-communities. Though we remain largely oblivious to the fact, ecological decisions involve choices as to whether or not we will seek to sustain entire mixed communities of plants, animals, and people. Since choices among elements, or between different communities, are not detachable, it should become clearer than ever that, in regard to those of us in power, who are likely outside the lifeworld in question or oblivious to the connections between it and those of its neighbours, the choices are not legitimately 'ours' to make.[13]

In science the question, 'What is life?,' no longer focuses on the organism, which has been abandoned as the object of investigation since the sub-phenomenal 'elements' have become the focus of microbiology, attended by the rhetoric of 'selfish genes' and the narrow but powerful conceptualization of numericized 'data' or 'code' as the raw material of bioinformatics.[14] Of course, this is critically important, given the concern we ourselves have as organisms confronting the instrumental disinterest in our phenomenal lives on the part of capital drivers and pharmaceutical bioengineering technologies.

In regard to the homecoming that is still underway, through the midst of the ever intense homelessness of such technology, Heidegger has much to say that is relevant and has much to offer as an originary counter to dominant reductive science, especially in his analysis of how the metaphysical epoch is turning from representations of objects to standing-reserve within the reign of *Gestell*, which strikingly presages artificial insemination, cloning, and genetic engineering.[15] Similarly, with the markets and services for procurement and transplantation of human cells, blood, tissues, and organs, we find that political and biological issues converge.[16]

Having moved from questions of lifeworld to life itself, and specifically to human life, we follow Heidegger into one of the most enigmatic neighbourhoods to be found in the search for home. If we think not of place but of time, the question of how we might dwell as mortals – that is, of the manner in which we come into our own and hold sway – hinges on thinking how it is that we linger. To be mortal is to linger for a while, but only for a certain while appropriate to us, a while that is different for a neutrino, a fruit fly, a mountain, or the immortal gods, if there be such.

Whether or not we achieve a homecoming or are always underway, living and passing through homelessness is critically a matter of time. This also takes us full circle back to the first question of what we are to do, of what we might be. Heidegger's story of homecoming enables us to follow part of what he says about passing out of the homelessness of the sphere of subject and object, even of the homelessness of humanism (in current terms, this is a movement through structuralism and post-structuralism to the post-humanist, or at least toward what comes 'after the subject').[17] Following the metaphysical road, we are pushing the limits of our capacities further and further, especially along the line of representational science-technology. For example, there is an emerging commercial world of life-supporting 'parts' and of engineering that do indeed treat the biomedical as stock (for those who can afford it). We do not want to die. Not now, certainly. In the dreams of many, not ever.[18]

On the other pathway, however, the one which Heidegger retrieves for us that runs alongside metaphysics but that originarily might lead home, we hear that mortals' essential manner of holding sway – as lingering for a while, as abiding for our time – is an affront, an injustice even. As Heidegger found, reading Anaximander, what tarries hangs on, clinging to itself, stubbornly hesitating and persisting in continuance, thus inconsiderately ignoring others of its kind that would come forth themselves, preventing a proper belonging with them and frustrating the order of passing (AF 41–6).

Here we would we have to ask, What is our appropriate time? When to let go? How to let go? Would we recover the importance of learning to die a good death?[19] Then, too, we have the complementary, What to guard and preserve? Whether to care for it at any cost: heavens and earth, divinities and mortals themselves (as dimensions), and the environment, the dispossessed, life itself (as concrete, tarrying things)?

Answers would need to be couched in the appropriate terms not only for ourselves individually, nor only for our own historical worlds, but as bearing on the trajectory proper (while open) to mortals. We are called to pursue homecoming to our utmost ability, striving to come into our own as fully as we might, opening and disposing ourselves by our capacities for originary thinking, saying, making, acting, and sacrificing to contribute appropriately to any gathering that might come – that would occur within the disclosing granting of what belongs together even when apart.[20]

Notes

Preface

1 At the social and historical scale, there have been fine descriptive and analytical studies of these phenomena for some time. Among the most enduring studies of intellectual history and modernization are Peter Berger's *Homeless Mind*, Erich Heller's *Disinherited Mind*, Simon Weil's *Need for Roots*, Leroy S. Rouner's edited volume, *Longing for Home*, Angelika Bammer's collection, *The Question of 'Home*,' Christopher Reed's edited volume, *Not at Home*, Arlen Mack's edited volume, *Home: A Place in the World*, and Anthony Vidler's *Architectural Uncanny*. The history of the United States is inseparable from the story of the sequences of dispossession and attempted recovery of identity and place: Paula M. Marks' *In a Barren Land*, Gener Weltfish's *Lost Universe*, David J. Weber's edited volume, *Foreigners in Their Native Land*, Disney Lemelle and Robin D.G. Kelley's *Imagining Home*, Oscar Handlin's *Uprooted* and Oscar and Mary Handlin's *Facing Life*, Mark Wyman's *Round-Trip to America*, and Valerie S. Prince's *Burnin' Down the House*.

2 The works that contribute most importantly to critical understanding and future action are considered in the afterword, where we return to these problems in light of what has been learned from Heidegger (and where a fuller bibliography is provided in the notes). The diffusion and availability of other-than-Western media, especially film and video, that struggles with the theme in a 'post-colonial' mode, is especially noteworthy.

3 For example, the recent – and often surprising – work of Badiou, *Saint Paul* (2003), as well as that of Laclau, *Elusive Universality* (2008), and Cheah, *Spectral Nationality* (2003); for a critique of this approach, in light of Heidegger's position, see Mugerauer, 'Double Gift.'

4 See Mugerauer, 'New Type of Medical Tourism.'

5 Intergovernmental Panel on Climate Change, *NOE 5*; Roaf et al., *Adapting Buildings and Cities* (2005), 190, 207–16.

6 *GAIA Atlas* (1992), 68, 73–4, 108.

7 Gore, *Earth in the Balance* (2006), 163; also see Mugerauer and Manzo, *Environmental Dilemmas* (2008).

8 Richardson, *Heidegger* (1963), and Mehta, *Martin Heidegger* (1967), though they did not develop the insights extensively. Father Richardson treated home, homelessness, homecoming, homeland, journey, and dwelling in his coverage of how Heidegger's Hölderlin interpretations thematize the moments of the poet's education 'in terms of one basic metaphor, sc. of Being-as-source' (*Heidegger* [1963], chapter 5, 'Homecoming,' 'Recollection,' 448; see also 440–72). In his analysis of both *Being and Time* and the later works, Mehta already observed that if we follow Heidegger's way of thinking, 'the alert, open-minded reader comes to the end of the journey ... with some understanding of how and why man today is homeless in the world, and of how in the midst of this homelessness, thinking as meditation is the true and only way to be at home again in the only home there is, the world (*Martin Heidegger* [1967], xii. Though the term is not indexed, he mentions the theme of home and homelessness ten times and further stresses its importance with the Heidegger quotation he chooses for the book's epigraph: '*Die Wanderschaft in der Wegrichtung zum Fragwürdingen ist nicht Abenteuer sondern Heimkehr*' [Traveling on the proper path of question-worthiness is not adventure but homecoming].

9 Sallis (1969, 1970), 'Nietzsche's Homecoming' (of 1969); 'Towards the Movement of Reversal' (of 1970); Schürmann (1987 [1982]), *Heidegger on Being and Acting* (1987); Beelemann, *Heimat als Daseinmetaphor* (1994); and Crownfield, 'The Last God,' 212–28; Bambach, *Heidegger's Roots*. Sallis continued a line of thought he opened in 'Nietzsche's Homecoming,' by examining how Heidegger utilizes the themes of rootedness and grounding to deal with contemporary science and technology and to portray our era as one in which 'home-coming becomes home-creation from out of the return to self' ('Towards the Movement of Reversal' [1970], 152; cf. 'Nietzsche's Homecoming,' 1969). Schürmann's insightful analysis remains consistently sensitive to the importance of the language of home, homecoming, belonging, rootedness, place, and dwelling for Heidegger's most radical thinking (*Heidegger on Being and Acting*, originally 1982, translated in 1987); he carefully attends to the ways Heidegger changes uses, for example, of 'rootedness' and 'place,' over the diverse periods of his thinking. Beelemann focuses on 'Heimat' as the master metaphor for Dasein in the early theological studies of the young Heidegger, in fact opening his analysis with the

remark that 'Heidegger's strong affinity for everything that had to do with "Homeland" is no secret' (*Heimat als Daseinmetapher* [1994], 13); cf. Marten, 'Heidegger's Heimat' (1980), 36–159.

Recently, further research has traced the origins and connections of the theme with the historical, cultural context within which Heidegger worked: for example, Charles Bambach lucidly succeeds in his project 'to explore the pastoral language of rootedness, homeland, and native soil in Heidegger's works from 1933–1945 and to show how deeply implicated it is in his own vision of a National Socialist Germany. By looking at Heidegger's texts and situating them within their own historical contexts, I hope to show the deep and abiding connection between the pastoral language of *Heimat* (homeland) and the militantly geo-political vision of German nationalism that come together to form what one contemporary called Heidegger's "Freiburg National Socialism"' (*Heidegger's Roots,* 4). Then, too, as the corpus becomes more completely available by way of the *Gesamtausgabe* and as more is translated, fresh readings are being generated. For example, David Crownfield's interpretation of *Contributions to Philosophy (From Enowning)* (which happily appeared before I finished writing) is fully congruent with that presented here: 'What is the gift of the god which, in its very passing away, calls and moves us outward to a higher homecoming than anything hitherto?'; 'My juxtaposition of "blessing and summons" here and "summons and promise" elsewhere relies on the indication in *Contributions* that the summons is not only a calling out but a calling home' ('The Last God,' 225, 227).

10 A great deal of interesting work remains to be undertaken. The figure needs to be traced through Heidegger's early works, through the philosophical tradition before and after him (obviously, in its German lineage, through Schelling, Nietzsche, Husserl, Schutz, and others). Nietzsche's persistent emphasis on the homesickness and homelessness of Western culture often is referred to and cited – by Heidegger too – but is not extensively analysed, despite the centrality of the figure in his thought, of which we are reminded by even a single quotation:

> German Philosophy as a whole – Leibniz, Kant, Hegel, Schopenhauer to name the greatest – is the most fundamental form of romanticism and homesickness there ever has been: the longing for the best that ever existed. One is no longer at home anywhere; at last one longs for that place in which alone one can be at home, because it is the only place in which one would want to be at home: the Greek world. But it is precisely in that direction that all bridges are broken – except the rainbow-bridges of concepts! And these lead everywhere, into all the homes and 'father-

> lands' that existed for Greek souls! ... One wants to go *back.* (*Wille zur Macht,* 419 [1885]; *Will to Power,* 225)

Another important locus is *The Gay Science,* where, for example, in book 5, section 377, Nietzsche says,

> We who are homeless – Among Europeans today there is no lack of those who are entitled to call themselves homeless in a distinctive and honorable sense: it is to them that I especially commend my secret wisdom and *gaya scienza.* For their fate is hard, their hopes are uncertain; it is quite a feat to devise some comfort for them – but what avail? We are children of the future, how could we be at home in this today? We feel disfavor for all ideals that might lead one to feel at home even in this fragile, broken time of transition; as for its 'realities,' we do not believe that they will *last.*' (*Gay Science,* 338)

There is somewhat more examination of the uncanny in Nietzsche but, again, not sustained treatments of the core motifs themselves. Clearly, Heidegger drew much from both Nietzsche's language and thinking about home and homelessness and in regard to the strategy of destruction and reconstruction, especially as a specific mode of active way-making to be performed; the vocabulary also illuminates the character of time. Nietzsche's powerful intersection of historical and cultural analyses reverberates with ontological-cosmic echoes in Heidegger, as we can see from the striking 'concluding' paragraphs of *Will to Power,* 1067, which contain lines almost describing the trajectory of Heidegger's journey from homelessness to the splendour of the simple (as we will see in this book): 'This world: a monster of energy ... a household without expenses or losses ... enclosed by 'nothingness' as by a boundary ... out of the simplest forms striving toward the most complex, out of the stillest, most rigid, coldest forms toward the hottest, most turbulent, most self-contradictory, and then again returning home to the simple out of this abundance, out of the play of contradictions back to the joy of concord' (Nietzsche, *Will to Power,* 550). Beyond formalistic analysis, the importance of 'the sociohistorical concepts of homeworld and alienworld' in Husserl's movement, for example, is well demonstrated in Steinbock, *Home and Beyond* (1995, 179), the breadth of which can in part be glimpsed from key phrases in some of his chapter titles: 'Liminal Experience as the Co-Generation of Home/Alien,' 'Liminal Experience as Appropriation: Making Ourselves at Home,' 'The Homeworld as Our World,' 'When is a Home a Home?' and 'Homecomrades.' See also his 'Homelessness and the Homeless Movement' (1994).

In *Home and Beyond*, Steinbock helpfully points to many of the other relevant works, though in many of them the theme is noted in passing rather than analysed: see, for example, Jan Patoèka's 'Le monde naturel' (1936), Alwin Diemer's *Edmund Husserl* (1956), Bernhard Waldenfels' 'Heimat in der Fremde' (1985) and *Das Zwischenreich des Dialogs* (1971), and Klaus Held's 'Heimwelt, Fremdtwelt, der eine Welt' (1991).

Schutz's work on 'The Stranger' and 'The Homecomer' also merits further exploration, as Helmut Wagner begins to argue, where explaining the importance of this line of inquiry for an understanding of community, detachment, and the construction of (non)acceptance – perhaps an even more pressing topic today, given current post-colonial reinterpretations of global movement. 'In his revealing study "The Stranger," [Schutz] analyzed the problems of orientation and adaptation which befall a person who, having been raised in one cultural community, is transferred to another one. He is forced first to become an observer of the ways of life of the host community and second to reconstruct, piece by piece, at least those rules for practical conduct without which everyday life would be impossible him' (Wagner, *Alfred Schutz* [1970], see the introduction, 18). Schutz's two most relevant essays – 'Stranger' and 'Homecomer' – appeared in the *American Journal of Sociology* in 1945.

Another equally large area to be fruitfully encountered lies in the German cultural production and interpretation of *Heimat* (almost an industry in itself in literature and film alone). From the huge literature on the Germanic tradition of *Heimat*, see especially the two-volume *Heimat* (*Analysen, Themen, Perspektiven* and *Lehrpläne, Literature, Filme*), published by the German Federal Centre for Public Education (Bundeszentrale für politische Bildung); Karl-heinz Rossbacher, *Heimatbewegung und Heimatroman*; Applegate, *Nation of Provincials*; Hermand and Streakley, eds., '*Heimat,' Nation, and Fatherland*; Rollins, *Greener Vision of Home*; Führ, ed., *Worin noch Niemand war*; Köstlin, *Heimat und Identität*; Wickham, *Constructing Heimat in Postwar Gemany*; Riedl, ed., *Heimat: Auf der Suche nach der verloren Identität*; Lindemann, ed., '*Heimat': Gedichte und Prosa;* Walser, *Heimatkunde*; Taurus Video, *Heimatfilm-Kollection*; Hofig, *Deutsche Heimatfilm*; Fiedler, *Heimat im deutschen Film*; Kaes, *From Hitler to Heimat*; Boa and Palfreyman, *Heimat – A German Dream*; and von Moltke, *No Place Like Home.*

The still-critical political analysis of Heidegger's use of home and homelessness needs to be continued, for example, from, as mentioned, Charles

Bambach's masterful investigations. On the political analysis of Heidegger's use of home and homelessness, see Bambach, *Heidegger's Roots* and 'Heidegger, Hebel, and the Politics of Homecoming'; 'Sophocles, Hölderlin, and the Politics of Homecoming' (2002); 'Heidegger, Technology, Homeland' (2002). See also Dallmayr, *Other Heidegger* (1993); de Man, *Romanticism and Contemporary Criticism* (1993); Bernasconi, *Heidegger in Question* (1993); Gosetti-Ferencei, *Heidegger* (2005); and Phillips, 'Toward the Uncanny Homeland' (2005).

Also beyond what I have been able to undertake, the complex of specialized analyses would need to be brought into a dialogue in order that we might benefit from the many diverse essays that already insightfully treat this theme in Heidegger's work. For example, on early analyses of the motif of *Heimat* and 'Dwelling' in Heidegger's works see Amar, 'Martin Heidegger' (1970); Alderman, 'Work of Art and Other Things' (1973); Allen, 'Homecoming in Heidegger and Hebel' (1977); Dauaenhauer, 'Heidegger, the Spokesman for the Dweller' (1977); Dubsky, 'Domov a bezdomovi' ('Home and Unhomeliness') (1966); Grugan, 'Thought and Poetry' (1972); Kelly, 'Earth as Home' (1972); Marten, 'Heidegger's Heimat' (1980); Wolff, 'Haus und Hütte' (1977); Derrida, *Margins of Philosophy* (1972), especially 130, where he 'famously' says that Heidegger's entire discourse is dominated by a 'metaphorics associating the proximity of Being with the values of neighboring, shelter, house, service, guard, voice, and listening'; and *Points ...: Interviews, 1974–1994* (1995), on German poetry aiming at a 'home port'; and Foltz, *Inhabiting the Earth* (1995). A feminist perspective is presented by Young, 'House and Home' (2001), 252–88.

From the large literature on the broader relation of Heidegger and Hölderlin see, in addition to the work of Bambach and others cited just above, the early work of Allemann, *Hölderlin and Heidegger* (1954); Schuwer, 'Nature and the Holy' (1977); Halliburton, *Poetic Thinking* (1981); Bruns, *Heidegger's Estrangements* (1989); Fóti, *Heidegger and the Poets* (1992); de Man, 'Les Exégèses de Hölderlin' (1955) and *Romanticism and Contemporary Criticism* (1993); Warminski, *Readings in Interpretation* (1987); Haar, *Song of the Earth* (1993); von Herrmann, 'Flower of the Mouth' (1989); Gosetti-Ferencei, *Heidegger* (2005); and the interesting reflection on their specific intersection by Skocz, 'Of Time and the River' (2004).

Further, many detailed comparative studies beg to be made, such as the way the *unheimlich* (uncanny, unhomey) is handled by Heidegger and Freud (comparison of the two remains a much underdeveloped area). Anthony Vidler treats the theme in his *The Architectural Uncanny*, where he also calls attention to Schelling's early interest in the aesthetic uncanny that persisted into his late *Philosophie der Mythologie*, as well as calling attention to E.T.A. Hoffmann as one of 'the foremost practitioners of the uncanny,' in that his stories are an 'almost systematic exploration of the relations between the homely and the unhomely, the familiar and the strange' (*Architectural Uncanny*, 27); see also 231nn22–4). Given the deeply Heideggerian current in most of Derrida, it is somewhat surprising that in proposing a rereading of Freud's essay, 'Das Unheimliche,' in a running series of footnotes in 'The Double Session,' Derrida makes no use of Heidegger, not even against the grain, though he is stressing Freud's ideas about how '*heimlich* is a word the meaning of which develops towards an ambivalence, until it finally coincides with its opposite, *unheimlich*' and, along the way, notes its connection with *Geheimnis* (secret) (*Dissemination* [1981], 220n32; see also 268–9n67, 248n52). In treating the next line of the same passage – '*Unheimlich* is in some way or other a sub-species of *heimlich*' – James Phillips develops the view of Heidegger's position as just the opposite, in that he holds the 'not-at-home' to be the more primordial phenomenon (*Heidegger's Volk* [2005], 199–203); on the basis of the experience of anxiety Phillips also critiques the reading of Heidegger's notion of *Heimat* in John Caputo's 'People of God, People of Being' (2000). Later, Derrida does say something more directly about *das Heimliche-Unheimliche* in *Specters of Marx* (1994): when treating ghosts, haunting (*es spukt*), and the stranger in Freud's 'Das Unheimliche,' he links Marx, Freud, and Heidegger in regard to not having begun where they 'ought to have "been able to begin," namely with haunting' (*Specters of Marx*, 172–6); see also his treatment of Freud's 'Das Unheimliche,' as well as of literary fiction, in *Postcard* (1987), 242–3. Of course, in thinking Heidegger in tension with Freud, Luce Irigaray not only takes to task both Freud and Heidegger for continuing the patriarchal oppression (in which men, seeking to make up for the lost first home of the mother, build themselves new homes where they place women, who themselves never gain a home of their own; see *Ethics of Sexual Difference* [1993]), but further criticizes Heidegger for refusing a way to resolve repression by insistently emphasizing 'nothing' and thus the notion that 'man' is 'always already separate ... in relation to the maternal whence he is born' (Irigaray, *Forgetting of Air*, 166).

11 *Heidegger, Hölderlin, and the Subject of Poetic Language*, 273n10. See also Luce Irigaray, *Foregetting of Air*, Kelly Oliver, *Reading Kristeva: Unraveling the Double-Bind*; and Nancy Holland and Patricia Huntington, eds., *Feminist Interpretations of Heidegger.*

Introduction

1 That the theme in Heidegger's work has long been recognized, even though not fully explored, is discussed in the preface, where early documentation and analysis is cited, especially in notes 8–10.
2 Harman, *Heidegger Explained* (2007), 106.

Chapter 1

1 A full study of the leitmotif in Heidegger's early work would be very rewarding but clearly a major undertaking. As but one instance of the depth of these themes, already in the 1925 summer course in Marburg, *Prolegomena zur Geschichte des Zeitbegriffs,* Heidegger devoted section 30 to 'Die Structure der Unheimlichkeit.'
2 He already begins the wordplay that becomes somewhat notorious and that culminates in the 1950s in his high originary mode of thinking and saying, with such phrases as 'the world worlds.' In *Being and Time,* where he is explaining that 'temporality is not a being at all,' he also says 'Temporality temporalizes' (*Zeitlichkeit zeitig*) (BT 328). Note, the custom in citing the text of English translations of *Being and Time* is to have the page references actually refer to the original German pages (not to those of the English translation) – the former are noted in the margins of both existing English translations.
3 After the first full reference by proper title to Heidegger's works, a standard abbreviation will be used for subsequent citations within the text (in this case BT for *Being and Time*). For a full list of the titles and abbreviations see xiii–xiv.
4 Heidegger introduces the terms 'region' (*Gegen* and *Gegnet*), as well as 'making room' (*einräumen*) in *Being and Time,* terms that later play a crucial role in his development of place in works such as 'Conversation on a Country Path,' 'Building Dwelling Thinking,' 'Memorial Address,' and 'Art and Space,' to which we will return in chapters 5 and 6. It does need to be noted that the development is not continuous. A striking example in which Heidegger himself acknowledges discontinuity from the other side of a leap occurs in 'Time and Being' (1962), where he says that 'The attempt in *Being and Time,* section 70 (pp. 367–9) ... to derive human spatiality from temporality is untenable' (TB 23).
5 This way of thinking being and dwelling together will appear again in the later essay BDT (146–7), which we will take up in chapters 5 and 6.
6 Heidegger uses 'over there' to mean the surrounding world: we find mean-

ing, ourselves really, over there, in our relation to the surrounding world. And, of course, he substantially considers death. But, in *Being and Time,* he does not put the two together as 'over there, on the other side' as he does in his Todtnauberg talk, incorporating Hebel's poetic language. This will be covered in chapter 6. 'The "here" of an "I-there" is always understood in terms of an "over there" at hand in the sense of being toward it which it de-distances, is directional, and takes care ... The over there is the determinateness of something encountered within the world. "Here" and "over there" are possible only in a "there," that is, when there is a being which had disclosed spatiality as the being of the "there"' (BT 132). The 'here' can be thought of as Da-sein's being here for itself, in contrast to the 'there,' where the others are with Da-sein and where understanding happens.

7 Nietzsche, *Birth of Tragedy,* sec. 7, p. 52; see also Schopenhauer, *World as Will and Idea.*

8 See, for example, Kiesel, *Genesis* (1993), esp. 228–44; van Buren, *Young Heidegger* (1994), esp. 271–82; Kiesel and van Buren, *Reading Heidegger from the Start* (1994), especially, Pöggeler, 'Destruction and Moment,' 137–56, and van Buren, 'Martin Heidegger, Martin Luther,' 159–74; McNeill, *Glance of the Eye* (1999), esp. 44–6, 116–17, 338.

9 This passage is from Rilke, *Notebooks of Malte Laurids Brigge* (1959), 46–7.

10 Two translations of 'What Is Metaphysics?' have been used here to provide the alternatives separated by a colon: they are, respectively, David F. Krell's, in Heidegger, *Basic Writings* (1977), 93–110, and Walter Brock's, in Heidegger, *Existence and Being* (1968), 325–61.

11 Heidegger often points out that 'orthodoxy' means 'being on the right way.' Literally, it comes from *ortho* (straight, right) and *doxos* (belief, opinion – long familiar from Plato).

12 Among the many thinkers and writers with whom Heidegger shares horizons that are not fully appreciated (partly because he does not acknowledge them), we find Kierkegaard. In the thinking in these passages in *An Introduction to Metaphysics* (see also *Being and Time*), which reflect upon a kind of 'being oblivious to being oblivious,' Heidegger would seem to be drawing upon Kierkegaard's ideas about the difference between being in despair beforehand but not knowing it, and knowing that one is in despair. This is what we find, reading Kierkegaard, 'So it appears that every aesthetic view of life is despair, and that everyone who lives aesthetically is in despair, whether he knows it or not. But when one knows it (and you indeed know it), a higher form of existence is an imperative requirement' (*Either/Or* 2:197).

13 'Falling out of being' is a complex phrase in Heidegger's work and echoes much of Western saying. As distinct from the language of 'being cast out,'

which dominates (and echoes Genesis and the thrownness of the potter and creating gods, for example), 'falling out' may bring to mind – as I wrote under a tree in the spring – 'falling out of the nest,' and the *attendant* figura of nest as home and site of gathering, as found in Heidegger's 'Dialogue on Language'). See my *Heidegger's Language and Thinking*, 33, 44–58, esp. 50.

14 Heidegger will return to Parmenides' saying, as we will see in chapter 4-A, with *What Is Called Thinking?*

15 See also what Heidegger says in *What Is Called Thinking?*, treated below in chapter 4-B and -C.

16 On the choice of 'apprehend' to render *vernehmen* see the translator's note on p. 116.

17 Hence the connection between Heidegger and Kierkegaard, as developed by many scholars. See, for example, Caputo, *Radical Hermeneutics.*

18 The classic articulation would be, of course, Francis Bacon's *Novum Organum* (1620), where he explains how we derive from nature itself the human knowledge that allows us the power to command nature by obeying nature. We find what nature does or can be made to do by submitting her to the rack, that is to the equivalent of judicial torture: in the proper – coded – legal vocabulary of testimony and trial he says he would focus upon 'nature under constraint and vexed; that is to say, when by art and the hand of man she is forced out of her natural state, and squeezed and molded ... seeing that the nature of things betrays itself more readily under the vexations of art than in its natural freedom' (Bacon, 'The Great Instauration,' 25; see also aphorism 98).

19 This is a major theme of Heidegger's *Hölderlin's Hymn 'The Ister,'* discussed below in notes 13 and 14 of chapter 5.

20 *Will to Power*, aphorism 419. A substantial part of the difference between homesickness and homelessness lies in the way that the former remains oriented to the past while the latter is directed to the future, as Heidegger points out, citing Ibid., aphorism 844: 'A romantic is an artist whose great dissatisfaction with himself makes him creative – who looks away, looks back from himself and from his world' (N, vol. 1, *The Will to Power as Art*, 132).

21 Bk 2, ch. 3, 'Critique of Highest Values,' aphorism 419.

22 See also Heidegger, *Contributions to Philosophy*, chapter 7, 'The Last God.'

23 Xenophanes had already argued that to find the 'One god, among gods and men the greatest, not at all like mortals in body or in mind, mortals need to open to difference, which requires passing beyond religious anthropomorphism: 'But if oxen (and horses) and lions had hands or could draw with hands and create works of art like those made by men, horses would draw pictures of gods like horses, and oxen of gods like oxen, and they would

make the bodies (of their gods) in accordance with the form that each species itself possesses' (Freeman, *Ancilla to the Pre-Socratic Philosophers* [1962], fragments 23 and 15).

Chapter 2

1 The translations of Heidegger's essays 'Wie wenn am Feiertage' and 'Andenken' are mine, done before Keith Hoeller's appeared; of course, comparison with his expert and subtle renderings in Heidegger, *Elucidations of Hölderlin's Poetry* (2000) is well worth while.

2 Recall, we saw in chapter 1 how Heidegger points out that our translation estranges us.

3 As the English translator notes, Heidegger switches from using the neuter form of the word, 'the serene' (*das Heitere*) to the feminine form (*die Heitere*) once he says 'this we call serene, after an older word of our mother tongue' (RP 363n1).

4 It would be interesting to develop the correlation with Aquinas' aesthetics: Aquinas' three criteria of beauty are integrity, proportion, and clarity (on *integritas*, see *Summa Theologiae* I, 91, 3, and II-II, 169, 2; on proportion as graceful ordering see *Commentary on* De Anima, I, 9, 144 and *Summa Theologiae* II-II, 141, 4; 145, 2; *Summa* I, 5, 4; on *claritas*, see *Summa* I, 67, 3; III, 45, 2. As Eco points out, when Aquinas writes 'To say that the appetite desires the good, and peace, and the beautiful, is not to say that it desires different things' (*De Veritate*, 22, 1), 'By peace he means the tranquility of order [*tranquillitas ordinis*]' (*Art and Beauty*, 82), which would seem to correlate with *serenitas* in the quotation above.

5 '*Ge-schichte*'; consider also '*Ge-birg*,' (A 106).

6 Also consider the role of witness in Heidegger's 'Dialogue on Language,' 6, 7, 9, 11, 19, 34–6; my *Heidegger's Language and Thinking*, 26.

7 There is a strong connection in German between 'home' and 'hearth' and the 'secret.' 'Home' and 'hearth' speak of the private and the interior. *Heimlich*, for example, means secret, secretive, concealed, private, and secluded, as well as comfortable and snug. *Geheimnis* means secret. These words connote mystery and the mysterious.

8 Heidegger's manner of moving occurs through the performance of 'passing over and back' as he both does and says, for example, in 'Dialogue on Language,' 44, 75, and *What Is Called Thinking?*, 26–7, 60, 106, as covered in my *Heidegger's Language and Thinking*, 2, 10, 31, 40, 48, 143, 155–6, 183.

9 Throughout, Heidegger is sensitive to Hölderlin's own poetic achievement. Hölderlin's corpus, according to Heidegger, is a journey: some poems are

part of the way out, others of the homecoming. As noted, 'Homecoming' and 'Andenken' are achievements of the latter; in another phase, for example, Hölderlin called the poetic letting beings appear in their truth and beauty in the presencing of *Beon* (*Seyn*), not Nature, but *Hyperion* (A 134).

10 To claim that he is 'such a one' is not to claim that he is 'the only one.'

11 Note the strong relation between this and Deleuze and Guattari's idea of a minor literature as a means whereby there occurs a 'becoming a people'; see, for example, Deleuze and Guattari, *Kafka* (1986).

12 Later, Heidegger folds this image of a bell in relation to poetry together with others by Goethe (considered in the essay 'Art and Space') and from his reflections on his own childhood ('Vom Geheimnis des Glockenturms'). See chapter 6, the section entitled, 'The Homey Works,' which continues from what we see at the end of this chapter to cover Heidegger's last meditations toward 'releasing the homey to a coming' (A 99).

Chapter 3

1 *Contributions to Philosophy* (*From Enowning*). For a description of the background of the work see von Herrmann, 'Editor's Epilogue,' 363–9.

2 For details on the difficult and the often perplexing novel words and syntax Heidegger uses, see translators Emad and Maly's foreword to *Contributions.* Also see Vallega-Neu, *Heidegger's* Contributions to Philosophy (2003).

3 Heidegger himself notes the continuity of speaking of the turning and the way he has long spoken of *Ereignis.* In 'Letter on Humanism' (1947), he writes concerning 'the turn,' 'in the publication of *Being and Time* the third division of the first part, "Time and Being," was held back. Here everything is reversed. The section in question was held back because thinking failed in the adequate saying of this turning [*Kehre*] and did not succeed with the help of the language of metaphysics. The lecture "On the Essence of Truth," thought out and delivered in 1930 but not printed until 1943, provides a certain insight into the thinking of the turning from *Being and Time* to "Time and Being." This turning is not a change of standpoint from *Being and Time,* but in it the thinking that was sought first arrives at the location of that dimension out of which *Being and Time* is experienced, that is to say, experienced from the fundamental experience of the oblivion of being' (LH 207–8). As von Herrmann notes, Heidegger then adds in a note, '"enowning" has been since 1936 the guiding-word of my thinking'; clearly, though it was not understood at the time given that the manuscript was then still kept secret, this reference is to the time and thinking of *Contributions* (CP 364). In 'The Turning' Heidegger densely utilizes a mature version of the thinking, there

connecting *eignen* (to be one, to belong to) and *erblicken/Einblick/Einblitz* (to bring to sight/flashing glance-insight), as the translator helpfully notes: 'Disclosing coming-to-pass (*Ereignis*) is bringing to sight that brings into its own (*eignende Eräugnis*)' (Tu 45).

4 The English translation uses 'being' to render *Sein* and 'be-ing' for *Seyn* – the distinctive eighteenth-century variation that Heidegger introduces. See translators Emad and Maly's foreword to *Contributions*, xxii–xxiv.

5 'Inabiding' is the translation of *Inständlichkeit* or *Inständigkeit*. See Vallega-Neu, *Heidegger's* Contributions to Philosophy, 33.

6 Emad and Maly translate *Abgrund* (and *Ab-grund*) as 'ab-ground' (see their foreword to *Contributions*, xxx–xxxii); others usually render it as 'abyss' (for example, see Vallega-Neu, *Heidegger's Contributions to Philosophy*, 88, and other English translations used in the rest of this book, such as Albert Hofstadter's of the essays in *Poetry, Language, Thought* and Reginald Lilly's of *The Principle of Reason*).

7 The thought and language here of a call that is a calling back that calls forth (*vorrufende Rückruf*) needs to be compared and contrasted with the call that calls Da-sein ahead and back in *Being and Time*, 251, 259 – though I cannot possibly do that here. Here is a good example of the problems of the encounter of my book project with *Contributions*: the explication of *Contributions* and Heidegger's later works in terms of homecoming requires a focus on both the leitmotif and the later works if it is to be done in my lifetime. Yet, *Contributions* (as many of Heidegger's other works, but to an extreme) moves in so many other directions – here toward *Being and Time*. I can only be thankful that many other scholars, more competent than I in these matters, are working out the relation of *Contributions* to the rest of Heidegger's corpus and, especially, to the earlier works.

Passages from *Being and Time* are as follows: 'The call calls from afar to afar. It reaches him who wants to be brought back' (BT 271); 'Where it comes from – the uncanniness of the thrown individuation – is also called in the calling, that is, is also disclosed. Where the call comes from in calling forth to ... is that to which it is called back ... The disclosive character of the call has not been completely determined until we understand it as a calling back that calls forth' (BT 280). The parallelism of these passages to *Contributions* is noted by Vallega-Neu in *Heidegger's* Contributions to Philosophy, 15–16.

8 Some time after I had written this section I discovered Crownfield's essay, 'The Last God,' 212–28. Though I have not focused on god in *Contributions*, it is gratifying to find Crownfield making the same argument. He argues, for example, that in *Contributions* 'summons is not only a calling out but a calling

home, with summons and blessing treated as coordinate modes of extremity' (227n7).

9 For treatment of Heidegger's use of religious, and especially biblical, language in his thinking, see my *Heidegger's Language and Thinking.*

10 Here Heidegger plays on *irren* and 'heterodoxy' as errant way, compared with 'orthodoxy' as right way/road. And truth as correctness is *adequatio*, or representation and correspondence. Thus, the 'right' way of representational orthodoxy in metaphysics turns out to be the *irren*, since it obscures *aletheia* and originary thinking as the 'really' right way.

11 On the technological and world as raw material, see my *Interpretations on Behalf of Place*, pt 2.

12 See chapter 1, note 11; see also *Umweg*, 'detour,' in Heidegger, *Contributions.* Recently, Jean Baudrillard develops the ideas of desire and production/consumption of the repeated, of the *similacra.* Though he does not acknowledge any special debt to Heidegger and is usually understood as thinking out of a Marxist approach, his use of Heidegger's ideas seems apparent and is worth further investigation. The entire recent French post-structuralist emphasis on 'desire' in Baudrillard, Deleuze, and Guatarri et al. could be fruitfully studied in relation to Heidegger's way of talking here.

13 So too, *Contributions to Philosophy* (complete with its joinings) would be another.

14 Obviously, here Heidegger is using a variation on the image of being as sun and of truth as enlightenment, with all its metaphysical heritage from Plato, Plotinus, and their line; see my 'Neglected Sources of Heidegger's Aesthetics.' Specifically, this is the 'shift' or 'inversion' that correlates with Hebel's figure of the moon as neighbouring, to be treated in the last chapter, on Heidegger's homey works.

15 Note the apparently Hegelian tone of this passage, a point that stimulates questions about the ways in which Gadamer is more Hegelian than Heidegger – a complex but worthwhile area for further investigation.

16 As discussed above (note 4 to chapter 1), Heidegger reflexively says this of himself in 'Time and Being' (1962).

17 In terms of the theological parallel, Heidegger is here avoiding the dualism and heresy of Manicheanism, where evil is reified and seen as equipotent with good.

18 The way Heidegger develops the issues of having a ground and of events unfolding without any ground will be treated below, in chapter 4-B.

19 See chapter 2, the analysis of Hölderlin's poem, 'Andenken,' and note 9.

20 Of course, Heidegger's own concern and earlier use of Hölderlin in regard to the German people is not so simple. This is a large and serious issue

beyond the scope of this work. In this regard, see especially Heidegger's *Hölderlin's Hymn, 'The Ister'*; the work of Charles Bambach (see Bambach in the bibliography; and chapter 5, notes 13 and 14; see also 24 on another focus).

21 See, for example, my treatment of this issue in *Heidegger's Language and Thinking* (1987), ch. 4, 195–247; and Schürmann, *Heidegger on Being and Acting*, sec. 38, on nearness/fourfold (pp. 223–5), for comparisons of Heidegger's language and thought with Meister Eckart's, and in identifying some of Heidegger's secularized versions of Christian doctrine, such as Augustine on providence (383n66).

22 My emphasis.

23 It is interesting to speculate whether Heidegger also has in mind something like the *Odyssey* as a paradigm, and if so, to consider how to compare Heidegger's thinking with Joyce's 'poetic' version.

24 Of course, for Heidegger the 'same' does not connote the 'identical'; see chapter 4-B on *What Is Called Thinking?*.

25 Note this image of ploughing in regard to Heidegger's earlier commentary on Sophocles' image of the violence of the human ploughing of the earth, and of the thoughts of technology and control connected with that.

26 Heidegger elaborates this enframing-homelessness in *Question Concerning Technology*; see chapter 4, below.

27 Later, Heidegger himself says this in *Question Concerning Technology*, 28, 34.

28 On the translation, the translators' note 4 on page 38 discusses how 'the phrase "comes to pass" renders the German verb *sich ereignet* (from *sich ereignen*, to happen or take place)' and connects what Heidegger says on p. 38 and pp. 45–6; also see note 3 just above.

29 Here we see yet another aspect of the passage from the early *Being and Time*, which still strives to overcome metaphysics, to the later 'Time and Being,' where as we have already seen, Heidegger notes that such attempts at overcoming remain within metaphysics; also compare releasement/*Gelassenheit* in Heidegger, 'Memorial Address,' as discussed in chapter 6.

30 Heidegger used the word 'world' already, for example, in 'Origin,' but there it had the usual metaphysical meaning, not the originary sense that appears here.

31 Heidegger thinks these themes originarily in 'The Thing,' see below, chapters 4, 5, and 6.

32 This is 'opposite' what Heidegger says in *Contributions*, sec. 126, that 'gods' are 'not at all' (p. 172). In *Contributions* Heidegger elaborates how the gods are not to be understood as beings and on how they '*do need* be-ing' (which itself also must be thought neither as a being nor as the sum total of beings),

as has happened in the course of metaphysics: 'be-ing "is" *not* a being: It is the not-being and thus, following the ordinary concept, the nothing' (sec. 126, p. 173. See also sec. 259, pp. 308–9; sec. 267, p. 335; sec. 279, p. 357).

Chapter 4

1 Of course, for its own purposes a specialized historical scholarship may wish to treat writings this way; but any thinking through and with Heidegger must accord with his own procedure and that of originary thinking, which though historical, is not historical in the sense which contemporary science or historiography take as their 'concepts.'

2 Though we cannot stop to develop the point here, here Heidegger continues to develop and use various modes of temporality that differ from the metaphysical, philosophical-scientific conception of time as flow and alternatives – a process that began with *Being and Time*'s elaboration of time non-metaphysically, with *Augenblick* understood as *kairos*. Further, in *Being and Time* he already developed a non-linear alternative wherein time was understood as bearing back and forth from future and past into present. So interpreted, the core of our uncompleted projects already lays claim to us and is that toward which we move in the course of our meaningful lives. As the primal nexus of that for which we already care and which claims us (our past), that which remains before us to be completed (our future), and our present moment of responsible choice, time is not reducible to chronology.

3 See, for example, Heidegger's comments in *What Is Called Thinking?*, 11, 31, 39, 41, 44–5, 139–40, 143–4, 150–1; and my *Heidegger's Language and Thinking*, 66–88.

4 On Heidegger and repetition, see Caputo, who analyses Heidegger in light of both Kierkegaard and Derrida with this theme, *Radical Hermeneutics*.

5 Despite the usual misunderstandings about the relation of Heidegger to the rest of the world, he was consistently clear on both the importance of recognizing the legitimacy of other worlds and the reasons for limiting himself to the West – because of his placement and ability, and because of the enormous dangers of moving from one language-world to another: 'no prophetic talents and demeanor are needed to realize that there are in store for planetary building encounters to which participants are by no means equal today. This is equally true of the European and of the East Asiatic languages, and, above all, for the area of a possible conversation between them. Neither of the two is able by itself to open up this area and to establish it' (QB 107). Of course, Heidegger thought out the issues of the 'inescapable' 'encounter of the Eastasian with the European.' He did so in dialogues with Eastern part-

ners, such as Count Kuki, on occasions when 'they made the Eastasian world more luminously present and the danger of our dialogues became more clearly visible,' even while Heidegger was keenly aware that 'here it was I to whom the spirit of the Japanese language remained closed – as it is to this day,' so that, most treacherously, 'the dialogue shifted everything into European.' That is, 'The language of the dialogue constantly destroyed the possibility of saying what the dialogue was about ... If man by virtue of his language dwells within the claim and call of being, then we Europeans presumably dwell in an entirely different house than Eastasian man ... And so, a dialogue from house to house remains nearly impossible ... Nearly. For still it was a dialogue' (DL 2, 3, 5; see also 9–10, 13–14).

That Heidegger was open to and interested in Asian thought is witnessed not only by the record of his enjoyment and persistence in substantial interactions with and learning from Japanese colleagues, but by his familiarity with Taoism and Chinese sources such as the aphorisms of Chuang-tzu, including the perhaps surprising and not–well-known project he initiated in 1946 to collaboratively translate Lao-tzu's *Tao Te Ching* with a Chinese colleague, Paul Shih-yi Hsiao (though the project was not completed, eight chapters were translated in their summer Saturday sessions, as Shih-yi Hsiao related in 'Heidegger and Our Translation,' 93–101). Beyond the extensive bibliography on the Japanese reception already recorded by Hans-Martin Sass in his 1982 *Martin Heidegger*, see, for example, Buchner, ed., *Japan und Heidegger*; on Heidegger's overall relation to Asian thought see especially Parkes, ed., *Heidegger and Asian Thought*; May, *Heidegger's Hidden Sources*; Petzet, *Encounters and Dialogues*; and J.L. Mehta's early comments in *Philosophy of Martin Heidegger*, 248–9, 253, as well as his 'Heidegger and Vedânta,' on the (still unfulfilled) need to attend more to the contribution to understanding Heidegger's thinking that would come by way of Indian thought.

6 In 'Moira' and *What Is Called Thinking?* Heidegger devotes some sections to an analysis of the representational thought of Leibniz, Berkeley, Hegel, and Nietzsche. Though this could be considered here or in the earlier section on homelessness (in this chapter), to follow the story which Heidegger tells these sections of Heidegger's work will be treated in the next section of this chapter, which takes up the passage through metaphysical homelessness – where the justification for doing so will be given.

7 See also *Introduction to Metaphysics* and the Hölderlin essays on *physis* (φύσις) such as WWAF.

8 In the interpretations of fire in the Hölderlin essays and in the story about Heraclitus at the stove in 'Letter on Humanism,' note that fire also means more than 'lighting governance' for Heraclitus. Though the meaning of

hearth is also central, 'Πῦρ names the sacrificial fire, the oven's fire, the campfire, but also the glow of a torch, the scintillation of stars. In "fire" lighting, glowing, belonging, blazing, soft shining hold sway and that which opens an expanse of brightness. In "fire," however, consuming, welding, cauterizing, extinguishing also reign' (Al 117).

9 See also Heidegger's Hölderlin essays where he discusses how the poet thought nature and his own growth in similar terms (for example, RP, A, and HEH).

10 Here Heidegger speaks about the early Greeks and 'the totality,' whereas earlier he had said that originary thinking did not think being as the sum or whole of beings. Apparently the 'totality' of which Heidegger is speaking originally meant something like the un-thought-out more primordial duality, which even before it was thought already slipped back into concealment as being and beings came forward in/as metaphysics. Support for this interpretation would be found in Heidegger's reading of Parmenides; for example, in 'Moira' and *What Is Called Thinking?* as treated below, pp. 256–64, 283–5.

11 Heidegger himself notes that we should compare the ideas here with his *What Is Called Thinking?* 203ff.

12 Note, at this point Heidegger begins to cease saying 'being,' instead increasingly writing 'duality'/'presencing of present.'

13 Recall, too, that language is the house of being, so thinking comes to the neighbourhood of being in language; see 'Letter on Humanism' 199.

14 As is Heidegger's habit, he goes over and over much of what he thinks and says. Clearly he had thought death and mortality, for example, in *Being and Time*; now he goes on to think the themes over originarily via the Greek.

15 Immortals/gods, of course, are not to be understood as persons. Heidegger says that because Logos (λόγος) is the sending/fateful, steering lighting, Heraclitus names 'Lightning' 'as an epithet of Zeus,' understood 'as the highest of gods' and therefore as 'cosmic sending,' though Logos 'is not in its innermost essence ready to appear under the name Zeus, i.e. to appear *as* Zeus' (Lo 72–3). 'The essence of λόγος thus would offer a clue concerning the divinity of the god' (*die Gottheit des Gottes*) (Lo 72 [18]) in presencing: that which gives the presencing of what is present would be degraded to the level of the existing if it was properly named Zeus, for even the highest of the gods is a present being whose presencing is granted from elsewhere (Lo 72–4).

Parmenides, in his long poem, thinks 'Αλήθεια as a goddess, though Heidegger contends that Parmenides neither says 'what the essence of ἀλήθεια *might be rooted in' nor thinks* 'in what sense of divinity ἀλήθεια is a goddess' (M 93). Here Parmenides' words hold a 'mythic experience.' But this is what needs to be understood lest we continue to speak rashly, 'as if we already possessed old and reliable knowledge about the divinity of the Greek gods – as if we were certain that it makes sense here to talk about "persons"' (M 94).

16 See also the end of 'The Turning'; we are called to take our place in belonging with the gods, under the heavens on the earth.

17 Recall that in treating Rilke ('What Are Poets For?,'), Heidegger needed to think beyond the Hölderlin essays, which were still thought from *Being and Time*, that is, which though beginning to be originary were still limited by metaphysical language. Just as Rilke and Hölderlin apparently used the same words, but actually did not do so (insofar as Rilke does and Hölderlin does not think metaphysically), so Heidegger needs to think 'realm' (*Bereich*) metaphysically and then non-representationally/originarily.

18 While focusing on the relationships between the not-yet-metaphysical Greek and metaphysical languages, Heidegger reminds us that we also – first of all, perhaps – live within dialect: 'We are bound to the language of the saying. We are bound to our mother tongue' (AF 19). For his further development of the latter, see chapters 5 and 6.

19 On the translation of 'the being of beings' as 'the presencing of what is present' see note 21 below.

20 For an elaboration of what Heidegger *does* here, see my *Heidegger's Language and Thinking*, especially the section 'The Style of the Thinking and Saying,' 111–46.

21 *Eon emmenai* (εον εμμεναι) is translated by Heidegger as '*das Anwesen des Anwesenden*,' which, in turn, is variously retranslated as the 'being of beings' or 'the presence of the presencing' and 'to "presence" of presencing' (Seidel, *Martin Heidegger* [1961]; as 'the presence of what is present' (Wieck and Gray's translation of *What Is Called Thinking?* [1968]), and 'the presencing of what is present' (Krell and Capuzzi's translation of 'Moira'). I follow Capuzzi's more felicitous 'the presencing of what is present' throughout this volume, changing those words in all English translations utilized.

22 For a fuller discussion of the way *Gestell* names the realm of systems, flows, and modular elements, see 'Taking Responsibility for the Technological Landscape,' chapter 7 of my *Interpretations on Behalf of Place*, 107–31.

23 Joan Stambaugh, in her translation of 'Onto-theo-logical Constitution of Metaphysics,' notes that 'There are three closely related terms in the German text: *begründe* (to account for), *ergründen* (to give the ground), and *gründe* (to ground). In a consultation Heidegger clarified the relation of these terms as follows: '"*Begründen*" has to do with beings and is ontic. "*Ergründen*" belongs to being and is ontological. "*Gründen*" is the relation-

ship of "*begründen*" and "*ergründen*" and encompasses both' (translator's note, OtlCM 57).

24 Heidegger's insight (via the poets) concerning the need to shift from 'inventing' language to learning how to think and say in 'ordinary' language will be developed in chapter 6

25 There is, of course, substantial commentary and disagreement on whether, and how, to translate *Ereignis*. Kenneth Maly and many others use 'enowning'; 'event of appropriation,' or simply 'appropriation,' is used by many; 'disclosing that brings into its own,' 'disclosing coming to pass,' and numerous other alternatives have been tried. Generally I employ whatever version is used in the existing English translation from which I am quoting a given passage; when translating myself, I normally use 'enowning' or leave 'Ereignis' to stand on its own – a good way to allow readers the interpret it as they see best.

26 See my *Heidegger's Language and Thinking*.

27 As we have seen several times, Heidegger already says this in *Being and Time*, which he glosses in 'Letter on Humanism,' 205–10, 217. See the translator's note (BT 5).

28 It is worth noting that David White argues that since 'whenever Heidegger enumerates the four sectors of the fourfold, he refers to the divine (*das Göttliche*),' the now standard English translation by Albert Hofstadter in *Poetry, Language, Thought* (for instance, in 'The Thing') conflates the distinction between the deity and the divine by rendering *die Göttlich*en as divinities: 'Heidegger says that '*Die Göttlich*en *sind die winkenden Boten der Gottheit*' from which it follows that the divine cannot be equivalent with the deity' (White, *Heidegger*, 126, 227n8). Hofstadter, of course, is following the standard approach of considering this dimension of the fourfold, complementary to the mortals, as the immortals – as gods or deities, in line with the rendering already in place, for example, in the early commentary by Vincent Vycinas (*Earth and Gods* [1961]). In any case, given the wide use of the translation, I have not altered Hofstadter's 'divinities' when I cite his translations.

Overall, Heidegger deploys a very elaborate vocabulary and posited relationships for the complex: It is not only a question of how to translate the critical words (for example, in their foreword to *Contributions to Philosophy* Emad and Maly consider '*Gott* and Related Words' in section 11, noting that 'The clue for translating *Gott, Götter, Göttern, göttern,* and *Götterung* ... is found in the word *Götterung*' (xxxv–xxxvi) – though the issue then shifts as to how to translate this key word), but of how to work out the tangle of relationships. These issues will be further considered in chapter 5 (see especially notes 3, 4, 6, and 7).

29 Even after his arrival, Heidegger uses the words 'being' and 'language' to make himself understood and to hold the earlier phases of the journey in thinking and saying. But the new language is clearly different, and the old words are phased out, or at least recede.
30 Of course, here 'corresponds' is not meant in the representational sense of 'correspondence,' where truth is understood in the correctness of correspondence; rather, it has the originary sense developed by Heidegger in the word constellation: say, hear, echo, re-spond, co-respond, attuned, etc.
31 The passages appearing in the English translation do not actually correspond to the German text at this point.
32 The connection can be developed with Western architecture, interpreted as the architecture of presence (the eternal present), via the way lingering, whiling, becomes presence, presence that may outstay its welcome in the allotted space. So the tracing and architecture may also be part of our character, hubris, and way of life in what becomes the series of metaphysical epochs. See my 'Heidegger and Architecture.'
33 In section B of chapter 4 we saw that the presence of what presences is what calls for thinking (e.g., in *What Is Called Thinking?* and sections of 'Dialogue on Language'); from the point of the experience of the arrival of *Ereignis,* however, Heidegger can name that which calls even more primally – as he already hinted was necessary in *What Is Called Thinking?*.
34 My emphasis. 'The Way to Language' was delivered and printed in 1959; twenty-five years before that would have been 1934, the period after which *Contributions* was begun (probably 1932) and just before its 'completion' (1936–7). On this usage and 'the paths to the appropriation' also see the notes in the summary of the seminar on 'Time and Being' (sTB 36).
35 See this chapter, section B; my *Heidegger's Language and Thinking,* chs. 1 and 3.
36 See my *Heidegger's Language and Thinking,* ch. 2.
37 Odysseus has also already quietly arrived home before he confronts the suitors and becomes himself again – the first, an almost unnoticed arrival, then the second, that blossoms forth.
38 Note, some of the lines on p. 112 are oddly translated.

Chapter 5

1 In addition to the distinctive character of this set of works, we can start to see the overall patterns within Heidegger's corpus, altogether the different sets work along a coherent network of pathways. As to this chapter, the fifth set of works is like the second set in that both are close to both the poetic and to

the originary. Further, just as the works treated in chapter 2 present the poetic homecoming which goes beyond the metaphysical homelessness of the works of chapter 1, so too the works and thinking of the poets now being taken up in this chapter go beyond those of the homecoming-wandering through metaphysics to an originary shore, considered in chapter 4. That is, the movement from set 1 → 2 is paralleled in that from 4 → 5. *In short, here we are in the midst of what can be considered a second phase or pulse, a second set of works.*

In terms of the entire body of works, the first and second sets of works generate the third; the fourth is like the first and the fifth is like the second; the fourth and fifth generate the sixth; the sixth is like the third:

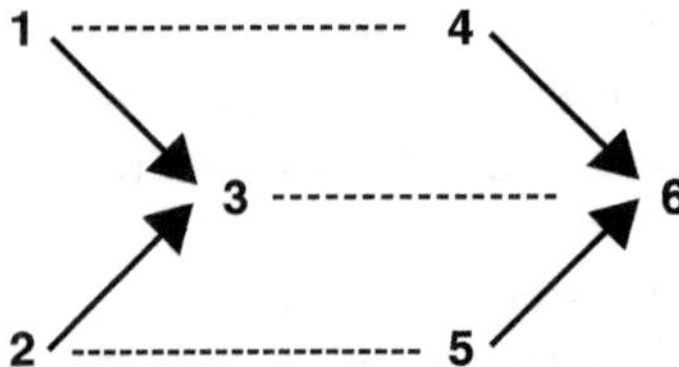

2 Beyond seminally treating this issue in *Being and Time*, from the difference between animals' perishing and the human capacity to die (as being capable of death), in *The Fundamental Concepts of Metaphysics* Heidegger develops the issues in terms of the thesis that 'the animal is poor in world' in contrast to the thesis that 'Man is world-forming,' (respectively, pt 2, chs. 3–5, pp. 186–273, and pt 2, ch. 6, pp. 274–366).

3 Normally Heidegger names the originary fourfold 'earth and sky (heavens), mortals and divinities' (BDT 149), but he also speaks of the divine (*das Göttliche*), divine (*göttlich*), God or god (*der Gott*), the gods (*die Götter*), half-gods/demigods (*Halbgötter*), half-god/demigod (*Halbgott*), godhead (*Gottheit*) (perhaps also translated as divinity), holiness (*Heiligkeit*), and the holy (*das Heilige*). For example, in 'Das Gedicht' (p. 187) he writes: '*Sie kommt aus des "Sphere des Gottes." Das Element des Göttlichen ist das Heilige. Darum sagt Hölderlin im Gesang* "Am Quell der Donau"'). In this regard, though David White may be still too metaphysical (too open to considering the gods as beings, the divine as divine presence, and totality-infinity in an onto-theo-logical sense), his analysis remains helpful where he comments on the lines 'The approach is the complete infinite relation in which earth and heavens belong with God and men [*Das Kommende ist das ganze un-endliche Verhältnis, in das mit dem Gott and mit den Menschen Erde und Himmel gehören*]' (HEH 175): 'God approaches the present within the flux of a past time when the gods were not lacking as

they are now. This is why Heidegger writes "God" and not the usual "the divine," that is, to stress the fact that the reality of the deity in past epochs was distinctly different than the reality of a lacking deity in our epoch' (White, *Heidegger*, 131). In the present chapter we will see Heidegger make special use of God/god (*der Gott*), which seems to occur in response to or as commentary upon the words of the poets, such as those of Trakl and Hölderlin. Note, in the quotations used here (and in related notes) I have left 'God' or 'god' as each translator had rendered *der Gott*.

4 To say that it is 'religious' is not to claim that it is connected with a specific 'religion.' 'Religious' is meant to connote a connection with or experience of the 'holy,' 'heavens,' and 'blue' of which Trakl and Hölderlin speak, not a sect's beliefs and practices much less any onto-theology. Because related terms such as 'sacred' are just as complex without having the benefit of being used by Heidegger and these poets, 'religious' seems the least objectionable term to use.

5 Hence, on occasion, especially when translating 'Hölderlins Erde und Himmel,' I render *Verhältnis* as 'belonging' instead of the more literal 'relation.' Note that using 'relation' parallels what Joan Stambaugh learned from her consultations with Heidegger, when he said that 'collection' was too mechanical to translate *Versammlung*, and that 'gathering' was much better. These are clearly related words and issues, since the operative underlying or 'master' phrase and thought is something such as 'the gathering together of what belongs together.'

6 Here, in commenting on Hölderlin, Heidegger seems to say 'God' and 'gods' for two reasons. First, Hölderlin's poem 'Greece' says 'God': second, Hölderlin and Heidegger probably say God and gods, rather than the divine, to emphasize the homecoming out of the time of darkness and to heighten the distinction between the Greek gods and the god to come: now, from this point, in the coming god, the divine will come. By saying 'god/God' they stress the belonging together of gods and mortals and the arrival of the lacking. This would emphasize the lack of fourfold now and its gathering in/as homecoming and giving prospect of becoming at home, as well as the way the gods and poets are the 'voices of sending': the god comes as 'prophet' – saying before – the divine and fourfold proper.

7 Again, Hölderlin here speaks of gods (*Göttern*) and god (*der Gott*), rather than the divine or divinities.

8 *Armen, heimisch, heimlich* ring together here (HEH 171–5): *armen* means poor, but more originarily needy and indigenous (our English indigenous and indigent together); *heimlich* means concealed, secret, hidden, as well as snug; *heimisch*, of course, means native, indigenous, and domestic and can connote

the secluded. Thus, the secret-homey is native, needy (of the fourfold's coming), and as closing round in coming, secluded into its own coming (consider also disclosure and concealment).

9 See White, *Heidegger*, 130.

10 Consider also Heidegger's interest in and effort to translate related passages from the *I Ching* concerning stilling and clearing muddy water, for example as related by Pezet, *Encounters and Dialogues*, 168–9, 181–3, and Paul Shih-yi Hsiao, 'Heidegger and Our Translation of the Tao Te Ching.'

11 The Greek χάρις is not etymologically related to Latin 'câris' ('charity').

12 See my *Heidegger's Language and Thinking*, ch. 4, pp. 195–247.

13 Heidegger consistently makes this sort of claim; in regard to the national and the political, see his *Hölderlin's Hymn* '*The Ister*,' where he holds that 'The πόλις [polis] cannot be determined 'politically' [*politisch*]. The πόλις [polis], and precisely it, is therefore not a 'political' [*politischer*] concept. This is indeed how things stand, provided that we wish to remain serious in our reflections and follow a clear train of thought' (80 [99]). Or, 'To the πόλις (polis) there belong the gods and the temples, the festivals and games, the governors and council of elders, the people's assembly and the armed forces, the ships and the field marshals, the poets and the thinkers. Yet we are never to think all these according to the civil state [*Kulturstaates*] of the nineteenth century' (82 [101]). In contrast to Heidegger's claim that all this needs to be understood as 'the pre-political [*Vor-politische*] essence of the πόλις [polis]' and not 'according to the fundamental modern form in which the specifically modern, self-framing self-consciousness of human beings orders all beings is the state' – where the latter indeed is the political and thus 'fundamentally different from the way of being' of the originary Greek and what might no-longer-metaphysically come (82 [102], 94), Charles Bambach argues the contrary, that Heidegger's work is political through and through – see the next note. Though Bambach's point is not the same as mine, he admirably develops the political dimension with expertise I do not have, though just as importantly, within a horizon that I am not ready to embrace before first trying patiently to hear what Heidegger says for himself – concerning which, also see the next note.

14 Here we find an important example of the complexity and importance of interpretation and translation. The many dimensions of the debates about Heidegger's relation to National Socialism are inextricably tied up with whether *vaterländische* should be translated originarily as 'native' (as fatherland, connoting native country-land) – as Heidegger contends and as I tend to follow – or as 'patriotic.' Hoeller renders both *patriotischen* (157) and *vaterländisch/Vaterländische* (158–9) as 'patriotic' in his translation of Heidegger's

comments on Hölderlin's 1802 letter to Böhlendorff (Hellingrath V2, pp. 327ff.; GSA VI, no. 240; VI, pp. 1086 ff.) in Heidegger's 'Hölderlin's Earth and Heaven' in *Elucidations of Hölderlin's Poetry* (183–4, 206). Bambach argues, for example in *Heidegger's Roots*, that it is naïve to ignore the charged political senses. There he discusses Heidegger on Böllendorf's letter and considers at length the shift that occurs in the 1942 *Ister* lectures (for these points, see *Heidegger's Roots*, 237–8, 232–6, respectively). One of the principle goals of Bambach's book is to treat the mythic origins of Hölderlin's *vaterländische Umkehr* and Heidegger's part in the 'decidedly political manner' of 'the German retrieval of this Greek myth,' including how 'Heidegger's own simultaneous retrieval and translation of autochthony as *Bodenständigkeit* ... excluded those who were rootless and non-autochthonic' (52; see also 185). Bambach is as explicit as is possible: 'Heidegger did not ... engage with Hölderlin primarily as an emissary of spiritual homecoming or as an envoy of poetic rebirth for the German language. Rather, I would argue, Heidegger's philosophical engagement with Hölderlin was always political. When he deploys the innocent language of "homecoming," "the uncanny," "poetic dwelling," "the hearth," and "commencement," he attempts to carry out his political designs by other means through an encoded discourse that works both as a subtle critique of National Socialism and as an urgent call for the instantiation of a more properly authentic National Socialism' (Bambach, *Heidegger's Roots*, 241).

Jennifer Anna Gosetti-Ferencei, in *Heidegger*, and Robert Bernasconi, in *Heidegger in Question*, also argue that Heidegger's claim about Hölderlin's being other than 'political' is not creditable (a stronger claim than Fred Dallmayr's, in *The Other Heidegger*, that Heidegger confuses Hölderlin's meaning, or Michel Haar's, in *Song of the Earth*, that Heidegger emphasizes the fatherland, rather than the land of the mother, which is more important for Hölderlin (142). Though she inexplicably ignores Bambach's contribution, Gosetti-Ferencei argues, for example, that 'Despite Heidegger's insistence that it is not political, his reading of Hölderlin and Sophocles is ripe with the heroism of nationalist ideology,' which 'obscures Hölderlin's understanding of the Greek of antiquity and of the German' by collapsing the two (180–1, 263–4, 287).

I suppose the idea that Heidegger is using an 'encoded discourse' would be a good basis for explaining why Heidegger means the same thing by both *vaterländisch* and *patriotisch.* Still, Heidegger does use both terms in 'Hölderlins Erde und Himmel,' and given his care in wording it would also be reasonable to contend that he uses the perfectly useful ordinary German word *patriotisch* if or when he means 'patriotic.' This interpretation would also take at its word what Heidegger explicitly says in a footnote to Hölderlins Erde und Himmel' that is the same as what he asserts about the national and the political in *Hölderlin's Hymn 'The Ister'* (as introduced in the previous note). In this note (using Hoellers' translation though leaving in the German rather than any English translation), with the poet's return from a journey in Southern France in mind, Heidegger discusses

> what has been named Hölderlin's 'occidental turn' and what Hölderlin himself, although with a different meaning, considers under the title 'die *vaterländische Umkehr*'. We must, of course, hear Hölderlin's discourse on the '*Vaterländischen*' and the 'national' according to the meaning of his thought, and that means that we must free it from out current narrow representations. The *Vaterländische*' means the relatedness of the land to the father as the supreme God, it means this life-granting 'relation' in which man stands because he has a 'sending.' Likewise, the 'national' means the land of birth (*nacsi, natura*) because it, as the beginning, determines what abides ... The fourth stanza of 'The Rhine' hymn contains an anticipation of the meaning of the names mentioned. Hölderlin's mediation upon 'die *vaterländische Umkehr*' and the 'national' remains outside our present consideration; not only because there is much that is difficult to explain and because the meaning of the whole has not yet been clearly resolved, but because Hölderlin finally left behind him, by overcoming it, that part of his way that he thought through under the title 'die *vaterländische Umkehr*'. Just the fact that this late poem 'Greece' exists – although only in drafts – confirms this for us. (206 [158–9])

As should be clear, my project does not read the leitmotif the way Bambach, Gosetti-Ferencei, and Bernasconi explictly exhort (and with which Hoeller may perhaps agree); rather my goal is to do an open reading-listening to as much of Heidegger's corpus as is possible via the leitmotif as he uses it, and to take with considerable deference the wording he so carefully lays before us, before engaging in the necessary critical scholarship. As to whether that can be done without first moving within the political context is no more possible to answer than is whether one can engage the political context without having attempted to hear what Heidegger says (tells us that he is saying) in his own terms – how he names his world as Paulo Freire would say. As with any enactment of the hermeneutical circle, neither any part nor the whole can be taken as 'entirely first'; rather, the project is to get underway from where one is and keep going from there, in Gadamer's terms, crossing among and fusing horizons. The readings may well come to the same in the end.

15 As Rüdiger Safranski nicely puts it, 'Meßkirch is a small town situated between Lake Constance, the Swabian Alb mountains, and the Upper Danube – a barren, previously poor region along the boundary between Alemannia and Swabia ... Heidegger had something of each in him, and the figures he chose for his patrons were the Alemannic Johann Peter Hebel and the Swabian Friedrich Hölderlin. He saw both as molded by the region while towering great in the world. This was how he also saw himself: he wished to "open up to the vastness of the sky and at the same time be rooted in the dark of the earth,"' (Safranski, *Martin Heidegger*, 3 [citing DM 38]).

Hebel himself locates the homeland of the dialect in the preface to the *Alemannic Poems*: 'The dialect in which these poems are composed might justify their title. This dialect predominates in the corner of the Rhine between the Frick Valley and what was formerly Sundgau, and it is spoken further in many varients down to the Vogesen and the Alps and all across the Black Forest in a large part of the Schwabian region' (cited in HFH 90).

16 *Her-vor-bringen* is variously translated as 'bring forth,' 'first bring forth,' and interestingly is interpreted by Christian Norberg-Schulz (a very sensitive reader of Heidegger's German) through the passages in 'The Origin of the Work of Art' in terms of 'setting-into-work' (*das Ins-Werk-Setzen*) and 'setting-forth' (*her-stellen*) (Norburg-Schulz, *Genius Loci*, 65–6, citing Heidegger, who says '"To set" means here: to bring to a stand' [OWA 36; see also 45, 74]). It seems reasonable to follow Heidegger's two-paths from the Greek via *her-vor-bringen*, so that *physus* is one way of bringing forth and human production another (as setting-forth: *her-stellen*) (see chapter 4-B). As discussed later, in 'Sprache und Heimat' Heidegger develops *her-vor-bringen* as 'bring forth out of hiding, into open disclosure' (SH 42). I often leave it as one of the untranslated words which, as with *Ereignis*, may be the most helpful way of understanding Heidegger.

17 In the explications of Heidegger's meditations on Hebel, dialect, and the homey in the rest of this chapter and the next, I follow the usual convention of using paraphrase when it helps the flow and quotations when the author's specific meaning is important. When I am using my own translations from the German, for paraphrases I simply note the page references, but use quotation marks when I am more precisely translating what he says.

18 As noted in passing in the first pages of chapter 4-B, when considering the leap between metaphysical language and the not-yet-metaphysical early Greek, Heidegger also calls our attention to the importance of dialect: 'We

are bound to the language of the saying. We are bound to our mother tongue' (AF 19).

19 Also connected with the *stimm* family of words is *Bestimmen. Bestimmung,* which normally means something like determine or diagnose, is more appropriately rendered for Heidegger by 'specify,' 'delineate,' or 'articulate,' so as to connote the aspect of choice and judgment, as might occur when one specifies or determines the boundaries of a neighbourhood, city, or region. Also see note 12 to chapter 6.

20 I follow Hofstadter in translating *Gebild* as 'image formed' to properly distinguish it from *Bild* ('The Thinker as Poet,' 7). Of course, while ordinarily *Bild* means picture or image or representation and *bilden,* 'to form, fashion, or shape,' as well as 'to compose, educate, or cultivate,' the contrast with *Gebild* (formation, form, figure) does not always help in following Heidegger. The question, '*Was kommt nun im Gebild des Gedichtes* "Der Sommerabend" *ins Bild?,*' contains all the terms, so their relation can be seen in the question about 'what comes in the formation (image formed) of the poem into focus/image' (SH 42).

21 Commenting on the final stanza of 'Summer Evening,' Heidegger moves from Hebel's *drum – darum* (for that reason) – treating why mortals must ask God for a 'good night,' to saying that the setting sun finds the quiet of the night and goes nearer the silent (or hushed, or peaceful) spirits (*den stillen Geisten*) (SH 46). Silent spirits are not, of course, necessarily the same as the more usual *Göttlichen,* divinities. Heidegger goes on in the next paragraph to speak of '*Menschen auf die Erde unter dem Himmel,*' noting that with such we do not yet have the entire formation (*Gebild*), but that Hebel himself barely says anything more. Heidegger boldly adds, however, that the mysterious, so to say, speaks between the lines of all that is said – speaks with the voice of those whom Hebel names the silent spirits, those who, along with the other three dimensions, compose the unified world that comes to appearance in the poem (SH 46–7). Without explanation, Heidegger stops speaking about the silent spirits, reverting on the last page of the essay to the usual fourfold: '*die Sterblichen auf der Erde unter dem Himmel vor den Göttlichen wohnen*' (SH 50) – the figure of the silent ones returns in 'Heimatfest beim Todtnauberg,' covered in the next chapter.

22 One of reviewers of this book manuscript disagreed with the degree of this positive assessment, on the grounds that Hebel's poetry is not very good. Certainly what I say would not make sense if judged in terms of traditional philosophy or aesthetics, since Hebel's poetry is not among the world's 'greatest' poetry. Whether the reviewer, who indeed did appreciate and

approach the issue from the viewpoint of originary thinking, is correct is for the reader to decide.

23 This can be compared to the analysis of the development of clock time in *Being and Time*, as covered in chapter 1.

24 Of course, Hölderlin is especially famous for his river poems. For another dimension of Heidegger's analysis of Hölderlin's river poems, focusing on journey and dwelling, see Skocz, 'Of Time and the River.'

Chapter 6

1 'The Origin of the Work of Art' has complex movements, as a result not only of the stopping and restarting through its theme eight times, but also of the diversity of styles of language/thinking that are woven together. A close analysis of the three modes of language shows that the essay is complexly constituted as follows in terms of modes of thinking and saying: straightforward, then two track; high originary, then two track; high originary, then two track; and high-originary, then straightforward.

2 In 'The Origin,' Heidegger is working out the 'different levels of knowledge' involved, and their differences, not from any reduction to a 'mere' or 'private experience,' where knowing as preserving is 'far removed from merely aestheticizing connoisseurship of the work's formal aspects' and 'the sphere of familiarity' that together capture works into 'the art business.' Even so, he still thinks knowing and willing together in the language of *Being and Time*, a problem for him later as he reconsiders matters in light of his own fuller insight that his efforts in *Being and Time* remained still metaphysical-representational (OWA 67–8). Hence, as noted above, his return in 1959 to rethink setting-into-work in language other than that of the misleading 'willing.' As also noted, such technical points, no matter how important in themselves, need not be taken up as part of our work and pathway; here, it is enough to appreciate the fact that he has managed an initial measure of originary understanding and then to follow that and how he proceeds, by using the figure of home and the play of the familiar and strange.

3 '*Die Stiftung ist ein Überfluß, eine Schenkung*' (OWA 62). We will return to the importance of preserving (*der Bewahrung*) when we take up two great themes – questions – that Heidegger defers until 'Building Dwelling Thinking' and 'Art and Space': things as places and the gathering that preserves.

4 This develops what Heidegger said in *Being and Time*, and that we covered in chapter 1, about being 'at home,' tranquilized in the familiar, where we are oblivious to how strange and question-worthy it is. More than ten years later

he continues to ponder whether 'another sojourn [*Aufenthalt*] might be granted to us'; 'Or, whether the technological world of science and industry would not, quickly and surely, manufacture growing possibilities, which have the consequence that the modern man feels everywhere at home [*zuhause*]? Thanks to that, the discussion about homeless-ness [*Heimatlosigkeit*] would have been proven a lie, branding it as the escape of an empty romanticism. What if, then, this groundless "home-ness" [*bodenlose … Zuhause*], secured only by means of technology and industry, abandons every claim to a home [*auf Heimat*] by being contented with the desert-like expansion of traveling?' (S 36–7 [22–3]).

5 The translator uses 'location' here, but to try to more appropriately convey the meaning in the complex of words and to be consistent across several articles, I use 'place.'

6 In addition to consistently investigating matters in a non-humanistic, non-anthropocentric manner, while still recognizing the distinctness of humans, Heidegger develops the dual dynamic in which things not only bring about world and world occurs as the horizon within which things might be things but also, and simultaneously with the fourfold, come to their own as in and through world: 'Men alone, as mortals, by dwelling, attain to the world as world. Only what conjoins itself out of world becomes a thing' (T 182).

7 Clearly, Heidegger develops 'region' from the early treatment in *Being and Time*. Perhaps somewhat surprisingly, he does not use the words *Gegend* or *Gegnet* in 'Building Dwelling Thinking'; it appears only once in 'The Thing,' and there only with a more general sense: 'If we think of the thing as thing, then we spare and protect the thing's presence in the region from which it presences' (T 181). There are more uses of the term in his reflections on language and poetry, as we have seen in chapter 5 (for example, there we saw the term used in 'Dialogue on Language,' 3, 37, 49; 'Language in the Poem,' 193, 195; 'The Nature of Language,' 69–70, 99–100, 104, 107; 'Hebel – Friend of the House,' 90; and 'Sprache und Heimat,' 29, 50). Heidegger, of course, also speaks of region by way of *Bereich*, for example with Hebel: '*offende Bereich*' (SH 42; see also 29); many other uses of related terms, such as references to administrative units such as counties (SH 8), are not so interesting in regard to our issues, though they do relate to the administrative dimension and skill of Abrahim a Santa Clara.

8 Compare this with *Being and Time*, for example, pp. 102–3, 111.

9 This correlates with translating *Wesen* as 'essential sway,' as commended by the translators of *Contributions to Philosophy* (*From Enowning*) in their forward, pp. xxiv–xxvi.

10 Though we cannot treat it here, the fusion of movement and rest takes up

one of the oldest and most primal issues concerning the basic principle (*arche*) of the cosmos, and though Heidegger would not go Aristotle's way, here he clearly seems to evoke the unmoved mover. The tension is clearly seen if we simply 'parse' the lines in terms of movement and rest. The teacher says, 'The region gathers [naming some originary 'movement'], just as if nothing were happening [*nichts ereigene*, itself combining 'nothing' with what is usually understood to name the core unfolding or primal source of what happens], each to each and each to all into an abiding [*in das Verweilen*], while resting [*Beruhen*] in itself [a double stillness, in itself no less]. Regioning is a gathering and a re-sheltering [*das versammelnde Zurückbergen* – again, an original event of world disclosure] for an extended resting in an abiding [*weiten Beruhen in der Weile* – again, a double staying-stillness]' (CCP 66 [39–40]). At the heart of what might help us understand the unfolding of the historical epochs of world, we hear about that dynamic, but as coming from and remaining at rest. Is this somehow thinking the not-yet-metaphysical or a reference to the earliest and founding metaphysical way of thinking?

11 For example, Heidegger variously reflects on how it is that the unity – oneness – of the fourfold is the fouring, and in that sense on the unitary realm out of which all comes (T 173 [46], 179 [52], and 180; BDT 149–51).

12 It is not really helpful to follow the translations of *bestimmen* or *bedingnis* as 'determine' because determine in English carries the sense of determinism, especially that of materialistic, naturalistic scientific explanation, which of course is quite the opposite of what Heidegger would convey. That meaning of determine would be carried by *Determinismus* in German. *Bedingung setzen* and *bestimmen* are more appropriately thought of by way of 'specify.' If this is understood, then we could use the English 'determine' in the sense of 'decide,' since that would convey the assumption that choices exist (as with *entscheiden/ung*); similarly it would be acceptable to speak of determining insofar as that would mean setting forth specifically.

The importance of thinking of specifying (not determining) becomes even clearer later where Heidegger uses *bedingen* to speak about the boundary around the polis. It is not that the polis needs to be (deterministically) this or that size, to have this or that shape, but that it be given bounds and differences that it might become a polis, both set into and off from the surrounding landscape (not to mention the more primal dimension of ordering the chaos). Each thing would be so specified, delineated, articulated, or rendered definite – each in its own way: temple and church, city and village, meadow and woodlot, research laboratory and hospital. Heidegger explicitly says such when he explains, for example, how rural villagers need to 'draw the boundaries [*ihre außergewöhnliche Bestimmung*] between themselves and life in the large cites and the gigantic areas of modern industrial complexes ... First, we must recognize alienation, recognize where it is active and determinative [*bestimmt*]' (700YM 234 [576]). Though the word is used in 'Sprache und Heimat' (SH 28), the appropriateness of rendering *bestimmen* as 'setting forth specifically' or 'rendering definite' can be seen in passages related to the setting into work of the belonging together of the fourfold in 'The Thing.' As two simple examples, consider the following texts: 'The presence of something present such as the jug comes into its own, appropriatively manifests and determines itself, only from the thinging of the thing' ('*Aus dem Dingen des Dinges ereignet sich und bestimmt sich auch erst das Anwesen des Anwesenden von der Art des Kruges*') (T 177; see also G 50), and 'we are bethinged – we spare and protect' (T 181). As we considered in chapter 5, there the thing and the four are thought in terms of 'proper jointure' (consider *Fug* and *Bezug*), which on a world-cosmic plane not only echoes 'the fateful' (*dike*), but the sense of *stimmen* as musical tuning and social-political voicing earlier noted in relation to *stamm* (see note number 19 to chapter 5).

13 'Allowing' here connotes that it happened as in the manner of a gratuitous act by a superior. Note that this language echoes much of that in the 'Dialogue on Language' with the Japanese colleague.

14 It remains to think through the relation of nothingness, the void, and death, for example, the way in which the jug's void might be homologous to 'Death (as) the shrine of Nothing' (T 178); compare that last phrase and Heidegger's characterization of Hölderlin's poetry (also considered here) as 'like a shrine without a temple' (RP 234).

15 As noted in the last chapter, in the case of this and the other yet untranslated essays of this section (such as 'Über Abrahim a Santa Clara,' 1964, 'Dankansprache am 26 September 1969 in Meßkirch,' 'Festansprache beim Heimatfest in Todtnauberg,' 'Vom Geheimnis des Glockenturms,' 'Statt einer Rede,' 'Verlust der Heimat,' 'Ein Wort des Dankes'), when I translate intending to pass on the precise wording or tone, I use quotation marks; however, I also regularly paraphrase sections of what Heidegger says in order to make the relevant points while letting the narrative flow. These paraphrases are not at all meant to be as serious as full translations, but to convey what Heidegger is remembering and saying without a tangle of quotation marks over this or that phrase, this or that sentence. In fact, I often do the same when using the English translations to tell the tale: though I do use quotation marks to indicate translated words, often I convey the general movement of the essay by paraphrase. Thus, unless otherwise noted or clear

from context, what is 'told' in these sections, which I then explicate, is a loose rendering of Heidegger's own words.

16 There are two English translations of 'Der Feldweg'; I utilize the one in each case that seems most illuminating. Both titled 'The Pathway,' they can be easily distinguished by the pagination: Thomas F. O'Meara's runs from page 88 to 91, while Thomas Sheehan's revision of O'Meara's translation runs from page 69 to 71.

17 In addition to Hugo Ott's account (*Martin Heidegger*, 129), a recent field trip and interviews by Adam Scharr provide interesting details (as well as a summary of what else has been written about the house). The description of the construction and the inscription are from Scharr, 'Professor's House,' 130–42. A longer version has now appeared: Sharr, *Heidegger's Hut* (2006).

18 From a description by Elfride Heidegger of how the house might be experienced by a visitor, translated in Petzet, *Encounters and Dialogues*, 186–7.

19 Of the many versions of this talk on Hebel, this one is perhaps the most complex and subtle and thus deserves more discussion than I can provide here.

20 Note the parallels between this description and that Hebel gave of his Wiesental village.

21 Heidegger refers to his 'Zur Heimatuniversität' in a 1951 letter to the Minister of Culture and Education, 'Zur Heimatuniversität in das gemäße Verhältnis.' In *Reden und andere Zeugnisse*, item 214, 477.

22 Ott, *Martin Heidegger* (1993), 312–17, 349–50, on the family house; 317, 364, on Heidegger's position and the subtleties of emeritus status.

23 My contention is simply that Heidegger is passing on the lessons of Abrahim a Santa Clara to his audience and thus helping to preserve local tradition and values; this does not ignore that what Heidegger originarily means by releasement from subjectivistic or objectivistic dimensions of a metaphysical world would differ from any positing of a transcendent realm of 'eternity' or the soul (though here Heidegger does not take up the issue of Abrahim a Santa Clara's relationship to onto-theo-logy). As Heidegger says in the epilogue to 'The Thing,' 'Thinking is perhaps, after all, an unavoidable path, which refuses to be a path of salvation and brings no new wisdom. The path is at most a field path, a path across fields, which does not just speak of renunciation but already has renounced, namely, renounced the claim to a binding doctrine and a valid cultural achievement or a deed of the spirit' (T 185).

24 On the details concerning the street, see 'Ein Wort des Dankes,' 35, and Ôhashi, 'Erinnerungen an Fritz Heidegger,' 203–6.

25 Petzet, *Encounters and Dialogues*, 199, 212–13, who says that among the many

gifts that Fritz gave to his brother is that he 'kept their native home for him all his life' (212); Safranski, *Martin Heidegger*, 428.

26 For reference to other works in the corpus treating *Gegend* and *Gegnet*, see note 7, above.

27 Recent books covering Heidegger's family life portray the lively humour of his brother Fritz, such as Zimmerman, *Martin und Fritz Heidegger*; some of his interactions with his parents (and the family history) are covered there and in Buchin and Denker, *Martin Heidegger und seine Heimat* (2005), as well as in the letters to Elfride (along with much else of course) which benefit extensively from the commentary of their granddaughter, Gertrud Heidegger (who now lives in the Heidegger Freiburg house), *Mein liebes Seelchen*. Interestingly, in these recent, fresh works, almost no mention is made of Heidegger's sister Marie, but on this topic, see my forthcoming, 'Marie Heidegger-Oschwald.'

28 Again, the reading here (which is first trying to hear, in his own terms, what Heidegger is saying) requires the parallel political reading and critique. As we know, and I have begun to discuss in notes 13 and 14 to chapter 5, Heidegger's interest in the peasant world and rootedness can be read in light of his connections to National Socialism – a point already made in 1964 by Adorno in *The Jargon of Authenticity* and since then developed by many others (from the huge and still-growing literature, see, for example, Milchman and Rosenberg, ed., *Martin Heidegger and the Holocaust*).

29 Letters to Jaspers, 24 July and 23 September 1925 and 24 April and 4 October 1926, cited in Ott, *Martin Heidegger*, 125, 351; and Safranski, *Martin Heidegger*, 129, 142–3. The hut and activities there are covered, for example, by Petzet, *Encounters and Dialogues*, 97, 190–6, 199, 202.

30 Some time before moving to Marburg, Heidegger purchased a small plot of land in Todtnauberg, where he had a modest cabin built. He took no part in the operation himself. Elfride organized and supervised everything. (Safranski, *Martin Heidegger*, 129.)

31 It seems reasonable to think that at this event, by engaging his audience in an especially intimate manner that includes deploying an exceptional sense of humour, Heidegger was coming as close as he could to enacting a belonging-together by emulating his brother Fritz, who remained 'a local' in Meßkirch his entire life and was renowned as a master of ceremonies and speech-maker – though, of course, Heidegger's own personal style of originary thinking/saying also operates, especially at the end of the talk. On Fritz's character, see the nice biographical work by Zimmerman, *Martin und Fritz Heidegger*.

32 Heidegger does not acknowledge the fact that apparently Elfride took com-

plete responsibility for overseeing the building of the cabin (as she did for all but the details of the study in the Freiburg residence and for the retirement house on the back of the lot, Fillibachstrasse 24), but see Safranski, *Martin Heidegger,* 129; Scharr, 'The Professor's House,' 132; Petzet, *Encounters and Dialogues,* 182. Scharr's article and book (*Heidegger's Hut*) contain a photos of the Todtnauberg cabin and a model he made of it; photos of both the Rötebuck house and the cabin can also be found in Gertrude Heidegger's edited collection of Heidegger's letters to Elfride, and in Marcovicz's album of photos (*Martin Heidegger, Photos,* 23).

33 Petzet, *Encounters and Dialogues,* 199.

34 As Oscar Handlin empirically discovered, in the following, about the difference between villagers' perceptions and the historical record, confirming Max Beloff's observation about the 'tendency to exaggerate "the stability and continuity" of that society': 'Here were the records and it turned out that no family had been there from time immemorial ... And that evidence conformed to the larger European pattern, which showed frequent thrusts to all the marches and a steady eastward drift of peasant population through the centuries. Yet the impression of sameness was not merely the product of distortion through the observer's eye. Nor did it spring simply from the romantic fancies of folklorists. The villagers themselves believed that they had always been there, always worn the same costumes, made the same lace, sung the same music and danced the same figures. That belief was not evidence that they and their ancestors had actually done so, but it was evidence that the community possessed institutional devices for absorbing the effects of change and preserving stability over very long periods' (in 'Encounters with Evidence,' a chapter added in 1972 to a new edition of Handlin, *Uprooted,* 308–9, and citing in passing Max Beloff, 'The Uprooted,' *Encounter* 1 [December 1953], 78).

35 This is the translation altered by Sheehan, not the original by O'Meara, which would be page 89.

36 Translator's note to 'Pathway,' 72.

37 This explanation is provided in a note by O'Meara, passing on what Heidegger explains, 'Pathway,' 90.

38 Heidegger reflects on the experience from the other side when writing about his first trip to Greece (made in 1962 when he was in his seventies), explaining how, though at first he became more and more perplexed, finally the place itself (aided by the friendly reception of the inhabitants) did give him the gift of opening up a bit of what Greece means (S 22). Practising two-track thinking, he says 'It never crossed my mind, during the journey, to question the usefulness and the pleasure of such (tourist) trips to Greece.

Neither, though, did the thought leave my mind that what matters is not us and our experiences of Greece, but Greece itself' (S 9). He reports that what he most deeply seeks – 'what is originarily [*anfänglisch*] Greek,' that is, 'its proper character' and 'that which determined the world of Greece in its proper character [which] remains concealed' – though only gradually and for a bit – nonetheless becomes disclosed (S 8). He sees something of what mountain and temple open (in a way that 'fulfils' what he has written in 'The Origin of the Work of Art' more than twenty-five years earlier): 'The wide floor of the valley, where the lone village of Nemea is nestled, is surrounded by terraced slopes, flocks of sheep stroll leisurely through the pastures. The entire region itself appears as a single stadium that invites festival games. Only three columns are left standing that still speak of the temple of Zeus that once was: in the breadth of the landscape they are like three strings of an invisible lyre on which perhaps the winds play songs of mourning, inaudible to mortals – echoes of the flight of the gods' (S 20).

We can follow the way Heidegger works to digest and articulate the core of what he has been given, for example as he describes his impression of the temple of Poseidon in Cape Sounion in almost the same words (S 42–3). Not surprisingly, the climax of the visit appears to happen at Delphi, after keen expectation, and then passing through the gauntlet of tourist hotels:

> By the time we reached the Castalian spring a shimmer of sacredness had again fallen over the place. Where did it come from?
>
> Not from the ruins of the temples, the treasures and buildings that stretched high along the hillside, but from the greatness of the region itself. The Phaedriades, the shining and gloaming ones, although at that time of the day had hidden their light; nevertheless the steep slopes of the ragged rocks and the cleavage of the dark gorge between them, in unison with the somber depth of the great valley of Pleistus surpassed any human work.
>
> Under the lofty sky, in the clear air of which the eagle, Zeus' bird, was flying in circles, the region [*die Gegend*] revealed itself as the temple of this place [*Ortschaft*]. The place itself before anything else unveiled for the mortals the hidden mystery of this location where it was allowed to erect their dedication. (S 51)

39 The gathering, and complex intertwining, of these dimensions was already underway from the beginning. For example, in that it wasn't very quiet when the whole family was at the cabin, Heidegger rented a room from some neighbours, the Brenders, and in their farmhouse, just down below, wrote *Being and Time* (*Mein liebes Seelchen*, 145).

Afterword

1 As stressed in the main text, though Heidegger continues to use the term 'essence,' he shifts its meaning away from the traditional sense of 'fundamental and unvarying features that "define" something as what it is.' (It needs to be noted, however, that all too many theorists fail to see that rejecting 'essentials' by referring to this [just cited] typical wording and 'correct' concept is rather misleading. For example, so taking 'essential' to connote the 'universal and frozen' is also inadequate to account for Aristotle's sophisticated theory, which certainly recognized differences and variations over against the univocal and that proceeded substantially by analogy.)
In any case, to say in Heidegger's more subtle sense that we can begin to understand, for instance, mortals becoming mortals in their capacity to say and think (their manner of holding sway and as a site of disclosure) is to propose the phenomena as dynamic, open, and unfolding via discontinuous historical-epochal disclosures. (Here what is 'essential' unfolds and thus changes over time, an understanding that is also critical to and used by Foucault.)

2 Skocz, 'Of Time and the River,' 303.

3 The burgeoning field of ecological and built-environment literature (including feminist reflections) and studies of the sense of place and identity make substantial use of, and in return add, insights to those of Heidegger's work on place, earth, and dwelling. To note just a few of the most important locations, in addition to the specific Deep Ecology movement associated with Arne Naess there is the International Association for Environmental Philosophy and its journal *Environmental Philosophy*. For the literature, see my *Dwelling, Place, Environment* (co-edited with David Seamon); and my *Interpretations on Behalf of Place*; *Environmental Interpretations*; and 'Deleuze and Guattari's Return to Science.' For examples of studies of the sense of place, see Kirkpatrick Sale's *Dwellers in the Land*; David L. Barnhill's *At Home on the Earth*. For feminist engagement with an ethics of place and ecology that significantly considers home and homelessness, as well as Heidegger, see especially Bigwood, *Earth Muse* (1993).

4 In classical terms, Aristotle similarly speaks of habitual action and virtue; in contemporary theories, the focus on disposition is prominent in the (feminist) ethic of care. See Mugerauer and Manzo, *Environmental Dilemmas*, 150–8.

5 There are some important differences between self-organization theory (such as Maturana and Varela's) and phenomenology on the issues of wholeness and identity, where a fruitful line of investigation is proceeding.

See my 'Deleuze and Guattari's Return to Science.' The motif is central, even to the new sciences of self-organization, as well as to ecological and sense-of-place studies; see Stanley Kaufman's *At Home in the Universe.*

6 See Mugerauer, 'The City.'

7 On these and other examples of successful designs and planning see ibid., and *Interpretations on Behalf of Place,* 107–50, 162–86.

8 This case is very nicely described and interpreted in Doevendans and Schram, 'Phenomenologies of Liquidity.'

9 These three modes by which meaning may enter our lives are specified in Frankl, *Doctor and the Soul,* a work compatible with Heidegger's.

10 Important contemporary attempts to work through the loss and recovery of home in literature include V.S. Naipaul's *Enigma of Arrival*; W.G. Sebald's *Austerlitz* and *Unheimliche Heimat*; N. Scott Momaday's *House Made of Dawn*; Fabiola Cabeza de Baca's *We Fed Them Cactus*; Aimé Césaire's *Notebook of a Return*; Ralph Ellison's *Invisible Man*; Ivan Doig's *This House of Sky* – and in film, Tvardarsky's *Nostalgia*; Marguerite Duras' *Nathalie Granger* and *La femme du Gange*; Satyajit Ray's *World of Apu*; Akira Kurosawa's *Ikiru*; Raúl Ruiz's *Dialogue d'éxilés.*

Post-modern analyses of globalization focus on mass displacement, diaspora, exile, emigration, and immigration: Becky Thompson and Sangeeta Tyagi's *Names We Call Home*; Wendy Walters' *At Home in Diaspora*; Li Zhang's *Strangers in the City*; M. Jackson's chronicle of the life of the nomadic Walpiri in the Tanami Desert of Australia in *At Home in the World*; memories of East Bengali native villages first appearing as a newspaper serial and later a book *Chhere asha gram* (*The Abandoned Village*) edited by Dakshinaranjan Basu; and Arjun Appadurai's 'The Production of Locality,' 178–99. (On Basu's work see Chakrabarty, 'Memories of Displacement,' 115–37.)

Post-colonial studies of transnational literature and media are appearing in rapid succession: Rosemary Marangoly George's *Politics of Home*; Arnold M. Eisen's *Galut*; Hamid Naficy's *Making of Exile Cultures* and *Making Films with an Accent*; and the journal *Diaspora,* edited by Kachig Tölöyan. (Hence, as I have argued elsewhere, the importance of and interest in the nomadic, since nomads are 'at home,' that is, belong in coherent social and natural patterns and rhythms without being settled or rooted in one place. Heidegger tends to conflate being rooted and being at home, thus failing to fully deploy his major insights into the continual, final force of 'staying underway'; see my *Interpretations on Behalf of Place,* 99.)

11 As we saw in the works covered in chapter 5 (especially those treating region-*Gegend*), Heidegger refuses to privilege one region over another, much less to support any sort of universalization (nationalism or globalization).

He affirms the importance of differences and relations at a local scale (for example, among Swabia, the Black Forest, Alemannia, and the Wiesental) and among more distant regions (Central Germany, East Prussia, Silesia, Bohemia). Similarly, though there remains the stubborn misconception that Heidegger's positive view of the Greek world or the West is chauvinistic, as we heard in chapter 4-C, he repeatedly says that he speaks of the origins of his world (also that of today's post-colonial global technology), the world which he might be capable of knowing. His actions and what he says show that he clearly respects Asian worlds, though, despite his partially successful efforts at dialogue with the Japanese, Indian, and Chinese traditions and colleagues a truly genuine conversation across languages-worlds has not taken place, and finally may not be possible. Perhaps even if such were successful, the greater danger would arise that in our supposed comprehension, the strange would not be let stay as strange and the different sources would not be kept back and sheltered as sources.

12 The reflections on animal and human life and the increasingly influential development and application of the Greek concepts of political life (*zoē*) and bare life (*bios*) to phenomena such as 'the camp' by Giorgio Agemben are of the first importance here, as is his recovery of the contributions of Hanna Arendt – both working in a Heideggerian vein. See his *Home Sacer* and *The Open*; Arendt, *Human Condition.* And as cited in note 3 of the preface, Badiou, *Saint Paul*, Laclau, *Elusive Universality*, and Cheah, *Spectral Nationality*, struggle with the issue of a post-Enlightenment need to come to terms with the absence of a basis to affirm human rights – from positions that I believe provide far less promise than Heidegger's. A case of the current environmental-political crises that stimulate such a search is compellingly described by Anna Tsing, *Friction*, in an account of the devastation of the rainforests of Indonesia.

13 Mugerauer, 'Theories of Sustainability.' The core of this argument is drawn from Ronald and Joan Gibb Engel's introduction to their wonderful book, *Ethics of Environment and Development.*

14 On the way organisms became 'empty' and thus 'irrelevant' since they have been seen as merely the vehicles for genes that use the former for their continuation/survival, and on how in turn genes became DNA, see Rose, *Lifelines*; Levins and Lewontin, *Dialectical Biologist*; Oyama, *Ontogeny of Information.* On the metaphorical and then literal understanding of biology and bioinformatics, see Kay, *Who Wrote the Book of Life?*; and Thacker, *Biomedia.*

15 Also relevant, but not included in our analysis of homelessness, are Heidegger's contentions that 'the stone is worldless, the animal is poor in world, and mankind is world-forming'; *Fundamental Concepts of Metaphysics,*

176; see all of chs. 2–6 of Part Two.

16 See Mugerauer, 'New Type of Medical Tourism'; Waldby and Mitchell, *Tissue Economies*; Goodwin, *Black Markets*; Scheper-Huges, 'Last Commodity.'

17 Note, the leading contender to answer the question, 'What comes after the subject?,' appears to be the 'gifted,' an approach especially developed by Jean-Luc Marion, whose work closely follows from Husserl's and Heidegger's. See Marion, *Being Given*; Mugerauer, 'Double Gift'; and 'Call of the Earth.'

18 See note 15, above, on the animal as world-poor; also important, but not treated in this book, is Heidegger's early treatment in *Being and Time* of 'being-toward-death' and scholarly study of how he modifies the idea during the course of his life. See Leman-Stefanovic, *Event of Death*.

19 As Luc Ferry points out, though secularization has all but ended the dominance of the great religions and wisdom traditions in preparing human beings for death, leaving the believer 'time to make peace with oneself and to commend one's soul to God,' we have not 'invented anything that can acceptably take their place' (*Man Made God*, 2–3). Additionally, the notion of there being 'a time to move on' would apply to the trauma of displacement, specifically to questions of when it is healthy, necessary, or otherwise appropriate to let go of the lost homeland and pass over without reserve into the new.

20 Here I have not treated divinity, because it is simply too complex and unsettled a topic, in addition to involving the difficulty of being clear on what Heidegger says. Many scientists and Marxists see the need to insist on the falsity of the idea of divinity or gods of any kind. But the bulk of humanity has believed in diverse sorts of divine forces since time immemorial (the current return to fundamentalism aside). Of course, the impact of various religions' beliefs also clearly is a source of conflict and pain in regard to our questions of what an individual should do, how we should respond to the environment, how to treat 'outsiders,' and how to comport ourselves in life and the issues of biomedical technology, from artificial inception, to cloning, to genetic engineering. The conflicts resulting from differences in views of divinity, occurring in any one place or in practices spread across other regions, make this a critical topic, but one beyond the scope of this afterword.

Bibliography

Works by Heidegger

Addendum to 'The Origin of the Work of Art.' In *Poetry, Language, Thought.*

'Age of the World Picture.' In *Question Concerning Technology.*

'Aletheia (Heraklit, Fragment 16).' In *Vorträge und Aufsätze.*

'The Anaximander Fragment.' In *Early Greek Thinking.*

'Andenken.' In *Erläuterungen zu Hölderlins Dichtung.*

Ansprachen zum 80 Geburtstag (am 26. September 1969 in Meßkirch).

'Art and Space.' Trans. Charles H. Seibert. *Man and World* 6, no. 1 (1973): 3–8.

Aufenthalte. Frankfurt am Main: Vittorio Klostermann, 1989.

'Aus einem Gesprach von der Sprache.' In *Unterwegs zur Sprache.*

Basic Problems of Phenomenology. Trans. Albert Hofstadter. Bloomington: Indiana University Press, 1982.

Basic Writings. Ed. David F. Krell. New York: Harper and Row, 1977.

'Bauen Wohnen Denken.' In *Vorträge und Aufsätze.*

Being and Time. Trans. Joan Stambaugh. Albany: SUNY Press, 1996.

'Brief über den "Humanismus."' In *Wegmarken.*

'Building Dwelling Thinking.' In *Poetry, Language, Thought.*

Contributions to Philosophy (From Enowning). Trans. Parvis Emad and Kenneth Maly. Bloomington: Indiana University Press, 1999.

'Conversation with Martin Heidegger.' In *Piety of Thinking.*

'Conversation on a Country Path.' In *Discourse on Thinking.*

'Dank an die Heimatstadt Meßkirch (27. September 1959).' In *Reden und andere Zeugnisse,* item 231. Originally 'Ein Wort des Dankes,' in *Zum 80. Geburtstag.*

'Dank bei der Verleihung des staatlichen Hebelgedenkpreises (10. Mai 1960).' In *Reden und andere Zeugnisse,* item 234.

'Dankansprache am 26 September 1969 in Meßkirch.' In *Ansprachen zum 80. Geburtstag.* Reprinted in *Reden und andere Zeugnisse,* item 263.

Denkerfahrungen, 1910–1976. Ed. Hermann Heidegger. Frankfurt am Main: Vittorio Klostermann, 1983.

'A Dialogue on Language.' In *On the Way to Language.*

'... dichterisch wohnet der Mensch ...' In *Vorträge und Aufsätze.*

'Das Ding.' In *Vorträge und Aufsätze.*

Discourse on Thinking. Trans. J.M. Anderson and E.H. Freund. New York: Harper and Row, 1966.

Early Greek Thinking. Trans. David F. Krell and Frank Capuzzi. New York: Harper and Row, 1975.

'Einleitung zu "Was ist Metaphysik?"' In *Wegmarken.*

Elucidations of Hölderlin's Poetry. Trans. Keith Hoeller. Amherst, NY: Humanity Books, 2000.

The End of Philosophy. Trans. Joan Stambaugh. New York: Harper and Row, 1973.

'The End of Philosophy and the Task of Thinking.' In *On Time and Being.*

'Das Ende der Philosophie und die Aufgabe des Denkens.' 1966. In *Zur Sache des Denkens.*

Erläuterungen zu Hölderlins Dichtung. 4th ed. Frankfurt am Main: Vittorio Klostermann, 1971.

Existence and Being. Trans. D. Scott, ed. Werner Brock. Chicago: Regnery Gateway, 1968.

'Der Feldweg.' In *Denkerfahrungen.*

'Festansprache beim Heimatfest in Todtnauberg.' In *Reden und andere Zeugnisse.*

Four Seminars. Trans. Andrew Mitchell and François Raffoul. Bloomington: Indiana University Press, 2003.

The Fundamental Concepts of Metaphysics. Trans. William McNeill and Nicholas Walker. Bloomington: Indiana University Press, 1995.

'Das Gedicht.' In *Erläuterungen zu Hölderlins Dichtung.*

Gelassenheit. 3rd ed. Pfullingen: Günther Neske, 1969.

'Gelassenheit.' In *Gelassenheit.*

'Hebel – Friend of the House.' Trans. Bruce V. Foltz and Michael Heim. *Contemporary German Philosophy* 3 (1983): 89–101.

'Heimkunft / An die Verwanten.' In *Erläuterungen zu Hölderlins Dichtung.*

(with Eugen Fink). *Heraclitus Seminar, 1966/7.* Trans. C.H. Seibert. Tuscaloosa: University of Alabama Press, 1979.

'Hölderlin and the Essence of Poetry.' In *Existence and Being.*

'Hölderlin und das Wesen der Dichtung.' In *Erläuterungen zu Hölderlins Dichtung.*

'Hölderlin's Erde und Himmel.' In *Erläuterungen zu Hölderlins Dichtung.*

Hölderlin's Hymn, 'The Ister.' Trans. William McNeill and Julia Davis. Bloomington: University of Indiana Press, 1996.

Hölderlins Hymne, 'Der Ister.' Ed. Walter Biemel. Vol. 53, *Gesamtausgabe.* Frankfurt am Main: Vittorio Klostermann, 1984.

Holzwege. 5th ed. Frankfurt am Main: Vittorio Klostermann, 1972.

'Homeland.' Trans. Thomas F. O'Meara. *Listening* 6, no. 3 (Autumn 1971): 231–8. Translation of '700 Jahre Meßkirch.'

Identity and Difference. Trans. Joan Stambaugh. Bilingual edition. New York: Harper and Row, 1969.

An Introduction to Metaphysics. Trans. Ralph Manheim. New Haven: Yale University Press, 1959.

'Johann Peter Hebel: Zähringer Rede.' *Reden und andere Zeugnisse.*

'Das "Kuinzige."' In *Reden und andere Zeugnisse.*

Die Kunst und der Raum. St Gallen: Erker-Verlag, 1969.

'Language.' In *On the Way to Language.*

'Language in the Poem.' In *On the Way to Language.*

'Letter on Humanism.' In *Basic Writings.*

'Logos.' In *Early Greek Thinking.*

'Logos (Heraklit, Fragment 50).' 1944. In *Vorträge und Aufsätze.*

Mein liebes Seelchen: Briefe Martin Heideggers an seine Frau Elfride, 1915–1970. Ed., with commentary by Gertrud Heidegger. Munich: Deutsche Verlags-Anstalt, 2005.

'Memorial Address.' In *Discourse on Thinking.* Translation of 'Gelassenheit.'

'Metaphysics as the History of Being.' In *The End of Philosophy.*

'Moira (Parmenides, Fragment VIII, 34–41).' In *Early Greek Thinking.*

'Moira (Parmenides, Fragment 8).' 1951–2. In *Vorträge und Aufsätze.*

'The Nature of Language.' In *On the Way to Language.*

Nietzsche. Trans. and ed. David Farrell Krell. 4 vols. New York: Harper and Row, 1979–87.

'Nietzsches Wort "Gott ist tot."' In *Holzwege.*

'On the Essence of Truth.' In *Basic Writings* and *Existence and Being.*

On the Way to Language. Trans. Peter D. Hertz and Joan Stambaugh. New York: Harper and Row, 1971.

On Time and Being. Trans. Joan Stambaugh. New York: Harper and Row, 1972.

'The Onto-theo-logical Constitution of Metaphysics.' In *Identity and Difference.*

'The Origin of the Work of Art.' In *Poetry, Language, Thought.*

'Overcoming Metaphysics.' In *End of Philosophy.*

'The Pathway.' Trans. Thomas F. O'Meara. *Listening* 2, no. 2 (Spring 1967): 88–91. Translation of 'Der Feldweg.'

'The Pathway (1947–1948).' Trans. Thomas Sheehan. In *Heidegger: The Man and the Thinker*, ed. Thomas Sheehan, 69–71. Chicago: Precedent, 1981. Translation of 'Der Feldweg.'

The Piety of Thinking: Essays by Martin Heidegger. Trans. James G. Hart and John C. Maraldo. Bloomington: Indiana University Press, 1976.

'Poetically Man Dwells.' In *Poetry, Language, Thought.*

Poetry, Language, Thought. Trans. Albert Hofstadter. New York: Harper and Row, 1971.

'Postscript to "What Is Metaphysics?"' In *Existence and Being.*

'The Principle of Identity.' In *Identity and Difference.*

The Principle of Reason. Trans. Reginald Lilly. Bloomington: Indiana University Press, 1991.

'Principles of Thinking.' In *Piety of Thinking.*

'The Problem of Non-objectifying Thinking and Speaking in Today's Theology.' In *Piety of Thinking.*

'Protokoll zu einem Seminar über den Vortrag "Zeit und Sein."' 1962. In *Zur Sache des Denkens.*

The Question of Being. Trans. William Kluback and Jean T. Wilde. Bilingual edition. New York: Twayne, 1958.

'The Question Concerning Technology.' In *Question Concerning Technology.*

The Question Concerning Technology and Other Essays. Trans. William Lovitt. New York: Harper and Row, 1977.

'Recollection in Metaphysics.' In *End of Philosophy.*

Reden und andere Zeugnisse eines Lebensweges. Ed. Hermann Heidegger. Vol. 16, *Gesamtausgabe.* Frankfurt am Main: Vittorio Klostermann, 2000.

'Remembrance of the Poet.' In *Existence and Being.*

'Der Satz vom Grund.' In *Der Satz vom Grund.* 4th ed. Pfullingen: Günther Neske, 1971.

'Science and Reflection.' In *Question Concerning Technology.*

Sein und Zeit. 12th ed. Tübingen: Max Niemeyer, 1972.

'700 Jahre Meßkirch.' In *Reden und andere Zeugnisse*, item 236. Translated as 'Homeland' by Thomas F. O'Meara. *Listening* 6, no. 3 (Autumn 1971): 231–8.

'Sketches for a History of Being as Metaphysics.' In *End of Philosophy.*

Sojourns: The Journey to Greece. Trans. John P. Manoussakis. Albany: SUNY Press, 1995.

'Die Sprache.' In *Unterwegs zur Sprache.*

'Die Sprache im Gedicht.' In *Unterwegs zur Sprache.*

'Die Sprache Johann Peter Hebels.' In *Denkerfahrungen.* Reprinted in *Reden und andere Zeugnisse*, item 225.

'Sprache und Heimat.' In *Hebbel Jahrbuch*, ed. Ludwig Koopmann and Erich Trunz, 27–50. Heide in Holstein: Westholsteinische Verlagsanstalt Boyens, 1960.

'Der Spruch des Anaximander.' In *Holzwege.*
'Statt einer Rede.' In *Reden und andere Zeugnisse,* item 275.
'Die Struktur der Unheimlichkeit.' In *Prolegomena zur Geschichte des Zeitbegriffs,* ed. Petra Jaeger. Vol. 20, *Gesamtausgabe.* Frankfurt am Main: Vittorio Klostermann, 1979.
'Summary of a Seminar on the Lecture "Time and Being."' In *On Time and Being.*
'The Thing.' In *Poetry, Language, Thought.*
'Time and Being.' In *On Time and Being.*
'The Turning.' In *Basic Works.*
'Über Abrahim a Santa Clara.' 1964. In *Zum 80. Geburtstag.*
Unterwegs zur Sprache. 4th ed. Pfullingen: Günther Neske, 1971.
'Der Ursprung des Kunstwerkes.' In *Holzwege.*
'Verlust der Heimat.' In *Reden und andere Zeugnisse,* item 247.
'Vom Geheimnis des Glockenturms.' 1954. In *Zum 80. Geburtstag.*
'Vom Wesen des Grundes.' In *Wegmarken.*
Vorträge und Aufsätze. 3rd ed. Pts 1–3. Pfullingen: Günther Neske, 1967.
Was heißt Denken? Tübingen: Max Niemeyer: 1971.
'Was ist Metaphysik?' In *Wegmarken.*
'The Way to Language.' In *On the Way to Language.*
'Der Weg zur Sprache.' 1959. In *Unterwegs zur Sprache.*
Wegmarken. Frankfurt am Main: Vittorio Klostermann, 1967.
'What Are Poets For?' In *Poetry, Language, Thought.*
What Is Called Thinking? Trans. Fred D. Wieck and J. Glenn Gray. New York: Harper and Row, 1968.
'What Is Metaphysics?' In *Basic Works.*
What Is Philosophy? Trans. William Kluback and Jean T. Wilde. New York: Twayne, 1958.
'Why Do I Stay in the Provinces?' In *Heidegger: The Man and the Thinker,* trans. and ed. Thomas Sheehan. Chicago: Precedent, 1981.
'Wie wenn am Feiertage.' In *Erläuterungen zu Hölderlins Dichtung.*
'The Word of Nietzsche: "God Is Dead."' In *Question Concerning Technology.*
'Words.' In *On the Way to Language.*
'Das Wort.' 1958. In *Unterwegs zur Sprache.*
'Ein Wort des Dankes.' In *Zum 80. Geburtstag.* Reprinted in *Reden und andere Zeugnisse,* item 23, under the title 'Dank an die Heimatstadt Meßkirch.'
'Wozu Dichter?' In *Holzwege.*
'Die Zeit des Weltbildes.' In *Holzwege.*
'Zeit und Sein.' In *Zur Sache des Denkens.*
Zum 80. Geburtstag von seiner Heimstadt Meßkirch. Frankfurt am Main: Vittorio Klostermann, 1969.

'Zur Erörterung der Gelassenheit: Aus einem Feldweggespräch über das Denken.' In *Gelassenheit.*

'Zur Heimatuniversität in das gemäße Verhältnis.' In *Reden und andere Zeugnisse,* item 214.

Zur Sache des Denkens. Tübingen: Max Niemeyer, 1969.

'Zur Seinsfrage.' In *Wegmarken.*

Other Sources

Agamben, Giorgio. *Homo Sacer: Sovereign Power and Bare Life.* Stanford: University of Stanford Press, 1998.

– *The Open: Man and Animal.* Stanford: University of Stanford Press, 2004.

Alderman, Harold. 'The Work of Art and Other Things.' In *Martin Heidegger in Europe and America,* ed. Edward Ballard and Charles Scott, 157–69. The Hague: Martinus Nijhoff, 1973.

Allemann, Beda. *Hölderlin and Heidegger.* Zurich and Freiburg: Atlantis Verlag, 1954.

Allen, Jeffner. 'Homecoming in Heidegger and Hebel.' In *Phenomenology of Man and of the Human Condition,* ed. A.T. Tymieniecka, 31–9. Dordrecht: Reidel, 1977.

Amar, A. 'Martin Heidegger: Der Magus aus Blut und Boden.' *Liberale Beiträge zur Entwicklung einer freiheitlichen Ordnung* (Neuwied) 12, no. 3 (1970): 174–86.

Appadurai, Arjun. *Modernity at Large: Cultural Dimensions of Globalization.* Minneapolis: University of Minnesota Press, 1996.

– 'The Production of Locality.' Pages 178–99 in *Modernity at Large: Cultural Dimensions of Globalization,* 178–99. Minneapolis: University of Minnesota Press, 1996.

Applegate, Celia. *A Nation of Provincials: The German Idea of Heimat.* Berkeley: University of California Press, 1990.

Arendt, Hannah. *The Human Condition.* Chicago: University of Chicago Press, 1958.

Bacon, Francis. 'The Great Instauration.' In *The New Organon and Related Writings.* Ed. Fulton H. Anderson, 3–29. New York: Liberal Arts Press, 1960.

Badiou, Alain. *Saint Paul: The Foundations of Universalism.* Stanford: Stanford University Press, 2003.

Bambach, Charles. 'Heidegger, Hebel, and the Politics of Homecoming.' Paper delivered at the German Studies Convention, Fall 2002, incorporated into 'Heidegger, Technology, Homeland.'

– *Heidegger's Roots: Nietzsche, National Socialism, and the Greeks.* Cornell: Cornell University Press, 2003.

– 'Heidegger, Technology, Homeland.' *German Review* 78, no. 4 (Fall 2003): 267–82.

– 'Sophocles, Hölderlin, and the Politics of Homecoming.' Incorporated into *Heidegger's Roots*.

Bammer, Angelika, ed. *The Question of 'Home'* Special issue of *New Formations: A Journal of Culture/Theory/Politics* no. 17 (Summer 1992).

Barnhill, David L. *At Home on the Earth: Becoming Native to Our Place, A Multicultural Anthology*. Berkeley: University of California Press, 1999.

Basu, Dakshinaranjan, ed. *Chhere asha gram* [The Abandoned Village]. Calcutta: Jugantur, 1975.

Beelemann, Axel. *Heimat als Daseinmetaphor Weltanschauliche Elemente im Denken des Theologiestudenten Martin Heidegger*. Vienna: Passagan Verlag, 1994.

Berger, Peter, Brigitte Berger, and Hansfried Keller. *The Homeless Mind*. New York: Vintage, 1974.

Bernasconi, Robert. *Heidegger in Question*. Atlantic Highlands, NJ: Humanities Press International, 1993.

Bigwood, Carol. *Earth Muse: Feminism, Nature, and Art*. Philadelphia: Temple University Press, 1993.

Boa, Elizabeth, and Rachel Palfreyman. *Heimat – A German Dream: Regional Loyalities and National Identity in German Culture, 1890–1990*. New York: Oxford University Press, 2000.

Bruns, Gerald. *Heidegger's Estrangements: Language, Truth, and Poetry in the Later Writings*. New Haven: Yale University Press, 1989.

Buchin, Elisabeth, and Alfred Denker. *Martin Heidegger und seine Heimat*. Munich: Deutsche Verlags-Anstalt, 2005.

Buchner, Hartmut, ed. *Japan und Heidegger: Gedenkschrift der Stadt Meßkirch zum hundertsten Geburtstag Martin Heideggers*. Sigmaringen: Jan Thorbecke Verlag, 1989.

Cabeza de Baca, Fabiola. *We Fed Them Cactus*. Albuquerque: University of New Mexico Press, 1954.

Caputo, John. 'People of God, People of Being: The Theological Presuppositions of Heidegger's Path of Thought.' In *Appropriating Heidegger*, ed. James Faulconer and Mark Wrathall, 27–41. Cambridge: Cambridge University Press, 2000.

– *Radical Hermeneutics*. Bloomington: Indiana University Press, 1987.

Césaire, Aimé. *Notebook of a Return to the Native Land* [*Cahier d'un retour au pays natal: Memorandum on my Martinique*]. Trans. M. Rosello and A. Pritchard. Newcastle, England: Bloodaxe Books, 1995.

Chakrabarty, Dipesh. 'Memories of Displacement: The Poetry and Prejudice of Dwelling.' In *Habitations of Modernity: Essays in the Wake of Subaltern Studies*, 115–37. Chicago: University of Chicago Press, 2002.

Cheah, Pheng. *Spectral Nationality: Passages of Freedom from Kant to Postcolonial Literatures of Liberation.* New York: Columbia University Press, 2003.
Crownfield, David. 'The Last God.' In *Companion to Heidegger's* Contributions to Philosophy, ed. Charles Scott et al., 212–28.
Dallmayr, Fred. *The Other Heidegger.* Ithaca: Cornell University Press, 1993.
Dauenhauer, Bernhardt. 'Heidegger, the Spokesman for the Dweller.' *The Southwestern Journal of Philosophy* 15, no. 2 (1977): 189–99.
Deleuze, Gilles, and Félix Guattari. *Kafka: Toward a Minor Literature.* Minneapolis: University of Minnesota Press, 1986.
de Man, Paul. 'Les exégèses de Hölderlin par Martin Heidegger.' *Critique* (September–October 1955): 34–43.
– *Romanticism and Contemporary Criticism.* Ed. Kevin Newmark, Andrzej Warminski, and E.S. Burt. Baltimore: Johns Hopkins University Press, 1993.
Denker, Alfred, and Holger Zaborowski, ed. *Martin Heidegger/Bernhard Welte: Briefe und Begegnungen.* Stuttgart: Klett-Cotta, 2003.
Derrida, Jacques. *Dissemination.* Trans. Barbara Johnson. Chicago: University of Chicago Press, 1981.
– 'The Double Session.' In *Dissemination,* 173–285.
– *Margins of Philosophy.* Trans. Alan Bass. Chicago: University of Chicago Press, 1992.
– *Points ... Interviews, 1974–1994.* Trans. Peggy Kamuf et al., ed. Elisabeth Weber. Stanford: Stanford University Press, 1991.
– *The Postcard.* Trans. Alan Bass. Chicago: University of Chicago Press, 1987.
– *Specters of Marx.* Trans. Peggy Kamuf. New York: Routledge, 1994.
Diemer, Alwin. *Edmund Husserl: Versuch einer systematischen Darstellung seiner Phänomenologie.* Meisenheim am Glan: Hain, 1956.
Doevendans, Kees, and Anne Schram. 'Phenomenologies of Liquidity – Perspectives on Water in the Netherlands.' Paper presented at Architecture and Phenomenology: An International Conference, Haifa, 17–21 June 2007.
Doig, Ivan. *This House of Sky.* New York: Harcourt Brace Jovanovich, 1978.
Dubsky, Ivan. 'Domov a bezdomovi [Home and unhomeliness].' *Filosoficky casopis* [Philosophy journal; Prague] (1966): 64–72.
Eco, Umberto. *Art and Beauty in the Middle Ages.* New Haven: Yale University Press, 1986.
Eisen, Arnold M. *Galut: Modern Jewish Reflections on Homelessness and Homecoming.* Bloomington: Indiana University Press, 1986.
Ellison, Ralph. *Invisible Man.* New York: Modern Library, 1992.
Emad, Parvis, and Kenneth Maly. Foreword to *Contributions,* by Martin Heidegger, xv–xliv.
Ferry, Luc. *Man Made God: The Meaning of Life.* Chicago: University of Chicago: 2002.

Fiedler, Manuela. *Heimat im deutschen Film: Ein Mythos zwischen Regression und Utopie.* Coppengrave: Coppi-Verlag, 1955.

Foltz. Bruce. *Inhabiting the Earth: Heidegger, Environmental Ethics, and the Metaphysics of Nature.* Atlantic Highlands, NJ: Humanities Press, 1995.

Fóti, Veronique M. *Heidegger and the Poets:* Poiésis, Sophia, Techné. Atlantic Highlands, NJ: Humanities Press, 1992.

Frankl, Victor. *The Doctor and the Soul.* New York: Vintage Books, 1986.

Freeman, Kathleen, trans. *Ancilla to the Pre-Socratic Philosophers.* Oxford: Basil Blackwell, 1962. Translation of Diehl.

Führ, Eduard, ed. *Worin noch niemand war: Heimat, Eine Auseinandersetzung mit einem strapazierten Begriff Historisch-philosophisch-architektonish.* Berlin: Bauverlag, 1985.

Fusco, Coco. *Internal Exiles: New Films and Videos from Chile.* New York: Third World Newsreel, 1990.

George, Rosemary Marangoly. *The Politics of Home: Postcolonial Relocations and Twentieth-Century Fiction.* Berkeley: University of California Press, 1999.

German Federal Centre for Public Education (Bundeszentrale für politische Bildung). *Heimat: Analysen, Themen, Perspektiven,* vol. 294.I. Bonn: Bundeszentrale für politische Bildung, 1990.

– *Heimat: Lehrpläne, Literature, Filme,* vol. 294.II. Bonn: Bundeszentrale für politische Bildung, 1990.

Gibbs, Ronald, and Joan Gibbs Engel. *Ethics of Environment and Development: Global Challenge, International Response.* Tucson: The University of Arizona Press, 1990.

Goodwin, Michael. *Black Markets: The Supply and Demand of Body Parts.* New York: Cambridge University Press, 2006.

Gore, Al. *Earth in the Balance.* New York: Rodale, 2006.

Gosetti-Ferencei, Jennifer Anna. *Heidegger, Hölderlin, and the Subject of Poetic Language: Toward a New Poetics of Dasein.* New York: Fordham University Press, 2004.

Grugan, Arthur. 'Thought and Poetry: Language as Man's Homecoming – A Study of Martin Heidegger's Question of Being and Its Ties to Friedrich Hölderlin's Experience of the Holy.' PhD thesis, Duquesne University, 1972.

Haar, Michel. *The Song of the Earth: Heidegger and the Grounds of the History of Being.* Bloomington: University of Indiana Press, 1993.

Handlin, Oscar. *The Uprooted: The Epic Story of the Great Migrations That Made the American People.* 2nd ed. Boston: Atlantic-Little, Brown, 1973.

Handlin, Oscar, and Mary Handlin. *Facing Life: Youth and Family in American History.* Boston: Little, Brown, 1971.

Halliburton, David. *Poetic Thinking: An Approach to Heidegger.* Chicago: University of Chicago Press, 1981.

Harman, Graham. *Heidegger Explained: From Phenomenon to Thing.* Chicago: Open Court, 2007.

Held, Klaus. 'Heimwelt, Fremdwelt, die eine Welt.' In *Perspektiven und Probleme der Husserlschen Phänomenologie*, ed. Ernst Orth, Band 24/25, 305–37. Freiburg: Alber, 1991.

Heller, Erich. *The Disinherited Mind.* New York: Harcourt Brace Jovanovich, 1975.

Hermand, Jost, and James Streakley, eds. *'Heimat,' Nation, and Fatherland: The German Sense of Belonging.* New York: Peter Lang, 1996.

Hofig, Willi. *Der deutsche Heimatfilm, 1947–1960.* Stuttgart: Enke, 1973.

Irigaray, Luce. *An Ethics of Sexual Difference.* Ithaca: Cornell University Press, 1993.

– *The Forgetting of Air in Martin Heidegger.* Austin: University of Texas Press, 1999.

Jackson, M. *At Home in the World.* Durham: Duke University Press, 1995.

Jaspers, Karl. *Notizen zu Martin Heidegger.* Munich: Hans Saner, 1978.

Intergovernmental Panel on Climate Change. *NOE 5 The Fourth Report of the International Panel on Climate Change.* http://www.ipcc.ch/SPM2feb07.pdf.

Kaufman, Stanley. *At Home in the Universe.* New York: Oxford University Press, 1995.

Kaes, Anton. *From Hitler to Heimat: The Return of History as Film.* Cambridge, MA: Harvard University Press, 1989.

Kay, Lily E. *Who Wrote the Book of Life? A History of the Genetic Code.* Stanford: Stanford University Press, 2000.

Kelly, D.A. 'The Earth as Home.' *Religious Humanism* 6 (1972): 178–85.

Kierkegaard, Søren. *Either/Or.* Trans. W. Lowrie. New York: Anchor Books, 1959.

Kiesel, Theodore. *The Genesis of Heidegger's* Being and Time. Berkeley: University of California Press, 1993.

Kiesel, Theodore, and John van Buren, eds. *Reading Heidegger from the Start: Essays in His Earliest Thought.* Albany: SUNY Press, 1994.

Köstlin, Konrad. *Heimat und Identität, Probleme regionaler Kultur.* Neumünster: Karl Wachholtz Verlag, 1980.

Laclau, Ernesto. *Elusive Universality.* Stanford: Stanford University Press, forthcoming.

Leman-Stefanovic, Ingrid. *The Event of Death: A Phenomenological Enquiry.* Dordrecht: Nijhoff, 1987.

Lemelle, Disney, and Robin D.G. Kelley. *Imagining Home: Class, Culture and Nationalism in the African Diaspora.* New York: Verso, 1994.

Levins, Richard, and Richard Lewontin. *The Dialectical Biologist.* Cambridge, MA: Harvard University Press, 1985.

Lindemann, Klaus, ed. *'Heimat': Gedichte und Prosa.* Stuttgart: Reclam, 1992.

Mack, Arlen. *Home: A Place in the World.* New York: New York University Press, 1993.

Marcovicz, Digne Meller. *Martin Heidegger, Photos, 23 September 1966, 17 und 18 Juni 1968.* Stuttgart: Fey, 1978.

Marion, Jean-Luc. *Being Given: Toward a Phenomenology of Givenness.* Trans. Jeffrey L. Kosky. Stanford: Stanford University Press, 2002.

Marks, Paula M. *In a Barren Land: American Indian Dispossession and Survival.* New York: William Morrow, 1998.

Marten, Ranier. 'Heidegger's Heimat: Eine philosophische Herausforderung.' In *Nachdenken über Heidegger: Eine Bestandsaufnahme,* ed. Ute Guzzoni, 160–75. Hildesheim: Gerstenberg Verlag, 1980.

May, Reinhard. *Heidegger's Hidden Sources: East Asian Influences on His Work.* Trans. Graham Parkes. New York: Routledge, 1989.

Mehta, Jarava Lal. 'Heidegger and Vedânta: Reflections on a Questionable Theme.' In Parkes, *Heidegger and Asian Thought.*

– *Martin Heidegger: The Way and the Vision.* Honolulu: University of Hawaii Press, 1976.

– *The Philosophy of Martin Heidegger.* New York: Harper and Row, 1971.

McCarthy, Cormac. *All the Pretty Horses.* New York: Knopf, 1997.

McNeill, William. *The Glance of the Eye: Heidegger, Aristotle, and the Ends of Theory.* Albany: SUNY Press, 1999.

Milchman, Alan, and A. Rosenberg. *Martin Heidegger and the Holocaust.* Atlantic Highlands, NJ: Humanities Press, 1996.

Momaday, N. Scott. *House Made of Dawn.* New York: Harper and Row, 1978.

Mugerauer, Robert. 'Call of the Earth: Endowment and (Delayed) Response.' In *Heidegger and the Earth: Essays in Environmental Philosophy,* ed. Ladelle McWhorter and Gail Stenstad. 2nd ed. Toronto: University of Toronto Press, forthcoming.

– 'The City: A Legacy of Organism-Environment Interaction at Every Scale.' In *The Natural City: Re-envisioning the Built Environment,* ed. Ingrid Leman-Stefanovic and Stephen S. Scharpe. Toronto: University of Toronto Press, 2008.

– 'Deleuze and Guattari's Return to Science as a Basis for Environmental Philosophy.' In *Nature Revisited: Environmental Philosophy in a New Key,* ed. Bruce Foltz and Robert Frodeman. Bloomington: University of Indiana Press, 2004.

– 'The Double Gift: Place and Identity.' Paper presented at Architecture and Phenomenology International Conference, Haifa, 17–21 June 2007.

– *Environmental Interpretations: Tradition, Deconstruction, Hermeneutics.* Austin: University of Texas Press, 1996.

– 'Heidegger and Architecture: Beyond the Architecture of Presence.' Keynote lecture at Heidegger Conference, North Texas State University, Denton, TX, 12–13 May 1994.

– *Heidegger's Language and Thinking.* Atlantic Highlands, NJ: Humanities Press International, 1988.
– *Interpretations on Behalf of Place:* Albany: SUNY Press, 1994.
– 'Marie Heidegger-Oschwald: A Sisterly Imitation of Mary and Martha.' *Praxis* forthcoming.
– 'Neglected Sources of Heidegger's Aesthetics: Schopenhauer, Plotinus, and Genesis.' In preparation, n.d.
– 'A New Type of Medical Tourism Emerges.' Paper presented at International Association for the Study of Traditional Environments conference, Bangkok, 11–15 December 2006.
– 'Theories of Sustainability: Environmental Ethics, Mixed-Communities, and Compassion.' Appendix 4 in Mugerauer and Manzo, *Environmental Dilemmas,* 312–20.

Mugerauer, Robert, and Lynne Manzo, eds. *Environmental Dilemmas: Ethical Decision Making.* Lanham, MD: Lexington Press, 2008.

Mugerauer, Robert, and David Seamon. *Dwelling, Place, Environment.* The Hague: Martinus Nijhoff, 1985.

Naficy, Hamid. *An Accented Cinema: Exilic and Diaspora Filmmaking.* Princeton: Princeton University Press, 2001.
– *The Making of Exile Cultures: Iranian Television in Los Angeles.* Minneapolis: University of Minnesota Press, 1993.

Naipaul, V.S. *The Enigma of Arrival.* New York: Vintage, 1987.

Nietzsche, Friedrich. *The Birth of Tragedy.* In *The Philosophy of Nietzsche,* trans. Clifton P. Fadiman. New York: Random House, 1954.
– *The Gay Science.* Trans. Walter Kaufmann. New York: Random House, 1974.
– *The Will to Power.* Ed. and trans. Walter Kaufmann. New York: Random House, 1968.

Ôhashi, Ryôsuke. 'Erinnerungen an Fritz Heidegger.' In *Japan und Heidegger: Gedenkschrift der Staat Meßkirch zum hundertsten Geburtstag Martin Heideggers,* ed. Hartmut Buchner, 203–6. Meßkirch: Jan Thorbecke Verlag Sigmaringen, 1989.

Oliver, Kelly. *Reading Kristeva: Unraveling the Double-Bind.* Bloomington: Indiana University Press, 1993.

Ott, Hugo. *Martin Heidegger: A Political Life.* New York: Basic Books, 1993.

Oyama, Susan. *The Ontogeny of Information: Developmental Systems and Evolution.* Durham, NC: Duke University Press, 2000.

Parkes, Graham, ed. *Heidegger and Asian Thought.* Honolulu: University of Hawaii Press, 1987.

Patoæka, Jan. 'Le monde naturel comme problème philosophique.' *Phaenomenologica* (1936). Trans. Jaromir Danek and Henri Declève. La Haye: Martinus Nijhoff, 1976.

Petzet, H.W. *Encounters and Dialogues with Martin Heidegger.* Chicago: University of Chicago Press, 1993.

Phillips, James. *Heidegger's Volk: Between National Socialism and Poetry.* Stanford: Stanford University Press, 2005.

Pöggeler, Otto. 'Destruction and Moment.' In Kiesel and van Buren, *Reading Heidegger from the Start,* 137–56.

Prince, Valerie S. *Burnin' Down the House: Home in African American Literature.* New York: Columbia University Press, 2005.

Reed, Christopher, ed. *Not at Home: The Suppression of Domesticity in Modern Art and Architecture.* New York: Thames and Hudson, 1996.

Richardson, William J. *Heidegger: Through Phenomenology to Thought.* The Hague: Martinus Nijhoff, 1963.

Riedl, Joachim, ed. *Heimat: Auf der Suche nach der verloren Identität.* Vienna: Verlag Christian Brandstätter, 1995.

Rilke, Rainer Maria. *The Notebooks of Malte Laurids Brigge.* Trans. M.D. Herter Norton. New York: W.H. Norton and Co., 1959.

Roaf, Sue, David Crichton, and Fergus Nicol, *Adapting Buildings and Cities for Climate Change.* Boston: Architectural Press, 2005.

Rollins, William H. *A Greener Vision of Home: Cultural Politic and Environmental Reform in the German Heimatschutz Movement, 1904–1918.* Ann Arbor: University of Michigan Press, 1997.

Rose, Steven. *Lifelines: Life beyond the Gene.* New York: Oxford University Press, 1997.

Rossbacher, Karlheinz. *Heimatbewegung und Heimatroman: Zu einer Literatursociologie der Jahrhundertwende.* Stuttgart: Klett, 1975.

Rouner, Leroy S., ed. *The Longing for Home.* Notre Dame, IN: University of Notre Dame Press, 1996.

Safranski, Rüdiger. *Martin Heidegger: Between Good and Evil.* Cambridge, MA: Harvard University Press, 1998.

Sale, Kirkpatrick. *Dwellers in the Land: The Bioregional Vision.* San Francisco: Sierra Club Books, 1985.

Sallis, John. 'Nietzsche's Homecoming.' *Man and World* 2 (1969): 108–16.

– 'Towards the Movement of Reversal: Science, Technology, and the Language of Homecoming.' In *Heidegger and the Path of Thinking,* 138–68. Pittsburgh: Duquesne University Press, 1970.

Sass, Hans-Martin. *Martin Heidegger: Bibliography and Glossary.* Bowling Green, OH: Philosophy Documentation Center, 1982.

Scharr, Adam. *Heidegger's Hut.* Cambridge: MIT Press, 2006.

– 'The Professor's House: Martin Heidegger's House in Freiburg-im-Breisgau.' In *Constructing Place: Mind and Matter,* ed. Sarah Menin, 130–42. New York: Routledge, 2003.

Scheper-Huges, Nancy. 'The Last Commodity: Post-Human Ethics and the Global Traffic in "Fresh" Organs.' In *Global Assemblages: Technology, Politics, and Ethics as Anthropological Problems*, ed. Aihwa Ong and Stephen J. Collier, 145–67. Oxford: Blackwell, 2005.

Schopenhauer, Arthur. *The World as Will and Idea*. Trans. R.B. Haldane and J. Kemp. New York: Doubleday, 1961.

Schürmann, Reiner. *Heidegger on Being and Acting: From Principles to Anarchy*. Trans. Marie Gros and Reiner Schürmann. Bloomington: Indiana University Press, 1987.

Schuwer, André. 'Nature and the Holy: On Heidegger's Interpretation of Hölderlin's Hymn "Wie wenn am Feiertage."' *Research in Phenomenology* 7 (1977): 225–37.

Schutz, Alfred. 'The Homecomer.' *American Journal of Sociology* 50, no. 5 (1945): 369–76.

– 'The Stranger: An Essay in Social Psychology.' *American Journal of Sociology* 49, no. 6(1944): 499–507.

Scott, Charles et al., eds. *Companion to Heidegger's* Contributions to Philosophy. Bloomington: Indiana University Press, 2001.

Sebald, W.G. *Austerlitz*. Munich: Hanser, 2001.

– *Unheimliche Heimat*. Salzburg: Residenz Verlag, 1991.

Seidel, *Martin Heidegger and the Pre-Socratics*. Lincoln: University of Nebraska Press, 1961.

Shih-yi Hsiao, P. 'Heidegger and Our Translation of the *Tao Te Ching*.' In Parkes, *Heidegger and Asian Thought*, 93–101.

Skocz, Dennis. 'Of Time and the River: Heidegger's Reading of Hölderlin's River Hymns.' In *Analecta Husserliana* LXXXII, ed. A.-T. Tymieniecka, 299–310. Boston: Kluwer, 2004.

Steinbock, Anthony J. *Home and Beyond: Generative Phenomenology after Husserl*. Evanston, IL: Northwestern University Press, 1995.

– 'Homelessness and the Homeless Movement: A Clue to the Problem of Intersubjectivity.' *Human Studies* 17 (1994): 202–23.

Thacker, Eugene. *Biomedia*. Minneapolis: University of Minnesota Press, 2004.

Thompson, Becky, and Sangeeta Tyagi. *Names We Call Home: Autobiography on Racial Identity*. New York: Routledge, 1996.

Tsing, Anna Tsing. *Friction: An Ethnography of Global Connection*. Princeton: Princeton University Press, 2005.

Vallega-Neu, Daniela. *Heidegger's* Contributions to Philosophy*: An Introduction*. Bloomington: Indiana University Press, 2003.

van Buren, John. 'Martin Heidegger, Martin Luther.' In Kiesel and van Buren, *Reading Heidegger*, 159–74.

– *The Young Heidegger: Rumor of the Hidden King.* Bloomington: University of Indiana Press, 1994.

Vidler, Anthony. *The Architectural Uncanny: Essays in the Modern Unhomely.* Cambridge: MIT Press, 1992.

von Herrmann, Friedrich Wilhelm. Epilogue to *Contributions*, by Martin Heidegger, 363–9.

– 'The Flower of the Mouth: Hölderlin's Hint for Heidegger's Thinking of the Essence of Language.' *Research in Phenomenology* 19 (1989): 27–42.

von Moltke, Johannes. *No Place Like Home: Locations of Heimat in German Cinema.* Berkeley: University of California Press, 2005.

Vycinas, Vincent. *Earth and Gods.* The Hage: Martinus Nijhoff, 1961.

Wagner, Helmut, ed. *Alfred Schutz on Phenomenology and Social Relations: Selected Writings.* Chicago: University of Chicago Press, 1970.

Waldby, Catherine, and Robert Mitchell. *Tissue Economies: Blood, Organs, and Cell Lines in Late Capitalism.* Durham, NC: Duke University Press, 2006.

Waldenfels, Bernhard. 'Heimat in der Fremde.' In *In den Netzen der Lebenswelt.* Frankfurt: Suhrkamp, 1985.

– *Das Zwischenreich des Dialogs: Sozialphilosophische Untersuchungen in Anschluß an E. Husserl.* The Hague: Martinus Nijhoff, 1971.

Walser, Martin. *Heimatkunde: Aufsätze und Reden.* Frankfurt am Main: Suhrkamp, 1968.

Walters, Wendy. *At Home in Diaspora: Black International Writing.* Minneapolis: University of Minnesota Press, 2005.

Warminski, Andrzej. *Readings in Interpretation: Hölderlin, Hegel, Heidegger.* Minneapolis: University of Minnesota Press, 1987.

Weber, David J., ed. *Foreigners in Their Native Land: Historical Roots of the Mexican Americans.* Albuquerque: University of New Mexico Press, 1973.

Weil, Simone. *The Need for Roots.* New York: Harper and Row, 1952.

White, David A. *Heidegger and the Language of Poetry.* Lincoln: University of Nebraska Press, 1978.

Weltfish, Gener. *The Lost Universe: Pawnee Life and Culture.* Lincoln: University of Nebraska Press, 1965.

Wickham, Chrisopher J. *Constructing Heimat in Postwar Gemany: Longing and Belonging.* New York: Mellen Press, 1999.

Wolff, Georg. 'Haus und Hütte: Eindrücke bei einem Speigel-Gespräch.' In *Erinnerung an Martin Heidegger*, ed. Günther Neske, 289–91. Pfullingen: Verlag Günther Neske, 1977.

Wyman, Mark. *Round-Trip to America: The Immigrants Return to Europe, 1880–1930.* Ithaca: Cornell University Press, 1993.

Young, Iris Marion. 'House and Home: Feminist Variations of a Theme.' In *Fem-*

inist Interpretations of Heidegger, ed. Nancy Holland and Patricia Huntington, 252–88. University Park: Pennsylvania State University Press, 2001.

Zhang, Li. *Strangers in the City: Reconfigurations of Space, Power, and Social Networks within China's Floating Populations.* Stanford: Stanford University Press, 2001.

Zimmerman, Hans Dieter. *Martin und Fritz Heidegger. Philosophie und Fastnacht.* Munich: C.H. Beck, 2005.

Index

www.ingramcontent.com/pod-product-compliance
Lightning Source LLC
LaVergne TN
LVHW020429080826
844660LV00034B/1375

9781442626812